# SUBMARINE GEOLOGY

HARPER'S GEOSCIENCE SERIES
CAREY CRONEIS, EDITOR

# SUBMARINE
# GEOLOGY SECOND EDITION

### FRANCIS P. SHEPARD

SCRIPPS INSTITUTION OF OCEANOGRAPHY
UNIVERSITY OF CALIFORNIA AT LA JOLLA

with chapters by

### D. L. INMAN AND E. D. GOLDBERG

HARPER & ROW, PUBLISHERS
NEW YORK, EVANSTON, AND LONDON

To RUTH YOUNG MANAR and JAMES MORIARTY
for many years of outstanding cooperation

# CONTENTS

## XI. Submarine Canyons, Deep Channels, and Other Marine Valleys

## XII. Coral and Other Organic Reefs

# EDITOR'S INTRODUCTION

Some fifteen years have elapsed since the publication of the first edition of Dr. Shepard's *Submarine Geology*. During this period there has been a remarkable global increase in the interest in marine geology, accompanied by spectacular improvements in the instruments and methods employed in both the qualitative and quantitative studies of the subject. For example, during the past decade the great oceanic depths have revealed notable new information through the use of the deep free diving Piccard bathyscaph, while the no less important continental shelves have been widely and intimately studied through the introduction, for geological investigations, of the self-contained underwater-breathing device known as SCUBA.

SCUBA diving has added an entirely new dimension to the geological exploration of the important segment of the oceanic floor which lies between the breakers and depths of about 150 feet. In this type of submarine research, Francis Shepard has been one of the pioneers. Likewise, the Scripps Institution of Oceanography, with which Dr. Shepard has now been associated for a score of years, has been the institutional pioneer in developing our geological and geophysical knowledge of the deep Pacific Ocean. The Scripps results have been interpreted and summarized by H. W. Menard. Meanwhile geophysical surveys of the Atlantic Ocean were being carried on through the notable research cruises of ships of the Lamont Geological Observatory. The Lamont investigations have been described by Ewing, Heezen, Tharp and others. The results of these classic Atlantic and Pacific studies were correctly judged to be of such general public interest that *Life* magazine, in its issue of November 7, 1960, presented an impressive color digest of them which attracted widespread attention.

The general interest in the oceans has now become so great that many nations maintain oceanic research vessels constantly at work, and the U.S.S.R. has at least two very large, completely self-contained, ocean-going laboratories. It is not surprising, therefore, that President Kennedy has seen fit to issue a very strongly worded statement concerning the importance of general oceanographic researches, and the pressing need for their financial support.

The growing awareness of the national significance of a well conceived research program in submarine geology has been translated into Congressional budgetary action. This in turn has resulted in increased National Science Foundation funds, and new Coast and Geodetic Survey appropriations for the construction of oceanographic vessels, and for the underwriting of new projects in marine geology.

Since *Submarine Geology* was first printed in 1948, off-shore drilling for oil and gas has become commonplace, and the equipment required has grown greatly in size and sophistication. Concurrently, the devices for ocean bottom coring have been constantly improved, and thus the cores which can now be obtained are greatly increased in length and perfection. All these and related technological advances have led by easy stages to the much discussed Mohole Project, also underwritten by the National Science Foundation. Its prototype drilling venture, conducted off Guadaloupe Island, in which a new type of drilling barge, the *Cuss I*, was employed, turned out to be notably successful. This has suggested that the greatly expanded Mohole Project, which is designed to drill through both the ocean bottom sediments and the earth's crust to the Mohorovičić discontinuity, can also be carried through to a successful conclusion. The Mohole Project, which is now engaging the active attention of a large group of American scientists and engineers, should, at the very least, prove an imaginative introduction to a new phase of marine geology. In fact, such investigations of the earth's inner space may well turn out to be as rewarding as our more highly advertised, and enormously more costly, researches into outer space.

When the first edition of *Submarine Geology* was being prepared, Dr. Shepard was on the Hawaiian island of Oahu where he witnessed the catastrophic effects of the Aleutian tsunami of April 1, 1946. By coincidence he was again spending several months on the Hawaiian Islands as the second edition of his text went to press. In the intervening years he also witnessed and, indeed, took an active part in the extraordinary changes in marine geology, geophysics, and oceanography which have had such a tsunamilike impact on the Earth Sciences—and sister sciences as well. In the present edition of *Submarine Geology* Dr. Shepard has taken full cognizance of the changes mentioned. As a consequence the text has emerged in an almost completely rewritten, modernized form which should receive the same full measure of acceptance which the first edition enjoyed.

CAREY CRONEIS

*Rice University*
*March, 1963*

# PREFACE TO THE SECOND EDITION

Since the appearance of the first edition of *Submarine Geology* in 1948, there has been a surprising growth of information in what was until recently a very small field of investigation. Field studies of the sea floor have gone beyond anything believed possible at the time the earlier edition was being composed. The literature has become enormous and continues to expand. It is impossible to do full justice to this great mass of writing without unduly increasing the size of this second edition. However, I have called attention to all the significant articles that I have encountered during a rather exhaustive combing of the literature. The necessarily brief mention of many of these articles and books can be supplemented by perusal of the works listed in the extensive bibliography located at the end of this book. Fortunately, a series of recent symposia on phases of oceanography, including the 1959 International Oceanographic Congress, has provided rather long abstracts in English of work that had hitherto appeared only in Russian, and hence had been of limited use because of language barriers.

In getting out a new edition covering a field that is expanding rapidly one cannot avoid the feeling that much of the information will have become dated by the time it is published. Hypotheses given favorable attention here may have been largely disproven by the latest discoveries coming from new exploration of the vast unknown areas of the sea floor. Similarly, objections offered to other hypotheses may have been removed. It is well to keep in mind that virtually all the hypotheses in submarine geology are highly speculative, and all one can do is to give the significant clues now available that have a bearing on the various ideas. It is to be hoped that the frank discussions herein will stimulate research that will produce more badly needed facts.

In the first edition I neglected certain technical aspects of submarine geology because they were beyond my field of study. The important information in such topics as wave mechanics, mechanics of sediment transportation, and geochemistry has been supplied in this second edition by my colleagues at Scripps Institution, D. L. Inman (Chapters III and V), and E. D. Goldberg (Chapter XVI). Chapter V is based on extensive studies by Brigadier R. A. Bagnold and Dr. Inman and was given the benefit of criticism by Brigadier Bagnold.

The discussion on methods and instrumentation in Chapter II has been supplemented by information from the active group of geologists at the U.S. Navy Electronics Laboratory with special sections supplied by R. F. Dill and D. G. Moore of that laboratory, and by G. G. Shor, Jr., and Victor Vacquier of Scripps Institution. Many helpful suggestions have been given me by friends who have kindly read portions or all of the manuscript. These include R. S. Arthur, E. C. Buffington, J. R. Curray, R. S. Dietz, R. S. Dill, K. O. Emery, R. L. Fisher, André Guilcher, E. L. Hamilton, D. L. Inman, H. S. Ladd, Ruth Y. Manar, H. W. Menard, J. L. Mero, D. G. Moore, W. R. Riedel, G. G. Shor, Jr., and J. I. Tracey, Jr. Drafting has been almost entirely the work of J. R. Moriarty, who has made many innovations. Appreciation is also expressed to Elizabeth Sanborn for the careful copying and recopying of the entire manuscript and to Helene Flanders for typing assistance. Finally, I should like to acknowledge the continual help provided to me by my wife, who has never been too busy to listen to the readings of the chapters and to offer her comments.

Assistance in preparing various phases of this book has come from contracts of the Office of Naval Research and from the National Science Foundation.

Francis P. Shepard

# CHAPTER I

# INTRODUCTION AND HISTORY

Geology is usually defined as the history of the earth but actually it has been largely limited to the history of the continents, which constitute only 28 percent of the earth's surface. The study of the other 72 percent is called submarine geology or alternatively either marine geology or geological oceanography. All these names seem equally acceptable and can be used as synonyms. Included, in submarine geology is the study of coasts and shorelines so far as they are related to the sea and its processes; the continental shelf, consisting of the broad platform that surrounds most of the coasts; the continental slope leading from the shelf down to the deeps; and the deep ocean floor beyond. Both the topography of the sea floor and the sediments are considered as well as the geophysical data that provide information on what is beneath the sea floor. The effect of marine organisms on the sea floor and on the accumulating sediments is also a part of the subject matter. Submarine geology is the newest and, until very recent years, it has been by far the least developed branch of geology. The interest in the subject has shown enormous growth since World War II and it is now not unusual to see one or more articles dealing with the geology of the sea and its shores in each new issue of the various geological journals.

Although Charles Darwin contributed to a considerable extent to the concepts which later became parts of submarine geology, the first really large backlog of information came from the history-making voyage of H.M.S. *Challenger* (1872–76). No geologists were included among the scientists on the vessel, but the study of the *Challenger* collections, along with some 12,000 samples from other expeditions (Murray and Renard, 1891), was made in part by a well-known geologist, A. F. Renard. The monograph that resulted is still of primary importance in connection with the study of marine sediments, particularly deep-sea sediments. Beginning in 1888 and continuing until 1920, the voyages of the United States Fish Commission steamer *Albatross* added greatly to the knowledge of the sea floor, particularly from the deep waters of the eastern Pacific. There was little participation of geologists even in the study of the *Albatross* samples, although Trask (1932) determined the percentage of calcium carbonate and organic matter of many of them; and Louderback (1914, 1940) described the samples from San Francisco Bay. Study of 343 of the *Albatross* samples was made by Murray and Lee (1909), and more general descriptions of most of the earlier samples were given by Agassiz (1906). The Dutch steamer *Siboga* in 1899 and 1900 made large collections of samples in the vicinity of the East Indies. These samples were described and discussed by geologists Böggild (1916) and Molengraaff (1916, 1922, 1930). Results of expeditions by the German steamers *Edi Stephan* and *Planet* early in the present century were reported by the geologist and oceanographer Andrée (1920).

Although most of the above references were made to the sample collections, all the voyages mentioned and many others resulted in the charting of ocean depths which began slowly to reveal the topography of the hidden three-quarters of the earth's surface. The charting of the continental shelves ran far ahead of that of the deep oceans. Shelf charts by the British Admiralty, the U.S. Coast and Geodetic Survey, and the Hydrographic Office of the U.S. Navy were the most complete and had the widest coverage in the early exploration, although other navies of the world added greatly to the information, particularly along the coasts of their own countries. The coastal charts constructed from the wire (and even rope) soundings, which preceded the development of echo sounding instruments, appear to have aroused little interest among geologists. They did, of course, recognize the presence of a terrace extending out from most coasts to a break in slope encountered at depths which they considered to be roughly 100 fathoms; and they called this terrace the continental shelf. The steeper slope beyond was given the name continental slope. Also, a few pioneer spirits called attention to the presence of valleys cutting the shelves and slopes. The early attempts of Spencer (1903) and others to explain these features, now known as submarine canyons, as the work of rivers resulting from huge continental uplifts during the glacial period were received coolly by the geological fraternity. The idea that canyons existed on the sea floor was subjected to the same scoffing as were the contemporaneous "horseless buggies" and the "flying egg crates."

A long period of comparative stagnation in submarine geology was broken a few years after the end of World War I. The development of echo sounding devices was one of the main reasons for the revival of interest in the sea bottom. With this new device the tedious lowering of weights to the bottom, taking hours of time for a single deep sounding, came to an end, and even the ocean abysses could be sounded without stopping a vessel's progress. The German steamer *Meteor* was among the first to carry out exploration by the new method. The extensive profiles across the South Atlantic (Stocks, 1933) added immensely to the knowledge of bottom configuration. The work of the U.S. Coast and Geodetic Survey aroused even more interest among geologists because their surveys extended along the continental slopes and revealed for the first time in considerable detail the submarine canyons (Veatch and Smith, 1939), which were known previously only from scattered soundings of doubtful validity. The U.S. Navy began in the 1920's to amass sounding data from the deep ocean. In recent years the installation of recording echo sounding devices on naval vessels has resulted in an enormous increase of sounding data, particularly from the Pacific. The numerous ocean charts compiled and published at the Navy Hydrographic Office show some of the results of this work. Helpful charts with a compilation of sounding data from the entire world have been published by the Hydrographic Office of Monaco. These Monaco charts have had new editions from time to time; but, because of the woefully inadequate staff, this organization has been unable to keep up with the latest developments and for that reason the world charts do not give more than a very generalized picture of the most interesting features of the relief.

The great breakthrough in knowledge of the deep oceans has come from the work of oceanographic institutions, most of it subsidized by grants from the U.S. Navy. The mapping of the Atlantic by expeditions of Lamont Geological Observatory has led to the interpretive diagrams of Heezen and Tharp (1959),[1] and the mapping of the Pacific by expeditions of Scripps Institution of Oceanography has led to interpretive diagrams by H. W. Menard. Both groups used U.S. Hydrographic Office soundings to supplement the scientific surveys. Spectacular color adaptions of these diagrams appeared in *Life* magazine for November 7, 1960. There is much yet to be learned of the topography in the vast oceanic areas and some of the preliminary interpretations of the soundings may prove to be erroneous. For example, the prolongation for a supposed 40,000 miles of the great rift valley discovered by the British on the Mid-Atlantic Ridge is highly speculative. Nevertheless, we now have a vast store of information concerning ocean floor relief and this should prove of great value in developing hypotheses concerning the origin and history of the oceans.

[1] In Heezen *et al.*, 1959; the Physiographic Diagram of the South Atlantic Ocean by the same authors was published by the Geological Society of America in 1962.

Exploration of ocean bottom deposits has been greatly extended since World War I, and virtually all expeditions have included geologists. The collections by the German ship *Meteor* in the early 1920's (Correns *et al.*, 1937; Schott, 1939) provided important information concerning the South Atlantic. About this time the Monaco Institution vessel *Pourquoi Pas* obtained collections along the European coasts (Dangeard, 1928), and the Dutch steamer *Snellius* collected extensively in the waters of the East Indies in 1929 and 1930 (Kuenen, 1935, 1942; Neeb, 1943).

In 1926 the American Petroleum Institute provided funds for a worldwide study of source sediments of petroleum, work conducted by Trask (1932). This led to extensive collections from shelf seas, enclosed basins, and deep open basins along various coasts of the world. The last cruise of the *Carnegie* terminating in the fatal explosion at Apia, Samoa, in 1929 provided deep-sea samples particularly in the Pacific (Revelle, 1944). Samples obtained by the Piggot gun sampler resulted in a line of relatively long cores across the Atlantic (Bradley *et al.*, 1942).

Investigations of sediments by Henry C. Stetson began at Woods Hole Oceanographic Institution in 1929 and were followed a few years later by studies at Scripps Institution of Oceanography. The work on the *Atlantis* (Fig. 1) along the east coast (Stetson, 1938, 1939) and on the *E. W. Scripps* (Fig. 2) off southern California (Revelle and Shepard, 1939) and in the Gulf of California (Anderson *et al.*, 1950) represented the principal pre-World War II field investigations. During the war, studies continued off California for military purposes (Emery *et al.*, 1952), and sediment charts were compiled from sample notations in the war areas (Shepard *et al.*, 1949).

After the war there was a great increase in marine sediment studies, and a considerable fleet of vessels was obtained by Woods Hole and Scripps Institutions (Fig. 3) and one relatively large vessel by Lamont Geological Observatory (Fig. 4), University of Washington, and Texas Agricultural and Mechanical College respectively. All these vessels have been equipped with sampling devices including piston corers that could take cores up to about 60 ft under ideal conditions, rock dredges, and large grab samplers. The extensive sampling accomplished by these vessels and by the round the world expedition of the Swedish vessel *Albatross* and the Danish ship *Galathea* has virtually swamped the sedimentologists with material in recent years. The problem at present is to get enough laboratory investigators to keep up with the constantly growing collection of cores. At the same time the Russians have a large program well under way for the study of sediments in their surrounding seas including the Arctic and the Black Sea, as well

Fig. 1. The 175-ft motor ketch *Atlantis* which conducted most of the investigations of Woods Hole Oceanographic Institution prior to World War II. Photograph by Woods Hole Oceanographic Institution.

Fig. 2. The 104-ft Scripps Institution motor schooner *E. W. Scripps* on which most of the Institution work in marine geology was accomplished prior to World War II.

Fig. 3. The 134-ft Scripps Institution motor ship *Spencer F. Baird* acquired after World War II and used extensively all over the Pacific in marine geology operations. Note the high **A** frame used in piston coring operations.

Fig. 4. The 202-ft motor schooner *Vema* belonging to Lamont Geological Observatory and used extensively in operations all over the North and South Atlantic and in the Indian Ocean. Courtesy of B. C. Heezen.

as in the ocean around Antarctica and in the principal oceans of the world. The two huge Soviet research vessels *Vitiaz* and *Lomonosov* have many large well-equipped laboratories for all the fields of oceanography. Most of their reports are in Russian but a number of brief summaries have now appeared in English (see for example *Marine Geology*, 1960).

Geophysical investigations began with Fridtjof Nansen's Polar Expedition of 1893–96 when he measured gravity while his vessel was frozen into the polar ice. Later Vening Meinesz (1932, 1934) made measurements in a Dutch submarine. This was followed still later by the use of charges of dynamite to probe by sound the substructure of the ocean floor (Ewing *et al.*, 1940). The geophysical operations have increased enormously since the end of World War II so that now we have a good foundation of records for determining the nature of the layers that underlie the ocean floor. The striking difference between ocean and continents in crustal thickness has been perhaps the most important discovery and has led to the initiation of the Mohole project to drill through the crust to the underlying mantle in the deep ocean where the crust is particularly thin. No less important has been the discovery that the sediments of the deep ocean constitute a relatively thin layer and in some places are virtually missing, a fact further confirmed by coring.

Photography of the sea bottom at depths of less than 150 fathoms was initiated by Ewing in about 1940 and was used during the war in the hunt for German submarines. Shortly after the war it was appreciated that no serious obstacle would be encountered in building camera cases that would operate at much greater depth without leaking. Beginning in about 1950 photographs have been taken at great ocean depths using strobe lights with cameras that will take a long series of flash shots of the bottom. Among interesting results has been the establishment that ripple marks occur at all depths, being particularly common on the summits of seamounts regardless of their depth.

The descent of man into the deep ocean has also progressed in an amazing fashion since World War II. As a result of secret developments by the Frenchmen Cousteau and Gagnon during the German occupation, aqualungs now generally called SCUBA allowing free diving with self-contained air supplies have become commonplace, and extensive exploration down to depths of almost 50 fathoms has been carried on by teams of geologists (Dill, 1958). Deep diving bells were developed by William Beebe as far back as 1930, but making contact with the bottom was not believed at all safe until the free diving bathyscaph was developed by Auguste Piccard. With this diving balloon using gasoline in its envelope the greatest depths of

the ocean have been reached (Piccard and Dietz, 1961). More maneu-
verable types of diving equipment like Cousteau's *soupcoupe* or diving
saucer are being developed and we should expect to see some important
advances in underwater exploration in the near future.

Important progress has been made in recent years in the understanding of wave mechanics and the mechanics of fluid motion as they
relate to sediment transportation and beach erosion. Geochemistry
has solved many problems concerning the nature of deep-sea clays and
diagenetic action on the sea floor.

One of the most difficult problems that confronts an oceanographer
is the choice of units of measurement. There is certainly a trend among
American scientists toward the use of the metric system. Unfortunately, however, the exclusive use of this system causes considerable
hardship to work in marine geology because virtually all the charts
from which observations are drawn have depths in fathoms and hence
the only practical method of contouring is with intervals in fathoms.
Furthermore, the greater part of the field work from oceanographic
institutions has involved the use of echo sounding devices with records
in fathoms. The conversion of all this information would be a stagger-
ing task. Accordingly, in most places fathoms have been used in text
discussions along with nautical miles equal to one minute of latitude
and approximately 1000 fathoms. This last relation allows easy
determination of percent slopes. Fathoms and nautical miles are well
known to most continental European scientists and are certainly
better known than feet and statute miles. In discussions of sediment
parameters and of units of force, the metric scale was adopted because
of general usage and convenience. Also charts taken from nations
using meters are given in the metric scales. On the other hand,
following the usual practice in the United States measures relative to
waves are given in feet, and currents are expressed either in knots or
feet per second. A convenient conversion is 50 cm/sec = 1 knot and
30 cm/sec = 1 ft/sec.

Thus there appears to be some inconsistency in the use of scales, an
inconsistency which is shared by most American writers dealing with
the ocean. This seems unavoidable, and conversion tables in Appendix
B will help to straighten out the difficulty.

# CHAPTER II

# METHODS AND INSTRUMENTATION FOR EXPLORING THE OCEAN FLOOR

### Introduction

Since the first edition of this book, there have been many new spectacular developments in instrumentation; yet many more are still needed. Thus accurate location of positions many hundreds of miles at sea is now possible; descent to the lowest depths of the ocean has been made; and, without the dangers inherent in diving, photographs of any place on the ocean floor can be taken by lowering cameras. Plans are being made to drill into the floor at great ocean depths; sound waves can be used to study the deep layers under the ocean even more effectively than is possible under the continents; and we have learned how to date various levels in the cores from the sea floor. On the other hand, the cores that we take on the ocean floor, although somewhat longer than they were in the early postwar years, are still likely to be disturbed by the coring process, particularly where sand is encountered.[1] Dredges still get hung up on the bottom, requiring great lengths of time for recovery or even their abandonment. Many ideas have been tried in the measuring of bottom currents, but there is still no good device that can give a lengthy record of the current conditions on the sea floor.

In the earlier edition, it was stated that simple devices were proving to be the most effective. In some respects that is not true any longer; but we are still having trouble with complicated instruments, and often have to fall back on the very simplest of types to get results.

### Obtaining Positions at Sea for Scientific Work

It is now much easier to obtain good positions in oceanographic work, but it has been the writer's observation that scientists commonly fail to get very good locations for their work even when such pinpointing is necessary for the problem they are investigating.

[1] This may now be avoided with the use of a box corer (Reineck, 1963), modified for great depths according to A. H. Bouma.

9

Almost all scientific laboratory vessels are now equipped with gyrocompasses and repeaters on each wing of the bridge. This greatly increases the accuracy when locating by bearings. For best results in using this method it is advisable to take three or more bearings so as to obtain an average position by the intersection of lines. Otherwise the unavoidable swinging of the compass during the operation or the misreading of one bearing may cause considerable inaccuracy. When operating in an area where land control points are based on old surveys whose accuracy was not likely to have been as great as in modern surveys, the best results are obtained by taking as many bearings as possible, plotting them all, and using the best concentration of line crossings.

A very accurate method comes from measuring the horizontal angles between three well-located objects by sextants. Unless the angles are small or the objects used in the angles are on or close to the circumference of a circle in which the vessel is also located (Fig. 5), sextant angles will provide great accuracy. These are plotted by means of a

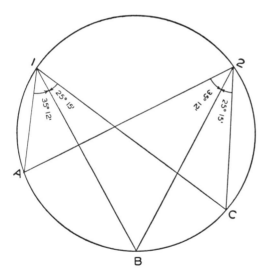

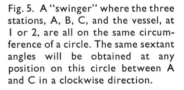

Fig. 5. A "swinger" where the three stations, A, B, C, and the vessel, at 1 or 2, are all on the same circumference of a circle. The same sextant angles will be obtained at any position on this circle between A and C in a clockwise direction.

three-arm protractor. Using two sextants which are "shot" simultaneously adds additional value to the method because there is no lag between the time of the observation and the mark placed on the sounding record whereas the pelorus bearings are necessarily taken at slight time intervals one from the other which produces inaccuracies when the vessel is moving. Also the rolling of the vessel is likely to swing the compass away from its correct azimuth, but a good sextant reader should have little if any inaccuracy as the result of rolling.

Even gyrocompasses may have an error and require frequent checking by astronomical bearings. To an experienced navigator the plotting of sextant angles is almost as fast as plotting bearings. In the use of the sextant it is important to see that there is no index error and that the sextant is in good adjustment.

When bearings and sextant angles are not possible, a good fix often can be obtained by means of radar out to the line of sight or farther under some refraction conditions. Most oceanographic vessels are now equipped with this device. Radar (short for radio direction and range) operates at 3000 to 10,000 megacycles a second with a wavelength of approximately 3–10 cm. With the typical ship radar considerable more accuracy is likely to exist in ranges (about 20 to 100 yd) than in bearings (several degrees) although both should be taken when possible. As in the case of bearings, it is very important to take three or more ranges and bearings so as to obtain the best intersection of the arcs of distance and of the lines of bearing. A large pair of dividers a meter or more in length should be available for plotting ranges. Checking of the radar should be made frequently by taking a series of points while the vessel is lying stationary. Most radars need considerable adjustment, and a technician trained in this work should accompany expeditions when possible.

Several other electronic position finders are now on the market. These have largely replaced the radio acoustic ranging method, referred to in the first edition of this book, which had rather large inaccuracies because it relied on sound waves in water that have somewhat variable speed and may fail to reach the target because of refraction, particularly where operating outside the good reflecting conditions that characterize the continental shelf.

The electronic system used most widely in navigation is Loran (*Electronics*, 1945). This uses hyperbolic lines of position and operates on 1700 to 2000 kc with a wavelength of 178 to 150 m. If land stations are located so as to subtend large angles from the vessel the method gives an accuracy similar to that of average star sights out to about 850 miles in the daytime and 600 at night when operating on ground waves, but up to 1600 miles at night using the sky wave. Shoran operates on 210 to 320 megacycles per second, with wavelengths of 1.43 to 0.94 m. Like radar it is limited to line of sight but extends to about 180 miles with 12,000-ft elevation of stations (found in Alaska, for example). It has a precision of ±50 ft. Two beacons have to be located on shore at high points. Considerable skill is required for operation. This accurate method has now been replaced by several other systems that are used extensively for aircraft, for marine surveying, and marine petroleum operations. These include Raydist,

Decca, Map, Lorac, and Moran. A brief description of two of them follows:

*Raydist* (Hastings, 1947) is based on a continuous wave system and on the counting of interference patterns of electromagnetic radiations. It measures distances to two stations and makes use of the Doppler effect. The basic frequency is 12 megacycles a second and the wavelength is 25 m. Normal range is about 35 miles but this can be extended to 200 miles. Accuracy is one part in 5000 ± 2 ft. Two land stations are necessary which will ordinarily require operators.

*Decca* (Anonymous, 1946) and *Delrac* are used for much longer ranges—out to about 1500 miles. This method measures hyperbolic distances by using a 20- to 200-kc wave with a wavelength of 1500 to 15,000 m. At least two continuous land transmitters are necessary with well-trained operators. The accuracy is large with a practical error estimated at 0.05 mile for a distance of 400 miles.

*Satellite navigation* is apparently going to be the method of the future for navigating out beyond shore station control. The satellites should become available soon, but it may be some time before practical methods have been devised so that the method can be put into operation for oceanographic work.

Where good sounding charts exist, and this applies to all the echo sounding surveys off the coasts of the United States despite any minor inaccuracies such as were discussed previously, it frequently is possible to obtain positions by running sounding lines between work stations. If these soundings are plotted on strips of paper to the same scale as the chart and the strips are superimposed onto the chart, a place where a fit can be made can be found by moving the paper strip around in the general vicinity, keeping it oriented along the line of course. The method is illustrated in Fig. 6. The fit often will not be accurate because the speed and course may not be properly estimated owing to some current. In this case the soundings can be stretched or compressed somewhat, and then a fit will be discovered. The method is totally impractical, of course, where horizontal bottom is encountered. Off the California coast no trouble of that sort has been found, so that in the work of Scripps Institution vessels the sounding method almost invariably has proved reliable when properly applied. In work with American Petroleum Institute Project 51 the sounding method proved very valuable on the continental shelf (J. R. Curray, personal communication). Navigators used to other methods may object at first to this innovation and prefer to use such methods as radio bearings, but comparison of results off southern California have shown that the sounding method is superior in most cases except in close proximity to radio stations. If the echo sounder is not working

it will be found helpful to take wire soundings at as frequent intervals
as practical in order to maintain a position.

When out of sight of land a navigator may have to rely on *dead
reckoning,* which means plotting the course, reading the ship's log to
tell how far the ship has run since a fix was obtained, and correcting
so far as possible for currents or wind drifts. It is important to know
the vessel's speed by testing on mile ranges with runs in both directions
averaged. When no shore control is possible in oceanographic work,
as is usually the case, the use of celestial navigation is necessary,

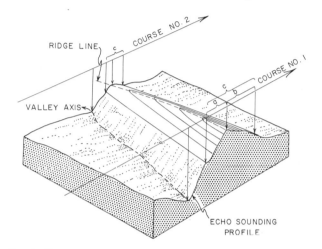

Fig. 6. Showing how a position can be obtained by sounding
lines where valleys and ridges are traversed. From Adams (1939).

although one should not expect high accuracy in this method except
when conditions are very favorable, that is, having a clear horizon,
little or no overcast sky, and a smooth sea. Star sights are taken at
dawn and dusk when the horizon and celestial bodies can both be seen.
At such times a position with an error of about a quarter of a mile
may be obtained under ideal conditions. Sun lines during the day are
quite inaccurate but better than nothing. Dead reckoning is often
more accurate, judging from closing errors, than celestial navigation
where courses of rather short duration are run out of touch with land
fixes.

**Sounding Methods**

Almost all soundings are now obtained by sound impulse, known as
echo soundings. The devices are ordinarily set at a speed of 4800 feet
(800 fathoms) a second. For precise echo sounding it is absolutely

necessary to have a frequency-regulated power source. Slight variations will cause the speed of the recorder drive motor to change and
result in relatively large errors in the recording of the travel time
between outgoing and incoming sound impulses. These errors appear
as sudden drops or rises on the echogram. Most survey echo sounders
now have electronic frequency and voltage control devices to prevent
such error. However, at sea, the scientist must be constantly aware of
the danger of the failure of these regulators and be able to distinguish
a power frequency shift from a topographic change on the bottom.
Many, perhaps most, of the lines of soundings taken across the ocean
up to about 1950 were obtained without a frequency regulator so that
the soundings are confusing because of errors, and therefore quite
useless in constructing good charts. It is only since the constant
frequency devices have been acquired that it has become possible to
obtain even reasonably good profiles of the deep ocean.

Another difficulty with earlier versions of echo sounders has been
that they record on too small a scale so that they do not show minor
irregularities. The older instruments generally had a large scale for
shallow depths and a small scale for great depths. The precision depth
recorders, PDR or PGR (Luskin *et al.*, 1954), show details of the
bottom with somewhat less than one fathom of relief at any depth.
A wide scale of 0–400 fathoms is used, and the record starts over again
at 400 running to 800 and so on to the greatest depth reached (Fig. 7).
The method does not give the absolute depths with this accuracy
because speed of sound is not well known throughout the water column.
However, with return to the same position and use of the same
frequency, the same depth should be obtained except for such minor
differences as may come from changes of temperatures or changes in
salinity and of course height of tide. So far as we know, significant
changes occur only in near surface water. Sound travels faster the
higher the salinity, the higher the temperature, and the higher the
pressure, but the differences are not very great.

**Correction of Soundings.**   One of the problems confronting both the
surveyor and the scientist relative to echo soundings is whether or
not to apply corrections so as to give true depths rather than the
depths recorded using a velocity of 4800 ft/sec. It is of considerable
interest to know the greatest depths in the ocean so that expeditions
that are investigating these depths should apply corrections for
sound velocities. On the other hand, to make soundings useful for
navigation for vessels operating with echo sounders set for 4800 ft/sec,
much can be said in favor of publishing uncorrected soundings. For
example, if a vessel wishes to obtain a position on an approach to a
harbor by means of echo soundings it may find that it is crossing a

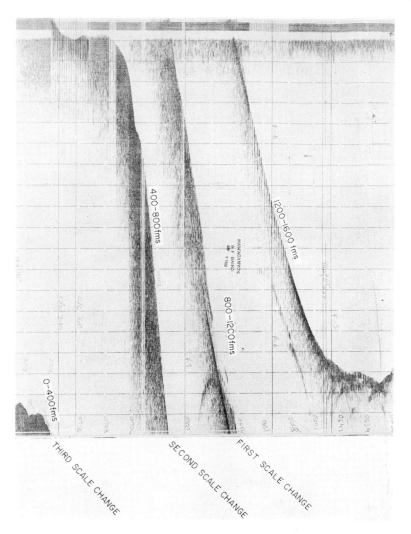

Fig. 7. Showing how continuous fathograms of a PDR are obtained beyond the 400-fathom depth of the lower margin. Three scale shifts (0–400, 400–800, and 800–1200) are included.

valley, a ridge, or a trough with an even axial slope, and hence it can determine its position by the depth of the crossing. If the published depths are corrected so that they do not agree with the fathometer of the vessel, the navigator may be thrown off position. As an example, the corrected depths in crossing San Diego Trough (Fig. 8) are offset by almost a mile from the uncorrected depths so a vessel using a good survey for this approach would be thrown off course by

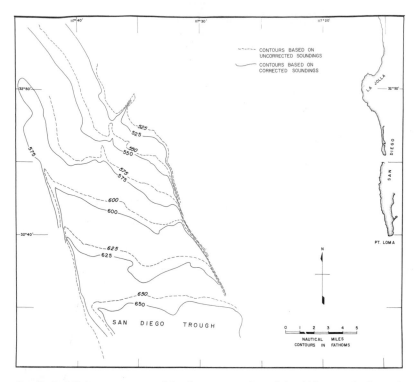

Fig. 8. A shift in contours resulting from correction of depth for speed of sound. Because ship fathograms used for navigation lack corrections, better positions would be obtained from chart with uncorrected soundings. In this case nearly a mile of position error could result from the corrected version.

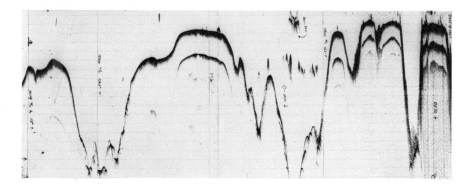

Fig. 9. The inverted V's which are commonly observed at the bottom of a submarine canyon or other narrow depression. The depth of the top of the inverted V is usually close to the true depth.

this distance unless the navigator went through the laborious task of applying corrections for sound. It is well for mariners to bear in mind that most charts, such as those of the U.S. Coast and Geodetic Survey, do apply corrections. Actually, however, there are few places where the corrections will interfere seriously with echo sounder navigation.

Another inaccuracy in echo soundings comes from the fact that the sound beam sent out by the transducer or sound head has a spread in most cases of about 30° from the vertical on both sides. As a result, where there is a steep submarine slope, the echo usually comes from the nearest point on the slope rather than from the bottom directly beneath the vessel. This can make a large difference. However, in crossing a valley it is often possible to get the true valley floor depth by observing a curved surface that often rises as an arc beneath the echoes coming from the walls (Fig. 9). This may come in with a strong echo when the center of the valley is crossed. Narrow beam echo sounders are now being constructed and the early tests show promising results.

### Sampling Devices

In recent years considerable progress has been made in sampling the bottom but there still are serious difficulties, particularly in obtaining good undisturbed samples on hard sand bottom. Also, the sampling of the deep-sea floor still takes so much time that a discouragingly small amount of material can come from a day's work. We have not yet learned to take more than one or at most two samples for each lowering. A device developed by D. G. Moore (1961c) may solve this problem to some extent. He drops free corers that contain expendable weights and casings (or barrels) and have core liners that are returned to the surface by a float after becoming detached from the core barrel by a release mechanism that actuates after a certain predetermined interval. This leaves the core barrel and weights in the bottom. With the free corer it is possible, also, to take closely spaced cores with accurately determined spacing.

**Grab or Snapper Samples.** For sampling by the grab or snapper method the clam shell snappers are still used extensively. Orange peel buckets (Fig. 10a) with a canvas top to stop stirring during the return to the surface have proved to be satisfactory down to depths of 100 and even 200 fathoms. The samples taken by the Navy Electronics Laboratory snapper (La Fond and Dietz, 1948) are somewhat less disturbed than those of the orange peel but generally not as large. For very large samples the van Veen or the Petersen grabs

A                                              B

Fig. 10. (*a*) An orange peel sampler in open position. The release shown at the top allows the sampler to close, and the canvas cover helps prevent the escape of sediment while returning to the surface. (*b*) Petersen grab sampler that permits the obtaining of a large bottom sample from near the floor.

(Fig. 10*b*) are quite effective. The van Veen sampler often preserves layering moderately well and the top can be opened so as to take a core of the sample before extruding it into a sieve or bucket.

The jaws of all snappers are likely to become bent or offset so they will not close tight. Most snappers will not work very well if there is a large wire angle because they tend to land on the side and hence do not dig into the bottom. Furthermore, snappers often fail to give a representative sample because of gravel holding open the jaws and allowing fine sediment to escape. An underway sampler like that described by Worzel (1948) and one developed by K. O. Emery and A. R. Champion (1948) are moderately successful in taking small samples without stopping the way of the vessel. They can be used only in shallow water and easily get out of adjustment.

**Coring Devices.**   Gravity corers are still used rather commonly despite the considerable advantage of piston coring. The Phleger corer (Fig. 11) is a small practical means of obtaining short core samples and can be used manually from small boats. Another light coring device was developed by Mackereth (1958). This makes use of "hydrostatic pressure operating on a cylindrical anchor chamber embedded in the sediment." It can be used only in relatively shallow water. The core is obtained in a plastic liner which allows easy storage. Most small gravity corers obtain a core of 2.5 cm diameter, but 5- or 6.5-cm core barrels can be used just as easily and will ordinarily obtain somewhat longer cores.

Because of danger of fouling wire it is unwise to lower a core tube at high speed. For this reason the free-fall method of coring (Hvorslev and Stetson, 1946) has proved helpful in increasing the velocity and momentum of the core tube at the time of hitting bottom (Fig. 12). The device is lowered rather slowly when near the bottom and a suspended weight hits first, releasing a lever arm that allows the core barrel to fall freely for a few feet and sink rather deeper into the bottom than a more slowly falling attached corer. Another advantage is that it is extremely difficult to tell when the bottom is reached in great depths except from the sudden loss of weight in a free-fall corer, unless a Sonar Pinger or a ball breaker is used (see below).

The piston corer invented by Kullenberg (1947) also falls freely after being released by the same method as the Hvorslev and Stetson corer. The piston in the inside of the core tube remains attached to the wire so that the core tube falls past the piston and hence avoids serious friction in taking a core (Fig. 12). A number of modifications of the Kullenberg device have been made by Maurice Ewing and by Silverman and Whaley (1952).

A serious difficulty in piston coring has existed whenever the core barrel is not completely filled during the free fall. In such cases the lifting of the apparatus by pulling on the piston tends to raise the core in the barrel and suck in bottom material or water from below. Thus the core is deformed by being pulled up through the barrel, and material of unknown length is added to the bottom. A common result is that the top of the core is lost, particularly if it consists of soft mobile mud overlying sand, and the lower portion has vertical flow lines indicative of the flow of material into the barrel during retraction. The result is that many cores have a deceptive appearance. The nature of the top of the core can often be ascertained by study of the material obtained in a small gravity corer used as a pilot weight. The two cores may be comparable provided the piston was at the top and the tube was filled before retraction. In this case the pilot core ordinarily will

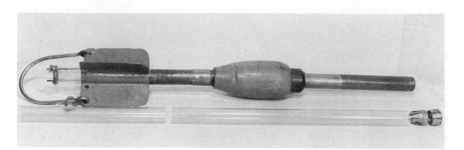

Fig. 11. Phleger bottom sampler which is used to obtain short cores. Note the core liner and core catcher (right) which helps prevent escape of sediment.

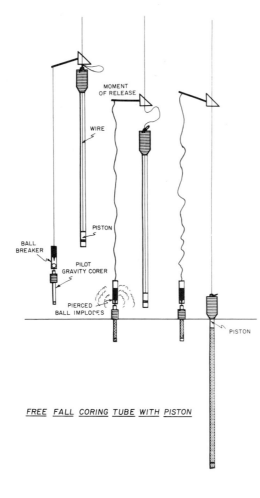

MOMENT
OF RELEASE

WIRE

PISTON

BALL
BREAKER

PILOT
GRAVITY CORER

PIERCED
BALL IMPLODES

PISTON

FREE FALL CORING TUBE WITH PISTON

Fig. 12. Operation of the free-fall method of coring and the action of the piston in producing a long core by reducing friction on the inside of the core tube. Ball breaker is also included.

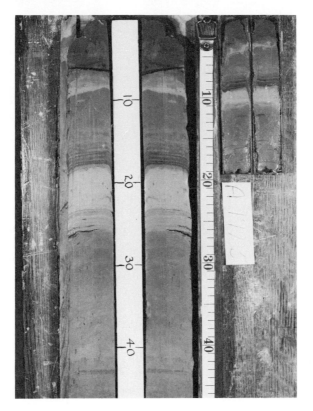

Fig. 13. An example of the shortening of layers in a gravity core (right) compared to a piston core (left). These cores were taken respectively with a pilot core and the piston core, as illustrated in Fig. 12. It is unusual that a piston core shows as much of the top layer as indicated in this core by Lamont Geological Observatory. Photo from Lamont Geological Observatory.

be considerably shorter than the piston core (Fig. 13). The difference is probably the result of shortening of the pilot core due to pushing aside some of the material (Emery and Dietz, 1941), whereas the piston core has had only minor changes of length.

To overcome the difficulty of sucking up the core into a partially filled tube it is necessary to have a device that will lift the core tube without pulling up the piston. A workable scheme to accomplish this has been devised by Emery and Broussard (1954) by immobilizing the piston after the core barrel has completed penetration of the sediments. This is accomplished by dropping a messenger on the winch cable after the corer hits the bottom in order to disarm the mechanism so that it is pulled from the bottom and to the surface by the top of the corer rather than by a cable attached to the piston. Preliminary investigations suggest, however, that such a method is limited to work in shallow water on continental shelves. A better method for deep water was devised by Bader and Paquette (1955). This includes a cable-clamping device which immobilizes the piston after the core barrel has penetrated into the sediments. As a result the core is not disturbed by upward movement of the piston during withdrawal.

When no core liner is used, considerable distortion comes from the extrusion of cores by forcing them out of the core tube with a hydraulic jack. This process tends to squeeze the more plastic layers along the sides and often deforms the sand layers by shearing. It seems likely that the advantage of obtaining a longer core because of absence of the extra friction from using liners is more than offset by the results of deformation. Furthermore, thick sand layers may prove impossible to remove without the use of a powerful stream from a hose which destroys the core. Even with a core liner a sand layer may be considerably deformed unless held in a vertical position, a difficult operation.

Kullenberg (1955) has maintained that it is possible to obtain extremely long cores in soft bottoms by the use of a piston coring device that trips only after it has penetrated for some distance. The friction which stops a core barrel from penetrating comes very largely from the walls rather than from the penetration of the lower end of the tube. Therefore, by building a very heavy corer without great length (Fig. 14) it is possible for a corer to penetrate until the sediment becomes sufficiently compact to stop the descent. A rope unwinds as the core tube sinks until a given depth is attained. At that point the piston is stopped and the core tube keeps falling, so that the piston action allows the taking of a core at a depth below the bottom roughly equivalent to the length of the rope. In this way only a deep section will be obtained in the core tube, but this can be supplemented by taking an ordinary piston core above or by using a shorter length of rope. Considerable experimenting will no doubt be necessary before the device can be operated successfully. Kullenberg has not reported results beyond some trial attempts, but it is to be hoped that further use of the device will be forthcoming.

Reports from the Soviet Union (Zenkevitch, 1955) indicate that cores up to 34 m in length have been obtained on the *Vitiaz* without any serious distortion. Their device is somewhat like that of an earlier model by Varney and Redwine (1937). It makes use of an evacuated chamber at the top which is opened from below when the corer hits bottom allowing the core to move up into the core tube to replace the

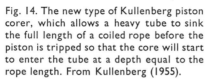

Fig. 14. The new type of Kullenberg piston corer, which allows a heavy tube to sink the full length of a coiled rope before the piston is tripped so that the core will start to enter the tube at a depth equal to the rope length. From Kullenberg (1955).

low pressure in the chamber above. The great problem in such a device must come from sucking in material from the sides due to the vacuum effect. Presumably this has been overcome by the Soviet scientists.

Obtaining cores from a hard surface with packed sand generally has proved impossible by either gravity or piston coring. This may be overcome by the use of a vibrator that operates on the corer after it has hit bottom. Such a device has been used by the Soviet Union in coring (Kudinov, 1957). The vibration acting like a jack hammer forces the corer into the sand. It may be necessary to have the device on a tripod that will hold it vertically during the operation on the bottom.

Another problem in coring has been to prevent the loss of the core by leakage from the bottom on the way to the surface. The building of a good core catcher has not proved easy. The common type consisting of plastic or metal leaves (Fig. 11) that fold in to prevent the core from escaping is fairly successful in mud cores but does not make a perfect seal so that sandy sediments are very likely to flow out through the leaves during the raising of the core tube to the surface. The use of a piece of cloth attached to the catcher on the inside is somewhat helpful, but not an entire success. The Soviets have a tight-fitting catcher that is said to be practical and G. O. S. Arrhenius has recently devised a somewhat similar catcher that also fills the tube during withdrawal sufficiently to stop sediment from escaping (Fig. 15). While operating in the Mediterranean on the French ship *Elie Monier*, I suggested another scheme that helped the situation. Having observed that much of the core escaped from the tube after it was pulled above the surface we had swimmers dive over with a large cork and push it

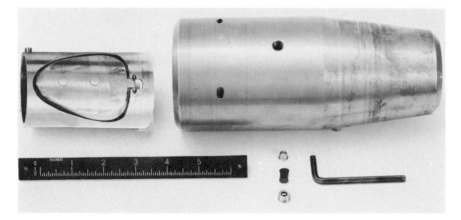

Fig. 15. Core catcher developed by G. O. S. Arrhenius which is effective in stopping most of the escape of sand from core barrels of various sizes. In returning to the surface the saucer-shaped plate fills the core nose.

into the bottom of the core tube before bringing the tube above the surface.

Rock has been cored largely where the core tube passed through the entire sediment thickness and still had sufficient velocity to take a very small core of the underlying rock. Ordinarily the core nose is damaged and often the barrel is bent. Off the California coast, however, rock has been cored intentionally by southern California oil companies without damage to the instrument. Here very short core barrels of hard steel are used and a few inches of rock obtained. For greater penetration a drilling rig will presumably be necessary (see p. 47).

In shallow water it is not difficult to jet into the bottom with a hose extending down from the surface. This can be used with or without SCUBA divers.

In summation, coring operations appear to be in a state of flux and there is much promise of obtaining better cores in the future. Unfortunately, the cores that are now available for study were mostly

A       B

Fig. 16. (*a*) The pipe dredge used successfully in coring crystalline rock from the walls of submarine canyons. In the foreground the barrel of a piston corer can be seen. (*b*) A large frame dredge with a chain bag used for catching rock samples broken from the sea floor.

taken by somewhat deficient methods and must be interpreted with care in order not to reach false conclusions.

**Dredging.** The most successful means of obtaining rock from the sea floor has been dredging. Several types of dredges have been devised (Fig. 16). All of these are quite simple in construction. Perhaps the most successful and certainly the least expensive is the pipe dredge consisting of a length of pipe of about 2 m with a diameter of about 50 cm. The front end is sharpened for cutting into the rock, and the rear has a grating built across it with enough space to allow fine sediment to pass through. A bridle is attached to the front end and this in turn to the cable with a swivel in between. A small cloth bag may be fastened into a part of the rear end of the dredge to collect sediment.

Some frame dredges have a solid sheet metal around them and others have a steel mesh bag attached. They vary in size from a jaw opening of about 2 m by 50 cm to about 1 m by 30 cm. The mesh bags have lengths of about 1.5 to 3 m.

The frame dredges have the advantage that they cover more ground than the pipes. On the other hand, they are far more likely to get caught under ledges that cannot be fractured than are the pipe dredges. The steel mesh bags are also rather easily caught and torn despite their strength. The mesh bags, on the other hand, have the advantage that they are likely to retain rock samples which may fall out of the solid dredges due to tipping over. The cost of the dredges is so small compared with operational costs that their loss is of no consequence, and the time factor is all that needs to be considered.

**Techniques in Coring and Dredging.** A few simple techniques have proved very helpful in shipboard operations involving coring and dredging. Relative to coring, it is often important to put the core in an exact position. For example, the center of a canyon may be very narrow so that to obtain a core on the canyon floor it is necessary to have the ship directly over the center at the time when the corer hits bottom. Unless electronic position control is available, this is difficult because of the problem of determining the location of the canyon bottom and because of drifting during the lowering of the device. The best way to find the canyon bottom is to run across the canyon, start up the far wall, and then stop the engines and make a turn first right and then left so as to come back into the wake of the earlier crossing (Fig. 17a). In this way the depth of the bottom as shown on the fathogram from the first crossing will be known and the speed will be so slow when the axis is reached that reversing the engines will bring the vessel to a halt at the deepest spot or, if there has been an overrun, a small amount of backing will bring the vessel into the desired locality. Backing, however, puts bubbles under the sound head and often stops the echo returns for a brief period.

If there is sufficient drift to throw the vessel out of position during the lowering, the winch should be stopped when the corer is fairly near the bottom, and then the vessel should be maneuvered back into position. This is relatively easy if the direction of drift can be determined by a fix or by noting the wire angle. If the wire is leading over the stern, as is true of the large winch wire in most of the Scripps Institution vessels, the vessel is slowly pushed ahead (never backed because of danger of tangling in the propeller) and turned if necessary in order to bring the ship to the desired spot. After getting into position again, the engines are cut, and the wire is allowed to settle to approximately a vertical position before lowering is continued. If the wire leads over the side of the vessel, the maneuver is much more difficult. However, even with such a lead it may be possible to bring the ship very slowly back into position turning only toward the

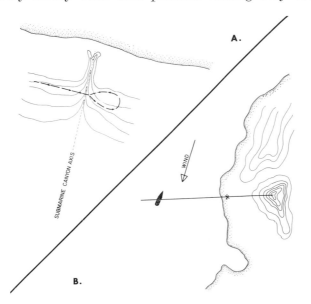

Fig. 17. Positioning methods for sampling. (*a*) A submarine canyon is crossed and the ship is turned in such a way as to get back into the ship's wake; then the ship proceeds very slowly until the same axis depth obtained previously is reached. (*b*) Illustrating how a position may be maintained by heading the vessel into the wind and steaming just sufficiently to keep shore points on range.

direction in which the wire leads, that is to port if the wire is on the port side or to starboard if on the starboard side. This is to prevent the wire from getting under the vessel or even worse into the propeller. Where good ranges are visible on shore, it is often possible to keep the ship in position during lowering by steaming slowly into the wind so as to counteract wind drift and keep the same range (Fig. 17*b*).

In dredging to save time in lowering to great depths it is advisable to have a heavy dredge. A weight attached to the wire in front of the dredge will help hold down the mouth as well as speed up the lowering. The difficulties likely to be encountered in dredging include (1) getting the wire coiled up on bottom by letting out too much or (2) getting

out of position by going ahead during the lowering and dragging
the dredge beyond the point where the sample is desired. To overcome
these difficulties the best plan known to the writer is to get into the
desired position and then let out a length of wire slightly less than
the depth. At that time the vessel is started ahead slowly in the direction in which dredging is desired, and more wire is let out. Speed
should be such that the wire lies at close to a 45° angle from the vertical. Wire is let out until a length of approximately twice the depth,
or at least 1.7 times the depth, is reached. Then the brake is set
sufficiently to stop the wire except when it pulls hard enough to
threaten breaking the cable. Dredging then proceeds with the wire
angle maintained at close to 45°, or more if a heavy weight is used.

Dredging is much easier over the stern than over the side because
dredging from the side of the vessel meets the difficulty that the wire
may get under the counter so that the wire has to be pulled against
the hull and wears off paint or even gets caught on some projection
of the hull. This will occur if the wind is blowing from the side
opposite that on which the wire is let out or if the current is coming
from the direction opposite the wire.

The letting out of wire from the side of the vessel, on the other
hand, may have one considerable advantage. In coring it is possible
to build a cradle aft of the winch that can be used for housing the
coring device and making it much easier to operate than by bringing
a heavy corer in over the stern. The coring operations by Woods
Hole's *Atlantis* and Lamont's *Vema* have been conducted from the
sides of the vessel, and the coring operation has been speeded thereby,
but maneuvering has certainly been hindered during the operations.
The very large A frame on the stern of the *Baird* (Fig. 3) has allowed
the raising of the core barrels sufficiently to get the corer on deck
without difficulty but only after many of the weights have been
removed between each operation. This is time consuming as well as
laborious.[2]

### Geophysical Methods

Great progress has been made in geophysical methods of exploring
the sea floor. The results are discussed in Chapters IX, X, and XV.
Here some of the latest methods will be considered.

**Seismic Refraction.**[3] The most extensively used method of geophysical exploration of the ocean basins has been seismic refraction.

---

[2] Having a movable cradle at the stern now eliminates this problem.

[3] This section was contributed by G. G. Shor, Jr., of Scripps Institution of Oceanography.

The fundamental principles and the field techniques used on land are well described in any standard text on exploration geophysics (see, for instance, Dobrin, 1960). In brief, elastic waves from an explosion are recorded by pressure-sensitive or velocity-sensitive detectors (hydrophones or geophones) with varying distances separating the shot and detector; travel times of the elastic waves recorded are then plotted against separation distance. From the travel-time plot thus obtained it is possible under favorable circumstances to determine the depth to any discontinuity at which there is an increase in velocity of the elastic waves and to determine the velocity in the rock and the dip of the interface.

Seismic refraction studies to determine geologic structure on land and at sea were first suggested by Mallet in 1846; the first successful use on land for exploration purposes was made by Mintrop in 1923 (see Weatherby, 1948). In 1937 Maurice Ewing and his associates, who had previously been studying structure of the Atlantic coastal plain by seismic refraction methods on land, carried their work out into the shallow waters of the continental shelf making little change in the techniques when they passed the shoreline (see Ewing *et al.*, 1940). In the land technique a single charge was placed in a borehole and numerous geophones were placed in a line outward from the shot point. This method proved difficult to use in deep water, although Ewing developed many ingenious methods of getting shots and recorders on bottom. Profiles were short and the depth penetration of the refracted waves was therefore small; in most cases it was sufficient to reach only the base of the sedimentary section.

In the years following 1946 refraction work at sea received a tremendous impetus from the availability of large quantities of high explosives left over from World War II and from the development of rapid methods of work in deep water. Extensive work in the deep ocean is now being done by Lamont Geological Observatory, Scripps Institution of Oceanography, Woods Hole Oceanographic Institution, Cambridge University, and the Soviet Academy of Sciences. The methods used vary in minor details but are essentially as follows.

Two ships participate. One lies to or steams slowly into the wind, with several hydrophones in the water alongside. Small floats to the hydrophones and to the portion of adjacent cables are attached. These floats are carefully adjusted to make the entire assembly either neutrally buoyant (as used by Scripps Institution and the Soviets) or slightly light (Lamont and Woods Hole). In the Scripps Institution apparatus there is an elaborate system of weights and floats used to decouple wave motion of the ship and the surface floats from the hydrophone; in the Lamont and Woods Hole system additional cable is payed out just before a shot is fired to make the hydrophone sink slowly through the water. All these adjustments are made solely to get a maximum signal-to-noise ratio to minimize the size of explosive charge needed. The second ship steams away from the recording ship, dropping explosive charges at close-time intervals, firing them at predetermined depths in the water to take advantage of the "bubble-pulse" phenomenon. When an explosion is set off under water, a gas bubble is created that expands and contracts several times with a period determined by the charge size and the water pressure. If the charge is placed at a depth that is a quarter wavelength for the period of the bubble oscillation, a large percentage of the energy is radiated at a single frequency, and the downward transmission is reinforced by the surface reflected energy. In utilizing this phenomenon and the higher efficiency of generation of elastic waves by a charge in water as compared with a charge in rock, it has been possible to receive refracted signals from a charge of a few hundred pounds of TNT at sea where many tons of explosive would be needed on land.

The arrangement of the lines of shooting depends on the complexity of the geologic structure to be expected. When a line of shots is fired in one direction from a single receiving point, the effects of dip of the refracting horizon cannot be separated from the determination of velocity, and false values for velocity and layer thickness will be obtained. Where the structures are extremely broad, as in the deep ocean basins, two lines of shots along opposing azimuths can be recorded at a single receiving station to eliminate dip effects. In marginal areas, near trenches, ridges, and the continental slope, a reversed profile (sets of shots received at either end of a single line of shooting) is required. Even in this case results can easily be ambiguous if there are changes of dip or faults within the length of the shooting line; the ambiguity can in some cases be resolved by executing several shooting profiles of varying lengths over the same track.

As indicated above, the solution for depth, dip, and velocity involves simplifying assumptions. The assumptions normally made are (1) that there is no layer in the bottom with lower velocity than the layer above it, (2) that all interfaces are planes, and (3) that the velocity of elastic waves varies only with depth, never with horizontal position. As all these assumptions are more or less inaccurate, the validity of a structural section from refraction work will depend a great deal on the simplicity of the underlying structure, the spacing of the shots on each profile, the number of profiles used, and the quality of the records. The interpreter of a set of refraction data should indicate in the body of his paper the degree of reliance that can be placed on the results from a given set of data; unfortunately too often a cross section or summary is taken as gospel and the qualifying remarks are ignored.

**Gravity Measurements.**[4] Measurements of the acceleration of gravity on land or at sea can be interpreted in terms of mass distribution within the earth and therefore in terms of geologic structure. Since gravity surveying requires merely the measurement of a natural field of the earth, it can be a rapid and relatively cheap method of surveying.

The problem of measuring the acceleration of gravity at sea is fundamentally the same as that of measuring it on land. One may measure either the period of a pendulum of constant size and weight, or one may accurately balance the pull of gravity against the pull of a spring of carefully calibrated characteristics. The problems of work at sea are merely those of the large accelerations of the platform on which the measuring device is mounted, accelerations caused by ocean waves. In shallow water this difficulty has been overcome by putting the meter on the sea floor and reading it by telemetering devices.

The problem of compensating for the motion of the ship on which the measuring device was mounted was first solved by Vening Meinesz, who devised a multiple-pendulum system that could compensate for small accelerations of the ship on which the apparatus was mounted. The small amount of motion that could be tolerated, however, limited gravity surveying to submerged submarines and required the use of several hours of ship time for each observation. Despite these limitations, an extensive network of gravity stations has been executed by Vening Meinesz using Netherlands submarines. Other scientists (mostly from the Lamont Geological Observatory) have used American submarines. In recent years several gravity meters have been devised that will record gravity from a large surface ship underway. With this innovation continuous recordings of the value of gravity can be obtained and far less time is needed for the interpretation of the readings.

A unique solution for sub-bottom structure can not be obtained from a gravity profile; for any set of data an infinity of interpretations is theoretically possible. When gravity data are combined with the results of seismic refraction work, however, the layering determined from the refraction studies can be used in the solution of the gravity profile, and the gravity data thus serve to fill in the gaps between the seismic lines.

[4] Also contributed by G. G. Shor, Jr.

**Continuous Acoustic Reflection.**[5]  The recent introduction of the
continuous recording acoustic reflection instrument, or acoustic probe,
has been of great significance in the study of the continental shelves
and upper slopes (McClure *et al.*, 1958). Through the use of these
instruments, previously unobtainable data can be collected that give
the approximate thickness and distribution of sediments and the
internal structure and surface morphology of buried bedrock. This
type of instrument consists essentially of three major units: the

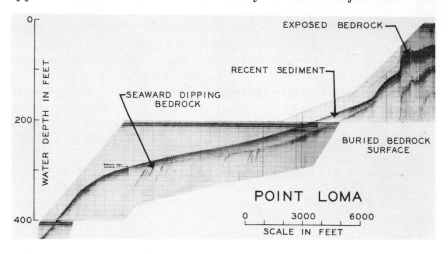

Fig. 18. Record obtained by sonic acoustic reflection that shows the sea floor and the buried
rock surface. Includes also the dip of the rock beneath. Note that the sediment thickens
away from shore but thins near the shelf margin where bedrock is exposed. From Moore
(1960).

sound source, together with its power supply; the receiving hydrophone, or phones, the accompanying amplifiers and receivers; and
the recorder. The short-pulse, high-power, low-frequency sound
sources used enable the sound pulse to penetrate several tens to
several hundreds of feet into the sea floor so that reflections are
received not only from the bottom, as with standard echo sounders,
but from sub-bottom layers as well. A typical record (Fig. 18) shows
reflections from the sediment covered sea floor, from a buried bedrock
surface, and from stratification within the bedrock.

The greatest variation among the several instruments designed for
detecting and recording sub-bottom reflections is the type of repetitive
underwater sound source used and the corresponding difference in
frequency. In general, the lower frequency devices result in greater

[5] This section was contributed by D. G. Moore of the U.S. Navy Electronics
Laboratory.

penetration into the bottom but give relatively poor definition of the smaller structural features. Sound sources currently in use include: (1) gas mixture exploders (Beckmann *et al.*, 1959), which give best results in the frequency range of 50 to 100 cps; (2) the discharge of powerful electric arcs (Arcer) using various underwater electrode systems, which give most effective reception in the range of 100 to 500 cps; (3) an aluminum disk piston transducer activated by an

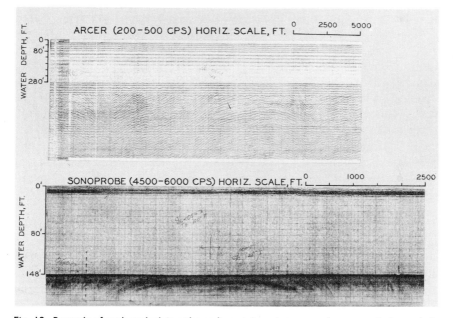

Fig. 19. Records of rock underlying the sediment by using a gas mixture exploder and the sonar probe. These records were obtained over folded Cretaceous rocks that underlie the Chukchi Sea north of the Brooks Range of Alaska. From Moore (1961a).

electromotive force (developed by H. E. Edgerton of Massachusetts Institute of Technology and marketed by Edgerton, Germeshausen and Grier of Boston, Mass. as "Thumper" transducer). This has a power peak in the range of 500 to 2500 cps; (4) a specialized magnetostriction transducer (part of the "Substrata Acoustic Probe" system developed by Magnolia Petroleum Company and known commercially as the Sonoprobe) that has its peak power at about 4000 cps and is effective in the range of 3000 to 8000 cps (McClure *et al.*, 1958); and (5) use of high explosives fired at short intervals. Because of the frequency differences, the records produced by these various systems are quite different in appearance (Fig. 19). The higher frequency records are more easily interpreted and more realistically represent individual stratification but generally show less penetration into the sea floor. No one single sound source is able to satisfy requirements for all acoustic reflection studies.

Because of the obvious application of acoustic reflection techniques to offshore oil exploration and engineering surveys, developments in the field have been very rapid. It seems quite probable that continued improvements in instruments and sound sources will make the continuous recording acoustic reflection instrument a standard and necessary tool in studies of the continental margins.

**Acoustic Sampler.** The nature of sediment can be determined to some extent by pulling a "sound fish" over the bottom (La Fond *et al.*, 1950). This consists of a hydrophone in a watertight container connected by a cable that houses an electric conductor of high tensile strength. This can be dragged along the bottom at the end of the cable. The different types of sound made by passing over rock, sand, gravel, and mud can be monitored with the listening equipment on the deck and hence differentiated. According to La Fond *et al.*, "Rock makes continuous bongs or clangs, sand makes a heavy scraping or rasping noise, and mud makes a quiet swishing noise." This instrument is particularly useful for drawing sediment boundaries which are very difficult to obtain from spot samples.

**Geomagnetic Measurements.**[6] The easiest and the cheapest method of geophysical investigation of the ocean floor consists of towing a total intensity magnetometer either by an airplane or by a ship. The ship has the advantage of taking an echogram at the same time. Much valuable information can be obtained from routine operation of the magnetometer when the ship is traveling to a distant destination or between oceanographic stations. As often as possible, the ship should be made to sail boxlike patterns so that the strike of the magnetic and topographic contours can be mapped. The sensitive element of magnetometer is towed about two or three ship lengths astern. It is usually hauled aboard when the ship is stopped so the cable does not foul with the screws or other oceanographic equipment. Bathythermographs, plankton nets, and midwater trawls can be towed while streaming the magnetometer. Since the magnetometer often has to be hauled in, it is convenient to roll up the cable on the drum of an electrically powered winch.

In the past a modified form of the World War II antisubmarine airborne magnetometer was used at sea. At present, various varieties of the proton-free precession magnetometer first developed by Varian Associates of Palo Alto, California, are being used. The sensitive

[6] This section was contributed by Victor Vacquier of Scripps Institution of Oceanography.

element of this instrument consists of a coil wound around a bottle filled with some hydrogenous liquid like water. A strong direct current is passed through the coil for about 5 seconds to align the axes of the protons generally in the liquid along the axis of the coil. After the current is shut off, the coil is connected to an amplifier and the frequency of a very weak signal, which persists for a few seconds, is measured by a counter. The signal is produced by the precession of aligned protons (which possess both magnetic and angular momenta) about the total magnetic field vector of the earth. The instrument is less complex than the modern echo sounding equipment and is no more difficult to operate and to maintain aboard ship. Oceanographic institutions that tow magnetometers have built their own instruments. The U.S. Coast and Geodetic Survey is using magnetometers manufactured by Varian Associates.

Geomagnetic measurements at sea can probe the constitution of the ocean floor several kilometers below its surface. From seismic refraction shooting we know that in the deep ocean the layer of mud and sedimentary rock is between about 200 and 2000 m thick. The larger figure is valid where the intermediate seismic velocity layer (5.1 km/sec) is limestone instead of volcanics. These sedimentary layers rest on highly magnetic igneous rock, which is probably basalt. When this basaltic shell is uniform in thickness and in its magnetic properties over areas that are large when compared to the depth of the ocean, the magnetic field measured by a ship-towed magnetometer is smooth. Quite often, however, it is rough, indicating abrupt lateral changes of magnetic properties in the crystalline basement which can only be the boundaries between igneous rock bodies, the horizontal dimensions of which are generally larger than the depth of the ocean. The thickness of these bodies can extend downward to where the rocks are too hot to be magnetic (575° C), but the curvatures of the magnetic anomalies produced by some of them require that they be not over a few kilometers thick and that their upper surface be no deeper than 2 km from the surface of the ocean floor. On the other hand, they cannot be less than 1.5 km thick, for that would call for an unusually large contrast in magnetic properties.

The only important magnetic mineral in igneous rocks is magnetite. A substantial magnetic anomaly can arise from a contact between two rock masses differing in their magnetite content by 1 percent. The magnetization of a rock also depends on the direction and the magnitude of the geomagnetic field at the time the rock cooled from dull red heat. The cooling magnetizes the rock proportionately to the magnitude of this ancient field, the direction of which may be quite different in a span of only 500 years from what it is now. Large magnetic anomalies can thus arise from contacts of rock units which are mineralogically identical.

## Underwater Mapping and Observations of the Sea Floor by Geologists[7]

**Diving in Geology.** The use of diving to obtain data from the sea floor is not new. Divers equipped with conventional "hard hat" diving gear have been making underwater geological observations of footings for bridges and other engineering structures at least since the early part of the eighteenth century. More recently, interesting results were obtained by Russian divers in the Black Sea (Klenova, 1948, p. 31) and by Shepard (1949), who, working with a diver equipped with underwater telephone communication to the surface, was able to investigate indirectly the geologic nature of sedimentation occurring in the head of Scripps Submarine Canyon. Geologists did not make the observations, and they were thus limited in their professional scope. It was not until the advent of self-contained underwater-breathing apparatus, SCUBA, that diving was used on a large scale in marine geology and proved what a great advantage it is for the geologist to make his own *in situ* observations. Its wide acceptance and use by geologists has shown that "it is much easier to teach a geologist to be a diver than a diver to be a geologist."

Compared with other methods of studying the oceans, diving with SCUBA to conduct scientific investigations of the sea floor is a relatively new technique. It began in the United States in the early part of 1949, soon after the first Aqua-Lung was introduced into this country from France by its co-inventor Jacques-Yves Cousteau (see Cousteau and Dumas, 1950). It was not, however, until 1951 that SCUBA came into general use as a tool for geologists (Dill and Shumway, 1954). The first use in the field of geology was in the study of sedimentation along the coast of southern California (Fisher and Mills, 1952) and of seasonal variation in sediment level in the heads of submarine canyons (Limbaugh and Shepard, 1957; Chamberlain, 1960). It became apparent to the early users of this equipment that it had useful commercial applications, especially in areas where there are rock outcrops and contacts exposed on the sea floor permitting the geologist to conduct underwater field mapping. One of the first organized field mapping projects by SCUBA-equipped geologists was conducted in 1953 for the purpose of studying in detail the sea floor geology at several offshore locations at San Nicolas Island, California,

---

[7] This section was contributed by R. F. Dill of the U.S. Navy Electronics Laboratory.

by the Sea Floor Studies Section of the U.S. Navy Electronics Laboratory (Menard *et al.*, 1954). Similar detailed studies, although limited in areal extent, have since been made on most of the continental shelves of the world. Nesteroff (1958) has used this technique extensively in the mapping and study of nearshore processes in the Mediterranean Sea.

Offshore mapping has been especially useful off southern California where extensive offshore oil-bearing structures have been found which have a surface expression in the sea floor exposures of bedrock. Previous to the use of SCUBA the examination of the geology of this area was stopped at the shoreline and a vast region of unmapped sea floor extended all along the coast between the shoreline and the closest approach that the seismic surveys could successfully investigate the subsurface geology. However, with SCUBA, underwater mapping was possible, and a correlation between offshore seismic and coring data and onshore geology became possible. At least three new oil fields were found and delineated by using this combined method for exploration. These discoveries were partly due to the extensive mapping of submarine surface outcrops by SCUBA-equipped geologists.

**Techniques of Underwater Geological Work.** Techniques used underwater are in many ways similar to those used by geologists on land. Attitudes are taken at various locations and plotted on a map, chart, or areal photograph. Rock samples are taken for paleontologic and lithologic information; the combined data are then analyzed for possible structural significance. Problems that are encountered in the field are worked out in much the same manner as on land, and the nature of the data collected depends on the amount of detail desired, the purpose of the mapping, etc. The diving geologist does, however, have many disadvantages compared to his dry land counterpart for he is limited by the depth to which he can go, by the length of time he can stay submerged, and to a great extent by weather conditions and the visibility of the water. Several advantages are his, however; mapping is always done with a partner or "buddy diver" who is or should also be a geologist. Observations at each outcrop are compared, and agreement is reached and recorded before the divers return to the surface. Another advantage is the great mobility the diver has underwater. It permits him literally to fly from outcrop to outcrop as he covers his area, for under water (as in space) he is essentially weightless. Problems of climbing mountains do not exist for the diving geologist—so long as his "mountains" are never over 250 ft high (or in this case, "deep").

For measuring attitude several instruments have been combined to make the underwater equivalent of a Brunton compass (Shumway,

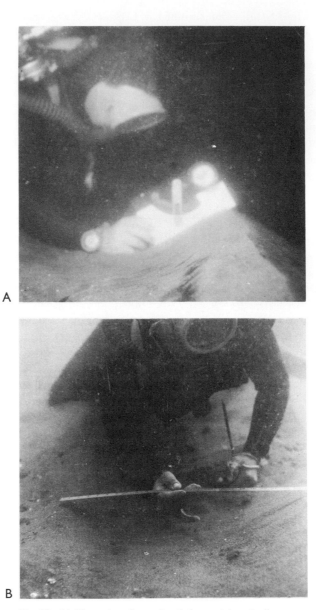

Fig. 20. (a) Measuring the angle of slope with an inclinometer; (b) measuring the wavelength of "giant ripple marks." Underwater photos by R. F. Dill.

1955). A small lucite pad with an attached compass in a watertight case, inclinometer, and a writing slate made of mat-finished plastic are combined and form the basic tool SCUBA geologists use for measuring dip and strikes of outcrops (Fig. 20). The writing slate is necessary because it has been found that man breathing air under high pressure forgets easily. Unless observations are recorded and checked by the "buddy diver" they cannot be considered dependable.

Fig. 21. Showing how SCUBA diving may be carried on with comparative comfort under Arctic conditions. Photo by R. F. Dill.

In addition to his underwater Brunton, the diving geologist usually carries a geologic hammer for rock sampling, sample bags, a knife, a depth gauge, an underwater watch, and small marker buoys to be sent to the surface if the exact locations of bottom features or samples are needed. He wears an exposure suit to protect him from the cold water in which he must often work. Fortunately, the problem of working in cold water has been almost eliminated with the development of extremely efficient exposure suits. Shumway and Beagles (1959) have shown by their dives under the ice in the Arctic that temperature is no longer a difficult problem for the diver even in water temperature as low as 30° F. (Fig. 21). This is not to say that a diver is invariably warm if he puts on an exposure suit; it merely means that he can still function primarily as a geologist and carry out his mapping duties in all the waters of the world, regardless of their cold temperatures.

The experienced underwater geologist can work to depths as great as 150 ft with relative ease. The number of dives he can make on any particular day depends on the depth of the water in which he is working and the amount of time that he stays down; the deeper a diver goes the shorter the period of time that he can spend underwater. For example, a day's work in shallow water of less than 30 ft may consist of as many as fifteen separate, 10-minute dives, but only two dives of 15 minutes' duration are possible at a depth of 150 ft. Fortunately, the geologist can plan his dives so that in many cases he can take advantage of the slope of the sea floor and by starting the day in deep water and by progressively moving into shallower water he can take full advantage of all the submerged time he has available. By using this method and taking into account the time necessary to record data, sort samples, and move to new locations, a diver can average six dives per day of approximately 15 minutes' duration on an average mapping project. This average value is based on the many dives that have been made at the U.S. Navy Electronics Laboratory, Scripps Institution of Oceanography, and Geological Diving Consultants, Inc.

The exact procedures that the geologist follows under water, although similar, are much more specialized than the geologic techniques used on land, because, in addition to the basic knowledge of geology, the geologist must have a working knowledge of diving physiology and be able to cope with the problems that can occur during his work under water. Terms like: bends, oxygen poisoning, nitrogen narcosis, air embolism, and decompression are as common in the vocabulary of the diving geologist as dip, strike, and contact. An excellent presentation of this physiological information is available in the U.S. Navy's Diving Manual (1960). In addition to the problems in diving physiology the geologist who ventures beneath the sea finds himself acting in much the same role as the early naturalist, for he is in a new environment and is forced to take advantage of every bit of information available to construct the geologic picture of an area. His rocks are in many instances honeycombed by boring organisms (Fig. 22) buried under a dense cover of calcareous algae or corals, and currents may cover an exposure that was prominent on one dive with enough sediment to make it unrecognizable and in many instances impossible to find within a few days. Currents continually sweep the divers back and forth across the bottom in areas of high swell and make it extremely difficult to navigate and determine the relative positions of objects on the bottom. Presently there is very little that is taught in the standard college course in marine geology, even those which have active diving programs, that prepares a student for what

Fig. 22. The honeycombing of rock surface by boring organisms. Ripple marks are shown on the left. Underwater photo by R. F. Dill.

he will encounter under water. Much remains to be learned about optimum field methods to be used by the diving geologist. This is a field where a vocabulary has not been fully developed and agreed upon for describing even the most common phenomena.

**SCUBA Photography.**    Many of the features seen under water have no surface counterpart, partly because of the lack of subaerial erosion. It is, therefore, difficult to convey their exact nature to persons not familiar with the sea floor. Underwater photographs often help to remedy this lack of direct contact and permit a recording of unfamiliar forms and processes. Unfortunately, the underwater world is not favorable for photography. Visibility in most instances is limited to less than 100 ft and averages about 10 to 20 ft on clear water days in most of the offshore areas of the continental shelves of the world. For this reason large-scale features cannot be photographed, and only

Fig. 23. A typical exposure of sedimentary rock with a talus slope in the foreground and undermining probably produced in part by echinoids like the one illustrated on the left. Underwater photo by R. F. Dill.

those features which are small enough to be encompassed at relatively short distances from the camera can be photographed. Regardless of these limitations underwater photography has been extremely useful in recording such features as ripple marks (Fig. 20), rock outcrops (Fig. 23), scour holes, organisms, and plants (Fig. 24), and time variations in sedimentation and erosion at given locations on the sea floor.

In many instances natural light can be used to expose the film, especially with the high-speed film. Extremely wide-angle lenses are almost mandatory as they permit photographs to be made at a minimum distance from the subject and thereby cut down the rapid attenuation of detail by turbid water. Many underwater cameras are now commercially available that meet the needs of the underwater geologist. Excellent cameras that are often used are the Rolli-Marine

Fig. 24. Growth of kelp plants largely covering the rock formations along the east slope of North Coronado Island, just south of the United States–Mexican boundary. Underwater photo by R. F. Dill.

manufactured by Rolliflex and a Hasselblad superwide camera in an underwater case. Discussions of the problems of underwater photography are presented by Cousteau and Dumas (1950), Schenk (1954), Cross (1954), and Dill (1961).

## Bottom Photography

The earliest report of bottom photography was made by Boutan (1900), who, in a diving suit, took photographs with a protected

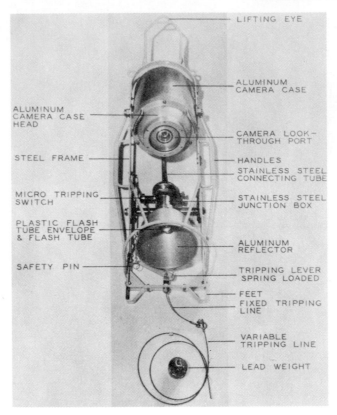

LIFTING EYE

ALUMINUM
CAMERA CASE

ALUMINUM
CAMERA CASE
HEAD

CAMERA LOOK-
THROUGH PORT

STEEL FRAME

HANDLES
STAINLESS STEEL
CONNECTING TUBE

MICRO TRIPPING
SWITCH

STAINLESS STEEL
JUNCTION BOX

PLASTIC FLASH
TUBE ENVELOPE
& FLASH TUBE

ALUMINUM
REFLECTOR

SAFETY PIN

TRIPPING LEVER
SPRING LOADED

FEET
FIXED TRIPPING
LINE

VARIABLE
TRIPPING LINE

LEAD WEIGHT

Fig. 25. The U.S. Navy Electronics Laboratory Type III deep-sea
camera designed and constructed by Carl J. Shipek.

camera in shallow water. During or shortly before World War II
an early model of the housed unmanned camera devices for photo-
graphing the bottom at greater depths was developed (Ewing *et al.*,
1946). This operated in water less than 100 fathoms deep by setting
off an unprotected flash bulb and synchronously taking a photograph
from a robot camera in a brass case mounted in front of a glass port-
hole. Now there are a considerable number of underwater cameras
that have strong enough cases to operate at all depths (Fig. 25). They
have electronic flash units and automatic film advancement that allow
the taking of a large number of photographs before bringing the
camera to the surface. The chances of losing the camera are increased
by taking multiple photographs as the camera moves over the bottom
but a tremendous time saving is involved in the case of deep water.
Taking photographs going down a slope rather than up a slope
considerably diminishes the chances of loss.

Fig. 26. Stereo pair of photographs obtained on board a Soviet vessel, *Vitiaz*, by N. L. Zenkevitch. Photograph obtained 200 miles north of New Zealand at a depth of 2040 m. Note dipping rock formation.

Corporation had been used for the drilling. This barge is 300 ft long and thus when held into the sea has very little motion so long as the waves are of relatively short length. The drilling, therefore, is from a relatively stable platform. It is carried out by use of a central well and a 98-ft derrick. The experimental phase of the project has been completed. The drilling has penetrated to a depth of 1000 feet into the large fan that enters San Diego Trough, and to 600 feet in the deep sea floor off Guadalupe Island. The Guadalupe hole passed through about 560 ft of upper Tertiary and then a few feet into a basalt.

The chief reason for the development of the drilling operations in the deep ocean is that the earth's crust is much thinner under the oceans than under the continents or under islands. Therefore, in order to find out what type of rock makes up the earth's mantle it is far easier to drill into the ocean floor.

### Bottom Current Measurement

Great progress has been made in measuring surface and inter-mediate depth currents (Swallow, 1955), but very little has been done with bottom current measurements, aside from some very elaborate devices that are classified as confidential. The Ekman current meters described in the first edition (p. 31) are still used occasionally and serve to give a rough idea of currents during a short period.

A useful device for measuring currents near the bottom consists of a current cross suspended from a floating buoy which offers little resistance. By suspending the cross near the bottom and watching the position of the buoy it is possible to track the bottom current. A difficulty comes from the float being carried into shoaler water where it will strike the bottom or into deeper water where it is no longer representative of bottom flow. Tracking can be visual or by radar (p. 11).

# CHAPTER III

# OCEAN WAVES AND ASSOCIATED CURRENTS

**BY DOUGLAS L. INMAN**

## Introduction

Ocean surface waves are of great importance to maritime and coastal engineers; the catastrophic effect of great storms on shipping and the loss of life and property resulting from inundation of coastal cities are well-known effects of waves. However, their most lasting effect results from their erosion of coastal formations, and their transportation and deposition of nearshore sediments. As a consequence, waves play the major role in determining the configuration of the coastlines and associated shoreline features of the world. Wherever beaches are found, whether they are hundreds of miles long as are some beaches on the east and gulf coasts of the United States, or a few feet long as is common in small lakes, waves usually have been the predominant agent in their formation. The magnitude and intensity of wave action become important features in determining the characteristics of the nearshore environment, both biologically and physically.

The study of waves is certainly not a new field of investigation, but has received the attention of prominent mathematicians, physicists, and engineers for over a century, and attempts to understand the nature of wave motion date back at least to the time of Leonardo da Vinci in 1480. Yet, in spite of the attention given by scientists throughout the ages, the understanding of waves and wave motion is still in a relatively immature stage of development, principally because of the nonlinear properties and the complex geometry of the water surface produced by wind waves at sea.

Before proceeding with the more complex aspects of wave motion, it is convenient to idealize the wave form as a sine wave (Fig. 28) in order to define some of the basic wave parameters. In this simplified picture we can define a wavelength $L$ as the horizontal distance between two crests; wave height $H$ as the elevation of the crest above the trough; and a wave period $T$ as the interval of time between

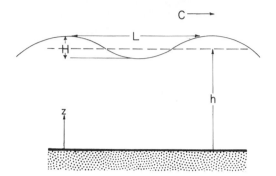

Fig. 28. Definition of terms. Schematic diagram of a sinusoidal wave of height $H$, and length $L$, traveling with phase velocity $C$ in water of depth $h$.

passage of successive wave crests by some position in space. The wave phase velocity, that is, the rate of propagation of the wave form, is then given simply as the wavelength divided by the period, $C = L/T$. A list of symbols and units for Chapters III and V is given in Appendix A.

### Waves Generated by the Wind

Waves are generated when wind blows over water (Fig. 29). However, the way in which the energy in the wind is transferred to the water to form ocean waves is not entirely understood. Energy is transferred to the water by the tangential stress exerted by turbulent flow of wind over the water surface, and once ripples and waves are formed, the sheltering effect produced by their crests causes a variation in wind pressure between the windward and lee sides that favors the propagation and growth of waves. These modes of energy transfer, developed respectively by Sverdrup and Munk (1947) and by Jeffreys (1925) and Miles (1960) do not appear to explain adequately the rate at which waves are generated by wind. It has been suggested by Eckart (1953) that energy is also transferred by the normal pressure fluctuations associated with the gustiness of the wind. This concept, extended by Phillips (1957) to include the development of a type of resonance in the random distribution of pressure fluctuations between wind and water, is a promising development in explaining the mechanism of generation of wind waves.[1]

The height of the waves generated and their period are functions of the velocity of the wind, $W$, the fetch or distance over which the wind blows, $F$, and the duration or time that the wind blows, $D$. This relation can be written symbolically as $H, T = f(W, F, D)$. For short fetches of 1 to 20 miles, the wave height increases directly with the

---

[1] An excellent summary and review of the theory of wave generation and forecasting is given by King (1959, pp. 54–93).

Fig. 29. Areal photograph of the sea surface for wind velocities of 70 knots. The irregular pattern of waves and white caps is indicative of the very complex geometry of the water surface. Analysis of these waves would show a very broad distribution of energy, corresponding roughly to the spectrogram for sea waves shown in Fig. 30b.

wind velocity $W$, and the wave period increases as the square root of $W$. The wave fetch is quite important in determining wave height and period, and long waves (long periods) can be generated only where the fetch is large. Thus the prominent part of the spectrum of waves generated in the southern oceans may include wavelengths somewhat in excess of 2000 feet (periods exceeding 20 seconds) whereas the lengths visible in small lakes are commonly not over 20 ft in length (periods of 2 seconds). Since the height of the wave depends on the wind velocity, fetch, and duration, it is apparent that the character of the waves generated in oceans, seas, and lakes will be quite different. In lakes, fetch usually becomes the limiting factor in wave size. The velocity, fetch, and duration of the wind all tend to be great in the southern oceans between latitude 40° S. and the Antarctic continent. Most of the largest waves are generated in the southern oceans, and it is not uncommon for these waves to travel great distances. The typical waves observed along the shores of southern California in the summertime were generated by storms in the South Pacific and have traveled 5000 miles or more before breaking on the beaches of southern California.

The propagation of ocean waves from distant generating areas was first clearly demonstrated by Barber and Ursell (1948) when their wave measurements from the southern coast of England showed the arrival times for waves of a specific period to be in agreement with the travel distances from storms in the Atlantic. The longest period waves arrived first, followed by waves of successively shorter periods. Their observations verified the fact that the energy of a group of waves travels with the wave group velocity, which for deep water waves is equal to one-half of the wave phase velocity. They present evidence of receiving one series of waves generated in the southern Atlantic Ocean some 6000 to 7000 miles from the coast of England. Using sensitive vibratron transducers to measure bottom pressure fluctuations Munk and Snodgrass (1957) have obtained the energy spectra of long period waves, the forerunners of swell, approaching the California coast from distant storm centers. They have attributed some waves to cyclones in the storm belt of the southern Indian Ocean, and estimate that these waves traveled over 8000 miles through the Tasman Sea and across the Pacific Ocean to the California Coast.

Although great waves at sea are impressive and of general interest, it is not clear to what maximum height wind-generated waves can grow because the measurement of wave height during storms is difficult. From the bridge of the liner *Majestic*, Cornish (1934) observed waves in the North Atlantic which he estimated to be 75 ft high. More recently, Deacon (1958) described a wave about 60 ft from crest to trough and with a period of about 15 seconds that was measured with a shipborne accelerometer-type wave recorder from the British weather ship *Ocean Explorer* in the North Atlantic Ocean in November, 1956.

For convenience, wind-generated waves can be divided into four types: sea, swell, forerunners, and surf. Waves which are in the generating area and are under the influence of wind, are referred to as sea waves. These waves are commonly very irregular, and it is usually difficult to observe a definite or systematic pattern.

After traveling from the generation area, waves are no longer under the influence of the wind, and the relatively regular long waves commonly outrun and lose the shortest and most irregular waves, so that a more uniform pattern of crest and trough becomes apparent; waves of this type are referred to as swell. Near shore, both sea and swell waves peak up and break into surf, and change from waves of oscillation to waves of translation. The longest and lowest waves, which outrun the main energy front of a disturbance, are frequently referred to as forerunners of swell. These waves may have periods of

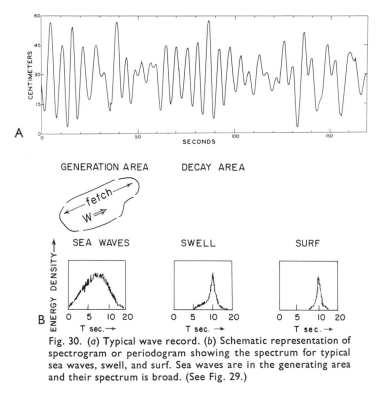

Fig. 30. (a) Typical wave record. (b) Schematic representation of spectrogram or periodogram showing the spectrum for typical sea waves, swell, and surf. Sea waves are in the generating area and their spectrum is broad. (See Fig. 29.)

the order of 30 seconds but since their amplitude is small, they usually give no visual manifestation on the beach and are detected only by sensitive instruments.

**Spectrum of Ocean Waves.**    If we look at the sea surface, especially when it is ruffled by wind, we see that its geometry is very complex (Fig. 29). We do not see a single wave with a single height and period, but rather an entire spectrum of waves. A record of the irregularities of waves on the surface can be obtained from surface gauges mounted on a pier or, indirectly, from such methods as stereophotogrammetry (Schumacher, 1952, p. 69; Ijima *et al.*, 1958), from shipborne accelerometers (Deacon, 1958), or by fluctuations of the wave pressure measured by instruments placed near the bottom. The latter is the more common procedure, but since pressure fluctuations decrease in accordance with the ratio of depth to wavelength the depth acts as a filter especially for waves of short period. Any of these methods results in a wave record such as Fig. 30a. The problem is to reduce the wiggly line representing the pressure or profile of the waves into meaningful data that tell us something about the magnitude and distribution of wave parameters such as height and period. There are two approaches to the problem, which are basically the same principle. They are (1) harmonic analysis, which consists of reducing the complex record into its fundamental constituents in terms of simple sine waves, and (2) statistical procedures such as the autocorrelation techniques (Rudnick, 1951). The harmonic analysis technique leads to a presentation of wave spectrum in terms of the relative frequency of occurrence of energy (energy density) for each wave period as discussed previously (Fig. 30b). The autocorrelation diagram is somewhat more difficult to interpret than the spectrogram and will not be further considered here.

The harmonic analysis of a wave record becomes quite tedious unless special equipment is employed, and in any event it can be obtained only from a continuous record, such as the wave pressure record previously described. Because small waves are difficult to observe or measure in the presence of high waves, and because high waves are of greater significance in the application of most wave data, a statistic called the "significant wave" was developed which is based on averages of the heights and periods of the highest one-third of the waves. The significant wave can be approximated directly from field observation, and it is a concept that has received rather widespread application, especially in engineering circles. The significant wave has a height which is defined as the average height of the highest one-third of the waves measured over a stated interval of time, usually 20 minutes. The number of waves to be averaged is obtained by dividing one-third of the time of duration of the wave observations by the "significant wave period." In turn, the significant wave period is defined as the average of the periods of the highest one-third of the waves, and it is usually determined by averaging the individual periods of the large well-defined groups of waves for the stated interval of time (Wiegel, 1953).

Observations of ocean waves showed that there tends to be a constant ratio between the various wave statistics such as the average wave height, $\bar{H}$, the root-mean-square wave height, $H_{rms}$, the significant wave height, $H_{1/3}$, the average of the highest 10 percent of the waves, $H_{1/10}$, and the maximum wave, $H_{max}$, which occurs during a given interval of time. It was found that the ratio between these wave height statistics remained relatively constant so long as the wave spectrum was narrow, that is to say, a swell from a distant source. Longuet-Higgins (1952) developed theoretical relations for these ratios, based on the assumption that the wave spectrum contains a single narrow band of frequencies,[2] and that the wave energy comes

---

[2] The wave frequency is the reciprocal of the wave period, and is usually expressed in cycles per second or per minute.

from a large number of different sources whose phase is random. A comparison of the theoretical with observed data is given in Table 1. The relatively good agreement between theory and observation extends the usefulness of the significant wave concept.

TABLE I. Relation Between Significant Wave Height and Other Wave Height Statistics

| $\dfrac{\bar{H}}{H_{1/3}}$ | $\dfrac{H_{\text{rms}}}{H_{1/3}}$ | $\dfrac{H_{1/10}}{H_{1/3}}$ | $\dfrac{H_{\max}}{H_{1/3}}$ | Nature of Investigation |
|---|---|---|---|---|
| 0.64 | 0.71 | 1.27 | 1.53–1.85[a] | Theoretical by Longuet-Higgins (1952); assuming narrow spectrum and source of random phase |
| 0.62 | | 1.29 | 1.87 | Observational by Putz (1952); analysis of 25 wave pressure records, each of 20 minutes' duration. |

[a] The ratio $H_{\max}/H_{1/3}$ varies with period and length of record. Waves with 6-second periods from records of 20 and 60 minutes' duration have ratios of 1.64 and 1.85 respectively, while waves with 12-second periods have ratios of 1.53 and 1.77 respectively for the same duration of record.

## Ideal Waves

Initially, progress in wave work was made from the application of certain broad and simplifying assumptions regarding the geometry of the waves, and by developing mathematical-physical relations for these simplified or ideal waves. This approach has provided the basis for our elementary equations of wave motion, and has furnished insight into the mechanics of wave motion. However, each of the ideal waves treated here has a limited application as regards either wave height, wave form, or the depth of water. While ideal waves provide a useful tool in wave work, they do not integrate into a single unified theory, equally applicable to all phases of ocean waves, and this fact should be constantly borne in mind in the following discussions. Three ideal waves which have been important in the development of wave theory, and to which we will have frequent occasion to refer are:

| Investigator | Wave Form | Application |
|---|---|---|
| Airy (1845) | Sinusoidal | Waves of small amplitude; irregular waves in deep water provided the slopes remain small. |
| Stokes (1847) | Trochoidal | Waves of finite amplitude, in deep and shallow water. |
| Scott-Russell (1844) | Solitary | Solitary or isolated crests moving in relatively shallow water. |

In deep water, waves of small slope can always be compounded from elementary sine waves which are propagated independently. The velocity of such waves is dependent on their length and is independent of depth. Wave velocity in shallow water, on the other hand, is less dependent on frequency and wavelength, and the wave height and depth of water are of primary importance. Waves in very shallow water tend to resemble the solitary wave of Scott-Russell, and his theory will be applied to wave action near the breaker zone. The wave concepts of Airy and Stokes apply best to waves in deep water where wavelength is the essential descriptive parameter. The general theory for waves of small amplitude, attributed to Sir George Airy in 1845 (Lamb, 1945, p. 368), is strictly applicable to waves of infinitely small height in water of any depth. The wave profile is sinusoidal and the particle orbits are closed circles in deep water and ellipses in shallow water. The first complete solution for waves of finite amplitude was derived by Gerstner in 1802. However, this solution, which assumes that the wave profile is trochoidal, applies only to waves in deep water. Of the theories for waves of finite height, that of Sir George Stokes (1847) has met with most success. The Stokes wave has flatter troughs and steeper crests than the Airy wave. The particle orbits are not closed but lead to a slight net transport in the direction of wave propagation. In general, the Stokes wave is a better approximation to natural waves than the Airy wave, because it allows for finite wave height, provides for wave-drift currents, and shows an asymmetry in wave profile and orbital velocity.[3] However, Stokes' waves cannot be superimposed to form, an irregular sea, while Airy waves can be generalized by means of a spectrum to irregular waves. For this reason, the small amplitude theory of Airy, which can be expressed in much simpler form, will be used in the following discussions with occasional reference to the Stokes wave where it applies.

It seems likely that the theory of cnoidal waves developed by Korteweg and de Vries in 1895 may prove to be more satisfactory than any of the above forms in providing a single continuous relation for expressing the properties of waves traveling in all depths of water. It can be shown that both the sinusoidal waves of deep water and the solitary wave of shallow water occur as special limiting cases of the cnoidal wave. Here again, however, the expressions for the cnoidal wave, which are given in terms of the Jacobian elliptic function cn $u$ (hence the term cnoidal), are beyond the scope of an elementary text. Wiegel (1959) has further developed the theory of the cnoidal wave and provided tables of functions so that it can be applied to a wider range of engineering problems.

[3] A recent compilation of Stokes wave functions to the third order of approximation has facilitated calculation of these wave properties (Skjelbreia, 1959).

**Airy Waves.** General considerations of hydrodynamic principles, when evaluated for the proper boundary conditions, lead to the equation of classical hydrodynamics in which the phase velocity $C$ is expressed as a function of the wavelength $L$ and the depth of water $h$:

$$C^2 = \frac{g}{k} \tanh kh \tag{1}[4]$$

where $g$ is the acceleration of gravity and $k = 2\pi/L$ is called the wave number and is a term commonly encountered in wave relations. This general expression for phase velocity is strictly applicable to waves of infinitely small height in water of arbitrary but uniform depth.

The effect of depth on the phase velocity can be readily deduced from the Airy expression for phase velocity, because the velocity varies only with the value of the hyperbolic tangent. The simplified expressions for the limiting values of the hyperbolic tangent, when the values of $kh$ are very large or very small, serve as the basis for the concepts of "deep" and "shallow water," which will be developed in the following discussion.

TABLE 2.　Hyperbolic Functions and Their Approximate Formulas for Large and Small Values

| Function | General Formula | Large Values of $x$ | Small Values of $x$ |
|---|---|---|---|
| $\sinh x$ | $\frac{1}{2}(e^x - e^{-x})$ | $\frac{1}{2}e^x$ | $x$ |
| $\cosh x$ | $\frac{1}{2}(e^x + e^{-x})$ | $\frac{1}{2}e^x$ | $1$ |
| $\tanh x$ | $\sinh x/\cosh x$ | $1$ | $x$ |
| Limiting condition | None | $e^x \gg e^{-x}$ | $e^x \doteq 1 + x$ <br> $e^{-x} \doteq 1 - x$ |
| Application | All depths | Deep water | Shallow water |

The general and limiting formulas for hyperbolic functions are given in Table 2, where $x$ is the equivalent of $kh$ in the relation for phase velocity, and $e$ is the base of natural logarithms. If the depth of water $h$ is large compared with the wavelength $L$, then $kh = 2\pi h/L$ is also large and the hyperbolic tangent of $kh$ becomes approximately equal to unity ($\tanh kh \doteq 1$). If this value is substituted in equation (1), it reduces to the following simple expression for the phase velocity of a wave traveling in deep water:

$$C_d{}^2 = gL/2\pi$$

or since $L = CT$, the deep water phase velocity can be expressed as a function of the wave period $T$:

$$C_d = gT/2\pi = 5.12T \text{ ft/sec} = 1.56T \text{ m/sec} \tag{1a}$$

[4] The corresponding expression for the phase velocity of a Stokes wave, excluding terms with exponents greater than 2 is, $C^2 = (g/k)(1 + \frac{1}{4}k^2H^2)$, for deep water.

Here, and in the following discussion, the subscripts $d$ and $s$ will be used to denote the specific case of waves traveling in deep or shallow water, and the symbols without such emphasis will apply to water of any depth. Although $C_d$ can be expressed as a constant, $g/2\pi = 5.12$, or 1.56, times the period $T$, it should be noted that this constant has the units of gravity and will have a different value if the velocity is expressed in different units.

By referring again to Table 2, it will be observed that for small values of $kh$, the value of the hyperbolic tangent of $kh$ is approximately equal to $kh$ ($\tanh kh \doteq kh$); i.e., when the depth of water $h$ is small compared with the wavelength $L$. Substituting $kh$ for $\tanh kh$ in equation (1) reduces it to the following familiar relation for the velocity of propagation of waves traveling in shallow water:

$$C_s = \sqrt{gh} \tag{1b}$$

In shallow water it is to be noted that the phase velocity is independent of wave period or length, and depends only on the depth of water.

Expressions for the wavelength of deep and shallow water waves can be obtained directly from the relation between phase velocity, wavelength, and period, $C = L/T$, which applies to waves traveling in water of any depth. Direct substitution in equations (1a) and (1b) gives the following expressions for wavelength[5]:

$$L_d = \frac{gT^2}{2\pi} = 5.12T^2 \,\text{ft} = 1.56T^2 \,\text{m} \tag{2a}$$

and
$$L_s = T\sqrt{gh} \tag{2b}$$

where $d$ and $s$ refer to deep and shallow water respectively.

In applying the above expressions for deep and shallow water, it remains only to decide the degree of approximation one is willing to accept, and from this to determine the limits for deep and shallow water. Expressions of the wave functions are commonly listed in terms of the ratio of the water depth to the deep water wavelength, $h/L_d$, rather than $L$, because $L_d$ can be computed directly from equation (2a). Values of $C/C_d$ as a function of $h/L_d$ are plotted in Fig. 31, and the numerical values for specific ratios of $h/L_d$ are listed in Table 3.

It is sometimes customary to refer to deep water where the depth exceeds one-half $L_d$. However, it is observed from Table 3 that the phase velocities computed using equations (1) and (1a) differ by only 0.37 percent for depths of $h/L_d = \frac{1}{2}$, and as a consequence, restriction

[5] Eckart (1952) gives the following very useful approximation for the wavelength in water of any depth: $L^2 = L_d{}^2 \tanh k_d h$.

of the application of the deep water equations to one-half the wave-length is too stringent for most practical purposes.

If a 5 percent error is acceptable, it is found that the limits of application for the deep and shallow water equations will occur at depths of approximately $\frac{1}{4}$ and $\frac{1}{20}$ of the deep water wavelength respectively. If a 10 percent error is acceptable, then these limits are found to occur at depths of approximately $\frac{1}{5}$ and $\frac{1}{10}$ of $L_d$. For our

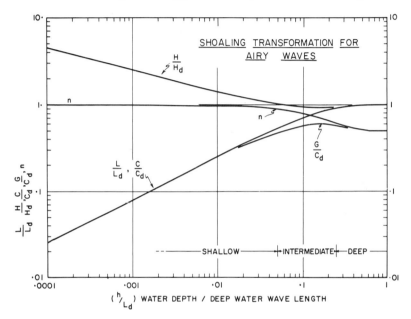

Fig. 31. Shoaling transformation for Airy waves as a function of the ratio of the water depth $h$, to deep water wavelength $L_d$. The range of relative depth for deep, intermediate, and shallow water waves is indicated.

purposes we will consider a 5 percent error as acceptable and reasonable and define deep and shallow water as applying to the following depth ranges.

Deep water: $h/L_d > \frac{1}{4}$

Intermediate water: $\frac{1}{4} > h/L_d > \frac{1}{20}$

Shallow water: $\frac{1}{20} > h/L_d$

In intermediate depths of water, that is in depths between $\frac{1}{4}$ and $\frac{1}{20}$ of the deep water wavelength, it is necessary to employ the complete general equation if errors are not to exceed 5 percent.

**Orbital Velocity.** If one follows a floating cork during the passage of a series of waves, it will be observed that it moves back and forth and up and down, undergoing an orbital motion that returns it to nearly the same position after each wave. A motion picture of the position of the cork at successive positions of the wave shows the trajectory of the cork to be nearly a closed circle, with a diameter equal to the wave height $H$ (Fig. 32a). Since the cork completes one revolution during each wave period, the orbital velocity is given simply by the circumference of the circle $\pi H$, divided by the wave period $T$

$$u = \pi H/T$$

For Airy waves the wave profile is sinusoidal and the orbits of water particles within the wave are closed circles in deep water and ellipses

TABLE 3. Error of Deep and Shallow Water Approximations for Various Relative Depths, $h/L_d$; $C$, $C_d$, and $C_s$ from Equations (1), (1a), and (1b) Respectively (After Arthur, 1952, Fig. 305)

| Relative Depth $h/L_d$ | | $\dfrac{C}{C_s}$ | $\dfrac{C}{C_d}$ | Percent Error | Depth |
|---|---|---|---|---|---|
| $\frac{1}{100}$ | 0.01 | 0.99 | | 1 | |
| $\frac{1}{50}$ | 0.02 | 0.98 | | 2 | Shallow |
| $\frac{1}{20}$ | 0.05 | 0.95 | | 5 | |
| $\sim\frac{1}{10}$ | 0.095 | 0.90 | | 10 | Intermediate |
| $\sim\frac{1}{5}$ | 0.21 | | 0.90 | 10 | |
| $\sim\frac{1}{4}$ | 0.28 | | 0.95 | 5 | |
| | 0.36 | | 0.98 | 2 | Deep |
| | 0.42 | | 0.99 | 1 | |
| $\frac{1}{2}$ | 0.50 | | 0.996 | 0.37 | |

TABLE 4. Limits for "Deep" and "Shallow" Water for Various Waves, 5 Percent Error

| Wave Period $T$, sec | Deep Water Wavelength $L_d = gT^2/2\pi$ | Deep Water (Depths greater than $\frac{1}{4}L_d$) | Shallow Water (Depths less than $\frac{1}{20}L_d$) |
|---|---|---|---|
| $\frac{1}{2}$ | 1.28 ft | 0.32 ft | 0.06 ft |
| 1 | 5.12 | 1.3 | 0.26 |
| 3 | 46.1 | 11.5 | 2.3 |
| 5 | 128. | 32. | 6.4 |
| 10 | 512. | 128. | 25.6 |
| 15 | 1152. | 288. | 57.6 |
| 20 | 2048. | 512. | 102. |
| 30 | 4608. | 1152. | 230. |

in shallow water. The orbital paths of particles in a Stokes wave are open circles, or curtate cycloids, so that the particle advances slowly in the direction of propagation of the wave. This gradual advance of the water particle leads to wave drift currents that will be discussed in a later section.

A more general expression for the maximum horizontal component of the orbital velocity for an Airy wave is given by the following equation:

$$u_m = \pi d/T \tag{3}$$

where $d$ is the horizontal diameter of the orbit and is given for water of any depth by the expression

$$d = H \frac{\cosh kz}{\sinh kh} \tag{4}$$

where $z$ is the distance above the bottom (Fig. 32). For deep water, both the hyperbolic sine and cosine reduce to a single exponential

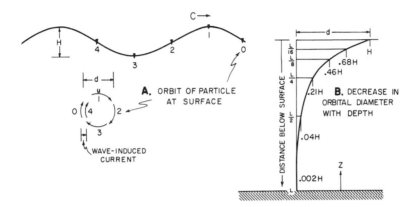

Fig. 32. Orbital velocity and diameter of an Airy wave traveling in deep water. (*a*) Trajectory described by particle at surface as successive parts of wave travel past point *O*. Note that at the surface the diameter of the orbit is equal to the wave height, $d = H$. (*b*) Decrease in orbital diameter with depth for a wave traveling where depth of water is equal to the wavelength *L*.

function (Table 2), and the simplified expression for the orbital diameter becomes

$$d = He^{-k(h-z)} \tag{4a}$$

This expression is plotted in Fig. 32*b*, where it can be seen that the orbital diameter $d$, is equal to the wave height $H$, at the surface, but decreases exponentially with distance below the surface, having a value of only 4 percent of $H$ at a half wavelength below the surface.

At the bottom $z$ is zero, $\cosh kz$ is equal to one, and the orbital diameter is given by

$$d_0 = H/\sinh kh \tag{4b}$$

where the subscript 0 refers specifically to conditions at the bottom. This relation has application to problems of sediment transport and the concept of "wave base." When this value is substituted in equation (3), the maximum horizontal orbital velocity at the bottom becomes

$$u_m = \pi H/T \sinh kh \tag{3a}$$

An example of the application of this equation can be made by comparing the orbital velocity and displacement associated with two different waves. Assume that each wave has a height of 2 ft and is traveling in water 50 ft deep, but that the first wave has a period $T$ of 5 seconds, and the second has a period of 10 seconds. For the first wave, equation (3a) and (4b)[6] give approximately 0.3 ft for the orbital diameter and 0.2 ft/sec for the maximum orbital velocity at the bottom; and the second wave would have values of 2.2 ft and 0.7 ft/sec respectively. It is doubtful that the first wave would cause any motion of sediment on the bottom, while the second wave would cause coarse sand to move.

In shallow water, the equation for the orbital diameter reduces to

$$d = H/kh \qquad (4c)$$

Since $kh$ always has values of 0.6 or less in shallow water, it is apparent that the orbital diameter will always be greater than the wave height when the wave is traveling in shallow water. This was indicated for the 10-second wave in the above example, which was traveling in water of intermediate depth and had an orbital diameter at the bottom just exceeding the wave height.

Also, for an Airy wave traveling in shallow water, the orbital diameter is constant from the surface to the bottom. Therefore, the maximum orbital velocity is also constant from surface to bottom, and equation (3) simplifies to

$$u_m = \frac{1}{2} \frac{H}{h} C_s \qquad (3b)$$

**Solitary Waves.**   In shallow water, and especially near the breaker zone, the sinusoidal or continuous frequency characteristics commonly associated with waves in deep water are lost and individual waves tend to retain their identity. Here, the length of the wave is less significant, and the depth of water and height of wave become controlling factors. In profile there is a tendency for the waves to consist of isolated crests separated by relatively flat troughs. For this reason the solitary wave concept of Scott-Russell will be used in describing waves near the breaker zone. Munk (1949b) has applied solitary theory to waves near the surf zone and his approach, which has met with some degree of success, will be employed in the following discussion.

Consider a wave with height $H$ traveling in shallow water of depth $h$, measured beneath the wave trough (Fig. 33). If the wave height is a

[6] Tables of sinh $kh$ as a function of depth divided by the deep water wavelength are given in Beach Erosion Board (1961), Appendix D.

significant portion of the water depth, then intuitively one reasons that the wave height can no longer be neglected in matters relating to wave phase velocity. Solitary theory gives the wave phase velocity for waves traveling through still water as

$$C = \sqrt{g(h + H)} \tag{5}$$

It will be noted that this has the same form as the relation for Airy waves in shallow water (equation 1b), and differs only in allowing equal significance to wave height and water depth.

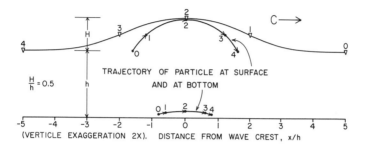

Fig. 33. Orbital velocity and displacement for a solitary wave traveling in still water. The trajectories show the position of a particle as successive parts of the wave travel past point O. Note that the surface displacement is twice that at the bottom. Solitary wave theory gives a displacement and orbital velocity only in the direction of wave propagation. A reverse motion is imparted to the orbital trajectory by assuming that the wave is traveling in water having a net reverse flow.

The orbital velocity associated with the passage of a solitary wave is given in its entirety by a rather complex equation. However, the equation simplifies to the following approximations for the maximum horizontal component of the orbital velocity at the surface:

$$u_m = \frac{H}{h} C \tag{6a}$$

and at the bottom under the wave crest:

$$u_m = \frac{1}{2} \frac{H}{h} C \tag{6b}$$

Again, these expressions for maximum horizontal velocity resemble the expressions for an Airy wave in shallow water. However, there are two fundamental differences; the orbital velocity of the solitary

wave decreases by one-half from surface to bottom, and the solitary
wave gives a velocity only in the direction of travel of the wave, i.e.,
there is no return or trough velocity. This can be illustrated by referring to Fig. 33. The solitary wave in theory, consists of a single isolated
crest traveling over an infinitely long flat bottom. Particles of water
are at rest prior to the passage of the wave crest; they partake in a
single forward and upward trajectory as the crest passes; and following
the wave they come to rest again at the same elevation above the

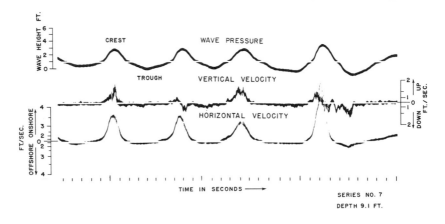

Fig. 34. Record of waves and their associated orbital velocities measured near the surf
zone off La Jolla, California. Measurements were made near the bottom in water 9 ft
deep. Waves have height and period of about 4 ft and 8 sec, respectively. From Inman
and Nasu (1956, Fig. 11).

bottom, but displaced forward a distance $r$ in the direction of wave
travel. A to-and-fro motion is imparted to the theoretical solitary
wave by assuming that the solitary wave is traveling in water that has
a steady net drift in the direction opposite to the wave travel. Near
the surf zone a net return flow is assumed to result when the shoreward
volume transport of water caused by the wave-drift currents impinges
on the relatively impermeable barrier of the shore. If the waves were
uniform, the shoreward volume transport, or discharge, would result
in a superelevation of the water surface near the beach, which in turn
would produce a uniform net return flow.

Observations (Shepard and Inman, 1950, Fig. 11) show that the
superelevation of water in the surf zone and the associated net return
flow are not steady, but pulsate in accordance with the grouping of
high waves followed by low waves. This pulsation of flow in the surf
zone is associated with a phenomenon called surf beat (Munk, 1949a;
Tucker, 1950) and results in considerable variation between the crest

and trough orbital velocities near the surf zone. Measurements by Inman and Nasu (1956) indicate that solitary theory on the average gives a reasonable approximation to the horizontal orbital velocities of water particles near the bottom when the waves are near the breaking point (Fig. 34). While agreement with theory was somewhat better for longer period waves, in general it was still quite good for most waves of simple profile so long as the relative wave height, $H/h$, was greater than about 0.4.

Since the solitary theory (equations 6a and b; Fig. 33) gives only the forward velocity $u_m$ associated with waves in still water, it is necessary to subtract the return flow velocity $v$ in order to obtain the maximum orbital velocity under the wave crest relative to a fixed position. The velocity of the return flow then becomes the maximum horizontal orbital velocity associated with the wave trough. Observations indicate that as an average rough approximation, $v = \frac{1}{3}u_m$, and consequently the maximum orbital velocities become

$$u_{m,(\text{crest})} \doteq \tfrac{2}{3}u_m$$
$$u_{m,(\text{trough})} \doteq \tfrac{1}{3}u_m$$

Values of $u_m$ are plotted as a function of wave height and water depth in Fig. 35.

**Breaking Waves.** From the relationship $u_m = (H/h)C$ (equation 6a), it is apparent that when the depth $h$ is equal to the wave height $H$, the wave phase velocity is equal to the orbital or particle velocity, and the form of the wave and the particles of water go forward together, and the wave collapses.

Equation (6a) is an approximation, and swell waves actually break on a gently sloping bed when $H/h$ equals about 0.78. However, sea waves and other very steep waves may break when the height to depth ratio is only about 0.6.

The wave steepness, the presence of supplementary or opposing wind, and the slope of the bottom bed all influence the nature of the breaking wave. Breaking waves can be roughly classified into three somewhat overlapping types: plunging, spilling, and surging (Fig. 36a). Plunging breakers tend to overtop all at once and collapse with a crash; they most commonly result from long, low swell, and their formation is somewhat favored by opposing winds. Spilling breakers tend to break and "spill" gradually over some distance; they commonly result from steep wind waves, and the tendency for the spilling breaker to occur is greater if the wind blows in the direction of wave travel. Surging breakers do not actually break in the sense of spilling or plunging, but surge up the face of the beach. They are usually associated with beaches having steep nearshore and shore face slopes.

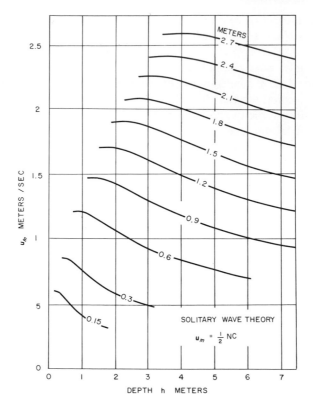

Fig. 35. Maximum horizontal orbital velocity near the bottom, $u_m$ for a solitary wave traveling in still water, according to the relation $u_m = \frac{1}{2}NC$ where $N$ is approximately equal to the $H/h$ as in equation (6b). In practice the still water orbital velocity is reduced by assuming the wave is traveling in water having a net reverse flow. From Inman and Nasu (1956, Fig. 27).

## Shoaling Transformations

The profiles of ocean swell in deep water are long and low, approaching a sinusoidal form. However, as waves enter shallow water the wave velocity and length decrease, the wave steepens and the wave height increases until the wave train consists of peaked crests separated by relatively flat troughs. Near the breaker zone the process of steepening is accelerated so that the breaking wave may obtain a height several times greater than the deep water wave. This transformation is particularly pronounced for long period swell from a distant storm. The profiles of local storm waves show considerable steepness in deep water, so that the shallow water steepening is not as pronounced as in the case of ocean swell. During the transformation from deep to shallow water, only the wave period remains essentially constant while all other properties of the wave change.

The shallow water transformation of waves commences at the depth where the waves "feel bottom," and cease to be deep water waves. As shown previously, this depth is equal to approximately one-quarter of the deep water wavelength.

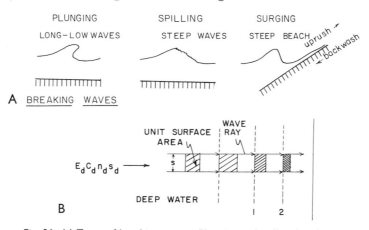

Fig. 36. (*a*) Types of breaking waves. Plunging and spilling breakers can occur on gently sloping beaches; surging breakers occur only on very steep slopes. (*b*) Concentration of energy in a shoaling wave. The density of shading between wave rays indicates the relative concentration of energy per unit of surface area.

Airy wave theory gives the wave phase velocity as

$$C^2 = (g/k)\tanh kh$$

from which it is apparent that the phase velocity, $C$, is influenced by depth when the depth is approximately a quarter of the deep water wavelength, and continues to decrease from this point shoreward. The change in wavelength with depth can be obtained from the product of the wave phase velocity and the period.[7] Since the wave period remains constant, the wavelength changes at the same rate as the wave velocity, and they can both be shown as a function of the relative depth, $h/L_d$ by a single curve (Fig. 31).

The shoaling transformation for wave height can most easily be

[7] Or the wavelength at any depth can be computed directly from the relation $L^2 = L_d{}^2 \tanh k_d h$ (Eckart, 1952), where again the subscript $d$ refers to the deep water wave condition.

explained from the standpoint of the conservation of energy in the advancing wave. Here it is not the energy alone, but the rate of travel of energy, or power, that becomes the important factor. The energy of a deep water wave is one-half potential, associated with the wave height, and one-half kinetic, associated with the orbital motion of the particles of water. In deep water the wave energy advances at a rate of only one-half the phase velocity of the wave. If one follows the crest of a wave traveling in deep water, it will be observed that the crest gradually diminishes in size and disappears. This occurs because the phase velocity of any individual wave travels faster and thus "outruns" the energy which is associated with the wave group. The rate of advance of energy is called the group velocity, $G$, and it is often expressed as some fraction $n$ of the phase velocity, such that $G = Cn$. In deep water, $n = \frac{1}{2}$ and increases in value as the wave travels into water of intermediate depth, until in shallow water it is equal to one, and the wave energy then travels forward with the phase velocity $C$.

In considering the energy transmission in a shoaling wave it is convenient to assume that the wave and its energy travel only in a straight line, so that the energy is contained between wave rays, where a ray is defined as a construction line pointing in the direction of wave travel (Fig. 36b). If $E$ is the energy in a unit surface area of a wave, and it is traveling forward with group velocity $Cn$, then the rate of propagation of energy between two wave rays must be the product $ECn$ times the distance $s$ between wave rays. Further, if energy is conserved, then this relation must be equal everywhere between the wave rays, and we can write

$$E_1 C_1 n_1 s_1 = E_2 C_2 n_2 s_2 = E_d C_d n_d s_d \tag{7}$$

where the subscript $d$ refers to deep water and 1 and 2 are successively shallower positions of the wave front as it advances towards the coast (Fig. 36b). Since the wave rays are assumed to be straight, $s_1 = s_2 = s_d$ and relation (7) reduces to $ECn = E_d C_d n_d$, etc. The condition where the spacing $s$ between wave rays is not constant will be considered under wave refraction.

Superficial considerations indicate that if energy travels into an area faster than it leaves, energy will become concentrated and the wave height will increase. In general since the wave form is slowing down as the water shoals, it can be expected that energy is entering a given sector more rapidly than it leaves, and hence there will be a concentration of energy which should be expressed as an increase in wave height. However, the explanation is complicated by the fact that during the first stages of shoaling the ratio of the group to the phase velocity undergoes a relatively rapid increase. Initially, this is expressed as an increase in the group velocity $G$, and consequently results in a slight reduction in wave height. As shown by the curve for $H/H_d$ in Fig. 31, the maximum reduction in wave height is about $8\frac{1}{2}$ percent and occurs at a depth equal to about one-sixth of the deep water wavelength. Thereafter the wave height increases continually as the wave shoals and exceeds the deep water wave height at a depth of about one-eighteenth of the deep water wavelength. Roughly, the reduction in wave height occurs within the zone of intermediate depths, ranging from about one-quarter to one-twentieth of the deep water wavelength.

The energy of an Airy wave per unit of surface area is proportional to the square of the wave height, $H$, and is given as $E = \frac{1}{8}\rho g H^2$, where $\rho$ is the density of water, and $g$ the acceleration of gravity.[8] If we substitute this value for the wave energy in the expression for energy transmission (equation 7) and let $n_d$ be equal to $\frac{1}{2}$, we obtain an expression for the wave height, $H$, at any depth in terms of the deep water wave height and the wave velocities:

$$\frac{H}{H_d} = \left(\frac{C_d}{2Cn}\right)^{1/2} \qquad\qquad (8)[9]$$

For the case of a very gradual shoaling bottom, Eckart (1952) derives a simplified expression for the wave height in shallow water;

$$\frac{H}{H_d} = \frac{\sqrt{\frac{1}{2}}}{(k_d h)^{1/4}}$$

where as before $k_d = 2\pi/L_d$.

Relation (8) is plotted in terms of the ratio of water depth to deep water wavelength in Fig. 31. Since this shoaling transformation is based on the small amplitude theory of Airy, it applies only so long as the wave height is small compared to the wavelength and depth of water. Thus, it is to be expected that this relation will have application to ocean surface waves of small height until they near the surf zone, where it will no longer apply.

Since waves near the surf zone exhibit many of the characteristics of the solitary wave, it seems more appropriate to estimate the wave height of long waves near the breaker zone from relations based on the solitary wave. Munk (1949b) developed the following relation for wave height by equating the Airy expression for energy transmission in deep water to the expression for the energy transfer of a

---

[8] The corresponding expression for the energy per unit surface area of a Stokes wave is $E = \frac{1}{8}\rho g H^2(1 - \frac{1}{8}k_d^2 H^2)$.

[9] Where $n$ = group velocity/phase velocity = $\frac{1}{2} + kh/\sinh 2kh$.

solitary wave[10] in shallow water:

$$\frac{H_b}{H_d} = 0.30 \left(\frac{L_d}{H_d}\right)^{1/3} \tag{9}$$

where $H_b$ is the breaker or near breaker height, $L_d$ and $H_d$ apply to the deep water wave, and the constant 0.30 is a dimensionless number. This shoaling transformation for breaker height is plotted as a func-

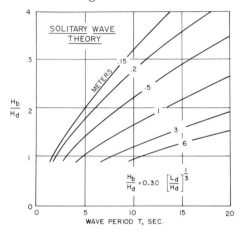

Fig. 37. Shoaling transformation in the height of a breaking solitary wave. The relation assumes that the deep water Airy wave of height $H_d$ is transformed to a breaking solitary wave of height $H_b$ without refraction.

tion of the wave period in Fig. 37. Values of the ratio of $H_b/H_d$ less than about 0.9 are unrealistic and indicate conditions where the waves are too steep for solitary theory to apply.

**Wave Reflection, Refraction, and Diffraction.**     Upon entering shallow water, waves are also subject to reflection, refraction, and diffraction, processes which are analogous to their counterparts in physical optics. The proportion of incident wave energy that is reflected from a coast increases with increasing slope of the bottom, and may approach the entire incident wave energy for the case of low waves reflected from a vertical wall. Diffraction results from the flow of energy along the wave crest in a direction at right angles to the direction of wave travel. Diffraction becomes an important mechanism for energy transfer when there is a pronounced gradient in wave height along the crest of a wave, as when a wave crest is abruptly terminated after passing beyond the breakwaters of a harbor entrance. In such a case diffraction is responsible for the occurrence

[10] The energy per unit surface area of a solitary wave is given as

$$E = \frac{8}{(3\gamma)^{3/2}} \rho g \frac{H^3}{CT}$$

where $\gamma$ equals $H/h$ is the relative wave height and is assumed equal to 0.78 in the derivation of equation (9).

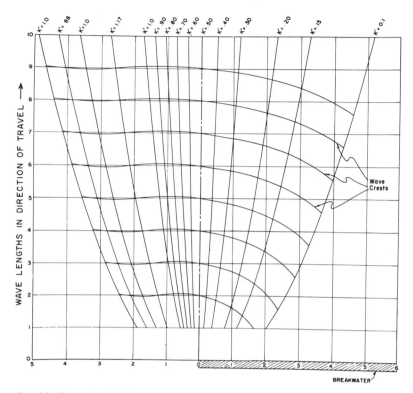

Fig. 38. Generalized diffraction diagram for waves passing a breakwater with uniform depth shoreward of the breakwater (after Dunham, 1951, Fig. 6; and *Beach Erosion Board Tech. Rept. 4*, Fig. 21). Each unit on the grid is equal to one wavelength of the undiffracted wave; curved crest lines show the position of successive wave crests after diffraction. The values of $K'$ give the proportion of the height of the undiffracted wave that is to be found in the lee of the breakwater.

of waves in the sheltered area behind the breakwaters, and thus is of importance in the design of harbors. Model studies of wave diffraction, or the graphic construction of diffraction diagrams (Fig. 38), are commonly utilized in determining the preferred positions for harbor entrances with regard to mooring and docking facilities. Where the bottom topography slopes, wave refraction usually becomes more significant in the distribution of energy in sheltered zones than diffraction.

Wave refraction is the process whereby the direction of travel of the wave changes with change in the depth of water. As waves travel into shallow water, refraction causes the wave rays, which are construction lines in the direction of wave travel, to turn into the shallow water so that the wave crests tend to parallel the depth contours

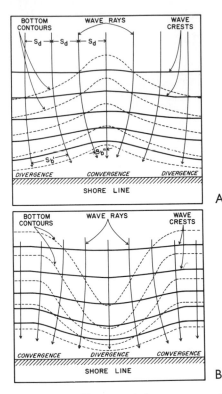

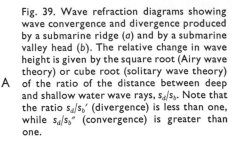

Fig. 39. Wave refraction diagrams showing wave convergence and divergence produced by a submarine ridge (*a*) and by a submarine valley head (*b*). The relative change in wave height is given by the square root (Airy wave theory) or cube root (solitary wave theory) of the ratio of the distance between deep and shallow water wave rays, $s_d/s_b$. Note that the ratio $s_d/s_b'$ (divergence) is less than one, while $s_d/s_b''$ (convergence) is greater than one.

(Fig. 39). For straight coasts with parallel contours, this decreases the angle between the approaching wave and the coast and causes a "spreading" of the energy along the wave crests. The wave height is decreased by this process but the effect is uniform along the coast. A submarine canyon or depression causes waves to be refracted or bent in such a manner that the waves over the canyon will diverge and decrease in height, and the wave crest will become convex toward the shore. When waves converge on either side of a submarine canyon, or over a ridge, the wave height will increase and the line of wave crests will be concave toward the shore. The amount of wave refraction and consequent change in wave height and direction is a function of both wavelength and the direction of wave approach.

The change in wave direction caused by refraction is related to the change in wave phase velocity, and is given by Snell's law:

$$\frac{\sin \alpha}{\sin \alpha_d} = \frac{C}{C_d}$$

where $\alpha$ is the angle between the wave crest and the bottom contours and the subscript $_d$ refers to deep water wave conditions. Used in the sense of physical optics, $\alpha_d$ is the angle of incidence, measured between the wave ray and a normal to the bottom contours, and $\alpha$ is the angle of refraction.

For waves traveling in intermediate depths of water, the change in wave height due to refraction is inversely proportional to the square root of the change in the spacing, $s$, between adjacent wave rays. By using the same reasoning which led to equation (7), we can write a refraction coefficient, $K$, for the change in wave height due to refraction for waves of small amplitude as follows:

$$K = \left(\frac{s_d}{s}\right)^{1/2}$$
(10a)

As in the case of the shoaling transformation for unrefracted waves, it seems more reasonable to use the expression for solitary waves when the waves are near the breaker zone. The energy in a solitary wave is proportional to the cube of the wave height, from which it follows that the change in wave height due to the change in concentration of energy per unit area becomes proportional to the cube root of the change of energy concentration. Thus, the change in wave height due to wave refraction must be inversely proportional to the cube root of the ratios of the spacing between wave rays. Near the breaker zone the coefficient for the change in wave height due to refraction becomes

$$K_b = \left(\frac{s_d}{s_b}\right)^{1/3}$$
(10b)

The complete expression for the height of waves near the breaker zone, considering changes related to both shoaling and to wave refraction, is given by the product of equations (9) and (10b)

$$\frac{H_b}{H_d} = 0.30\left(\frac{L_d}{H_d}\right)^{1/3} K_b$$
(11)

## Wave-Drift Currents

The orbital motion of a water particle during the passage of a wave traverses an open curve rather than a closed orbit (Fig. 32). This produces a gradual advancement of the water particle with the passage of each wave, which results in a net current in the direction of wave propagation. For a Stokian wave traveling in deep water the velocity of the wave-induced current $u_\theta$ at any depth $h - z$ below the water surface is given in terms of the maximum orbital velocity $u_m$ and the wave phase velocity $C$ as[11]

$$u_\theta = \frac{u_m{}^2}{C} e^{-2k(h-z)}$$
(12)

[11] Lamb (1945, p. 419).

When this relation is integrated from the surface to sufficient depth, the discharge $q$, in terms of the volume transported forward per unit of wave crest length per unit time becomes

$$q = \frac{\pi}{4} \frac{H^2}{T} \tag{13}$$

Although this is a useful relation for predicting the volume transport induced by waves traveling in deep water, observations indicate that it does not give satisfactory results for depths shoaler than about one-quarter of a wavelength. Longuet-Higgins (1953) developed a relation for wave currents applicable to shallow water waves of low amplitude that gives a volume transport of water in the direction of wave propagation at the water surface and at the bottom, with a reversal in the direction of flow at intermediate depths (Fig. 40a). Russell and Osorio (1958) found that even though the theory was developed for waves of small amplitude and for laminar motion, their model experiments made over a smooth bottom agreed fairly well with theory when the depth of water was between about one-tenth and one twenty-fifth of the wavelength (Fig. 40b). The velocity of the bottom current was in agreement with theory down to the shoalest depths measured, where the depth was only 3 percent of the wavelength.

Longuet-Higgins gives the velocity of the discharge as a complex function, which for the most rapidly moving layer of water near the bottom simplifies to the form

$$u_\theta = \frac{5}{4} \frac{u_m{}^2}{C} \tag{14}$$

where $u_m$ is the maximum horizontal component of the orbital velocity near the bottom, and $C$ is the wave phase velocity. $C$ and $u_m$ are given by equations (1) and (3a) respectively. Longuet-Higgins, in an appendix to the 1958 paper shows that his relation should also apply to turbulent flow; however, this has not been verified by model experiments. For given values of depth to wavelength ratio, the model experiments showed that the lowest wave produced the highest ratio of observed to theoretical drift velocities (Fig. 40b). Wherever the depth was small compared to the width of the tank, a circulation with a horizontal axis was observed to form. In cases where the waves were almost steep enough to break, the bottom velocities were reduced to about one-half of the theoretical value. Here again, it seems unlikely that this relation will apply to the case of a breaking wave.

No theory for breaking waves has been advanced to the point of

THEORETICAL  WAVE-DRIFT  PROFILE

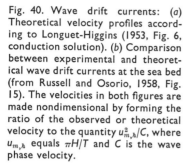

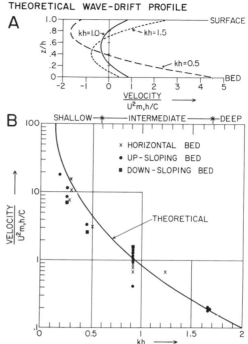

Fig. 40. Wave drift currents: (a) Theoretical velocity profiles according to Longuet-Higgins (1953, Fig. 6, conduction solution). (b) Comparison between experimental and theoretical wave drift currents at the sea bed (from Russell and Osorio, 1958, Fig. 15). The velocities in both figures are made nondimensional by forming the ratio of the observed or theoretical velocity to the quantity $u^2_{m,h}/C$, where $u_{m,h}$ equals $\pi H/T$ and $C$ is the wave phase velocity.

prediction of wave-induced currents. However, it is of interest here to apply the solitary theory to the surf zone. If one assumes that the total volume of the wave above the trough moves forward with the breaking wave, then solitary theory (Munk, 1949b) gives the discharge of a breaking wave as

$$q = \frac{4}{\sqrt{3\gamma^3}} \frac{H_b^2}{T} \tag{15}$$

where as before $q$ is the volume transported forward per unit of wave crest per unit of time and $\gamma$ is the relative depth, $H/h = 0.78$. It is interesting to note that the variables in the expression for volume transport in both solitary and Stokian wave are $H^2/T$.

### Currents in the Surf Zone

Waves in deep water cause a volume transport, or discharge of water in the direction of their travel. This discharge increases as the waves pass into shoaling water near shore. The beach, however, presents an almost impermeable obstacle which must reduce to zero the entire component of the discharge normal to the shore. The superelevation of the water surface produced by the wave-drift currents against the shore constitutes a normal outward force which,

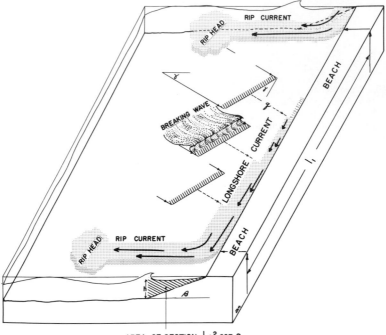

Fig. 41. Schematic drawing showing the generation of longshore and rip currents by waves breaking on a beach. The current increases along the beach until it flows seaward as a rip current.

in effect, superimposes an outward discharge balancing the inward discharge by the waves. Such a state of equilibrium must exist on the average over a sufficient length of shore. However, it is uncertain to what extent the equilibrium is stable at any given point, i.e., to what extent the water transported shoreward at any point may return seaward elsewhere.

If the direction of wave travel is not normal to the shore the accompanying discharge has a longshore component in any case, over and above that due to any local disequilibrium in the force components normal to the shore; and a definite longshore current must result. For some as yet unexplained reason this longshore current is found to be confined largely within the surf zone.

The waves discharge water into each unit length of the surf zone. Therefore, assuming the resulting longshore current to be confined to the surf zone, the velocity of the current would go on increasing indefinitely with distance along the shore, were it not for the existence of outward flowing *rip currents* at discrete places (Fig. 41). Because of this build-up the existence of outward flowing rip currents is inevitable.

Assume that waves breaking at an angle $\alpha$ with the beach produce a volume discharge of water $q$ per unit time and unit length of wave crest (Fig. 41). Since $q$ is in the direction of travel of the breaking wave, the discharge must result in a longshore component $q \sin \alpha$ per unit of wave crest. This longshore component, in turn, becomes $q \sin \alpha \cos \alpha$ per unit of beach length, and would produce a longshore current increasing indefinitely with distance along the beach if it were not released by rip currents. If the average spacing between rip currents is $l_1$, then the average longshore discharge $q_l$ must equal

$$q l_1 \sin \alpha \cos \alpha / 2$$

The sectional area of the water inshore from the breaker zone can be expressed as $\frac{1}{2} h^2 \cot \beta$, where $h$ is the water depth at the point of breaking and $\beta$ is the average slope of the beach (shaded area in Fig. 41). If the discharge $q_l$ is uniformly distributed over the inshore waters, then the average longshore current $\bar{u}_l$ will be given by the ratio of the longshore discharge divided by the area of the section:

$$\bar{u}_l = \frac{q l_1}{h^2} \tan \beta \sin \alpha \cos \alpha$$

or

$$\bar{u}_l = 4 \sqrt{\frac{\gamma}{3}} \frac{l_1}{T} \tan \beta \sin \alpha \cos \alpha \tag{16}$$

where the latter equation results from the substitution of the value of $q$ from solitary wave theory (equation 15).

Other expressions for the velocity of the longshore current have been developed by Putnam et al. (1949) and have been modified by Inman and Quinn (1952). While these latter expressions give useful empirical relations for the velocity of the longshore current, they all lack the necessary rigorous testing.

The net onshore transport of water by wave action in the breaker zone, the lateral transport inside the breaker zone by longshore currents, the seaward return of the flow through the surf zone by rip currents, and the longshore movement in the expanding head of the rip current, all constitute a nearshore circulation system (Fig. 42). The pattern that results from this circulation commonly takes the form of an eddy or cell with vertical axis. The positions of the rip currents are dependent on the submarine topography and configuration of the coast and on the height and period of the waves. An example of a circulation cell in relation to the refraction produced by submarine canyons is illustrated in Fig. 43. Periodicity or fluctuation of current velocity and direction is a characteristic of flow in the

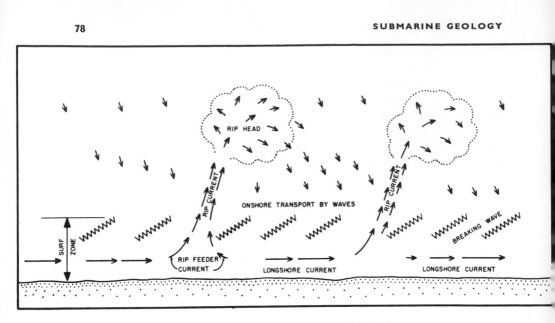

Fig. 42. Nearshore circulation system and related terms.

nearshore circulation system. This variability is due primarily to the grouping of high waves followed by low waves, a phenomenon which gives rise to a pulsation of water level in the surf zone.

### Summary of Wind-Generated Waves and Associated Currents

The foregoing treatment of waves and their associated currents has presented, in somewhat technical form, the nature and fluid mechanics of ocean waves and their associated currents. A summary of the results of this treatment of a large field of research follows with emphasis on applications. A summary of useful equations and their range of application is given in Table 5. Waves are generated by wind blowing over the water surface and are propagated as swell in the direction of the wind but far beyond the area where the wind produced the motion. As a result large waves with long periods spread from storm centers to the farthest limits of the oceans, and some of the energy even returns from the shore as reflected waves. Thus many large waves occur along coastlines at a time when no local storms exist. Because waves often approach a coast from several different generation areas there may be a great difference in their height as they approach the shore, depending on whether the waves of the different trains are in phase so that they reinforce one another (causing large waves) or in opposition (resulting in small waves). Because several large waves come in succession followed by several

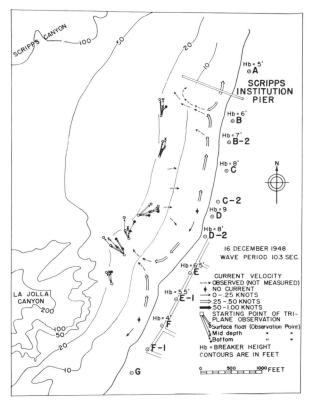

Fig. 43. Cell-like features of the circulation pattern during relatively long-period waves along the beach south of Scripps Institution. The rotary currents are related to the wave convergence between canyons and divergence at canyon heads. Velocities were measured by tracing movement of suspended and surface floats. Letters refer to ranges used in the work. From Shepard and Inman (1950).

small waves, it is usually possible to time a landing through the surf to coincide with the smaller waves.

Upon entering shallow water the open ocean swell undergoes a shoaling transformation. This may include refraction which causes a change in direction of the wave front so as to conform somewhat to the contours of the shallow sea floor. One result of this change in direction of wave travel is to cause energy to concentrate in areas over shallow submarine ridges, producing what is called a wave convergence, while energy is reduced over sea floor valleys, producing a wave divergence (Fig. 39). On entering shallow water the speed of propagation of the wave is decreased whereas the height of the wave crest is increased. The trough between waves is flattened and the crest

Table 5. Summary of Wave Equations

| FUNCTION | DEEP WATER | INTERMEDIATE | SHALLOW WATER | NEAR-BREAKER |
|---|---|---|---|---|
| PHASE VELOCITY, C | $\dfrac{g}{2\pi}T$ | $\left[\dfrac{g}{k}\tanh kh\right]^{\frac{1}{2}}$ | $\left[gh\right]^{\frac{1}{2}}$ | $\left[g(h+H)\right]^{\frac{1}{2}}$ |
| WAVE LENGTH, L | $L_d = \dfrac{g}{2\pi}T^2$ | $L_d\left[\tanh k_d h\right]^{\frac{1}{2}}$ ⟶ | | $CT$ |
| WAVE HEIGHT, H | $H_d$ | $H_d\left[\dfrac{C_d}{2Cn}\right]^{\frac{1}{2}}$ | $\dfrac{H_d}{[4k_d h]^{\frac{1}{4}}}$ | $0.32\,H_d\left[\dfrac{L_d}{H_d}\right]^{\frac{1}{3}}$ |
| ORBITAL DIAMETER, d | SURFACE $d = H_d$ <br> BOTTOM $d_o = 0$ | $d_z = H\,\dfrac{\cosh kz}{\sinh kh}$ | $d_z = \dfrac{H}{kh}$ | $d_o \doteq \dfrac{3}{2}H$ |
| MAXIMUM ORBITAL VELOCITY, $u_m$ | $\dfrac{\pi d}{T}$ ⟶ | | $\dfrac{1}{2}\dfrac{H}{h}C$ | $u_{m,o} \doteq \dfrac{1}{3}\dfrac{H}{h}C$ |
| LIMITS OF APPLICATION | | | | |

$\dfrac{h}{L_d} > \dfrac{1}{4}$    $\dfrac{h}{L_d} \longrightarrow \dfrac{1}{20} > \dfrac{h}{L_d}$    $\dfrac{H}{h} > \dfrac{1}{4}$

sharpened. When the long low swell type of wave gets to a point where the wave height is approximately equal to the water depth, the wave collapses or breaks. In the case of the short steep waves breaking occurs when the wave height is just over one-half of the water depth. The long swell wave usually breaks with a hollow front called a plunging breaker, while the wind wave with a steep front breaks as a spilling type of breaker (Fig. 36a). If the beach is very steep a surging type of breaker will form with strong uprush and backwash.

It has often been reported that breaking waves are accompanied by undertow, a current supposed to return seaward under the advancing wave fronts. This is essentially an erroneous interpretation, probably resulting from the observation on steep beaches that strong backwash flow may carry a swimmer toward the oncoming breaker. However, within the breaking wave all water moves toward the shore. The on-shore transportation of water associated with the breaking wave tends to pile water against the shore and to produce currents that flow along the shore called "longshore currents." After flowing parallel to the beach, the water is returned seaward in narrow flows called "rip currents" (Figs. 41–43). In and near the breaker zone, the seaward flow of water in the rip current extends from the surface to the bottom. Outside of the surf zone and in slightly deeper water the seaward flow of the rip current rides over the bottom water which may have a net onshore motion. Rip currents are the cause of most drownings along open coasts where large swell come in to the shore. Rip currents often occur on the up-current sides of points, but they also occur on either side of convergences where the water moves out from the center of the convergence and then turns seaward. Rip currents tend to carry swimmers out to sea, but most of the drownings could be avoided if the swimmer would swim laterally out of the rip rather than trying to swim against it. Rips can be observed by bathers because of their agitated roiled up water with foam lines at their boundaries and because of the roughness of the bottom in the feeders that lead to the outflowing rip.

# CHAPTER IV

# CATASTROPHIC WAVES AND OCEAN CURRENTS

## Tsunamis (Tidal Waves)

The Japanese word *tunami* (written *tsunami* by American scientists because of the *ts* sound) is used to cover the rare type of sea waves that accompany some of the large submarine earthquakes as well as explosive submarine volcanic eruptions. Some of these waves, popularly known as tidal waves, are far larger where they break against the coast than any waves raised by wind. The water from tsunamis has been driven for two miles or more across coastal plains, and the uprush of the waves is said to rise to heights of as much as 135 ft, a rise of 50 ft being reported in many cases (Johnson, 1919, p. 41). In some localities the coastal erosion of tsunamis may greatly exceed that of ordinary waves during the intervals of many decades between the tsunamis. These tremendous waves cause an enormous amount of damage to coastal communities that are in their paths.

**The Hawaiian Tsunami of April 1, 1946.** Although it has been known that tsunamis traverse the widest oceans, up to 1946 it seems to have been generally supposed that serious damage from the waves occurred only relatively near the source of disturbance. This is certainly not the case. On the morning of April 1, 1946, while working on the first edition of the present book at a remote locality on the north shore of Oahu, my wife and I had to run to escape waves that swept into the Hawaiian Islands after traversing 2300 miles of ocean. This experience was followed by an investigation of the coastal damage on the five main islands (Shepard *et al.*, 1950). This represented such an unusual opportunity to learn about the nature of tsunamis that these particular waves will be used as an illustration of the phenomenon in general.

At 2:00 a.m., Hawaiian time, an earthquake took place with an epicenter in the elongate deep off the Aleutian Island of Unimak. It is probable that this earthquake was associated with a deepening of the floor of the fault trough in this area. The trough runs approximately east and west, so that the waves moved with greatest effect in a north-south direction. Hawaii lay to the south. Since a giant oscillation was set up within the ocean at this locality, the first wave was followed by others. These waves, moving across the open ocean, were imperceptible to vessels that lay in their path because they had a height of only about one foot in the open ocean. Since they are known to have reached the islands, a distance of 2000 nautical miles, in less than 5 hours, they moved at an average speed of 470 miles an hour. With the speed given and knowing that there was about 12 minutes between the arrival of each wave, there should have been about 90 miles between the crest of each passing wave in the open ocean.

The fact that at least the first three waves showed a progressive increase in height was a fortunate thing so far as the islanders were concerned. It would have been still more fortunate if the inhabitants of beach houses and of the coastal strip at Hilo had known that such a sequence was a common occurrence. The waves showed a decided increase on the two Hawaiian tide gauge records, from the first to the fourth at Honolulu, and from the first to the sixth in an estuary on the south side of Kauai. Also, numerous observers of the waves report that such increases took place. In my experience, an increase in the first three waves was noted which produced high-water marks above tide level of 13, 17, and 19 ft, respectively. This compares with 0.8, 1.5, and 2.3 ft above normal for the Honolulu tide gauge which was in the harbor and on the protected side of the same island.

Many people were warned of the coming of the waves by the withdrawal of the water from the reefs and from the shallow coastal platforms. To some people the withdrawing water became apparent because it removed the sound of breakers, leaving a strange quiet. This alarmed many natives who were used to the constant sound of the sea. It is uncertain whether the sea withdrew before the first advancing wave or whether the first wave was so small as to fail to attract attention. The tide gauges show a small rise preceding the first fall in sea level, although no record was obtained on the open coast. In a tsunami the first withdrawal should provide a warning to people of the coming of dangerous waves.

It was most difficult to estimate the actual height of the wave which came in along the shore. The evidence which Shepard *et al.* (1950) were able to find in the Hawaiian Islands showed the height to which the water rose, causing damage or leaving debris behind in its retreat. The waves were probably low as they came in to the coast. Where I was living I observed the second wave as it broke over the outer coral reef, and it was just possible to see over the advancing wave (Fig. 44) from a height of eye of about 18 ft above the tide.

Fig. 44. Photograph of the second wave of the tsunami of April 1, 1946. Note the large breakers in the ordinarily quiet lagoon inside a coral reef. Taken at 6:45 a.m. at Kawela Bay on the north coast of Oahu.

Unlike normal waves the tsunami kept on coming rather than dissipating its energy where it encountered the reef. Views taken of the waves breaking near Hilo on the Island of Hawaii show that the breaking waves rose approximately 30 ft above still-water level. In both of these areas the wave run-up reached heights on shore that are comparable to the height at which they were breaking. In some other cases, however, where the waves encountered steep slopes the run-up exceeded their breaker height. Where the waves entered valleys with straight walls, as along the northeast coast of Hawaii, there is evidence that they rose as they crossed the beach and then subsided somewhat as they passed inland. In one of these valleys, Pololu, the wave left debris at an elevation of 55 ft, and in a valley on the north coast of Molokai a high-water mark of 54 ft was measured.

Tremendous differences in wave heights were found along the coasts of the Hawaiian Islands (Fig. 45). As would be expected the heights decreased in passing around from the north side of the islands to the south. In encircling round islands like Kauai the waves showed less loss in height than in encircling angular islands like Molokai. Another cause of variation was the submarine topography. In the case of the tsunamis, as in ordinary wind waves, the heights were greatest inside submarine ridges and less inside valleys (Fig. 46).

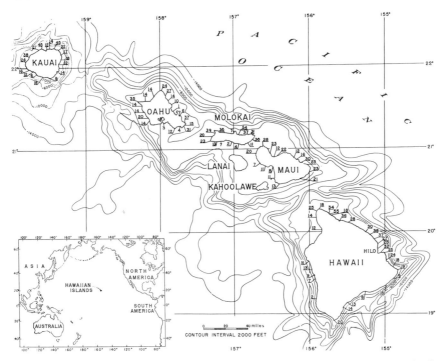

Fig. 45. Maximum heights reached by waves from the 1946 tsunami in the Hawaiian Islands. Heights expressed in feet. From Shepard *et al.* (1950).

Another important effect came from the coral reefs. Where the reefs were wide and particularly where there was an appreciable lagoon inside the reef, the heights were much less. An extreme case of the latter comes from Kaneohe Bay in Oahu where almost no wave was experienced inside the broad reefs. The reefs are well offshore in this area. The importance of reefs is also demonstrated by the great contrast in the heights on the north side of Oahu, where the reef is fairly continuous, with the heights on the north side of all the other main islands where reefs are largely negligible except locally off Kauai.

**The April 1, 1946, Tsunami in Other Areas.**    Although the greatest damage occurred in Hawaii, the 1946 tsunami rose to its greatest heights in the Aleutians. At Scotch Cap in Alaska a lighthouse was destroyed at about 100 ft above sea level.

Along the California coast the tsunami was reported by members of the Department of Engineering of the University of California as rising to a maximum of 10 ft above still water. This rise, which was observed at Half Moon Bay, resulted in slight damage. Elsewhere, more moderate rises were observed. From the available data it

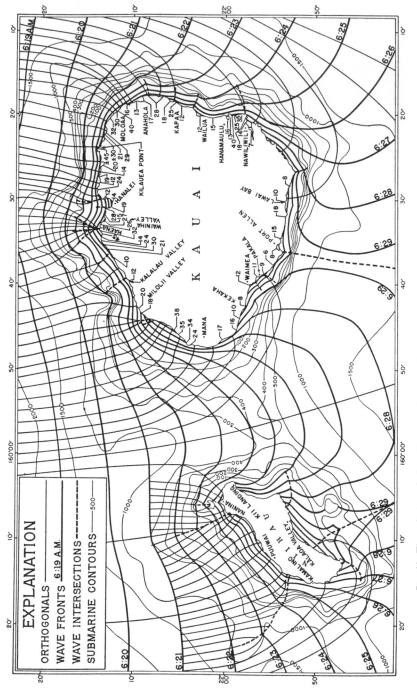

Fig. 46. The relation of advancing wave fronts and convergence of orthogonals in producing high water levels along the north coast of Kauai during the 1946 tsunami. Note that the two portions of the wave that passed around the Island of Kauai became reinforced on the south coast. From Shepard et al. (1950); based on computations by D. C. Cox.

appeared that the rises may have been greatest on the south side of points for which no reason is evident. The data to the north of California are scarce, but tide gauges suggest that the waves were negligible. The gauges along the South American coast showed larger waves than those of British Columbia and Alaska.

The available evidence indicates that the waves had a line source rather than a point source. Evidently this line ran essentially normal to the orthogonals coming to the Hawaiian Islands. This caused the great effect in that area.

**The 1952, 1957, and 1960 Tsunamis in Hawaii.** Prior to 1946 no large tsunami had hit the Hawaiian Islands since 1877, but subsequently in 14 years three series of waves have caused severe damage to the islands. In 1952 (Macdonald and Wentworth, 1954) the waves coming from Kamchatka were distinctly lower at Hilo as well as elsewhere in the islands except in Maui, where they rose to greater heights on the east side of the Isthmus than in 1946. In 1957, after another Aleutian trough earthquake, Hilo was again spared serious damage but the north coast of Kauai was hit worse than in any known tsunami. Fortunately, the warning system based on seismograph records had been developed by the U.S. Coast and Geodetic Survey sufficiently that the island police, were able to move along the coast and warn people to get to high ground ahead of the waves. No fatalities resulted. The waves along the northeast coast of Hawaii were almost as high as in 1946 and distinctly higher than in 1952 (Fraser *et al.*, 1959). On May 23, 1960, the first of a series of tremendous earth movements along the coast of Chile sent waves of great destructive power all the way across the Pacific and caused very serious damage to the Japanese coast. Hilo, Hawaii, was again devastated, and the water rose in the city to a height of 37 ft, well above the 1946 level, and sixty-one people were drowned. Unlike the tsunami of 1946 the breakwater was not damaged despite the great rise in water level, yet the highest water levels were attained within the harbor rather than in the city outskirts as had been the case in 1946. At Waikiki Beach the water rose sufficiently to produce minor damage in some of the basements of the new hotels along the waterfront, the first time on record.

The history of all these inundations has been different in each locality although some areas, notably Hilo and the north side of Maui Isthmus, appear to be vulnerable to waves coming from both the north and south.

**Tsunami Effects Along the West Coast of United States.** The west coast has had virtually no damage from tsunamis. This is partly because of the long diagonal approach of waves coming both from the Aleutian and the South American trenches. This causes the waves to lose energy in crossing the long distance of shallow water before coming to the shore. The waves originating in Chile in 1960, however, did produce moderate damage to yachts and coastal engineering works both in San Diego and in Los Angeles harbors. Both of these face toward the south, and thus the waves had a more direct approach. The amplitude of the waves coming into San Diego reached at least 5 ft and continued to be measurable for the entire day with considerable variation in heights. Strong currents moved up the entrance of both harbors and caused ships to break their lines and crash into the pier pilings.

**Wave Heights in Bays and on Points.** According to Imamura (1937), tsunamis are said to be particularly violent at the heads of deep funnel-shaped bays. The study of the Hawaiian waves, however, does not entirely bear out this statement. The wave heights at Hilo, which have been considered as an example of this funneling action, do not show that the water rose higher at the head of the bay than near the entrance. In fact, the greatest consistent high-water marks are on the south side of the bay halfway from the bay head to the outer point. A study of the numerous heights reported by the Japanese for the tsunami of 1933 off the Sanriku coast (Tokyo Imperial University, 1933) shows that the water rose higher at the heads of small bays than on the adjacent points, but that the heights at the heads of long indentations were low. Also, some of the greatest heights were relatively near prominent points but not at the very end of these points. On the other hand, in 1946 where a prominent point extends out beyond the north side of Molokai and is bordered by deep water, the water rose only about 7 ft in contrast to 54 ft a few miles to the northeast. Many factors enter into the picture.

**Conclusions Concerning Tsunamis.** The preceding discussion, which referred largely to the 1946 Hawaiian tsunami, appears to serve as a basis for drawing some general, if tentative conclusions, because the Hawaiian waves gave such an unusual opportunity to trace the phenomenon around islands and to check the relations of high-water marks to the nature of the submarine approaches. The only other waves of this nature which have been given considerable study, those of the Sanriku coast of Japan, are not related to such a variety of submarine topography, although the numerous recorded heights have yielded useful data.

The following points come from the studies of the 1946 waves and from other information:[1]

---

[1] These conclusions should be re-evaluated after the publication of the symposium on tsunamis held in Honolulu in 1961 at the Tenth Pacific Science Congress.

1. The waves in the Pacific that follow earthquakes are probably the result of movement along a line rather than in a narrow zone such as might have been the result of submarine landslides.
2. The above suggests that faulting is the cause. According to van Dorn (1961) the "absence of a bore and the leading trough suggest a source aligned with the axis of the Aleutian Arc, with downthrust on the south side."
3. Tsunamis can travel for thousands of miles and retain enough energy to rise for a score or more feet on an unprotected coast facing the direction of wave approach.
4. A withdrawal of the water from the coast is likely to be the first substantial manifestation of approaching waves, although a slight crest often precedes.
5. The first wave is not likely to be the largest.
6. In general the waves are relatively high inside submarine ridges and relatively low inside submarine valleys, provided these features extend into deep water.
7. The waves may be small where they hit a projecting point which is bordered by deep water.
8. The waves are greatly decreased by the presence of coral reefs bordering the coast.
9. The waves have a funneling effect in some small bays but are generally small at the heads of long estuaries.
10. The waves can bend around a circular island without great loss of energy but are considerably reduced in height in encircling an elongate angular island.

## Landslide Surges

The falling of a mass of rock or part of a glacier from a cliff into a bay or lake may cause tremendous waves. Like tsunamis these are impulsively generated waves but to date have been observed only in restricted waters. The largest so far recorded took place on July 9, 1958, in Lituya Bay on the south coast of Alaska (Miller, 1960). As the result of an earthquake a rockfall estimated as containing 40,000,000 cu yd of rock fell from an altitude of up to 3000 ft into upper Lituya Bay and caused the water to rise 1700 ft up the mountainside across the fiord. A wave moved out of the bay at an estimated speed of 100 miles an hour and crossed the spit at the bay's entrance with a height of about 50 ft carrying a small fishing boat over the tops of the trees on the spit and dropping it outside where it sank although the fishermen were miraculously saved and able to get away in their skiff.

Miller (1960) lists various other waves also due to falling masses of rock. The most destructive was that of May 21, 1792, in Shimbara Bay of Kyushu Island of Japan. Here a huge rockfall came down into the sea during a series of earthquakes and generated three large waves that drowned 15,000 people living along the shores of the bay. At Loen Lake in Norway a series of slides occurred producing surges up to 230 ft above lake level in 1936 as the result of large rockfalls into the lake from the cliffs.

### Storm Surges (Storm Tides)

The large inundations that often accompany great storms have been referred to as tidal waves, but the term is no more applicable than it is for tsunamis. *Storm surges* or *storm tides* are better names for this phenomenon. Storm surges are largest near the heart of a storm but at least in the Gulf of Mexico they are pronounced at distances of as much as 400 miles from the storm center. The water level in the Gulf of Mexico at hurricane centers has risen as much as 5 to 20 ft and a 15-ft rise was observed on more than one occasion in the hurricanes that swept up the east coast of the United States between 1938 and 1954. Such a rise may have devastating effects on coastal communities where the ground is low-lying, as in Louisiana and Texas. The Galveston catastrophe in 1900 drowned 6000 people after the sea had topped the sea wall and rushed into the town. In 1957 Cameron Parish on the west side of the Mississippi Delta was completely inundated, the sea extending many miles inland (Morgan *et al.*, 1958). In the Bay of Bengal in 1737 a great storm swept the sea across the lowland and is said to have drowned 300,000 people (Carson, 1951).

The storm surges unlike tsunamis do not have rhythmic rising and falling of the water level. Usually one or two great surges come in, rising rather slowly above an already high tide. At distances of a hundred miles or more from the storm center the water may rise three or four feet, which is quite significant in a low coastal area where the tides have a small range.

### Ocean Currents

Almost all the water in the ocean is in a constant state of movement. Stagnation exists only at the bottom of some deep basins with shallow sills. Elsewhere the water is flowing, mostly at a very slow rate but in some places with a velocity at least as great as is found in the rivers on the continents. Aside from the currents in the surf zone, already considered, ocean currents are the result of (1) wind stresses on the surface of the open ocean, (2) tidal forces, and (3) differences of water density. The last are due to evaporation, differential heating, freezing of sea water, melting of ice, introduction of fresh water from the lands, and development of dense sediment-laden water due to slumping or other stirring of the bottom sediments.

**Wind-Drift Currents.** Indirectly the wind is responsible for most of the currents in the surface and near surface waters. The wind produces these currents by frictional drag at the surface. Because of the earth's rotation and the resulting Coriolis force, the wind-induced currents in the open ocean have a mean transport approximately 45° from the direction of the wind (somewhat less at the surface and greater at depth). The direction is to the right of the wind in the northern hemisphere and to the left in the southern hemisphere.[2] In the shallow water along the coast the deflection is very slight so that the water may flow essentially in the direction of the wind stress, particularly in a strait or long narrow bay.

The depth of wind-induced currents (aside from the permanent currents discussed below) depends on the velocity and constancy of the wind, and is generally quite negligible below 25 to 50 fathoms. If the wind blows at a fast rate for a long time in the same direction, it develops a thick homogeneous layer of isothermal water. In general, thick isothermal layers develop best during cold periods because there is less of a thermal gradient below the surface. Very thick isothermal layers are found, however, in portions of the tropics where strong steady trade winds exist.

**Permanent Currents and the Prevailing Winds.** The large permanent ocean currents, like the Gulf Stream, are all related to the density distribution of the oceans but are maintained by the prevailing winds.

These great streams of water have a surface slope to the left in the northern hemisphere and to the right in the southern hemisphere. The water on the higher side is always warmer and hence lighter. The major gyrol currents turn to the right in the northern hemisphere, and to the left in the southern hemisphere (Fig. 47), The westward movement at low latitudes is the result of the trade winds and the easterly movement the result of the west winds at higher latitudes. The most concentrated currents occur along the east side of the continents of Asia and North America because of the pile up of water due to the trade winds. The level is raised sufficiently in the Pacific Ocean to cause a strong countercurrent flowing east to the north of the equator, and a weaker countercurrent to the south of the equator. Within a narrow band along the equator (2° N–2° S) an even stronger,

[2] For a more detailed discussion see Sverdrup et al. (1942, pp. 489-503).

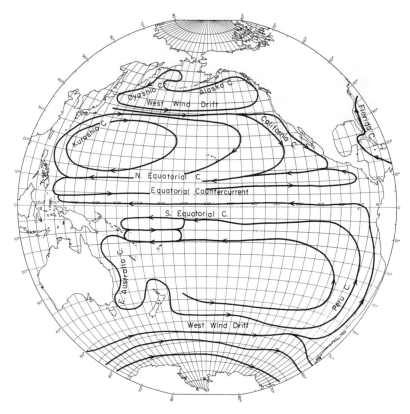

Fig. 47. Principal permanent oceanic currents of the world.

but subsurface, eastward flow exists, called the Pacific Equatorial Undercurrent by its discoverers Cromwell, Montgomery, and Stroup. These countercurrents are also well developed in the Atlantic. At high latitudes on the east side of the Atlantic and Pacific a branch of the east flowing current which is driven by the westerly winds, extends north along the west coasts of Europe and North America with considerable warming of the adjacent lands. Cold currents come down the northeast coasts of Asia and North America extending as far south as New England (Labrador Current) and northern Japan (Oyashio Current). Similarly cold currents in the southern hemisphere extend well north along the west coast of South America (Humboldt Current) and Africa (Benguela Current).

Some of these great streams actually move hundreds of times as much water as does the Mississippi or the Amazon River. For example, the Gulf Stream off eastern and southern Florida has a flow of 26 million cu m/sec. It is about 95 miles wide and flows at the surface

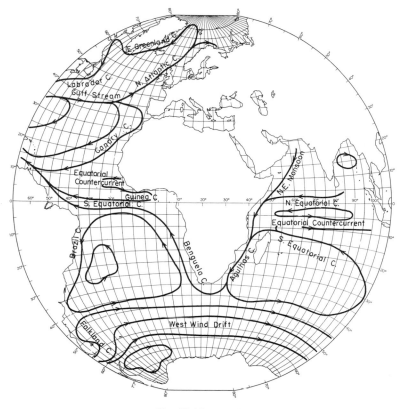

Fig. 47 (Continued).

with maximum speed at from about 3 to 6 knots. The flow has sharp
boundaries that shift from time to time and throw off large eddies.
The Gulf Stream evidently has a sufficient force in crossing the Blake
Plateau (Fig. 131) to scour the bottom at 400 to 600 fathoms and
prevent the deposition of fine sediment on much of this plateau.
Similarly, the Kuroshio (Japanese current) in flowing along the east
coast of Japan evidently scours the bottom accounting for the
numerous localities where rock is reported even out to depths of as
much as 700 fathoms.

The fast flowing currents like the Gulf Stream develop countercurrents along the sides that have an important influence on the
coastal configuration of Florida and the Carolinas where there is a
series of capes and concave bights. Similar features along the east
coast of Japan may have some connection with countercurrents from
the Kuroshio.

**Tidal Currents.**   The tides have a more important effect on the sea floor and on coastal configuration than do the permanent currents. The tides result from the gravitational attraction of the moon and to a smaller degree of the sun. If the earth were covered with an even layer of water, the tides would be high when the moon was overhead and on the opposite side of the earth, and low when the moon was near the horizon. Actually the time of high and low tide is far more complicated. The continents interfere with the free movement of a tidal bulge around the earth and embayments greatly retard the time of the tides moving up them. As a result the high tides are many hours later in the upper part of some embayments than in the lower, and the time of high tide becomes progressively later in moving along a continental coast, even in a north-south direction. The greatest tides occur when the moon and sun work in conjunction (that is, on the same or opposite sides of the earth), producing large tidal ranges called spring tides. When the moon and sun are in opposition or quadrative (that is, at right angles to each other in respect to the earth) the low tidal ranges called neap tides result.

The effect of the tides on the sea floor and coasts is more pronounced in places where constrictions such as narrow entrances to large bays cause strong flows because of the differences of water level on the outside and inside of the bay. Currents are equally strong in straits or water level canals which connect different bodies of water such as Tsugaru Strait between Hokkaido and Honshu, Japan, (Fig. 124), the Seymour Narrows in British Columbia, and the Cape Cod Canal in Massachusetts. At the Seymour Narrows velocities up to 15 knots were recorded prior to the blasting out of a huge rock from the middle of the channel. At the Bungo Strait entrance to the Inland Sea of Japan the effect of these strong currents is shown by a scour hole with a depth of 215 fathoms (Fig. 114). At the Golden Gate entrance of San Francisco Bay there is a scour basin with 60 fathoms of water depth (Fig. 113).

Tides are very long period waves, with periods of about $12\frac{1}{2}$ hours or twice that amount, called respectively semidiurnal and diurnal tides. If the moon were always directly over the equator, that is with zero declination, there would only be semidiurnal tides, but since it has varying degrees of declination another force comes in which produces the diurnal tide. The effect of the diurnal tide is greater in some bodies of water than in others depending on the natural period of the basin. Thus a typical tide curve at times of high declination in the Atlantic, Pacific, and Gulf of Mexico is shown in Fig. 48.

Two types of tidal oscillations occur. One is the progressive wave type which has the maximum flow at the crest of the wave in the direction of propagation and in the trough in the opposite direction.

This type occurs in the open ocean and does not produce high current velocities, the highest being at high tide and low tide. The other type is the standing or stationary wave in which the crest and trough remain fixed in position. This type is due to the reflection of the progressive waves against a barrier or to the oscillation of the water in an enclosed basin. The water oscillates about a nodal line with the tidal stream at zero velocity when the water reaches its maximum

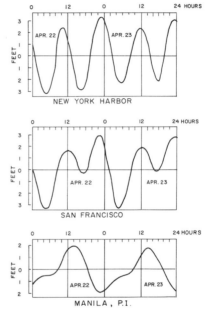

Fig. 48. Three principal types of tidal curves; semidiurnal (New York), mixed (San Francisco), and diurnal (Manila).

slope and at its maximum velocity when the surface is flat. The natural period of oscillation of any basin depends on its horizontal and vertical dimensions.

Since most shallow-water tides are standing waves the strongest tidal flows are usually not at the points of largest tidal ranges but in the modal points in between. For example, the tidal range is small in the entrance of San Francisco Bay as compared with the range in the upper bay, but the currents are much stronger at the entrance.

Tides reach their greatest vertical amplitudes in rather long funnel-shaped bays, like the Bay of Fundy where they reach a world maximum of 60 ft and in the Bay of St. Michel on the Normandy coast of France. The tides in such inland seas as the Gulf of Mexico and the Mediterranean have very low amplitude as do the tides in the Great Lakes. However, large tidal currents exist locally in the inland seas where there is a narrow strait between two sizable bodies of water. For example, the entrances to Barataria and Terrebonne bays in Louisiana have strong currents and the Straits of Messina have whirlpools, known as the Charybdis in Greek mythology, due to the tide.

Since tidal waves are shallow water waves, their current or orbital velocity tends to produce the same velocity from top to bottom of the water column, except where density stratification is found in the water. Also, directly at the bottom the friction reduces the tidal flow to a considerable degree, as it does in the case of river flow. Currents measured during a spring tide at the entrance to San Francisco Bay showed a velocity at the surface of 6 knots and within about 2 ft of the bottom of 3 knots.

The importance of tides in contributing to sediments of the ancient seas may be greater than generally supposed by geologists. Wherever straits debouched into the ancient seas, tides may have been a major factor in bringing in the sediments. Similarly, tides may have moved up into the fingerlike mouths of partially drowned deltas and produced a considerable redistribution of the sediments. This might account for some of the channel sand deposits in the cyclothems of the Late Paleozoic. If the moon was torn from the earth and is receding as suggested by George Darwin (1881) and believed by many geologists, the early tides may have been much more powerful than those of the present day. The friction produced by the tides lengthens the day so that in the early history of the earth the shorter tidal periods were another cause of greater tidal erosion than now takes place. It is not now possible to say whether greater tidal forces had a major effect on sedimentation, erosion, and on evolution of life in the early geological periods, but this can be considered as a possibility to be investigated.

**Currents Induced by Internal Waves.** Internal waves, sometimes referred to as boundary waves, are oscillations that have their maximum amplitude within the water body, e.g., at a density discontinuity, rather than at the surface. They were first discussed by Stokes in 1847 but were not applied to oceanographic conditions until Ekman (1904) made use of the theory to explain the "dead water" encountered in the Arctic. Here vessel keels reach below a thin layer of melt water into a more saline layer where alternating currents, not found at the surface, are encountered. At about the same time Otto Pettersson was making his measurements in a fiord on the Swedish coast and finding that the temperature stratification at depth moved up and down at regular periods. The phenomenon can also be seen in a small tank by using liquids of different density and different color, and moving the ends of the tank. Pulsating boundary waves will be observed at the contact that do not agree in period with surface waves and are much larger.

Beginning in World War II extensive studies of internal waves were made by the use of the bathythermograph that allowed the obtaining of temperature gradients below a vessel at frequent intervals. Ufford (1947) found oscillations as frequent as 5-minute periods in the area near San Diego. The most recent studies have been made by La Fond (1961) using a tower built up from the sea floor off Mission Beach in southern California. He was able to measure the variation in wave form from the surface to the bottom and found, as had been expected by theory, that, while the wave height of internal waves is greatest in intermediate depths, the horizontal velocity is greatest at the bottom and at the surface. The horizontal velocities obtained by La Fond indicate that erosion or at least prevention of deposition on high areas of the sea floor may be caused by internal waves.

**Turbidity Currents.** When sediment is suspended in water, the resulting combination is more dense than the clean water. As a result such a mixture will descend an aqueous slope. Currents produced in this way in the laboratory are very turbid. It has become very clear that these currents are important in carrying sediments, even coarse sands, down the submarine slopes, particularly along submarine canyons, and they may even erode the slopes. The problem of the speed of turbidity currents requires special consideration and is discussed in Chapter V, pp. 138–140, and in Chapter XI, pp. 338–343.

**Observed Bottom Currents.** Despite all the advances in other phases of submarine geology that have occurred since the writing of the first edition of this book there is almost nothing to report on direct measurement of bottom currents.[3] The earlier measurements (1st ed., pp. 62–65) showed that currents up to about half a knot occur on shelves, canyon floors, continental slopes, and in basins and troughs. The measurements give no indication that there is any appreciable decrease in velocity with depth nor in relation to topography. It seems highly probable, however, that more adequate coverage will show some very definite relations. SCUBA observers have found very strong currents in some localities on the shelf (R. F. Dill, personal communication). Also, attempts to sample on some hills of the outer Texas shelf have indicated that there are powerful currents near the bottom. Furthermore, fishermen report having their bottom trawls pulled out ahead of them by the bottom currents over these highs. In working along the slopes off Canton Island in the central Pacific, W. G. Van Dorn reports that strong bottom currents, possibly 5 or 6

---

[3] The currents measured by Swallow (1955) are mostly some distance above the bottom.

Fig. 49. Medium foraminiferal sand with concentration of coarse particles in troughs of sharp-crested ripple marks. Ripple length approximately 8 in. Field coverage: approximately 20 sq ft. Location: Southwest flank of Eniwetok atoll near the outer break in slope. The depth is 1100 fathoms. Courtesy of Carl J. Shipek, U.S. Navy Electronics Laboratory, San Diego, Calif. Official photograph U.S. Navy.

knots, existed at depths of about 30 fathoms with no appreciable current near the surface. Other evidences of strong bottom currents come from the finding of relatively coarse sediment in deep water that must have been carried seaward along the axes of deep submarine canyons (Chapter V, p. 138; Chapter XI, p. 338).

Until the measurements with current meters at great depth were made during the *Meteor* expedition (Wüst, 1935) it was generally supposed that only slow drifts of water took place over the deep ocean floor. Heezen (1959b) has presented an interesting picture of the

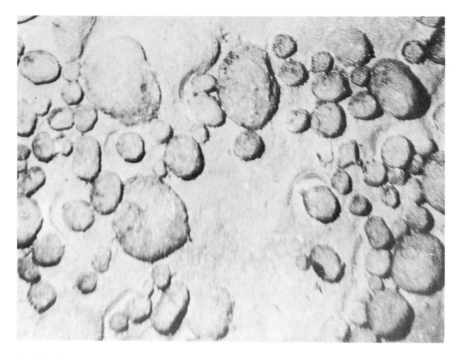

Fig. 50. Photograph taken at 3000 fathoms in basin 300 miles east-southeast of Bermuda. Shows current scour next to round objects, which are probably manganese oxide nodules. This Woods Hole Oceanographic Institution photograph by David Owen.

gradual disappearance of this erroneous idea and has shown how even in the last century Milne (1897) in his work on submarine cables began to bring up information suggesting deep ocean currents had worn or broken the cables. In addition to the turbidity currents discussed above, there are many other types of currents that operate on the deep sea floor. Submarine photographs on seamounts (Fig. 49) provide substantial evidence of these currents even at depths of as much as 1000 fathoms. According to Heezen (1959b) all photographed seamounts have shown the presence of ripple marks. Furthermore, virtually all dredged seamounts have yielded rock or evidence of the existence of rock.

The suggestion that substantial currents may occur at depths of the order of 500 fathoms first came from the work of Agassiz (1888), who found that Blake Plateau off the southeast coast of the United States was "swept clean of slime and ooze and is nearly barren of animal life." Cores taken by Lamont geologists have shown that rocks of Tertiary age occur near the surface at various places along the plateau (Ericson *et al.*, 1961, p. 235).

The existence of currents, definitely not turbidity currents, along the deep ocean floor has come from various sources in addition to the measurements of the *Meteor* expedition. Bottom photographs have shown scour around manganese nodules (Fig. 50) at localities where turbidity currents were out of the question. Cores of the *Albatross* expedition and of various Scripps Institution expeditions have shown that there are Tertiary formations at or near the surface in many places in the Central and South Pacific. This was found principally from the study of radiolarians (Riedel, 1959) but was confirmed by the study of the Foraminifera and coccoliths.

That there may be currents even in the bottom of a trench was shown by the photographs of Cousteau (1958) showing rock bottom in depths of 4000 fathoms in the Romanche trench. Thus there appears to be no definite depth limit to appreciable currents on the sea floor. The dive to the bottom of the deepest trench in the world revealed the presence of forms of life requiring oxygen (Piccard and Dietz, 1961). This discovery shows that there must be circulation of the water here as had been determined previously in many other deep basins.

# CHAPTER V

# SEDIMENTS: PHYSICAL PROPERTIES AND MECHANICS OF SEDIMENTATION

**BY DOUGLAS L. INMAN**

## Introduction

The classification of sedimentary deposits by mechanical, chemical, and biological analysis appears to be much advanced over our understanding of the mechanics of sedimentation. However, classifications that neglect the dynamics leading to the ultimate formation of a deposit must remain to some extent arbitrary. Further, the existence of traditional classifications and well-established procedures of analysis should not lead to the complacency that such classifications and procedures will necessarily yield measures that are relevant to sedimentary dynamics. One must continually strive for an understanding of what is basic in nature's scheme, while at the same time avoiding the pitfall, which is all too common in the natural sciences, of building concepts upon other concepts which have not been tested by critical experiment. Both the physical properties of sediments and the concepts of sedimentary mechanics presented here should be interpreted in the light of the above considerations.

Certain physical properties of sediments appear to be fundamental to the marine geologist in his study of the classification of sedimentary deposits, as well as to the student of sedimentary mechanics in his groping to understand the natural dynamics by which the sediment was transported and ultimately deposited. Density, size, and size distribution are controlling parameters in almost all the physical properties of sediments. Settling velocity, while fundamental to sedimentation and suspension, is also an important measure in determining the size of fine sediments; in which case the "equivalent size" is that of a quartz sphere having the same settling velocity as that of the less spherical natural grain. Packing and permeability become important considerations in transport by waves and currents, and the slopes of beach faces are, to a certain extent, controlled by the permeability of the beach sand. Permeability in turn, is determined by the packing, size, and size distribution of the sediment grains.

Fluids and fluid properties are discussed separately from those of a mixture of granular and fluid material because the mixture has properties differing quite widely from those of the fluid alone. Fluid stresses alone are of importance in settling velocity and the initiation of grain movement. However, when the grains constitute about 9 percent or more of the grain-fluid mixture, the tangential grain-to-grain stresses dominate, and the mixture acquires a normal dispersive stress that is not possessed by the fluid alone. Considerations of these normal grain stresses and their relation to the horizontal or tangential shear (Bagnold, 1954) have opened new horizons in the field of sediment transport. This concept has led to a rational approach to the quantitative prediction of sediment transport by waves and currents and to the formulation of general relations which may govern the flow and dimensions of phenomena such as turbidity currents.

### Sediment Size

Sediments are frequently referred to as sand, silt, or clay. These terms, of course, refer to the *size* of the sediment particles which is one of the fundamental physical properties of any sediment. The size distribution or range in size of the particles that make up the sediment aggregate is also of importance. Size and size distribution are frequent variables in determining most sediment properties, i.e., they enter in basic concepts of settling velocity, transportation, permeability, sorting, etc. It is the purpose of this section to discuss size, the concept of size scales, and measures for describing the distribution of sediment size.

**Grade Scales.**    Early in the study of sediments it was found that a linear or arithmetic scale was not the most convenient one in treating sediments. Most properties of sediments, such as settling velocity and permeability to fluid flow, were found to vary as some power of sediment size rather than directly with size.

If the size distribution of a sediment aggregate is considered on an arithmetic scale, it is found that the distribution is very skewed, so that the bulk of the sediment occurs in one of the fine sizes of an arithmetic distribution. Thus, a representation of this type is difficult to use because sediments differing widely in physical characteristics appear somewhat similar. From the nature of the size distribution curve and from the settling relations discussed later, it is apparent that a logarithmic or geometric scale is better suited for describing sediment distributions.

TABLE 6.   Grain Size Scales for Sediments

| | | | | |
|---|---|---|---|---|
| **GRADE SCALES** | | | | |
| WENTWORTH (1922) after Udden (1898) | Phi $\phi = -\log_2$ (m.m.) | (m.m.) | MICRONS $\mu$ | U.S. BUREAU OF SOILS |
| BOULDER | | | | |
| | — 8 | 256 | | |
| COBBLE | — 7 | 128 | 100 | |
| | — 6 | 64 | | |
| | — 5 | 32 | | LARGE |
| PEBBLE | — 4 | 16 | 10 | |
| | — 3 | 8 | | |
| | — 2 | 4 | | MEDIUM |
| GRANULE | — 1 | 2 | | |
| SAND — VERY COARSE | 0 | 1 | 1000. | FINE |
| COARSE | + 1 | 1/2 | 500. | COARSE |
| MEDIUM | + 2 | 1/4 | 250. | MEDIUM |
| FINE | + 3 | 1/8 — 10 | 125.0 | FINE |
| VERY FINE | + 4 | 1/16 — 20 | 62.5 | VERY FINE |
| SILT — COARSE | + 5 | 1/32 | 31.3 | |
| MEDIUM | + 6 | 1/64 | 15.6 | SILT |
| FINE | + 7 | 1/128 | 7.8 | |
| VERY FINE | + 8 | 1/256 — 200 | 3.9 | |
| CLAY — COARSE | + 9 | | 1.95 | |
| MEDIUM | + 10 | 1/1024 | 0.98 | CLAY |
| FINE | + 11 | | 0.49 | |
| VERY FINE | + 12 | 1/4096 | 0.24 | |
| COLLOID | | | | |

A geometric series is a progression of numbers, such that there is a fixed ratio between successive elements of the series. The first geometric scale for sediment size to receive extensive use was developed by Udden (1898). Udden used powers of 2 mm in his scale. In 1922 Wentworth extended Udden's scale and gave names to the various elements of the series. This scale is now in common use in the United States. Wentworth's scale as well as several others are illustrated in Table 6. A useful chart correlating twenty-one grain size scales in common use in this country and Europe was compiled by Truesdell and Varnes (1950).

Krumbein (1936) used the exponents, that is, the powers of two in the Wentworth series, as the basis for a logarithmic scale of sediment size. Because most sediments are finer than one millimeter, and thus would have a negative exponent which is cumbersome to use in computations, he used the negative logarithm to the base two. Krumbein defined a phi unit as the negative logarithm to the base two of the particle diameter in millimeters; $\phi = -\log_2$ ($D$ in millimeters). This notation has the disadvantage that large sizes have

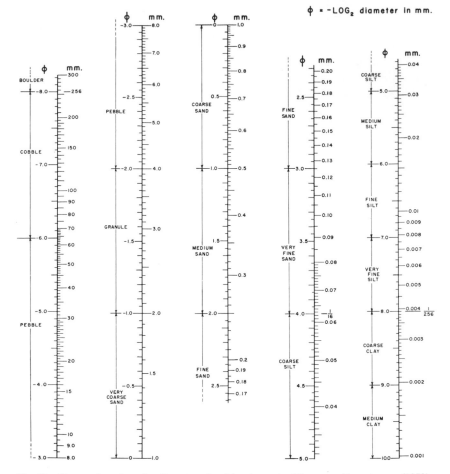

Fig. 51. Conversion chart for diameters in phi units and millimeters. From Inman (1952).

negative values and small sizes are positive. On the other hand, it is convenient in that each whole phi unit designates the boundary between a single Wentworth size; thus very fine sand, which includes sizes from 0.125 to 0.0625 mm, is contained between $+3.0$ and $+4.0\phi$. Also, the phi scale considerably simplifies plotting of frequency distribution and cumulative frequency curves of sediments, and the computation of standard deviations and skewness of sediment distribution. A conversion chart from millimeters to phi units is given in Fig. 51; a detailed conversion table is also compiled by Paige (1955).

**Measures of Size Distribution.** Numerous descriptive measures obtained from the grain size analysis of sediments are used in the literature to indicate the salient features of the size-frequency distribution of a sediment. These measures range in complexity from those obtained by computing the various moments[1] of the sample distribution about some central measure of sediment diameter, to those obtained by selecting a few points from the central 50 percent of the cumulative frequency curve of the sediment.[2]

In the preceding section it was observed that the size-frequency distribution curves of sediments become more symmetrical when the logarithm of the diameter instead of the diameter is plotted as the independent variable. In many cases these curves approach normal distributions or one of the family of curves derived from a normal distribution.[3] This is advantageous because it allows the properties of the distribution to be described in terms of deviations or anomalies from the normal distribution, which is a procedure well established in mathematical statistics.

Measures such as the mean, standard deviation, and skewness, obtained from moments, provide a convenient and concise notation which yields the general features of the size-frequency distributions of sediments. However, the dependence of moment measures on the entire distribution is a limitation to their practical application to sediments, since mechanical analyses of sediments frequently result in open-ended curves, and thus do not give the coarse and fine limits of the distribution. Another disadvantage of moment measures is the complex and time-consuming procedure required to compute them, although, where available, modern computer techniques make the handling of large quantities of data quite rapid.

In a normal frequency distribution curve approximately 68 percent of the population occurs between plus and minus one standard deviation either side of the mean (or median, since these two measures are equal for a normal distribution), and 95 percent occurs between two standard deviations either side of the mean. Thus the 16th and 84th percentiles of a normal sediment cumulative frequency curve represent diameters one standard deviation either side of the mean.

---

[1] In mathematical statistics the moment is used to denote the product of the frequency of occurrence within a given (size) class and the difference (or the difference raised to some power) between the class size and that of some origin, such as the mean of the distribution. The sum of the products for all classes divided by the number of classes is the moment of the distribution. The first four moments, when converted to the proper form, are referred to as the mean, standard deviation, skewness, and kurtosis.

[2] Trask (1932) defined the sorting coefficient as $So = \sqrt{Q_1/Q_3}$, and the skewness coefficient as $Sk = Q_1 Q_3/Md^2$, where $Q_1$ and $Q_3$ are the diameters in millimeters corresponding to the 25th and 75th percentiles respectively of a cumulative percent (coarser) curve, and $Md$ is the median diameter.

[3] A normal distribution is one whose frequency distribution curve is "bell-shaped" and symmetrical. A more complete description may be obtained from any text on statistics, such as Dixon and Massey (1951, p. 47).

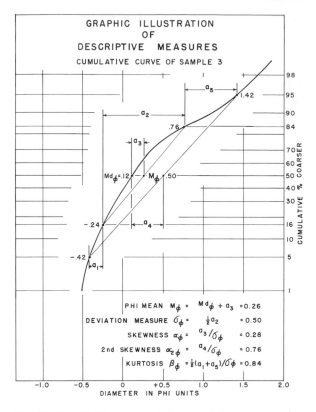

Fig. 52. Graphic illustration of the descriptive measures for
the size distribution of sediments as obtained from the
cumulative frequency curve. From Inman (1952).

The above considerations led Inman (1952) to develop expressions
for the particle size distributions of sediments in terms of phi measures
that serve as approximate graphic analogies to the moment measures
commonly employed in statistics. These parameters include a measure
of the median diameter, standard deviation, kurtosis, and two
measures of skewness, the second being sensitive to skew properties of
the "tails" of the sediment distribution. They are computed from
five percentile diameters obtained from the cumulative size-frequency
curve of the sediment and are defined in Fig. 52 and Table 7.

The phi median diameter $Md_\phi$ is a measure of central tendency. It is
sometimes used in preference to the mean because it may be obtained
directly from the cumulative curve without interpolation and because
it is less influenced by extreme values of skewness than the mean.
The phi deviation measure, $\sigma_\phi$, is a measure of sorting or spread and is
approximately equal to the standard deviation of statistics. Since

TABLE 7.   Descriptive Measures
(from Inman, 1952)

| Measure | | Nomenclature | Definition |
|---|---|---|---|
| Central Tendency | 1[a] | Phi Median Diameter | $Md_\phi = \phi_{50}$ <br> $= M_\phi - (\sigma_\phi \alpha_\phi)$ |
| | | Phi Mean Diameter | $M_\phi = \frac{1}{2}(\phi_{16} + \phi_{84})$ <br> $= Md_\phi + (\sigma_\phi \alpha_\phi)$ |
| Dispersion (Sorting) | 2 | Phi Deviation Measure | $\sigma_\phi = \frac{1}{2}(\phi_{84} - \phi_{16})$ |
| Skewness | 3 | Phi Skewness Measure | $\alpha_\phi = \dfrac{M_\phi - Md_\phi}{\sigma_\phi}$ |
| | 4 | 2nd Phi Skewness Measure | $\alpha_{2\phi} = \dfrac{\frac{1}{2}(\phi_5 + \phi_{95}) - Md_\phi}{\sigma_\phi}$ |
| Kurtosis (Peakedness) | 5 | Phi Kurtosis Measure | $\beta_\phi = \dfrac{\frac{1}{2}(\phi_{95} - \phi_5) - \sigma_\phi}{\sigma_\phi}$ |
| Diameter in Phi Units corresponding to a given percentage | | 5th Percentile Diameter | $\phi_5 = Md_\phi - \sigma_\phi + \sigma_\phi(\alpha_{2\phi} - \beta_\phi)$ |
| | | 16th Percentile Diameter | $\phi_{16} = Md_\phi - \sigma_\phi + (\sigma_\phi \alpha_\phi)$ |
| | | 50th Percentile Diameter | $\phi_{50} = Md_\phi$ |
| | | 84th Percentile Diameter | $\phi_{84} = Md_\phi + \sigma_\phi + (\sigma_\phi \alpha_\phi)$ |
| | | 95th Percentile Diameter | $\phi_{95} = Md_\phi + \sigma_\phi + \sigma_\phi(\alpha_{2\phi} + \beta_\phi)$ |

[a] In reporting data, it is sufficient to list only one measure of central tendency, since the second may easily be computed from the other parameters.

one phi unit is equivalent to one Wentworth division, the phi deviation measure gives the standard deviation of the curve in terms of Wentworth units.

In a symmetrical distribution, the mean and the median coincide, but if the distribution is skewed, the mean departs from the median, and the extent of this departure is a measure of skewness. The phi skewness, $\alpha_\phi$, gives the departure of the mean from the median in terms of the phi deviation measure, and is therefore a dimensionless measure of skewness, independent of the spread or deviation of the distribution.

The phi skewness measure is zero for a symmetrical size distribution. If the distribution is skewed toward smaller phi values (coarser diameters), the phi mean is numerically less than the median and the skewness is negative. Conversely, $\alpha_\phi$ is positive for a distribution skewed toward higher phi values. This measure of skewness is related to the moment skewness, $\alpha_3$, of statistics by the approximate relationship, $\alpha_3 = 6\alpha_\phi$.

The secondary skewness, $\alpha_{2\phi}$, has the same form as the primary skewness, only it is based on the 5th, 50th, and 95th percentile diameters. While the primary skewness is sensitive to skew properties occurring in the bulk of the particle size distribution, the secondary skewness is most sensitive to the distribution within the tails of the sediment. Also, $\alpha_{2\phi}$ serves as a check on the continuity of skewness indicated by $\alpha_\phi$. Since $\phi_5$ and $\phi_{95}$ are 1.65 standard deviations from the mean, $\alpha_{2\phi}$ divided by 1.65 would equal $\alpha_\phi$ if the distribution were normal. The inclusion of the second skewness, together with the other measures, allows five significant points ($\phi_5$, $\phi_{16}$, $\phi_{50}$, $\phi_{84}$, and $\phi_{95}$) of the cumulative curve of a sediment distribution to be obtained from the phi measures without resort to the original mechanical analysis of the distribution.

The phi kurtosis measure, $\beta_\phi$, is a parameter sensitive to the relative lengths of the tails of a distribution compared with the spread of the central portion, and is thus a measure of peakedness. This measure may be thought of as the ratio of the average spread in the tails of a distribution, that is the average value of $\phi_{16} - \phi_5$ and $\phi_{95} - \phi_{84}$, to the phi deviation measure, $\sigma_\phi$. For a normal distribution $\beta_\phi$ has a value of 0.65. If the tails have a greater spread than in the case of a normal curve, $\beta_\phi$ is greater than 0.65, Conversely lower values of $\beta_\phi$ indicate that the tails have less spread than for a normal curve with the same deviation measure. The limitations and the departure of the graphic phi measures from their moment equivalents is discussed by Inman (1952).

In reporting sediment size distributions it is sometimes convenient to convert the mean and median to their equivalent micron or millimeter value, since these metric units are directly applicable in sediment transport relations. On the other hand, the phi deviation and skewness, etc., should remain in the phi notation since they give sorting and skewness directly in Wentworth units and have no meaningful linear equivalents. Also such relations as the Krumbein and Monk expression for permeability use $\sigma_\phi$ directly (see section on permeability). The phi deviation measure can be computed directly from a cumulative frequency curve plotted in millimeter or micron notation by the relation

$$\sigma_\phi = 1.66 \log_{10} \left[ \frac{D_{16}}{D_{84}} \right]$$

where $D_{16}$ and $D_{84}$ are the 16th and 84th percentile diameters in mm or microns and $D_{16} > D_{84}$.

The procedures and measures of size distribution discussed above provide a convenient notation which in turn yields a reasonably accurate description of the mean, standard deviation, and skewness of the distribution of sediment sizes; i.e., the broad outline of the spectrum of sediment size. However, this provides no assurance that such measures are necessarily the most relevant in terms of sediment transport. For example, it may be that a minor mode obscured within the coarse portion of the distribution is the more relevant measure in so far as the threshold of grain movement at the bed is concerned.

### Constituents and Shape of Sediment Particles[4]

Grain size gives only one part of the sediment picture. Of equal interest to the geologist is the nature of the constituent grains. Thus in a sand the grains may be dominantly *terrigenous*, that is, derived from the lands and transported to the sea in solid form; *biogenous*, that is, the product of marine organisms built from the material taken out of solution by the organisms; or *authigenic*, that is, deposited on the sea floor as the result of chemical reactions not due to organisms. In sands the terrigenous sediments consist largely of quartz with moderate amounts of feldspars, ferromagnesiums, and other minerals. The biogenous constituents are largely calcareous organisms, principally molluscan shells or shell fragments with moderate amounts of Foraminifera, Ostracoda, Byrozoa, echinoids, and in tropical areas large quantities of coral and algal fragments. The authigenic constituents include principally glauconite and various forms of phosphatic nodules and grains.

It is obvious that the nature of the current or wave motion necessary to account for the erosion, transportation, or deposition of a sediment cannot be deduced entirely from the grain size. For example, a sediment consisting largely of shells could be deposited in the absence of current if the animals lived where the shells accumulated. The fluid stresses required to transport solid mineral grains are greater than that necessary to transport hollow foraminiferal tests of the same size and shape. An even greater stress is needed to transport heavy minerals such as magnetite. Also the settling velocity varies with the excess density $(\rho_s - \rho)$, of the grain over that of the fluid. Thus the excess density of a quartz sphere $(\rho_s = 2.65)$ settling in water $(\rho = 1.00)$ is 1.65 g/cm$^3$, while that of a hollow foraminifer with, say, one-half of the effective density $(\rho_s = 1.32)$ would have an excess density of only 0.32 or approximately one-fifth. In the range of viscous settling (see section on settling velocity) such a foraminifer would fall with a velocity of only one-fifth that of the quartz sphere.

---

[4] For methods of determining constituents by coarse fraction analyses and of determining roundness, see Appendix at the end of this chapter, pp. 147–151.

The shape of the mineral grains is also an important characteristic of granular sediments. Spherical grains are easily dislodged or set in motion on the sea floor whereas angular grains may be more difficult to dislodge, and flat tabular grains may offer considerable resistance where they are resting on a smooth surface or sunk into a finer grained matrix.

Once dislodged the spherical grains are not likely to be transported as far as are the platy grains, because mica settles slowly once it has been carried into suspension. Mica is carried away from the shore by rip currents (see Chapter III, p. 76) and in offshore moving currents of muddy water.

The shape of grains of sand size is particularly important in sedimentation because of the wide range in shape from thin flat grains such as mica to spherical foraminiferal tests. Somewhat less significant are the differences between spherical and cubic or other angular grains with three roughly equivalent axes.

There are numerous articles discussing methods of determining roundness and sphericity. In general usage, roundness refers to the ratio of radius of curvature of the corners of a solid to the radius of curvature of the maximum inscribed sphere (Waddell, 1932). Sphericity, on the other hand, refers to the degree to which the shape of a fragment approaches that of a sphere. Thus a perfect cube has high sphericity whereas the corners are sharp, giving it poor rounding.

### Packing, Porosity, and Dilatation

There are numerous possible spacial arrangements of neighboring grains in a granular mass at rest, and the aggregate property is referred to as packing. The type of packing becomes of importance in such considerations as fluid stress on a granular bed, spontaneous liquefaction of granular masses, porosity, and permeability. Graton and Fraser (1935) showed that there are six cases of simple systematic packing in spheres, in addition to several "haphazard" cases. Systematic packing of uniformly sized spheres ranges from the "loosest" possible or cubic packing to the "densest" or rhombohedral packing (Fig. 53). In cubic packing the centers of the spheres form the eight corners of a cube, an arrangement producing a maximum of pore space between spheres. Rhombohedral packing is the most stable and the most compact possible arrangement of spheres. It is an arrangement where the centers of the spheres are situated at the eight corners of a regular rhombohedron. The volume concentration, $N$, of the solids in these two cases, i.e., the ratio of solid to whole space, is 0.524 and 0.740, for cubic and rhombohedral packing respectively. The porosity, the ratio of pore space to whole space, in the above two cases is $1 - N$ or 0.476 and 0.260 respectively.

In nature, packing is complicated by the occurrence of nonspherical shapes and by nonuniformity of size, factors which produce a considerable degree of disorder in packing. Departure from a spherical shape may produce an increase in porosity, whereas nonuniformity of size decreases porosity. In general, the greater the effects of gravity on the grains at the moment of final settlement in relation to the effects

Fig. 53. Two extreme cases of systematic packing of uniformly sized spheres, ranging from (a) the "loosest" possible or cubic packing to (b) the "densest" or rhombohedral packing. After Graton and Fraser (1935).

**A.** CUBIC PACKING

**B.** RHOMBOHEDRAL PACKING

of fluid flow over the bed, the looser the packing and the greater the porosity. Thus the denser rhombic packing tends to be found where the bottom bed is actively subjected to current or wave stresses, as on the shallow portions of sandy continental shelves, and on the beach face. Loose packing is more common where sediments settle from suspension into still water.

Chamberlain (1960, Table 7), working with fine sand from the beach face, measured an *in situ* porosity of about 0.42 as compared with a porosity of 0.40 for the same sand when compacted by vibration to its densest packing. On the other hand, sand settled into the less active waters of the adjacent submarine canyon head had *in situ* porosities of about 0.47, while micaceous sand from the canyon had porosities as great as 0.73. Hamilton *et al.* (1956) found similar ranges in porosity for sediments from the shelf and bay in the vicinity of San Diego.

When a dense grain aggregate is at rest, the packing arrangement cannot be changed without moving and rearranging the grains. Since grains at rest are in contact with their neighbors on all sides, rearranging them requires that there be at least a temporary expansion or dilatation in the volume of the aggregate. Reynolds (1885) first investigated the "dilatancy" of a granular mass and pointed out that it is a property not possessed by known fluids or solids. He showed that a change in bulk occurred when the shape of the granular aggregate was changed. In other words, whenever a granular mass is sheared, a change in volume is produced, and hence a change in porosity.

The instantaneous "drying" of the surface of a wet beach when stepped upon is a good example of the dilatation of a dense-packed sand due to shear. The dilatation produces a sudden increase in pore space and a local deficiency in pore water. Capillary action causes water to flow toward the area of dilatancy, and an excess of water is observed when the weight causing the shear is removed.

If a loosely packed granular mass is subjected to a shear or shock, a slight dilatation causes each grain to be separated from its neighbor and the entire mass may collapse toward a denser packing arrangement. If the loosely packed granular mass is water saturated, the sudden collapse produces a dense granular suspension, and the entire mass may flow. This sudden collapse and flow of rigid granular structure is called "spontaneous liquefaction" and is probably associated with many avalanche-like phenomena in nature, including turbidity currents. Spontaneous liquefaction may also be caused by an increase in pore water pressure rather than from an external mechanical stress or shock (see Terzaghi and Peck, 1948, p. 100). For example, an underground spring issuing into a sand body may produce a local excess in pore water pressure over that due to the hydraulic head of water immediately above the sand. An excess pore pressure acts as a dispersive grain pressure, permitting grains to flow in response to other forces such as gravity. The concept of dispersive grain pressures produced by the shear of grain-fluid mixtures in motion will be discussed under the flow of high granular concentrations.

**Permeability**

The resistance of the bottom bed to the discharge of liquid through it in part determines the dissipation of energy of waves moving over the bed, and enters into considerations of sediment transport by waves. Permeability is a major factor in determining the slopes of the foreshores of beaches.

The discharge rate of a liquid through a porous granular bed depends upon grain and liquid properties as well as upon the impelling force or pressure head producing the flow. The complete expression for the discharge is known as Darcy's law and is valid for all directions of flow and for all velocities small enough that forces of inertia are negligible compared to those of viscosity. Following the presentation of Hubbert (1958), the volume discharge, $q$, of fluid crossing unit area in unit time is given by:

$$q = (GD^2)(\rho/\mu)(-gdh/dz) \qquad (1)$$

where $G$ is a dimensionless factor of proportionality depending upon the geometry of the pore space; $D$ is a measure of size of the pore space such as the mean grain diameter; $\rho$ and $\mu$ are the density and dynamic viscosity, respectively, of the liquid; $g$ is the acceleration of gravity; and $dh/dz$ is the rate of change of the pressure head in the direction of flow. If the flow were through a cylinder, $dh/dz$ would be the decrease in pressure as indicated by fluid height in the manometers divided by the flow distance between manometers.

Of the three factors on the right of equation (1) $GD^2$ depends only on properties of the porous media, and $\rho/\mu$ are properties of the liquid only. The combined geometrical factor $GD^2$ is often expressed by the symbol $K$ and is called the permeability of the porous media. The permeability has the units of length squared and is sometimes given in darcies where one darcy equals approximately $10^{-8}$ cm$^2$.

Krumbein and Monk (1942), experimenting with water flow through

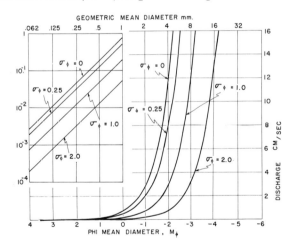

Fig. 54. Perpendicular discharge $q$ in centimeters per second through unit area of the bottom bed of thickness equal to the applied head of water. Computed from the relation of Krumbein and Monk (1942, eq. 17) for sea water at 15° C, salinity 35°/$_{00}$, and for sediments with phi deviation measures of $\sigma_\phi = 0$ (single size), $\frac{1}{2}\phi$, 1$\phi$, and 2$\phi$. The very low discharge through sands less than 1 mm is shown on the logarithmic scale in the insert.

sands of differing sizes and standard deviations, obtained the following empirical expression for the permeability $K$ expressed in darcies:

$$K = 760 \; D^2 e^{-1.31\sigma_\phi}$$

where $D$ is the geometric mean diameter expressed in millimeters, $e$ is the base of natural logarithms, and $\sigma_\phi$ is the deviation measure in phi units. From this relation it is seen that the permeability increases with the square of the grain diameter and decreases exponentially with increasing standard deviation. Thus for a given mean size, well-sorted sands are more permeable than poorly sorted sands.

The permeability of bed material may be expressed, independently of the scale of the impelling force, as the perpendicular water discharge through a unit area of a bed of thickness equal to the perpendicularly applied head of water. This gives a value of unity to $dh/dz$ in equation (1) and permits the discharge of any given liquid to be expressed in centimeters per second as a function of the permeability. This discharge, using the relation of Krumbein and Monk (1942) for the permeability, is graphed in terms of sediment size and phi deviation measure in Fig. 54. The relatively low discharge through sands of less than 1 mm mean diameter as compared with coarser material is readily apparent. A typical beach sand has a phi deviation measure of about $\frac{1}{4}\phi$.

### Flow of Liquids and the Transportation of Granular Material

The transportation of granular solid material has been widely studied by the hydraulic engineer and in general it has been assumed that the laws of fluid flow could be applied directly to sediment transport. However, as Reynolds (1885) and Bagnold (1954) have shown, a mixture of granular and fluid material has properties differing quite widely from that of the fluid alone. Thus the laws of fluid flow can apply only when the concentration of granular matter is very low, as in a very dilute suspension of solids, or to the granular bed boundary directly, before many grains are set in motion.

In by far the majority of cases—when appreciable solid granular material is in motion—the laws of fluid flow alone are inadequate.

In this section the aggregate phenomena that occur when a fluid moves over a granular bed will be considered first, followed by discussions of: the principles of fluid flow; the free fall of isolated particles through a fluid; the threshold of grain movement; and finally, a discussion of the suspension of dilute concentrations of granular material. The transport of a swarm of discrete solids will be considered in the section under the flow of granular solids in high concentrations.

**Fluid Flow over a Granular Bed.**    The nature of the motion in a moving fluid can be either laminar (i.e., composed of thin fluid elements each moving uniformly relative to its neighbor) or turbulent (i.e., each fluid element moving at random in relation to its neighbors). If the initial motion of the flow is gradual and steady, and the flow is shallow, its motion will probably be laminar throughout. Turbulence results whenever there is tangential shear at a fluid boundary, and spreads to other parts of the fluid if the Reynolds number[5] of the flow is sufficiently large.

In a shallow flume turbulence is commonly initiated when an eddy or vortex forms in the lee of some bottom irregularity such as a large granule or pebble. If the eddies are sheared and carried upward into the fluid they transport their motion to other layers of the fluid. If the bed is sufficiently rough to produce turbulence, the turbulence is transferred to successively higher layers until at some downstream point the entire flow becomes turbulent. Motion in large rivers and in ocean currents is inherently turbulent because of the very large Reynolds numbers of the flow and the presence of numerous tangential stresses exerted at the surface boundary by winds and at the bottom boundary by flow over bed irregularities.

At this point it is helpful to give an elementary description of the nature of the grain movement and flow conditions observed in a simple flume as the velocity of the water is gradually increased. Consider a flat bottom bed of sand, as in a river or flume, with water flowing above at a velocity so low that none of the bed grains is moved. If the flow rate is gradually increased, the following sequence of sediment movement will be observed.

The first grain movement will consist of an intermittent rolling and sliding of individual grains. This motion, intermittent in time and space, indicates the random nature of the turbulence in the fluid flow and the irregularities in grain packing on the bed. This first incipient sediment motion is referred to as the initiation or threshold of grain motion (Fig. 55).

As the flow rate is increased, the number of particles moved increases, and some particles are lifted off of the bed, executing short trajectories or saltations before falling back. Saltation is an indication that the transportation of material on the bed as bedload has reached a more advanced stage. If the flow is turbulent, some of the grains

---

[5] The Reynolds number is a dimensionless criterion expressing flow intensity. It is given as $R = \overline{u}h/\nu$ where $\overline{u}$ is the mean velocity of flow, $h$ is the depth, and $\nu$ is the kinematic viscosity equal to the molecular viscosity $\mu$ divided by the density of the fluid. For water at 20° C, $\nu$ has a value of about 0.01 cm²/sec. For flow where the width is large compared with depth, turbulence can become general throughout the flow when $R$ is 600 or greater.

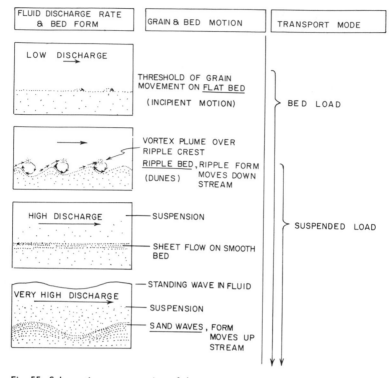

Fig. 55. Schematic representation of the various modes of transport and types of grain motion as observed through the glass window port of a flume as the liquid velocity is gradually increased.

may be lifted higher above the bed by the random motion of the water, and the grains are then said to be in suspension. In well-developed suspension the sediment grains deviate from the even low-angle "cannon ball"-shaped trajectory, the mark of true saltation, and partake in the more random motion of the turbulent water. Thus turbulence is a necessary condition for suspension.

As the velocity and flow rate are increased further, the amount of material transported in suspension increases, and, if the sediment is fine, suspension becomes an important mode of transport. If one looks down on a flume where suspended transport is well developed, it will be observed that the suspended material moves in clouds or billows in a random manner rather than in a uniform and constant concentration. Here again the turbulent nature of the fluid flow is reflected in the motion of the suspended particles.

If grain motion continues, the flow will produce the familiar bed irregularities known as sand ripples. At low velocities the grains roll up the gentle upstream face of the ripple and slide down or are deposited on the steeper lee face. At somewhat higher velocities the sand may jump or saltate from one ripple to the next. In the regimen of bedload transportation the velocity of the sand is always slow compared with the velocity of the fluid, and the form of the ripple moves in the direction of the current. In deep rivers, a much larger bottom feature termed a dune is eventually formed under flow intensities similar to those forming ripples. Aqueous sand dunes are analogous to the dunes of wind-blown sand and differ greatly in scale from ripples. Ripples are the small scale features that can be observed moving up the windward face of sand dunes.

Ripples attain a maximum length and height at some intermediate velocity range. If the flow is increased beyond this range, a condition will be reached where the ripples decrease in height and vanish and the bed becomes smooth again. Since the bottom is nearly flat after the ripples vanish, this flow condition is sometimes referred to as "sheet flow." The entire bottom is in motion, and it can be observed that the motion extends several grain layers into the bed. The intense bed shear produces a marked increase in sediment transport. In this sediment regime the laws of fluid flow alone are inadequate to describe the sediment transport, and it is necessary to introduce the grain-to-grain shear forces discussed under the flow of granular solids in high concentrations.

At still higher flow rates, undulations again form on the bottom if the flow is shallow. Unlike the ripples, the new undulations which are called sand waves, are more sinusoidal in profile than ripples, and their form moves upstream instead of down. This is because the sand that is eroded from the lee face of the sand wave is deposited on the upstream face of each succeeding wave crest. Sand waves were termed anti-dunes by Gilbert (1914) and are usually accompanied by waves at the water surface above the sand wave. However, there is considerable doubt if sand waves occur in deep rivers; the large-scale features observed in such cases are more appropriately called dunes.

Certain fundamental similarities and differences are worth noting between the phenomena occurring at the granular bed boundary under unidirectional flow and that occurring under oscillatory motion due to wave action. In both flows there is a threshold below which grain motion does not occur; only under wave action, the threshold is further complicated by the presence of acceleration and deceleration. In both types of motion, after local turbulence develops behind ripple crests, there is a phase when the turbulent vortex produces a scour in the ripple trough moving grains in counter direction to the flow over the crest (Fig. 55). The convergence of flow at the ripple crest causes a plume of sediment to rise in the vortex above the ripple. In the oscillatory case the sediment plume forms suddenly at the end of the forward or backward motion. This is because deceleration of flow enhances the formation of turbulence whereas acceleration inhibits its formation. Also, oscillatory flow tends to inhibit the upward spread of turbulence from the bottom, because the oscillation does not allow sufficient time for the turbulence to spread. In both unidirectional and oscillatory flow, providing the orbital diameter of the oscillation is large compared to the ripple wavelength, intense shear causes ripples to disappear and the bed becomes smooth. The similarities in boundary layer phenomena between the two types of flow suggest that the same basic principles apply to both.

**Fluid Stress**

In the preceding section it was shown that large-scale natural water flows are inherently turbulent. It is customary to describe

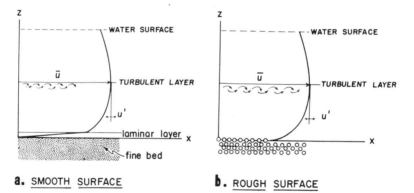

Fig. 56. Turbulent flow over (*a*) smooth surface, and (*b*) rough surface.

turbulent flow in terms of the average velocity $\bar{u}$, and a random fluctuation related to turbulence, $u'$. The velocity at any instant, $u$, is the vector sum of these two. This may be written:

$$u = \bar{u} + u'$$

If the bottom is considered to be hydrodynamically smooth, there will be a thin layer of laminar flow on the bottom even though the main flow is inherently turbulent (Fig. 56). If the surface is hydrodynamically rough, then the turbulence effectively extends to the very bottom.

Flow in the laminar layer is characterized by the absence of random velocity fluctuation. In flow of this type, thin fluid layers are considered as moving parallel to each other in such a manner that a stress or shear is exerted between layers. Since all fluids possess resistance to change of form, this property is a form of internal friction and is called (dynamic) molecular viscosity. The viscosity of a fluid is analogous to the shear modulus of elasticity of solids where the magnitude of deformation of the solid is replaced by the rate of deformation in the fluid. Newton defined the coefficient of molecular viscosity as:

$$\mu = \frac{\text{Shear stress}}{\text{Rate of deformation}} = \frac{\tau}{du/dz}$$

from which the viscous shear stress per unit area becomes

$$\tau = \mu \frac{du}{dz} \tag{2}$$

where $du/dz$ is the rate of change of velocity $u$ with respect to the distance $z$ above the bed. The stress $\tau$ has the dimensions of force per unit area, or momentum per unit area and time, and is usually expressed in dynes per square centimeter. The coefficient of dynamic viscosity $\mu$ has dimensions of momentum per unit area and in the metric system is expressed in grams per centimeter per second or poise. Fresh water at $20°$ C has a $\mu$ of $10^{-2}$, and this value is modified only slightly for salt water and for changing pressure due to depth. The viscosity increases to twice this value when the water temperature decreases to zero degrees centigrade.

**Eddy Viscosity.**    In the turbulent layer (Fig. 56) there is an exchange of momentum on a very much larger scale. W. Schmidt and G. I. Taylor, using Prandtl's mixing length concept, and arguing by analogy from kinetic theory, formulated the concept of the *Austausch* or momentum transfer coefficient which in form is analogous to the molecular coefficient $\mu$. The details of this concept and its importance in development of more recent concepts are given in modern texts on the fluid boundary layer (see Priestley, 1959, Chapters 1–3).

In turbulent motion, small fluid masses are carried back and forth across any given fluid surface. If there is a velocity gradient this gives rise to a positive transfer of momentum when particles of higher velocity enter a region of lower velocity. Because of this exchange, fluid in a region of higher velocity will be retarded and fluid in a region of lower velocity will be accelerated. Therefore a shearing force is exerted on a surface across which momentum transfer takes place, and it can be shown that the stress is equal to the rate of momentum transfer across the surface. This reasoning leads to the formulation of an equation for turbulent flow which in form is analogous to (2):

$$\tau = A_z \frac{d\bar{u}}{dz} \tag{3}$$

where $\bar{u}$ is the average velocity, and $A_z$ is the value of the eddy viscosity $A$, applicable in the vertical direction. $A$ is the exchange coefficient introduced by Schmidt (1917) as a result of the space exchange of momentum due to random fluctuation in turbulent flow. Both $\mu$ and $A$ have the dimensions of $ML^{-1}T^{-1}$. It should be noted that the molecular viscosity is independent of the state of motion and is a characteristic property of the fluid. Observations show that the eddy viscosity is not a constant in natural currents, but depends upon the nature of the fluid movement. The eddy viscosity is many orders of magnitude larger than the molecular viscosity. For ocean currents $A$ has been found to range between one and 1000 cgs units (Sverdrup et al., 1942, p. 91).

Prandtl's Mischungsweg theory leads to a definition of $A_z$ as

$$A_z = \rho l^2 \left| \frac{d\bar{u}}{dz} \right| \tag{4}$$

where $l$ is the mixing length, $\rho$ is the density of the fluid, and $|d\bar{u}/dz|$ is the absolute value of the shear. Over a rough surface $l$ must have a definite value, since turbulence extends to the very bottom, and for a fluid of indifferent stability may be written

$$l = k_0(z + z_0)$$

where $k_0$ is von Kármán's constant, and has been found to be equal to nearly 0.4, $z$ is measured positive upwards, and $z_0$ is the roughness length and is related to the height of the roughness elements.

By combining equations (3) and (4) and considering the stress to be constant, one obtains the von Kármán-Prandtl equation for boundary currents over a rough surface:

$$\bar{u} = \frac{u_*}{k_0} \ln \frac{z + z_0}{z_0} \tag{5}$$

where the factor $u_*$ is equal to $\sqrt{\tau/\rho}$ and is called the "friction velocity"; $u_*$ has the dimensions of a velocity and is proportional to the average velocity $\bar{u}$ at some distance $z$ above the bottom. Since $u_*$ is proportional to $\bar{u}$ and has the same dimensions, they can be equated in terms of a constant of proportionality $c$, such that $u_*^2 = c\bar{u}^2$. If $u_*$ is replaced by its equivalent $\sqrt{\tau/\rho}$, the relation can be written

$$\tau_0 = \rho u_*^2 = c\rho\bar{u}^2 \tag{6}$$

and it can be seen that $c$ is a drag coefficient relating the stress $\tau$ to the square of the velocity. Comparison with equation (5) shows that $c$ is a function of the height at which $\bar{u}$ is measured above the bottom, and the degree of bottom roughness.

Equation (5) can be written

$$\ln(z + z_0) = \frac{k_0}{u_*}\,\bar{u} + \ln z_0 \tag{5a}$$

which is in the form of a straight line when the logarithm of $(z + z_0)$ is plotted against the average velocity $\bar{u}$ (Fig. 57). The slope of the

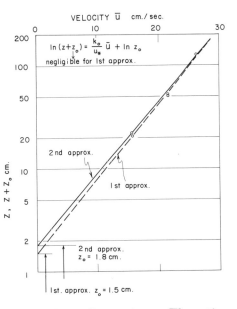

Fig. 57. The procedure of successive graphic approximation for the computation of the stress exerted on the bottom bed by a tidal current flowing over a sand bottom. In the first approximation the abscissa $\bar{u}$ is plotted against $\ln z$, and the ordinate axis intercept gives an approximate value of 1.5 cm for $z_0$. In the second approximation $\bar{u}$ is plotted against $\ln(z + z_0)$ giving a value of $z_0$ of about 1.8 cm. Basic data is from Sverdrup et al. (1942, p. 480).

line is $k_0/u_*$, and its intersection with the ordinate is $z_0$. Thus the bottom stress $\tau_0 = c\rho\bar{u}^2$ can be approximated over a rough bed from a plot of the velocity profile. An example of the procedure for computing the bottom stress exerted by a tidal current flowing over a sand bottom (Sverdrup et al., 1942, p. 480) is given in Fig. 57 using the procedure of graphic approximations. For the first approximation it is assumed that $z_0$ can be neglected in $\ln(z + z_0)$, and that $\ln z$ can be plotted as the ordinate, and $\bar{u}$ as the abscissa. This first plotting gives an approximate value of 1.5 cm for $z_0$. This value of $z_0$ is then used in a second approximation in which $\ln(z + z_0)$ is plotted against the mean velocity $\bar{u}$. The second approximation gives a value of 1.8 cm for $z_0$. Successively higher approximations could be made, but the observational variation in the data does not usually warrant more than a second approximation.

Once the value of $z_0$ is obtained, the stress $\tau$ can be computed for any given velocity and distance above the bottom from equation (5a). For the example in Fig. 57 the average stress computed for the three elevations is about 6.5 dynes/cm². In turn, the drag coefficient $c$ can be evaluated from equation (6) when the stress $\tau$ and the mean velocity are known. Available data from velocity profiles over sandy bottoms indicate that $c$ has values that range from $2.5 \times 10^{-3}$ to $11.6 \times 10^{-3}$ when computed for velocities measured at 100 cm above the bottom. For the velocity profile in Fig. 57, $c$ has a value of $11.0 \times 10^{-3}$ at 100 cm above the bottom. These data include velocities at 100 cm ranging from 15 to 55 cm/sec and for $z_0$ ranging from about 0.1 to 1.8 cm.[6]

Francis (1957) developed a semi-empirical relationship which gives the mean velocity of flow $\bar{u}$ of a stream in terms of the whole depth of flow $h$ and the roughness length $z_0$:

$$\bar{u} = \frac{u_*}{k_0} \ln \frac{13.2h}{z_0}$$

This relation appears to be consistent both with the von Kármán-Prandtl theory, as a comparison of its form with that of equation (5) shows, as well as with practical flow relations applicable to uniform flow in open channels. Francis' equation can be put in the form of equation (6):

$$\tau_0 = \left( \frac{k_0}{\ln \dfrac{13.2h}{z_0}} \right)^2 \rho \bar{u}^2 = c \rho \bar{u}^2 \tag{6a}$$

where the square of the quantity in parentheses is analogous to the drag coefficient $c$ of the former equation, only applying to the mean velocity of the whole flow rather than that at a specified height above the bottom. Over a wide range of values for $h$ and $z_0$, values of about $10^{-3}$ are obtained for the drag coefficient;[7] i.e., ones comparable to those obtained from equation (6) with velocity measured 100 cm above the bottom.

For the case of steady flow in streams or laboratory flumes where the water and the bed surface slope at the angle $\beta$, the stress on the bed can be approximated directly from the relation

$$\tau = \rho g h \tan \beta \tag{7}$$

[6] Personal communication from R. S. Arthur, based on data from Sverdrup et al. (1942), Lesser (1951), Bowden and Fairbairn (1956), Charnock (1959), and Bowden, Fairbairn, and Hughes (1959).

[7] For example, the drag coefficient $c$ of equation (6a) has the following values: $0.84 \times 10^{-3}$ for $h = 1000$ m, $z_0 = 0.1$ cm; $1.04 \times 10^{-3}$ for $h = 100$ m, $z_0 = 0.5$ cm; $1.4 \times 10^{-3}$ for $h = 20$ m, $z_0 = 0.5$ cm.

where $\rho$ is the density of the water, $g$ is the acceleration of gravity, and $h$ is the depth of water.

## Settling Velocity

The settling velocity of particles has a basic relation to the concept of size. Classification of sediments by settling velocity is customary and is an efficient procedure for segregating the finer sediments into size classes. Size in this sense is usually reported in terms of the size of a quartz sphere having the same settling velocity. Such sizes are referred to as hydraulically equivalent, or simply as equivalent diameters. Settling velocity is also useful in some cases as a measure of dynamic similarity, and is a necessary consideration in dilute suspended sediment transport. The settling velocity as developed here applies only to individual, isolated grains falling through still water. If the concentration of grains is high, the bulk density and overall size of the aggregate must be taken into consideration as in the case of a turbidity current. The effect of high concentration is all too frequently overlooked when settling velocities are measured.

Newton proposed that a particle falling in a fluid will accelerate under force of gravity until the frictional drag of the fluid approaches the value of the impelling force, after which a constant velocity $w$, called the settling velocity, will be reached. The frictional drag relation is proposed on the assumption that the drag force $f$ is proportional to the square of the velocity:

$$f_d = \tfrac{1}{2}c_d a_2 D^2 \rho w^2$$

where $c_d$ is a dimensionless drag coefficient; $a_2 D^2$ is the projected area of the particle in the direction of motion ($\pi D^2/4$ for spheres); and $w$ is the relative velocity between the particle and the fluid.

When a particle settles in a fluid, it is acted upon by the force of gravity acting downward, and by a buoyant force (given by Archimedes' principle) acting upward. The difference between these two forces is the impelling force and is given by

$$f_i = a_3(\rho_s - \rho)g D^3$$

where $a_3 D^3$ is the volume of the particle ($\pi D^3/6$ for spheres), $(\rho_s - \rho)$ is the difference between the density of the solid and of the fluid, and is therefore the excess density, and where $g$ is the acceleration of gravity.

By equating the impelling force to the drag force, the settling velocity is found to be

$$w = \sqrt{\frac{2a_3}{c_d a_2}\frac{\rho_s - \rho}{\rho}gD} \tag{8}$$

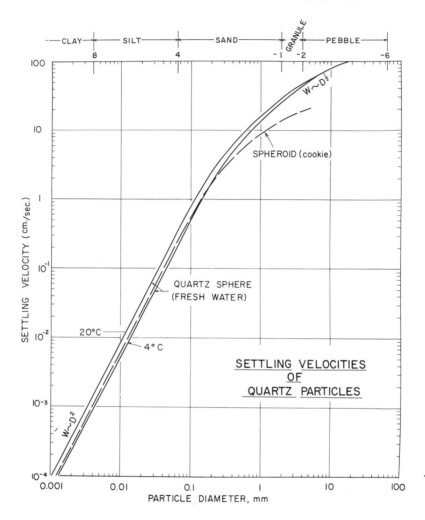

Fig. 58. Settling velocity of quartz spheres and of a quartz spheroid with a major to minor axis ratio of 4:1. The spheroid is assumed to fall in the direction of the minor axis, and the diameter is taken as that of a sphere with the same volume. Note that the settling velocity w is proportional to the square of the diameter for viscous or Stokes settling (diameters less than 0.2 mm) and to the square root of the diameter for inertial settling (diameters greater than about 1 mm).

Instead of being a constant as Newton assumed, the drag coefficient $c_d$ is found to be a function of the Reynolds number, $R = \rho w D / \mu$, where $\mu$ is the coefficient of molecular viscosity. Inspection of the settling velocity curve (Fig. 58) shows that there are two general modes of settling: inertial settling for particles larger than about

2 mm, and viscous settling for small particles less than about 0.2 mm. Between those sizes there is a transition zone.

In inertial settling the shape of the particle and its projected area in the direction of propagation become important factors in determining the settling velocity. For spheres, $c_d$ equals approximately one-half and $a_3/a_2$ is two-thirds, and the settling velocity is given approximately as

$$w \cong \sqrt{\frac{8}{3} \frac{\rho_s - \rho}{\rho} gD} \qquad (8a)$$

from which it is evident that the settling velocity varies as the square root of the grain diameter. An ellipsoid with major axis four times greater than the minor axis will have only one-half the settling velocity of a 2-mm quartz sphere of equal volume (when falling parallel to the minor axis). Settling velocity for such a spheroid or cookie is shown by the dashed line in Fig. 58. In the region of inertial settling temperature has but little effect, and shape and density are controlling. Natural grains with shapes departing from spheres will always have settling velocities somewhat less than that for spheres.

In the region of viscous settling (diameters less than about 0.2 mm), $c_d$ is equal to 24/Reynolds number. Substituting this value of $c_d$ in equation (8) gives Stokes' law for the settling velocities of small particles

$$w = \frac{1}{18} \frac{\rho_s - \rho}{\mu} gD^2 \qquad (8b)$$

from which it is seen that the settling velocity varies as the square of the particle diameter. In viscous settling the velocity is dependent on the ratio of the immersed weight of the particle to its total surface area. Within this limit, shape in itself influences settling velocity only as it effects this ratio. Thus a spheroid has almost the same settling velocity as a sphere of equal immersed weight. On the other hand, long spines or other appendages, such as marine plankton have, appreciably decrease settling velocity because they increase the surface area with little increase in immersed weight.

In the range of viscous settling, temperature is important because it effects the viscosity $\mu$ which enters directly into the velocity equation (8b). A decrease in temperature of fresh water from $20°$ C to $4°$ C causes a reduction in the settling velocity of a 0.02-mm quartz sphere from 0.035 cm/sec to 0.022 cm/sec, a factor of one-third. Pressure has almost no effect on settling velocity, while salinity reduces the velocity only slightly. In the above case, the 0.02-mm quartz sphere would have a settling velocity of 0.020 cm/sec at 4° C if the water had a salinity of 35‰.

### Threshold of Grain Movement

Experiments by Shields (1936), White (1940), Bagnold (1942), and others indicate that movement will not take place until a critical drag force that is a function of grain size is exceeded. The expression for the critical or threshold stress can be derived by equating the fluid forces

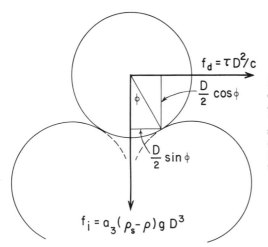

Fig. 59. Schematic representation of equilibrium conditions at the threshold of movement of a spherical grain. When the moment of the drag force about the pivot point $f_dD \cos \phi/2$ just exceeds that of the gravity force holding the grain in place, $f_iD \sin \phi/2$, the grain will move.

that just cause the motion of a grain to the gravity force that holds the grain in place. The latter force is given by

$$f_i = a_3(\rho_s - \rho)gD^3$$

where $a_3$ is a shape coefficient such that $a_3D^3$ is the volume of the grain (Fig. 59). If the drag per unit area on the bed is $\tau_0$, the total drag exerted on the grain by the fluid will be $f_d = \tau_0 D^2/c$, where $c$ is a packing coefficient and is defined as $D^2$ times the number of grains per unit area exposed to the fluid drag. As the drag force on the grain increases, the grain will begin to pivot about a fulcrum point at its contact with the adjacent grain. If both drag and gravity forces can be considered as operating on the center of the grain, the grain will become unstable, and hence the threshold is reached when the moment of the drag force about the fulcrum point equals the moment of the gravity force about the same point:

$$f_d\left(\frac{D}{2} \cos \phi\right) = f_i\left(\frac{D}{2} \sin \phi\right)$$

where $\phi$ is the angle of internal friction of the grains and is approximately equal to the angle of repose. Substituting for $f_i$ and $f_d$ gives the threshold value of the drag as

$$\tau_t = a_3 c(\rho_s - \rho)gD \tan \phi \qquad (9)$$

Thus the maximum size grain moved under any given fluid drag on the bed is proportional to the drag, and from relation (6), the size is also proportional to the square of the drag velocity $u_*$, and the mean velocity of flow $\bar{u}$. It should be noted that the value of the mean fluid flow $\bar{u}$ for any given drag $\tau_0$ will vary with varying distance above the bed, and is meaningless as an index of bed stress unless the distance above the bottom and the flow conditions are specified. This led Bagnold (1942) and others to express the threshold of grain movement in terms of a critical value of the drag velocity

$$u_{*t} = \sqrt{\tau_t/\rho}$$

This critical value of the drag velocity at which sand movement commences, owing to the drag force of the fluid, is sometimes referred to as the threshold velocity (Bagnold, 1942: Inman, 1949a). However, this frequently leads to confusion between the mean velocity $\bar{u}$, which is a true velocity, and the drag velocity $u_*$, which is a measurement of bed stress with the units of velocity. Hereafter, $u_{*t}$ will be referred to as the "threshold *drag* velocity" to minimize the confusion. A comparison between the mean velocity $\bar{u}_t$, measured at one meter above the bottom and the approximate corresponding value of the threshold drag velocity, $u_{*t}$, is shown in Fig. 60a and b.

It should be noted that Hjulström (1935, 1939) in reporting the threshold of grain movement in terms of the mean velocity $\bar{u}$ measured at a distance of one meter above the bottom states, ". . . the choice of the average velocity as an independent variable must be regarded as a temporary substitute until more data are available." The average or mean velocity is easy to visualize and measure, but it is not equally applicable to all conditions and must in general be redefined for each condition of flow.

We have dealt in general terms with a critical drag force or its equivalent threshold drag velocity which may be computed from the average velocity profile (see equation (5a)). However, it should be remembered that if even momentarily the value of $u_{*t}$ is exceeded, movement will result. Thus we are interested in the instantaneous velocity $u$, consisting of the average velocity $\bar{u}$, plus the velocity related to random fluctuation $u'$. Kalinske (1943) shows that the instantaneous drag force may be many times that computed from the average velocity.

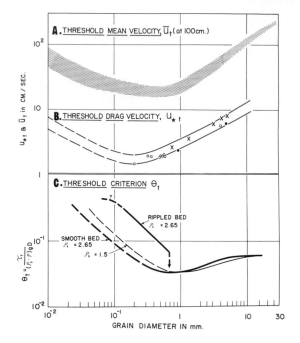

Fig. 60. Threshold criteria for initiation of grain movement as a function of grain diameter. (*a*) Mean velocity $\bar{u}$,
measured at one meter above the bottom, required to
initiate sediment movement (after Hjulström, 1939). This
is an arbitrary measurement dependent upon flow condition and depth of water. (*b*) Threshold drag velocity
$u_{*t} = \sqrt{\tau_t/\rho}$ required to initiate sediment movement (after
Inman, 1949; circles, dots, and crosses are data from U.S.
Waterways (1935), White (1940), and Gilbert (1914). (*c*)
Threshold values of the generalized friction coefficient $\theta_t$
for rippled and smooth beds (after Bagnold, in press;
Shields, 1936).

A broad curve, including some of the experimental values of the
threshold drag velocity, for various grain diameters is shown by
parallel solid lines in Fig. 60*b*. These threshold velocities were computed from the experimental critical drag forces obtained by White
(1940), the U.S. Waterways Experiment Station, and from Nevin's
(1946) analysis of data obtained by Gilbert. The threshold drag
velocity gradually decreases with decreasing grain diameter until
a diameter of approximately 0.18 mm is reached. At this value of the
threshold drag velocity, $u_{*t}$, the bottom becomes effectively smooth,
and individual grains cease to shed small eddies. The drag, instead of
being carried by a few grains, is more evenly distributed over the
whole surface. As a result of these changes the velocity necessary to

start surface movement increases as the grain diameter decreases below approximately 0.18 mm. This startling fact was experimentally demonstrated (Bagnold, 1937) by blowing a stream of air over a loosely scattered layer of fine portland cement powder. It was found that no movement occurred even when the wind was strong enough to move pebbles 4.6 mm in diameter.

It should be noted that while the relationship $u_*{}^2 = c\bar{u}^2$ holds for a smooth surface as well as for a rough surface, the value of $c$ may not be the same in both cases. The use of a constant value of $c$ in computing threshold velocity from the average stream velocity may not give accurate values when the bottom changes from rough to smooth. However, the stream velocity required to move the finer material does increase with decreasing grain size for water as well as wind transported sediments (Hjulström, 1939). This fact is illustrated in Fig. 60b by dotted lines representing the *apparent* threshold drag velocity. The data for this section of the curve were obtained from average stream velocities tabulated by Hjulström (1935).

The threshold of grain movement can also be expressed in terms of a generalized friction coefficient $\theta_t$. Bagnold (1963), following the work of Shields (1936), defines $\theta_t$ as the dimensionless ratio of the threshold shear stress $\tau_t$ to the immersed weight of the bed grains, as expressed by $(\rho_s - \rho)gD$. Thus $\theta_t$ takes both grain size and density into consideration. For similar bed conditions of size and packing, $\theta_t$ should be a constant, varying only with the excess density $(\rho_s - \rho)$. Because of their form drag, rippled beds have much higher values of $\theta_t$ than smooth beds. The threshold values of $\theta_t$ for smooth and rippled beds, and for grains with densities of 2.65 and 1.5 gms/cm$^3$ are shown as a function of grain size in Fig. 60c.

## Suspension

The suspension of granular material is a problem both in diffusion and advection. A qualitative relationship for dilute suspensions under conditions of equilibrium was first developed by Schmidt (1925) for air and later applied to silt in water by O'Brien (1933). Schmidt assumed that the mass of sediment particles carried downward by gravitational settling must equal the amount carried upward by turbulent motion:

$$\text{(down)} \quad wN_z = -\frac{A_s}{\rho}\frac{\partial N}{\partial z} \quad \overset{\uparrow}{\text{(up)}} \tag{10}$$

where $w$ is the settling velocity, $\rho$ the density of the fluid, $N_z$ is the grain concentration by volume at distance $z$ above the bottom and $A_s$

is the dynamic eddy viscosity applicable to sediment transfer. Both sides of the above relation have the units of sediment mass per unit of area and time, when multiplied by the density of the sediment, $\rho_s$.

The above relation can be integrated from a distance $z_1$ just above the sediment bed to some distance $z$ to give

$$\ln \frac{N_z}{N_1} = -\rho \frac{w}{A_s} (z - z_1)$$

or

$$\frac{N_z}{N_1} = e^{(-\rho w/A_s)(z-z_1)}$$  (11a)

where $N_z/N_1$ is the concentration ratio of sediment having a settling velocity $w$ at height $z$ to that at a constant height $z_1$ above the bottom, and ln and $e$ are the natural logarithm and the base of natural logarithms respectively.

The theory of the vertical distribution of sediment in dilute suspension is dependent on a concentration gradient. It should be noted that under similar flow conditions, the ratio of the sediment concentrations is proportional to $e^{-w}$. Thus fine material has a more uniform distribution with depth, and hence a smaller concentration gradient than coarse material. If the height $z_1$ is considered to be infinitely close to the bottom, and the turbulence is sufficient to cause suspension, then the concentrations of the various grain sizes at height $z_1$ are proportional to the amount of each grain size on the surface of the bottom.

The significance of the suspension relationship may be better understood by substituting for $A_s$ in equation (10), the equivalent value $a\rho k_0 u_*(z + z_0)$, where $a$ is a constant of proportionality in equating $A$ of equation (3) to $A_s$. Integrating (10) now gives

$$\ln \frac{N_z}{N_1} = - \frac{w}{a u_* k_0} \ln \frac{z + z_0}{z_1 + z_0}$$

or

$$\frac{N_z}{N_1} = \left( \frac{z + z_0}{z_1 + z_0} \right)^{-w/a u_* k_0}$$  (11b)

If $z_0$ is small compared to $z$ and $z_1$, it can be neglected and the relation reduces to

$$\frac{N_z}{N_1} = \left( \frac{z}{z_1} \right)^{-w/a u_* k_0}$$  (11c)

and the logarithm of the concentration ratio becomes proportional to $-w/u_*$ times the log of the ratio of the heights above the bottom.

This relation holds quite well for dilute suspensions of sediment under conditions of steady flow. However, as Vanoni (1953, p. 144) shows, the presence of suspended material in a fluid flow (1) has the apparent effect of reducing the friction factor, and (2) produces an increase in the fluid velocity and the discharge rate of suspended sediment. Of course, decreasing water temperature increases sediment suspension and transport rates, principally by reducing the settling velocity of the sediment.

Under the influence of wave action suspended material is not necessarily in equilibrium, and the flow is an extremely complex periodic variable depending upon wave height, period, depth of water,

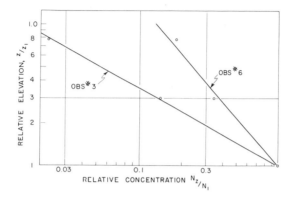

Fig. 61. Measurement of sediment concentration at elevations of 10 cm ($z_1$), 30 cm, and 78 cm above the bottom caught in a sediment trap placed outside of the surf zone at La Jolla, California (Inman, 1949b). Water depth, wave height, wave period, and the mass of sediment trapped at the 10-cm elevation are as follows: (Obs 3), 1.2 m, 67 cm, 10.8 sec, and 3.8 g/cm²/hr; (Obs 6), 2.9 m, 120 cm, 7.6 sec, and 7.6 g/cm²/hr.

distance from the plunge point of waves, and roughness of the bottom. Even though the flow conditions are extremely complex near the surf zone, the results of preliminary observations with a sediment trap (Inman, 1949b) indicate that the relationship of concentration of suspended material to height above the bottom is similar to that expressed in equation (11c). Figure 61 shows curves with the relative concentration of suspended material trapped by the orbital velocity of waves near the surf zone, as a function of the relative distance above the bottom. The relative height above the bottom is expressed in terms of $z/z_1$, and the relative concentration of suspended material in terms of $N_z/N_1$, where $N_1$ is the volume concentration of material trapped at the 10-cm elevation. The computed maximum horizontal orbital velocity, the wave period, and height, the depth of water, and the amount of material trapped at the 10-cm elevation for each observation are given in the caption of Fig. 61.

Inspection of this figure shows the effect of the maximum orbital velocity and the wave period on the slope and form of the concentration curves. The relative amount of material in suspension between the 10-cm elevation ($z/z_1 = 1$) and the 30-cm elevation ($z/z_1 = 3$) increases with increasing orbital velocity. The shape of the curve, based on material trapped at three elevations, appears to depend in part upon the period of the waves. During short-period waves (Observation 6) the curve is steeper and there is a relative increase in the concentration of material at the upper elevation. During longer period waves (Observation 3) the curve is less steep, indicating a relative decrease in the concentration in the upper elevation. This finding may be explained by the placing in suspension of the greatest amount of material during the maximum orbital velocities accompanying the wave crest and trough. With long-period waves a large percentage of the suspended material settles to the bottom during the intervals between crest and trough. During short-period waves the frequency of maximum velocity is greater and relatively more material is maintained in suspension.

## Flow of Granular Solids in High Concentrations

The following discussion of the transportation of high concentrations of granular material (i.e., a swarm of discrete solids) follows closely that given by Bagnold (1963), and has profited by his critical review.

When the concentration of granular material is high in fluid flow, the principles of fluid flow alone do not apply to the mixture, and it is necessary to consider the grain-to-grain stresses as well as the fluid stress. In the static case a shear stress applied to a granular mass in its densest contact packing causes a dilatation of the grains as first observed by Reynolds (1885). In this static case a tangential grain-to-grain shear stress $T$ produces a normal dispersive grain stress $P$ in the ratio of $T/P = \tan \phi$, where $\phi$ is the angle of internal friction and is a measure of the mean angle of contact between the grains, and is approximately equal to the angle of repose of the granular mass (Fig. 62).

In the flow of dispersed granular solids in fluid, Bagnold shows that the grain-to-grain contact produces a dispersion of grain momenta and a dispersive pressure $P$ which is proportional to the tangential shear $T$ in the same ratio $\tan \phi$ as in the case of the static granular shear. For this case, the total applied fluid stress $\mathfrak{J}$ necessary to maintain the shearing of the combined flow is equal to the sum of the grain-to-grain stress $T$ and the fluid stress on the bottom $\tau_0$, such that

$\mathfrak{J} = T + \tau_0$. The general relation of the total applied stress to the rate of grain shear $dU/dz$ can be written

$$\mathfrak{J} = T + \tau_0 = \mu(f'N)\frac{dU}{dz}$$

where $\mu$ is the fluid viscosity and $(f'N)$ is a function of the volume concentration $N$ of the granular material, and $U$ is the transport velocity of the grains.

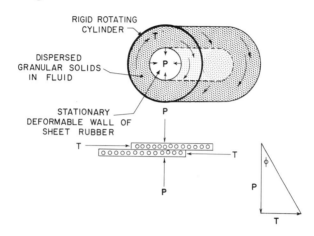

Fig. 62. Schematic representation of Bagnold's (1954) experiment for measuring the tangential shear $T$ and the resulting normal dispersive pressure $P$ produced by shearing a dispersion of granular solids in a fluid. The grain-fluid mixture is contained between two concentric cylinders, the outer one rigid and free to rotate, thus producing a tangential shear $T$, which causes a deformation of the stationary sheet rubber wall equal to the normal dispersive pressure $P$. The stress relations are shown schematically and vectorially in the lower half of the figure, where $\phi$ is the angle of internal friction and is approximately equal to the static angle of repose of the grains.

Bagnold (1954) demonstrated in an ingenious experiment of grain and fluid mixtures that the tangential grain-to-grain stress $T$, is commonly of the order of 100 times the fluid stress $\tau$, and that the fluid element did not begin to dominate until the volume concentration $N$ of the grains had been reduced to less than 9 percent.

In his experiment, Bagnold selected grains and liquid of exactly the same density in order to eliminate differential effects of gravity and other acceleration forces that would otherwise exist between the particles and the liquid. The mixture of liquid and grains was sheared between two concentric drums (Fig. 62); the wall of the inner one was stationary, and was constructed of deformable rubber, while the wall of the outer was rigid and free to rotate. The shear applied to the grain-liquid mixture was accurately measured from the torque required to rotate the outer drum, and the dispersive or normal stress produced by the tangential stress in the shearing was measured as an increase of static pressure in the inner stationary drum, which had a deformable periphery. There is no dispersive pressure associated with the shear of a viscous Newtonian fluid in the absence of solid granular particles. The presence of solid grains introduces a dispersive pressure $P$, which acts normal to the direction of tangential stress $T$. The concept can be illustrated by analogy to a lubricating fluid, which would more effectively separate moving parts (neglecting the scouring effect of the grains), if it contained sand grains. In the field of sedimentation the presence of the dispersive pressure $P$ and its relation to $T$ are fundamental concepts in considerations of work done in transporting a sediment load.

It is well to pause here and point out the significance of Bagnold's findings, and to emphasize the fundamental difference between fluid stress and grain-to-grain stress. In fluid flow the friction coefficient $c$ relates the stress $\tau$ over unit horizontal area of flow to the square of the flow velocity (see equation (6)) $c = \tau/\rho u^2$, and is completely independent of any normal stress exerted on the flow. On the other hand, in solid physics the friction coefficient is the ratio of the tangential stress $T$ necessary to just maintain motion of one solid element over the other, in the presence of the normal stress $P$ across the plane. In the case of cohesionless grains, as Bagnold showed, this takes the form of $\tan \phi = T/P$.

**Bed Load Transport.** Consider the equilibrium conditions of fluid and grain stresses when sediment is transported in a stream. For the present consider that the sediment bed is horizontal and that transport occurs principally as bed load near the surface of the bed. If the sediment is in motion, the applied stress from the fluid flow, $\mathfrak{J}$ acting over unit area of the bed, is balanced by the tangential grain-to-grain shear stress of the moving grains, $T$, and by any residual fluid stresses exerted directly on the bed by the fluid, $\tau_0$. If the system is in equilibrium, $\mathfrak{J}$ must be equal and opposite to the sum of $T$ and $\tau_0$ and following the notation of Fig. 63a we can write

$$\mathfrak{J} = \tau_0 + T \tag{12}$$

Before grain motion commences, $\tau_0$ may be as large as the threshold drag necessary to initiate grain motion. However, once an appreciable number of grains is in motion, the solid phase shear stress $T$ may become a hundredfold or more greater than $\tau_0$. In such a case the fluid

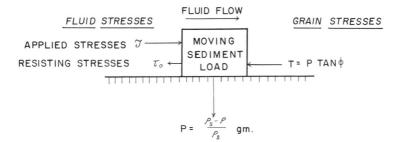

**A.** HORIZONTAL BED

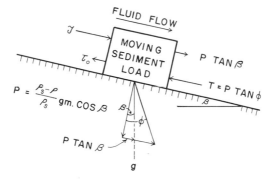

**B.** SLOPING BED

Fig. 63. Schematic diagram showing the stress equilibrium for bed load motion of sediment for (a) a horizontal bed and (b) a bed sloping in the direction of motion at an angle $\beta$.

shear can be neglected, and the simple relation between $\mathfrak{J}$ and $T$ can be considered.

Since the ratio between the tangential grain shear $T$ and the normal dispersive pressure $P$, $\tan \phi = T/P$, has been shown by Bagnold to remain nearly constant, even when the grain concentration in the liquid is as low as 9 percent, we can substitute $P \tan \phi$ for $T$ in equation (12). This substitution is of considerable importance because the normal dispersive pressure can be evaluated directly from a knowledge of the immersed weight of grains in motion. If $m$ is the dry mass of grains in motion per unit area of bed, then their immersed weight is $m$ times $[(\rho_s - \rho)/\rho_s] g$, and is equal to the normal dispersive pressure $P$ which is required to maintain them above the bottom.

The tangential grain shear stress required to maintain the grains in motion becomes

$$T = P \tan \phi = \frac{\rho_s - \rho}{\rho_s} gm \tan \phi$$

If the grains move with a velocity $U$, then the work done by the fluid in moving the grains is the product of the tangential shear $T$ and the velocity of grain motion; thus

$$\text{Work done in grain transport} = TU = \frac{\rho_s - \rho}{\rho_s} gmU \tan \phi \qquad (13)$$

It is convenient here to consider the sediment transport rates in terms of the work, or power expended in transporting the sediment. It will be observed that the product $mU$ of equation (13) is the sediment transport rate in dry mass per unit time and unit width of the stream. However, dry mass is not directly applicable to transportation by the fluid, and it is convenient to define a dynamic transport rate in terms of the immersed weight of the sediment by applying the factor $[(\rho_s - \rho)/\rho_s]g$ to the dry mass transport rate $(mU)$:

$$i = \left( \frac{\rho_s - \rho}{\rho_s} g \right) (mU) \qquad (14)$$

The quantity $i$ is the dynamic transport rate and is the immersed weight of sediment transported in unit time per unit width of flow, and has the dimensions of grams per cubic second.

Comparison of equations (13) and (14) shows that the power expended in transporting the sediment is the product of the dynamic transport rate and the tangent of the angle of internal friction, $i \tan \phi$. However, all the available power does not go into transporting sediment, and it is of interest to consider the efficiency of the stream as a transporting machine. If the total power available for sediment transport is $\omega$, then the efficiency $\epsilon$ of the stream is the ratio of the applied power $i \tan \phi$ to the total available power,

$$i \tan \phi = \epsilon \omega$$

or

$$i = \frac{\rho_s - \rho}{\rho_s} gmU = \epsilon \frac{\omega}{\tan \phi} \qquad (15a)$$

If the bed slopes at an angle $\beta$, then the complete equilibrium condition would be that expressed schematically by Fig. 63$b$. The complete expression for the bed load transport over a sloping bottom then becomes:

$$i = \frac{\rho_s - \rho}{\rho_s} gmU \cos \beta = \epsilon \frac{\omega}{\tan \phi - \tan \beta} \qquad (15b)$$

However, the slope of most streams is of the order of $2 \times 10^{-3}$ and both $\cos \beta$ and $\tan \beta$ in equation (15b) usually can be omitted for bed load considerations.

**Suspended Load Transport.**   The transport relations for a stream carrying a dense suspended load can be formulated from reasoning similar to that leading to the expression for the work done in transporting a bed load (equation (13)). If a dry mass of grains $m$ is maintained in suspension over unit area of bed, then the dynamic transport rate $i_s$ of the grains as they are carried along by the stream at grain velocity $U_s$ must be

$$i_s = \frac{\rho_s - \rho}{\rho_s} \, gmU_s \qquad (16)$$

Since the immersed weight of the grains per unit area of the bed is

$$\frac{\rho_s - \rho}{\rho_s} \, gm = \frac{i_s}{U_s}$$

the fluid must exert an equivalent normal dispersive stress in order to maintain the grains in suspension. If the grains have a settling velocity, $w$, relative to the fluid that supports them, then the stream must expend power in supporting the grains equal to the product of the normal stress and the settling velocity:

$$\text{Power expended in suspension} = Pw = \frac{\rho_s - \rho}{\rho_s} \, gmw = i_s \frac{w}{U_s} \qquad (17a)$$

However, if the bed slopes at an angle $\beta$ from the horizontal, additional gravity components are introduced (refer to Fig. 63b) which reduce the power expended by the stream by the amount $P \tan \beta$, and modify the normal stress to

$$P = \frac{\rho_s - \rho}{\rho_s} \, gm \cos \beta$$

If these changes are introduced into equation (17a), the power expended by the stream in transporting a suspended load down a sloping bed at the dynamic transport rate $i_s$ becomes

$$i_s \left( \frac{w}{U_s} - \tan \beta \right) = \epsilon_s \omega \qquad (17b)$$

where $\epsilon_s$ is the fraction of the total available power $\omega$ that is applied to suspended load transport.

There is a similarity between the ratio $w/U_s$, which affects the transport rate of suspended sediment, and $w/u_*$ which determines the slope of the concentration gradient of suspended sediment. $U_s$ is proportional to $u_*$ since the latter in turn is proportional to the mean velocity $\bar{u}$ of the stream (see equations (6) and (11)).

**Autosuspension and Turbidity Currents.** Following the reasoning leading to equations (17), it is observed that the power expended by the fluid in supporting a suspended load over a horizontal bed is $i_s w/U_s$, while the power expended by gravity directly on the sediment suspended over an inclined bed is $i_s \tan \beta$, where $\beta$ is the slope of the bed. The difference, $i_s(w/U_s - \tan \beta)$, is the net power the fluid must expend in the presence of a sloping bed. From this it follows that if $\tan \beta$ exceeds the ratio $w/U_s$, the suspended grains must impart energy to the stream and cause it to flow faster. Just as a boat floating down a river moves slightly faster than the water, and thus tends to push the water along.

This concept, which is termed autosuspension, was first suggested by Knapp (1938), but was generally overlooked. It was later derived independently by Bagnold (1956) and further developed to include turbidity currents (Bagnold, 1963). Since the principle operative only where $\tan \beta$ exceeds $w/U_s$, its most frequent application is either (1) to very fine sediments as in rivers or (2) to larger particles flowing down somewhat steeper slopes, as in an avalanche or a turbidity current.

Contrary to the assumption of a gradient in the concentration of suspended material, which is a necessary requirement in the development of the usual suspension relation (see equations (10) and (11)), autosuspension would give a uniform distribution of grains throughout the fluid. This relation is observed in rivers, where it is well known (Bagnold, in press) that fine silt does not tend to concentrate toward the bed, but is uniformly distributed throughout the flow.

There is insufficient data to test the application of the principle of autosuspension to turbidity currents, but Bagnold has derived the following relations in a form suitable for testing.

Consider the conditions necessary for the self-maintenance of a turbidity current of thickness $h$ flowing with mean velocity $\bar{u}$ down a bed inclined at angle $\beta$ with the horizontal (Fig. 63$b$). Following the notation of the previous section, the immersed weight of grains in suspension over unit area of bed is $(\rho_s - \rho)gm/\rho_s$. If the grains have a uniform concentration $N$ throughout the thickness $h$, the immersed weight can be written $(\rho_s - \rho)gNh$, by replacing $m/\rho_s$ with its equivalent value $Nh$.

In this case the fluid imparts no power to the flow. The total power available is that derived from the gravity component, $\sin \beta$, of the immersed weight of the suspended grains, multiplied by the velocity of flow of the grains $U_s$. If it is assumed that the grains and the turbidity current have the same velocity $\bar{u}$, one may write

$$\text{Available power} = \omega = (\rho_s - \rho)gNh\bar{u} \sin \beta \qquad (18)$$

If this power is to drive the turbidity current, it must supply both the power required to maintain the grains at a constant height above the bed, and the power needed to overcome the bed and surface drag resistance to maintain the flow velocity $\bar{u}$. The power required to maintain the grain suspension over the bed is simply the immersed weight of grains times their settling velocity $w$,

$$(\rho_s - \rho)gNhw$$

Neglecting, for the time being, the drag exerted at the upper flow boundary, the power required to maintain the flow velocity is the product of the bottom boundary stress $\tau_0$ and the flow velocity; $\tau_0 \bar{u}$.

Therefore, the condition that a turbidity current be self-maintaining is that the available power $\omega$ equal or exceed that required to maintain suspension and overcome the boundary resistance of the flow:

$$(\rho_s - \rho)gNh\bar{u} \sin \beta = \text{or} > (\rho_s - \rho)gNhw + \tau_0 \bar{u} \qquad (19)$$

The bottom boundary stress $\tau_0$ can be approximated from the semi-empirical expression of Francis' (equation (6a)) which gives $\tau_0 \bar{u}$ as approximately equal to $2 \times 10^{-3}\rho\bar{u}^3$. Little is known regarding the drag at the upper flow boundary, but doubling the value of the coefficient does not seem out of order for the value of the combined bed and upper boundary stresses. Using this value of $4 \times 10^{-3}$ for the drag coefficient and rearranging terms gives

$$\frac{\rho_s - \rho}{\rho} \frac{gNh}{\bar{u}^3} (\bar{u} \sin \beta - w) \geq 4 \times 10^{-3} \qquad (19a)$$

As an equality, relation 19a forms a cubic equation with three real roots. Two of these have physical meaning and give the limits of the range of flow velocities within which the available power equals or exceeds that required for self-maintenance of the turbidity current. The lower velocity fulfills the suspension requirement, $\bar{u} = w/\sin \beta$, while the higher velocity gives the upper limit at which all remaining available power is expended in overcoming boundary drag. Velocities above this upper limit would result in the boundary drag exceeding the available power, and cause the current to degenerate. Thus, it seems likely, considering the assumptions leading to relation (19), that a turbidity current flowing down a constant slope with a velocity within the limits set forth, would accelerate under the influence of the excess power until its velocity approaches the upper limit and a steady state is reached.

The mechanisms initiating turbidity currents are not clear. In many instances, such as in Scripps Submarine Canyon off La Jolla, California (Chamberlain, 1960), it seems likely that spontaneous liquefaction (see section on dilatation) resulting from excess pressure of associated storms at sea, or with earthquake shocks, initiates the motion of the sediment mass. In Scripps Submarine Canyon there is an initial slope exceeding 45° down which the sand avalanches before flowing on the more gentle slopes of 4.5° which extend from 65 to 165 fathoms, or the 1.1° slope that extends out to depths of about 550 fathoms.

If it is assumed that the avalanche of sand out of Scripps Submarine Canyon had attained, by the time it reaches the more gentle 4.5° slope, a thickness $h$ of 10 m, with a uniform volume concentration $N$ of 5 percent of fine sand having a settling velocity $w$ of 1 cm/sec, then the permissible velocities of propagation $\bar{u}$ from relation (19a) are found to range from 13 cm/sec to 13 m/sec.

In like manner the Grand Banks turbidity current (Heezen and Ewing, 1952) could also be tested, but here again it is necessary to make assumptions as to the thickness of the flow and the concentration of suspended material. If it is assumed that the flow had a thickness of 100 m with a 5 percent concentration of very fine sand flowing down an initial incline of 1.8°, the permissible flow velocities are found to range from 3.3 cm/sec to 24 m/sec.

It should be recognized that these figures in themselves may have little meaning quantitatively. The velocities are based on assumptions of thickness of the flows and on concentration of suspended material that may be far from correct. Also the computed velocities are not necessarily those at or even very near the sea floor. At present the only means of checking velocities is from the study of cable breaks. Some indication of the nature of the flows may be inferred from the nature of deposits left on the sea floor by turbidity currents (see pp. 341–343). These deposits have been cored extensively both along the axes of submarine canyons and out on the sea floor fans that extend below the canyons. Conclusions concerning velocities along the bottom of submarine canyons are not warranted without taking this evidence into consideration. In the future evidence should become available from measurements being made along the axis of Scripps Submarine Canyon at La Jolla.

### Total Load Transport in a Stream

The total sediment load transported by a stream can be expressed formally as the sum of the bed load (equation (15b)) and the suspended load (equation (17b)). Their sum gives the total dynamic transport rate

$i$ as:

$$i = i_b + i_s = \left( \frac{\epsilon_b}{\tan \phi - \tan \beta} + \frac{\epsilon_s}{(w/U_s) - \tan \beta} \right) \omega \qquad (20)$$

or $$= K\omega$$

where $K$ is a dimensionless coefficient equal to the complex expression within the brackets. $K$ equates $i$ to the total available power $\omega$, and may have values greater than one, especially for suspended load transport. Its value will generally be several times greater than the sum of the individual bed and suspended load efficiency coefficients, $\epsilon_b + \epsilon_s$. On empirical evidence from flume experiments and from natural rivers in the United States (Bagnold, in press) it appears that both $\epsilon_b$ and $\epsilon_s$ attain constant values at some critical value of flow so that the total sediment transport becomes proportional to the power $\omega$.

The validity of the above formal relation follows directly from the fact that the total load is the sum of the bed and suspended loads. However, it is not possible experimentally to separate one from the other, even under controlled laboratory experiments. In nature, the difficulties of measurement are much greater, and it is indeed rare when estimates of the total load can be assumed as reliable. The usual assumption is that all material trapped "above the bed" is suspended load while the remainder is bed load.

The power $\omega$ of a stream per unit of area of its bed is the product of the applied fluid stresses $\mathfrak{J}$, and the mean velocity of flow, $\omega = \mathfrak{J}\bar{u}$. The applied power is the decrement of the flow energy per unit distance traveled by the stream, and is equal to $\rho g h (dH/dx)\bar{u}$ where $h$ is the depth of water, and $dH/dx$ is the energy gradient. The energy gradient is approximated by equation (7), from which the applied fluid stress becomes $\mathfrak{J} = \rho g h \tan \beta$. The actual applied stress is probably somewhat greater for fully developed flow since the turbulent fluid stresses applied to the suspended load are not necessarily included in this relation. With this substitution the total dynamic transport rate becomes

$$i = \frac{\rho_s - \rho}{\rho_s} g(m_b U_b + m_s U_s) = K\rho g h \tan \beta \bar{u} \qquad (21)$$

where the expression for the dry mass transport rate within the parentheses is based on the assumption that $\cos \beta$ is approximately one and $\tan \beta$ is much less than $w/U_s$.

An estimation of the value of the coefficient $K$ can be obtained for field conditions by using the data of Colby and Hembree (1955) for the Niobrara River. In the vicinity of Cody, Nebraska, the character of the Niobrara River changes abruptly from a wide sandy stream to a natural flume. The natural flume has a constricted cross section of about 3 by 3m with solid rock walls and bottom. The solid rock permits a reasonable estimate of the total sediment discharge to be obtained from measurement of suspended load throughout the section. Since there is no net erosion or accretion between the natural flume and the upstream gauging station, the total load can be assumed the same in both localities. Estimations of the bed load at the upstream gauging station can then be made by subtracting the suspended sediment discharge at the gauging station from the total discharge measured at the natural flume (Table 8).

TABLE 8.    Stream Flow Conditions and Sediment Discharge
for the Gauging Station Section of the Niobrara River
on March 3, 1950

| | |
|---|---|
| Stream width | 21.3 m |
| Mean depth, $h$ | 50. cm |
| Total water discharge | 11.1 cu m/sec |
| Average stream velocity, $\bar{u}$ | 109 cm/sec |
| Stream slope, tan $\beta$ | $1.7 \times 10^{-3}$ |
| a. Suspended sediment discharge (measured at gauging station) | $1.17 \times 10^4$ g/sec |
| b. Total sediment discharge (measured at natural flume) | $1.96 \times 10^4$ g/sec |
| c. Bed load sediment discharge (b — a) | $0.79 \times 10^4$ g/sec |
| The median diameters of the suspended load and the bed load were about 0.125 and 0.25 mm respectively | |

Source: Colby and Hembree (1955, pp. 46, 101).

The stream flow conditions and the sediment discharge can now be used to evaluate $K$ from equation (21), where the quantity in brackets is the total sediment discharge ($1.96 \times 10^4$ g/sec) divided by the stream width. This substitution gives a value of 0.62 for $K$, which, considering the limitation and assumptions leading to its formulation, is probably somewhat too high. If it is assumed that the power $\rho g h \tan \beta \bar{u}$ is expended on the bed load alone, then $\epsilon_b$ is found to have a value of 0.15, or an efficiency of 15 per cent. In the latter case, no data are available for estimating $\epsilon_s$. No claim to accuracy is made in these single evaluations of $K$ and $\epsilon_b$. They are presented here to illustrate possible procedures for evaluating $K$, with the hope that data will eventually become available so that the discharge of sediment can be related to the power of the stream.

### Transport of Sediment by Waves

Waves traveling in shallow water dissipate power on the granular bed by the direct tangential stress of the to-and-fro motion of the water over the bed, and by the percolation of water in the porous bed induced by the pressure field of the passing wave. Both of these effect the transportation of sediment; the former by causing a to-and-fro motion of the sediment and the latter by producing upward currents which help to initiate motion and suspension of bed grains. In the following development it will be assumed that tangential stresses of wave motion constitute the principal mechanism for setting sediment in motion. The theory for tangential stress and for bed percolation are developed respectively by Putnam and Johnson (1949) and Reid and Kajiura (1957), and tables for their computation are presented in Bretschneider and Reid (1954). Tables relating to percolation in the latter reference should be modified in accordance with Reid and Kajiura (1957).

Assume that a fraction $K$ of the power $\omega$ expended by waves in tangential shear on the bottom is used in moving sediment on a horizontal bed. From the principles leading to the formulation of equation (15a), the instantaneous dynamic transport rate $i$ of grains near the bed can be expressed as

$$i = \frac{\rho_s - \rho}{\rho_s} gmU = K\omega$$

where $U$ is the to-and-fro velocity of grain motion produced by the waves. However, if the to-and-fro wave stresses on the bed are equal in magnitude and opposite in direction there can be no net displacement of grains, and the power is simply expended in a back and forth motion of a mass of grains of immersed weight,

$$\frac{\rho_s - \rho}{\rho_s} gm = i/U$$

Since the sediment is already supported by the wave stresses, no additional stress is required to move it. Thus if a current $u_\theta$, in any direction $\theta$, is superimposed on the to-and-fro movement of sediment by the waves, a net transport of sediment will occur

$$i_\theta = iu_\theta/U$$

in the direction $\theta$. Thus the wave motion supplies the power to keep the sediment in motion, and the magnitude and direction of the current $u_\theta$ determines the resulting magnitude and direction of sediment transport. If the to-and-fro velocity of the sediment grains $U$ is proportional to the maximum horizontal component of the wave orbital velocity $u_m$, then the relation for sediment transport becomes

$$i_\theta = \frac{\rho_s - \rho}{\rho_s} gmU = K'\omega \frac{u_\theta}{u_m} \tag{22}$$

where $K'$ is an efficiency coefficient modified to include the assumption that $U$ is proportional to $u_m$.

In the case of waves traveling over a shallow bottom Longuet-Higgins (1953) shows that the waves induce a current in the direction of wave travel, which, for the most rapidly moving layer of water near the bottom bed, simplifies to the form of equation (14) of Chapter III

$$u_\theta = \frac{5}{4}\frac{u_m^2}{C}$$

where $u_m$ is the maximum horizontal component of the orbital velocity near the bottom, and $C$ is the wave phase velocity (refer to "Wave-induced Currents," Chapter III). If this value of the wave-induced current is substituted for $u_\theta$, equation (22) simplifies approximately to

$$i_\theta = \frac{5}{8} K'' \omega \gamma \tag{22a}$$

where $K''$ absorbs the additonal numerical approximations[8] in the above relation and $\gamma = H/h$ is the relative depth in terms of the wave height $H$ and the water depth $h$. Equation (22a) expresses the dynamic transport rate in the direction of wave travel in terms of the available wave power and the relative depth. This relation could be expected to apply only in very shallow water where $\gamma$ equals about $\frac{1}{2}$ or greater.

The power $\omega$ that the waves expend by tangential stress on unit area of bed can be approximated by assuming that the general relation $\tau = c\rho\bar{u}^2$, as defined in equation (6), can be applied to wave stresses. Then the instantaneous rate at which power is dissipated per unit area of bed is the product of the stress and the velocity,

$$\omega = \tau\bar{u} = c\rho\bar{u}^3 \tag{23}$$

This relation is quite general, but can only be applied to the waves traveling over a sandy bottom if values of the drag coefficient $c$ are known, and if it is assumed that the energy dissipation can be obtained by substituting the orbital velocity of the waves for the velocity $\bar{u}$ of equation (6). Also, in applying equation (23) to waves it should be noted that both $\tau$ and $\bar{u}$ are fluctuating quantities, and that a phase difference between them will decrease their product.

Putnam and Johnson (1949) used this approach to compute the dissipation of wave energy by bottom friction as waves travel over a shallow bed. They assumed that the instantaneous orbital velocity of an Airy wave, averaged over a wave period, could be substituted

[8] In arriving at the above approximation it was assumed that $u_m = \frac{1}{2}\gamma C$.

in equation (23) giving the relation

$$\omega = c\rho\left[\frac{4}{3\pi}\,u_m^{\,3}\right]$$

where $u_m$ is the maximum orbital velocity as given by equation (3a), Chapter III, and the factor ($\frac{4}{3}\pi$) results when the instantaneous velocities are averaged over a wave cycle.

An estimation of the drag coefficient can be obtained from Bagnold's (1946, p. 12) relations for the drag over a rippled sand bed. He found the drag coefficient $c$ to have a constant value of 0.08 when the orbital diameter of wave motion was equal to about twice the ripple wavelength. When the wave orbital diameter exceeded twice the ripple length, the coefficient varied as the $\frac{3}{4}$ power of the ratio of the ripple wavelength $\lambda$ to the half-amplitude of the orbital diameter $\frac{1}{2}\,d_0$

$$c = 0.072\left[\frac{d_0}{2\lambda}\right]^{-3/4} \tag{24}$$

Putnam and Johnson (1949) evaluated $c$ for given ripple and wave conditions,[9] and concluded that a value of $c$ equal to $10^{-2}$ would apply for most ocean waves where the wave orbital displacement is large compared with the ripple wavelength.

The total power of a train of Airy waves traveling in shallow water is given as $\frac{1}{8}\,\rho gH^2Cn$ (equations (7) and (8), Chapter III), where $\rho$ and $g$ are the liquid density and the acceleration of gravity respectively, $H$ is the wave height, and $Cn$ is the group velocity of the waves. The power $\omega$ per unit of bed that is available for sediment transport is the decrement of the total wave power per unit of distance traveled $x$,

$$\omega = \frac{1}{8}\,\rho g\,\frac{d}{dx}\,(H^2Cn)$$

which for the condition of constant depth becomes approximately

$$\omega = \frac{1}{4}\,\rho g\,H\,\frac{dH}{dx}\,Cn \tag{25}$$

where $dH/dx$ is the rate of change of wave height with distance of wave travel.

Little laboratory data are available with which to evaluate $\omega$, and natural data from the ocean are unknown. However, the power decrement $\omega$ of real waves should be approximately equal to that given by equation (23), using Bagnold's relation (equation (24)) for

---

[9] Putnam and Johnson found $c = 10^{-2}$ for the condition of ripple wavelength $\lambda = 5$ in., and ocean waves with a period of 12-second, height of 4 ft, and a water depth to deep water wavelength ratio of 0.03.

the value of the coefficient $c$. Regarding the decrement in wave height to be expected, Savage (1953) working in a flume with waves a few inches high and periods near $1\frac{1}{4}$ seconds obtained values of $dH/dx$ varying from about $10^{-3}$ to $2 \times 10^{-3}$ over rippled sandy bottoms. This, of course, includes all losses due to tangential stress, percolation, and sidewall effect of the flume. The relations tabulated by Bretschneider and Reid (1954, plate IB) and based on the work of Putnam and Johnson (1949) give values of $dH/dx$, due to the tangential stress alone, of about $5 \times 10^{-4}$ for ocean waves 1 m high with periods varying from 5 to 15 seconds traveling in water depth equal to twice the wave height ($\gamma = \frac{1}{2}$).

In order to make a sample computation, indicating the possible order of magnitudes of the wave-induced sediment transport, it is necessary to know the value of the efficiency coefficient $K''$. No data are known for this coefficient in nature. However, in the interest of illustrating the possible importance of wave-induced transport, an arbitrary value of one percent ($K'' = 0.01$) will be assumed in the following calculation.[10] Consider a 1-m high, 10-second period wave traveling in water 2 m deep ($\gamma = \frac{1}{2}$), over a horizontal sandy bed, and assume that $K'' = 0.01$, $c = 0.01$, and the orbital velocity $u_m = 150$ cm/sec. Under these conditions the wave would result in a wave-induced dynamic transport of sediment, $i_\theta$, in the direction of wave travel of 170 g mass per cubic second. This is the equivalent of a dry mass transport of quartz sand

$$mU = i_\theta \left/ \frac{\rho_s - \rho}{\rho_s} g \right.$$

of 0.5 g per centimeter of wave crest per second; or of a volume transport, assuming a bulk density $\rho'_s$ of 1.5 g/cm³, of $mU/\rho'_s$ equal to about $\frac{1}{3}$ cu cm per centimeter of wave crest per second. Over a longer time this converts to a volume transport rate of 600 cu m per meter of beach per year.

The wave-induced transport in shoaling water would be decreased by the slope of the bed. By analogy, the $\tan \beta$ term in the denominator of equation (15b) would become positive rather than negative, and the power available for transport would thus decrease. In the case of breaking or near-breaking waves, as near a beach, the wave-induced transport would be expected to produce an increase in the bed slope until an equilibrium condition of no net transport resulted.

Although the quantitative aspects of the wave-induced transport rates developed here for purposes of illustration may have little direct

[10] Evidence from experiments by Inman and Bowen (1963) of wave-induced transport of quartz sand suggests that $K''$ has values of about 1 to 10 percent.

application, the possible importance of this mechanism should be given serious consideration in matters pertaining to the formation of beaches and barrier beaches in areas where waves travel in relatively shallow water.

## Appendix[11]

**Coarse Fraction Analysis.**    In the investigation of the sediments of the coastal area along the northwest Gulf of Mexico various methods were used to determine the characteristics of sediments in the different environments. One of the most useful methods for distinguishing these environments proved to be the estimation of the constituents of the coarse fraction, that is, of the sediments that were coarser in size than 62 microns.

To estimate the constituents of the coarse fraction the most practical method appears to be to sieve the sand fraction into the standard sizes > 1 mm, 1–0.5, 0.5–0.25, 0.25–0.125, and 0.125–0.062 mm. Each fraction is then weighed, and a cut is taken from each sieve and spread over a gridded tray. Then one hundred or more grains are classified; bias is avoided by choosing the grains nearest grid inter-sections. The cut can be taken by a sample splitter, but it has been proved by careful tests in the Scripps Institution laboratory that just as effective a method and one consuming much less time results from spreading the sample over a large tray and taking small scoop samples from various parts of the tray. The counting of the grains is accomplished very satisfactorily by using a "Denominator" blood counter of the type with eight keys that can be operated by the touch method without taking one's eyes from the field of the binocular microscope. When one hundred grains have been counted, the device stops automatically and the figures give the percents of each type up to eight. If larger numbers are required, another counter can be added, but each grain recorded on the additional counter should be included on the right-hand key of the Denominator in order to get the count to stop at 100 (or a multiple of 100 if this is desired).

When the counts have been made, the percents of constituents in each size should be multiplied by the weight percent for the respective grade sizes, and thus the percent of each constituent in the whole sample can be determined using any standard computer. The average for a particular environment can be obtained by adding percentages of all analyzed samples in that environment.

The plotting of results can be made in various ways. Figure 64 illustrates two of the methods that were used for certain Gulf Coast

[11] This section is by F. P. Shepard.

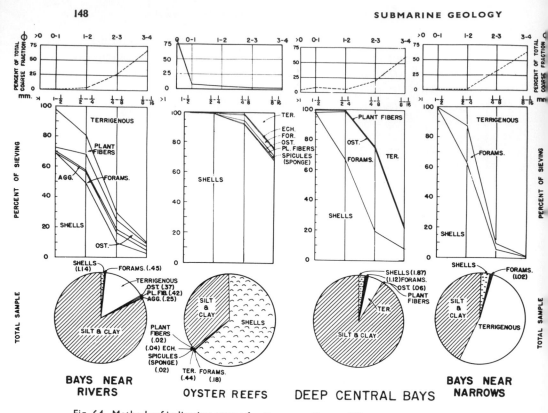

**Fig. 64.** Methods of indicating coarse fraction according to different environments in a Texas bay. This shows average percentage of material in different sizes of coarse fraction, percentages of constituents in each sieve size, and percentage of materials in total sample (shown in pie diagram along with percentage of silt and clay).

environments. In the pie diagrams the percent of fines is included to give another means of distinguishing the several environments, but the pie diagrams can also be made by using only the coarse fraction. The results of each sieve size are given in the middle bracket, and the upper bracket shows the weight percents in each size.

The choice of the constituents to be counted should of course depend on the capability of the investigator and on the relative importance of the various constituents in the area under investigation. The groups that have proved most useful in the work at Scripps Institution have included terrigenous minerals (often separating these into a quartz-feldspar group, ferromagnesians, and mica); rock fragments; authigenic minerals (often separating these into glauconite, phosphatic grains, and pyrite); Foraminifera (separating, if possible, into planktonic and benthonic); echinoids; ostracods; diatoms; bryozoans; and aggregates (describing these as to color, etc.). Although the above list exceeds eight and hence the capability of the counter, in most samples a group of eight seems sufficient for the purpose. The number of aggregates will depend considerably on the type of disaggregation that is practiced in preparing the sample. The use of sodium oxalate 67 g with sodium carbonate 10.6 g per 100 liters, or sodium hexametaphosphate is helpful in breaking up most of the aggregates, although some are very persistent and may have genetic significance. For some purposes it is best not to try to disaggregate the sediment because certain features that may be preserved in sedimentary rocks such as fecal pellets are usually disaggregated by a good peptizer. Preparing two samples for study, one with disaggregation and the other with only washing in distilled water, will help solve this difficulty. Percentages of less than three are deceptive unless a considerable number of samples is averaged. In some cases it might be better to look over the whole field and estimate by eye the percents of the rarer constituents.

The coarse fraction method is definitely not a highly accurate method and it suffers somewhat because it gives discontinuous distributions that are arbitrarily cut off at 62 microns, and because values are given as weights but are based in large part on numbers of individuals in the counts. Counts of mineral or organic species that have modes near the cutoff size of 62 $\mu$ could be very misleading when compared with similar samples. The grains of constituents such as mica or Foraminifera obviously weigh much less than terrigenous grains, and much less than magnetite, but this can scarcely be avoided and the results appear to justify the means. In fact, such tests as have been made on unknowns from various environments by other tests such as the foraminiferal population, the macroorganisms or the ostracods show that the coarse fraction method ranks fully as high as any other.

**Roundness Analysis.** Because of the difficulty of developing good three-dimensional methods of comparison of the shapes of grains, most methods of evaluating grain shapes have been based on two dimensional analysis (see for example Waddell, 1932; Krumbein, 1941; and Riley, 1941). The scale proposed by Powers (1953) is primarily two dimensional but the photographs of models which he uses give some indication of the third dimension. Since the third dimension is obviously of great importance in sedimentation, it seems important to have a method that is more applicable to the third dimension even if it is mathematically less exact. With the idea of checking the roundness of grains, a series of classes was developed (Shepard and Young, 1961) somewhat akin to the Powers models. These are illustrated in Fig. 65.

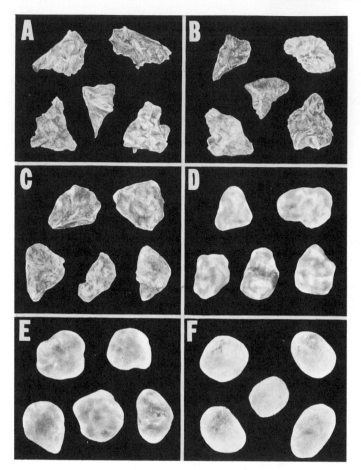

Fig. 65. Examples of the six classes used for roundness determinations. Modified from Powers (1953). A = very angular, B = angular, C = sub-angular, D = subrounded, E = rounded, F = well rounded. Photographs by Ruth Y. Manar, retouching by J. R. Moriarty.

The analysis of the roundness of grains using the models in Fig. 65 can be accomplished in approximately the same way as that described for coarse fraction constituents. One hundred grains of the same mineral, quartz being preferred, are classified under the binocular microscope, and the numbers are multiplied by the same factors used by Powers, that is, 0.14 for very angular; 0.21 for angular; 0.30 for subangular; 0.41 for subrounded; 0.59 for rounded, and 0.84 for well rounded. For some studies it may be advisable to count grains of all types. Bias is more of a problem than in coarse fraction analysis because of the ease of putting marginal grains in a higher or lower bracket following a subconscious desire to find a sample rounder or more angular in order to fit some preconceived hypothesis. As a result it is very important to study all samples as unknowns using a code system. It is also very advisable to have a second operator to offset a common tendency to call grains more rounded on certain days than on others. When two operators show distinct differences in results, the sample should be rerun to see if a closer agreement can be reached.

The use of shape analysis lies in its application to differentiating sedimentary environments. The application to beach and dune studies has been repeatedly demonstrated (MacCarthy, 1935; Beal and Shepard, 1956; and Shepard and Young, 1961) but not much attempt has been made to apply the method to other environments where there may well be important correlations. Shape may also tell something about the distance of transportation of grains, although roundness does not necessarily increase with distance of travel and may decrease as shown by Russell (1939) and Kuenen (1958).

# CHAPTER VI

# DEFINING AND CLASSIFYING
# SHORELINES AND SEA COASTS

The marine and land phases of geology meet at the shoreline. Because the sea has influenced the development of shorelines and of the coasts, it is important to include in a treatise on submarine geology a discussion of the character and origin of the shore and coast. The classification of coasts is made easier by the numerous excellent air photographs that have appeared in recent years. Among the photographs that have proved particularly useful should be included those of Putnam *et al.* (1960) and the Hydrographic Office (1947).

### Nomenclature for Coastal and Shoreline Features

Definitions relative to beach terms are given in Chapter VII, pp. 168–170, but a few terms will be discussed here. Much of our nomenclature on coastal and shoreline features dates back to Johnson's *Shore Processes and Shoreline Development* (1919). Some revisions have been suggested in recent years (Price, 1951, 1955, and 1956; Shepard, 1952b; Beach Erosion Board, 1954), and we are indebted to Wiegel (1952) for a very complete glossary of terms with definitions related to shores and shore processes. The *shoreline* is generally defined as "the line where land and water meet," whereas the *shore* is the zone from mean low tide (or lower low tide) line to the inner edge of wave transported sand, and the *coast* is the broad zone directly landward from the shore. The coast includes the sea cliffs and elevated terraces as well as the lowlands inside the shore. Since the shoreline is dependent on the state of the tide, the direction and force of the wind, the height of the breakers, and the effect of seiches, as well as the slope of the shore, it is only a line for any particular moment and may migrate over a belt miles in width, as at Mt. St. Michel on the Normandy coast of France. Similarly, high tide or mean tide line is not a constant but an average position for a certain period. The interplay between shoreline and coast makes it impractical to classify them separately.

Among other terms which are useful to define in the present

chapter are *barriers* and *bars*. The word "bar" has been used rather indiscriminately. Among mariners a bar is a slightly submerged ridge, usually of sand or other type of sediment. This usage seems desirable. On the other hand, the term "offshore bar" for an elongate sand island or peninsula as used by Johnson (1919) is confusing. Some of these sand masses have lengths of scores of miles, widths of more than 10 miles, and heights above sea level of 100 ft or more, hardly suitable for the term "bar." The word "barrier" seems far more applicable for the feature and the combined terms *barrier islands*, *barrier spits*, or *bay barriers* (see Fig. 73) can be used where appropriate. *Barrier beaches* are suggested where the sand mass consists only of a beach lacking both the dunes and marsh flats which form a part of the larger barriers.

### Purpose of a Shoreline and Coastal Classification

There have been some recent attempts to classify broad coastal belts according to their general geological or topographic character (Valentin, 1952; McGill, 1958). This goes somewhat beyond the scope of the marine aspects of geology and will not be considered here. The purpose of the classification in the present volume is to help the interpretation of the most recent geological events which have transpired along the coast. A classification which can be applied successfully to a combination of coastal charts, topographic maps, and aerial photos would appear to be the most useful and, therefore, these sources will be used to illustrate the types.

### Difficulties with Earlier Classification

For many years the classification developed largely by Johnson (1919) was taught widely in the schools and is no doubt still used by some. It is a genetic classification which is, of course, desirable, but depends largely on the supposed recent history of the coast, that is, shorelines of submergence where the coast has sunk, shorelines of emergence where it has risen, neutral shorelines where it has been stable, and compound shorelines that have emerged and submerged. This is unfortunate because all coasts of the world have been subject to the rise in sea level at the end of the last glacial episode, which was so recent that it has left its effects on virtually all coastal areas in one way or another. Furthermore, there is abundant evidence that the sea level has stood higher than now in interglacial episodes, and therefore all relatively stable coasts have evidence of this higher stand.

Accordingly, an investigation of almost any coast of the world may show that it is both a coast of emergence and submergence, or a compound shoreline according to Johnson. The typical neutral shoreline of Johnson was that of the delta. Most large deltas, however, are areas of general subsidence quite independent of the recent rise of sea level so that the word neutral does not appear to be applicable regardless of changing sea levels.

Perhaps the worst feature of the Johnson classification has been the use of barriers (called "offshore bars") as the principal criterion for distinguishing a shoreline of emergence. It is well known that barrier islands form along the sinking shorelines of abandoned deltas (R. J. Russell, 1958). Also they appear to have grown upward during the last part of the postglacial sea level rise along the Texas coast (Shepard, 1960c), and in fact occur along most of the lowland coasts which have had their valleys drowned by the rising sea level (see also pp. 264–268). Barrier islands also have been seen to develop in periods of a few years along stable coasts such as that of west Florida (Shepard, 1952b). Barriers with sloping crests may develop during emergence (Curray, 1960), but these are not the type referred to as examples of coasts of emergence. Equally deceptive is the use of the straightness of a coast as an indication of emergence. Straightness, as will be shown, is a product of wave action and has little to do with emergence.

A very different type of classification from that of Johnson is given by Valentin (1952), although they both make considerable use of coasts of emergence and submergence. Valentin takes the data for the basis of his emergence and submergence from worldwide tide gauge records. As a result the physiographic criteria used by Johnson are not used. The Valentin classification is of an entirely different nature from that which is attempted here. It may be useful for some purposes but it is only as good as are the tide gauge records. Actually, there are not many places in the world with records extending back more than a few years in which tide experts have any great confidence. The principal feature of the Valentin classification, therefore, is that it shows the areas of well-known emergence surrounding the formerly glaciated territories. Much of the rest is subject to uncertainty.

### Nature of Proposed Classification

The classification provided here represents a revision of one which I first suggested (Shepard, 1937a) and slightly revised in the first edition of *Submarine Geology*. Use has been made of a more complex classification by Price (1953, 1955), which is based on many of the same underlying principles as that of my earlier classification. Some of the names have been suggested by D. L. Inman.

The classification has as its two principal subdivisions *Primary coasts* and *Secondary coasts*, the former representing coasts and shorelines which are essentially the result of the sea resting against a land mass that owes its topography to a terrestrial agency, whereas the latter are largely the result of present day marine processes or marine organisms. Further subdivisions of each group are made according to the specific agent, terrestrial or marine, which has had the greatest influence. Actually, there are few coasts and shorelines where the influence of only one agent is indicated. As a result many coasts should be given a dual or triple classification, and any relatively large area is likely to belong in more than one category. Most coasts, however, appear to show one dominant influence.

Although the classification may at first sight seem to offer many more complications than the simpler groupings of the old Johnson scheme, it will be found that most shores can be classified quite satisfactorily from charts and aerial photographs. This has become evident from use of the classification in its various evolving forms for the past twenty-five years in class work. After some practice, students can apply the groupings with considerable success.

## Classification of Shorelines and Coasts

I. *Primary (Youthful) Shorelines and Coasts.* Configuration due to the sea coming to rest against a land form shaped by terrestrial agencies rather than marine.

    A. *Land Erosion Coasts.* Shaped by subaerial erosion and partly drowned by rise of sea level or by downwarping, or inundated by melting of an ice mass from a valley along the shore.

        1. *Ria coasts (drowned river valleys)* (Fig. 66(1)). Usually recognized by the relatively shallow water of the estuaries which indent the land. Commonly have a V-shaped cross section and a deepening of the axis seaward except where interfered with by a barrier built across the estuary mouth.

            (a) *Dendritic type.* Pattern resembling an oak leaf and due to river erosion in horizontal beds or homogeneous material.

            (b) *Trellis type.* Due to river erosion in inclined beds of unequal hardness (Fig. 67).

        2. *Drowned glacial erosion coasts.* Recognized by being deeply indented with many islands. Charts show deep water (commonly over 50 or 100 fathoms) with the cross section of the bays U-shaped and with much greater depth within the bays than near the entrance. Hanging valleys and sides commonly parallel and

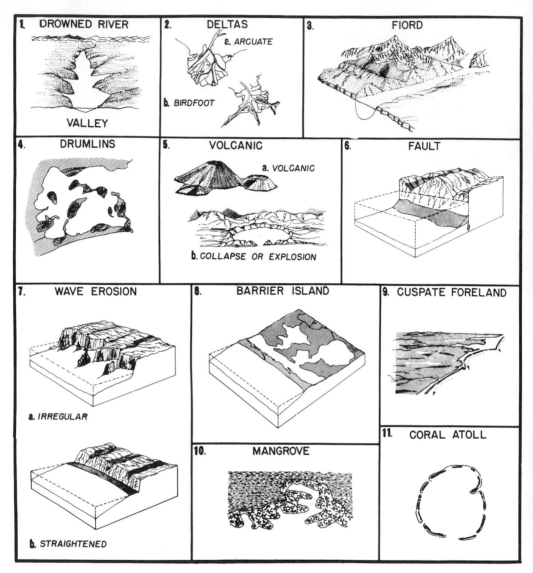

Fig. 66. Thirteen types of coasts and shorelines included in the classification.

relatively straight in contrast to rias. Almost all glaciated coasts have these criteria.

(a) *Fiord coasts*. Relatively narrow inlets cutting through mountainous coasts (Fig. 66(3)).

(b) *Glacial troughs*. Broad indentations like Cabot Strait and the Gulf of St. Lawrence or the Straits of Juan de Fuca.

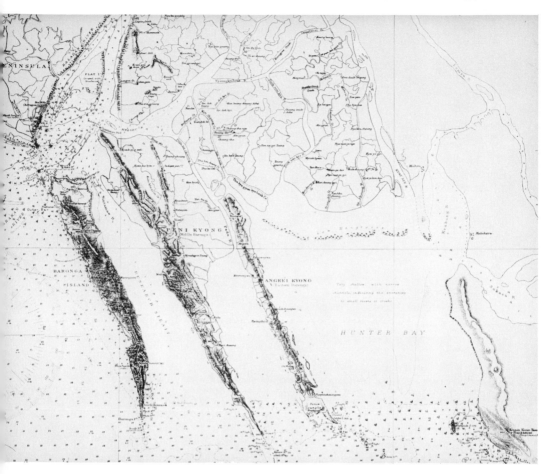

Fig. 67. Trellis dip coast formed by the erosion of inclined layers of rock of different resistance. From U.S. Hydrographic Office Chart No. 3705 of the coast of Burma at 20° N. Lat.

    3. *Drowned Karst topography.* Embayments with oval-shaped depressions indicative of drowned sink holes. This is an uncommon type. It exists locally as along the east side of the Adriatic (Fig. 119), and along the Asturias coast of North Spain.

B. *Subaerial Deposition Coasts.*

    1. *River deposition coasts.* Largely due to deposition by rivers extending the shoreline.

        (a) *Deltaic coasts:*

            (i) *Digitate (birdfoot)* the lower Mississippi Delta (Fig. 66(2*b*)).

            (ii) *Lobate* western Mississippi Delta, Rhone Delta.

            (iii) *Arcuate* Nile Delta (Fig. 66(2*a*)).

            (iv) *Cuspate* Tiber Delta (Fig. 68).

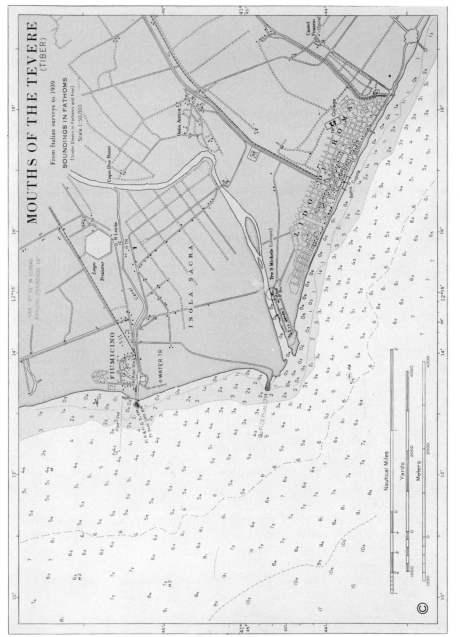

Fig. 68. Cuspate delta. From U.S. Hydrographic Office Chart No. 3493.

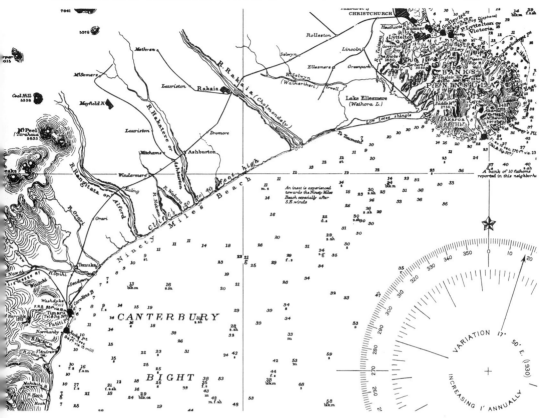

Fig. 69. Alluvial coast straightened by deposition of a series of rivers coming from the New Zealand Alps. Banks peninsula represents an eroded and partially submerged volcano.

(b) *Alluvial plain coasts.* Relatively straight gently sloping coasts being prograded by a group of braided streams, ordinarily coming from a nearby mountain range. Example is the east coast of South Island, New Zealand (Fig. 69).

2. *Glacial deposition coasts.*

(a) *Partially submerged moraines.* Usually difficult to recognize without a field study to indicate the glacial origin of the sediments constituting the coastal area. Usually modified by marine erosion as, for example, Long Island.

(b) *Partially submerged drumlins.* Recognized on topographic maps by the elliptical contours on land and islands with oval shore lines. Example: Boston Harbor (Fig. 66(4)).

(c) *Partially submerged drift features.*

3. *Wind deposition coasts.* An unusual type found principally in the tropics where calcareous dunes have been lithified and drowned by rising sea level.

Fig. 70. Distribution of fossil dunes along the north coast of Puerto Rico. These constitute a special type of coast found in tropical areas. From Kaye (1959).

Fig. 71. Landslide coast, Palos Verdes Hills. Note buckling of pier where slide has advanced into the Pacific Ocean. Photo courtesy of R. R. Benedict.

 (a) *Dunes.* Where deposition of wind-blown sand is in excess of wave erosion.

 (b) *Fossil dunes.* Examples: along the north coast of Puerto Rico (Fig. 70) and along the west coast of Morocco.

 (c) *Sand flats.* Form in front of advancing dunes; found only in embayments.

 4. *Landslide coasts.* Recognized by the bulging earth masses at the coast and the landslide topography on land (Fig. 71).

C. *Volcanic Coasts.*

 1. *Lava flow coasts.* Recognized on coastal charts by land contours showing cones, by convexities of shoreline, or by conical slopes continuing from land out under the water. Slopes of 10° to 30° common above and below sea level. Found in many oceanic islands (Fig. 66(5a)).

Fig. 72. Mud lump islands off Pass a Loutre, Mississippi Delta. These islands are rapidly worn away by the waves. Photo courtesy of J. P. Morgan.

    2. *Tephra coasts.* Where the volcanic products are fragmental. Roughly convex but much more quickly modified by wave erosion than are lava flow coasts.

    3. *Volcanic collapse or explosion coasts.* Recognized in air photos and on charts by the concavities in the sides of volcanoes (Fig. 66 (5b)).

D. *Shaped by Diastrophic Movements.*

    1. *Fault coasts.* Recognized on charts by the continuation of relatively straight steep land slopes beneath the sea. Angular breaks at top and bottom of slope.

      (a) *Fault scarp coast.* Example: northeast side of San Clemente Island, California (Fig. 66(6)).

      (b) *Fault trough type.* Example: Gulf of California and Red Sea.

      (c) *Overthrust type.* No examples recognized, but probably exist.

    2. *Fold coasts.* Difficult to identify on maps or charts but probably exist.

    3. *Sedimentary extrusions.*

      (a) *Salt domes.* Occur as oval-shaped islands in the Persian Gulf.

(b) *Mud lumps.*   Small islands due to upthrust of mud in the vicinity of the passes of the Mississippi Delta (Fig. 72).

II. *Secondary Coasts.*   Shaped primarily by marine agencies or by marine organisms. May or may not have been Primary Coasts before being shaped by sea.

A. *Wave Erosion Coasts.*

1. *Wave straightened cliffs.*   Bordered by a gently inclined sea floor in contrast to fault coasts.

(a) *Cut in homogeneous materials* (Fig. 66(7b)).

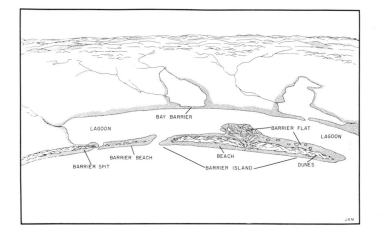

Fig. 73. Various types of barriers and the component parts of a barrier island.

(b) *Hogback strike coasts.*   Where hard layers of folded rocks have a strike roughly parallel to the coast so that erosion forms a straight shoreline.

(c) *Fault line coasts.*   Where an old eroded fault brings a hard layer to the surface allowing wave erosion to remove the soft material from one side leaving a straight coast.

2. *Made irregular by wave erosion.*   Unlike ria coasts in that the embayments do not extend deeply into the land.

(a) *Dip coasts.*   Where alternating hard and soft layers are exposed to the waves; not easily distinguished from trellis coasts (see Fig. 67).

(b) *Heterogeneous formation coasts.*   Where wave erosion has cut back the weaker zones leaving great irregularities.

B. *Marine Deposition Coasts.*   Coasts prograded by waves and currents.

1. *Barrier coasts* (Fig. 73).

(a) *Barrier beaches.*   Single ridges.

(b) *Barrier islands.*   Multiple ridges, dunes, and overwash flats.

(c) *Barrier Spits.*   Connected to mainland.

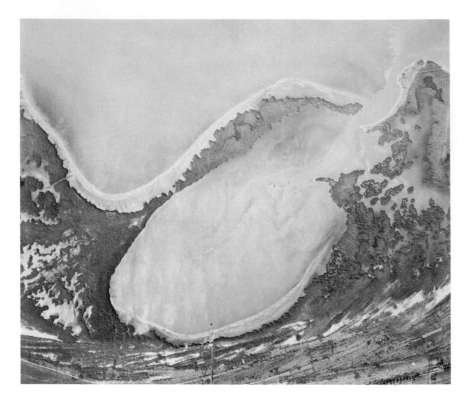

Fig. 74. A mangrove shoreline on the east side of Sanibel Island, west coast of Florida. Beach or dune ridges are shown at the extreme base of the photograph. Photo by D. L. Inman

     (d) *Bay barriers.*   Sand spits that have completely blocked bays.
     (e) *Overwash fans.*   Lagoonward extension of barriers.
   2. *Cuspate forelands.*   Large projecting points with cusp shape. Examples include Cape Hatteras and Cape Canaveral (Fig. 91).
   3. *Beach plains.*   Sand plains differing from barriers by having no lagoon inside.
   4. *Mud flats* or *salt marshes.*   Formed along deltaic or other low coasts where gradient offshore is too small to allow breaking of waves.
C. *Coasts Built by Organisms.*
   1. *Coral reef coasts.*   Include reefs built by algae. Common in tropics. Ordinarily reefs fringe the shore and rampart beaches are found inside piled up by the waves.
   2. *Serpulid reef coasts.*   Small stretches of coast may be built out by the cementing of worm tubes onto the rocks or beaches along the shore. Also found mostly in tropics.
   3. *Oyster reef coasts.*   Where oyster reefs have built along the shore and the shells have been thrown up by the waves as a rampart.

4. *Mangrove coasts.* Where mangrove plants have rooted in the shallow water of bays and have collected sediment so as to extend the coast (Figs. 66(10), 74). Also a tropical development.

5. *Marsh grass coasts.* In protected areas where salt marsh grass can grow out into the shallow sea and like the mangroves collect sediment so as to extend the land. Most of these coasts could be classified also as mud flats or salt marsh.

Fig. 75. A coastal platform elevated at the time of the great Japanese earthquake of 1923. Location at the island of Enoshima. From Yamasaki (1926).

## Discussion of the Classification

The classification has been made much more nearly complete than previously, but it still may lack types of unusual or complex nature. Some omissions have been made on purpose such as *coasts of emergence.* Objection to this omission has been presented by King (1959, pp. 236–240). There are, to be sure, coasts which are dominated by their elevated terraces, but these terraces are found in various degrees along most coasts of the world, and if they are relatively low (less than about 60 m in elevation), they may be due to the high stands of sea level during interglacial or preglacial times and are, therefore, difficult to separate as a genetic coastal type. If there has been faulting in historical time that has elevated a coastal terrace, there would appear to be good grounds for reference to *coasts of emergence* but this is almost impossible to tell from maps and charts or even photographs. A few cases are known, notably a portion of the coast at Sagami Bay to the south of Tokyo, Japan (Fig. 75). This coastal strip certainly has neither straightness nor barrier islands to indicate the uplift. There are some raised terraces, but the recency of their uplift is not apparent in photographs. The small rocky promontories to the west of the bay that represent the elevation of what were slightly submerged rock reefs prior to the earthquake of 1923 had no indication, when examined by the writer in 1957, that they represented a recent uplift.

Most glaciated coasts have been rising in historical times so that they might be termed coasts of emergence. The striking characteristics of these coasts, however, are mostly those of glacial erosion. Their recent elevation has not greatly influenced the shape of the coast. Therefore, even in this case the introduction of coasts of emergence adds a confusing element to the classification and does not seem warranted. At least from a practical point of view it is better to leave out these complications and thus maintain a workable classification.

# CHAPTER VII

# BEACHES AND RELATED SHORE PROCESSES

## Introduction

The deposits of sand and gravel that cover the shore in many places are known as beaches. Although they appear stable under conditions of small waves, beaches are eroded so rapidly when attacked by heavy surf and storm waves that they may completely change their character or even disappear in a few hours. Less spectacular but cumulatively important are the slow changes mostly in the form of growth that accompany small waves. In addition to these cyclic changes, beaches undergo large permanent modifications as the result of the works of man. Hardly a jetty is built that does not cause the loss of some beach and the overexpansion of another. As a result the understanding of the causes of beach development and destruction is of considerable economic importance.

Largely because of heavy beach erosion along various coasts, much progress has been made in recent years in studying the underlying processes. Notable has been the establishment of the Council on Wave Research at the University of California, Berkeley, an organization that has published a series of conference symposium reports covering beach erosion and related aspects all along the coasts of the United States. The same group has also produced a glossary of terms that contains much helpful information (Wiegel, 1953). The Beach Erosion Board of the U.S. Army Engineers has continued its investigations of various beach problems and has issued numerous reports including its summation in 1954 (Rept. 4) on "Shore Protection, Planning, and Design."

For many years Douglas Johnson's *Shore Processes and Shoreline Development* (1919) was the only textbook related to beaches, but this has now been supplemented by C. A. M. King's *Beaches and Coasts* (1959). Other books supplying helpful information include André Guilcher's *Coastal and Submarine Morphology* (1958) and J. A.

Steers' *The Sea Coast* (1953). Zenkovitch (1958) has written another book on beaches and shore processes based on the Black Sea area.

New information of importance is in Inman and Frautschy's (1966) investigation of compartments of beach transport along the southern California coast with their relation to sources and submarine canyon heads and reports by Inman and Bagnold (1963) on beach mechanics. Along the east coast extensive studies of the beaches of Cape Cod have been made (summarized in Stetson *et al.*, 1956), and other studies have concerned the coast of New Jersey (McMaster, 1954). In Europe, in addition to the new books, a host of short articles has appeared covering beaches, notably by English, French, Dutch, German, Russian, and Danish authors.

### Beach Terminology

The nomenclature of beach features is now quite well established as a result of coordinated efforts by engineers and geologists (Fig. 76). This has been important in connection with legal practice coming from the disputed ownership of beaches and the lawsuits over the erosion of beach property. Among the terms the following (in alphabetical order) appear to be the most pertinent:[1]

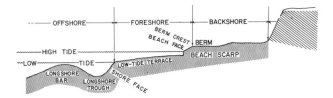

Fig. 76. The principal subdivisions of beaches and of the adjacent shallow water area.

*Accretion*   The building up of a beach either by natural processes or artificial works of man.

*Backshore*   The zone of the beach lying between the foreshore and the coastline (Fig. 76).

*Backwash ripples*   Low amplitude ripple marks formed on fine sand beaches by the backwash of the waves. Commonly about 50 cm apart (Fig. 98a).

*Bar*   An elongate slightly submerged sand body. May bare at low tide.

*Barrier* (Fig. 73)   A sand beach (barrier beach), island (barrier island), or spit (barrier spit) that extends roughly parallel to the general coastal trend but is separated from the mainland by a relatively narrow body of water.

[1] For more complete definitions see *Beach Erosion Board* (1954), Wiegel (1953), and *Glossary of Geology* (1957).

*Beach*   The zone of unconsolidated material extending landward from the mean low water line to the place where there is a change in material or physiographic form as, for example, the zone of permanent vegetation, or a zone of dunes, or a sea cliff. The upper limit of the beach usually marks the effective limit of storm waves.

*Beach face*   The sloping section of the beach below the berm normally exposed to the wave uprush (Fig. 76).

*Beach ridge* (storm beach)   A low extensive ridge of beach material piled up by storm waves landward of the berm. Usually consists of very coarse sand, gravel, or shells. Occurs singly or as a series of more or less parallel ridges. Should not be confused with dune ridges that form particularly where the sand is fine and resemble beach ridges locally called "cheniers."

*Beach scarp*   An almost vertical slope along a beach. It is caused by unusually large waves or developed where a beach is retrograding with moderately large waves.

*Berm* (beach berm)   The nearly horizontal part of a beach inside the sloping foreshore (Fig. 76).

*Berm crest* (berm edge)   The seaward limit of a berm (Fig. 76).

*Bight*   A slight indentation of the shoreline with a crescentic shape.

*Cusp*   One of a series of short ridges on the foreshore extending transverse to the beach and occurring at more or less regular intervals depending in spacing on wave height (Fig. 82).

*Cuspate foreland*   A large sandy cusp-shaped projection of the coast (Fig. 91).

*Cuspate sandkey*   A cusp-shaped sand island.

*Cuspate spit*   A sandy cusp-shaped projection of the shoreline, found on both sides of some lagoons (Fig. 92).

*Feeder beach*   An artificially widened beach serving to nourish downdrift beaches by littoral currents.

*Foreshore*   The sloping part of the beach lying between the berm and the low water mark (Fig. 76).

*Groin* (groyne, British)   A short wall built perpendicular to the shore for the purpose of trapping littoral drift (Fig. 96).

*Jetty*   A structure extending into open water with a greater length than a groin and designed to prevent the shoaling of a channel by confining stream or tidal flow (Fig. 94).

*Longshore bar* (ball or ridge)   A sand ridge or ridges, extending along the shore outside the trough, that may be exposed at low tide or may occur below the water level in the offshore (Fig. 76).

*Longshore trough* (runnel or low)   An elongate depression or series of depressions extending along the lower beach or in the offshore zone inside the breakers.

*Mole*   In coastal terminology refers to a massive solid-fill structure (generally revetted) of earth, masonry, or large stone.

*Nearshore*   A relatively narrow zone extending seaward of the shoreline and somewhat beyond the breaker zone. The zone of wave-induced nearshore currents.

*Offshore*   The breaker zone directly seaward of the low tide line (Fig. 76).

*Overwash*   The portion of the uprush that carries water over the crest of the berm.

*Revetment*   A facing of stone, concrete, etc., built to prevent shore erosion.

*Rill marks*   Small drainage channels forming in the lower portion of a beach at low tide.

*Rip channel*   Channel cut by seaward flow of rip current, usually crosses longshore bar.

*Sand domes*   Small domed-up surfaces of the beach due to entrapment of air. Erosion of the domes usually produces ring structures.

*Shingle*   Defined variously as a beach with flattish pebbles or consisting of smooth well-rounded pebbles.

*Shore face*   The narrow zone seaward of the low tide shoreline over which the beach sands and gravel oscillate most actively.

*Swash mark*   The thin wavy line of fine sand, mica, or fucus left by the uprush along a beach.

*Tombolo*   A sand zone above ordinary high tide level that connects an island or rock to the mainland or another island.

*Uprush* (swash)   The rush of water up onto the beach face following the breaking of a wave.

**Beach Classification**

Beaches may be classified in various ways. A differentiation can be made between the variety of features found on the beach profiles (Fig. 77). The profile may show a continuous slope, may have one or more berms, or may have a low tide terrace with or without bars and troughs that are exposed at low tide. The same beach, however, may develop all these characteristics at different times so that this does not serve very well as a fundamental classification of beach types. More striking differences exist between the gravel or shingle beaches, coarse sand beaches, and fine sand beaches. The typical gravel beach has a beach ridge on the inside where the waves have piled up the gravel sometimes as much as 20 ft above normal high tide. In some areas the ridge consists of shells like the "cheniers" of the Gulf Coast (Russell and Howe, 1935). Ordinarily there is no appreciable berm in the gravel beaches and the foreshore slopes continuously seaward. Often the slope, however, is interrupted by a step near the low tide line. In many places this step is sand covered.

Coarse sand beaches may have berms but these berms slope landward, often at considerable angles. The foreshore is steep, although somewhat less so than found in gravel beaches (Table 9).

The slope of the beach face results from a dynamic equilibrium between the run-up or swash of water up the beach face and the return flow or backwash of water down the face. Although primarily related to the beach permeability, the slope shows a strong correlation with

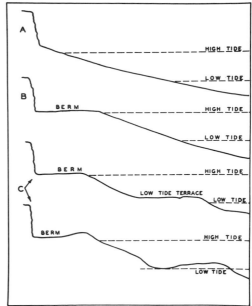

Fig. 77. The principal types of beach profiles.

grain size because the permeability is determined by grain size. It will be noted that the loss of run-up due to discharge into the beach is ten times greater for beach grains 4 mm in diameter than for 1 mm, and that the discharge through sand less than 1 mm in diameter is almost negligible for times as short as a wave period (see Fig. 54). Thus there is almost as much water in the backwash of a fine sand beach as in the swash, and as a result the beach face cannot stand at a steep angle. All the coarse sand beaches are soft so that they are equally poor for walking and for traffic. The offshore commonly has bars and troughs.

Fine sand beaches differ from the others chiefly in having very gentle foreshore slopes. The sand is generally packed hard on the foreshore so that one can walk along the beach without sinking in and,

TABLE 9.   Average Beach Face Slopes Compared to Sediment Diameters

| Type of Beach Sediment | Size | Average Slope of Beach Face |
|---|---|---|
| Very fine sand | 1/16– 1/8 mm | 1° |
| Fine sand | 1/8– 1/4 mm | 3° |
| Medium sand | 1/4– 1/2 mm | 5° |
| Coarse sand | 1/2–  1 mm | 7° |
| Very coarse sand | 1–  2 mm | 9° |
| Granules | 2–  4 mm | 11° |
| Pebbles | 4– 64 mm | 17° |
| Cobbles | 64–256 mm | 24° |

Source: Data compiled by D. L. Inman and F. P. Shepard.

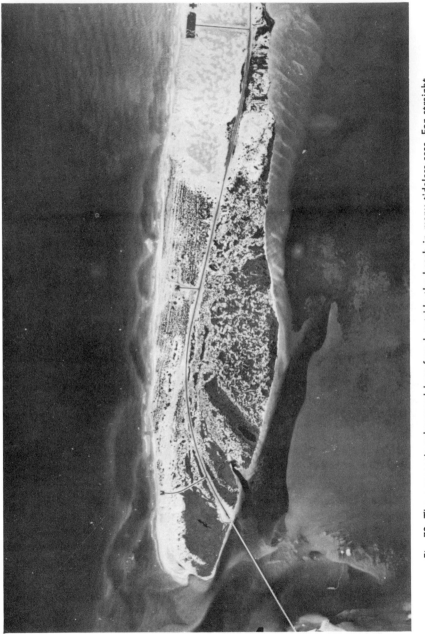

Fig. 78. The crescentic submerged bars found outside the beach in many tideless seas. For straight bars see Fig. 89.

unless the tide has recently retreated, the foreshore is likely to be hard enough to support an automobile or to land a small plane.

Beaches also vary somewhat according to the amount of tide and to their exposure to wave attack. In tideless or nearly tideless seas beaches are often bordered by a series of longshore bars and troughs whereas seas with large tidal ranges are likely to have a broad terrace with at most one large bar exposed at the low tide level. In some tideless seas the bars adjacent to the beach are crescentic (Fig. 78) with the points between the crescents faced toward the land. Where the same type of sand is exposed to larger waves along one portion of a beach than another, the inclination of the foreshore is lower inside the zone of large waves. This difference is more striking in the case of coarse sand beaches than in fine.

Another fundamental difference in beaches is related to their ground plan. Thus there are the long continuous and relatively straight beaches of the barrier type in marked contrast to the short crescentic beaches in the coves between rocky headlands (Fig. 79). Along some cliffed coasts, as in much of southern California, there are long relatively straight beaches extending between widely separated rocky points. Of these types the cove beaches are likely to contain coarse sand because it has been locally derived from the sea cliffs whereas the long beaches are more commonly fine-grained because here the sand has come largely from streams, and the coarser products of the streams do not commonly reach the coast.

## Mechanics of Beach Development

Beaches receive their nourishment of sand almost entirely from the sediment of the adjacent sea floor. The studies of orbital velocities in the surf zone (Inman and Nasu, 1956) have confirmed the data from tank experiments (*Beach Erosion Board*, 1941) that velocities of onshore motion are greater under the advancing wave crests than the velocities of offshore motion under the troughs. The studies have also shown that during periods of low waves the differential velocity is sufficient so that the sand tends to move onshore except in zones of rip currents. The onshore migration is particularly large during long-period waves when there is more opportunity for the sand to be deposited. Conversely with high waves of short period, which keep sand in suspension, the beach retreats largely because the sand washed off the foreshore by the backwash does not settle until it is carried into a rip current and has moved seaward to relatively deep water.

Fig. 79. A cove beach showing typical summer (upper) and winter (lower) conditions at Boomer Beach in La Jolla, California. Some of the sand in winter has shifted along the beach to the right of the photograph.

Beaches develop their well-sorted condition partly due to the common presence of oscillation ripples in the surf zone (Inman, 1957). The turbulence and hence lifting force is greatest at the crest of the ripples, and therefore only the coarsest sediment is deposited there. This material tends to move shoreward particularly with small waves as it is only placed in suspension during the passage of a wave crest. The fine material of the troughs is carried into suspension only during large waves, and hence is carried seaward in the rip currents.

### Sources of Beach Sands

Almost all the sand that goes to make up beaches has come from the sea floor. Most of the sand had been previously brought into the ocean by runoff from the lands, although in some areas a larger source comes from the products of cliff erosion and in many tropical areas the largest portion of the sand is derived from the erosion of coral and algal reefs that exist along or near the shore (see for example Inman et al., 1963).[2] Another important source of sand is from the Pleistocene deposits of the inner continental shelf which in turn may have been stream-derived but have been buried by the rise in sea level accompanying the melting of the continental glaciers (see Chapter IX). Finally, a small source of sand is introduced more or less directly from the lands by offshore winds carrying dune sand into the sea where it is picked up by the waves and may be transported back onto the shore to form beaches.

In California many streams carry sand directly into the ocean, whereas other streams during times of flood move with sufficient velocity across the small estuaries at their mouths so that sand is introduced. Wherever there are longshore currents (see p. 75), this sand is carried along the shore so that it provides a source for nourishing the beaches.

The importance of runoff as a supply to beaches was clearly indicated in some measurements made by U. S. Grant, IV, and his assistants along a mountainous coast in southern California. He found that certain beaches varied in width directly with the variation of the rainfall during the preceding winter. Thus, when there was a large winter rainfall, the streams from the mountains provided a large sand supply which was carried up onto the beaches during the following summer. A greater lag between supply and beach nourishment is observed elsewhere.

In many areas little runoff goes into the open ocean because the rivers are entering estuaries, and the sand is deposited near the river

[2] Shells of organisms may be an even greater source of sand in tropical regions.

mouths forming bayhead deltas. To some extent this sand may be carried to the open sea by tidal currents but usually very little gets out of the bays. This partially accounts for the lack of beaches in many coastal areas between estuaries.

Sand introduced into the ocean does not always have an opportunity to be carried along the shore to form beaches. Some of the finer sand may be carried so far seaward by the strong outflow of entering rivers that the wave action is too weak to carry it back to the land. Powerful rip currents may exist near the points where the sediments are introduced and these currents also may carry the sands too far from the shore for their subsequent return. Where waves are large, sand and gravel may move in from considerable depths. Johnson (1919, p. 93) has cited cases where shingle and chalk ballast have been dumped 7 to 10 miles out from the shore and in 10 to 20 fathoms depth, and yet were subsequently recovered on the shore.

Cliff erosion is an important source of beach sand where the cliffs face the open sea and consist of unconsolidated sands or weakly cemented formations high in sand content. Such cliffs often retreat at rates of one or more feet a year (Johnson, 1919, p. 295; 1925, p. 318; Shepard and Grant, 1947; King, 1959, pp. 294–305, 357–361). In many glaciated regions these sand cliffs are exposed to the action of the open sea. A notable example of retreat is found at Cape Cod where historical records show that some cliffs have retreated as much as 1000 ft in the past 100 years. The nature of this retreat in recent years is well covered in the work of Stetson et al. (1956). The result of cliff erosion at Cape Cod is the supplying of vast quantities of sand that are transported both north and south along the Cape causing beaches to grow at both ends.

Cliffs of more consolidated rock are not important as a source of beach sands. Some solid rock cliffs are retreating at a rate that can be measured, but for the most part old photographs of rock cliffs show that little or no change has occurred during the past 50 to 100 years (Shepard and Grant, 1947). In many places glacial striations can be traced down a rock slope into the ocean, even where the rock faces are exposed to rather heavy surf (Johnson, 1919, pp. 184–195). This is still another reason for the lack of beaches along many deeply indented coasts. Small cove beaches, however, usually receive their supply from rock cliffs.

Evidence that old shelf deposits constitute the source of beach sands is found in areas where streams are not introducing any appreciable amount of material and where there are no alluvial or soft rock cliffs to supply the sand; yet the beaches are forming actively, and the sand is migrating along the coast. A good example is furnished by the beaches of the barrier islands along the coasts of Alabama and Mississippi, west of Mobile Bay (J. C. Ludwick, unpublished manuscript). It is almost certain that the great bulk of the sand brought in by the Mobile River, at the head of Mobile Bay, is deposited at the bayhead delta because the lower bay has predominantly muddy sediments. Cliffs are virtually nonexistent on the open coasts of Alabama and Mississippi, which are bordered by sand islands. These islands are migrating westward under the influence of the easterly winds, but new supplies keep re-forming at the east ends of the islands. This sand must come from the extensive sand shelf deposits to the south and east. Another example of a shelf source may exist in Monterey Peninsula, California, where dunes have been quarried for years for their sands used in road building. The local beach continues to keep up the supply of dune sand owing to the onshore winds, and yet the beach persists despite the fact that to the north it is bordered by a bold granite coast with no beaches. It is doubtful if any appreciable amount of sand comes around the rocky coast and rocky nearshore toward Monterey Bay. Thus the sand apparently comes largely from deposits on the open sea floor to the north. In his study of the minerals in the beach sands of New Jersey, McMaster (1954) concludes that the southern beaches must have had their source of sand from the continental shelf. In their study of the mineral assemblages of the northwest Gulf of Mexico, van Andel and Poole (1960) found evidence that some of the Texas beaches had received their sands from erosion of the old sediments on the adjacent continental shelves. Thus there is evidence that beaches can receive their sediments from offshore sources.

## Beach Cycles

Almost all beaches are in a constant state of flux. Some beaches develop only during seasons with small waves and disappear during the seasons of high waves (Fig. 79), whereas other beaches change in height and width during the stormy season. The width diminishes but the height of the top of the berm may increase. In most areas the periods of large waves occur in winter although hurricanes with their enormous cutting power are more likely to occur in late summer or fall, in both the Atlantic and Pacific ocean areas.

Examples of the winter and summer cycles are shown in Fig. 80. It will be seen that the berm is cut back or disappears entirely during the stormy season. As a result the beach foreshore becomes more gently sloping although on some occasions a beach scarp may form on the foreshore as the result of excessive cutting at one level. The

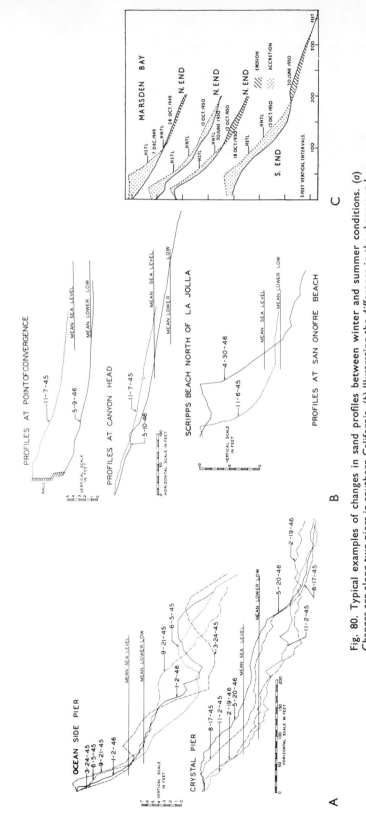

Fig. 80. Typical examples of changes in sand profiles between winter and summer conditions. (a) Changes are along two piers in southern California. (b) Illustrating the difference in the changes at La Jolla, California, between points of high wave convergence and of wave divergence (at submarine canyon head). Shows also a change at San Onofre Beach, southern California, where a considerable lateral shift has taken place so as to build up the beach at the south end as the result of northwest approaching waves. (c) Profiles of Marsden Bay, County Durham, on the English coast, showing the development of berms. From King (1959, Fig. 8-1).

offshore ordinarily develops rather deep channels due to strong long-shore currents, and bars develop outside due to the combined effect of offshore creep of sand inside the breaker line and onshore creep outside. The net effect on the offshore is deposition that takes care of most of the loss of sand on the inside.

The return to small wave conditions tends to reverse the sand shift so that the longshore bars migrate shoreward and fill the inner trough, and the sand starts to pile up on the beach to form a new berm that is almost always lower than any remnant of an old one. The new berm will ordinarily build up gradually to the level of the old berm as the result of occasional rather large waves that cut back the berm crest and carry the sand up to the higher level left by the old berm.

In addition to the winter and summer cycles there are cycles of shorter period. These may come from an isolated unseasonal storm followed by small waves or they may develop on account of the change from neap to spring tides. The storm cycle is similar in its effects to seasonal cycles. The tidal cycle is the result of the change of elevation of erosion and deposition on the upper beach. Ordinarily deposition occurs at the highest level reached by the waves because at this point the water sinks into the sand and leaves behind some of the products of the uprush. Thus, given waves of the same magnitude, deposition will occur at a certain level during neap tides, but during spring tides the waves will reach a higher level, and in the zone where deposition had occurred during neap tides, the backwash will tend to cut away the deposits of the neap tide period. The small sardine-like fish called *grunion* make use of this cycle by laying their eggs in shallow holes dug in the sand at the upper levels reached by high tides at the end of a spring tide period. This allows the waves to deposit sand over the eggs and keep them covered during the next fortnight, after which the eggs hatch during a period of erosion so that the young can return to the sea (Walker, 1952). The nature of the instinct that allows the grunion to be familiar with a process only recently discovered by man is not yet clear.

Another important effect of seasonal changes is the shifting of sand along the beach as a result of a change in wave approach. The tendency in beaches is for the shore to form as closely as possible at right angles to the direction of wave approach (King, 1959, p. 169). This is the most stable beach form because longshore drift is at a minimum under this condition. As a result a wide beach facing the wave approach develops on the side of an embayment away from the wave approach (Fig. 81). If the wave approach changes to the opposite direction, the wide beach will tend to shift to the other end of the embayment. A good example of such a shift is found at La Jolla Point in southern

California where Boomer Beach (Fig. 79) on a north-south coast builds up in summer on account of the southerly approach of the waves. This same beach entirely disappears during the fall or winter because the large waves usually approach from the northwest. At this time much of the sand of Boomer Beach goes to the south end of the small embayment and forms another beach at that point.

Fig. 81. Growth of a beach on the downcurrent side of a coastal indentation. Photograph of Pt. Dume, Calif., by D. L. Inman.

Seasonal cycles are sometimes very erratic. As an example the writer had observed for many years that the sand beach just south of Scripps Institution became denuded during the winter and for a considerable period the underlying gravel was exposed (Fig. 82). Since 1947, however, the gravel condition has only once developed as it did in former years, and except for small patches of gravel that have been uncovered locally the sand cover has persisted. Furthermore, the extensive exposure of rock directly north of Scripps Institution pier that formerly occurred every winter has been greatly reduced in magnitude in recent years.

The fact that except in 1951 the beach has largely maintained its sand every winter since 1947 is not easy to explain, particularly since the rainfall has been very light ever since the March flood of 1938. As a result, there should have been far less sediment brought into the ocean

Fig. 82. (a) Gravel cusps that formerly appeared every winter at La Jolla, California. (b) The same beach after sand has covered the gravel. Since 1947 the exposure of the gravel has occurred only once.

to supply the beach from the north. A minor source of sand coming from the retreat of the alluvial cliffs on either side of Scripps Institution has also decreased, partly because of a new sea wall and partly because the rodents that were causing a large amount of the erosion have been controlled. Nor is there much evidence of decreased wave activity during these years of beach maintenance. The erosion of fine sand beaches at low tide by heavy rains may have been partially responsible for the former winter denudation.

## Subpermanent Loss of Beach Sand

Since beaches receive new supplies from runoff and from cliff erosion and since the waves are effective both in setting up currents that move the sand along the shore and in bringing the sand up onto the shore to form the beaches, it should follow either that beaches would grow continuously wider or that some means exists of disposing of the excess sand. The latter is rather clearly indicated, and sand is disposed of in several ways and is lost to the beaches either temporarily or permanently. One such means is evident from airplane pictures of the downcurrent extremity of some elongate beaches. Dunes can be seen in many land valleys inland from the downcurrent end of these beaches (Fig. 83). These dunes often extend in from the shore for several miles. The sand may eventually cross divides and return to the shore downwind from the dunes by stream transportation. Alternatively it may be carried inland into desert basins and hence become lost to the beaches.

Some of the sand that is carried downcurrent along the shore is deflected seaward at the lower end of the beach where a point results in strong rip currents. If carried seaward far enough across the shelf by such a current, it may not return to the shore. However, the studies by Trask (1952, 1955) show that sand can bypass rocky points and continue along the shore provided that the water off the points is not very deep near shore. Thus the sand coming down the California coast passes Point Conception, turns at a large angle, and continues on down to the Santa Barbara breakwater, where much of it is temporarily trapped.[3] The nature of the wave refraction at a projecting point is such that the sand is deflected and swept around the point rather than continuing seaward unless caught in a rip current. Trask found that very active bypassing occurs in the zone out to a depth of 30 ft off southern California and that some transfer takes place to a depth of about 60 ft. This agrees with the changes observed in measurements

[3] The pumping operation set up by an Army Engineer project now allows the sand to continue moving down the coast.

Fig. 83. Development of dunes from the excess sand carried to the downcurrent side of an embayment. This sand migrates inland and is lost to the shore. Photo by Spence Air Photos; taken at southern end of Santa Monica Bay, southern California.

of sand changes made on stakes off La Jolla (Inman and Rusnak, 1956).

A very important loss of sand occurs where submarine canyon heads extend in toward a beach. Study of profiles of the canyon heads along the California coast (Shepard, 1951b; Chamberlain, 1960; and Inman and Frautschy, 1966) shows the rapid fill in these localities. Computations have indicated that the rate of this fill is approximately equal to the amount of supply of sediment being carried down the coast from the runoff in the entire area that lies between canyon heads. The sand would fill rapidly and hence eliminate the canyon head if it were not for mass movements that carry the sediment out along the canyon axis, presumably in the form of sand flows and turbidity currents (see p. 338).

According to Inman and Frautschy (1966) there are many essentially closed beach compartments along the California coast. At the south end of each compartment a submarine canyon heads close to the coast and catches most of the sand supply that is drifted toward it from the north (Fig. 84). Directly south or a short distance to the south of each canyon head there is a rocky shoreline usually in the form of a projecting point. Farther south the beaches re-form and become progessively wider because of an increasing supply from entering streams. These beaches persist with few if any interruptions until a canyon head is reached. In southern California one compartment extends essentially from Point Conception to Hueneme and

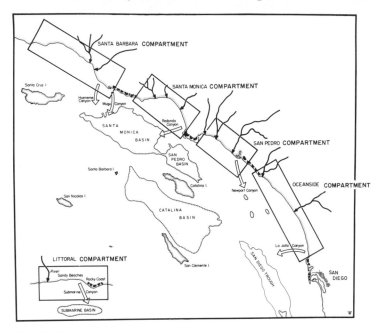

Fig. 84. The compartmentalization of beaches along the southern California coast with loss of sand into the heads of submarine canyons at the southern end of each compartment. Inman and Frautschy (1966).

Mugu canyons. This compartment receives most of its supply from the Santa Ynez Mountains along the Santa Barbara coast although, as shown previously, some sand comes from the north around Point Conception (Trask, 1952). During times of small runoff, as in recent years, the continental shelf has supplied the sand for the beaches (Trask, 1955). In the second compartment from Mugu Canyon to Redondo Canyon the sand comes largely from the runoff of the Santa Monica Mountains and bypasses Point Dume because the submarine canyon at this point does not extend in close to the coast.

The third compartment extends from the Palos Verdes Hills to Newport Canyon. Here a beach exists as a spit for a short distance beyond Newport Canyon and forms Newport Harbor. This spit, according to Inman, remains almost static in size because after periods of small runoff of the Santa Ana River, the chief source of supply, most of the sand bypasses the canyon head, whereas after periods of heavy runoff the canyon head receives an excess of supply, and hence the beach beyond does not grow. It seems possible that bypassing of the Scripps Canyon head, at the southern end of the next compartment, may be regulated in somewhat the same way or that even more sand goes past the canyon head during periods of low runoff and, hence, may account for the increased sand on the beach south of Scripps Institution during the drought of recent years.

### Composition of Beach Sands

Beach sands, like all other sand deposits, include a wide variety of constituents. Quartz, however, is certainly the most abundant component of most beaches, and other terrigenous minerals such as feldspars, ferromagnesians, and mica make up the bulk of the residue. In areas where mica is available, the mica is frequently interbedded with the quartzose sands. Magnetite and ilmenite are also interbedded with terrigenous sand layers in many beaches, particularly at the base of the sand on the inner backshore. Along with these heavy minerals some minerals of economic importance may be found such as tungsten, scheelite, and wolframite. Locally these are quarried as a source of these rare minerals. Most terrigenous beaches consist dominantly of fine sand with a resulting gentle slope and hard-packed foreshore.

Beaches with nonterrigenous sands are found principally in tropical areas and in oceanic islands. In approaching the tropics from higher latitudes, calcareous constituents in the sands show a great increase and in the tropics there appear to be more calcareous sands than terrigenous. Calcareous sands are largely the product of shoreward wave transport of the thriving masses of invertebrate organisms living directly off shore. In reef areas the sands consist largely of coral and algal reef fragments, usually with a considerable percent of Foraminifera, the latter often so worn that they are difficult to recognize. In tropical areas where offshore reefs are absent, the beaches commonly consist of shell sands like the Coquina beaches of eastern Florida. These shell beaches also contain many Foraminifera, Bryozoa, and echinoid fragments. Shell beaches are rare in extratropical areas except where there is little terrigenous material present (Raymond and Stetson, 1932). Here fragments of shells and barnacles may be detached from rocks by the waves and carried shoreward to form beaches. The shell beaches are usually of coarse material and, hence, are steep and soft so they are poor for traffic. In several places along the east coast of Florida the beaches change character abruptly between the soft, steep shell beaches and the broad, hard, gently sloping quartz sand beaches. The latter have pavement-like surfaces, such as Daytona Beach where auto races have been held for decades.

Oceanic islands, in addition to the calcareous sands that are prevalent in the tropics, have many beaches with volcanic sand. Olivine is particularly common because it is abundant as phenocrysts in the basic lavas of oceanic islands and because it is a hard mineral with poor cleavage and hence is better preserved than the phenocrysts of basic feldspars and ferromagnesian minerals found also in the basalts. A study of the beaches of Kauai in the Hawaiian Islands (Inman et al., 1963) shows that the olivine sands[4] are found largely on the dry side of the island and calcareous sands on the wet side. This is despite the fact that olivine must come from the erosion of the volcanic rocks, and the calcareous sands come entirely from the offshore area. The streams on the north and east sides of this island drain areas of tremendous rainfall but do not carry a large quantity of volcanic sand because of the very heavy vegetation cover and because of the deep chemical weathering undergone by the rocks. Hence, the bordering reefs supply most of the sand. On the dry side of the island there are a few rather large streams coming from the interior, and these streams, deriving their material from somewhat drier areas, have sediments that are less weathered and include an abundance of olivine. Around canyon mouths, such as Waimea, the olivine sands are transported by wave action for considerable distances along the coast.

### Beach Stratification

Under conditions of small waves beaches acquire layers of sand that contain easily transported materials such as mica or small shells. Under more powerful waves the sands are more commonly quartz or other relatively round terrigenous minerals. With still more severe waves the beach may undergo attrition with the concentration of the heavy black minerals from previously deposited sands. Both of these processes develop beach stratification. This may be seen either where runoff during a heavy rain has cut a channel across the beach or where a trench has been dug in the sand. The stratification is not infrequently disturbed by small folds (Fig. 85). These are likely to be due to the escape of trapped air as was shown by Stewart (1956). The

---

[4] The writer's recent studies show that olivine is not as abundant in the volcanic sands as had been supposed. These sands consist predominantly of small fragments of basalt.

Fig. 85. Typical beach stratification with dark layers due to heavy minerals. At the right the disturbance in the stratification is probably produced by entrapment of air. Foot rule is included for scale.

stratification is best developed on the foreshore of the beach and usually slopes parallel to the surface slope.

## Barrier Beaches and Beach Ridges

The barrier type of beach (formerly called offshore bars) is probably the most common variety. These beaches and the associated barrier islands and barrier spits (Fig. 73) are found along most lowland coasts of the world. In the United States almost all the beaches of the Gulf Coast are of this type, and they are found commonly on the east coast from Long Island to Florida. Along the west coast they occur only in a few scattered localities and are best developed in Washington.

The barriers of the Gulf Coast of the United States have been studied in connection with American Petroleum Institute Project 51 (Shepard, 1952b, 1960b; Rusnak, 1960b; Shepard and Moore, 1955). They have also been discussed recently by Le Blanc and Hodgson (1959), Russell (1959), and J. C. Ludwick (unpublished manuscript). Studies have been made of the barriers of west Africa (Guilcher, 1959a). These investigations have provided information that is helpful in explaining both the barrier beaches and barrier islands.

Johnson (1919, p. 348–392) was of the opinion that most barriers result from the emergence of a flat gently sloping continental shelf that allows the waves to break at a considerable distance from the shore where a bar is formed that in turn is built up into a beach. Previously, Gilbert (1885, p. 87) had attributed barriers to longshore drift with the sediment derived from cliffs or other sources and built in the direction of the current as longshore spits. Later storms may cut through the spits leaving isolated barrier islands. On the other hand, de Beaumont (1845) suggested that erosion of the bottom in the breaker zone piled up ridges on the inside making the barriers. Johnson compared the two hypotheses by profiles (Fig. 86) and found results favorable to de Beaumont's hypothesis. However, Johnson did not have available the information from recent borings showing that at least some of the barrier islands have grown upward as the sea level rose with deposition of fine sediments on either side (Fig. 87). Therefore the Johnson profiles are not necessarily valuable in answering the

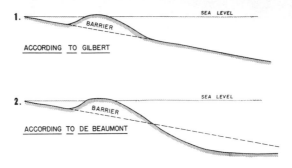

Fig. 86. The hypotheses of Gilbert and de Beaumont on the origin of barrier islands. Gilbert believed the barrier, introduced by longshore currents, was simply added to the slope and de Beaumont believed that the waves excavated the sea floor on the outside and built the barrier on the inside.

question. Actually there is much evidence to support both de Beaumont and Gilbert. Thus, spits are developing and being enlarged along the coasts in many places and many, perhaps most, barriers can be traced upcurrent to a source either in a sea cliff or a sandy delta. Nor can there be any doubt but what sand is carried along the shore in

Fig. 87. The upgrowth during submergence of barrier sands between deposits of shelf muds on the seaward side and bay muds on the lagoon side.

great quantities as the result of diagonally approaching waves. On the other hand, barriers like those of the Mississippi islands develop from offshore sand sources as has been indicated previously. One cannot avoid the conclusion that barriers result from both onshore creep of shelf sands and from longshore drift.

The development of new barrier beaches is not an unusual event, particularly along the west coast of Florida (Fig. 88). Equally common

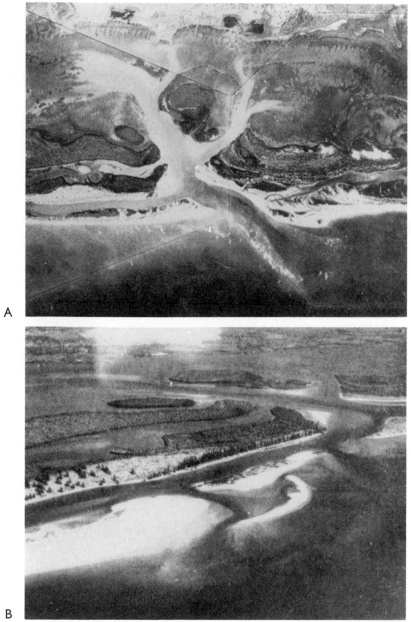

A

B

Fig. 88. The development of a new barrier island along the west coast of Florida between 1939 and 1951. Photograph (a) by U.S. Coast and Geodetic Survey; photograph (b) by D. L. Inman.

Fig. 89. The major physiographic divisions of a large barrier island. The foreground shows the Gulf of Mexico and the background a bay shore along the Texas coast. Two types of dunes are illustrated: stabilized longitudinal dune ridges and transverse migrating dunes. Longshore bars are indicated by the breaker lines, and on the inside, bars can be seen through the temporarily clear water. Photograph courtesy of Edgar Tobin Surveys.

is the breaching of old barrier islands by storms. In general, barrier beaches grow seaward during times of small waves like other beaches, and are cut back during storms. As barriers are built forward, dune ridges are likely to be built inside the beach and, rising above the beach level, these ridges may become covered with vegetation and hence stabilized. If the beach continues to build seaward, a new dune ridge may form closer to the new shoreline and this in turn may become stabilized. Thus a series of ridges, commonly referred to somewhat erroneously as beach ridges, may develop as in Fig. 89. By using the various tests to differentiate between beach and dune sands (Shepard and Young, 1961) it is, in the writer's opinion, possible to distinguish beach and dune ridges. Tests made to date indicate that the ridges in fine sand like those in Fig. 89 are dune ridges. On the other hand, ridges of gravel or shells are in general true beach ridges thrown up by the waves. The reason that beach ridges do not commonly form in fine sand is that such material does not pile up like coarse sediment but, rather, is swept inland by the storm tides forming overwash fans (Fig. 90).

Fig. 90. One side of a fanlike projection into Aransas Bay made by storm-tide overwashes crossing St. Joseph Island, Texas. Photo by D. L. Inman.

Barrier islands are still explained in many textbooks as the result of coastal emergence, bringing gentle slopes into the offshore area, but this idea of Johnson (1919) does not fit the facts that have come from recent studies. Low slopes in the offshore area can develop as well from submergence as from emergence. The borings along the Texas coast (Shepard and Moore, 1955, p. 1555; Shepard, 1960b) show clear indications of the effects of the rising sea level at the end of the glacial period (see Fig. 126). At least some of the barrier islands of Texas appear to have grown up as the sea level rose, as for example St. Joseph Island where shallow inlet shells with a carbon-14 age of 6500 years are found interbedded with barrier island sands at a depth of 46 ft below sea level. The upgrowth of the Chandeleur Islands and Breton Island east of the Mississippi Delta has quite clearly occurred during the submergence of the sea floor (Russell, 1936; Lankford and

Shepard, 1960). Since the evidence is so overwhelmingly in favor of a general submergence of the coasts of the world extending from about 20,000 years before the present until at least 3000 years ago (Fig. 126), and since barriers are extremely common around the coasts of the world, the conclusion seems almost inevitable that they must have developed during general submergence. On the other hand, they may grow also to some extent during emergence as suggested by Curray (1960) for the drowned barriers off Texas. Also, the fact that new barriers are now growing outside of old along some coasts shows that they probably can develop and have developed during periods of stability. The perpetuation of the barriers, on the other hand, is somewhat facilitated by very slow submergence or sea level rise such as has apparently occurred during the past 6000 years. This prevents the fill of the lagoons inside the barriers but still permits the upgrowth of the islands keeping pace with the submergence.

### Cuspate Shorelines

Cusp sizes along coasts are of all gradations, varying between the small beach cusps (discussed on p. 201) and the huge cuspate forelands like Cape Hatteras. The latter is from 60 to 150 miles across (depending on how much one includes of the barriers on the sides) and protrudes about 30 miles beyond the general coastline. Since a rather special process appears to have led to the development of the small beach cusps, here we shall confine the discussion to the larger features.

**Cuspate Forelands.** The huge cuspate projections of the open coast, called cuspate forelands, are confined to a few areas in the world. Thus on the southeast coasts of the United States the large cuspate forms begin east of the Mississippi Delta extending to North Carolina. The cusp forms are sometimes associated with deltas like the Tiber but for the most part occur quite independently. Johnson (1919, p. 324) has pointed out that there are two types of cuspate forelands, one with beach ridges (or dune ridges) that are truncated by one side of the foreland and extend parallel to the other side, and the other type with beach ridges or simple barriers that conform to the two sides of the foreland (Fig. 91).

Outside most of the cuspate forelands there are shoals or rocky islands, the latter represented by Lauvi Point, Guadalcanal (Fig. 91b). According to Tanner (1960), these shoals develop where wave energy is too low to handle the large supply of sand introduced by littoral drift. As an example he refers to the shoals off Cape San Blas and Cape George in northwest Florida which have a supply from the Apalachicola River that lies just to the east.

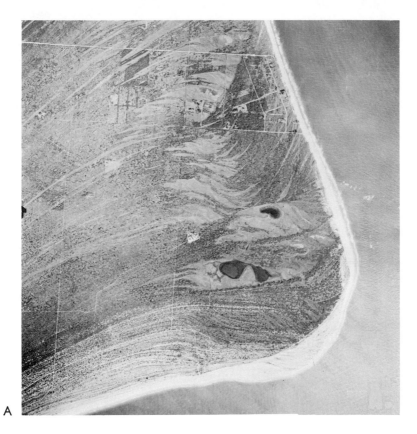

A

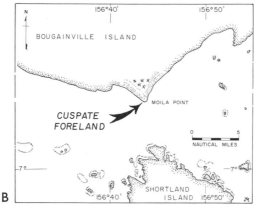

B

Fig. 91. (a) A cuspate foreland, Cape Canaveral, on the east coast of Florida, showing the beach or dune ridges truncated on the north side and parallel to the coast on the south side. Photograph by U.S. Coast and Geodetic Survey in 1943 (CYS-1C). (b) Growth of a symmetrical cuspate foreland in Bougainville Island resulting from the different wave approach on the two sides of the point produced by Shortland Island. From U.S. Hydrographic Office Chart No. 2926.

An alternative origin suggested in part by Johnson (1919, p. 322) and by King (1959, p. 371) is that a shoal or an island lying offshore deflects the wave approach on both sides so that sediment is washed toward a point inside the obstruction and builds barriers with beaches facing the wave approach on either side (Fig. 91b). Favoring such an origin is the fact that the cuspate forelands of southeastern United States are confined to areas where the water is clear enough and warm enough so that some sort of organic reef may develop on the shelves, although true coral reefs are not found. Investigation of the shoals off the cuspate forelands should serve to confirm or deny this possible origin.

Cuspate forelands may also be formed by outgrowth in the slack water between two giant eddies inside a current that is moving parallel to the coast. Cape Fear and Cape Hatteras, off North Carolina, appear to be at least in part due to the eddies inside the Gulf Stream.

Where the supply of sand is coming primarily from one direction, as at Cape Canaveral, Florida, the cuspate foreland is likely to grow in the direction of the current. This takes place by erosion of the barriers that formed on the upcurrent side and transfer of the sand to new ridges on the downcurrent side. Hence, the ridges are largely parallel to one side (Fig. 91a).

The formation of double tombolos is allied to the question of cuspate forelands. These represent forelands that have grown seaward to the island that was responsible for their development. One of the best known is Cape Verde on the west coast of Africa.

**Cuspate Spits.** The cusps that form on both sides of lagoons inside barriers (Fig. 92) have been discussed by many authors (see particularly Johnson, 1925, p. 445; Fisher, 1955; Price and Wilson, 1956; and Zenkovitch, 1959). These spits are somewhat more common on the barrier island side but often are as well developed next to the mainland. Like cuspate forelands they may have a solid form or may have only barrier beaches with a lagoon on the inside. Where the water is clear in the lagoon it is common to find a submarine ridge extending out from the cuspate point.

Johnson explained the cuspate spits on Nantucket Island as the result of the elongation of the barrier spit on the outside with the development of recurved spits at a succession of points. These hooks were later modified by the eddies of tidal currents. Fisher suggested that the breaching of barriers by storms carries sediment over into the lagoons forming a deposit. This deflects the currents moving along the lagoon and results in further deposition. Price and Wilson, on the other hand, considered that standing wave oscillations or seiches in a lagoon develop the paired spits at nodal points. Zenkovitch

Fig. 92. Cuspate spits in the east arm of Pensacola Bay, Florida. Note the underwater bars extending out beyond the spits. Cuspate bars are shown in the offshore area (foreground). Photograph by U.S. Coast and Geodetic Survey in 1945 (C-3258).

considered that the spits were due to shore drifting processes but thought that they may represent a remnant of slightly lower sea conditions. Each of these more or less overlapping ideas may explain the cuspate spits, different processes operating in different localities. Gierloff-Emden (1961) has observed that all of these lagoonal cuspate spits occur in areas with small tidal range. They are evidently destroyed by strong lagoonal currents.

**Giant Cusps.** Along many open beaches there are projecting points spaced at intervals of scores or hundreds of feet. Elsewhere these cusps occur as solitary points (Fig. 93). An explanation for one of these cusps near Scripps Institution has been determined. Currents diverge from the zone of wave convergence north of La Jolla Submarine Canyon and are turned seaward where they encounter weaker currents that are due to the diagonal approach of the waves away from the head of La Jolla Canyon (p. 79). The back eddy from these seaward moving water masses causes deposition producing a point.

Fig. 93. Typical giant cusps along the outside of Cape Cod, Massachusetts, near Highland Light.

Probably other points are related to zones where there are similarly conflicting currents that turn seaward.

### Effect of Engineering Structures on Beaches

The building of jetties or other types of projecting walls to develop harbors along straight coasts has had disastrous effects on many beaches. The usual result is illustrated in Fig. 94 where a pair of jetties has been built seaward from Lake Worth Inlet, north of Palm Beach, Florida. The prevailing current is from the north so that the sand has been trapped next to the north jetty and greatly widened the beach. Directly to the south of the south jetty the beach has a somewhat normal width due to wave refraction with resulting north drift; but farther south the beach has been lost and property undermined because of absence of the normal supply of sand from the

Fig. 94. The effect of building jetties at Lake Worth Inlet, east Florida. The current approaches from the north and has built up the sand on that side, whereas erosion is occurring on the south side of the jetty (lower right). Photograph by U.S. Coast and Geodetic Survey in 1945 (C-1511).

Fig. 95. The effect of the Santa Barbara breakwater. Note the large accumulation of sand on the near side of the breakwater due to the wave approach from that side; also the sand bar that has built into the harbor after the sand has bypassed the end of the breakwater. Photograph by J. H. Filloux.

north. Numerous similar examples have developed in southern California, notably at Santa Barbara and Redondo. At the latter an entire city block was destroyed as the result of the trapping of sand north of a curving jetty. Waves approaching from the west and south-west were refracted toward the shore north of the Redondo Canyon head and caused the cutting away of the beach. No new supplies came from the northern sources until pumping was adopted. At Santa Barbara (Fig. 95) the sand built up along the entire west side of the jetty and then built around the end to form an island in the entrance to the harbor. It has been necessary to pump this sand to the east in order to nourish the beaches in that direction that were being robbed of their supply. The Army Engineers first deposited the sand as a bar separated from the shore by water with a depth of 15 ft. This proved ineffective as the sand did not migrate toward the shore so that it had to be dumped in shallower water.

At Santa Monica a jetty was built parallel to the shore (Fig. 96) with the hope that the sand would be carried through the harbor and hence supply the downcurrent beaches. This system did not work because the wave shadow caused by the jetty allowed the sand to build up on the inside very much like a cuspate foreland. This threatened to fill the harbor and caused loss of beach downcoast. Accordingly pumping had to be resorted to at this place also.

Not all jetties cause beach problems. If they are put in at points where rocky headlands project on the downcurrent side, there are no beaches to be ruined locally and the effect on beaches considerably farther south is not very great. This is the situation for example at Newport Harbor south of Long Beach. At the entrance to San Diego Harbor the existence of a rocky point to the north and west has meant that sources of sand are to a considerable extent from the south side, due to wave refraction by Point Loma. Hence the harbor jetty has not caused much trouble, although the slight readjustment of shoreline next to the jetty caused some temporary erosion near the Coronado Hotel shortly after the jetty was built.

Groins (groynes) (Figs. 96, 97) cause much less trouble than jetties. They have been built along many beaches where erosion threatened. They stabilize the sand rather than causing the building out of the broad beaches characteristic of the upcurrent side of jetties. Beaches downcurrent from groins may have slight losses but the effects can often be largely offset by building groins at these places also. A special form of groin has been suggested by Rivière and Laurent (1954) that leaves a gap between the inner and outer portions allowing a flow of current between the two and hence prevents excessive building out of the sand.

Fig. 96. The parallel breakwater built at Santa Monica, California. The wave shadow has caused deposition of sand on the inside which threatened to fill the harbor until it was removed by pumping to the beaches on the downcurrent side. Note the groins at various points along the coast. Photo by U.S. Coast and Geodetic Survey in 1934 (E-5753-22).

Fig. 97. The undermining of beach cottages at Newport Beach, California, as a result of a storm tide on October 10, 1934. Note the large rip current carrying sediment seaward from the area that is being undermined. Photo by U.S. Air Force.

## Beach Changes Produced by Tsunamis and Storm Tides

As explained previously (p. 82) the most significant effects of both tsunamis and storm tides come from the rise in sea level. During tsunamis,striking results occur in the normally protected areas in harbors or behind coral reefs when the protection is largely removed owing to the high water level. The waves can attack unconsolidated deposits where there has been no adjustment in the form of a cliff and terrace that would retard erosion. As a result, large shifting of the soil and alluvium may occur in the very few minutes during which the waves are active at the high level. The cutting may also greatly extend the beach in an inland direction. The runoff that follows the rise may also cause considerable erosion leaving channels in alluvium where it was concentrated. Another important effect observed in the Hawaiian Island tsunami of 1946 (Shepard *et al.*, 1950) was the transportation of coral blocks up onto the shore that left them strewn both on the beaches and inland for considerable distances. The quarrying of these blocks was the result of waves breaking violently over the reefs after a temporary build-up outside. The beaches were sometimes left quite untouched because they were adjusted to erosion at normal sea level, and therefore the rapid up-and-down movement of the water did not allow time for any unusual effect other than leaving blocks of rock or coral quarried from lower levels.

Storm surges (storm tides) have the combined effect of raising the sea level and bringing the huge storm waves in to attack the coast (Fig. 97). As a result very extensive changes have been produced.

Storm surge effects have been studied from the unusual storm of January-February, 1953, that funneled water into the North Sea, raised the sea level to a maximum of 10 ft, and flooded the coastal lowlands of Holland and England (King, 1959, pp. 283–312; Robinson *et al.*, 1953). Along the coast of Suffolk, cliffs 6 ft high were cut back as much as 90 ft, and cliffs 40 ft high regressed 40 ft. At the same time many breakthroughs occurred in beach ridges with flooding of the marshes inside. The effects of hurricanes along the east and Gulf coasts of the United States have been widely studied (see for example Morgan *et al.*, 1958; Nichols and Marston, 1939; Chute, 1946). The raising of sea level as much as 15 ft has caused numerous breakthroughs to occur in barriers and has eroded the dunes behind the beaches along the coasts where these storms have occurred. Lower beaches have been built up by some of these hurricanes because of removal of great quantities of sand from high levels followed by deposition at the low levels. In June of 1957 hurricane Audrey striking southwest Louisiana spread some of the beaches widely over the marshlands and allowed later wave attack to cut back the coast (Morgan *et al.*, 1958). The sheltering effect of well-developed shell-sand ridges in the western part of the storm area prevented important changes, but temporary inlet channels were developed across the ridges that were soon sealed by littoral drift. Large mud arcs were produced locally from the eroded mud flat material.

## Minor Beach Features

Johnson (1919, pp. 457–520) has given a complete account of the minor structures found on beach surfaces. However, some additions to the types have been made along with new interpretations.

**Beach Cusps.** Small cusps with points facing the sea and rounded embayments in between (Fig. 82) are found commonly on coarse sand and gravel beaches whereas they are more sporadic on fine sand beaches. The cusps are usually rather evenly spaced with distances from about 1 ft to several hundred feet between. The spacing of cusps is clearly related to the height of the waves when they were produced. This is shown by tracing cusps from the zones of high waves at a convergence along the Scripps Institution beach to zones of low waves at the divergence formed by the submarine canyon (Fig. 43). The cusps show a progressive decrease in size. It is often possible to find widely spaced cusp remnants on beaches left from storm waves at a high level where normal waves do not reach, whereas the more closely spaced cusps occurring at lower levels are the result of smaller waves. Cusps in bays, along the shores of small lakes or inside coral reefs where there is little fetch, are very closely spaced.

Cusps on fine sand beaches show a strong tendency to develop during neap tide periods, when there is less tidal range, and to disappear during spring tides. In the long beach north of La Jolla the cusps are most common during the fall when the beach berm is first being cut back.

Johnson (1919, pp. 457–486) explained cusps as the result of normal approach of waves to the coast and thought their destruction was due to diagonally approaching waves. Although this contention appears to be fairly well supported, observations at La Jolla show that intersecting patterns of waves approaching the beach diagonally from both directions may be accompanied by cusp development. The important factor is to have conditions that prevent strong longshore drift since this destroys the cusp shape. The cusps are evidently due to piling up of water on the berm or on the upper beach with return along rather evenly spaced channels. The interchannel ridges are sharpened into points, and the channels are rounded by the waves. Directly

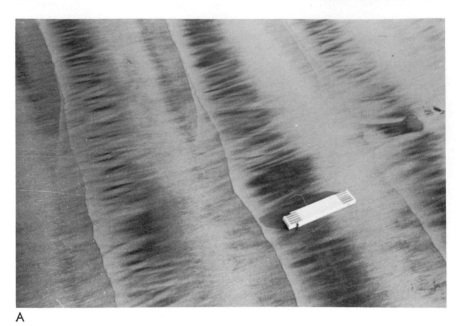

A

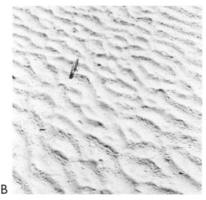

B

Fig. 98. (a) Backwash ripples with a typical 18 in. wavelength. These develop only on fine sand beaches. (b) Typical current ripples produced in a channel along the lower foreshore by longshore currents. Wavelength approximately 3 in.

seaward of the indentations there are usually small rises on the beach where the material from the indentation is deposited. Diagonally approaching waves are much more effective in destroying cusps on fine sand beaches than on coarse.

**Beach Ripples.**   At low tide most beaches exhibit ripple marks of several types left by the receding water. These include the following. On the foreshore, backwash ripples (Fig. 98a) develop on fine sand

C

Fig. 98 (*Continued*). (c) Giant ripples on one side of a tombolo along the Oregon coast. The wavelength is approximately 6 ft. Photo by Ph. H. Kuenen.

beaches as a result of the backrush of the waves which sets up a turbulent motion. These ripples are usually about 50 cm apart and extend parallel to the contours of the beach. They are low-amplitude ripples and frequently have concentrations of mica in the troughs whereas heavy black sands are more common on the crests. At lower levels, where rip current channels are exposed by the low tide, current ripple marks are seen that trend roughly normal to the beach (Fig. 98*b*). These ripples have wavelengths of a few centimeters in fine sand beaches and up to 30 cm in coarse sand beaches. In some places giant ripples that are several feet across are found in the larger channels in areas of strong currents (Fig. 98*c*). Intersecting patterns of ripples are often developed as the result (1) of longshore currents moving parallel to the shore producing current ripples and (2) of normally approaching waves producing oscillation ripples. As indicated by Trefethen and Dow (1960) superposed current ripples may intersect earlier generation of ripples where one set is produced by a strong flood tide and a superimposed set is due to weaker cross drainage currents during the ebb (Fig. 99).

**Miscellaneous Features.** Various other features characterize beach surfaces. Where there has been entrapment of water by the high tide, the water returning to the sea at low tide cuts miniature channels called rill marks. Where the top of the wave comes to a halt the water sinks into the sand and leaves behind lines of beach debris or mica, called swash marks (Fig. 100a). These are destroyed by each wave that extends to a higher level. Another type of marking develops where the backwash encounters obstacles such as pieces of gravel, shells, or occasionally the projecting antennas of little burrowing sand

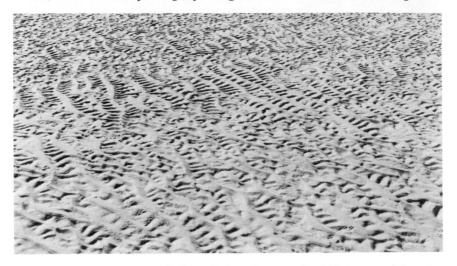

Fig. 99. An example of cross ripples formed where the strong flood tide has caused the major ripples (roughly normal to the photograph base), and lateral drainage into an estuary during the ebb tide has caused the smaller ripples (roughly parallel to the base). From Trefethen and Dow (1960).

crabs (*Emerita*). These obstacles divide the flow and leave streaks of dark sand in a diagonal pattern called backwash marks (Fig. 100b). Where the sand is very porous, pockets of air are often formed. This air may coalesce and raise the overlying sand surface into a minute dome, called a sand dome (Emery, 1945). Erosion of the top of these domes often develops ring structures because of the alternating black and white sand layers. Where the air has escaped, small holes are observed with minute craterlike rims.

Organisms traversing beaches or burrowing under them make distinctive markings. The craters made by digging crabs are particularly common in the tropics. Sand hoppers make raylike patterns (Emery, 1944), and many trails are found due to invertebrates moving along the beach (Fig. 100c). Also shore birds leave many tracks and may leave numerous small holes due to their digging for worms.

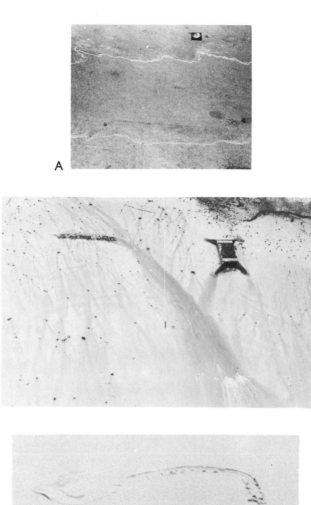

Fig. 100. (a) Swash marks, debris left at the highest point reached
by a wave along a beach. (b) Large backwash marks produced by the
tsunami of 1946. For scale note the object in the upper right which
is a displaced bridge. Smaller backwash marks are shown in Fig. 98a.
Air photo by U.S. Navy. (c) Trail left by an echinoid crawling along
a beach. Photo by D. L. Inman.

# CHAPTER VIII

# CONTINENTAL SHELVES: TOPOGRAPHY AND SEDIMENTS

## Introduction

The shallow platforms or terraces which surround the continents are called *continental shelves*. Almost all these shelves are terminated with a sharp break in slope, called the *shelf edge* or *shelf break*. In the past it has been common practice to define continental shelves as the zone inside the 100-fathom curve. This, however, does not fit the name because the shelves rarely terminate at 100 fathoms. The margins of some shelves are as shoal as 10 fathoms whereas others are much deeper than 100 fathoms. Furthermore, some shelves have large inner zones that are deeper than 100 fathoms and yet have depths less than 100 fathoms on the outside. Accordingly, it seems reasonable to limit the shelves to the area inside the shelf break, except that some depth limit has to be found in order not to include extensive deep plateaus which border a few coasts (Figs. 131, 134). An arbitrary depth of 300 fathoms was chosen for this limit by a group of marine geologists in making a report to the United Nations (Guilcher *et al.*, 1957). Using this limit we can consider as a shelf those platforms bordering a continent which terminate oceanward at depths of less than 300 fathoms. Where two breaks are seen, the most marked of the two should be chosen provided it is less than 300 fathoms in depth.

The topography of the greater part of the continental shelves has been rather well known for more than half a century. Important additions, however, have been made in recent years as the result of echo soundings located by precision electronic methods that provide accuracy beyond where visual fixes can be obained from the land.

## Description of the Continental Shelves

It has now become evident that there are various distinct types of shelves and these same types are repeated in a considerable number of localities geographically quite remote from each other.

To give some background for discussing the various types of shelves and their origin it should be helpful to take a tour around the continents and to describe the shelves along the way. The reader can find the greater part of the names referred to in this tour on the Chart of the World (inside back cover). The circumnavigation will be made clockwise around the western and eastern hemispheres starting along the east coast of North America. In the descriptions to follow, nautical miles (6080 feet) and fathoms (6 ft) will be used.[1] Conversion of the scales to meters and kilometers can be made by reference to Appendix B.

**Eastern North America.** The best known shelves in the world are found along eastern North America because of the very detailed and accurate charting of the U.S. Coast and Geodetic Survey and because of the extensive studies of the sediments especially in the Gulf of Mexico.

Along the Labrador coast the soundings are not very detailed but are sufficiently numerous to indicate some definite characteristics. Holtedahl (1958) has shown the general nature of the relief. The shelf has an average width of 70 nautical miles. There are discontinuous troughs and basins extending along the inner shelf with depths of 100 to 300 fathoms (Fig. 101). Beyond is a shoaler portion, and then another line of basins is passed before reaching the irregular shelf edge which lies around 200 fathoms.

The width of the shelf increases greatly off Newfoundland and averages more than 200 miles. On the outer shelf there is a mass of irregular banks averaging about 30 fathoms in depth. This area, known as the Grand Banks, is famous as a fishing ground. The abundance of fish is apparently the result of the good circulation produced by the Labrador Current whereas the rock-strewn character of the bottom gives small fish a chance to hide. The banks also have extensive sand-covered areas. The general character of the bottom is shown on maps published by the French Institute of Fisheries.

Inside the Grand Banks the bottom is mostly deeper than 100 fathoms, and the deep water extends up into most of the bays of Newfoundland. A wide, deep channel known as Cabot Strait Trough crosses the entire continental shelf just south of Newfoundland (Fig. 102). This continues landward up the Gulf of St. Lawrence, with depths from about 100 to 300 fathoms as far as the mouth of the Saguenay Estuary just below Quebec. The St. Lawrence Trough borders the land in its upper portion so that deep water lies near the shore, but lower down it cuts across the broadened Gulf coming in

---

[1] In the first edition of this book statute miles were used. The reasons for the change are discussed on p. 8.

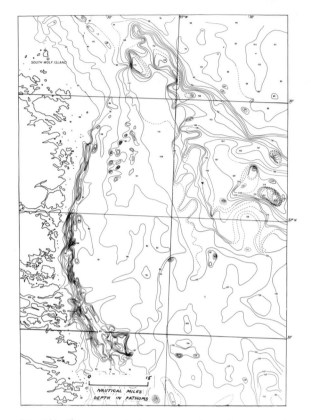

Fig. 101. Troughs and depressions along the coast of Labrador. Other irregularities and great depth are indicated. From Holtedahl (1958).

contact with the land again at Cabot Strait before extending across the broad outer shelf.

South, along the coast of Nova Scotia, the shelf exhibits more deep troughs and basins on the inside with banks extending along the outer portion (Fig. 103). One of the banks rises above the surface as Sable Island. These highs appear to represent a continuation of the Grand Banks interrupted by Cabot Strait Trough. Similarly the banks off Nova Scotia are continued to the South of Northeast Trough[2] as Georges Bank, which finally terminates near Cape Cod. Georges Bank comes almost to the surface in Georges Shoal where the water is only 2 fathoms deep. The topography of the shoal areas is indicated by the very detailed Coast and Geodetic Survey charts (Fig. 104). Two sets of sand bars extend respectively northwest-southeast over

---

[2] Referred to as Eastern Channel by Torphy and Zeigler (1957).

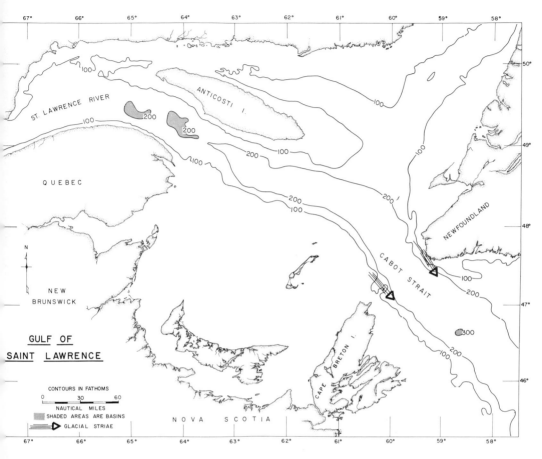

Fig. 102. Cabot Strait Trough where deep water extends up the Gulf of St. Lawrence and crosses the entire shelf. Striae discovered by the writer in 1930 indicate glacial motion through Cabot Strait. See also Fig. 103.

the shoalest portions and northeast-southwest in slightly deeper water. These have been shown by Stewart *et al.* (1959) to be related respectively to the tidal currents which sweep across the Bank into the Gulf of Maine and to the approach of the major set of swell from the east.

A reconnaissance study of the sediments of Georges Bank was made by Shepard *et al.* (1934), and they were found to consist largely of sand although fishermen bring up gravel and even boulders from portions of the bank. Evidence of glacial till underlying a portion of the bank came from anchor samples obtained after a storm had caused the large anchors of a Coast and Geodetic Survey vessel to

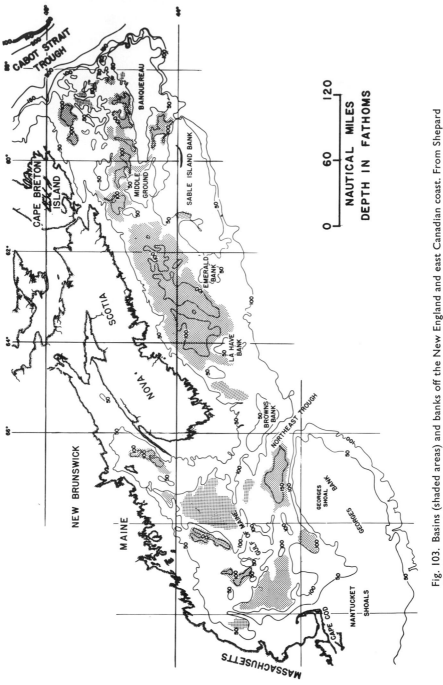

Fig. 103. Basins (shaded areas) and banks off the New England and east Canadian coast. From Shepard (1959b, Fig. 31).

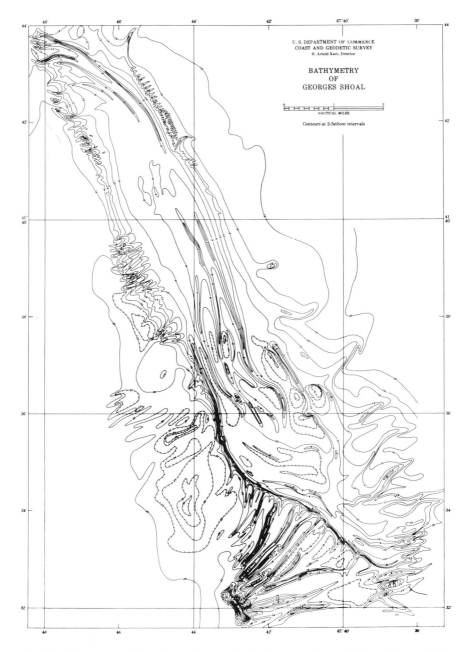

Fig. 104. Underwater "dunes" on Georges Bank. Two trends are indicated. From H. B. Stewart, U.S. Coast and Geodetic Survey.

dig deep into the sand cover. Elsewhere, however, the bank is underlain by a thick mass of sand. This was discovered from a study of the borings at the site of the Texas Towers used for radar (J. M. Zeigler, personal communication). This sand is clean, well-rounded quartz. Studies by the writer have shown that some of it is better rounded than sands in most present-day beaches and coastal dunes. In fact, it is rather comparable in general appearance, if not origin, to the St. Peter Sandstone of the Middle West.

The Gulf of Maine bears a close resemblance to the Gulf of St Lawrence. The northern arm, the Bay of Fundy, is also trough-shaped although the water is not nearly as deep as in the Gulf of St. Lawrence. Farther south there is a rocky ridge extending seaward of Cape Ann, and many other rocky ridges and hills rise above the inner portion of the Gulf of Maine (Fig. 105). If the sea level were considerably

Fig. 105. Detail of irregularities in the Gulf of Maine, east of Cashe Ledge, based on closely spaced soundings. From U.S. Coast and Geodetic Survey.

reduced, there would be extensive lakes in the Gulf of Maine as well as on the exposed shelf along the coast farther north and in the Gulf of St. Lawrence. The largest of these basins lies off Nova Scotia with a length of about 150 miles and a width of 50 miles.

The large basins of the Gulf of Maine have sediments which are high in silt and clay but have also a scattering of gravel and stones of various sizes. No long cores have been described from the Gulf as yet, so that we do not know whether this poor sorting extends deep in the sediments or is merely a surface expression.

In the Boston area a band with rocky and gravel bottom occurs along the coast and is succeeded seaward by mud bottom in the inner basin. This basin is rimmed by the sand-covered Stellwagen Bank, a northward extension of Cape Cod, although it is separated from the Cape by a narrow channel kept open by the strong tides. Directly east of Cape Cod the bottom slopes continuously from the shore to the deep southern extension of the Gulf of Maine. This slope is sufficiently smooth so that it is easy for a navigator to determine his distance off the Cape by soundings.

South of Cape Cod and its bordering islands of Nantucket and Martha's Vineyard the shelf undergoes a remarkable transformation. There are no more deep basins and broad banks. In their stead there is a comparatively smooth gently sloping shelf extending out to marginal depths of about 60 fathoms. Near the Cape there are small hills consisting locally of a series of sand waves. These appear to be a seaward continuation of the shifting shallow bars constituting Nantucket shoals. All these shoals represent a broad sheet sand suggestive of those found in various ancient formations.

Off the Mid-Atlantic States, north of Cape Hatteras, the shelf continues as a relatively smooth plain averaging 100 miles in width. There are numerous minor ridges and troughs (Fig. 106) comparable to the barrier islands and their inner lagoons which extend along much of the present coast south of New York. Another striking relief feature of the shelf is the shallow channel extending from the entrance of New York Harbor almost to the shelf break. This channel differs from a typical river valley in its straightness and from submarine canyons in its low relief and in having many basins along its course. A similar but less extensive channel occurs off both Delaware and Chesapeake bays. The shelf edge is around 70 fathoms but becomes shoaler to the south until it is only 40 fathoms deep at Cape Hatteras. Using an acoustic probe Ewing *et al.* (1960b) found a reflecting horizon at 80 fathoms along the shelf margin between Hudson and Wilmington canyons. This horizon truncates the inclined beds and appears to be a wave-cut terrace.

The sediments on the Mid-Atlantic shelf have been described by Stetson (1938) and by Shepard and Cohee (1936). The most striking characteristic is the patchiness of sediment distribution, gravel occurring sporadically at all distances from the land. To the north there is a general decrease in grain size seaward, but the sediment coarsens at the shelf break. Farther south in crossing the shelf the sediment becomes alternately finer and coarser.

Fig. 106. Shelf topography south of New York showing low ridges comparable to the barrier islands along the coast. Shallow transverse valleys are also indicated and the heads of several submarine canyons. From Veatch and Smith (1939).

At Cape Hatteras the shelf is reduced in width to 19 miles. This Cape is bordered by a shoal which extends almost to the shelf edge. To the south the shelf increases in width to 60 miles off Georgia, but farther south it narrows until it virtually disappears south of Palm Beach, Florida. The shelf edge deepens from 20 fathoms in the north to 56 fathoms off Savannah, Georgia, then shoals to about 15 fathoms at Palm Beach. A series of cuspate forelands extends from Cape Hatteras to Cape Canaveral, all built over the inner shelf. Off each foreland there are shoals on the outside which appear to control the location of the forelands (see p. 192). Gorsline (1959) has shown that the sediments on this part of the shelf are largely sand, some of it authigenic. The sand has an increasing proportion of shell and other organic debris to the south and seaward. At the break in slope Foraminifera become important. Oolites are abundant on the outer shelf (Stetson, 1938) and both authigenic glauconite and phosphorite occur in appreciable quantities.

The virtual elimination of the shelf to the south in the Miami area is clearly related in some manner to the Gulf Stream which closely hugs the coast in this area. South of Miami narrow coral reefs extend along the east margin of the Florida Keys. Outside the reefs the bottom slopes steeply to 100 fathoms and then gradually to 150 fathoms, the shelf edge. Ginsburg (1956) has studied the reefs and found three subdivisions: fore reef, outer reef, and back reef, all calcareous but each having rather distinctive faunal assemblages. Inside the Keys the shallow Florida Bay, with water less than 2 fathoms deep, has a rock floor which is covered in part with mud banks. The latter are irregular masses that develop where marine grass (Thalassia and Halodule) is growing on the rock surface forming an obstacle which leads to the deposition of calcareous mud. When the mud reaches to or near the surface, mangroves become rooted and develop a peaty soil on top of the mud, forming low islands. Some of these are famous for their unusual bird life.

**Gulf of Mexico.**   With the possible exception of the southern California shelf, the shelf along the northern Gulf of Mexico has been studied more than any other shelf in the world, largely because of its relation to the Texas and Louisiana oil fields. The topography has been well outlined by the U.S. Coast and Geodetic Survey, and the sediments studied by American Petroleum Institute Project 51 (Shepard et al., 1960), by special investigations of the oil companies (Fisk, 1956; Ludwick and Walton, 1957), and by the U.S. Geological Survey (Gould and Stewart, 1955).

The west Florida shelf has a width of about 100 miles in contrast to the narrow shelf on the east side of the peninsula. Across much of this

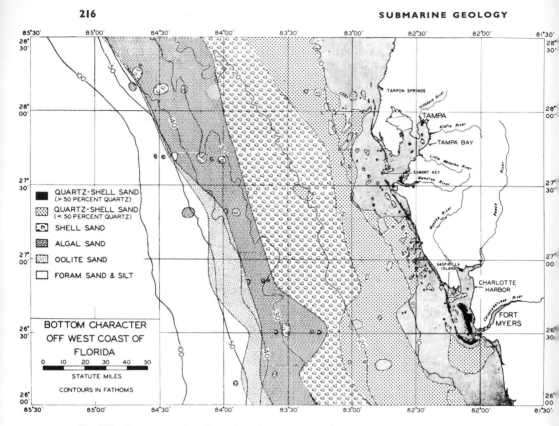

Fig. 107. The progressive change in sediment types in crossing the west Florida shelf. From Gould and Stewart (1955).

width there are small sporadic hills, representing coral reefs or other types of bioherms, the deeper banks no longer having active growth. The outermost reefs occur in 80 fathoms (Jordan and Stewart, 1959). Otherwise the shelf is quite smooth. The sediments were studied by Gould and Stewart (1955). They found a sequence out from shore consisting of quartz and shells, shell sand, algal sand, oolite sand, and finally, at and beyond the shelf margin foraminiferal sand and silt (Fig. 107). The quartz shell sand also extends well up into the large bays along the west coast. In places along the inner shelf diving by geologists of the Florida Geological Survey has revealed that the sediments are very thin and rock outcrops are fairly common. The oolites, like those off eastern Florida, are certainly relics of an earlier condition and are not being deposited at present. Running parallel to the outer edge of the shelf between latitudes 25° and 26° there is a low sand ridge with depths between 60 and 100 fathoms (Jordan and Stewart, 1959).

To the north of Lat. 29° the calcareous outer shelf gives way to a quartz sand with zones containing abundant shells. This sand extends all along the shelf virtually to the Mississippi Delta (J. C. Ludwick, personal communication). It is a medium-grained sand with the same mineral assemblage as that of the southern Appalachians and contrasts with the finer Mississippi River sands that have a much lower quartz content and different mineral assemblages (Goldstein, 1942). Along some of the outer portions of this shelf there are hills which represent bioherms (Ludwick and Walton, 1957). These hills have a covering of algal balls, with some living algae, and relic coral growth of an earlier period.

The shelf is virtually cut in two by the Mississippi Delta (Fig. 108). At South Pass the river has built entirely across the shelf and is now providing most of its sediment to the continental slope. At Pass a Loutre the distributaries have also nearly crossed the shelf and are contributing to the slope but also have contributed to a wedge of sediment extending east along the shelf for 40 miles. This sediment can be divided into topset for the shallow platform near the margin of the Delta, foreset for the sediment on the gentle slope, and bottomset for the sediment on the flat shelf beyond (Fig. 109). There is some intermixing at the boundary between the east Gulf sands and the Mississippi Delta muds shown by the presence of east Gulf sand in the outer fringe of the muddy Delta deposit. This indicates that shifting of sand by the waves and currents has occurred at depths of at least 40 fathoms in this relatively protected area.

The shelf west of the Delta has been extensively studied by Curray (1960). He has found that there are a number of elongate ridges which he believes represent old drowned barrier islands. Escarpments suggesting wave-cut cliffs are present as deep as the edge of the shelf at 65 fathoms. A considerable group of hills rise above the outer shelf with relief of as much as 40 fathoms. These have been found to be partly covered with algal deposits and various types of shell sands along with *Amphistegina* Foraminifera. At least two of the banks have bedrock showing at the surface. Dredging showed that some of this rock was as old as Miocene (Lankford and Curray, 1957) despite the tens of thousands of feet of sediment which are known to cover the Miocene in the general vicinity. There seems to be little doubt but what salt dome activity is responsible for at least some of these hills (Shepard, 1937b; Murray, 1960). On the other hand, some of the hills found on the inner shelf appear to be drowned barrier islands.

Sediments on the shelf west of the Mississippi Delta (Fig. 110) are largely silty clays particularly in the neighborhood of the Delta and off the central Texas coast. Off Galveston, however, there are extensive

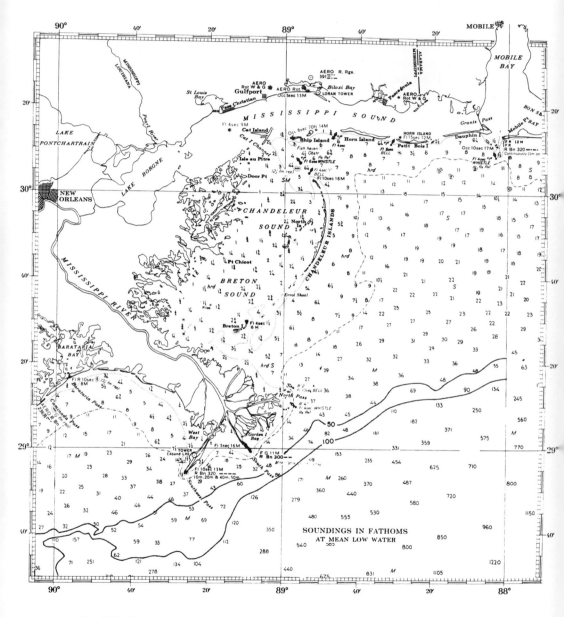

Fig. 108. Elimination of the continental shelf by the outbuilding of the Mississippi Delta.

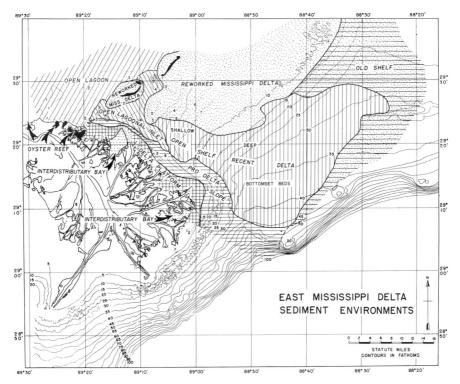

Fig. 109. Sediment environments east of the Mississippi Delta. From Shepard (1956).

areas where a silty sand predominates and much of the sand contains an abundance of shells. Carbon-14 dates taken from a number of the shells which were of shallow water or estuarine origin (Curray, 1960) have shown that they are old, dating as far back as 17,000 years for the outer portion of the shelf and successively younger toward shallow water. However, the shells on some of the inner banks are thought to be about 30,000 years old, which adds a complication to the history. In some places the sands with old shells have Foraminifera related to present-day depths. Since these Foraminifera have been found as deep as 4 ft below the surface of the sand, this suggests that present-day currents are capable of shifting the sands along the deeper shelf so that old sands are being reworked. Postglacial deposition of fine sediments has amounted to about 15 ft along much of the outer-most shelf and locally to as much as 100 ft.

The studies of the Texas bays (Shepard and Moore, 1955, 1960) have shown that they are filling at the rate of about one foot per century. The sediments are predominantly mud although sand is brought in particularly through the passes in the barrier islands and is common

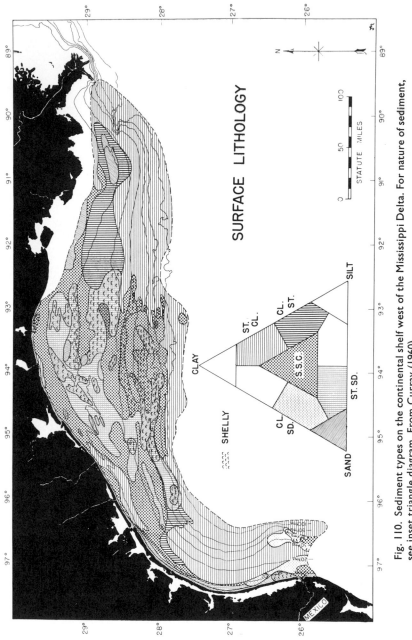

SURFACE LITHOLOGY

Fig. 110. Sediment types on the continental shelf west of the Mississippi Delta. For nature of sediment, see inset triangle diagram. From Curray (1960).

in portions of the lower bays. Oyster reefs are found in the relatively low salinity conditions of the middle bays. The sediments differ from those of the continental shelf in a general lack of glauconite and echinoid fragments which are common on the shelf. The clay minerals show a change from high montmorillonite near the river mouths to higher illite and chlorite in the lower bays (Grim and Johns, 1955). The faunas differ particularly in their small number of species although the numbers of individuals are often higher than on the shelf. The Laguna Madre (Rusnak, 1960b), lacking entering streams, has high salinity, and the sediment differs from the northern bays in having better preserved stratification, higher sand content, and in having lime coatings of the sand grains along with oolites near the shore. Lamination in the northern bays is well preserved only near river mouths and apparently is eliminated by boring organisms elsewhere in the bays.

The study of Foraminifera (Phleger, 1960b) and macroorganisms (Parker, 1960) has indicated that the various ecological facies along the Gulf Coast can be recognized by the faunal assemblages.

South of the Mexican border the shelf narrows and the sediment becomes progressively more calcareous. Off Yucatan, a shelf some 140 miles wide is said to be almost entirely calcareous, including small coral reefs but largely fragmental shells. The shelf margin here also has numerous hills, presumably related to coral reefs. On the east side of Yucatan, as on the east side of Florida, the shelf virtually disappears. This is also an area where the Gulf Stream approaches the coast. Beyond Yucatan, the shelf widens to 130 miles off eastern Honduras but consists almost entirely of a mass of shoal coral reefs. These banks continue to the south in the narrow shelves that skirt Costa Rica, Nicaragua, and the north side of Panama.

**Gulf of Batabano, Southwest Cuba.**   The shelves in the West Indies are mostly very narrow, but a wide shelf exists off the southwest coast of Cuba where Batabano Bay[3] has an area comparable in size to that of the Big Horn Basin in Wyoming. This has been studied by the Jersey Production Research Company (Daetwyler and Kidwell, 1959). The shelf here has a width of 70 nautical miles and a length of 150 miles with a depth averaging about 4 fathoms and many banks and shoals rising to the surface. Along the outside there is an almost continuous rim of shoals. These constitute coral reefs to the east and the large Isla de Pinos lies along the outer shelf in the south center of the bay.

The sea bottom is largely covered with calcareous sediment despite the supply of terrigenous material from the entering streams. According to Daetwyler and Kidwell the water is carried in from the east

[3] This is the "Bay of Pigs" where the unfortunate landing attempt was made in 1961.

by the wind-induced currents and is warmed over the banks causing precipitation of $CaCO_3$. This produces an ovoid nonskeletal carbonate with a local zone of oolite. These chemical precipitates grade into a zone with relatively high skeletal content and locally into calcareous muds. Along the shores of the mainland there are zones high in molluscan fragments. The grain size in the calcareous sediments shows no relation to depth of water nor to distance from the coast. Locally along the north side of Isla de Pinos there are small patches of quartz sand coming from the metamorphic rocks of the island. The calcareous sediments are not very thick, and local borings have shown that there is an underlying platform of limestone containing large cavities apparently the result of solution during the low sea level stages of the Pleistocene.

**Northern and Eastern South America.**    Activities of the Woods Hole Oceanographic Institution and of the Royal Dutch Shell have produced considerable information concerning the bays and shelves of northern South America. The Gulf of Maracaibo (Redfield, 1958) has muddy sediments with a low oxygen content. The 9-fathom bar separating the gulfs of Maracaibo and Venezuela is sand covered. Zeigler (1959) refers to the heavy sedimentation in the Gulf of Venezuela but notes that a submerged arch, persisting across the Gulf despite this sedimentation, indicates the importance of orogenic movements.

To the east the Gulf of Paria has been extensively studied (van Andel and Postma, 1954). The Cano Mámano arm of the Orinoco River, which is believed to have started about 700 years ago, supplies muddy sediments to neighboring portions of this Gulf, but the strong currents that flow through the eastern Serpents Mouth entrance prevent deposition of the Orinoco fines, and Pleistocene sediments are preserved on Soldado Bank just inside this pass. A notable contrast exists in the clay minerals of the Gulf of Paria with those reported by Grim and Johns (1955) from Texas bays. Instead of montmorillonite being most abundant near the river mouth and decreasing out in the Gulf, the reverse is true and illite is most common off the river entrance. The glauconite found in portions of the Gulf also might appear to contrast with the glauconite-free bays of Texas, but van Andel and Postma suggest that the glauconite is Pleistocene in age so that estuarine conditions of deposition may not have existed at that time.

Off the main mouths of the Orinoco, Nota (1958) found conditions that are in many ways similar to those off the east side of the Mississippi Delta. A broad shallow platform off the river has laminated silty sediments which become clayey (pelitic) beyond and lose their lamination. Halfway across the shelf, sand increases and calcareous sediments become important. The calcareous sands of the outer shelf represent old deposits like those of the northern Gulf Coast. Near the outer edge a series of calcareous-covered banks, said to be bioherms, rise above the general level. To the north off Trinidad actively growing reefs are found on the shelf (Koldewijn, 1958). Unlike the Mississippi, the Orinoco has not built appreciably across the shelf. Farther south the Amazon, despite its enormous sediment transport, also has failed to build its delta across the shelf and, in fact, is now engaged in filling the last remnant of a large estuary. A submarine delta is being built on the inner continental shelf (Russell, 1958). According to the charts the shelf off the Amazon has sand sediments on the outside and mud on the inner shelf. This is confirmed by the investigations of Ottman (1959), who sampled the area.

To the south and east of the Amazon the generally wide shelves of the northern lowlands shrink and become largely calcareous, with many coral banks and other types of shoal water reefs. South of Cape San Roque a shelf only 10 miles wide extends along the south-eastern length of Brazil as far as Queen Charlotte Bank where a large coral reef with abundant shoals extends the shelf width to 65 miles and produces a serious danger to navigation. Farther south, the shelf is irregular both in width and depth. Off the large Rio São Francisco del Norte there is again a mud zone near shore, and sand is found on the outer shelf. South of Rio de Janeiro the shelf widens and has increased to about 100 miles off the large estuary, Rio de la Plata. Here also mud is found inside and sand outside. From latitudes 39° S to 49° S the shelf break lies around 70 to 80 fathoms, commonly reaching 100 fathoms, whereas to the north it is rarely over 50 fathoms. The Gulf of San Matias south of the Rio Plata was investigated by the *Vema* (Granelli, 1959). "Ripples" 4 fathoms high were found at the entrance, and "giant ripples" 8 fathoms high were discovered in the Gulf with numerous smaller ripples in between. Strong tidal currents up to 8 knots are found. These are related to the large tidal range up to 7 m. Despite the currents and ripple marks, fine sediment is reported. According to Granelli a core showed 9 m of clay over 3 m of sand.

The southern tip of South America was covered by glaciers during the Pleistocene. This is reflected by the topography. Apparently there are troughs off Patagonia and heterogeneous types of sediment are indicated. A trough with depths between 100 and 400 fathoms extends up along the south and west sides of the Falkland Islands. This is bordered to the south by Burwood Bank. The Straits of Magellan are similar to the deep inlets in the glaciated zones of eastern North America.

**Western South America.**  Beyond Cape Horn, the irregularity of
the shelf shows a considerable increase, and a whole series of troughs
extends across it with depths quite comparable to those off Labrador
and Newfoundland. The deepest fiords in the world[4] (maximum depth
900 fathoms) indent the coast, and these inlets are found as far north
as 42° where evidently the glaciation stops. To the north the shelf
becomes relatively flat but quite deep, mostly over 50 fathoms, and
very narrow. The slopes of the inner shelf are mostly quite steep as far
north as 7° S. Lat. As off Argentina, the shelf edge is deep, mostly
close to 100 fathoms. From 14° S. to 6° S. Lat. the shelf is wider,
about 30 miles across, and at the Gulf of Guayaquil it reaches 40
miles. Here sand bottom is found whereas not much is reported along
the rest of the west coast shelves. Neaverson (1934) collected scattered
samples along the shelves of Chile. In some places he found that the
sediment coarsened outward from shore and elsewhere it became finer.

**Western North America.**  At the Gulf of Panama the shelf widens
to about 75 miles. Flat bottom with depths around 50 fathoms is
conspicuous in this gulf. The shelf terminates near the 100-fathom
contour. The Gulf of Panama has been well charted for bottom
character, and there is little doubt but that the sediments are increasingly coarse away from the shore. Mud occurs in the inner gulf,
and sand and shells become increasingly more common away from the
shore and out beyond the lee of the Perlas Islands. Near the shelf edge,
rock is reported at several places. To the north of Panama the shelf is
narrow or nonexistent up to 11° 15′ N. Lat. Beyond this point, the
shelf widens to 30 miles and continues wide on the west side of the
Gulf of Tehuantepec, where it has a maximum width of 55 miles.
The soundings are scarce, but one gathers that this is a deep shelf with
some zones over 100 fathoms. From Tehuantepec to the entrance of
the Gulf of California the shelf is virtually nonexistent. Along the
east side of the Gulf of California there is a narrow shelf of variable
depth but having conspicuously deep soundings along steep portions
of the coast, notably at Guaymas. At the head of the gulf there is a
broad shelf off the Colorado Delta, depths of 10 fathoms being found
20 miles from land. This shelf off the Colorado River is covered with
mud having an appreciable content of sand. At the southern limit of
this shelf, between Tiburon and Angel de la Guarda Islands, there is a
basin about 200 fathoms deep which has stratified sands and gravel
overlying mud. The west side of the gulf is notable for the absence of
shelves. Water hundreds of fathoms deep is found close to the peninsula of Baja California and adjacent to the islands.

[4] Except perhaps Antarctica where most fiords are still ice covered and only explored
sporadically.

The shelf and lagoons along the west coast of Baja California have been studied rather extensively during and since World War II. The sediments of San Cristobal, Sebastian, Viscaino, and Todos Santos bays are described by Emery *et al.* (1957). The wide open San Cristobal Bay has a sand shelf with little or no relation of grain size to distance from shore. Phosphorite is found in most of the samples. Viscaino Bay, partially protected by Cedros Island, has much larger quantities of mud sediment with some decrease in grain size outward. The coarsest sediment is found in the strait at the south end of Cedros Island where the currents are strong. Todos Santos Bay at Ensenada is also protected by several islands and by Punta Banda to the south. The shelf on the inside of the islands grades out from clean, fine-grained sand along the shore to micaceous silt in the deeper water, but to the north of the islands the outer shelf is rocky with sand and gravel deposits, and the strength of the currents is indicated by the giant ripple marks shown in bottom photographs. Some of the deep outer sand is definitely shown to be relict by the presence of extinct shallow water Foraminifera (Walton, 1955).

The shelf off San Diego was extensively studied during World War II (Emery *et al.*, 1952). This shelf is only 10 miles wide, but it includes many features of interest (Figs. 111, 112). On the outside it is flanked by a rocky submarine bank which continues north as a submarine ridge. To the south the bank is cut by a canyon (Fig. 146), but beyond the canyon it rises to form the Coronados Islands (just across the Mexican line). Inside the bank a shallow longitudinal valley borders the coastal shelf. The sediment distribution off the Tijuana River, near the Mexican border, shows in a seaward direction alternating coarse and fine sediments. The sediments now introduced may grade outward from coarse to fine, but relict, and hence presumably Pleistocene sediments, are represented (Fig. 112) over extensive areas where, according to R.F. Dill (personal communication) currents are only strong enough to introduce fine clays and these are too fine to accumulate in the shallow water. Thus an extensive cobble and boulder patch is found a mile outside the Tijuana River, and apparently the same deposit underlies a much larger area to the west and north. Farther seaward there is an extensive deposit of semi-oxidized, medium-grained sand which is also clearly relict and like the boulders was probably subaerial in origin. During World War II a large amount of sediment was dredged out of San Diego Harbor and dumped onto the inner shelf by a pipeline. This formed an oval patch of sandy mud which persisted for about five years but was gradually subjected to the attrition of currents until now there is a fine sand in the area comparable to that of the surrounding deposits. Similarly, after

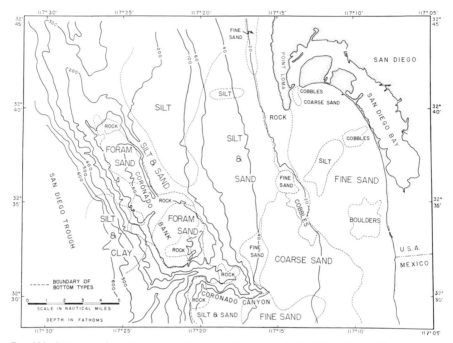

Fig. 111. Bottom sediment types and topography on the shelf off San Diego. The silt zone near shore has now disappeared, having been a temporary result from dredging of San Diego Bay. See also Fig. 112.

rainstorms muddy sediments settle temporarily on the coarser sediments outside but are carried away after a short interval. The bank outside is not receiving any appreciable amount of sediment from the continent at present. Between outcrops of rock on this outer shelf there are sediments consisting of Foraminifera along with some relict terrigenous material, partly silt. Many of the Foraminifera have tests filled with glauconite. Phosphorite nodules are also found, especially on the deeper parts of the bank beyond depths of about 75 fathoms.

Inman (1953) investigated the nearshore sediments north of Point La Jolla where the narrow shelf is cut by two canyons. Except in the canyon heads most of the shelf sediments are fine sands like the local beach except south of La Jolla Canyon where the medium-grained sand from the pocket beaches is found. The effect of the canyons on the sediment is discussed in Chaper XI. Wimberley (1955) investigated the sediments directly north of Scripps Canyon. He found that the sediment texture is in general related to water depth with a decided increase of mud at about 30 fathoms. However, a sand suggesting a former beach was located at 40 fathoms at the shelf margin.

Farther north the shelf is only a few miles across as far as the Long

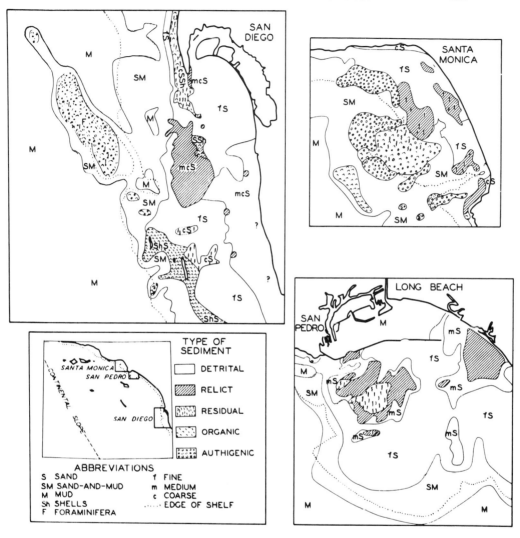

Fig. 112. Types of sediments of three areas in southern California, classified as to origin. Dotted line is shelf break. After Emery (1960, Fig. 180).

Beach area where it again widens. Here, Moore (1954) has indicated that there are also rocky areas along the central and outer portions and areas of Pleistocene sediments surround the central rock area (Fig. 112). Both relict and residual sediments are found. The central shelf has Miocene rock with residual coarse brown sand flanking it. To the southwest is a large zone of relict sands which have a Pleistocene fauna. This relict sediment is recognized by a content of Pleistocene fauna, lithological resemblance to Pleistocene dunes bordering Santa Monica Bay, and the existence of the brown iron-stained sand like that off San Diego. Both sand and mud are found fringing the shore. The shelf gives out off the Palos Verdes Hills as one would expect because of the recent uplifts (Woodring *et al.*, 1946). In Santa Monica Bay a well-studied shelf exists (Terry *et al.*, 1956; Emery, 1960, p. 200) with again rock and coarse relict sediment on the outside (Fig. 112). Some of the relict sand in Santa Monica Bay is brown-stained like that off San Diego. Terry *et al.* (1956) compared the sediment of Santa Monica Bay reported by Shepard and Macdonald (1938) with that collected twenty years later and concluded that the grain size had definitely decreased. They attributed this to the diversion of the mouth of the Los Angeles River and various other artificial changes reducing the supply of sand sediment introduced into the bay. Oil and gas seeps occur in this area. The southern California shelf sediments are also discussed by Stevenson *et al.*, (1959). The shelf edge averages about 43 fathoms and, in fact, is almost as shallow along the entire southern California coast.

To the north and west of Santa Monica the shelf is mostly narrow, much of it either rocky or covered only with a thin veneer of sediments. Oil exploration, particularly in the Santa Barbara area, has shown that rock structures underlie much of this shelf and active drilling is now being carried on in the area. From Ventura to Point Conception great amounts of oil and bitumen are seeping out of the underlying rocks, and the water surface over extensive areas is oil-covered especially near Coal Oil Point, west of Santa Barbara. In places the SCUBA divers reported streams of oil 30 ft high, and asphalt domes 10 ft high and 50 to 100 ft across (R. F. Dill, personal communication). Smaller seeps occur in Santa Monica Bay and in other places along this part of the California coast (Emery, 1960, Fig. 244). Nearing Point Conception the bottom currents are so strong on occasions that little sediment is found on the shelf and it is often difficult for SCUBA divers to work against these currents (R. F. Dill, personal communication).

Studies with an acoustic probe of sediment thickness and shallow structure on the shelf off southern California (Moore, 1960) show that relatively thin lenticular masses of sediment cover smooth sloping rock platforms. In general the sediment thickens landward of the shelf margin as well as down the slope beyond. Pleistocene as well as Recent sediments occur in some places. A great local variation in sediment thickness on the southern California shelves is caused by topographic control and proximity to sources. Most of the mid-portion of the shelves has 30 to 50 ft of sediment except off La Jolla where the shelf is nearly barren of sediment. Large stretches in this southern California area have more than 40 ft of Recent sediment cover. The rock structure is very evident in the acoustic probe sections showing anticlines and synclines in some places.

Near San Francisco the shelf again widens and maintains its width off most of the northern United States and British Columbia. Off Pigeon Point (about 40 miles south of San Francisco) Moore and Shumway (1959) studied the 15-mile wide shelf. Samples and acoustic probe data led them to conclude that the broad flat outer shelf was cut into Pleistocene sediments and that the inner steep shelf is cut into rock. The only Recent sediments are on the inner shelf. The Golden Gate, the entrance to San Francisco Bay, is a locus of strong currents with resulting rock and gravel bottom. Outside the Gate there is a sand bar some five fathoms deep which forms an arc with natural openings only at the south and north ends (Fig. 113). This bar is constantly shifting in position and depth. Inside the Gate, San Francisco Bay is also influenced by tidal currents showing the coarsest sediment in the deep outer bay and finest in the upper ends of the bay (Louderback, 1940). Beyond the Gate the shelf has mostly a sand cover but near the outer edge a rocky rim rises to the surface to form the Farallon Islands. Cordell Bank to the north has littoral zone shells at 34 fathoms, and Miocene rocks have been dredged from the area (Hanna, 1952). North of Drakes Bay the shelf shows an alternation seaward of sand, then mud, and then sand as do so many other shelves.

In the San Francisco area and to the north the shelf edge is deeper than off southern California. Instead of terminating near 50 fathoms, as along most of the southern California shelf, depths of 70 to 80 fathoms are the rule. The shelf narrows north of San Francisco to about 10 miles at Point Arena, and the inner part is steep. Evidence of even greater depth of margin comes from the acoustic probe studies of Moore and Shumway (1959). Off Pigeon Point south of San Francisco they found that the sloping rock terrace terminates seaward at about 90 fathoms whereas the Recent sediment terrace that overlies the rock has a margin at about 60 fathoms. Another rock terrace near shore terminates at about 50 fathoms where the rock outcrops. These records show the difficulty of estimating depth of terrace cutting from topography alone.

Along the Oregon and Washington coasts the shelf widens again to about 20 miles but has an even deeper outer margin, around 100 fathoms, except where there are banks along the outer margin as at Cape Blanco, Oregon, and at Hecate Bank off the Washington coast farther north. The latter, according to the charts, has a hard clay bottom rather than rock which is found on most other West Coast

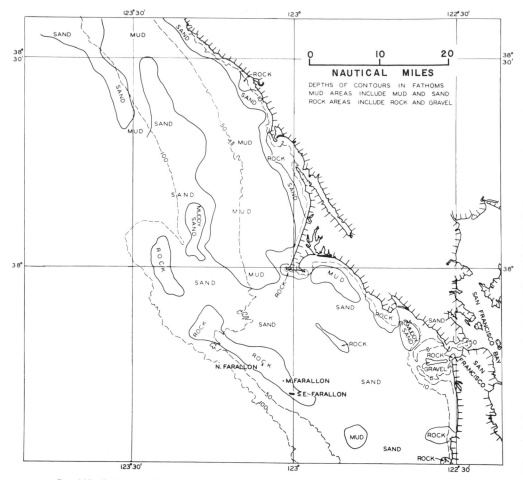

Fig. 113. Sediment character off San Francisco and to the north. A crescentic bar is shown off the deep entrance to San Francisco Bay.

banks. The shelf topography is relatively smooth although rock knolls rise locally above the flat portions. According to oil company reports the shelf has only a thin cover of sediment. The sediments on the shelf have not been studied but are given on the charts as alternating sand and mud without any noticeable relationship in grain size to depth or distance from shore.

Off the Straits of Juan de Fuca a trough resembling Cabot Strait Trough, but not as deep, cuts across the shelf in a southwesterly direction, terminating in a submarine canyon. The trough has the typical heterogeneous sediment distribution characteristic of glaciated shelves. It extends deeply into the land connecting with the network of deep fiords in Puget Sound and north among the islands. Along the coast of British Columbia the glacial characteristics continue with the usual fishing banks and deep troughs on the adjacent shelf. Again, as off Labrador and Nova Scotia, some of the troughs extend parallel to the shore while others cross the shelf. In general there is a wide shelf off British Columbia and southern Alaska but it definitely narrows in approaching the Aleutian Islands.

North of the Aleutians the land was not glaciated and the broad Bering Sea shelf, with an average width of 400 miles, has no troughs or basins to indicate glaciation. Aside from a few islands and rocky banks near the shelf margin there is an amazing lack of relief. Some of the echograms show absolute flatness (Buffington *et al.*, 1950), and there is no known area of comparable extent which has this same degree of flatness anywhere on the surface of the earth.

Sonoprobe studies (Moore, 1961a) show that much of the flatness is due to smoothing by a thin (5–20 ft) sediment cover over what in many places appears to be an irregular rocky platform having local relief of up to 30 ft. The sediments are muddy near the Yukon River and in Morton Sound but largely sandy farther out. The shelf edge has depths around 70 fathoms.

**Eastern Asia.**    The Sea of Okhotsk has been extensively surveyed and studied by the Soviet Union. According to Bezrukov (1960) the northern part was glaciated and contemporaneously the central and southern part received terrigenous deposits. The northern third of the sea appears to be a relatively deep, somewhat basined continental shelf with a rather gradual increase in slope to the south. The deep outer part of the sea is bordered by the ridge containing the Kurile volcanic islands. Thus there is some resemblance to the Bering Sea with its Aleutian Island rim. The Gulf of Sakhalin, lying off the Amur River at the north end of the Tartary Straits, is relatively shallow, mostly less than 20 fathoms, and the bottom has little relief.

The elongate Gulf of Tartary, south of Tartary Straits, is largely a shelf sea covered with mud, probably supplied by the Amur River. The shelf terminates to the south at a depth of over 100 fathoms. Off Vladivostok, on the Sea of Japan, the shelf is 30 miles wide and contains irregular patches of sand, mud, and rock. Mud occurs in the bays and sand predominates on the open shelf, whereas rock bottom is found off the projecting points of land. South of Vladivostok a narrow shelf extends down to the Korean (Tsushima) Strait. This shelf is dominantly sand-covered to the north but mud increases and predominates in the approach to the strait. This strait is part of the shelf, although there is a relatively deep zone along the west side of Tsushima

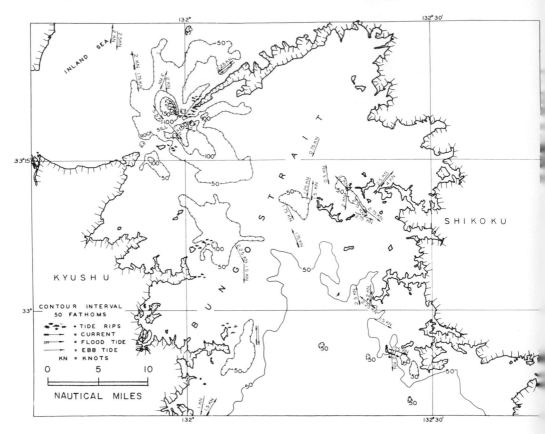

Fig. 114. The unusually deep hole resulting from tidal action at the southeastern entrance to the Inland Sea of Japan. Based on Japanese Navy charts.

Island. The sediment in the strait is principally sand, although mud occurs on the west side and rock bottom skirts the islands and is reported from the banks.

The nature of the sediment on the shelf and slopes around Japan is indicated on the Japanese bottom sediment charts published in 1949 by the Maritime Safety Board. The work by the writer and his associates during World War II resulted in more detailed charts of the same area (Shepard *et al.*, 1949). In both cases the basis for the sediment charts is largely the sediment notations made in great detail by the Japanese surveyors and included on the Japanese navigational charts. Except off the island of Hokkaido, sediments show little indication of decreasing grain size gradation in a seaward direction. The predominant sediments are sand on the open shelf with mud

represented in the bays particularly in the Inland Sea. All the peninsulas are bordered by rocky bottom, and rock occurs also in the three
entrances to the Inland Sea as well as in the straits between islands and
in local patches along the open shelves. Bungo Strait between
Kyushu and Shikoku has a hole with a depth of 215 fathoms (Fig. 114).
This is the deepest cut in the world that can be attributed to tidal
action in a narrow bay entrance. In the large Kagoshima Bay at the
southern end of Kyushu an active volcano has grown up across the
northern end of the bay and has apparently contributed much of
the bottom sediment (labeled as volcanic ash).

Along the Chinese coast and to the south some of the widest shelves
in the world are found. These platforms are perhaps the closest parallel
which we have to the ancient shelf seas in which most sedimentary
rocks are thought to have been deposited. The east Asiatic shelf is
partly protected by outlying islands, and there are also large deeply
indented gulfs. Some of the largest rivers of the world, including the
Yellow, the Yangtze Kiang, and the Mekong, contribute sediments
more or less directly to these shelves. Despite these large sediment
sources the eastern Asia shelves (Fig. 115) do not show the outward
gradation from coarse to fine sediment supposed to be characteristic
of ancient seas. Instead muddy sediments are found almost everywhere
along the coast and sand along the outer shelves (Shepard *et al.*,
1949). Collection of about 1000 samples by the Japanese led to some
study of the sediments in the East China and South China seas (Niino
and Emery, 1961). On the west side, the sediments are fine-grained
consisting largely of reworked loess from the Hwang Ho and Yangtze
Kiang rivers. On the east, off Korea, coarser grained sediments come
from the high gradient rivers. The outer shelf sand zones consist of
sands high in calcareous content, containing considerable authigenic
material, especially glauconite. Niino and Emery consider that the
sediments are thickest in the Gulf of Po-hai and central China seas
where no outcrops are found. These they consider as zeugo geosynclinal seas following the classification of Kay (1951). At the entrance
to the China Sea many rocks are exposed and form a connection
between Korea and South China. Therefore, they think that the open
shelf from Korea to Indochina has only a thin blanket of sediment on
top of bedrock. To the south the Gulf of Tonkin has fine-grained
sediment.

Recent explorations by Scripps Institution off South Vietnam and
in the Gulf of Thailand (James Faughn, personal communication)
have given some important new information on the shelf. Just south
of Hainan Island the outer shelf becomes very deep and contains an
elongate depression about 300 fathoms deep inside a marginal depth

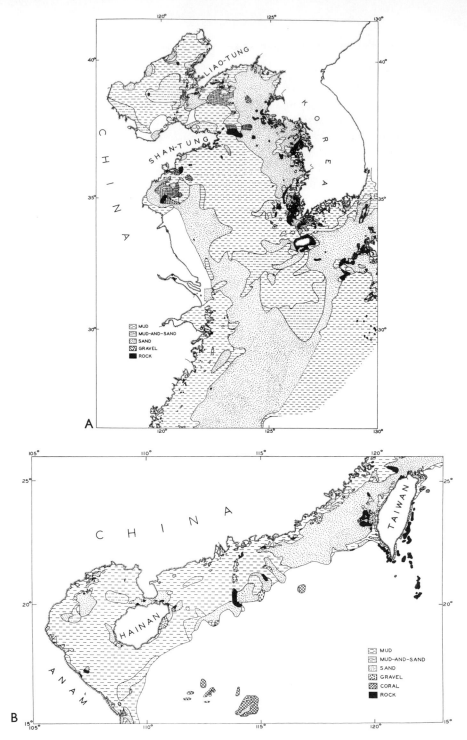

Fig. 115. Bottom sediment charts from Niino and Emery (1961) showing the extensive sand zones along the China coast north (*a*) and southwest (*b*) of Taiwan. Based on 53,000 bottom notations, partly from Shepard *et al.* (1949).

of from 230 to 250 fathoms. Some of the profiles indicate rather rough topography. To the south this deep margin is in line of continuity with a shoaler shelf margin of somewhat less than 100 fathom depths off Saigon. The outer shelf continues sandy[5] all the way south across the mouth of the Gulf of Thailand, but mud covers most of the bottom within the Gulf and occurs also off the mouths of the Mekong River. Cores taken by the writer on a Thai Navy vessel in 1957 showed that in the head of the Gulf the mud is very soft but about 100 miles to the south the mud layer is only a few inches thick and is underlain by a hard clay, apparently a Pleistocene formation.

Farther south there is an extensive shelf sea between Sumatra and Java on the one side and Borneo on the other. The northern approaches to this sea are mud-covered except in the narrows between the islands of Bangka, Billiton, and Borneo where sand and even rock bottom is reported. The petrology of the Java Sea sediments has been investigated by van Baren and Kiel (1950). They found that there are ten petrological provinces including: (1) a Java group which borders the north coast of Java, except to the west where the Krakatau group shows the influence of the volcano; (2) an extensive Borneo group covering almost half of the Java Sea; (3) a Molucca group; and (4) a South China Sea group. Relations to the broad land masses of the Tertiary and Pleistocene were observed and there is not much cover of Recent (Holocene) sediments.

**Australia.**   To the north of Australia the Sahul Shelf represents one of the largest shelf seas in the world. Including the Gulf of Carpentaria and the shallow part of the Arafura Sea, this has an extent of 700 miles in a northwest-southeast direction and 350 in a northeast-southwest direction. This shelf is still poorly surveyed, and little is known of the bottom character. Apparently most of it is less than 50 fathoms deep and much of it only 30 to 40 fathoms. Coral reefs rise locally. The Aroe (Aru) Islands have been described by Fairbridge (1951) as crossed by old river channels now below the surface. According to Verstappen (1959), however, the channels are the result of diagonal shear joints and Recent warping of the Aru rise and have no relation to river courses.

Along the Queensland coast the shelves are narrower than to the north particularly off the York Peninsula but broaden again to the south, reaching a maximum of about 180 miles. This Queensland shelf is about half covered with coral constituting the Great Barrier Reef. Along much of the coast there is a somewhat discontinuous channel about 20 to 30 fathoms deep inside the reefs. Here the bottom is

---

[5] Apparently this is calcareous sand according to preliminary examination of the Scripps samples by K. O. Emery and Hiroshi Niino.

largely mud covered. The reefs have a maximum width of 70 miles at 22° S. Lat. and have what are generally considered the finest growths of coral in the world. Most of this portion of the shelf is very shallow because of the coral, but outside the reef the shelf in some portions has depths up to at least 220 fathoms.

South of Sandy Cape near the Tropic of Capricorn the reef ends, and a narrow shelf continues along the entire southeast coast. Most of this portion appears to have depth terminations around 55 to 70 fathoms although the outer part is not well sounded. The average width is around 20 miles. Most of the shelf is sand covered although gravel and rock are also reported from various places and some of the rocks actually come to the surface such as the Solitary Rocks, around 30° S. Lat., near the outer edge of the shelf. Off some of the rivers mud bottom is indicated but only in narrow bands. A fairly consistent terrace occurs at about 16 fathoms along much of this coast. The sandy shelf continues and apparently coarsens in texture as far as Bass Strait, although approaching the strait many of the bottom notations are indicated as shell and coral. On the west side of the strait the bottom grows muddier, apparently where the islands form some protection from the waves of the open sea.

The south coast of Australia is poorly charted in most areas. Where shown, the shelf edge is variable in depth but averages about 70 fathoms. Almost all bottom notations indicate sand with abundant shells. This sandy shelf reflects the absence of muds introduced from rivers as expected along this arid coast.

The Rowley Shelf of western Australia is described by Carrigy and Fairbridge (1954) as dominantly covered with a shell sand derived from fragments of mollusca, corals, Bryozoa, Foraminifera, and algae. There are small amounts of insoluble residue sand, largely quartz. Here also the arid conditions of the land mass prevent the development of a mud shelf. Great differences in depth are found along this shelf. North of 20° S. Lat. there are extensive areas well over 100 fathoms in depth and in some zones the shelf extends out to about 250 fathoms, like the shelf off parts of Queensland. Coral reefs rise as isolated bioherms above some of these considerable depths. The 200-mile-wide Sahul Shelf off northwest Australia extending almost to Timor has the large Bonaparte Depression, a basin comparable in area to the largest basins off glaciated coasts (Fig. 116). The maximum depth, however, is only 84 fathoms, 30 fathoms below the rim, far less in both respects than basins of typical glaciated shelves. This basin which may still be tectonically active occurs outside an ancient basin which has been receiving sediments intermittently since early Paleozoic (Teichert, 1958b). The bottom of the Bonaparte Depression is

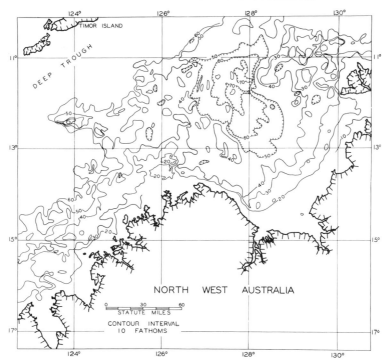

Fig. 116. A large shelf depression along the Australian (Sahul) Shelf. Contours do not go below 70 fathoms.

predominantly mud but is surrounded on all sides by sand-sized sediments. According to preliminary reports by Tj. H. van Andel and J. R. Curray from extensive sampling the inner sands are predominantly terrigenous and the outer predominantly calcareous. A local sediment study of interest is that by Carrigy (1956) in Warnbro Sound of southwest Australia. This is a partly barred basin, and the sediments are largely calcareous sands and silts with the finer sediments near shore farthest away from the bar source. The fine sediments are high in organic carbon and nitrogen.

**Southern Asia.** The Malacca Strait between Sumatra and Malaya is shallow, mostly less than 40 fathoms. The bottom is given as a heterogeneous mixture of mud and sand with small patches of rock. Toward the outer margin sand, presumably calcareous, increases and becomes dominant. To the north the shelf narrows to 40 or 50 miles, and extensive islands and passageways occur along the coast with partly submerged ridges out beyond the islands. On the inner shelf the bottom is dominantly muddy reflecting the many rivers which flow into the sea in this area. The outermost shelf, where the depths run close to 50 fathoms, is rocky up to 12° N. Lat. and becomes muddy farther north where the effect of the Irrawaddy and Rangoon rivers becomes important. In the Gulf of Martaban the shelf widens to 150 miles but narrows to 70 miles off the overlapping Irrawaddy Delta. In the wide portion there is an extensive area about 10 to 15 fathoms deep. The Gulf of Martaban is similar to other shelves off large rivers in having extensive mud bottom near shore whereas sand covers the entire outer shelf. To the west, off the Irrawaddy Delta, some of the notations on the outer shelf are sand and mud. The shelf margin has depths of from 60 to 70 fathoms. Along the western margin of the shelf the currents apparently prevent mud deposition and coral banks are found on a shelf elsewhere labeled as sand, probably a calcareous sand.

Up the Burma coast beyond the Irrawaddy the shelf narrows to 20 miles and is generally mud-covered. The same irregular islands fringe the coast. Some of the islands are elongate and appear to be hogbacks with submarine continuations to the south (Fig. 67). The marginal depths around 60 fathoms continue outside the 100-mile-wide shelf off the Ganges. This shelf is partly overlapped by the Ganges Delta causing it to narrow to 60 miles. The shelf is largely covered with mud off the Ganges but fine sand bottom is reported along much of the coast and extends out as a sand tongue outside the main mouth. Sand is found among the elongate shoals on the west side of the delta where subsidence due to faulting and tilting appears to have taken place (Morgan and McIntire, 1959). Off the middle of the delta a troughlike valley cuts across most of the shelf.

On the narrow shelf along the east coast of the Indian peninsula the typical sediment distribution (Mahadevan and Rao, 1954; Rao and Mahadevan, 1959) is terrigenous sand near shore with some black sand concentrates, turning to mud at about 30 fathoms and then to calcareous sand along the outer portion beyond 40 fathoms. The outer sand includes oolites similar to the oolite band off both sides of Florida. The Foraminifera in these oolite sands, according to F. B. Phleger and R. R. Lankford, have an abundance of shallow–water types even at depths of about 100 fathoms that suggest deposition under low sea level conditions and nondeposition since the sea rose. The narrow shelf is almost entirely overlapped by the Godavari and Kistna deltas, and the margin runs comparatively straight despite these deltas. The shelf edge is around 50 to 70 fathoms except off the deltas where it shoals to 20 fathoms. Most of the shelf is 20 miles in width, but near Pondichéry at the south end of the peninsula the 100-fathom curve bends near to the coast in several places. Palk Strait separating India and Ceylon has a width of 40 miles with water almost entirely 5 to 7 fathoms in depth except where local coral reefs rise above this shallow floor, particularly to the northwest near Adams Bridge. The latter, judging from its appearance from the air, is a coral reef virtually cutting off the southern end of Palk Strait.

Ceylon has a fairly consistent 10-mile shelf cut in several places by submarine canyons. An average depth at the margin is about 35 fathoms. The canyon at Trincomalee Bay comes right into the estuary and extends across quartzite ridges. The Ceylon shelf is largely covered with sand and coral.

Off the southern tip of India the shelf widens to 60 miles and shows depths of as much as 120 fathoms. To the north the shelf narrows to about 30 miles at 11° N. Lat. but widens farther north to as much as 190 miles off the Gulf of Cambay. Much of this western shelf has a shelf margin between 50 and 60 fathoms and a broad, flat 50-fathom terrace (Fig. 117) extends from 17° to 21° N. Lat. The outer shelf is largely sand-covered, but mud occurs along the coast and during the southwest monsoons this mud is stirred up into the water to such an extent that it actually disrupts the wave trains sufficiently that small boats can land behind a "breakwater" of soupy mud called a mudbank (Hiranandani and Gole, 1959). This phenomenon is apparently unique.

The Gulf of Cambay and the Gulf of Cutch are suggestive of the indentation on the west side of the Ganges Delta and they may both represent delta flank depressions. The former has parallel bars shaped by the tide, also like those west of the Ganges. A terrace at 17 fathoms occurs off the Gulf of Cambay and somewhat shoaler terraces are found to the north, notably the Kori Great Bank on the south side of the Indus submarine trough. The latter is not represented on the north side of the trough where the shelf is considerably deeper. Approaching the Indus River the shelf becomes more and more mud covered, although here again there are indications of sand on the outer shelf. As off the Ganges, the shelf is cut in two by a long submarine trough which heads near the Baghiar Mouth. Strong currents run parallel to the trough axis, and at the edge of the trough their effect is seen by rips at the surface. The shelf remains 100 miles or more in width up to Karachi where it narrows abruptly with the change in trend but has a deeper edge. Off Baluchistan the width averages 20 miles with gradual decrease to the west. The shelf continues to be mud-covered according to the sparse bottom notations. The edge is much shoaler along this east-west coast and averages about 20 fathoms. Continuing west along the coast of Iran the shelf is still narrower, about 10 to 15 miles wide, but the edge appears to have deepened to about 60 fathoms.

The Gulf of Oman has a broad shelf at its head, and this leads into

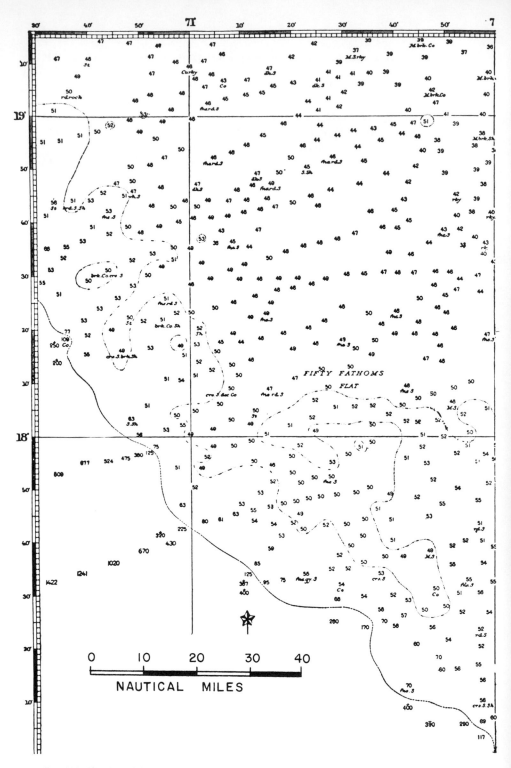

Fig. 117. The broad flat terrace on the outer shelf of western India just south of the Indus Delta. From U.S. Navy Hydrographic Office Chart No. 1590.

the shallow water of the Persian Gulf. The Gulf of Oman is largely mud-covered as is also the northern and northeastern portion of the Persian Gulf (Emery, 1956). The Tigris and Euphrates rivers are the source of these muddy sediments. These rivers are said to have built their combined delta forward into the Gulf for 90 miles during the past 4000 years. The submarine slope of the delta at the head varies from 00′ 50″ to 01′ 40″. The southern and western portion of the Persian Gulf has sandy sediment, much of it calcarenite as shown by Houbolt (1957). Along the Arabian desert coast, on the other hand, most of the sand is terrigenous and of eolian derivation. Small coral reefs grow along portions of the Qatar Peninsula. Emery found relatively high organic contents in the sediment especially near the lower end of the Gulf where plankton blooms occur in the Strait of Hormuz owing to mixing of the Arabian Sea water with the underlying saline water from the Persian Gulf. The mixed water is carried into the Gulf where the plankton sinks to the bottom. A considerable number of hills and islands occur in the southern Gulf, and these have been found to be salt domes.

Along the coast of Arabia the mud bottoms disappear, and sand along with rock is indicated on the generally narrow shelves. The edge of the shelf runs fairly straight, but the land shows a number of projecting points and islands which virtually or entirely eliminate the shelf since there is no appreciable outbend around them. Approaching the entrance to the Red Sea the shelf is more regular in width, averages about 20 miles across, and terminates at around 40 fathoms. At the entrance to the Red Sea there is a long channel with axial depths of a little over 100 fathoms.

**Eastern Africa.**   The shelf on the east coast of Africa is narrow for the most part and poorly surveyed. In places there appears to be no shelf along the straight coast, suggestive of a fault coast (p. 162). As along the Arabian coast the indentations are accompanied by a widening of the shelf and narrow zones are found off the points and islands. A coral-covered shelf occurs at Zanzibar and Mafia islands. Off the Zambesi, one of the large rivers of Africa, the shelf widens and continues to increase in width to the south until it attains 70 miles off Beira at 20° S. Lat. Most of this shelf is shallow with marginal depths around 30 fathoms. Following a narrow stretch the shelf again widens to about 70 miles between 25° and 26° S. Lat., but here the increase is related largely to a double shelf with depths of the outer portion around 200 to 300 fathoms. The shelf is narrow again to the south except for a bulge north of Natal where an unusually even shelf terminates at about 50 fathoms.

Off South Africa the shelf shows a considerable bulge reaching a width of 130 miles. The slope is steep along the coast to about 40 fathoms. The soundings on the outer shelf are not very abundant, but there are indications that the shelf extends out to well over 100 fathoms. The outer shelf, known as Agulhas Bank, is particularly irregular with many hills and basin depressions. Most of this outer portion is between 70 and 100 fathoms in depth. The irregularities occur in the area with the strong westerly currents reported from this shelf. The shelf sediment is predominantly sand with abundant shells. Small areas of mud occur to the west and rock is also reported in a number of places especially on the outer shelf.

**Western Africa.**   The shelf narrows temporarily west of the Cape of Good Hope, but it deepens considerably. Extending from 32° to 28° S. Lat. the shelf is about 100 miles wide with the outer portion ending at around 270 fathoms according to sparse soundings. The deepening occurs rapidly near shore in most places. The equally sparse bottom notations show mud on the inside with sand and rock on the deep outer shelf. Aside from Antarctica this shelf is perhaps the deepest in the world, if one rules out the Blake Plateau which is entirely deeper than the arbitrary 300-fathom limit set for shelves in general. North of 28° S. Lat. the shelf narrows to 50 miles in width and continues at about that width for almost 600 miles to the north. All along this portion the inner shelf is steep, whereas terraces occur around 70 fathoms or deeper. It is difficult to determine the exact depth of the shelf break.

Farther north the shelf narrows and virtually pinches out in some places, but approaching the equator it widens again off the mouth of the Congo to about 50 miles. At this point the Congo submarine canyon crosses the entire shelf and enters a deep estuary on the inside. The terraces on this shelf continue to be more than 100 fathoms deep in some places, but the margin adjacent to the Congo submarine canyon is at about 100 fathoms. The sediments are muddy around the Congo mouth but dominantly sandy to the south. To the north the shelf shoals and has a width of 20 to 30 miles as far as the Niger Delta, except where it is bisected by Cape Lopes (1° S. Lat.). Muddy sediments are reported from most of the shelf between the Congo and the Niger.

The shelf off the Niger Delta is virtually unique in conforming with the outer curve of the broadly arcuate delta margin (Fig. 118). The width continues about the same as it is to the south. The inner slope to 5 fathoms is relatively steep but the inner shelf is all shallow. There is some indication of terracing on this shelf at about 15 to 17 fathoms. The outer margin is apparently deeper than to the south, about 50 to 70 fathoms, but because of the gentle slope beyond, it is not easy to be sure of this edge depth at any point. The sediment, as would be expected, is muddy. Extensive sediment collections by R. Allen and Percy Allen have been made and are being studied as this is written.[6] All along this stretch around the Niger Delta the currents set to the east and south.

West of the Niger, the shelf narrows to 20 miles, a condition that continues as far as the Greenwich Meridian. It shows a slight outward

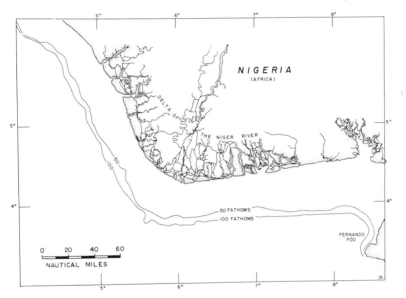

Fig. 118. The outbending of the continental shelf in conformity with the margin of the Niger Delta.

bulge, however, off the Volta Delta. Muddy bottom continues and the edge depth is around 50 fathoms. Here also the inner shelf is shallow. The shelf widens off Ghana to 50 miles but narrows again beyond. West of the Volta Delta the mud bottom is replaced by sandy sediment with some mud. This mixture continues along the Ivory Coast, Liberia, and Sierra Leone, but off Guinea the sand increases and becomes the dominant sediment as far as Cape Verde. Off Guinea the shelf widens to 70 miles and has many minor hills and depressions including submarine valleys in continuity of the drowned coastal valleys. Edge depths are around 50 fathoms with shoal inner portions. The width decreases slightly beyond, and finally is reduced to about 5 miles off Cape Verde. This Cape resembles Cape Hatteras except

[6] A paper has now appeared (Allen and Wells, 1962) describing a group of submerged coral banks around the outer margin of the shelf. This is reminiscent of the banks along the outer shelf of the north Gulf of Mexico and off the Orinoco.

that the 50-meter elevation at the end of the point represents an old volcano that has been tied to the land by a tombolo. The edge shows no outward bend to conform with the Cape, and the latter encroaches over the shoal inner shelf. North of Cape Verde the 50-fathom contour hugs the shore but the shelf widens to 20 miles or more having an outer margin at 70 to 80 fathoms. Around 20° N. Lat. Arguin Bank extends out for 40 miles with shoal soundings where wrecks have occurred. Outside the bank there is another 20 miles or more of normal shelf with depths up to 60 fathoms. North of Cape Blanco the shelf varies from 30 to 50 miles in width and is almost entirely covered with sand up to 29° N. Lat. Farther north the sand hugs the shore with mud outside. At 31° N. Lat. rock and stony bottom notations become abundant especially near the shore, and in places this type of bottom extends across the entire shelf, as for example, in the vicinity of Magador. This shelf has been surveyed recently in great detail by the French. The rocky patches continue as far as Gibraltar. Along this northern portion the width runs close to 20 miles. The shelf edge varies around 100 fathoms.

**Mediterranean Sea.**    The activity of SCUBA divers (Rosfelder, 1955) in various parts of the shelf around the Mediterranean has indicated the widespread presence of beds of Posidonia, a common type of marine grass. These cover much of the zone between 3 and 25 fathoms. Information concerning the character of the sea floor in the Mediterranean is available from the charts of the Deutscher Seewarte made by the Germans during World War II.

A narrow shelf is found from the Strait of Gibraltar along the north coast of Africa almost to the Gulf of Tunis. This area has recently been surveyed by Jacques Cousteau's *Calypso* for Gas de France. The rock and gravel bottom continues around the east side of Morocco Peninsula. Farther east as far as Algeria the shelf is muddy in and around all the embayments but has rock, sand, and gravel off each of the peninsulas. In the vicinity of Oran the shelf is largely sand-covered with many zones of rock. The Gulf of Arzeu has a mud zone on the inner shelf with a belt of sand outside. Beyond, most of the shelf is mud-covered with some rock along the shore. From Dellys to Bone the shelf is mostly quite narrow and very rocky. Beyond Bone the shelf widens, and there are a considerable number of rocky banks along the outside as far as the Straits of Sicily. The Gulf of Tunis is largely mud-covered but wide sand areas are found off the points on either side. The Sicily Strait scarcely exceeds 200 fathoms in depth so that there is essentially a shelf extending from Tunis to Sicily and separating the Mediterranean into two parts. The study of Sicily Straits by expeditions of the *Calypso* (Blanc, 1954) has shown that there are extensive calcareous sands with shells, Bryozoa, and Foraminifera. There is some "hard ground" with ferruginous coatings found on the banks. At the greater depths muds are encountered. South of the straits the shelf widens to as much as 170 miles off the Gulf of Gabes. The shelf edge is rather indefinite but is apparently around 200 fathoms in much of this area. The shelf around the Gulf of Gabes is largely sand, but mud and clay bottom are reported in the deeper water.

Beyond the Gulf of Gabes the shelf continues as a 10- to 20-mile band along the desert coast. The sediments are, as would be expected from the source area, predominantly sand with local rock patches. The first mud appears on the outer shelf at 28° E. Long. and becomes the dominant sediment approaching the Nile although off Alexandria the inner shelf is still sandy, but becomes mostly a sandy mud farther east with mud outside. Mud alone is deposited directly off the Rosetta and Damietta mouths, but sand zones are found at various depths on the outer shelf (d'Arrigo, 1936). The shelf edge curves out around the Nile Delta as off the Niger Delta. The shelf here is relatively steep from the shore to five fathoms, followed by a gentle slope to 15 fathoms, and then somewhat steeper to about 50 fathoms, the shelf break.[7]

The shelf along the coast of Israel has been studied by Rosenan (1937) and Emery and Bentor (1960). Along the shore there is a relatively steep descent to about 10 fathoms. The shelf edge shoals to the north from 65 fathoms to about 40 fathoms, and the flat areas also shoal in that direction. This suggests the influence of the Nile Delta in depressing the southern end. The sediments are largely derived from the Nile although they are patchy as on so many other shelves. In general there is sand near the shore and mud outside, but rock bottom with shells and coral often occurs between the two. Some rock also occurs along the outer shelf. The same type of narrow and mostly mud-covered shelf extends north around Lebanon and hence along the south coast of Turkey.

Shelves continue to be narrow along most of the northern side of the Mediterranean. An exception is the broad shelf extending for 300 miles along the inner portion of the Adriatic Sea and mapped in detail by Captain Debrazzi and Professor Segrè (Fig. 119). This shelf terminates at a depth of slightly more than 100 fathoms, but well inside the edge there is a transverse basin with depths up to 148 fathoms (270 m). This appears to have no continuation into the land on either side and looks like a fault scarp on the north side. Other basins are found along

---

[7] A profile by Dietz and Menard (1951) indicated that there was no shelf break off the Nile, but the charts suggest that this profile may have been atypical.

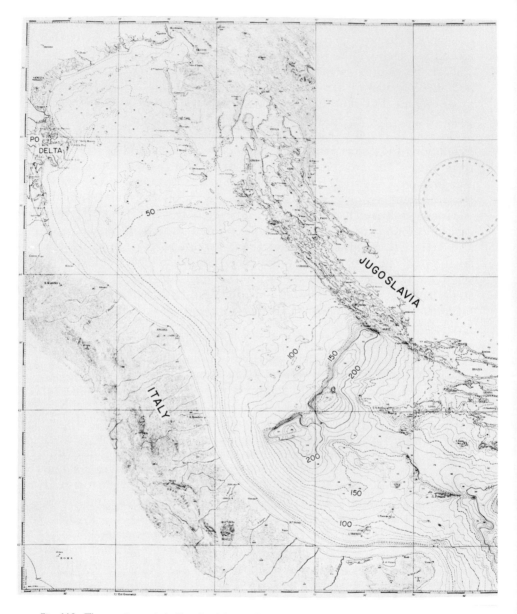

Fig. 119. The continental shelf in the Adriatic Sea. Note the large transverse depression and the deep water along the coast of Jugoslavia. From E. Debrazzi and A. G. Segrè. *Pubblicata dall' Instituto Idrografico della Marina-Genova*, August 1960. Depths in meters.

the bays of the Karst coast of Yugoslavia. The bottom is of hetero-geneous character including large areas of mud along with sand, shells, and rock in various scattered areas. The chief evident source of sediments is the Po Delta entering south of Venice and overlapping onto the inner shelf. Relatively deep water is found along much of the coast of Yugoslavia and along the Italian coast of Abruzzi, in contrast to the gentle slopes off the Po Valley. Off the latter there is a rapid change from sand to mud, but sand occurs again in depths of about 15 fathoms (d'Arrigo, 1936).

The remainder of the Italian peninsula has narrow shelves. The south portion has been mapped by d'Arrigo (1959), and off Naples the shelf has been described by Müller (1958). The narrow shelves con-tinue along the French Riviera and, as Bourcart (1954a, p. 31) has indicated, shelves are missing in some of this area. From the Italian border to Marseille according to Nesteroff (1958, 1959) there are four sediment zones extending out from the shore. These consist of: (1) *terrigenous sand and gravel* along the shore; (2) *Poseidonia beds* (les herbiers) (Fig. 120) between three and 25 fathoms, wherever terrigenous sediments are scarce; (3) *shelly sands* between 15 and 30 fathoms; and (4) *mud* covering almost all the sea floor below 30 fathoms except along portions of canyons. West of Marseille the shelf widens off the Rhone Delta area to 40 miles. It is notable, however, that the shelf edge does not bend out here as off the Nile on the other side of the Mediterranean. The laminations in the foreset beds due to variation in discharge extend to a depth of 40 fathoms quite unlike the Mississippi foresets. The outer shelf, however, is largely covered with mud off the Rhone Delta. Van Straaten (1959a) describes a small delta front platform. The sediments discussed by Kruit (1955), van Andel (1955), and Duboul-Razavet (1956) are sandier than those off the Mississippi. The generalized Carte-Bathy-Lithologique published by Thoulet in 1912 shows the sediment distribution west of the Rhone Delta. Sand follows the shore except off points where rock occurs. The sand-mud boundary is located mostly between 10 and 15 fathoms. A few patches of rock are found on the middle shelf.

Along the Spanish coast the shelf shows several bulges and in-dentations. The latter are found off the mountainous portions of the coast. Off the Ebro Delta and for 60 miles to the south the shelf is about 45 miles across, much wider than along the rest of the east coast of Spain. Muddy zones occur off the Ebro, but gravel is also reported well out on the shelf and a group of islands, Islotes Colum-bretes, is found to the south at the shelf margin.

**Western Europe.** Around the rest of the Iberian Peninsula there are narrow shelves with widths averaging less than 20 miles. In the

Fig. 120. *Poseidonia* beds along the French coast near Nice. The plants
have a height of about two meters. Underwater photo by R. F. Dill.

Gulf of Cádiz there are extensive areas of mud bottom apparently
associated with the large rivers Guadalquivir and Guadiana, but there
are also considerable areas of rock and sand bottom, the latter showing
little relation to distance from the shoreline. Around the Portugese
coast and the north coast of Spain the shelf has large areas of rock
bottom. These are shown in the Carta Litologica Submarina published
by the Portugese Navy. Most of the rest of the shelf is sandy with only
small areas of mud. The shelf edge deepens to the north along the
Portugese and Spanish coasts. To the south it lies at around 90 to 100
fathoms but beyond the Spanish border it deepens to approximately
200 fathoms with some indication of deep terrace levels. To the east
along the north coast of Spain the edge comes back to about 100
fathoms. The shelf is somewhat muddier off the Spanish coast than off
Portugal, but sand and gravel continue to be common at all distances

from land. The irregularity of the outer shelf margin is striking off the relatively straight north coast of Spain.

Along the western coast of France the shelf widens almost continuously to the north and increases from 30 miles off Biarritz to 100 miles off the Loire. This widening is related to the northward widening of the coastal plain on land. The French coast forms a marked contrast with the more mountainous coasts of the Iberian Peninsula. On the shelf rather extensive areas lie around 70 fathoms in depth and the 50-fathom curve is relatively close to the coast especially to the north. The relatively straight shelf margin has depths of around 80 to 100 fathoms. The sediment is a mixture of sand, mud, shells, and gravel with the coarser sediment a little more common on the outer shelf. The samples on the shelves were described by Berthois and Le Calvez (1959). They found thin mud deposits overlying sand. Some of the sands appear to represent a continuation of the wide dune belt of Gascony apparently deposited during glacially lowered sea level. There has been no significant sedimentation on the outer shelf during postglacial times.

The widening of the shelf along the French coast continues off the English Channel and culminates seaward off Lands End where it is 200 miles across. Marginal depths run from about 80 to 110 fathoms. The shoals around Finistère were found to contain migrating underwater dunes related to tides which reach surface velocities of 9 knots (Guilcher, 1959b). The sediments in the Bay of Mont St. Michel (Bourcart and Boillot, 1959) show an increase in grain size offshore and a decrease in calcareous content. The strong tidal currents carry the sediment in from the English Channel. Very great irregularity is found in the area off both the English Channel and the Irish Sea (the Celtic Sea). Rising above an otherwise deep shelf numerous banks trend parallel to the channels on the inside and suggest relations to currents as in the shoals of Georges Bank. The sediments are largely sand, shells, and gravel with very little mud. The banks differ from those of New England and Nova Scotia in having much greater depth, largely 50 to 70 fathoms. Berthois and Le Calvez (1959) suggested that the banks are related to currents during a lower sea level stage. Furthermore, there are no deep troughs on the inside although the elongate Hurd Deep in the English Channel extends more than 30 fathoms below its outer rocky rim. The English Channel has numerous rock outcrops (Dangeard, 1928; King, 1948; Hill and King, 1954). The elongate sand banks in Dover Straits rest on rock outcrops (Van Veen, 1936). The rocks underlying the channel are Paleozoic, Mesozoic, and Tertiary in age. The influence of the tide on the channel is very evident from the elongate banks.

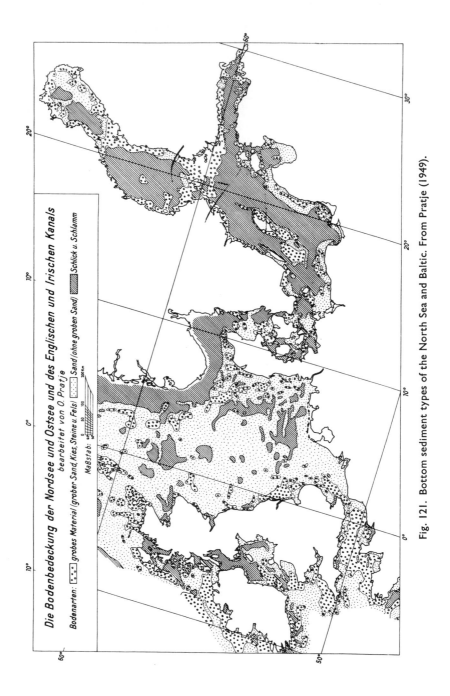

Die Bodenbedeckung der Nordsee und Ostsee und des Englischen und Irischen Kanals
bearbeitet von O. Pratje

Bodenarten: grobes Material (grober Sand, Kies, Steine u. Fels) | Sand (ohne groben Sand) | Schlick u. Schlamm

Maßstab: 0  50  100  200 km

Fig. 121. Bottom sediment types of the North Sea and Baltic. From Pratje (1949).

Along the coast of Ireland and Scotland the open shelf narrows to about 60 miles, although there are in addition various channels inside the islands. The 50-fathom curve hugs the Irish coast but farther out there is a considerable platform with depths of 60 to 70 fathoms, corresponding with a similar platform off western France. Along the coast of Scotland there are indentations with troughs and basins similar to those off other glaciated coasts but not as deep. The general bottom character (Fig. 121) is shown on the map by Pratje (1949), which includes also the North Sea and the Baltic. The most conspicuous feature of the whole area is the scarcity of mud bottom. Sand dominates with extensive gravel deposits.

The North Sea is notable for the elongate banks in the southern portions (Fig. 218) (Stocks, 1956; Jarke, 1956) and the deep trough to the northeast, called the Skagerrak. Some of the banks in the south are asymmetrical and according to Guilcher (1951) have been deformed by the wind waves. The Skagerrak extends around the southern Norwegian coast. The rest of the North Sea shelf is relatively deep with low relief hills and basin depressions. To the south the banks are especially well developed in the approaches to the English Channel and extend along both the Low Countries and the English coasts, but continue farther north along the latter. These banks represent shifting underwater dunes comparable to those of Nantucket Shoals off Cape Cod, Massachusetts. Farther north a more stable shoal, Dogger Bank, an important source of fish, has yielded human artifacts and the remains of Pleistocene mammals. These show that the area was inhabited during the times of glacially lowered sea level, although the southern limit of the Pleistocene glaciers must have been very close. The "Wadden" (tidal estuaries) along the Dutch coast have been extensively studied by van Straaten and Kuenen (1957) and other Dutch geologists. They have shown that the sediments in these embayments are derived largely from the North Sea and that the grain size grows finer toward the heads of the bays with coarser grained material in the channels and fines on the tidal flats and in the marshes. Van Straaten (1951) has compared the minor sedimentary structures developed in these environments with ancient sediments. Farther north along the Danish coast similar Wadden are described by Hansen (1951).

The deep Skagerrak which follows the Norwegian coast is the first of a series of troughs found all along the peninsula (Fig. 122) and very similar to the troughs off other glaciated areas. These have been contoured by O. Holtedahl (1940) and have been discussed more recently by H. Holtedahl (1955, 1959). The shelf off Norway has off-lying banks that are mostly deeper than Georges Bank and the Grand

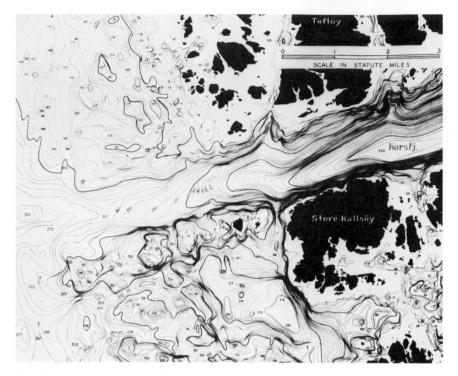

Fig. 122. The outer part of the Carlsfiord depression (southwest of Bergen, Norway). Depths in meters. The location of the center of the figure is Lat. 60°08′ N., Long. 5°00′ E. From Holtedahl (1940, pl. V).

Banks, but they have similar irregularities and the same topographic contrast with the deeper shelves on the inside. The shelves off Norway average about 100 miles in width and more than half of their areas are deeper than 100 fathoms. The sediments (Holtedahl, 1955) are poorly sorted like those of the Gulf of Maine and other glaciated areas.

The Baltic includes some basins over 100 fathoms in depth, but it is mostly shoaler than the typical indentations in glaciated regions. The floor is quite irregular with a considerable number of banks and islands. The northern Baltic Sea was studied by Gripenberg (1934, 1939), Pratje (1948), and Segerstråle (1957). The southern part of the sea and also the German coast have been investigated by Gröba (1953). The German Navy bottom sediment charts made during World War II show many detailed compilations of the bottom character. The general impression received from these charts is of sediment which decreases from sand near shore to mud in the interior of the basins (Fig. 122). There are, however, many exceptions to this

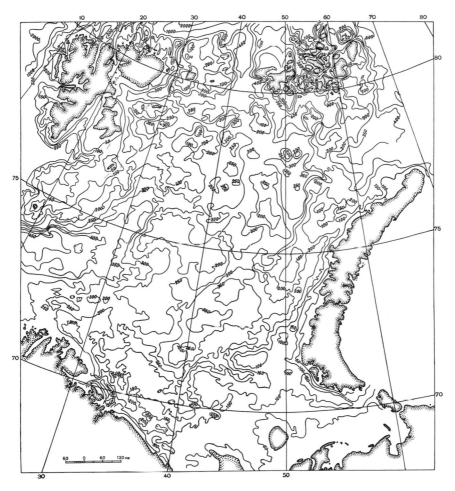

Fig. 123. Submarine contours of the Barents Sea north of Russia. Contours in meters. Basins do not have depression contours. From Klenova (1960a).

rule, and Gripenberg showed that much of the North Baltic has late glacial clays without any cover of recent sediments. These older clays can be recognized by their varved structure in contrast to the homogeneous postglacial clays. Some of the calcareous sediments of the western Baltic are said to be derived directly from the erosion of old limestones.

**The Arctic.**   North of Norway and the adjacent part of the Soviet Union there is a very deep shelf in the Barents Sea area. This is the widest shelf in the world, being over 700 miles across. Most of it is deeper than 100 fathoms but very little exceeds 300 (Fig. 123). Along the north border of the shelf there are two large groups of islands, Norway's Spitsbergen and the Soviet Union's Zemlya Frantsa Iosifa. The Barents Sea has many deep troughs. The sea has been extensively explored by Russian submarine geologists, notably Klenova (1940, 1960a,b). The sediment is largely mud but contains an abundance of stones (Bissett, 1930) as in the other deep areas off glaciated coasts. The Kara Sea on the east side of Novaya Zemlya has a deep trough running along the coast of the island.

East of the Kara Sea the shelf undergoes a marked change. Aside from some deep troughs around the presently glaciated outlying islands of Severnaya Zemlya (100° E. Long.) the Siberian and Alaskan shelf is very flat and largely less than 40 fathoms in depth. Very shallow zones extend out beyond most of the large rivers of northern Siberia. The shelf is decidedly narrower where it is overlapped by Severnaya Zemlya Islands (95° E. Long.), but widens again to about 300 miles off northeastern Siberia, and then narrows in the Chukchi Sea off Alaska to about 50 miles, still maintaining its general flatness. An exception to the flatness is found in the Barrow Sea Valley which penetrates the shelf west of Point Barrow, Alaska. Otherwise the flatness of the shelf north of Bering Straits corresponds with that of the Bering shelf on the south side. According to the fathograms in both places, the shelf appears to be as flat as any from which echo soundings are available. Locally there are, however, small hills about 1 to 2 fathoms high that are found near shore in depths out to about 15 fathoms (Rex, 1955), and other hills found at greater depth on the side of the shelf sea valleys (Carsola, 1954c).

The sediments of the Chukchi Sea (Carsola, 1954a) are dominantly mud, apparently related to the MacKenzie River. Along with the mud is an abundance of sand and gravel, apparently rafted into the sea by drift ice. This mixing produces a bimodal sediment, characteristic of all high-latitude shelves off both glaciated and unglaciated areas. The brown color of the Chukchi sediments suggests oxidizing conditions of deposition. Decomposable organic material is present to the extent of about 1.5 to 2.0 percent. These sediments appear to be similar to those described by Böggild (1916) for the northeast Siberian shelf.

At the eastern end of the Beaufort Sea some deep troughs appear and farther east all the glaciated lands are cut up into islands and deep troughs similar to those off virtually all other glaciated territory. As far as known the depth of the passageways between the islands is no greater than those around Norway and Newfoundland. Hudson Bay seems to be very much the same sort of deep basin. Not much is known about the sediments of these embayments nor of the irregular continental shelves on the outside. There are, however, indications that stones are found along with finer material in Hudson Bay.

**Antarctica.**     As this edition was being written a vast amount of new information was being analyzed from the many explorations of Antarctica during the International Geophysical Year. The results published to date have strengthened the previous indications that the shelves around Antarctica (Zhivago, 1959; Lisitzin and Zhivago, 1960) are unusually deep, even right next to the ice barrier where depths of several hundred fathoms are found. Near the continent there are depressions probably like those off other glaciated land masses, some of them running parallel to the coast. Along some of the outer shelf inside the break in slope there has been discovered a flat area locally around 300 fathoms in depth. According to Zhivago, moraines can be traced along the shelf showing a more northerly stand of the ice. It seems likely that this is the deepest shelf in the world and, in fact, much of it may be too deep to be classified as a shelf at all. Poorly sorted sediments have been found on this shelf similar to those in other glaciated territories except that they still are being deposited by icebergs in this area.

**Insular Shelves.**     The platforms bordering oceanic islands have been appropriately termed insular shelves. Such shelves do not exist around all oceanic islands but at least narrow platforms are found commonly. The widest insular shelves are shallow banks found in the tropics. Many are covered with coral, partly grown up to or near the surface. Some of the insular shelves show very good terraces, in part extending well below the typical terrace levels of the continental shelves. The insular shelves around Iceland are crossed by troughs similar to those off other glaciated areas.

The islands lacking shelves include many of those which have had recent volcanic activity, and many of those where coral reefs are growing actively, notably around atolls. The island of Hawaii with its active volcanoes is almost entirely free of marginal platforms.

**Shelves in Landlocked Bodies of Water.**     The description of submerged shelves would not be complete without consideration of the deep landlocked bodies of water within the continents. Of these the Great Lakes have been most extensively sounded (Hough, 1958). A study of the Great Lakes charts shows that they virtually lack shelves. Johnson (1919, Figs. 201–204) has presented a series of profiles off the shores of Lake Michigan. It is notable that these profiles do not show benches even off wave-cut cliffs which are retreating rapidly at the present time.

Charts are available from some of the large glacially excavated lakes in the Alps. The soundings show that the lake margins are for the most part precipitous, lacking shelves. Off the deltas of some large rivers there are shallow platforms of moderate width.

The Caspian, a large inland sea, has been charted and investigated by the Russians (Klenova, 1956). At the northern end off the Volga Delta the Russian charts show an extensive shelf with very shallow water. On the other hand, shelves appear to be narrow or missing around the remainder of this inland sea.

The Black Sea is connected to the ocean by a shallow passage only 30 fathoms deep. This sea is of special interest in the shelf study since it is a deep sea and has a shelf around most of its margin. The shelf is very wide in the bight near Odessa, having a maximum width of about 120 miles. This wide area is related to the delta of the Danube, which enters on the western side of the bight. The shelf depths appear to be entirely less than 50 fathoms. The Black Sea shelves, however, are inconspicuous except in the Gulf of Odessa. Most of the others do not exceed 5 or 10 miles in width, according to available soundings. Unlike most shelves off large rivers in the open ocean, the shelf off the Danube is reported as having sand and sandy mud near shore, and mud on the outside. The same indication of decrease of grain size away from the shore is found on the shelves around much of the remainder of the Black Sea.

## Summary of Shelf Topography

It should not have been necessary to complete the preceding *tour du monde* to have learned that the old concept of nicely graded continental shelves extending out to a so-called wave base belongs in a museum for antiquities. The profile of equilibrium, with its gentle concavity near shore and convexity outside, may apply reasonably well to the beach and the shallow water along the shore but has little relation to the shelves as a whole. Instead, one is confronted with extremely variable features, including an abundance of terraces, hills, and depressions. There are some localities where the shelf slopes out evenly from the shore to its outer edge, but a study of areas with closely spaced shelf soundings shows that these are very exceptional. Cross sections constructed from a few widely spaced soundings connected by straight lines may give the illusion of an even slope, where in actuality there are all sorts of intervening hills and valleys. On the other hand, even though the bulk of the shelves are sparsely sounded, they provide abundant evidence of irregularities.

Statistical averages of such a variable feature as the continental shelf should be used with caution in the search for causes, although it may be helpful to have a few averages for the record. The following figures were compiled in preparation of the first edition from contoured charts and profiles obtained from thousands of charts covering all parts of the world, using measurements for each 10 miles along the shelf.[8]

1. The continental shelf has an average width of 40 nautical miles.
2. The average depth at which the greatest change of slope occurs at the shelf margin is 72 fathoms.
3. The average depth of the flattest portion of the shelves is about 35 fathoms.
4. Hills with a relief of 10 fathoms or more were found in about 60 percent of profiles crossing the shelves.
5. Depressions, 10 fathoms or more in depth, were indicated in 35 percent of the same profiles. Many of these are basins, but others may represent longitudinal valleys.
6. The average slope is 0°07′, being somewhat steeper in the inner than in the outer half.

**Shelf Marginal Depths in Relation to Width.**  A comparison of the depth of the shelf margin with groups of shelf widths gives some interesting information. The narrowest shelves (0 to 25 miles wide) have somewhat shoaler terminations than those of greater width, but the difference is not striking and there is no progressive deepening in the 25- to 50-, 50- to 75-, and 75- to·100-mile groups. Many of the narrow shelves with shoal margins are found in regions of active coral growth. Omitting these cases, no marked relation between width and depth is found. South of the glaciated areas the shelves off the west coast of the United States are, on the average, slightly deeper than those on the east coast. This may seem surprising since generally it has been supposed that the west coast is rising, whereas the east coast is subsiding. In some cases a local narrowing of a shelf is accompanied by shoaling. For example, where the Mississippi Delta encroaches onto the shelf in the Gulf of Mexico, the uncovered portions directly adjacent to the delta are shoaler than the areas to the east and west, respectively. The same shoaling is found adjacent to the great cuspate foreland of Cape Hatteras.

**Shelf Marginal Depths in Relation to Exposure to Storm Waves.** Attention has been called to the greater depth of the shelf on the exposed east side of Madagascar than exists on the west side.[9] Since this has led to some generalizations, it is important to see whether the same depth relation holds true for the shelves in general. We have

---

[8] It is to be hoped that some investigator will make a new compilation from more up-to-date sources.

[9] According to André Guilcher (personal communication) this is the result of down-faulting on the east.

already found various factors which seem to control the depth of the shelves, such as relation to glaciation, to coral growth, and to mouths of large rivers. Many other influences, such as earth movements and resistance of rocks to erosion, also confuse the picture so that it is difficult to form any opinion relative to exposure to waves. However, evidence could be provided by tracing shelves along unglaciated and supposedly stable coasts, where neither rivers nor coral appear to be important. To complete the case it is also necessary to cross from a storm belt to a zone of small surf. There are few such places but Southwest Africa appears to represent the best case. At the south end where storms are particularly severe we find a deep shelf. However, proceeding northward to where the southerly storm winds cease and the waves are much smaller, we find the shelf is far deeper than the average for the world. This finding suggests that diastrophism is more important than wave erosion even in a supposedly stable area such as South Africa. Another test is provided by the Island of Santa Catalina off southern California, which apparently lacks the elevated wave-cut terraces of all the other islands (Lawson, 1897; Shepard et al., 1939) and has narrow insular shelves on both the exposed southwest side and the protected east side. These shelves have marginal depths of about 50 fathoms on both sides (Shepard and Wrath, 1937) so that here again we can find little indication of the importance of wave exposure in determining the level of the shelf margin.

Another attack on this same problem comes from comparing the marginal depths off coasts with prevailing onshore winds to those off coasts with prevailing offshore winds.[10] It was found that the median depth for windward coasts was 59.2 fathoms and for leeward coasts was 72 fathoms. Obviously, other factors than wind direction are involved, and we have no evidence that shelf edges are deeper where waves are high.

### Summary of Shelf Sediments

The description of the bottom materials found on the shelves of the world should provide no particular surprise to anyone who has followed the literature of the past twenty-five years relative to marine sediments (see particularly *Recent Marine Sediments*, 1939). However, the idea that sediments grade outward across the shelf with coarse near shore and fine at the outer edge has become so much of a geological dogma, that it has been slow to yield ground. A perusal of the descriptive part of this chapter will show how far from the truth is this

[10] Since glaciation has been shown to have such an important bearing on marginal depths, the glaciated shelves were left out of these averages.

generalization. It is certainly the exceptional area which provides evidence of the supposed outward decreasing gradation of sediment texture. The actual picture which comes from both chart notations and from the collection and analysis of shelf samples is that of irregularly distributed sediment zones which show little relation either to depths of water or distance from the shore. The colored bottom sediment charts have a mass of irregular patches suggestive of the splashes of color on some of the worst of the modern paintings.

Another commonly expressed opinion of the shelf has been that it represents the top of an encroaching sediment mass, building out over the deep ocean floor. However, the occurrence of rock bottom in so many places on the outer shelf should prove somewhat disconcerting to those holding such views. Also, the presence of gravel and coarse sand on the outer shelf in places where there are fine materials inside requires an explanation.

The finding of the irregular sediment distribution and the rocky bottom or coarse sediment on the outer shelves may serve as a means of dispelling old notions relative to shelf genesis, but these observations by themselves are not very helpful in developing new hypotheses. The next step, therefore, is to look for some relations which may bring order out of the apparent chaos. Considerable encouragement in this undertaking comes from comparison of bottom types with elements of the genetic coastal classifications of Chapter VI. Also, the nature of the bottom relief on the shelf has a marked relation to the sediment types and more particularly to rock bottom. Furthermore, the bottom types have some relation to indications of current strength shown by the arrows on many of the charts. Finally, a marked change in sediment distribution is found between the open shelves and enclosed shelf seas. All generalizations which come from these relationships have exceptions, but often these can be explained by the interaction of several different influences.

# CHAPTER IX

# ORIGIN AND HISTORY OF THE CONTINENTAL SHELVES

In Chapter VIII the continental shelves were described with little attention to the origin of the characteristics which were portrayed. The information is still rather scarce, but it provides a basis for discussing the problem of shelf origin. First, however, it seems advisable to classify the shelf types as far as is possible from available information.

**Shelf Classification**

It might be supposed that an important item in shelf classification would be the emergence or submergence involved in the shelf history. As in the case of the classification of shorelines, however, dividing shelves into emerged and submerged categories provides many difficulties. In fact, there seems to be little indication that coasts with drowned valleys have more deeply submerged shelves than are found off coasts with prominent elevated marine terraces. Again the effects of low sea level during the Pleistocene and the recency of the rise in sea level at the end of the last glacial stage (Wisconsin, Würm) have confused the situation so that other types of subdivision seem necessary. Despite the difficulties involved in diagnosing submergence and emergence, an adequate classification requires some consideration of the recent history of the area along with a knowledge of the processes operating on the shelf now and during the Pleistocene.

**Shelves Bordering Glaciated Land Masses.**   The most distinctive and clear-cut shelf type is found off most of the glaciated lands of the world. These shelves are generally wide, and they contain deep basins and troughs where the water depths commonly exceed 100 fathoms. These deeps trend both parallel to the coasts and transverse to them. In most cases the transverse troughs of the open shelf connect with fiords extending for many miles into the land masses and containing depths at least as great as any of those found on the adjacent open shelf. Most of these troughs which cut across the shelves have shoaler water near their outer margin than inside. There are numerous banks extending along the outer portions of this type of shelf. Some of the banks rise to where they form dangerous shoals or even islands. None of these outer banks is known definitely to have rock ledges, although rocky knobs are common on the inner shelves.

The sediments in the basins and troughs are unique in having a mixture of muddy sediments along with a scattering of coarse debris including gravel up to boulder size. The banks are largely covered with sand but also have coarse sediment including boulders.

**Shelves with Parallel Sand Ridges and Troughs.**  Almost all the shelves which lie off unglaciated land masses are smoother than those off glaciated. There are, however, many departures from complete smoothness, and few shelves have what is often referred to as a "profile of equilibrium," that is, a concavo-convex but continuous outward slope from coast to shelf break. Among the irregularities recognized on many shelves are elongate sand banks. On the inner shelf these extend roughly parallel to the shore and on the outer shelf parallel to the shelf margin. These banks rise only a few fathoms above the general shelf level, and in some places there are shallow troughs or basins between successive sand banks.

**Smooth High-Latitude Shelves.**  So far as can be told from presently available fathograms, the smoothest of all continental shelves are found in high northern latitudes off land masses that were not glaciated (Carsola, 1954a; Carsola *et al.*, 1961). Only very minor irregularities, related to grounded sea ice, are reported (Rex, 1955). Most of these shelves have shoaler depths than the average for shelves in general.

**Shelves Associated with Strong Currents.**  There are various coasts along which the permanent oceanic currents flow. It is notable that almost all the zones where these currents are particularly concentrated are also areas where the shelves are narrow or missing. As noted previously, Florida, a low flat area, has a broad shelf on the west and virtually no shelf on the south and southeast. The shelf is also inconspicuous off Cape Hatteras. Along these shelfless areas the Gulf Stream impinges with speeds commonly attaining 3 knots and often 4 to 6 knots at the surface (Stommel, 1958). The same situation may exist in Yucatan where a stronger current impinges on the east side than on the west and north, and where no shelf is present on the east, in contrast to the wide shelf on the west. Yucatan is also a low, flat land, but has more relief than Florida. In each of these cases the slope adjacent to the shore descends to depths excessive for a shelf but not as great as those of the ocean basins. Off eastern Florida this intermediate depth area (Blake Plateau, discussed in Chapter X) terminates outwardly with an escarpment which is in line with the edge of

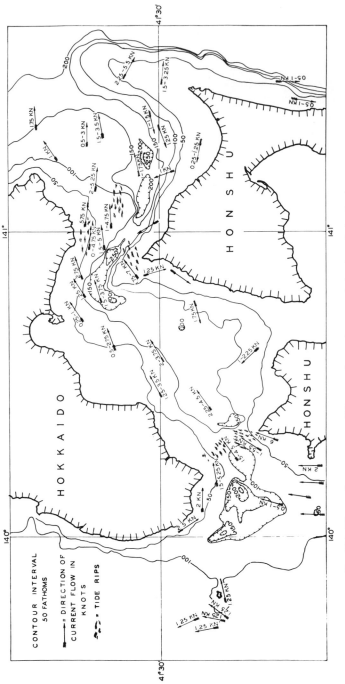

Fig. 124. The surface currents of Tsugaru Strait, Japan, and the deep holes in the two narrows.

the continental shelf north of Cape Hatteras. Most of the narrow shelves associated with strong currents have either rock bottom or coarse sediment and water-worn shells along with authigenic minerals, particularly glauconite and phosphatized gravel-sized particles.

**Current Effects at Bay Entrances.**    Aside from the deeps associated with glaciated coasts the most remarkable relief on the inner continental shelves is found at narrow entrances to bays. Charts show that wherever there are sizeable bays separated from the ocean by narrow straits, deep holes exist either in the narrows or directly adjacent to them. In the entrance to San Francisco Bay (Fig. 113) the bottom attains a depth of 64 fathoms with a sill of 10 fathoms outside and a rock sill at about 25 fathoms. Even more pronounced bottom depressions are found at the Pacific entrances to the Inland Sea of Japan. In Bungo Strait, the southern entrance to this sea, there are depths of as much as 228 fathoms (Fig. 114). So far as can be told from the bottom character notations, this deep hole has a rock rim on the outside at depths of 78 fathoms. Along the east coast of South America the narrow entrance to Rio de Janeiro has a depression with a depth of 26 fathoms and a sill of 8 fathoms, and Bahia Nueva in southern Argentina also has a depression, with 95 fathoms inside a narrow entrance having a sill of 28 fathoms. All these localities are associated with strong tidal currents. The deep depressions in Tsugaru Strait (Fig. 124) are also associated with strong currents, in this case a combination of tidal and permanent oceanic currents.

Outside the Golden Gate there is a lunate sand bar which rises to within about 5 fathoms of the surface (Fig. 113). Bars of this type exist off various bottleneck bay entrances, excellent examples being found along the west coast of North Island, New Zealand. They seem to be clearly related to the deeps within the narrows. They are found also off river and estuary mouths, such as the Columbia River. Smaller asymmetrical dunelike features are found on the bottom on either side of a tidal scoured basin in the entrance to San Diego Bay (R. F. Dill, personal communication).

**Shelves Bordering Large Deltas.**    Most continental shelves bordering large deltas are very wide despite encroachment onto the shelves resulting from delta building. The delta front shelves have many flat terraces that extend to depths of at least 50 fathoms (Fig. 117). Almost all the shelves off deltas have muddy sediments along the coast and sandy sediments on the outer portion of the shelf. The muddy sediments along the shore are unusually high in wood fibers, mica, and iron-stained aggregates. On the other hand, organisms are less numerous than off other types of coasts.

**Shelves in Clear Tropical Seas.** In virtually all portions of the tropics where the water is not clouded by the entrance of nearby rivers, coral or algal reefs rise above the general shelf level and often constitute dangerous shoals. In many places these reefs are found on the outer shelf with a navigable channel inside along the coast.

**Narrow Shelves with Rocky Banks Outside.** Off many mountain ranges there are narrow shelves with rock banks rising above the general level. The dredging of these banks has shown that the rock is of various ages, although largely Tertiary. In some places the sediments found on the inner shelves are known to be thick.

## Origin of the Continental Shelves

**Earlier Suggestion.** The classical hypothesis that the continental shelves represent a combination of wave-cut and wave-built terraces related to present conditions (Fig. 125a) does not fit the facts which we have reviewed in this and the previous chapter. If such outbuilding had been general, the outer shelves should be underlain by thick masses of fine sediment, but we find extensive areas of rock bottom on the outer shelves, especially at the shelf margins. Furthermore, if this simple explanation were correct, it would be difficult to account for the fact that the outer shelf depths are not related to the wave heights of the area. Nor do the sediments show the expected gradation outward from coarse to fine that would be anticipated under the wave-cut, wave-built terrace hypothesis. It is only a rare stretch of shelf where the topography and sediments are at all compatible with such an origin. Possibly the shelves off the Niger and Nile deltas, where the shelf margin curves outward in conformity with the front of the delta (Fig. 118), may represent wave-built terraces, but even here it would seem more likely that we are dealing with slightly submerged deltas rather than with wave-built terraces.

The shortcomings of the wave-built embankment idea are considered further in the chapters on the continental slopes and submarine canyons.

**Effect of Glacially Lowered Sea Levels.** There can be no doubt but what the lowered sea levels resulting from continental glaciation must have been tremendously important in developing the continental shelves. It is a basic principle of geology that erosion and depositional processes seek to bring land levels either down to or up to sea level. It seems probable that the amount of sea level lowering during maximum glaciation was of the order of 60 to 90 fathoms. This is based on the following information:

1. The average marginal depths are about 72 fathoms and in view of the unlikelihood of wave-built terraces and thinness of modern

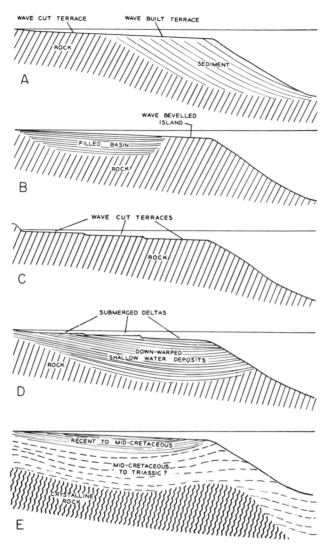

Fig. 125. Several modes of origin for continental shelves.

sediments these may well represent approximate lowest sea level. If warping movements are neglected, some of the margins would be slightly lower because of wave erosion in the surf zone and others slightly higher because of postglacial deposition.

2. Many borings along coasts have shown that valleys extend to depths of 60 to 100 m (33 to 50 fathoms) below sea level. Allowing for valley slope in crossing the shelf, this would suggest that the low sea level was somewhat more than 50 fathoms below the present.

3. The use of an acoustic probe off the east coast of the United States (Ewing *et al.*, 1960b) showed the presence of a broad terrace with depths of 80 fathoms that cut across the dipping formations of the outer shelf. This is in a relatively stable area and is also in rather close agreement with the marginal average.

4. Almost all studies of glaciated areas have shown that the ice extended farther and was thicker than had been supposed in deriving the basis for the 100-m (55 fathoms) estimates of lowering (Flint, 1957). The margins clearly crossed the greater part of the wide shelves off glaciated areas including Antarctica (Thomas, 1960).

5. The thickness of the ice may have been considerably greater than estimated judging from the amount of postglacial rebound, such as 220 m for Canadian Arctic islands in the past 7500–9000 years (Donn *et al.*, 1962).

There are reasons to believe that the low levels had a duration of many thousands of years (Emiliani, 1955; Ericson and Wollin, 1956). This being the case most portions of the continents that were surrounded by soft rocks or unconsolidated sediments must have had terraces cut into the margins at the low levels. Contemporaneously, streams were reducing the neighboring lands toward the temporary base level. Furthermore, large rivers must have produced deltas at elevations corresponding to the low stands.

As Dietz and Menard (1951) have demonstrated, most of the energy of wave erosion is exerted within a score of feet of sea level so that all but the shoalest wave-cut terraces of the continental shelf must have been produced by wave erosion when the sea stood lower or alternately the land higher.

The chief evidence for effective erosion during a glacially lowered sea level is a rather general uniformity of the depth at the shelf break. In most well-surveyed areas this break is found near 70 to 80 fathoms. This must indicate first that the sea stood for a considerable period at this low level and, second, that most shelves including those of much of the unstable Pacific coasts have not undergone large vertical movements since the glacial period when the sea level was lower. The shelf margins around 50 fathoms off southern California might imply 20 fathoms of uplift, but the shelves off northern California have marginal depths close to the world average, and off Oregon and Washington the margins are deeper than average. Off part of eastern United States the discovery of a broad wave-cut platform at about 80 fathoms (Ewing *et al.*, 1960b) indicates general stability or possibly a minor subsidence.

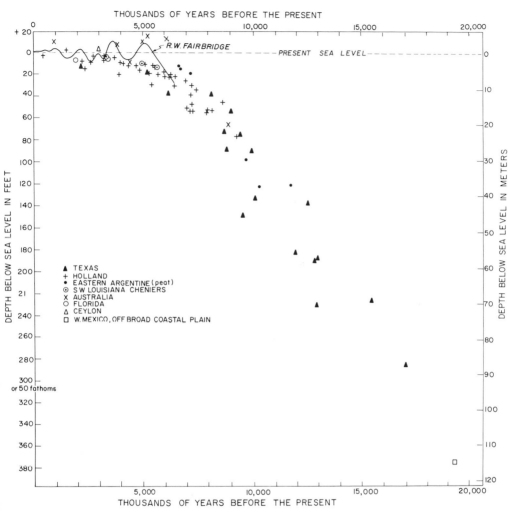

Fig. 126. Chronology of sea level rise in the last 19,000 years shown by carbon-14 dates on peat and nearshore types of shells. These were all obtained in stable areas where earth movements can probably be considered negligible during the period involved. The Australian dates form an anomaly suggesting possible instability, but the most recent work suggests that some or all of these dates are based on kitchen middens.

**Time Table of Rising Sea Level.**    One of the results of the extensive shelf and bay studies along the Texas coast has been the establishment of a tentative time table of sea level rise at the end of the glacial period (Curray, 1960; Shepard, 1960c). Samples collected from various parts of the shelf and from cores drilled into the bays have yielded shells of shallow-water or estuarine organisms. When these have been subjected to carbon-14 tests they have yielded a chronology of the sea level rise (Fig. 126). Since these dates fit nicely with most dates from other relatively stable areas of the world (Jelgersma and Pannekoek, 1960; Godwin *et al.*, 1958), it can be assumed that this actually shows the sea level rise rather than a downwarping movement of the Texas shelf. The rapid rise from 17,000 to 7000 years before the present seems well established. The slow rise which seems to have followed is disputed by other workers who believe either in a stillstand for the past 3000 to 5000 years (Gould and McFarlan, 1959; Fisk, 1959) or considerable up and down movement during the past 6000 years, including several stands higher than the present (Fairbridge, 1958, 1960, 1961). Most or all of the evidence for a postglacial higher stand comes from the stable Australian block or from coasts known to be unstable. The Australian evidence is thrown into doubt by finding dates for the 12-ft terrace of respectively 900 years, 2000, 4000, 6000, and more than 25,000 years. The reality of a stand at plus 12 or even plus 5 ft in postglacial times has yet to be proved.[1]

**Terrace Levels on the Shelf.**   Various suggestions have been made of stillstands during the sea level rise which would produce terraces and flat-topped banks (Shepard and Wrath, 1937; Heezen, 1959a; Emery, 1958a; Parker and Curray, 1956; Ewing *et al.*, 1960b). The only one of these levels which is represented widely on the shelves of the world is found at about 10 fathoms. This terrace is also clearly evident on the topography both inside and outside several of the Marshall Islands coral reefs (Emery *et al.*, 1954, pp. 50, 95). This level seems to represent a time when glaciers stopped retreating and may have even slightly readvanced, causing temporary slight lowering of the sea level (Curray, 1960).

**Glacial Erosion Versus Faulting off Glaciated Territory.**   Glaciation appears to have had a more direct role in shaping the shelves off glaciated territory. The fact that virtually all the shelves off glaciated lands have deep troughs and basins not found elsewhere strongly suggests that glaciers from the lands moved across them, dug into the soft rock formations and sediments, and produced depressions like those resulting from glaciation on land. There would be no reason for glaciers to stop at the present sea coasts. The sea was lower during glaciation, but even if it had not been, the ice could have moved out over the shelf reaching bottom as soon as it had a thickness of about 1.1 times the water depth. Much of the ice in Antarctica is resting on land below sea level. The banks off the various glaciated coasts are equally easy to explain since the eroded portions must have been dumped at the margins of the ice. It is not unlikely that some banks represent ploughed up portions of the sea floor just as portions of

[1] The 12- and 5-foot terraces in Oahu have proved to be from 24,000 to 32,000 years in age.

Martha's Vineyard Island off the Massachusetts coast are due to the glacial scooping of soft sediments, forming ridges instead of true moraines. Possibly the thick orthoquartzite sand of Georges Bank shown by the boring at the site of the Texas Towers (J. M. Zeigler, personal communication) can be explained in part in this way, representing ploughed up Tertiary sand.

In the early days of geology it was commonplace to explain breaks in slope on land as fault scarps. In geological studies of lands such interpretations are now confined to cases where substantiating evidence exists, but the fault scarp origin is still resorted to by geologists in the interpretation of the continental shelf off glaciated areas. Examples include the Bay of Fundy (Johnson, 1925, pp. 204–296; Koons, 1941), the Gulf of St. Lawrence (Keith, 1930; Hodgson, 1930), the Norwegian shelf (O. Holtedahl, 1950; H. Holtedahl, 1955, 1958, 1959), and the shelf around Antarctica (Lisitzin and Zhivago, 1960). After Olaf Holtedahl had described the shelf scarps off Norway, which he considered as faults, Hans Holtedahl marshalled evidence to show that the same features exist off Laborador and British Columbia. Hans Holtedahl was impressed by the fact that many of the troughs extend parallel to the land rather than cutting across the shelf. Although he appreciated that there had been glacial erosion, he thought that glaciation would have cut troughs across the shelf rather than along it. However, an examination of the trends of the basins now occupied by lakes and of the fiords in glaciated areas seems to indicate that glacial ice does not always move directly out from glacial centers. As Bretz (1935) observed around Greenland, some of the present ice tongues are moving at right angles to the general front of the ice. In fact, there is not much reason to believe that glaciers should act very differently from rivers in choosing their valleys. The latter cut valleys in soft formations with little relation to their trend.

Further evidence against fault origin of the shelf troughs and escarpments is the failure of geologists to report any recent tectonic activity on land in the adjacent areas of Norway and Laborador. It would be surprising if the faulting was limited to the sea floor. On the other hand, there is no proof that at least some of the troughs are not of fault origin, and it may be that a special type of diastrophic activity has resulted from the recovery of the earth's crust from the weight of the ice. It is perhaps more likely that the margins of some of the troughs are related to old fault lines.

**Sand Ridge Shelves Versus the Smooth High-Latitude Shelves.**   The reason that many shelves in intermediate latitudes have low sand ridges, whereas unglaciated high latitude shelves are usually very flat, may hinge on the effects of glacial stages. Just as barrier islands are now forming along many coasts where the waves build up sand ridges, so also barrier islands may have formed on the deeper portions of the shelves during the glacial stage low stands of the sea. One might question whether such sand ridges could be preserved as the sea rose, but evidently many of them have been preserved since the sands in the ridges appear to be of the barrier type (Curray, 1960, pp. 256, 264; Shepard, 1960b), and the shells found on the inside are not uncommonly lagoonal resembling the shells in the bays inside the present barriers.

In the high latitudes, where the shelf was not plowed up by glaciation, the lowered sea level conditions might not have been favorable for developing barriers because of continuous sea ice present along the coasts. This would have prevented the development of waves and also may have prevented the formation of barriers by floating ice being pushed against the shore. It would appear that these flat Arctic shelves raise another argument against the hypothesis of an ice-free Arctic during glacial stages, claimed by Ewing and Donn (1956, 1958).[2] If the seas were ice-free, barriers should have formed ridges on what is now the outer shelf.

**Narrow Shelves Due to Wave Erosion.** The terraces which are found incised into the slopes of many coastal hills and mountain ranges are explained as the work of wave erosion prior to uplift. There are also many wave-cut rock benches exposed at low tide (Fig. 127). Other terraces of this sort can be seen by swimming with SCUBA equipment beyond the base of sea cliffs. Still other terraces have been exposed by sonoprobe profiles (Moore, 1960; Ewing et al., 1960b). The seaward extent of these terraces is indicated in many areas by kelp beds, since these plants usually grow only on rocks.[3] So far as is known, the terraces do not extend for many miles into the ocean without a break in slope. Those cut in rock are largely confined to relatively weak rocks. Coasts with resistant rocks, like granite, are not ordinarily bordered by rock terraces. Since the widening of the bench and the shoaling of the bottom outside the coast would impede wave erosion, the cutting into any type of rock coast would be most rapid in the early stages. Therefore, oscillations of level, either of sea or land, increase the rate of shelf cutting. The rate of erosion in soft rock is not well known. Comparison of old pictures with the present

[2] Other objections are given by Livingstone (1959) and Ericson and Wollin (1959). These are partly answered by Ewing and Donn (1959).

[3] These rocks are known to include boulders, so that they are not necessarily indicative of bedrock. According to J. R. Curray and R. F. Dill, kelp may also grow on top of dead kelp as the sediment buries the bedrock on which older kelp was growing. Thus the rock may not occur directly under the kelp bed.

Fig. 127. A wave-cut bench cut across inclined layers of Eocene rock at La Jolla, California. Photograph taken during a low spring tide.

coast shows very little change in many places (Shepard and Grant, 1947). Elsewhere rather large points have disappeared (Johnson, 1925, Fig. 152).

Where the shore formations are unconsolidated, the erosion benches appear to take a rather different form. Evidence regarding this point comes from Cape Cod, Massachusetts. The outer cape lies next to one of the deep areas which characterize shelves off glaciated areas. Erosion has been cutting into this coast at an average rate of 3.2 ft per year (Johnson, 1925, p. 400). Because this erosion has presumably been at least as fast since the sea reached almost its present level, about 6000 years ago, we might expect to find a terrace of about 4 miles width off the exposed east side of the Cape. Figure 128a shows that there is actually no terrace at all, but the slope continues seaward to the glacial trough below without any appreciable interruption. This case, however, may not be typical because strong currents are known to exist along the entire coast, and these currents may have prevented the terracing of the slope beyond the retreating coast.

An area north of Point La Jolla, southern California, illustrated in Fig. 128b, lacks strong longshore currents. Here the 20-ft-high cliffs of alluvium were being eroded at a rate of about 1 ft per year from 1918 to about 1945 when, for various reasons, erosion virtually ceased. Therefore, we might anticipate finding a much wider terrace here than that off nearby weak rock cliffs. Actually, no terrace is found and the slope of this area (Fig. 128b) is at about the same angle and as continuous as off Cape Cod. The outer edge of this incline has a depth of

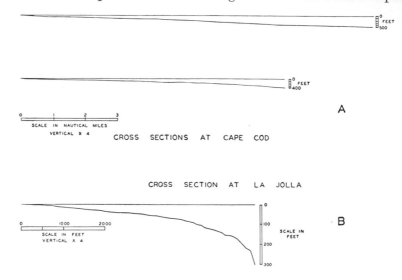

Fig. 128. (a) Profiles off outer Cape Cod where wave erosion has cut into the fluvio-glacial cliffs at about 3 ft per year for the past century. Note absence of wave-cut terrace. (b) Profile off La Jolla, California, just south of Scripps Institution, where the waves have been cutting back the alluvial cliffs at about 1 ft per year except for a recent cessation. The gentle slope terminates outwardly with a steep descent into a submarine canyon.

30 fathoms where it intersects the precipitous wall of a submarine canyon. Other cases show similarly even slopes. One can conclude, therefore, that sloping terraces are cut rapidly into unconsolidated formations and that much gentler terraces are cut more slowly across weak rocks.

What happens to resistant rocks is less certain. There are numerous places along glaciated coasts where granites with striated surfaces extend right down to sea level, indicating the absence of appreciable marine erosion at these places after the sea level reached approximately its present stand. The small amount of postglacial cliffing in the crystalline rocks of New England has been stressed by Johnson (1925, Chapter VI). Old photographs show a decided absence of cutting along other exposed hard rock coasts. Certainly, bench cutting in hard rocks is an extremely slow process, and it can be doubted if the continental shelves owe much of their formation to such processes. It may be significant, however, that most dredgings on the continental shelves have yielded weak rather than resistant rocks.

**Marine Terrigenous Deposition.** We have seen that there are vast areas where deposition on the shelf is inhibited apparently by currents which keep the fine sediment in transit. The outer edge of the shelf is in general a place where deposition is negligible. Relatively fast deposition occurs locally on central or inner shelves and in broad inner shelf basins where the sediments are dominantly silt or silt and clay. This is well illustrated by sub-bottom acoustic reflection studies off California (Moore, 1960). Some of the basins, such as those off southern California, are too deep to be properly included with the shelves, but in time they may become filled so that a broad shelf may develop in these areas, particularly if the outlying islands are reduced by waves to below sea level (Fig. 125b). This process can be considered as cause for the formation of many of the existing shelves.

The building of a shelf upward toward sea level by general deposition can occur only where deposition exceeds removal. This condition appears to be common on the central or inner shelves, but somewhat unusual on the outer shelves. Wherever such deposition is proceeding, a general outward graded slope should be found, and there should be a gradation from coarse sediment inside to fine outside. There are few shelf areas where such conditions exist across the entire shelf, but gradations across zones of active deposition are not uncommon.

**Delta Deposition.** Although delta deposition takes place both on the sea floor and subaerially, there seems to be little doubt that the net effect of the deposition is to build out the land. However, the delta investigations of Russell (1936, p. 162) in Louisiana and the history of other deltas show that these surfaces have a tendency to subside. How much this subsidence is due to a weighting of the earth's crust by deposition, how much to compaction and squeezing out of the underlying sediments, and how much to diastrophism is uncertain, but the subsidence is well established. Accordingly, the shallow flat surfaces in the vicinity of deltas or off large rivers without deltas may be explained as submerged delta flats. The deeper flat surfaces may represent either deltas that have undergone large sinking movements or the deltas of the glacial stages when the sea level was lower than it is at present.

We have learned that shelves near the mouths of large rivers are considerably wider than the average, despite the overlap resulting from delta deposition. If this width were due largely to the building

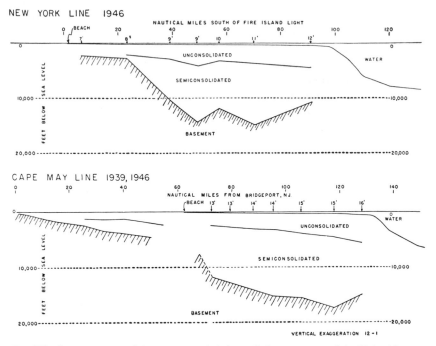

Fig. 129. Cross sections of the continental shelves off the east coast of the United States, based on geophysical measurements by Lamont Geological Observatory. See also Fig. 139.

out of deltas over the deep adjacent ocean basins followed by submergence of these deltas, the shelf margins off deltas should protrude. Bulges are found off the deltas of the Niger and the Nile, but the margins appear to be little affected off most other deltas. Where the margins are straight, there are grounds for the belief that deposition has not built the shelf out appreciably onto the deep ocean floor.[4] Borings and geophysical prospecting in the Mississippi Delta show that tremendous thicknesses of sediment have been deposited there, but there is no proof as yet that these deposits were built out over the deep Gulf floor and well cuttings are said to indicate shallow water deposits. Sinking may have kept pace with deposition, as is said to have happened in the ancient geosynclines on the continents. The geophysical measurements off the United States east coast by Ewing *et al.* (1950), and Officer and Ewing (1954) have produced evidence that this shelf may have undergone such a history. Discontinuities are shown at two levels (Fig. 129). The upper unconsolidated beds are

[4] The Arcer profiles made recently by Moore and Curray (1963) in the northwest Gulf of Mexico show quite clear evidence that the Pleistocene and Holocene deposits have built out the shelf margin with deposition on both the outer shelf and slope. Similar evidence was obtained by the same authors along the west coast of Mexico south of Mazatlan (personal communication).

believed by Ewing to include formations from Holocene (Recent) to Middle Cretaceous and the semiconsolidated beds, from Middle Cretaceous to the crystalline basement. It will be noted that none of the sections from the Lamont studies is indicative of wave-built terrace accumulations.

Deltas must certainly have played an important role in the filling of deep areas inside islands and banks. In view of the known rapid rate of delta growth, this process may have far exceeded in importance other marine deposition. During times of lower sea level, these deltas may have been built into lakes and thus have flattened extensive stretches of an otherwise irregular shelf.

The fact that subaerial deltas are not more widespread across the present continental shelves can be explained both by local subsidence and by the relatively recent rise of sea level which followed the last glacial epoch. After the several hundred feet of postglacial submergence a delta growth of such a rate as 10 ft a year during postglacial time should have resulted in the filling of embayments to the extent of many miles. Some large deltas are advancing as much as 100 ft a year, although these advances are found only in rather protected gulfs and bays. On the other hand, the rise in sea level of several hundred feet must have drowned very wide tracts in most of the large deltas. Accordingly, it is not surprising that only a few rivers have built across the shelf and that wide shelves exist off most river mouths.

**Explanation of Shelf Sediment Distribution.** The fact that coarse sediment occurs outside fine sediment in so many places on the continental shelves can be explained largely as the result of non-deposition on much of the outer shelves since the sea level rose and drowned the extensive river deposits of the glacial stages laid down on the exposed shelves. Sand barriers and other relict coastal deposits were also formed during the rising sea level stage. Wherever currents have been relatively strong the finer shelf deposits have bypassed these older sands.

In some places the strong currents of the outer shelf are reworking the glacial stage sands so that residual sands with present day faunas are found outside muddy inner shelf deposits of the same age. The muds can accumulate wherever weaker currents are found on the inner shelf. Locally, coarse sediments are being deposited on the outer shelf in the vicinity of shallow banks where wave action or strong currents yield a supply.

## Conclusions Concerning Shelf Origin

The preceding discussion has indicated the multiple origin of continental shelves as they now exist. The importance of the low stands of sea level during glacial stages is undeniable. Most of the outer terraces of the shelves can be accounted for as either the result of low-level wave abrasion or as deltas built during the low stands. Most of the wide shelves, however, must have a history that is only partly explained by the glacial sea levels. Some of them appear to have resulted from the filling of relatively deep basins, such as exist along many coasts, along with the beveling of outlying islands which border many of these basins. Other shelves, such as those off the east coast of the United States, have undergone a long history of submergence and deposition, probably much of the latter being accompanied by delta building, but the final product being largely due to the low sea level stages. Still other shelves have been built far out over the continental slope or even the deep ocean floor, but these cases appear to be unusual and occur at the juncture of two divergent continental trends, as off the Niger where the strength of the two adjacent segments may be sufficient to withstand the crustal load imposed by such outbuilding. Many of the wide shelves are probably in part the result of downwarping processes along the continental margins which have carried the land below the level of the sea, in part by loading and isostatic adjustment.

## The Existence of Continental Shelves Without Glacial Control

The importance of the low stands of sea level in the development of the continental shelves has been indicated. This raises the question of whether shelves would exist without glacial control. Since there is no clear evidence of the existence of large ice caps between the Precambrian and the Permian and between the Permian and the Pleistocene, this problem assumes considerable importance in considering the genesis of ancient marine deposits.

It has been shown that shelves can be cut by wave action producing wave-cut terraces. In the case of erosion of soft rock coasts these shelves should be very shallow, when judged from the present day terraces. These features would not be the type of shelf on which significant deposits would form. Shelf cutting in hard rock is apparently so slow that no appreciable shelves could be expected as a result of their erosion by waves unless an infinitely long time were available. Waves working on unconsolidated material may produce shelves, although there is no available evidence to support the existence of this particular type.

Very large shelves would have formed where coastal lowlands were submerged either by diastrophism or by sea level rise that operated faster than alluviation. This cause of shelves has no doubt been important along many of the coasts of the world over much of geological time. All the thick sediment masses underlying coastal plains contain abundant evidence of submergence during their formation. Whenever the submergence was faster than deposition, shelves would have developed.

Where coasts were rising, even at a slow rate, shelves could not have formed, and therefore presumably did not exist during most of the Pleistocene period. At these localities it seems probable that the continental slope would have adjoined the coast. Deposition on slopes, therefore, would have been more rapid and submarine slumping with turbidity currents more common than is now the case.

## Economic Resources of the Continental Shelves

When the three-mile limit of territorial waters was agreed to many years ago, little thought was given to the possibility that the shelves contained large natural resources. The geologists of the last generation, believing as they did in continental shelves consisting largely of great wave-built terraces encroaching over the deep ocean, would not have believed it possible that large oil accumulations would be found under the shelves. Now that we know that wave-built terraces are not important, it is not surprising that structures favorable to the accumulation of oil should exist beneath shelves adjoining land areas that have yielded oil. The large developments of oil off Louisiana and Texas (Pepper, 1958) have added greatly to the reserves of the United States. Considerable oil has also been obtained from the shelf off southern California. To date most of the Huntington Beach oil has come from offshore by slant drilling. Exploration off the east coast of South America has yielded some promise of oil with one show of oil off the Amazon (Pepper, 1958, p. 57). The west coast of South America despite its narrow shelf may also have considerable oil under the shelf. In fact Richfield Oil Company has an underwater well completed in that area. Along the Gulf Coast of the United States sulfur may well prove to be a valuable product from the sea floor (Pepper, 1958, p. 49). Sulfur occurs as cap rocks to salt domes, and the latter are now well established as existing in considerable number on the shelf west of the Mississippi Delta.

Iron ore is mined from under the shelf off Newfoundland (Pepper, 1958, p. 52). Monazite and other heavy minerals found in beaches above sea level can also be expected in some of the many beach deposits now out on the continental shelf.

As this is being written several companies are considering the advisability of dredging phosphate deposits on the shelves and shallow banks off southern California and Baja California. These deposits, largely phosphorite, were found in abundance on Coronados Bank off San Diego (Emery *et al.*, 1952). Photographs show that in some areas phosphorite nodules occur in great profusion so that these deposits may be profitable to recover.

# CHAPTER X

# CONTINENTAL SLOPES

## Introduction

Since writing the first edition of this book the greatest advances in sea floor studies have come from the investigations of the deep ocean and the continental shelves. Much less has been learned about the continental slopes where large areas are still quite unexplored despite the ease with which such studies can be made. During this interval the U.S. Coast and Geodetic Survey has completed the sounding of the slopes in the Gulf of Mexico and since then has concentrated mostly on surveys of Alaskan waters. A few lines have been run along the European slopes, particularly along the coasts of France and Great Britain. Various portions of the east coast slopes have been explored by the Lamont Geological Observatory, and extensive studies have been made of the slopes off southern California by the Hancock Foundation, and off western Mexico by Scripps Institution. Some information also has come from the area around Japan and New Zealand, and the slopes around Antarctica and in the Arctic have been surveyed extensively. In these high-latitude explorations the United States Navy and the Soviet Union have played leading roles.

Most continental slopes have a definite upper limit at the contact with the continental shelf, whereas the juncture with the abyssal ocean floor is usually hard to define. Several types of slope are illustrated in Fig. 130. In many places there is a broad zone of gentle slope in approaching the deep ocean floor. It has been suggested that this lower slope be called the *continental rise,* and that it be separated from the much steeper continental slope above. In some places the continental rise is a relatively narrow band that is rather closely related to the continental slope, but elsewhere it extends for hundreds of miles out into what clearly seems to be a part of the deep ocean territory. Another complication in defining the continental slope comes from the existence of an intermediate depth zone, part way down some continental slopes, in which there are either basins and ranges, as off southern California (Figs. 130*f* and 134), or a plateau, as

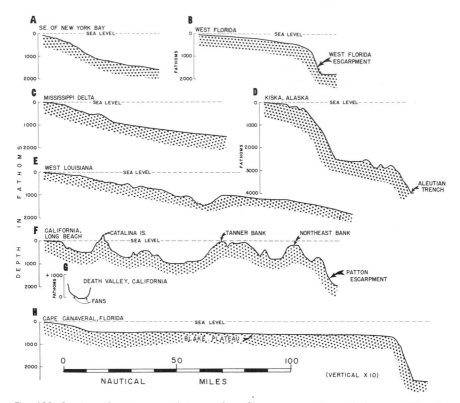

Fig. 130. Sections showing several types of profiles across continental slopes and Death Valley. Same vertical exaggeration in all.

off the southeastern corner of the United States (Figs. 130*h* and 131). This intermediate zone has been given the name *continental borderland*.

No discussion of the continental slopes which omitted mention of the various sorts of submarine valleys would be complete since these valleys are found on most of the slopes and constitute one of their most striking characteristics. The valleys, including many deep rock-walled canyons, are considered more extensively in Chapter XI, where an attempt is made to explain them. The continental border-lands appear to come definitely into the continental slope province, but the continental rises will be considered mostly in the discussion of the deep ocean basins (Chapters XIII—XV).

### Description of the Continental Slopes

In describing the continental slopes special attention will be paid to those slopes off the United States where detailed soundings are available along with many bottom samples, bottom photographs, and extensive geophysical measurement of the underlying layers. Elsewhere information comes mostly from scattered soundings, from a few widely separated fathograms, and from local sampling of the bottom.

**Eastern North America.** Little is known about the continental slopes of northeastern Canada. The series of right-angled bends around Newfoundland and off the Cabot Strait Trough are of interest particularly since this is the area where so many cables were broken by the huge earthquake in 1929 (Fig. 162). A few profiles (Heezen *et al.*, 1959, Pl. 24) show that there are slopes as steep as 5° marginal to the shelf off Newfoundland and Nova Scotia. These steep slopes terminate at less than 1000 fathoms in most places and are either bordered by or include jagged peaks and depressions. Below lies the gentle continental rise. There are indications that the slopes have submarine canyons, but they are poorly sounded.

From Georges Bank to Cape Hatteras the slopes are relatively well surveyed down to a little over 1000 fathoms (Heezen *et al.*, 1959, Fig. 1; Veatch and Smith, 1939). The base of the continental slope is found at depths from 1000 to 1500 fathoms and is bordered by a continental rise that continues down to abyssal depths. The continental slope has fewer hills than off Canada. However, the slope is apparently more dissected off the United States where there are innumerable valleys, many of them as large and deep as most land canyons. These canyons continue at least as far south as Cape Hatteras where one was discovered by the Lamont scientists (Heezen *et al.*, 1959, pl. 20).

South of Cape Hatteras there is a radical change in the character of the continental slope (Fig. 131). One or more broad steps are found leading down to the deep ocean floor. Also the base of the continental slope is no longer bordered by a continental rise. Instead, the steep slope beyond the terraces ends in a trough. From the latitude of South Carolina to the Bahamas there is one principal terrace, called Blake Plateau, with depths ranging from about 400 to 600 fathoms. It has long been known that this plateau had little if any sediment cover. The slope inside Blake Plateau is gentle, only about 1.5°. Precision Depth Recorder fathograms show the presence of small hills on this slope off Daytona Beach (Heezen *et al.*, 1959, pl. 4). The plateau also has minor irregularities including grabenlike depressions on the western side (Heezen *et al.*, 1959, pl. 7). Outside the plateau there is an abrupt drop with a slope described as 50 percent in some profiles (Heezen *et al.*, 1959, p. 33), and perhaps much steeper since steep slopes are impossible to detect except with the new narrow beam echo sounders initiated in 1960. Cores from this escarpment revealed

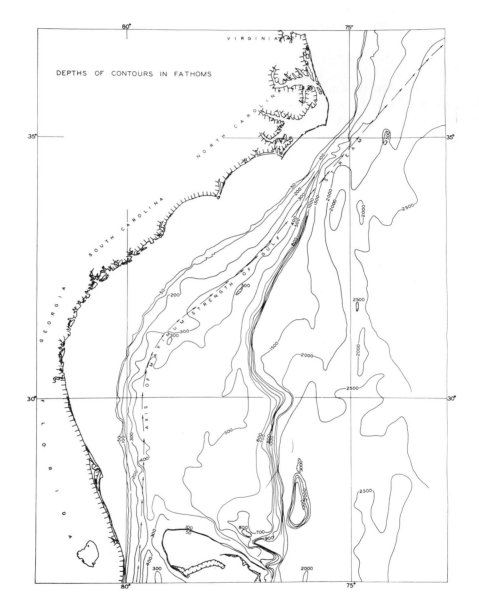

Fig. 131. Change in the continental slope at Cape Hatteras and the broad Blake Plateau to the south. Note the relation of the Gulf Stream axis to the inner margin of Blake Plateau. The Gulf Stream axis shifts from time to time.

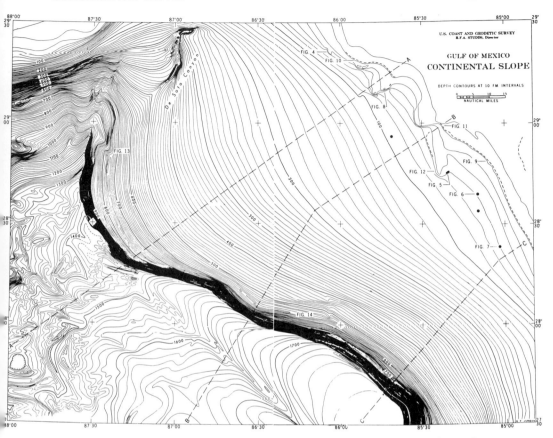

Fig. 132. The continental slope west of Florida. The steep escarpment continues to the south. From Jordan (1951). See also Fig. 193.

formations from Recent to Upper Cretaceous age (Ericson *et al.*, 1952). The geophysical studies of the Blake Plateau (Hersey *et al.*, 1959) have indicated the probability that thick Cretaceous formations underlie much of the surface. Lamont cores from the plateau (Ericson *et al.*, 1961, pp. 235, 236) have yielded firm sediment of upper Cretaceous, Oligocene, Miocene, Pliocene, and Pleistocene ages. A ridge extending southeast from Cape Fear is underlain by thick, low-velocity layers indicating a sediment-filled trough. The ridge is thought to have been a former chain of islands that subsided by faulting.

Near the southern end of Florida the Blake Plateau grades into a channel along which the Gulf Stream and its reciprocal subsurface currents are flowing. This channel separates Florida from the Bahamas and from Cuba to the south and west and deepens toward the Gulf of Mexico. Off Key West the north side of the channel was found to

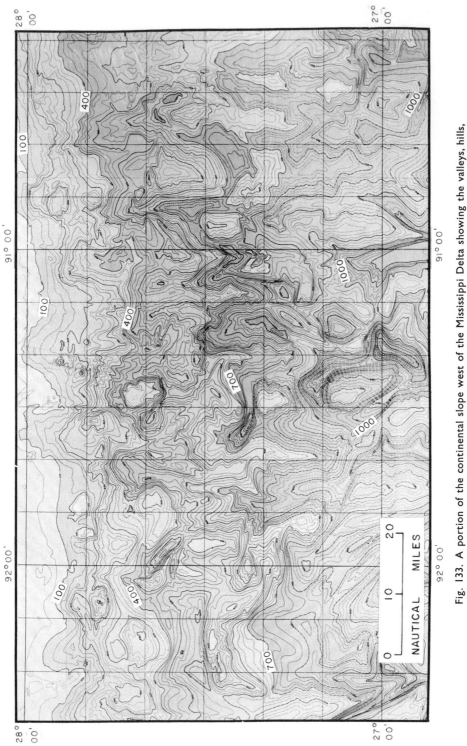

Fig. 133. A portion of the continental slope west of the Mississippi Delta showing the valleys, hills, and basins typical of this slope. Contour interval 25 fathoms; shade changes at 100, 400, 700, and 1000 fathoms. From Gealy (1956). See also Fig. 193.

have a series of basins just below the 100-fathom line (Jordan, 1954). These are described by Jordan as drowned sink holes. On the slope below these sinks there is an escarpment of small dimensions but with a slope of as much as 20°.

Seaward of the broad western Florida continental shelf the descent is very gentle out to about 600 fathoms, but beyond that there is a steep escarpment, fully as steep as that outside the Blake Plateau (Figs. 130*b* and 132) (Jordan, 1951; Jordan and Stewart, 1959). In some places this escarpment drops 1000 fathoms in about two nautical miles, a 27° slope. At the southern end of the escarpment there are submarine valleys starting at about 800 fathoms and terminating in basins at over 1800 fathoms. The northern end of the escarpment probably lacks these valleys. A photograph of the slope by David Owen (Jordan, 1951) showed the presence of rock bottom. These Florida slopes are among the steepest in the world, almost as steep as the scarp off southeast Cuba, a fact of especial interest since unlike the Cuban escarpment there is no sign of tectonism on either side of Florida.

Another right-angle change in direction of slope takes place at the northern end of the west Florida escarpment. The slope extends west-southwest past the Mississippi Delta with little if any indication of an outward bend resulting from the sedimentation. East of the delta the slope is relatively smooth but is interrupted by a troughlike valley off the western delta. Farther west begins an area of numerous hills, valleys, and basins (Fig. 133) (Gealy, 1956). Unfortunately, the trend of the sounding lines, mostly north and south, makes the basins a little suspect, but some of them are well established by the east-west lines. The average slope here is slightly less than 1°. It is worth noting that this rather unique type of topography is found off the area where salt domes form hills on the continental shelf margin. The irregular slope stops at a depth of about 1000 to 1100 fathoms and is succeeded by an escarpment 500 fathoms in height, below which there is a long even slope continuing to the Sigsbee Deep.

Off Tabasco, in the southwest corner of the Gulf, profiles (Creager, 1953, and in press) showed the same sort of hills and depressions as found west of the Mississippi Delta. Another steep escarpment west of Yucatan was charted by the oceanographers of Texas Agricultural and Mechanical College (Creager, 1958). This escarpment extends from the shelf edge to over 1700 fathoms and forms one side of a submarine trough.

**South America.**   Little is known about the slopes off South America. Off the Magdalena River Delta of Colombia there are irregular submarine valleys, and there must be considerable instability judging from the frequent cable breaks (Heezen, 1956). Farther east the U.S. Navy Hydrographic Office has charted other irregular escarpments.

Off the great deltas and the broad lowlands of Venezuela, the Guianas, and Brazil the small amount of available information suggests that there are very gentle slopes as off the Mississippi Delta. South of Cape São Roque, however, the slopes steepen and for 1500 miles show an inclination from about 4° to 20°, well above the average. This appears to be the longest stretch in the world with rather consistently steep slopes. As off Florida this is an area with no indications of recent diastrophism, and the Brazilian Highlands are considered to have been formed into mountains as far back as in the late Paleozoic. Off southern Brazil the scarce soundings indicate the presence of a number of banks along the slope. In recent years portions of the slope off the Argentine have been charted. Advance sheets supplied through the courtesy of the Argentine Hydrographic Department show that there are submarine canyons cutting this slope north of 46° S. Lat., but the slope apparently lacks canyons farther south. The slopes off most of the Argentine have inclinations around 2° but are much gentler off the Falkland Islands.

Off the west coast of South America the continental slopes are notable for their great vertical range (Zeigler *et al.*, 1957). Many of them extend down to 3000 and even 4000 fathoms. Including the adjacent slopes of the Andes, these slopes have the greatest vertical extent of any in the world, amounting to about 43,000 feet (13,100 m) in one place. However, despite these great vertical ranges the slopes are for the most part not particularly steep, averaging about 5° out to 1000 fathoms. The slopes beyond 1000 fathoms are somewhat steeper than inside, particularly near the base, which is in great contrast to the east side of the Americas, where slopes are considerably reduced at depth. In a few places, sounding lines normal to the shore show very even slopes of around 4° to 6°, extending to several thousand fathoms. To the north the slopes are less regular and there are some indications of the presence of continental borderlands.

**Western North America.**   The slopes off the west coast of Central America and Mexico are comparatively well known largely from the charting operations of Scripps Institution (Fisher, 1961; Shepard, in Anderson *et al.*, 1950), and of the U.S. Navy Electronics Laboratory.

In the Gulf of California the area has been surveyed recently in considerable detail by several groups from Scripps Institution with numerous sounding lines, many bottom samples and extensive geophysical prospecting, and magnetometer studies. As this is written the information from some of this work is fragmentary, but some of the first results amplify earlier indications of great fault scarps along the west side of the Gulf and provide evidence of equally great escarpments on the east side. The latter are partly buried by unconsolidated sediments but are indicated in the magnetometer studies made from the Scripps Institution *M/V Horizon*. The slopes around the end of Cape San Lucas, the southern end of the peninsula, are carved into an intricate series of granite-walled canyons (Shepard, 1961b). So far as known these canyons do not persist north of La Paz and are found only off Topolobampo on the east side. The escarpments are largely rocky, but muddy sediments were found on some slopes of at least 20° inclination. In the northern part of the Gulf near Tiburon Island layers of coarse sand and fine gravel are found in depths as great as 225 fathoms. These coarse sediments are not graded and have no indication of turbidity current origin. It is not unlikely that they are carried down from shallow water along the Sonora coast by the strong bottom currents related to the large tidal flows in this area.

North along the west coast of Baja California only miscellaneous lines of Scripps Institution, Hancock Foundation, and U.S. Navy soundings are available as far as Cedros Island. These slopes are cut in some localities by submarine canyons. Elsewhere they are remarkably even. South of Cedros Island there is an escarpment leading down to a small trench (Fisher, personal communication). These slopes are said to contain metamorphic rock (K. O. Emery, personal communication). Somewhat to the north of Cedros Island this trench terminates and a continental borderland comparable to the basin and range topography of southern California begins (Krause, 1961), continuing to Point Conception west of Santa Barbara, California.

The southern California basin and range province has a width of about 150 miles (Figs. 130*f* and 134), terminating westward with an escarpment that is comparable in height and declivity to that of the eastern Sierra, but differs in the absence of the great canyons that cut the land escarpment. This area has been discussed by Shepard and Emery (1941), Shepard and Einsele (1962), and Emery (1960). All the borderland basins are shoaler than typical deep ocean basins. To the south off San Diego a former basin has been filled to its brim and hence is referred to as San Diego Trough, but the other basins are only partly filled (Emery, 1960, p. 52). The ranges rise partly as high islands above the surface, such as San Clemente and Catalina, or form shallow banks, such as Cortes and Tanner, and near the outer escarpment the banks have several hundred fathoms of water above them. According to Moore (manuscript) studies of the Tanner Bank area indicate an anticline with the topography a reflection of the structure. Others of the basin-range highs owe their

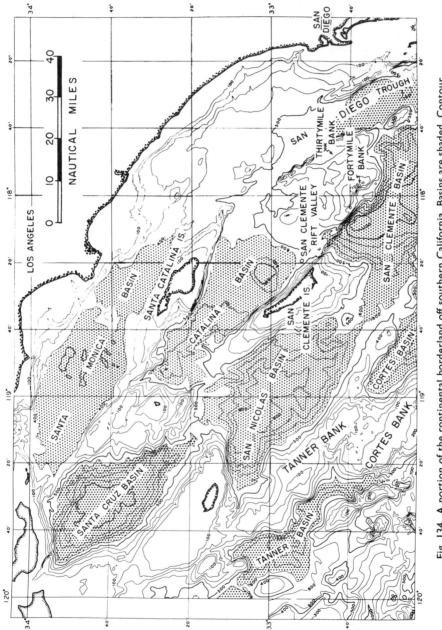

Fig. 134. A portion of the continental borderland off southern California. Basins are shaded. Contour interval 100 fathoms. Modified from Shepard and Emery (1941).

topographic expression to faulting, and their internal structure is discordant with their topography. On the sides of the basins there are relatively straight escarpments in most places. Near the continents and around some of the islands and banks these escarpments are cut by valleys. The lower portions of these valleys cross fans which terminate at the base of the slope and which look very much like submerged equivalents of alluvial fans.

Along the continental borderland of southern California the sediments found in the basins and in San Diego Trough are predominantly a silty clay, but contain also layers of sand, especially around the fans that lie outside submarine canyons. The sand layers in the outer basins are predominantly calcareous as are also the sands on the outer banks (Emery, 1960, pp. 210–227). These calcareous sands are a mixture of Foraminifera and shells of other types. In many places the foraminiferal sands are associated with glauconite and phosphorite. Rather extensive areas on the banks have rock bottom, and well-rounded gravel up to cobble size is found on many of the banks, even the deeper ones.

To the north the outer escarpment of the borderland is interrupted but continues somewhat to the east beyond a small gap. This gap lies west of the east-west ranges in the Santa Barbara and Los Angeles area. The northward continuation of the continental slope off the Santa Barbara Islands shows an offset of the escarpment to the east. Farther north there is no borderland inside but instead a gentle 1° slope extending in almost to the land. A slope up to 12° occurs beyond depths of 800 fathoms. This change in slope seaward compares with the gentle slope and outer escarpment off west Florida.

North of San Simeon (35° 40′ N. Lat.) the steep portion of the slope moves in toward the coast displacing the gentle slope that exists farther south. Approaching Point Sur a series of large canyons with numerous tributaries is found cut into the slope. These canyons culminate in the great Monterey and Carmel canyons, but continue intermittently almost to the northern border of California. At Punta Gorda, just south of Cape Mendocino, the entire continental slope is offset and an east-west escarpment extends seaward for more than 40 miles (Fig. 135). Many epicenters of earthquakes are known to have occurred along this escarpment (Tocher, 1956; Shepard, 1957). Furthermore, the inner end of the scarp bends to the southeast and points toward Shelter Cove where the northernmost observed displacement occurred at the time of the San Francisco earthquake. To the south of the escarpment a submarine canyon terminates headward directly against a blank mountain wall rather than opposite the land valleys. This appears to give evidence of a large horizontal

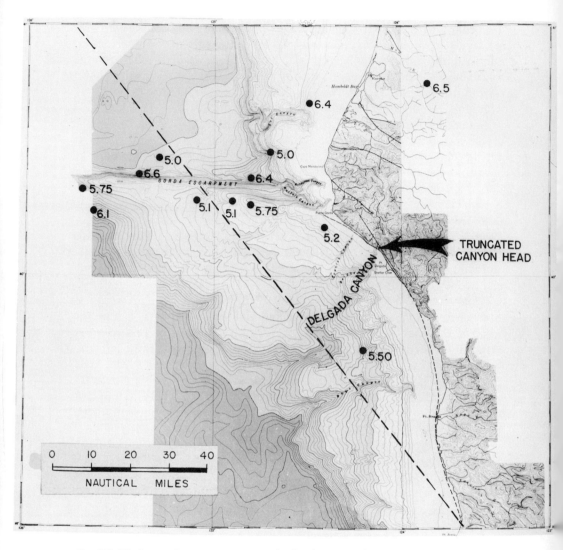

Fig. 135. The large submarine escarpment that bends westward in continuity with the curving coastline of California. This escarpment is believed to represent a northward continuation of at least one branch of the San Andreas fault because it connects with the fault zone that extends south from Punta Gorda along the coast passing through Shelter Cove where a displacement occurred in 1906 at the time of the San Francisco earthquake. Major earthquakes are indicated with their amplitude from Tocher (1956). The abrupt termination of Delgada Canyon along this coast against a mountain wall suggests that it has been displaced by a strike slip fault. The dashed line is a common interpretation of the northward continuation of the San Andreas but obviously no strike slip faulting could have occurred along this line without displacing the Gorda escarpment.

movement similar to that of the San Andreas fault to the south (see also p. 383).

To the north of Gorda escarpment there is a considerable change in the character of the continental slope. Outside of a gentle inner slope there is a broad terrace around 500 fathoms with hills rising from its outer edge. This further example of a continental borderland has less relief than that off southern California. West of the borderland a relatively steep escarpment drops to depths of about 1500 fathoms. Farther north the borderland is less conspicuous, but as far as the Columbia River the slope is almost entirely gentle, rarely exceeding 2°. A conspicuous absence of submarine canyons is found between Eel Canyon off the Eel River, and Columbia Canyon[1] off the mouth of the Columbia River. Various hills are seen on the slope in this portion.

From the Columbia River north to the limit of detailed slope surveys off southern Vancouver Island there are a series of canyons extending virtually to the base of the slope and in fact some of them connect with channels that extend out over the broad fans of the adjacent continental rise (Fig. 188). The continental slope in this area averages about 3° out to the 1000-fathom line. The slope contains small terraces and ridges, some of the latter rising 200 fathoms above surroundings. The continental slope terminates at depths of about 1300 fathoms.

North of the Canadian border the slopes are comparatively straight as far north as the large bend in the Alaskan coast near Mt. St. Elias. Canyons are found off Vancouver Island where a good survey is available, but they are unknown to the north. The slopes are steeper than most of those to the south averaging about 5° to 6°. The steep portion of the slope terminates from 1000 to 1300 fathoms, and is followed by a gentle continental rise with fans similar to those off Washington. Off Graham Island a long ridge rises above a 1600-fathom trench.

Beyond the bend in the coast at Yakutat Bay the situation changes. The east-west slope (Fig. 187) extends down to the Aleutian Trench where there are depths of 3000 fathoms or more. The lower part of the slope leading to the trench is steeper than the upper part reaching as much as 30° inclinations in some places. Along the Aleutian Island chain where detailed soundings are available the slope is cut by a series of trough-shaped valleys (Fig. 161) which are apparently related to the faulting of the area (Gibson and Nichols, 1953; Gates and Gibson, 1956). Directly north of the Aleutian Islands the slope outside the broad Bering shelf is cut by a large canyon, but farther north the slope is apparently quite straight having inclinations of about 8°.

[1] Name established in Shepard and Beard (1938) with approval of U.S. Coast and Geodetic Survey, but renamed Astoria Canyon on Survey chart a few years later.

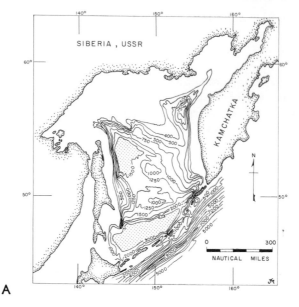

Fig. 136. (*a*) Contours of the Sea of Okhotsk. Depths in
meters. After Bezrukov (1960).

**Eastern Asia.** The slopes off northeastern Asia have been charted
in considerable detail by the Soviet expeditions (Bezrukov, 1960;
Udintsev, 1957, 1960). They found a great ridge extending off Cape
Olyutorsk. To the south the slope into the Bering Sea has inclinations
up to 20° to 25°, one of the steepest known submarine slopes. Farther
south, off Kamchatka, the Soviets discovered a deep trench starting
south of the submarine continuation of the Aleutian Island chain.
This trench extends south along the Kurile Island arc. In the Okhotsk
Sea a very uneven slope was discovered, and the area is of the continental borderland type with various basins and ridges, the former
attaining depths up to 1600 fathoms (Fig. 136*a*). Bezrukov (1960) has
mapped the sediment distribution in this borderland area (Fig. 136*b*).
Much of the area is covered with a mud containing a large diatom
content. Sand and gravel deposits occur on some of the highs.

Along the Japanese coast a great variation in slope declivity is
found. North of Tokyo, so far as the soundings show, the slopes are
quite gentle, about 2° out to the 1000-fathom contour, but the slope
steepens at greater depth, particularly on the walls of the Japan
Trench where slopes of about 10° are found. The few available soundings give no indications of canyons on either the inner or outer slopes
in this area except near Tokyo where there are a series of canyons.

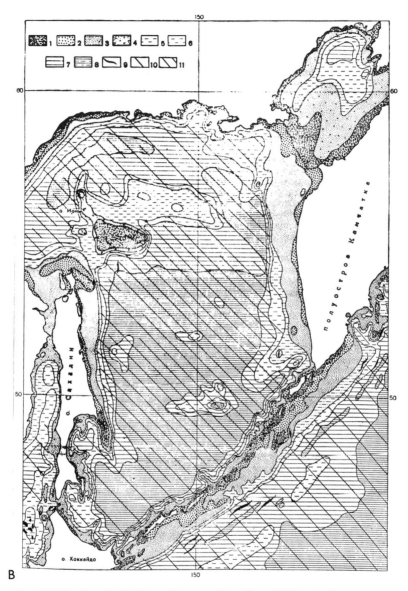

Fig. 136 (*Continued*). (*b*) The sediments of the Sea of Okhotsk. Interpretation of pattern in upper lefthand corner: 1, shingle-gravel sediments; 2, coarse sands; 3, fine sands; 4, unanalyzed sands; 5, coarse silt; 6, fine silt oozes; 7, silty clayey mud; 8, clayey mud; 9, area of rock outcrop; 10, slightly siliceous-diatomaceous oozes; 11, siliceous-diatomaceous oozes. From Bezrukov (1960).

Other slope indentations, like those in Sagami and Surugu bays, are not strictly canyons, since they have a broad trough shape. The slopes along the southern coast of Japan are variable in declivity, largely between 2° and 10°. Rock bottom is reported in numerous places along the slopes off Japan, even at depths up to 1000 fathoms. Sand and gravel are common notations, although here, as in most other places, mud is the most common type.

South of Japan, off the Yellow Sea, the slopes are gentle and hilly but apparently free from valleys. The slopes steepen off Formosa and are creased by a considerable number of canyons. These slopes are very rocky and have high hills, some rising as banks or even islands. Few data are available off southern China and Indo-China, but the slopes appear to be gentle and have a few hills partly topped by coral banks.

On all sides of the Philippines the slopes are unusually steep, averaging 11° down to 1000 fathoms. The slopes extend to great depth around Samar and eastern Mindanao but do not appear to steepen at depth. Off Mindanao the slopes have a vertical range of 5000 fathoms which, added to the land height of 2000 ft (610 m) makes a total of 32,000 feet (9754 m). The slopes around eastern and northern Luzon are cut by numerous canyons, although valleys are not shown elsewhere. Along the west coast of Bougainville Island the slopes extend to depths of 5000 fathoms, but the few soundings suggest that these slopes are not steeper than about 12°. Along the east coast of Australia the slopes are somewhat steeper than average, particularly to the south of the Great Barrier Reef. In this south-eastern section the slope inclination commonly increases beyond the 1000-fathom line.

**Indian Ocean.** Some steep slopes are found south of southwestern Australia. In one place the slope to 1000 fathoms is indicated as 27°, another of the steepest slopes of the sea bottom. To the north the slopes decrease and are less than 1° off northwestern Australia.

Along the southern side of Java and Sumatra, so far as could be determined, the long slopes leading to the trench floor are relatively gentle; most of them 5° or less in declivity. These low angles are surprising since the slopes lead to the greatest known depths in the Indian Ocean. Off northwestern Sumatra there is a small borderland area and a much larger one occurs north of Malacca Strait, extending all the way to Burma. The narrow shelf along the southern Burmese coast is bordered by a gentle slope and a broad basin, mostly less than 1500 fathoms in depth, but with a maximum depth of 2270 fathoms. This basin is separated from the main Indian Ocean by a row of islands and shoals, the Andaman and Nicobar island groups. Off the Irrawaddy and Ganges rivers, slopes vary between 1° and 2°. Along the eastern Indian Peninsula the slope steepens to 4° and locally to 6°, and off Ceylon the slopes are mostly 10° or more, being comparable to those off the Phillippines and off the Brazilian Highlands. These steep Ceylon slopes are cut by a few canyons. Western India has slopes of 2° to 3° for the most part. To the south the slopes have submarine hills with coral reefs rising above them.

Along the coast of Arabia and Italian Somaliland, where shelves are very narrow or nonexistent, most of the slopes are apparently gentle although east African charts have little information. There are, however, enough soundings to show a series of valleys cutting across the slope north of Mozambique. Off South Africa, slopes average 5°, and an irregular borderland is observable at one point.

**Western Africa.**    The slopes bordering the deep shelves of Southwest Africa are mostly not over 2°. There is a slight steepening to the north of 20° S. Lat., and at one place a 10° slope extends down from the shore without any intervening shelf. Off the Congo, the slopes scarcely exceed 1°. The slopes are gentle also off the Niger, but to the west along Ghana and the Ivory Coast the slope steepens to 5° or 6° which continues as far north as Sierra Leone. A few valleys are known to cut these slopes. North of 10° N. Lat. the slopes are consistently low mostly around 2°. A continental borderland is in evidence around the Canary Islands and extends somewhat to the north. The slopes around Casablanca are slightly steeper than those to the south.

**Mediterranean Sea.**    Along the Atlas Mountain coast, the narrow shelf is bordered by slopes averaging 6° (Rosfelder, 1955). These slopes are cut by many canyons or troughlike indentations. No data are available to the east as far as Cyrenaica where the slopes are only 2° or 3°, but include hills and some valleys. The slopes along the Israel coast are gentle to the south about 1.5°, and increase to 5° farther north. They are cut by many valleys. Off Lebanon and Syria the slopes run about 10° and these steep inclines continue along the coast of Turkey, with many irregularities in the nature of fault troughs. Steep slopes are common also off the Greek peninsula. The slopes around the Italian peninsula are mostly quite low but show a marked increase around the Italian and French Riviera (Bourcart, 1959), where they are cut by many canyons and troughs (Fig. 137). These slopes are mostly covered with mud (Bourcart, 1954b). Somewhat gentler slopes occur off the relatively broad shelf of the Gulf of Lyons. Along the coast of eastern and southern Spain the slopes are variable and in some places as steep as 10° to the 1000-fathom line. These slopes also have a considerable number of canyon indentations.

**Western Europe.**    The Gulf of Cádiz is notable for having a remarkably low smooth slope beyond the shelf, less than 1°, so that there is little if any break evident at the shelf edge. Beyond Cape St.

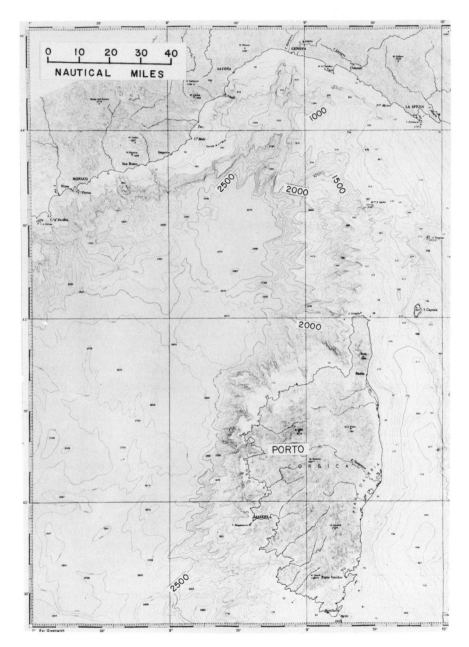

Fig. 137. Deeply eroded continental slopes of West Corsica and of the Italian and French Riviera. Contour interval 100 m. From E. Debrazzi and A. G. Segrè, *Pubblicata dall' Instituto Idrografico della Marina-Genova*, August 1960.

Vincent the situation differs in that the slope is cut by many canyons, but the angle is increased only to about 3° and this relatively low inclination continues all along the west coast of Portugal. Off northern Spain the slopes are much steeper, attaining inclinations of as much as 15° and averaging about 8°. These slopes are very irregular, having canyons, troughs, hills, and ridges. The soundings are not sufficiently detailed to show the exact nature of the topography.

Berthois and Brenot (1960) found a series of canyons along the slopes off western France north of the previously known Cap Breton Canyon which approaches the coast near the Adour River. The slopes in this area were found to have coarse sediments with sand, gravel, and pebbles in the 250–400 fathom zone. Rock of Mesozoic age was dredged in one place. Ripple marks (probably due to currents) were discovered in submarine photographs along this slope (Heezen et al., 1959, pl. 11). The slopes average about 5° in inclination but decrease to about 2° off the English Channel to the north. In this area the bottom is labeled on the charts as gravel or rocky in many places. Recent surveys show that the submarine valleys continue to Lat. 49° (Day, 1959). A terrace was found at 1500 fathoms and a scarp at 2300 fathoms. Along the west coast of Ireland the slopes are variable and there is a continental borderland with the 100-fathom Porcupine Bank rising above it. The same condition exists off western and northern Scotland with a series of shallow banks and islands separated by channels 500 to 1200 fathoms deep. Rock bottom is common off both of these areas. The slopes north of the North Sea are notable for their gentleness, averaging around 1° to 1000 fathoms. Along the Norwegian coast (Holtedahl, 1940) the gentle slope continues to 67° N. Lat., where the slope increases and there is a change in trend north of the Lofoten Islands. Off the latter a maximum slope of 4° is observed (Holtedahl, 1940, Chart III). The slope north of the Lofoten Islands is cut by one or more submarine canyons.

The continental slope of the Arctic is being explored although little detail is as yet released probably because of military considerations. North of Point Barrow, Alaska, a continental borderland was discovered with a detached ridge 100 miles long and a 23° slope beyond (Fisher et al., 1958). To the east of the borderland the slope is gentle, about $1\frac{1}{2}°$ although cut by a series of submarine valleys, some of canyon dimensions (Carsola, 1954b; Carsola et al., 1961).

The continental slope off Antarctica was extensively studied during the International Geophysical Year operations. The principal published source of this material comes from the Soviet explorations (Lisitzin and Zhivago, 1960). In Davis Sea the Soviets found an elongate depression with a continental borderland (deeper than 300 fathoms) outside, although it has been called a part of the continental shelf by the Soviet geologists. Beyond the borderland the slope to the rather flat sea floor is about 5°.

## Summary of Continental Slope Characteristics

The description of the slopes has shown that although there are many gaps in the soundings, some definite characteristics can be assigned to them. The typical continental slope is not precipitous, averaging 4°17' for the first 1000 fathoms of descent. The trend of the typical continental slope is straight or gently curving. However, the canyons cut into these slopes are comparable in dimensions with the canyons of mountain slopes but are by no means as abundant. The slopes also have a smaller number of hills than are found on the flanks of mountains. The typical slopes of the Atlantic and Indian oceans are relatively steep near the top and gentle at the bottom, but in the Pacific many of the slopes steepen in the deeper portions. Where soundings on the lower slopes allow contouring, a large number of basin depressions are indicated. According to the surveyors who lack geological training, mud is the most common sediment, forming about 60 per cent of the chart bottom notations while sand comprises about 25 percent; rock and gravel are reported from numerous areas and constitute about 10 percent of the notations. Shells and ooze make up most of the remaining 5 percent.

## Continental Slopes Related to Coastal Types

**Coasts with Deltas and Large Rivers.** There seems to be little doubt but that the continental slopes have characteristics which vary with many of the types of coast discussed in Chapter VI. The slopes are clearly influenced by the deposits from large rivers and especially by those with protruding deltas. Off large rivers the average slope to 1000 fathoms is only 1°21', less than a third that of continental slopes in general. Virtually all the slopes off the large rivers are gentle. The slopes are not very even in inclination, but include a considerable number of hills and depressions. Also, some small valleys are found and a few large submarine canyons. The sediments are predominantly mud.

**Fault Coasts.** The slopes off the supposed fault coasts (where appreciable shelves are lacking) contrast with those off deltas in being the steepest of any group. Their average slope is 5°40' to 1000 fathoms, although there are a number of localities where slopes up to 25° or more are indicated. On the other hand, great stretches of fault coasts, notably off the Andes, are bordered by continental slopes rather close to 5° in inclination. Such slopes extend into some of the great trenches of the deep oceans. Judging from available soundings, the slopes off fault coasts are relatively smooth and even in inclination. Submarine canyons are rare but small valleys common. In many places the slopes increase with depth. Rock bottom is more common off fault coasts than on other continental slopes, although mud, as elsewhere, dominates.

**Young Mountain-Range Coasts (Other Than Fault Coasts).** Off young mountain ranges bordered by shelves the continental slopes are slightly more gentle than off fault coasts. The median slope is 4°40' to 1000 fathoms. Unlike the fault coasts the slopes are cut by many submarine canyons. Continental borderlands are somewhat more common off the young mountains than elsewhere.

**Stable Coasts, Lacking Large Rivers.** Most types of coasts other than the three discussed above are usually considered as stable since such mountains or hills as exist have not been involved in any recent mountain-making movements. Many of these coasts are bordered by wide shelves, although some have conspicuously narrow shelves. The slopes outside these supposedly stable coasts have a median inclination of 3°, which is less than average. However, there is a wide variation in slopes, and included in this group are four of the areas with the steepest continental slopes in the world; west Florida, the Brazilian Highlands, southwestern Australia, and Ceylon. It is significant that the slope inclinations are steeper in these four areas than those found off many fault coasts. Except for west Florida the shelves are relatively narrow in these four cases and there are low mountains near the coast.

### Slopes in Relation to Ocean Basins

In the Pacific the slopes, which follow one of the great earthquake belts of the world, might be expected to be strikingly different from those of the Atlantic and Indian oceans. A difference does exist: the median slope along the margin of the Pacific is 5°20' to 1000 fathoms, as contrasted with a median of 3°05' in the Atlantic and only 2°55' in the Indian Ocean. The Mediterranean Sea is intermediate between the Pacific and the other oceans, having a median slope of 3°34'. Despite these medians, the steepest submarine slopes of the world appear to be in the Atlantic south of Cuba, and the longest stretch of more steep slope is also found in the Atlantic off the Brazilian Highlands. The Pacific slopes, however, are unique in several respects. They contain virtually all the slopes of great vertical range. Also, there are a remarkable number of areas in the Pacific where the slope lies between 5° and 6°, and where the inclination, based on rather widely separated soundings, does not vary greatly from top to bottom. Furthermore, almost all slopes that are steeper below the 1000-fathom contour than above it are found in the Pacific. All three of the principal oceans have about the same abundance of submarine valleys, but the slopes of the Mediterranean Sea have valleys more closely spaced than in any of the oceans. Continental borderlands are found along the slopes of each of the principal oceans as well as in the Mediterranean.

Such differences as exist between the slopes of the different oceans appear to be more related to the coastal types than to the particular ocean basin. Fault coasts and young mountain coasts with their steeper slopes are most abundant in the Pacific, and the Mediterranean stands second in this respect. Other unknown factors certainly enter the picture, however.

The bottom composition of the slopes appears to be about the same for the different oceans, being again somewhat more related to coastal types than to the specific ocean.

## Origin of the Continental Slopes

**General Considerations.** Before discussing their origin it is important to remember that the continental slopes represent the link between the two principal levels on the earth's surface, one close to sea level and the other approximately 2000 fathoms below sea level. The narrowness of this transition zone is impressive. If the continental rise that fringes the base in some areas is disregarded, the slopes have a general width of 10 to 20 miles. This is somewhat narrower than typical transition zones between the high plateaus and the low plains of the continents.

It is of considerable significance that most of the continental slopes are rugged. Valleys, often of canyon proportions, are common along most slopes, the chief exceptions being found where the slopes are very gentle and where no large source of sediment is available to build them seaward. The origin of these canyons will be reserved for consideration in the next chapter, but their presence must be taken into consideration here. Quite aside from their origin, the canyons are important in the interpretation of the slopes because they cut below the surficial sediment cover and, hence, provide a means of finding the thickness of the sediment mantle and of the character of the underlying rock. The canyons are also important in funneling sediment from the shelves down to the deep ocean floors.

The slopes are also uneven in transverse profile having many hills and basins along with broad plateaus or terraces along their length. It is probably of some significance that the well-surveyed slopes of the United States have strikingly different characteristics one from another, there being eleven quite distinct provinces.

Some portions of the continental slopes are important areas of sedimentation. Much of the fine sediment coming out from the lands is kept in suspension by the currents of the continental shelves but comes to rest on the slopes except where it is bypassed along the axes of valleys. Recent studies indicate a somewhat greater rate of deposition on the slopes than on the outer shelves (Curray, 1960, p. 252; Phleger, 1960b, pp. 92–95). When the sea levels were considerably lowered owing to the growth of continental glaciers, the rivers must have emptied their sediment directly onto the slopes in most areas providing a much greater source of slope sediment than now exists where broad shelves border the land. Much of the sediment provided at that time, however, may have slid down from the upper to the lower slopes because rapidity of deposition prevented normal consolidation in the soil mechanics sense (Terzaghi, 1956). The continental borderlands of the southern California type catch most of the sediments moving towards the deep ocean floor.

With these considerations it is possible to compare the various hypotheses which have been suggested as explanations of the continental slopes. These include: frontal slopes of wave-built terraces, delta foreset beds, downwarped continental surfaces, fault scarps, and fault zones.

**Wave-Built Terraces.** By far the simplest explanation for the slopes is that they represent the front of wave-built terraces (Fig. 138) developed outside wave-cut terraces. Although it has become evident in recent years that the outer portions of many of the narrow continental shelves include extensive areas of rock bottom so that they could not represent the top of a wave-built terrace, there is still a common impression that the wider shelves such as those off the northeast coast of the United States and off the British Isles and northern France are wave-built terraces because geophysical prospecting has shown that there are thick masses of sediment underlying the shelves (Drake et al., 1959; Hill, 1957). This impression of the wave-built terrace may be quite erroneous, however, because dredging of the walls of canyons along these slopes has shown that there are outcrops of Tertiary and even Cretaceous rocks at intermediate depths showing that the slopes could not have been built forward to any great extent. The acoustic probe measurements off the east coast (Ewing, J., et al., 1960a) show further indication of the presence of a truncated surface closely underlying the sediments at the shelf break. Prouty (1946) explained the outcrops along the slopes south of Cape Hatteras as the result of the Gulf Stream, but this could not account for the rocks along the slope off New England where there is no known current. It seems highly probable that the formations are truncated at the slopes, although they commonly have a thin covering of recent sediment.

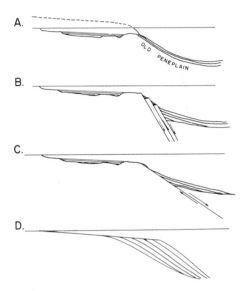

Fig. 138. Showing several possible origins of the continental slope: A, downbending of an old peneplain; B, step faulting; C, low-angle normal fault; D, wave-built terrace.

Strong evidence that the continental slopes are not the fronts of wave-built terraces comes from their irregular topography. Depositional slopes should decrease in inclination outward and should be smooth except where cut by small slump valleys (Fig. 159). The numerous instances of an increase in slope with depth and of escarpments at intermediate depths are decidedly contrary to what would be expected of deposition.

**Foreset Beds of Deltas.** Delta foreset beds are no better explanation than wave-built terraces for the slopes as a whole. However, there seems to be a considerable likelihood that the slopes off the Niger (Fig. 118) and the Nile are the foreset beds of those respective river deltas. The conformation of the shelf margin and of the slope contours to the delta front in each case could scarcely be explained in any other way. These cases, however, are virtually unique. Elsewhere the shelf margin shows little if any bulge beyond the large river deltas. The Niger and Nile both empty into the ocean at a juncture between north-south and east-west trending coasts. The continental sectors form supports on either side of these deltas and may provide crustal strength to the intervening deep sea floor and allow the outbuilding of delta fronts over this portion of the sea floor without appreciable crustal yielding. This hypothesis might be checked by gravity measurements to see if these delta areas are out of isostatic balance.

The possibility exists that the slopes in other areas are in part foreset slopes of deltas built during the glacial stages of low sea level. The almost universally gentle foreset slopes off large deltas, however, are in contrast to typical continental slopes which are several times as steep. The absence of bulges off most of the large rivers is also an argument against a foreset bed origin.

**Downwarped Continental Surfaces.** Geological literature has many references to the disappearance of old land masses, such as Appalachia and Cascadia. These are thought to have supplied geosynclines with sediment and then to have sunk and been incorporated into the ocean basins. Veatch (Veatch and Smith, 1939) suggested that the continental slopes on both sides of the Atlantic were downwarped remnants of Miocene peneplains (Fig. 138a). Downwarping of the continental shelves bordering the Atlantic appears to be established both by geophysical prospecting, drilling in Cape Hatteras (built out over the shelf), and by rocks of shallow origin dredged on the canyon walls off the east coast of the United States. However, the picture coming from this information is not that of a downwarped peneplain, but of a geosyncline with a rise of the basement toward the outer edge of the shelf and another syncline outside (Fig. 139a). There is certainly no evidence favoring the downwarping of the slope independent of the shelf. Formations appear to outcrop along the slope (Prouty, 1946; Heezen *et al.*, 1959). Furthermore, the downwarping of a former continental mass would presumably bring a light crustal segment into the deep ocean province which should be indicated in gravity and geophysical prospecting studies, but has not been found.

**Fault Scarp or Fault Zone.** It is now clearly recognized by all geophysicists that there is a striking difference between the earth's crust under the oceans and under the continents. The continental shelf appears to be more related to the continents than to the oceans although the continental borderland off southern California is gradational between the two (Shor and Raitt, 1958). Since the topographic relations apparently fit the juncture between the heavy crust under the ocean and the light crust under the continents, it can be assumed that the contact between the different levels is maintained by isostasy. Since it is known that sediments are carried from the continents to the deep ocean floor there must be some movement to compensate for the weighting of the oceanic crust. This in turn could be expected to

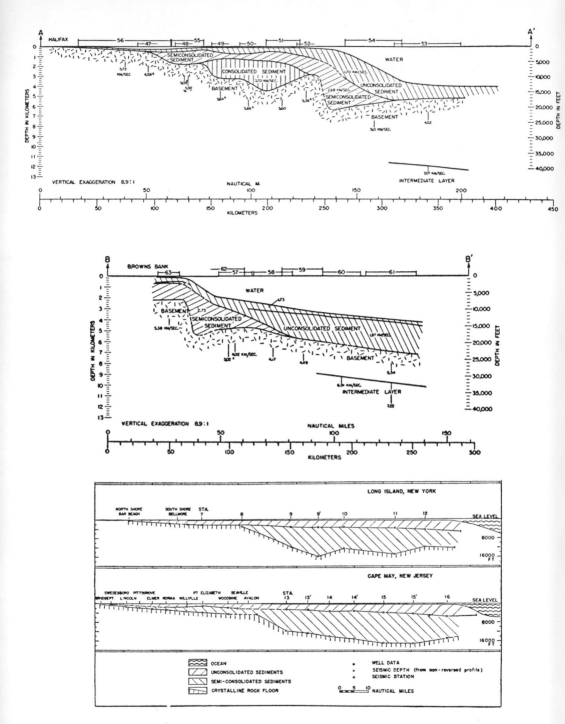

Fig. 139. Sections across the eastern United States continental oceanic margin showing the various layers underlying the shelf and slope and the basement. From various reports by Lamont Geological Observatory scientists. See also Fig. 205.

produce faulting perhaps accompanied by warping at the continental margin. If the continental slopes are essentially fault scarps, however, it is clear that the faulting is not very active in most places. Earthquakes have not been recorded from the slopes along the greater part of the Atlantic Ocean and Indian Ocean margins although they are quite common along the borders of the Pacific. Nor are the slopes in general as steep as typical fault scarps on land. Thus it would seem that fault origin or fault maintenance of the slopes must mean that only occasional fault movements occur in addition to what may be called an original faulting. Step faults rather than a single fault would be likely (Fig. 138b).

That something in the nature of faulting accounts for the bulk of the continental slopes is indicated by the following:

1. Deep narrow trenches occur along the base of about one-half of the continental slopes of the world and these trenches are the most unstable portion of the earth's crust. Geophysical measurements show that buried trenches may exist along portions of the Atlantic slopes[2] (Fig. 139) and indicate that these slopes may have been more active tectonically in the past. Trenches are also found at the base of many continental fault scarps in the Pacific.

2. Earthquakes occur along some of the slopes where no trenches exist. An example is the tremendous earthquake of November 19, 1929, which led to the breaking of so many transatlantic cables south of the Grand Banks of Newfoundland (Fig. 162).

3. The continental slopes bordered by trenches are similar to most of those lacking trenches. They both have relatively straight trends terminating with sharp angular, rather than curving, changes of direction. Many of the continental slopes not bordered by trenches are steeper than those with trenches, for example, the lower slope off western Florida and the slopes off Brazil, southwest Australia, and Ceylon.

4. The continental slopes off a number of narrow shelves and off coasts without shelves cut transversely across the strike of formations running into the coast as, for example, off central California (see California State Geological map).

5. The numerous outcrops of rock dredged from the slopes are difficult to explain by any other hypothesis than recurrent faulting.

6. The fact that most of the shelf margins do not bulge seaward off the great river deltas of the world seems to indicate that the margins are maintained in position by recurrent faulting.

7. The presence along the shelf margin off Louisiana and Texas of

---

[2] These are interpreted by R. S. Dietz (personal communication) as downwarped geosynclines depressed by isostasy owing to the load of sediments.

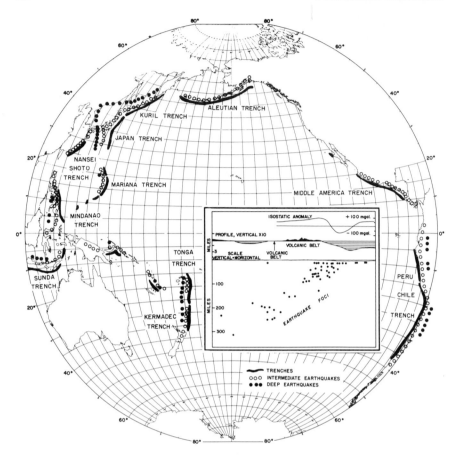

Fig. 140. The relation of trenches to the Pacific margin and the depths of earthquake foci in relation to the continental margins. After Gutenberg and Richter (1954) and Fisher and Revelle (1955).

hills that are now generally attributed to salt dome origin (Lankford and Curray, 1957; Murray, 1960) indicates that there may be faults at this margin which allow the linear arrangement of so many of these domes. A similar row of hills off the Orinoco Delta are considered as having reef origin (Nota, 1958), but they might possibly be due to salt domes along a marginal fault.

An alternative fault interpretation for the slopes was given by Emery (1950). He suggested that there are high-angle thrust faults extending from the continental shelf margin down under the continents. This agrees with the earthquake epicenters which also increase in depth under the continents (Fig. 140). Emery further suggested that the thrust faults elevated the margins and allowed the cutting of submarine canyons into them before they were again submerged.

## Origin of Gulf of Mexico Slopes

The two rather unique slopes of the northern Gulf of Mexico require some special discussion. That off western Louisiana and Texas (Fig. 133) with the hills and basins has been attributed to landsliding by Gealy (1956). This may be the explanation, but it seems rather strange that landsliding of such gigantic dimensions should occur along a slope of less than 1°. This is far below the world average so that it would be somewhat surprising if large-scale sliding should occur here but not on the steeper slopes. Furthermore, deposition is very slow here now, and the clay content of the sediments is high. Therefore, it is probable that the sediment is normally consolidated, which in turn should inhibit slumping or other types of mass movements[3] (Terzaghi, 1956). On the other hand, slumping may have resulted from faulting along the Sigsbee scarp as suggested by Dietz (1952).

A more satisfactory explanation for this special type of slope west of the Mississippi Delta may be salt dome action similar to that of the continental shelf. The valleys of the continental slope may have been partially blocked by salt doming developing basins and hills. Such an explanation, however, requires geophysical investigation before it can be given as more than speculation.[4]

The other Gulf of Mexico slope of special interest is that off western Florida (Fig. 132). This is located in a very stable area, and yet it is one of the steepest slopes so far discovered on the entire ocean floor. At the south end of the escarpment there is a trench of moderate depth which may indicate that the escarpment is of fault origin despite the absence of any other evidence of faulting. To the north the trench may have been filled because sediment appears to have come from that direction, partially filling the lower portion of some deep valleys.

An alternative origin of the west Florida escarpment is that it represents the drowned front of a coral reef. Such an explanation has been given by Newell (1959b) for the escarpments of the Bahamas and the escarpment bordering Blake Plateau. It could also apply to the

[3] The equally gentle slopes off the Mississippi birdfoot delta are subject to sliding because of rapid deposition.

[4] The recent Arcer sonic profiles made by Moore and Curray (1963) in this area give substantial evidence of the existence of salt domes underlying the slope.

steep slopes off west Florida, Yucatan, Brazil, and Ceylon. A submerging shelf of coral may grow upward with very steep slopes. If the shelf has been gradually submerged, such an origin for the escarpments is possible. Evidence for such a submergence comes from the borings in the Bahamas and has been given for the Blake Plateau (Ericson *et al.*, 1961). Against this idea for tropical submarine escarpments is the straightness of the west Florida scarp that is more suggestive of faulting. Before coming to any conclusion concerning the origin of these low-latitude escarpments it would be well to carry on extensive dredging to find out whether or not the exposed rocks consist of coral.

## Modification of Continental Slopes

The discovery that slides and turbidity currents are operating in the submarine canyons which cut the continental slopes (see Chapter XI) raises the question as to the importance of the same processes on the continental slopes in general. The outcrops of rock on the slope certainly imply either a nondepositional environment or sliding and flowing of material down a considerable portion of the upper slopes particularly when the sea level was low. Otherwise the slopes should be much more completely covered with the sediments that are certainly brought to them from the continents. Submarine currents, however, may explain some of the rock surfaces although Ericson *et al.* (1961, p. 242) think that slumping accounts for most submarine exposures. Archanguelski (1927) was the first to report evidence of such slumping on submarine slopes other than canyons. He found that the cores on the slopes of the Black Sea were considerably confused as if by slumping. Further evidence has come from cable breaks on the slopes although many of these have occurred in submarine canyons, and the breaks have been attributed to turbidity currents by Heezen and Ewing (1952) (see pp. 339–341).

Laboratory experiments by Moore (1961b) on samples obtained from the slopes off southern California indicate that wherever deposition is slow and clay content is high the sediments develop stability even on slopes up to 14°. The sediments are, in soil mechanics terminology, normally consolidated under their overburden pressure. This means that no excess pore water pressure is present and sediments increase in strength with burial depth so that they may maintain their stability.[5] However, during the times of lowered sea level when sedimentation was much more active on the exposed

[5] The possibility should be considered that the tested samples have been normally consolidated by the coring process.

upper slopes, it can be assumed that slides would have taken place keeping many of the slopes free from sedimentation. Possibly the bare rock still found in places has not been covered in the short time since the sea level rose.

## Continental Slope Evolution

The interesting discussion of the evolution of continental slopes by Dietz (1952) provides suggestions of various stages of development in the history of slopes. He describes the Pacific slopes of North America as youthful, the slopes off the east coast of United States as mature, and the slopes off a portion of Antarctica as old, whereas the Gulf Coast of the United States is thought to have slopes rejuvenated after reaching late maturity. In the early stages, according to Dietz, the sediment which reached the upper continental slope is carried downward by sliding and turbidity current action. This action in turn erodes gullies into the slope which may become canyons. The investigations by Moore (1961c), however, suggest that even in the initial stages represented by the United States west coast slopes, sediments are quite generally stabilized except where there are canyons crossing the shelf and coming near the shore and hence receiving a considerable supply of sediment. Sonoprobe studies (Moore, 1960) show that off California the shelf break is usually free of a sediment cover and that the sediments thicken both downslope and shoreward from the break with the greatest thickness on the continental shelf (Fig. 18). The upper slope along the Gulf Coast is known to have received somewhat larger deposits in postglacial time than the outer shelf (Phleger, 1960b, pp. 292–295; Curray, 1960); this suggests absence of sliding. Despite this objection, it may well be that much of the sediment has slid off the upper slopes, particularly during times of lowered sea level or whenever the rivers have built deltas across the shelf so as to allow rapid upper slope deposition like that now occurring off the Mississippi River.

Dietz further speculated that the sediments which slid or were carried down the slope by turbidity currents would build fans at the base and that eventually these fans would coalesce with the deltas built out from the lands. In this way the margins would be extended, and a very gentle slope to the deep ocean, such as occurs in the MacKenzie Sea sector of Antarctica, would be left. This is thought to complete the cycle. Dietz considers a rejuvenation has taken place off the northwest Gulf Coast because of a small scarp of possible fault origin which occurs at the base of the basin and hill province discussed above. He thought that this faulting has allowed slumping which in turn produced the topography (Fig. 133) as described by Gealy (1956). Objections to this mode of origin have been given above so that it seems to the writer rather questionable that this irregular slope can be explained by rejuvenation.

## Conclusions Concerning Slope Origin

As in the case of continental shelves, it seems unwise to conclude that the continental slopes have all had the same origin. From the available evidence, however, a diastrophic origin of the greater part of this juncture between oceans and continents is indicated. This is favored by the general straightness of the slopes, the angular changes in trend, the excessive steepness, the association with earthquake belts and deep trenches in the Pacific, and the outcrop of rocks along the slopes in various parts of the world. On the other hand, at least the Niger and Nile deltas appear to be bordered by depositional slopes because of the outbend of the shelf margin, but off almost all other deltas there is no evidence of appreciable building forward of the shelves. Origin of some of the slopes in the tropics by upbuilding of coral reefs on submerging platforms must be seriously considered and is certainly the explanation for the steep slopes around many coral reefs. Similarly, steep volcanic slopes occur around many or perhaps most oceanic islands, and the possibility cannot be overlooked that some of the continental slopes in volcanic areas are explained in this way although as yet there is no substantial evidence to support this type.

# CHAPTER XI

# SUBMARINE CANYONS, DEEP CHANNELS, AND OTHER MARINE VALLEYS

## Introduction

Although the origin of submarine canyons has been discussed for generations (see for example Spencer, 1903, and Lawson, 1893), very little field work has been carried on to establish their characteristics. Most information still comes from a few detailed studies of canyons along the California and Baja California coast. Since writing the first edition of this book a few rather spectacular results have come from French reconnaissance studies in the Mediterranean and from the Lamont Geological Observatory's coring and sounding operations in canyons off the east coast of the United States and in the Congo Canyon. The writer has had the opportunity to investigate and trace out to their termini the La Jolla and Coronado canyons of the San Diego area along with a number of canyons around the tip of Baja California and a few along the east coast of Japan. Studies of the small delta front valleys and of the fault scarp ravines in several areas have also provided useful information. Reconnaissance surveys have indicated that canyonlike features exist in the Arctic. All this new information has helped to clarify the picture, but it is still premature to make any statements that "the canyon problem is now solved" such as have appeared recently in at least one geology textbook.

## Types of Marine Valleys

Land valleys include a number of types of diverse origin such as fault, river cut, glacially excavated, and landslide valleys. With this in mind in discussing the valleys of the sea floor it is important to distinguish between the various marine types. These include: (1) the relatively straight broad-floored, trough-shaped valleys which follow structural trends, have basin depressions, and few, if any, entering tributaries; (2) the shallow, rather discontinuous elongate depressions

311

that cross the shelves; (3) the small gullies that cut the forward building submerged slopes of great deltas; (4) the ravines that extend part way down steep submarine fault scarps; (5) the relatively large troughs cutting the shelf and slope outside some large deltas; (6) the rock-walled, V-shaped, winding valleys with many tributaries that extend down the continental slopes; and (7) the outward continuations of the sixth type which exist as partly leveed fan-valleys crossing the great fans at the base of the slopes. It is only the sixth type to which the word canyon seems applicable because these are the only submarine valleys which have true canyon proportions and characteristics. The name "submarine ravines" for the canyons used by Kuenen (1953a) may be appropriate in some cases, but it fails to convey the truly majestic proportions which characterize a large number of canyons cutting the continental slopes.

### Description of Canyons

The description of a few of the submarine canyons may be deceptive since they may be atypical, but unfortunately it is only these few canyons which have been studied in sufficient detail to warrant their inclusion. Since the canyon type of submarine valley is closely connected with the outer leveed channels, some of the descriptions will include both types. The other varieties will be described separately.

**La Jolla and Scripps Submarine Canyons.**    Partly because of their location close to Scripps Institution of Oceanography, La Jolla Canyon and Scripps Canyon, a prominent tributary (Fig. 141), are the best known in the world. The three tributaries at the head of Scripps Canyon have been explored extensively by SCUBA divers, and with the help of their photographs and descriptions along with extensive soundings and bottom sampling an accurate picture is now available (Fig. 142). The innermost head of South Branch of Scripps Canyon lies only 230 m from the low tide shoreline directly off Sumner Canyon on land, and jetting through the sand fill inside the canyon head, Chamberlain (1960, Fig. 2) has shown that a rock gully continues to within 60 m of the shoreline. The head as it now exists is a sand chute which can be traced outward for about a hundred meters to where rock appears on the walls and the valley enters a narrow gorge with a steeply sloping floor usually covered with sand, surf grass, and kelp. Beyond the depth of wave agitation there is a zone where the kelp and surf grass are concentrated. The rock on the canyon walls is stratified and is partly covered with marine growths. Wall slopes are commonly vertical or even overhanging. Tributaries enter the sides either as hanging valleys or as steep-floored ravines.

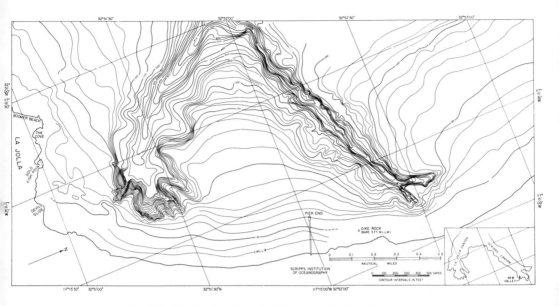

Fig. 141. The heads of La Jolla Canyon and Scripps Canyon.

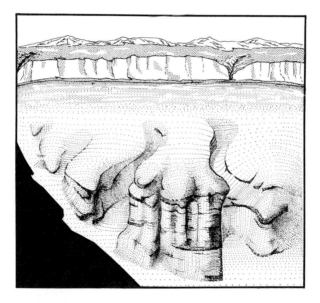

Fig. 142. Aqualung view of two of the tributaries to Scripps Canyon showing the vertical and overhanging walls and the sand chutes leading down into the rock gorges. Sketch by James R. Moriarty from descriptions and sketches of Earl Murray. Steep canyon wall in foreground is removed.

Fig. 143. Underwater photo of a gully tributary at the head of Scripps Canyon after
a deepening has exposed the smoothed and eroded base. For scale see knife. Photo
courtesy of R. F. Dill, U.S. Navy Electronics Laboratory.

The depths on the floors of these tributaries are subject to constant changes. Building up of sediment occurs for about a year and
then rapid deepening takes place which amounts to as much as 50 ft
in extreme cases. It has been possible to connect several of these
deepenings with earthquakes (Shepard, 1952a; Chamberlain, 1960,
Appendix V). Others have occurred which could be related to unusually
large waves, and still others for no apparent reason. The exact nature
of the removal of sediment that causes the deepenings is not definitely
known although the sand has moved out of some of the tributaries,
probably as a sand flow, and exposed channels that according to
Dill (1962) appear to have been freshly scoured by some sort of
abrasion (Fig. 143), probably the result of creep.

The cliffed walls continue out to the point where Scripps Canyon
joins La Jolla Canyon a mile from shore and at a depth of 150 fathoms.
Pictures of some of the outer cliffs have been made by pulling a

Fig. 144. The alluvial walls at the head of La Jolla Canyon.
Underwater photo by Frank Haymaker at 30 m.

submerged camera toward the wall with a projecting rod so as to
obtain a flash photo at proper focus when the rod makes contact
(McAllister, 1957) (Fig 27).

La Jolla Canyon has much less precipitous walls. At its head there
are alluvial formations (Fig. 144) which appear to be weathering back
at an appreciable rate although the surveys over the past twenty-five
years do not show marked changes. A considerable number of branches
come into this canyon head. Diving observations show that large
blocks are breaking away from the wall, and the alluvium is being
eroded. Farther down, the walls have rock outcrops, some of them
Cretaceous and some Eocene (Emery and Shepard, 1945). A number
of dredge hauls on the walls beyond where the canyon reaches 300
fathoms failed to yield rock. At approximately this depth the profiles
(Fig. 145) show that the true canyon has apparently ended and is
replaced by a channel with natural levees. Locally the channel has
terraces on the side. Traced outward into San Diego Trough a fan with

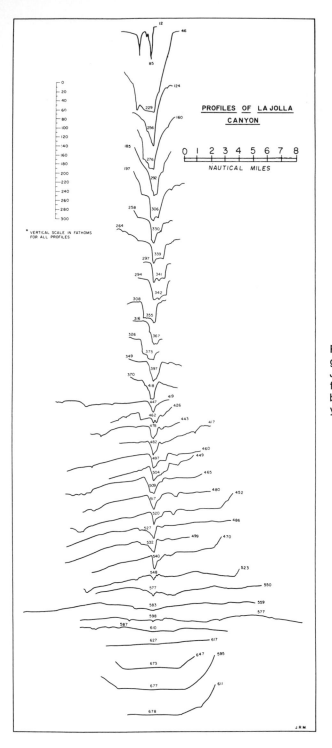

Fig. 145. Profiles from fathograms along the length of La Jolla Canyon and across the fan-valley that cuts the fan out beyond the rock-walled canyon.

a channel becomes evident. The fan-valley decreases in depth until, merging with the fan, it disappears in the flat floor of the trough.

Cores along the length of La Jolla Canyon beyond the confluence with Scripps Canyon show alternating layers of sand and silty clay. The same types continue all the way out to the end of the channel. Sand layers, however, are found also in the fan and on the levees on either side of the channel although the sand is somewhat less common.

**Coronado Canyon.**   A canyon occurs off the United States–Mexican border starting at a distance of 8 miles from the Tijuana River mouth. Near its head there is a northern tributary called Loma Sea Valley with a divide, beyond which the slope is reversed (Fig. 146). Apparently Coronado Canyon has cut across the rocky Coronado Bank and pirated a valley which formerly drained to the northwest along Loma Sea Valley. Where Coronado Canyon extends west across the ridge it has steep rocky walls and a narrow V-shaped gorge but beyond, where it turns rather abruptly to the south, its outer wall consists of a sediment-covered ridge with irregular hummocks suggesting landsliding although a little shale was found in dredgings near the base of the bank. The outer wall was formerly interpreted as an old delta, but it might also represent a high natural levee built on top of a low rock ridge. Slumping of either a former delta or levee has taken place. The valley floors both in the rock canyon and in the channel beyond contain a fill with layers of sand alternating with silty clay. Beginning directly west of North Coronados Islands there are layers of shell and shallow water foram sand on the channel floor which closely resemble the sediment found on the narrow shelf off this island (Phleger, 1951a). On the other hand, some coarse sand containing fine gravel found on the canyon floor nearby is distinctly different from that on the adjacent shelf (Shepard and Einsele, 1962).

Traced seaward the valley leaves the base of the rocky slope off the Coronados Islands and is found to have low natural levees on both sides. This valley winds across the southern end of San Diego Trough. As it approaches a rocky ridge the channel is cut considerably deeper below the floor than upstream, but this gorge does not persist all the way down into San Clemente Basin. It appears that the local deepening of the valley is related to the crossing of the ridge.

**Cape San Lucas Canyons.**   Off Cape San Lucas at the southern tip of Baja California there are a series of canyons which can be traced out to where they end at a depth of about 1300 fathoms (Fig. 147). These canyons, like those off southern California, slope outward continuously so far as could be told from echo soundings. They are winding and V-shaped and have numerous tributaries entering along their entire length. The walls have been dredged in a number of places

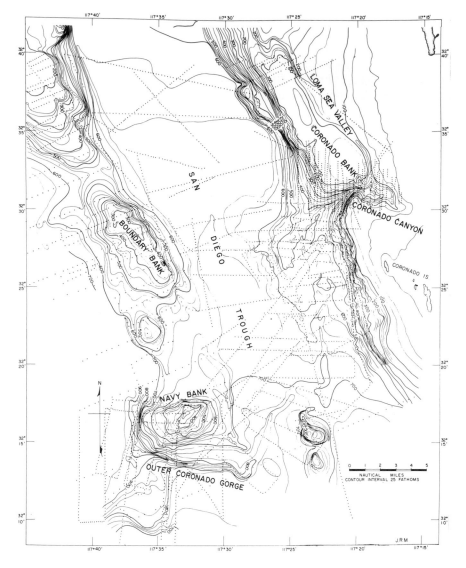

Fig. 146. Contour map of Coronado Canyon and its outer continuation across San Diego Trough and across a rocky ridge west of the Trough. Note the increase in depth as the valley crosses the outer ridge but the disappearance of all trace of the valley on the slope extending into San Clemente Basin. The canyon head crosses a ridge very much as do antecedent streams. It appears to have captured the drainage of Loma Sea Valley. Sounding lines shown by dots. For regional relations see Fig. 134.

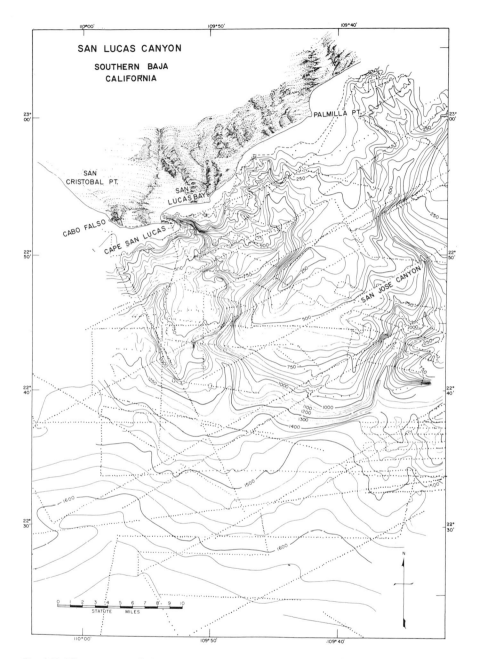

Fig. 147. The granite-walled canyons south of Cape San Lucas. Note their numerous tributaries, their relation to a submarine structure 8 miles south of the Cape, and their termination at approximately the same depth (1325 fathoms). A large submarine fan is shown seaward of the canyon terminations. Sounding lines shown by dots. Contour interval 50 fathoms out to 1250 fathoms and 25 fathoms beyond.

Fig. 148. Underwater photograph of sandfall in a tributary of San Lucas Canyon. Photograph taken by natural light at a depth of 175 ft by Conrad Limbaugh.

and granite, along with other intrusive igneous rocks, has been recovered. Near the bottom of one of the outer canyons breccia was dredged which had in its cement Foraminifera suggestive of the present day depths. The breccia is probably due to local cementation of slide material after the canyon was cut. There is nothing about these canyons that seems to differentiate them topographically from the land canyons found in the nearby mountains (Shepard, 1961b).

Where cored, the canyon floors provided sand with mud layers, and the sand layers[1] continue to some extent out beyond the canyon termini onto an irregular fan. The latter lacks definite channels. One photograph by Carl J. Shipek showed what appeared to be ripple marks on the canyon floor.

The most spectacular find coming from the investigation of a small tributary of the San Lucas canyons was made by SCUBA divers. They found a moving river of sand (Fig. 148) which was cascading over a

[1] Two cores obtained in 1962 from these canyon floors recovered several feet of coarse sand containing gravel up to 2 cm in diameter.

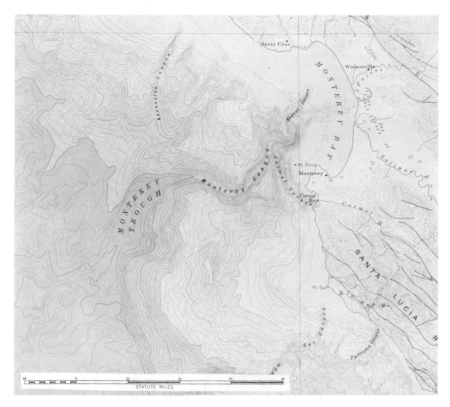

Fig. 149. The winding canyon heads in Monterey Bay and vicinity. Carmel Canyon is cut in granite, and granite was also found on the east wall of Monterey Canyon. From Shepard and Emery (1941). Contour interval 300 ft (50 fathoms).

cliff and continuing on below their zone of observation. The flow of the sand river above the fall was slow enough so that fish could submerge into it and swim away from the divers who were pursuing them. The source of the sand was very evident since, on the night before the dive, sand had been washed over a narrow tombolo and carried directly toward this canyon head. Dives made subsequently showed no sand flows in operation.[2] Smaller scale sand flows have also been seen in Scripps Canyon by E. F. Murray and R. F. Dill.

**Monterey Canyon.** In vertical dimensions Monterey Submarine Canyon off central California is perhaps the largest in the world (Fig. 149), although it is not the longest. Its head is located at Moss Landing where oil company drillings have revealed the presence of a 5000-ft canyon filled with Miocene and younger sediments (Starke,

[2] Another large flow was reported by R. F. Dill in 1962, along with evidence of erosion.

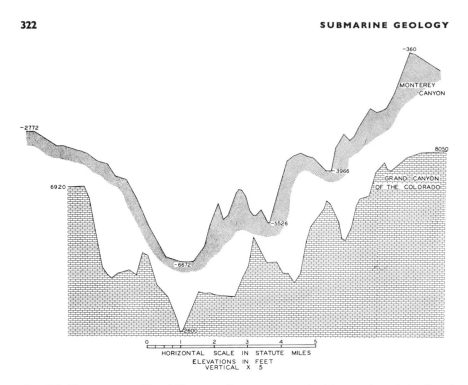

Fig. 150. Transverse profile of Monterey Canyon compared with a section of the Grand Canyon by using the same number of points of elevation.

1956). According to available information the present sea floor valley shows no rock until a depth of about 300 fathoms has been attained. The upper portion is clearly cut into alluvium or other unconsolidated sediments. Cores obtained by Frank Haymaker and later by R. R. Lankford and E. F. Murray in the canyon head show that here also there are alternating layers of medium-grained sand and silt. Traced outward the canyon acquires rock walls and farther out granite is found at least on one side overlain by sedimentary formations (Shepard and Emery, 1941). The shape of the canyon is similar to that of the canyons in the adjacent mountain ranges with an evident control exerted by the northwest trending structures. Carmel Branch comes out of Carmel Bay and extends along the coast as a narrow V-shaped gorge with granite walls. One branch of Carmel Canyon appears to be a direct continuation of a land canyon. A cross section taken near the place where Carmel Canyon enters Monterey Canyon shows that the latter is quite comparable in dimensions with the Grand Canyon of the Colorado (Fig. 150). A core from the canyon axis at a depth of 840 fathoms showed a graded sediment with mud overlying sand and rounded gravel up to 5 cm in diameter at the bottom. Seaward, the canyon loses its V shape at about 850 fathoms and becomes more of a trough. This in turn becomes a channel with natural levees on the side and can be traced out to depths of over 2000 fathoms (Dill *et al.*, 1954). A core along the outer channel obtained by H. W. Menard (personal communication) also was found to have gravel.

**Tokyo Canyon.** This canyon (Fig. 151) extends into the outer portion of Tokyo Bay. It has been extensively studied by Japanese investigators and most recently by the writer on the *Spencer F. Baird* with the collaboration of Professor H. Niino of the Tokyo College of Fisheries on the *Umitaka Maru*. The canyon has a winding course, innumerable tributaries on both walls, and a V-shaped profile with a small flattening of the floor. The walls have relatively soft sedimentary rock with some hard lava near the upper rim although most of the slopes appear to have a sediment cover. The floor out to about 400 fathoms is covered with mud containing a few sand layers, but farther out cores yielded only small quantities of sand and fine gravel. No fan was found where the canyon terminates in the Sagami Bay fault trough at 800 fathoms. The small canyon just to the south is narrower and has steeper walls. A series of bottom photographs show that the walls of this canyon are very rocky with occasional ripple-marked surfaces, and that the canyon floor is covered with current ripples of coarse sand with gravel and small pieces of rock in the troughs. The surface currents in the vicinity of this small canyon are periodically very strong, causing "overfalls" above the south rim of the canyon.

Investigations of other canyons in the vicinity of Tokyo Bay showed that except for the upper portion of Tokyo Canyon the absence of muddy sediments on the canyon floors was characteristic of the group. All these canyons have numerous tributaries and winding courses except for the Tateyama Bay tributary of Tokyo Canyon. No canyon head extends in beyond the 30-fathom line. Off Kamogawa to the east of Tokyo Bay, a winding V-shaped canyon extends out to about 1200 fathoms where it enters an easterly extension of Sagami fault trough. Rock was found on the walls of this canyon out to at least 1000 fathoms.

**Trincomalee Canyon.** This enters the only appreciable bay on the east side of Ceylon and has not been studied by geologists, but deserves special attention because of the fact that it definitely enters an estuary and cuts through hogbacks of Precambrian gneiss and quartzite (Adams, 1929). The soundings show that it has precipitous rock walls, and this is attested to by SCUBA divers (with whom the writer has talked) who have made dives into the canyon. The canyon shows a gradient at its head of 31° and an average gradient of 7.3°, which makes it among the steepest in the world (Shepard and Beard, 1938).

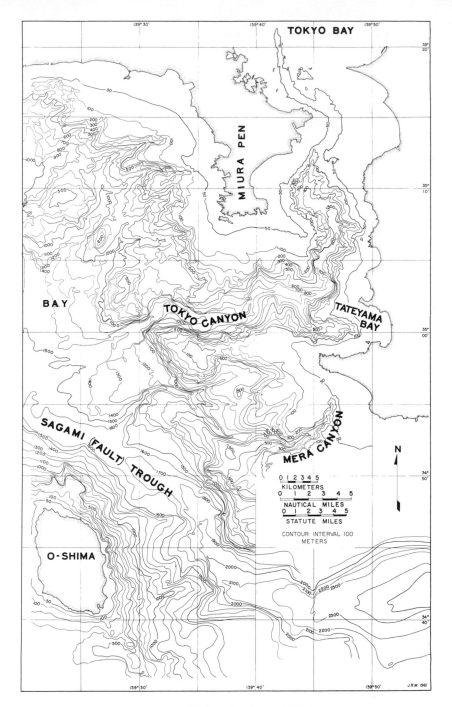

Fig. 151. Canyons in the vicinity of Tokyo, based on a 1960 Scripps Institution survey and on a Japanese survey of recent date. Note the fan at the lower end of Tokyo Canyon. Contours at the head of Tokyo Canyon are from Japanese interpretations and the rest from work by the writer. The contours are in meters.

It has been traced out only to 800 fathoms but no doubt continues to much greater depth. There are other Ceylonese canyons of smaller dimensions, all of them occurring off a straight coast.

**Mediterranean Canyons.** Numerous canyons are found along the slopes of the Mediterranean, all extending below the 155-fathom-sill depth of the sea. The Corsican canyons (Bourcart, 1959), found entirely along the west coast, are unique in that they enter every bay along that side of the island and give the impression of being a direct continuation of the land canyons (Figs. 137, 152). In places along the Corsican coast it is possible to swim past small land ravines and look down through the remarkably clear water into submarine canyon heads. The canyons of the Corsican sea floor are certainly cut into the hard crystalline rocks found on the adjacent land. Tributaries on the sea floor appear to be as common as those on land. The canyons extend down to depths of at least 1100 fathoms and probably to 1400 fathoms. A core from St. Laurent Canyon near the north end of the island revealed the characteristic canyon sand layers along with a considerable thickness of sand with plant fibers at the base of the core.

The French and Italian Riviera is bordered by slopes cut by as many canyons as the slopes off West Corsica (Figs. 137, 153). These are found off land valleys in most places but differ from the Corsica canyons in that most of them do not extend into estuaries. One valley comes into the bay at Villefranche, but this differs from other submarine canyons in having a basin depression. Off Nice there is a series of ravine heads which come in close to the straight gravel beach. These must have been cut into the unconsolidated sediments of the Var Delta. According to Nesteroff (1958), Vengeur Canyon in the Gulf of Juan has walls which locally come up above the surface. Vertical cliffs on the submerged wall are identical with the subaerial stream-cut cliffs on Isle de Santa Marguerite, and the submerged cliffs have no sign of recent erosion. They are protected by calcareous algae growths. According to Nesteroff (1958) the formations off the Var are alluvial and the morphology identical to that of the Pleistocene formation of the hills of Nice. In deeper water many of the canyons have been found to have rock walls (Bourcart, 1950). Between Cannes and Toulon there are rock-walled canyons with heads running roughly parallel to the coast. Here structural control of these erosion valleys is as clearly indicated as in the Monterey submarine canyon. The outer ends of the canyons are said to have fans with channels (Bourcart, 1959). Cores in depths of more than 1000 fathoms reveal sand and gravel layers (Bourcart *et al.*, 1960).

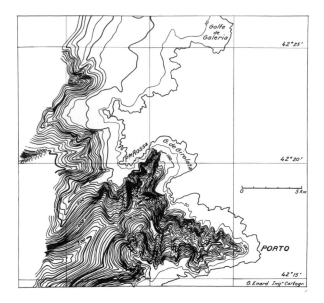

Fig. 152. The relation of canyons on the west side of Corsica to the coastline. Contour interval 50 m. From Bourcart (1959).

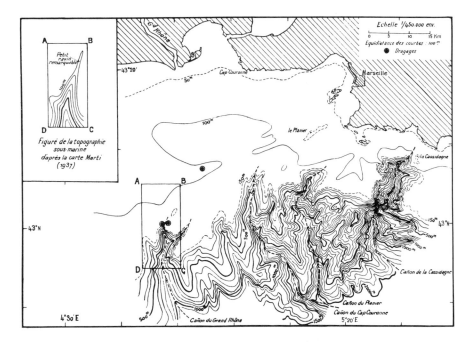

Fig. 153. Comparison of the canyons off the Côte d'Azur (right) with those off the Rhone Delta (left). No indication of a break between the two is indicated, contrary to what might be expected according to the interpretations of Kuenen (1953a). From Bourcart (1959).

Lowering of sea level did not cause the canyons. There can be no doubt but what both the Corsican and the Riviera canyons extend well below the 155-fathom-sill depth of the Mediterranean. Kuenen (1953a) claimed that the canyons west of Marseille differ from those off the Riviera, the former being compared to the Corsican canyon "ravines" and the latter to the canyons off eastern United States. From Bourcart's contours, however, it is difficult to see any decided difference between the types (Fig. 153). At least Arrigo Canyon near the Spanish border seems to be clearly of the same type as those off the Riviera (Bourcart *et al.*, 1948). The minor differences may be related to the general change in the land character from the Riviera mountainous coast to the lowland of the Rhone delta coast.

**Eastern United States Canyons.** The east coast of United States is bordered by a wide shelf, and the outer portion of this shelf is indented by a series of canyons which run down the slope beyond. These canyons are also considered by Kuenen as differing from such canyons as Corsica, Tokyo, the French Riviera, and California. None of the east coast canyons has been studied in as much detail as have the California canyons, and the data concerning their outer termini are based on rather poorly located sounding lines. However, the inner canyons have been fairly completely surveyed so that it is possible to contour a number of them with some degree of confidence, and Hudson Canyon has been traced seaward across the broad submarine fan (Fig. 154). The contours by Veatch and Smith (1939) have been referred to widely but, as has been pointed out by various geologists, the contouring shows far more small valleys than can be justified from the available soundings. Another interpretation is given in Fig. 155. Kuenen claims that the east coast canyons, which he calls "the New England type," differ from the "Corsican ravines" in extending straight down the submarine slopes except for some diversion at the canyon heads. As pointed out by Kuenen, there are no canyons that run parallel to the slope.[3]

The inner canyons are cut into rock formations, some as old as the Cretaceous (Stetson, 1936). Probably the walls are precipitous in places, as was reported by Stetson, as the result of the notching of a block of sandstone by the dredging wire. It may be correct, however, to state that most of these east coast canyons are cut into soft rocks or unconsolidated sediments. Hudson Canyon appears to have many small tributaries although no major tributaries enter it so that this

[3] A canyon off southern France, claimed by Kuenen to be of the "New England type," does have a bend making it run parallel to the general slope for a short distance (see Fig. 153).

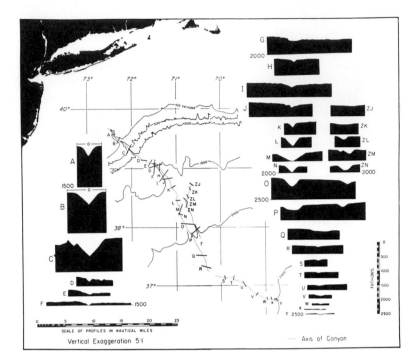

Fig. 154. Cross sections of Hudson Submarine Canyon. From Heezen *et al.* (1959, Fig. 17).

and most other east coast canyons differ from the California and Baja California submarine canyons in this respect. As Stetson once pointed out to the writer, there are ridges bordering the sides of the lower portions of the charted canyons. This appears to make these portions fan channels with the ridges interpreted as natural levees like those described for California.

The floors of the east coast canyons have been cored by Stetson (1936) and by Lamont Geological Observatory scientists (Heezen *et al.*, 1959). Stetson found that there were sediments of postglacial age overlying glacial age sediments as indicated by the faunal changes in the planktonic Foraminifera. The Lamont cores show sand layers up to 7 m in thickness (Ericson *et al.*, 1961). Some of these layers grade upward from fine sand to a very fine sand containing silt (Shepard, 1961a). Two cores obtained in Hudson Canyon had a gravel layer, but a recent examination of these cores by Ericson and the writer showed that the gravel is set in clayey sediment and probably represents a mud flow down the canyon wall or glacial marine sediment. The finding of a block of Miocene rock well out along the axis of the

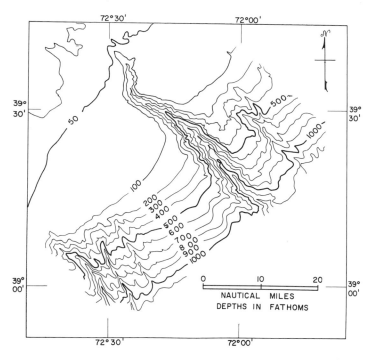

Fig. 155. Submarine contours of Hudson Canyon and vicinity.

Hudson deep-sea channel might also be indicative of relatively power-ful current action, but alternatively it may only represent an iceberg deposit of Pleistocene age.

## Delta Front Submarine Troughs

Outside the deltas of the Ganges, the Indus, the Niger, and the Ventura of southern California there are troughlike valleys which cut across the continental shelf and extend down the slopes beyond. The Pakistan Navy made detailed surveys off the Ganges and Indus (Fig. 156) out to the edge of the continental shelf (Hayter, 1960). The Ganges Trough was traced seaward by the *Galathea* expedition (Kiiler-ich, 1958). These surveys show a trough-shaped cross section with a floor about 4 miles wide in the place of the V shape of typical sub-marine canyons. The walls of the trough are essentially straight, have only minor indentations, and so far as known have no rock outcrops. Similarly off the Niger Delta and off the Ventura Delta at Hueneme, California, the submarine valleys do not have rock walls or trib-utaries.

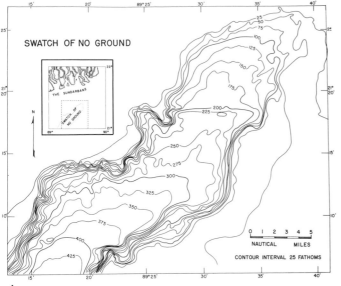

A

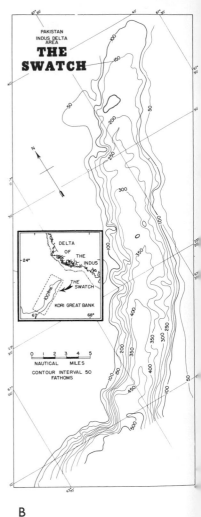

B

Fig. 156. (*a*) Troughlike valley off the Ganges Delta. Based on detailed survey by Pakistan Navy. (*b*) Submarine trough off the Indus Delta. Based on detailed survey by Pakistan Navy.

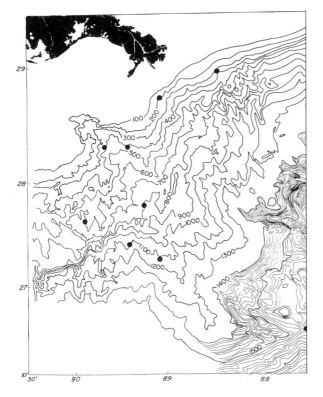

Fig. 157. Submarine trough and fan off the western portion of Mississippi Delta. Depths in fathoms. Contour interval 100 fathoms to 1400, then 10 fathoms. From Ewing *et al.* (1958).

Off the western side of the Mississippi Delta another troughlike valley is found which does not approach the coast although borings and geophysical prospecting show that it connects with a filled channel that extends into the edge of the subaerial delta. The floor of this trough is about 5 miles across. It can be traced seaward to a depth of about 900 fathoms where it apparently connects with a submarine fan (Fig. 157). Phleger (1955) found displaced Foraminifera in cores along the axis of the trough.

## Congo Submarine Canyon

At the mouth of the Congo (Fig. 158) there is an estuary with a canyonlike valley extending into the estuary for about 15 miles. This is particularly interesting because the Congo transports enormous

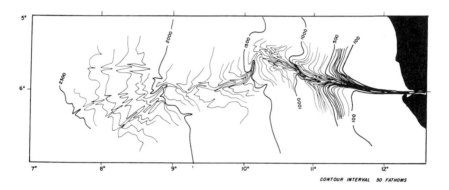

Fig. 158. The Congo Submarine Canyon showing the outer fan and fan-valleys. From Heezen *et al.* (1959).

loads of sediment that could fill the estuary in a few years. Heezen's studies (Heezen *et al.*, 1957, 1959) have shown that the head is constantly changing and that attempts to maintain cables across the canyon outside the coast have met with repeated failures especially after the rainy season. Slides or turbidity currents occur about fifty times a year. Heezen's survey showed a very large fan on the outside with channels cutting across it. The entire length of the canyon and its outer channel is 500 miles, one of the longest known in the world. The canyon has a few short tributaries on the inside and is V shaped. If rock is present on the walls, it has not yet been reported. Sand, silt, and organic debris including leaves were found in cores from the floor. The sandy layers are high in silt and all the coarsest material consists of plant fragments.

## Foreset Slope Valleys

The small valleys on the foreset slope of deltas are quite different from the delta-front troughs. They occur only on the upper slope and are found principally where deltas have built across a shelf or are building into a fiord with steep sides so that there is no frontal shelf. The best known are those off the Mississippi Delta (Fig. 159). Here the valleys are concentrated around the active mouths but occur also at points where the mouths have been abandoned recently as off Grand Pass (now sunk below the Gulf waters) and off Southeast Pass, formerly an important distributary. The valleys extend down to a depth of about 200 ft (60 m) and terminate on the slope in a zone containing small hills. The valleys are not cut deeper below their surroundings than about 10 fathoms and have almost no tributaries. Occasional basins of small dimension are found on the floors. Off the Fraser Delta (Mathews and Shepard, 1962), the valleys occur only near the main mouth but are found also off Canoe Pass (a mouth largely abandoned by 1919), and at the point where the river emptied before the jetty was complete. Unlike the valleys off the Mississippi the Fraser valleys have some indication of natural levees along the side. The hills at the base of the valleys along the front of the Fraser Delta are very pronounced. The Rhone's Mediterranean delta also has very small valleys which stop midway down the slope (van Straaten, 1959a). The Rhone Delta in Lake Geneva, on the other hand, contains a very different type of valley. Here en echelon channels are found down the entire slope of the delta front although decreasing in amplitude until they virtually disappear at the base. Near the subaerial delta the lacustrine valleys are bordered by high, steep-sided natural levees, but the levees gradually merge outward into the fan. The topography closely resembles the channel crossing the fan outside La Jolla Canyon (Fig.145). Dives into the Rhone Channel near the river (Dill, 1961) showed strong currents were flowing down to at least 35 m and asymmetrical ripples were advancing down the floor of the channel.

The sediments of the foreset slope valleys in oceanic deltas are, so far as known, free from any concentration of coarse material. The cores in the Mississippi and the Fraser delta valleys show the same types of material as are found on the ridges in between. Any appreciable current should concentrate the coarse fraction so that one can assume that such currents do not exist in these ocean valleys. In Lake Geneva, on the other hand, the channel floor has a well-sorted sand, whereas muddy sediments occur at the surface of the levees.

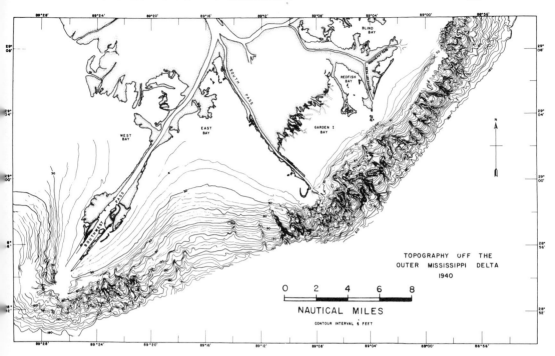

Fig. 159. Gullies in the foreset slope of the Mississippi Delta that are concentrated off the most advanced distributaries. These gullies are apparently the result of slides in the advancing slope. They terminate at depths of 200 ft (33 fathoms).

Here there can be no doubt about the concentration of currents in the channel and such currents were observed by Dill (1961) in a dive into the valley.

### Fault Scarp Valleys

Emery and Terry (1956) have described small ravinelike valleys cutting the submarine fault scarp off the Palos Verdes Hills near Los Angeles. These valleys have few if any tributaries and are not known to have rock walls. The same type of valley is found on the submerged fault scarps of the Gulf of California where a detailed survey by the writer showed that the valleys are discontinuous on the slope (Fig. 160).

### Fault Trough Valleys

There is no doubt but what some of the valleys of the sea floor are fault troughs and hence are not primarily related to erosion. It is often difficult to decide which valleys should be put in this category because

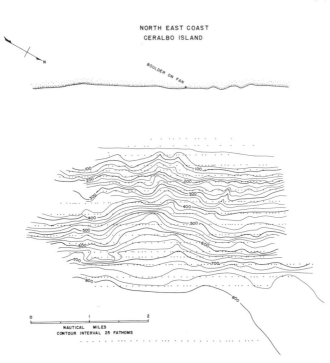

Fig. 160. Landslide valley on the fault scarp slope northeast of Ceralbo Island in the Gulf of California. Dots indicate sounding lines.

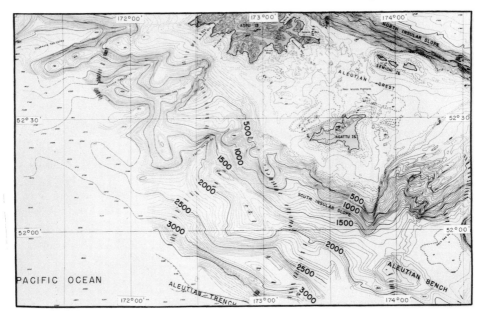

Fig 161. The trough-shaped valleys south of the Aleutian Islands. The trough shape and the depression contours suggest fault origin. Contour interval 50 fathoms. From Gates and Gibson (1956).

of inadequacy of the surveys. Perhaps the best examples of the fault type are found around the Aleutian Islands where some very deep valleys extend down into the Aleutian Trench (Fig. 161). These fault valleys have steep straight sides but have a broad floor with basin depressions at the bottom. They are, therefore, somewhat similar to glacial troughs, differing from the latter in extending down or along the slopes to very deep water and in being confined to unstable areas.

## Origin of Submarine Valleys

**Miscellaneous Types.**  Some of the sea floor valleys are easy to explain and their origin should cause little controversy. Where the soundings are sufficiently abundant for recognition the fault trough type is, of course, self-explanatory. The foreset slope valleys in marine deltas and the ravines on fault scarps appear to be due to mass movements on the sea floor (Shepard, 1955). According to Terzaghi (1956), rapidly accumulating silty sediments can slide on slopes as low as 1 percent, thus accounting for the gullies bordering the Mississippi Delta. The hummocks found outside the foreset slope of the Fraser Delta provide good supporting evidence for slide origin of the valleys at that place. The giving out of all the well-sounded foreset slope valleys part way down the front of the marine deltas is strong evidence against a turbidity current origin because turbidity currents continue to the base of slopes, and there should be little reason for cutting to stop in midslope. The absence of a concentration of coarse sediments on the valley floors provides further evidence against turbidity currents. On the other hand, the heavy cold water currents are clearly the cause of the delta front valley in Lake Geneva and probably in many other lacustrine deltas. These density currents are, of course, more possible where the rivers enter fresh water.

The delta-front troughs which cross the shelf outside several deltas and extend down the slope constitute more of a problem. Because of the scarcity of available information concerning these troughs one can only speculate on somewhat insecure grounds. The rivers must be introducing a huge mass of sediment which is highly mobile and hence may move down the gentle slopes as a mass movement. Currents of some sort must be in operation along these valleys to prevent their fill by sediments from the nearby river mouths. Possibly these currents develop during flood stages in the river when great quantities of sediments are introduced.

**Submarine Canyons: Turbidity Currents Versus Subaerial Erosion.**
By far the most difficult problem in valley origin is to explain the cause of the rock-walled canyons which cut many of the continental slopes

to great depths. In the first edition of this book the suggestion was made that the canyons might have been cut by rivers during a low stand of sea level caused by continental glaciers that were much larger and thicker than generally thought to have been the case. This idea has been discarded for the following reasons which became evident shortly after the first edition was published:

1. If the sea level was greatly lowered there should be shallow-water deposits of Pleistocene age on the flat-topped seamounts (guyots). These have not been found although older shallow-water formations have been dredged here (see Chapter XIII).
2. The huge glaciers suggested by the earlier hypothesis would presumably have had to fill the entire Arctic basin, but much of the Arctic shelf was not glaciated.
3. Submarine canyons found cutting some of the Arctic slopes (Carsola, 1954b) indicate the absence of the hypothetical Arctic ice cap.

*Facts Requiring Explanation.* Before attempting to find a satisfactory explanation for submarine canyons it is very important to review some of the facts which have been learned from their exploration by geologists and from the available hydrographic surveys. Some difficulty is encountered in this tabulation because there is no assurance that all the canyons which have been described have the same type of origin. Kuenen may be correct in separating the rock-walled canyons into the "New England type" and into what he calls "Corsican ravines." However, as has been pointed out previously, the difference between the two is very slight, if it exists at all. Accordingly, the facts to be given can be said to apply to both of Kuenen's types. The following points seem to be pertinent:

1. The canyons have rock walls of all degrees of hardness including granite and quartzite, but are more commonly of softer types.
2. The canyons have winding courses although they have straight stretches where influenced by structural control.
3. Many of the canyons have dendritic tributary systems.
4. So far as known, all rock-walled submarine canyons terminate part way down the continental slopes, although many of the valleys continue as leveed channels across the fans at the slope base.
5. The canyon floors are roughly V shaped although there are some indications of narrow flat floors at the base of the V.
6. The canyon floors are largely covered with sediment containing an abundance of sand, usually consisting of sand layers alternating

with clayey sediments. Many of the sands are graded. Gravel is found locally on the floor of a few canyons.

7. The canyons occur off both stable and unstable coasts, are essentially worldwide in distribution, and occur even in the Arctic and off some oceanic islands.
8. In many places the canyons extend in across the shelf to the coast.
9. A number of canyons extend deeply into estuaries whereas other canyons start off straight stretches of coast.
10. Some canyons have their rock walls extending into shore whereas other rock-walled canyons have their heads cut into Pleistocene or even Holocene alluvium.
11. Contrary to previously expressed opinions the canyons are not closely related to large rivers although canyons and trough-shaped valleys are found off some of these rivers.

*Discredited Hypotheses.* When the first edition of this book was written there was a large number of hypotheses used by geologists as canyon explanations. In recent years most of these hypotheses have been gradually discarded, leaving only the turbidity current hypothesis and another which combines subaerial erosion with drowning and maintenance of the canyons by turbidity currents, submarine slides, and sand flows.

The idea that canyons are the product of artesian springs coming out along the slopes (Johnson, 1939) was based on the east coast canyons which appear to be related to seaward-dipping coastal plain formations, and these were thought to act as aquifers. The hypothesis does not explain the canyons cut in granite and other resistant rocks nor is there even any likelihood of there being sufficient underground circulation to produce the deep canyons beyond the wide shelf off the east coast of the United States. The absence of sink holes or other basins along the length of the canyons adds another serious difficulty.

Tsunamis were suggested by Bucher (1940) because of the fact that these long period waves transmit some of their energy to the deep ocean floor. These currents, however, are significant only in shallow water and on the slopes could be concentrated only on ridges. Finally the canyons are definitely not confined to the areas where tsunamis are common.

Canyons have been explained by diastrophic movements (Wegener, 1924, p. 177). No doubt both faulting and folding can produce valley-like depressions on the continental slopes. The winding pattern and V shape of the cross section of submarine canyons, however, shows clearly that most of them are not diastrophic. Fault valleys would not show as much sinuosity nor would they show the dendritic tributaries which enter many canyons of the sea floor. Furthermore, there is no indication that canyons are more common in unstable areas.

Landsliding has certainly produced many land valleys and should be effective on all steep submarine slopes having unconsolidated sediments. The shape of landslide valleys, however, is very different from the typical submarine canyons. The dendritic tributary system and especially tributaries extending parallel to the coasts for many miles are hard to attribute to land slides. Slides leave hummocky topography and would certainly give out along the slopes where the gradient decreased. The deep granite-walled gorges form an overwhelming difficulty for an hypothesis which relates canyons only to mass movements.

_Turbidity Currents._ Turbidity currents have found energetic support in recent years as an explanation for the erosion of submarine canyons. They are considered either as one of the major causes (Kuenen, 1953a) or as the sole cause of submarine canyons (Heezen, 1956). The idea was first suggested by Daly (1936) but was not given much credit until Kuenen performed his experiments at Groningen University (Kuenen and Migliorini, 1950) and showed that sand mixed with mud and water could travel down the length of a long tank without losing much of the suspended load. The discovery, made first by Scripps Institution geologists (Shepard and Emery, 1941; Ludwick, 1950) but later greatly amplified by Maurice Ewing and his associates, that sand sediments were commonplace in submarine canyons and even out on the sea floor beyond, demonstrated that the currents could carry sand. The succession of cable breaks in a seaward direction after the Grand Banks earthquake of 1929 (Fig. 162) led Heezen and Ewing (1952) to the conclusion that there were turbidity currents moving down the slope at a high speed. This was widely hailed as the final needed proof that turbidity currents had the velocity necessary to cut canyons.

The theory of turbidity currents is discussed elsewhere (p. 138). Observations in nature are confined to lakes where entering streams have water that is of higher density than lake water because it is colder and/or contains more sediment. Turbidity currents in the ocean are probably due to the development of spontaneous liquefaction in water-saturated slope sediment, as for example, after an earthquake, or perhaps are due to storm waves stirring up large quantities of mud on the upper part of a slope.

Unfortunately no turbidity currents have been observed in the ocean nor measured by current meters. That they exist, however, appears highly probable because of the finding of many layers of sand

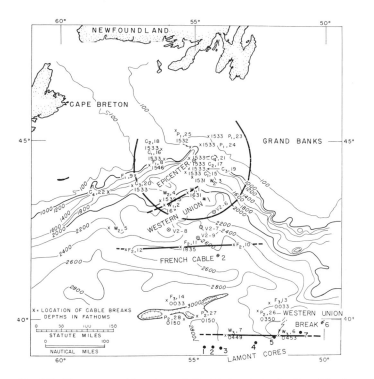

Fig. 162. The times and locations of all cable breaks in the Grand Banks area after and during the earthquake in 1929. The arc of a circle (100 nautical miles from epicenter) circumscribes the area in which most cable breaks occurred simultaneously with the earthquake. The station numbers represent cores taken by Lamont Geological Observatory with stratigraphy indicated in Fig. 165. Numbers 1 to 7 were all on cruise A-180 but numbers 3 to 6 obtained no core. See also Fig. 163.

out on the deep fans at the base of the continental slopes, particularly around the mouths of submarine canyons. Many of these sand layers contain shallow water organisms. Furthermore, it is known that the material accumulating at the heads of submarine canyons is unstable and slides or flows from time to time, and causes considerable deepening of the floors (Shepard, 1951b).

Favoring the existence of powerful turbidity currents is the evidence deduced from the breaking of cables. The most striking incidence of this occurred south of the Grand Banks after the earthquake of 1929. Heezen and Ewing (1952) first called attention to the possible significance of the fact that these cables broke in an orderly sequence down the slope away from the earthquake epicenter (Fig. 162). They thought that these cable breaks were the result of a great turbidity current moving down the entire slope in the area. They postulated that the

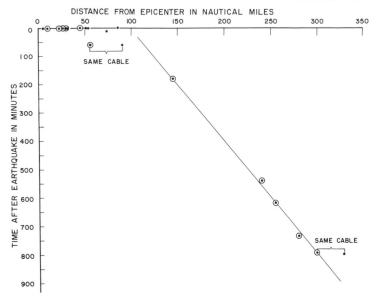

Fig. 163. The relation of distance from epicenter to time of cable break. Note that the outer cables broke principally along a line which represents a velocity of 15 knots. See also Fig. 162.

early stages of flow attained an average speed of 50 knots because of the two-hour interval between breaks 100 miles apart. The speed according to Heezen and Ewing was gradually reduced but averaged almost 25 knots an hour for the 350-mile journey to the outermost broken cable. Other cable breaks in the Mediterranean led Heezen and Ewing (1955) to infer rapid currents. In both cases, however, it is difficult to differentiate between breaks due to landslides and those due to turbidity currents, nor is the velocity demonstrated.

An examination of the cable break data south of the Grand Banks shows that the evidence for high speed is subject to doubt because the cables broke for a distance of as much as 100 miles from the epicenter at the time of the earthquake (Fig. 162) and thus the currents could have started immediately at least that far away. Therefore, the assumption of a point or a line source of the currents is not justified. By plotting the times of break as abscissa and the distances from the epicenter as ordinate one finds that the best fit for velocities is for 15 knots starting at a 100-mile distance (Fig. 163). Such velocities are reasonable from the point of view of energetics at least some distance above the bottom (p. 138). However, in the investigation of the subject, Terzaghi (1956) suggested as an alternative that a progressive and temporary spontaneous liquefaction of slope sediments, moving like

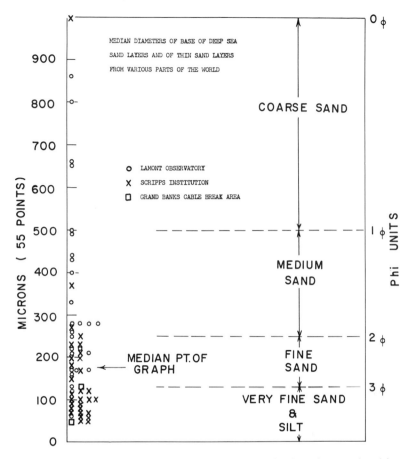

Fig. 164. Fine size of the turbidity current deposits that have been analyzed by Lamont Geological Observatory and Scripps Institution. Note the analyses of the cores obtained in the area in which the Grand Banks cables were broken. All these analyses represent the lowermost analyzed portion of coarse sediment layers.

a wave down the slope after the earthquake, caused the cables to sink deeply into the temporarily liquefied slope and break as the result of distortion and stretching. This avoids the difficulty of explaining the 15-knot bottom speed implied by the turbidity current origin. The nature of the cable breaks is believed by Terzaghi to exclude the possibility of turbidity current action.

Perhaps the most convincing evidence concerning the velocities of turbidity currents comes from a study of the nature of the sediments left by these currents. Figure 164 shows the mean diameters obtained by a group of analyses of the sand layers collected by Lamont Geological Observatory and Scripps Institution. In all cases of thick sand layers the analysis is taken from the bottom which was the first deposit formed and is therefore most indicative of the nature of the highest velocity attained by the current. The results show that virtually all the sands are fine-grained with only one in the very coarse sand range. A few gravel deposits are known but almost all these appear either to represent mud flows of material coming from the canyon walls and hence not moving at high speeds or to consist of glacial marine sediment.[4] Nor is there any evidence that gravel

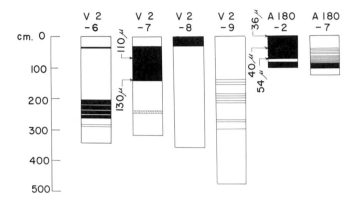

Fig. 165. The nature of cores obtained in the area where Heezen and Ewing believe that currents had a velocity of 50 knots (V2-6 to V2-9). Note that only V2-8 has a coarse layer, shown by black, at the surface, and this has a median in a fine sand size. The other two cores (A180-2 and A180-7) were taken in the outermost part of the cable break area and one shows a silt layer at the surface and the other a mud layer. Numbers A-180-2 and A-180-7 are shown as numbers 2 and 7 in Fig. 162. From Ericson et al. (1961).

or cobble beds are found in the inner zones near the point of origin of the turbidity currents. The cores from the Grand Banks cable break area collected by Lamont either have mud layers at the surface or have layers of fine sand or silt (Fig. 165). Cores along La Jolla Canyon (Shepard and Einsele, 1962) do not show any appreciable change in sand size outward along the canyon and, in fact, the only cores with coarse sand are from the outer channels. Also, as shown by Ericson et al. (1961, p. 259) the "well preserved but fragile tests of Foraminifera in graded layers indicate that transportation by turbidity currents does not entail much abrasion by sand-size particles," and hence one can conclude that the currents along the bottom are of a mild nature, or the concentration of abrasive sand in the current is very low.

Furthermore, there is every reason to believe that a powerful current, such as 50 knots or even 15 knots acting along the bottom,

[4] An exception referred to previously was found off Baja California.

would erode actively and would find available a large amount of coarse debris on the continental slopes because they are all underlain by rock and the canyons through which turbidity currents move toward the outer fans are largely rock walled. Therefore, the data from the sediments indicate that turbidity currents near the bottom are probably slow moving, certainly no faster than the currents in the lower reaches of rivers where equally fine sand is transported. Faster currents higher in the water column seem reasonable according to theory (see pp. 138–140).

Accordingly, it appears that turbidity currents, although capable of cutting through soft sediments and perhaps in some cases through unconsolidated formations, are quite clearly not the type of currents necessary to erode granite gorges and probably have as their chief function the transportation of fine sediment down canyons, over the slopes, and out over the adjacent plains of the ocean floor. On the other hand, they either maintain or erode the channels in the submarine fans below the canyons.

*Favoring Subaerial Erosion.* The characteristics of most of the well-sounded submarine canyons provide a strong argument for their having been originally cut, or at least shaped, by river erosion rather than turbidity currents. Dendritic patterns are the result of an erosional agency attacking the entire surface whereas turbidity currents, set off either by slides or possibly by floods at a river mouth, would concentrate their attack down the slope along lines in continuity with the point of origin. The various types of valleys associated with deltas which have had a point source are conspicuous in their lack of dendritic tributaries. The relief in Cape San Lucas canyons (Fig. 147) and in the Corsican canyons (Fig. 152) is most difficult to explain as due to turbidity currents.

Equally troublesome to the turbidity current hypothesis is the V shape of the typical submarine canyon. The narrow rocky ravines around La Jolla, for example, are much more suggestive of river origin. If these ravines stopped abruptly at a depth of 60 to 90 fathoms, thought to be the approximate Pleistocene glacial low stand of sea level, no one would hesitate to say that they were river cut during glacial low stands. However, they definitely continue well below such a level. This seems to indicate the diastrophic submergence of a coast of high relief cut by river gorges.

The rather considerable number of submarine canyon heads extending into bays along the coasts of the world is also a strong argument that these are of subaerial origin as Kuenen (1953a) has admitted. Where the submarine canyon is essentially a continuation of the land canyon, as is the case off Corsica and off portions of California,

Baja California, and eastern Japan, the subaerial origin appears to be well established. Since these submarine canyons are not strikingly different from many others, the same origin is implied.

The granite walls of the submarine canyons of California and Baja California, the crystalline rocks of the Corsican canyons, and the gneiss and quartzite walls of Trincomalee Canyon of eastern Ceylon offer considerable difficulties to the turbidity current hypothesis as has been generally admitted even by some of its strongest advocates. Even if turbidity currents can attain high velocities in the broad outer channels, for which there is some possibility, no one has suggested a method whereby such velocity could develop at the canyon heads. Hence, these crystalline-walled canyons are far more reasonably explained by submergence of river canyons. The possibility cannot be overlooked that important headward erosion is resulting from sand flows or sand creep (see R. F. Dill (1962), and Figs. 143 and 148).

*Objections to Subaerial Erosion.*   The most common objection to the idea that the canyons were cut by streams is that such an hypothesis calls for far too widespread marginal submergence. Actually, the amount of submergence necessary has been greatly exaggerated by the failure of the critics of the river erosion hypothesis to realize that the outer parts of the valleys where the great depths are found are not canyons but channels cut through fans outside the rock-walled canyons. For example, the rock canyon off La Jolla extends only to a depth of about 300 fathoms, beyond which there is a large fan crossed by one or more channels.

There is ample evidence from wells along most coasts of the world that subsidence has taken place. This is certainly true of the east and Gulf coasts of the United States and can be as easily supported for the California coast, especially in the Los Angeles area and at the head of the Monterey Canyon in Salinas Valley. The formations penetrated by wells along all these coasts have no indication of having been deposited at as great depth below sea level as that at which they are now found. The evidence for submergence of atolls is now clearly established (Ladd *et al.*, 1953; Ladd and Schlanger, 1960). As Landes (1959) has aptly remarked, geologists have no objection to mountain ranges being elevated thousands of feet but they are greatly disturbed by canyons having sunk to the same degree.

The objection referred to by Woodford (1951) and others that there is a decided nick point between the profiles of canyon heads and adjacent river valleys would be significant if the submarine canyons had been submerged in recent times and little had happened subsequently. If submerged at a remote period, however, the land valley should show little relationship to the valley beneath the sea because in the latter, river erosion has ceased. Furthermore, the heads of many submarine canyons, such as the one in Monterey Bay, appear to have had a complex history and their present form may be largely related to submarine slides and turbidity currents. The real connection with the deep rock-walled Monterey submarine canyon is more likely to be found in the deeply buried Miocene gorge of the lower Salinas Valley (Starke, 1956).

Another objection related to nick points was offered by Kuenen (1953a). Referring to the writer's two-phase development of canyons (Shepard, 1952a), Kuenen pointed out that the profiles of such canyons as that of the Hudson should show a change in slope at the contact between the old consolidated formations (into which the writer claimed that the canyons were cut subaerially) and the overlying unconsolidated formations deposited on the shelf after canyon cutting. The failure to find such a hiatus convinced Kuenen that these canyons were cut after the soft formations were deposited. This had always seemed to be a serious objection until the results of acoustic probes used by Lamont Geological Observatory (Ewing, J., *et al.*, 1960b) showed that there are inclined formations underlying the walls of the canyon (Fig. 166). These records indicate that the

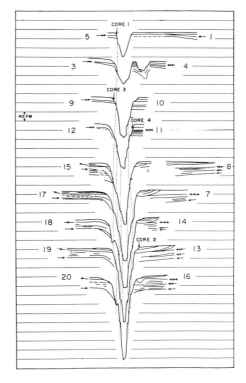

Fig. 166. Profiles of the Hudson Canyon showing the inclined beds underlying the south wall as indicated by use of an acoustic probe. From Ewing *et al.* (1960a).

younger unconsolidated formations have built up the walls until the slope is essentially uniform. Further examination with acoustic probes seems advisable before this new evidence of two-phase development can be well evaluated.

**Origin of Outer Channels.**   The channels that cut the fans outside submarine canyons are evidently the result of turbidity currents that have moved out along the canyons and carry sediments that were deposited as fans. The channels cross the fans in the locus of the most powerful flow. Directly outside this flow,levees are found giving the channels greater depth below their immediate surroundings.

**Time of Origin of Submarine Canyons.**   The advocates of turbidity currents as the principal or entire cause of submarine canyons have in all cases considered that the Pleistocene stages of low sea level were the times when the canyons were cut. It is argued that the lowered sea level brought the rivers out to the outer shelf and provided the sediments for canyon cutting.

If this were the case, the canyons should be confined to the continental slopes. This is by no means true, as an examination of the various illustrations in this chapter will show. Most of the major submarine canyons head well into the continental shelf and many of them extend essentially to the shore or even enter estuaries. Furthermore, the evidence suggests that turbidity currents were only slightly more important in glacial stages than in postglacial time. Examination of the many excellent cores obtained by Lamont scientists shows that the difference in abundance of sand layers between the two periods is slight. The existence of canyons on the slopes leading to the Arctic basin (Carsola, 1954b) is also hard to explain if the canyons were cut during glacial stages.

Another difficulty with the idea that the canyons were cut during the short glacial intervals comes from their huge dimensions. Where cut into granite, for example, a canyon thousands of feet deep would require a very long period of time for its excavation, even if cut by streams. It seems hardly conceivable that enough turbidity currents could have developed in these geologically rather short epochs to produce such profound erosion. Finally, there are fans lying outside the submarine canyons which give every indication of containing many times as much material as would have come from the cutting of the entire canyon (Menard, 1960a). It is highly probable that the canyons have existed through rather long periods, probably many millions of years, in order to have allowed the movement of so much material along the canyon axes. Computations of movement along the California coast by D. L. Inman (personal communication) would seem to indicate that several millions of years are involved.

If the canyons were originally river cut, it is obvious that they must be older than Pleistocene. The lands have certainly changed considerably since they were submerged.

## Conclusions

The detailed study of the valleys of the sea floor makes it constantly more evident that they cannot be explained by any one process alone. There can be little doubt but that some types of valleys are now forming and have formed in the past on the sea floor. A rather considerable group appears to be the result of diastrophism, particularly faulting. Submarine mass movements even on very gentle slopes have produced valleys in between hydrographic surveys. Other valleys, such as those on submarine fans, are in all probability the result of turbidity currents. Each of the above types is quite different in form from the winding rock-walled gorges of the sea floor with their many entering tributaries. It seems likely that this latter group was originally excavated by stream erosion at some time in the rather remote past although they have probably been considerably modified by marine processes and have acted as chutes down which turbidity currents have moved from time to time for millions of years and have built up the huge fans at the base of the canyons. The crystalline-walled canyons of Baja California, Carmel Bay, Trincomalee Bay in Ceylon, and west Corsica belong clearly in this category and probably many others cut into sedimentary rocks such as those of southern California, eastern Honshu, and the French Riviera. Most of the valleys of the sea floor, however, require more study before determining the class to which they belong.

## Unsolved Problems

From the foregoing discussion it will be evident that there is much yet to be learned about submarine canyons. The surveys in most areas are still too poor to know what sort of valley exists. Many of the valleys referred to as canyons may be only fault troughs. We have little idea how far out the rock-walled canyons continue. Almost all the rocks have been obtained in relatively shallow water. More collections should be made of the sediment on the canyon floors to look for coarse debris. Acoustic reflection surveys in the future should yield much information on the shape and structure of buried formations.

Much experimental and observational work is necessary before we can find out about the speeds which are developed in turbidity currents. Plans are set up at Scripps Institution for studying these currents and their speed if they actually occur at the times of the periodic landslides in the canyon heads. Cables with radio or direct wire connection with the shore should be put out in various canyon heads for timing the movements. It is possible that artificial slides can be set off by explosives jetted into the bottom. Vessels or deep-diving submarines like Cousteau's diving saucer (or *soucoupe*) could be relatively near the spot and move in to make measurements and observations of the effects.

**Recent Explorations.**   After the above had been written and readied for publication, the results of an intensive study of canyon heads, by R. F. Dill, appeared in a thesis on "Submarine Erosion." Extensive documentation in this field yields new evidence strongly favoring abrasion by creep of the mats of sediment containing embedded rock, and by kelp, in canyon heads. This erosion is apparently taking place even in the crystalline canyons of Baja California. Whether or not this type of erosion is confined to the shallow heads, with their steep inclinations, is not yet known. The results of box cores obtained in 1963 in the deep parts of the Baja California canyons suggest that erosion may also be occurring there. A few samples brought up freshly broken fragments of granite rock, from floors lying under a mixture of gravel and sand. This evidence, along with photographs of current ripples and rocks on the floor of a Japanese canyon, at 200 fathoms, certainly favors submarine erosion of canyons. The processes producing such erosion are not yet clearly understood. Many features, such as the boulders embedded in mud seen by Dill from the bathyscaph *Trieste* along the axis of La Jolla Fan-Valley, are hard to reconcile with traditional ideas of turbidity currents.

# CHAPTER XII

# CORAL AND OTHER ORGANIC REEFS

## Introduction

The past decade has been very fruitful in the study of organic reefs. The penetration by drilling through an atoll into the deep underlying volcanic rock was finally accomplished in 1951 (Ladd *et al.*, 1953; Ladd and Schlanger, 1960). The other results of the extensive coral reef investigations which accompanied the preparations for the Bikini and Eniwetok nuclear bomb tests have now been largely published in U.S. Geological Survey Professional Paper 260. In addition the Pacific Science Board and the U.S. Geological Survey have made extensive studies of the reefs that surround the United States mandate islands of the western Pacific (Cloud, 1952, 1958, 1959; McKee, 1958, 1959). N. D. Newell and his associates at the American Museum and Columbia University have investigated many of the Bahama reefs (Newell, 1959a; Newell *et al.*, 1951, 1959), along with reefs in the Pacific (Newell, 1956). Almost all this recent work has been greatly assisted by SCUBA diving which has brought most reefs into the zone where exploration by man is practical.

These recent results add to an impressive array of earlier reports and books about coral reefs and their origin beginning with Darwin (1842), who first gathered significant facts about these greatest of all structures built by organisms. Important studies followed early in the present century, including laboratory investigations that provided indications of the rates at which colonies of corals could build up their reefs (Vaughan, 1916; Mayor, 1924). Voluminous information came from the work of Davis (1928) and Daly (1910, 1915), who aroused great interest in the subject of reefs by their articles and debates but did not make any detailed field studies. In the field the early work of Gardiner (1931), Ladd and Hoffmeister (1936), Hoffmeister and Ladd (1935), and Yonge (1940) laid much of the ground work for the larger scale investigations that followed. The detailed studies by various scientists of the information coming from the cores of the 1897–1899 borings into Funafuti Atoll also have proved very fruitful.

## Factual Information

**Organic Reefs Defined.**  Organic reefs, usually referred to collectively as coral reefs, can be defined as structures built by organisms with a framework strong enough to withstand the attacks of ordinary wind waves by a baffle effect (Ladd, 1961). Unusually large waves break fragments off the front of the reef, and often pile up the fragments, some weighing tons, above sea level so as to produce islands, but an actively growing reef will soon recover from the storm and rebuild its damaged frame.

The most common frame builders of present day reefs are the hermatypic corals, the coralline algae, and the hydrocorals. During the remote past the reef framework included sponges and Bryozoa in addition to corals and algae. Besides the frame an important constituent of a reef includes the binding material that consists largely of coralline algae, hydrocorals, Bryozoa, and Foraminifera. Emery *et al.* (1954) estimated that in the Marshall Islands 30 percent of the total reef consists of the framework. The frame and binding material together make a rigid stable structure but leave large cavities in between. This produces a mass high in pore space, for example, 25 to 50 percent was estimated by Newell (1956) for Raroia Island. As the reef grows upward, the cavities generally have communicating passages with the sea, and sediment from the reef is carried into them. It has been suggested (Cullies, 1904, p. 396) that after being buried by approximately 20 ft of coral the cavities are filled by chemical precipitation from the circulating sea water and that deeper in the upgrowing reef solution may take place. This may attack the original coral framework leaving the filling of the old cavities as the new framework. In this way the coral reefs may remain almost as porous after deep burial as they were when first formed. Alternatively the solution and reprecipitation may occur as the result of intermittent uplift of the reefs during the long period of gradual submergence of the reef platform. Such alternations have been found by Ladd and Schlanger (1960) in the study of the Eniwetok borings. This, of course, is important in providing the space for oil accumulation in ancient reefs.

**Types of Reefs.**  The most common types of reefs in the present seas are: (1) fringing reefs which grow out from a land mass but are connected with it; (2) barrier reefs which are separated from a land mass by a lagoon; (3) atolls, oval-shaped reefs rising from deep water and surrounding a lagoon in which there is no land mass; (4) faros, ring-shaped reefs located on banks or shelves; (5) table reefs or coral banks that rise above the adjacent sea floor as a shallow bank without

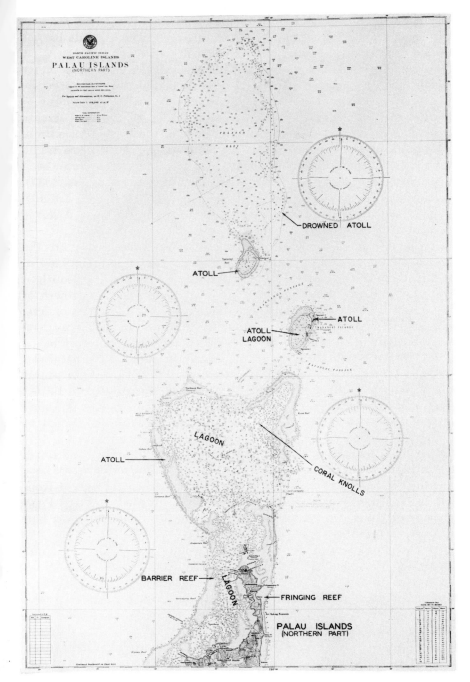

Fig. 167. The various types of coral reefs. From U.S. Hydrographic Office Chart No. 6074.

any appreciable rim, and (6) coral knolls, also called pat
pinnacles, small masses that rise above the lagoon floor ins
reefs or atolls. All these are illustrated in Fig. 167.

**Reef Ecology.** It is important to understand the condit
which modern reefs are capable of growth in order to int
significance of ancient reefs. It is commonly held that the
ancient reefs in such places as Spitsbergen indicates that tl
was tropical and that the water was shallow at the time of f
This is not necessarily true. Ahermatypic corals in which th
symbiotic flagellates (zooxanthellae) occur at all depths and l
found at temperatures as low as $-1.1°$ C (Vaughan and Wel
As Teichert (1958a) has emphasized, ahermatypic coral reef
living along the coast of Norway and elsewhere in the North
at various depths all greater than 35 fathoms.

By far the most common reef formers of the present day
hermatypic corals and coralline algae which are largely co
their growth to the tropical belts, extending a little north or
the tropics where conditions are favorable. The vigorous gr
these reef formers takes place only in depths of 25 fathoms
although some hermatypic reef corals have been found living
as 90 fathoms. The winter temperatures in reef areas are rarel
$18°$ C. In the Persian Gulf, however, where the summer tempe
are well above $30°$ C small reefs are growing where there are
temperatures of relatively short duration as low as $13°$ to
Maximum temperatures of above $35°$ C will kill most corals b
temperatures are rarely, if ever, attained in present seas ex
extremely shallow water where there is negligible circulation.

Reef corals are also dependent on the proper salinity con
They live within margins of about 27 to 40‰. As a result a re
be killed by a great flood of fresh water that sweeps out over i
the land. According to Mayor (1924) this happened in Pago
Harbor of American Samoa after a rain of 37 in. in four day
deluged the area.

The studies of coral reef platforms by Vaughan (1916) and
meister and Ladd (1935) have shown that reefs develop on a
variety of surfaces, although Vaughan claimed they cannot grow
soft mud bottom. Their absence on muddy deposits is explained b
deleterious effect of the mud in the water. Actually coral reefs
found by borings in west Sumatra to overlie mud deposits (Umbg
1947). Studies of the reef at Waikiki, Oahu, suggested to Edmon
(1928) that the mud from a stream which had formerly entered at

[1] From records of the Arabian-American Oil Company at Dhahran, Saudi Ar

place had prevented growth in the immediate vicinity. His experiments showed that most reef-forming corals would not stand burial in silt except for a short period. The absence of reefs along the coast at the southern end of the Queensland Great Barrier Reef is apparently related to the muddy water coming out from the land in this zone. However, the effect of the mud in the water may not be very important by itself. Ladd and Hoffmeister (1936, p. 82) have called attention to the existence of reefs off the Rewa River in the Fiji Islands ". . . in spite of the tremendous amounts of silt brought to the sea in this area." Kuenen (1933, p. 65) also refers to floods covering a reef with silt without killing it. Reefs exist off the south coast of the Hawaiian Island of Molokai despite the muddy water which characterizes this area.[2] On the north side of the same island, where the water is generally clear, there are few reefs. It may be that the freshness of the water off some entering rivers is a more important factor in preventing reef formation than the mud in suspension.

The general impression has been that corals and algae grow somewhat more actively on the outer edge of the reef, particularly on the windward side because of the large supply of food and the clear water. Actually, there is little evidence to show either that there is more food or that corals are growing more actively at this place than elsewhere. The studies of Odum and Odum (1955) on Eniwetok suggest that this reef may not obtain any net gain from the larger plankton that are swept across it. Zones of different types of coral extend in roughly parallel bands from the outer reef to the inner lagoon (Wells, 1954). Mayor (1924) found that *Acropora* thrive at the reef margin, whereas *Porites* and some other genera thrive along shores in rather silty water away from the breakers. The plankton tows in coral reef areas indicate that copepods, which are a particularly important source of food for corals, are more abundant in lagoons than on the marginal reefs. Also, some of the most thriving reefs are found in the lagoons. Where there is a good food supply in the lagoons inside barrier reefs, fringing reefs are developing actively and filling the lagoons so that the entire reef is evolving into a fringing reef. Also, the actively growing coral pinnacles within the lagoons of many atolls (Fig. 168) indicate that these will be completely filled in a few thousand years unless some change of conditions takes place. Figure 169 illustrates an atoll with a lagoon largely filled.

Experiments by Vaughan (1916) and Mayor (1924) have shown that under extremely favorable conditions corals may be able to build their reefs upward toward the surface at rates of as much as 19 fathoms

[2] During relatively dry weather I swam over a reef off Kaunakakai and found living coral at a point where visibility through a glass face mask was limited to one foot.

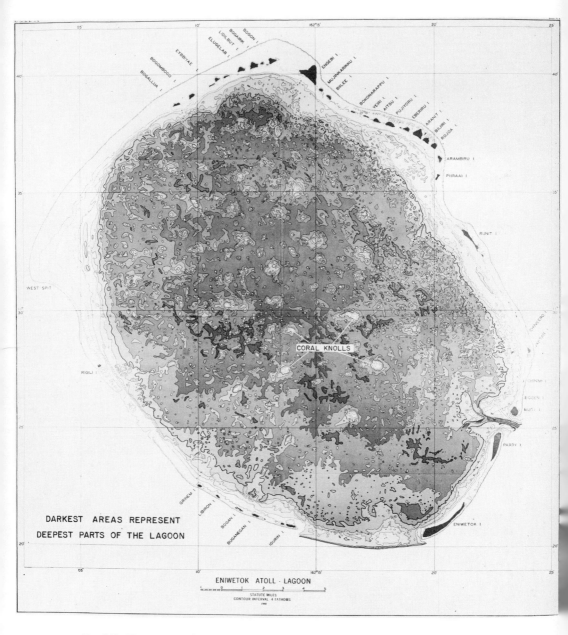

Fig. 168. The relief in the lagoon on Eniwetok Atoll. The darkest shades have depths of 32-36 fathoms. Note the large entrance channel on the east side of the island. From Emery et al. (1954).

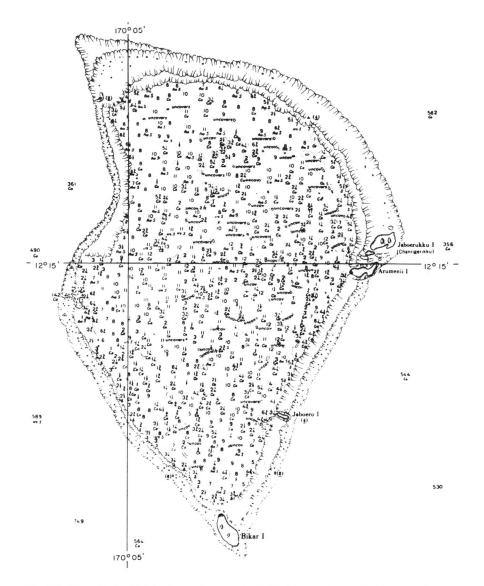

Fig. 169. Bikar Atoll which has been almost entirely filled by coral growths. Note the absence of circular shape.

in a thousand years for *Acropora* (of the reef margins) and 9.5 fathoms for *Porites* (of the lagoons). This is based on growth rates respectively of about 10 and 5 cm per year but the growth is not necessarily upward. However, the corals form only one constituent of the reefs so that these rates are probably excessive, although a relatively fast rate can be assumed. This must have been important in allowing both the reefs and the lagoons to keep pace with either slow sinking of islands or with slow rise of sea level. As a result, wherever the food supply and other conditions were favorable, the reefs have maintained themselves despite submergence.

## Atolls

Atolls are unique in exposing none of the foundation on which they grew. The interest in discovering this basement has led to many borings which finally yielded basement rock (olivine basalt) at a depth of more than 4000 ft (1200 m) in the atoll of Eniwetok (Ladd *et al.*, 1953).

Atolls are by far the most common type of coral reef and the best known. According to Cloud (1958) there are at least 330 atolls. Over half are included in the Tuamotus (62), eastern Indonesia (37), the Carolines (32), the Marshalls (29), and the Fiji Islands (25). Only about 10 modern atolls lie outside the Indo-Pacific tropical area. These exceptions include Midway in the central Pacific, two atolls in the Red Sea, the Dry Tortugas (west of Key West, Florida), and Hogsty Reef in the Bahamas.

Excellent maps of atolls are found in the extensive reports on the Marshall Islands (Emery *et al.*, 1954). The atolls vary in outline from circular (Fig. 168) to highly elliptical or even rectangular with bulging corners (Figs. 169 and 177). The rims vary from submerged banks surrounding lagoons of greater depth to lagoons completely enclosed by an island. Where the rims are not continuous, islands are somewhat more common on the windward side of the atolls, but there is great variation in this respect.

A cross section of a typical atoll is shown in Fig. 170. Bordering the steep talus slope leading to deep water is a growing reef often fringed by an algae ridge (called the *Lithothamnion ridge*, not a correct generic name) emerging above sea level (Fig. 171). The outer growing reef has an abundance of *Acropora*. A partly dead reef flat lies farther in, followed by a growth zone near shore where *Porites* is particularly common. A calcareous sand and gravel beach flanks a low island consisting largely of rubble but in some localities containing old

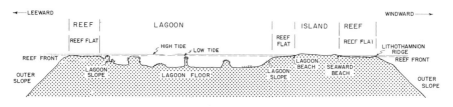

Fig. 170. Cross section of a typical atoll. Modified from Tracey *et al.* (1955).

slightly elevated reefs. A study of an inter-island reef on the windward side of Eniwetok (Odum and Odum, 1955) showed that there are
six zones represented in a traverse from the open ocean to the lagoon.
These consist of (1) a windward buttress about half coral, (2) a coral
algae ridge, (3) an encrusting coral zone, (4) a zone of small coral
heads, (5) a zone of large coral heads, and (6) a zone of sand and
shingle carried in by the waves. On the lagoon side there is another
reef flat, a slope with live coral, a terrace at about 10 fathoms, then a
further descent to the sediment-covered lagoon floor. The floors have
some flat surfaces, but detailed surveys show that they are usually a
far cry from what R. A. Daly once described as "flat as a billiard table."
Some atolls have hundreds or even thousands of knolls rising above
the rather irregular floor (Fig. 168), many of them approaching the

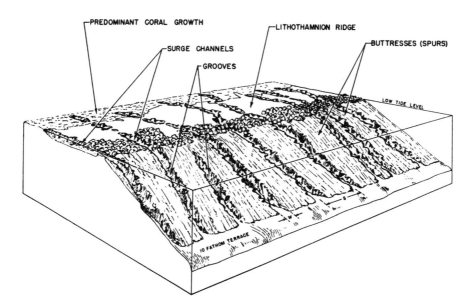

Fig. 171. Typical growth and erosional features of the reef front. From Munk and Sargent
(1948).

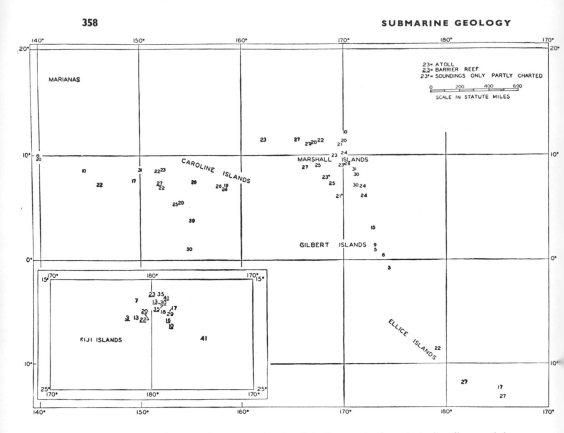

Fig. 172. Chart showing the average depths of the lagoons in the principal atoll area of the southwest Pacific.

surface and almost all of them supporting live reefs, with steep sides consisting largely of talus.

The lagoon depths were described by Daly (1910, p. 300) as having average depths of about 35 fathoms. This estimate is certainly too high as can be seen in Fig. 172 where the average depths for each lagoon in the main atoll area in the Pacific are given. A better world average is 25 fathoms exclusive of those atolls that are so nearly filled as to make soundings difficult. The deepest atolls are of the order of 50 fathoms. Most of these have sunken rims. In atolls in general it can be seen that the principal channels crossing the reefs have depths that are rather close to those of the central lagoons.

An interesting characteristic of the outer margins of atolls was first reported by Hanzawa (1940) and has been seen in recent years by numerous geologists from planes flying over them. The margin, particularly on the windward side, is found to have numerous grooves (Fig. 171). These may be related to wave action and have been explained by Munk and Sargent (1948) as representing the form with the greatest natural breakwater effect. Some of them, however, are apparently being covered over by coral growth, and their origin by ridge growth off Jamaica has been clearly demonstrated by Goreau (1959). In many places it is possible for a SCUBA diver to swim from a surge channel on the reef flat through a tunnel and come out on the reef face in one of the grooves. Grooves occur also on the front of other types of reefs, although less commonly.

The floors of the lagoons have been extensively sampled (Emery et al., 1954; McKee, 1958). Beyond the growing reefs at the margin there are in general belts with a dominance of coral debris or foraminiferal sands, followed toward the center by a dominance of the debris of the alga *Halimeda*, then by a second band of Foraminifera, and in the deeper lagoons by coral mud. This order is greatly complicated by the irregularity of the floors.

## Slopes Outside Coral Reefs

Coral reefs usually terminate outwardly with a steep slope but this slope may or may not extend to oceanic depths. Around many coral islands the reefs descend precipitously for a few fathoms, with a more gradual slope or a narrow shelf beyond. In one section at Bikini the slope on the leeward side was essentially vertical to 30 fathoms (Emery et al., 1954). At Eleuthera Island, in the Bahamas, Schalk (1946) found a "cliff" extending from 30 to 100 fathoms. The outer slopes are likely to be far steeper than the slopes around volcanic islands. Kuenen (1933, pp. 95–98) has called attention to the extremely steep slopes off a series of coral reefs in Indonesia. He found that "Practically all atolls are partly surrounded by slopes of more than 45° down to 200 meters. In many cases these angles are continued down to 500 and 600 meters." He even refers to some slopes which approach the vertical. According to Kuenen, the steepness of the slopes was not dependent on the size of the atolls nor on the presence or absence of a lagoon inside the coral reef nor on the completeness of the atoll rim. The detailed soundings around Bikini indicate that the slopes outside the marginal cliffs are close to 25°. The charts in the Marshall Island area show many other examples of slopes of about 25° to approximately 1000 fathoms.

Although the slopes outside most atolls extend down to oceanic depths there are a considerable number of cases where the atolls rise only from a platform or continental shelf. Examples of the latter are found among the reefs off the northeast coast of Australia and among the Fiji Islands.

## Australian Barrier Reef

The Great Barrier Reef of northeast Australia is by far the largest reef in the world. This extends for 1500 miles along the continental shelf and has an average width of about 100 miles. Wide ship channels occur inside the southern portion of this reef, separating it from the mainland. In these channels there is little or no sign of reef growth, and the bottom is covered with fine sediment. The reefs have spread widely over the outer shelf in the southern portion and over the entire shelf to the north. Their extent has been well indicated by the studies of Fairbridge (1950b) and is based in part on aerial photographs taken during World War II. There are faros on the shelf resembling atolls but having only minor lagoonal depths. These faros have been explained by Fairbridge (1950b, p. 357) as due to prevailing winds spreading the coral debris from a bank in the form of a horse-shoe that may connect at the leeward end.

The corals of the Great Barrier Reef are said to be the finest in the world and have many different colors. They make up a larger pro-portion of the reef material than in most of the island atolls where coralline algae are more abundant. The biology of the Great Barrier Reef corals has been studied extensively by Yonge (1940), and the physiography of the reefs has been given considerable study by Steers (1937).

## Borings into Reefs

Charles Darwin first suggested that it would be a fine thing if some wealthy man would provide funds to have a deep hole bored into an atoll to find out about the basement. Although the cost has been taken care of by various other means, a considerable number of borings have now been made into reefs including atolls. First, in 1897 and 1898 borings were made into Funafuti Atoll (Fig. 173) in the Ellice Islands by the Royal Society and the government of New South Wales. The main hole passed through 1100 ft (360 m) of coral reef material which is described by Hinde (1904) as follows:

1. 0–150 ft (0–45 m), corals growing in place and surrounded by Foraminifera and other organisms.
2. 150–748 ft (45–228 m), largely fragmental material with a small percent of coral and consisting largely of Foraminifera and organic debris.
3. 748–1112 ft (228–340 m), a mass similar to that from 0–150 ft (0–45 m) except that it was dolomitized.

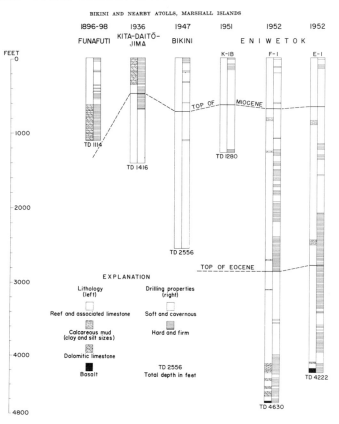

BIKINI AND NEARBY ATOLLS, MARSHALL ISLANDS

Fig. 173. Borings into a series of Pacific Ocean atolls. From Ladd and Schlanger (1960, Fig. 287).

Hinde considered that the entire section represented continuous deposition of reef material. Subsequent study of the cores (Grimsdale, 1952) has shown that only the 560- to 770-ft (171–235 m) zone consists of submarine talus. Hinde found that a 70-ft (21 m) boring in the lagoon of Funafuti Atoll had cores consisting entirely of uncemented joints of *Halimeda* akin to the present lagoonal sediment, but a short section below showed rubble limestone with coral and Foraminifera similar to the upper part of the main boring. There is no certainty that the main boring penetrated beyond Pleistocene, but Pliocene and Pleistocene are difficult to differentiate by the Foraminifera, the chief source of information.

Borings at two points in the Queensland reefs showed that the coral extended to depths of 400 and 450 ft (120 and 137 m) respectively, where the bit passed into a coarse terrigenous sand and grit that was bored for another 200 and 280 ft (61 and 85 m) respectively (Richards,

1940). A Bermuda boring (Pirsson, 1914) penetrated through the coral cap at 245 ft (76 m) and penetrated a weathered rock extending to 455 ft (139 m), below which there is a volcanic sand and gravel zone traced to 560 ft (171 m) where basaltic lava was encountered. Borings penetrated to 1416 ft (432 m) in the elevated atoll, Borodino Island (Kito-Daito-Jima), 210 miles east of Okinawa (Hanzawa, 1940). This well penetrated 700 ft (214 m) of hard limestone and encountered the Miocene at about 500 ft (152 m). A boring into Maratoa, a small elevated atoll island on the shelf northeast of Borneo, extended 1407 ft (427 m) into reef material suggestive of lagoonal fill without hitting the bottom (Kuenen, 1947).

In 1947 four holes were drilled in Bikini Island by the Navy in cooperation with the U.S. Geological Survey (Emery et al., 1954, pp. 80–85). One of these reached a depth of 2556 ft (780 m) (Fig. 173) and all of this appeared to represent a shallow water lagoonal or near reef environment. Some of the sections at various depths probably consist of what was a growing near-surface reef. According to Rita Post and Ruth Todd, shallow water Foraminifera were found throughout the section. No *Globigerina* oozes nor any deep water organisms were found to indicate that an environment such as the deep outer slope was involved. It was discovered that the holes penetrated Miocene rock at about 850 ft (259 m), and the deepest hole reached Oligocene at close to 2000 ft (610 m).

In 1952 two holes were drilled into opposite sides of Eniwetok Atoll by the Atomic Energy Commission and the Los Alamos Scientific Laboratory in cooperation with the U.S. Geological Survey (Ladd *et al.*, 1953; Ladd and Schlanger, 1960). Both of these penetrated to sufficient depth to reach the basement rock at respectively 4158 and 4610 ft (1267 and 1405 m) (Fig. 173). Each hole encountered several hundred feet of Quaternary reef before entering the Tertiary section where the hole encountered Eocene at about 2800 feet (853 m). In the shoaler hole unweathered basalt was recovered but the other hole did not yield a sample of the hard rock at the bottom. The sections were very similar down to 1400 ft but strikingly different below. The deeper hole encountered Globigerina-rich limestone, apparently deposited in somewhat deeper waters than those in which the lagoonal sediments of the shoaler hole were laid down. The deposition of the entire limestone section was in relatively shallow water and represents a submerging coral reef. During some of the period of accumulation the reef was exposed, producing weathered rock in which the aragonite of the corals was removed. These zones contain pollen and land snails indicative of islands hundreds of feet high (Ladd, 1958, 1961; Ladd and Tracey, 1957).

In both the Bikini and Eniwetok drillings large amounts of soft rock were encountered as was also the case at Funafuti. Much of it was a poorly cemented coral sand. Large caverns caused difficulties with loss of tools. Dolomites occurring at different depths in all the holes (Fig. 173) indicated no regularity in the limestone-to-dolomite sequence.

## Geophysical Prospecting

Attempts have been made to determine the character of the basement under the atolls of Eniwetok, Bikini, and Kwajalein (Raitt, 1952, 1957). The results are indicated in Fig. 174. The rock with velocity of 4.15 km/sec occurs at depths of 1.6 to 1.8 km under a north-south section of Eniwetok which is somewhat too deep for the 1267 m and 1405 m at which the basalt was found in the two holes. Raitt explains this either by the assumption that the velocity of the second layer may have been increased by the presence of thin layers of consolidated material or that the upper part of the volcanic material may have been highly fractured and hence showed no greater velocity than the overlying reef material.

Raitt's section across Sylvania Seamount and the adjacent Bikini Atoll shows an irregular surface of the volcanic rock (3.68–4.13 km/sec). Somewhat more than a kilometer of supposed coral was found, enough to account for the failure of the Bikini drilling to penetrate to the basalt. In a northeast-southwest section across Bikini Atoll the velocities showed that the volcanic rock comes to the sea floor on the side of the island and this was confirmed by dredging.

## Origin of Atolls and Barrier Reefs

Since the time of Darwin the greatest interest in coral reefs among both geologists and biologists has concerned the origin of atolls and barrier reefs. The knowledge that, aside from the unusual ahermatypic corals, reef growth is limited to shallow water indicates that virtually all the reefs must have started on shallow platforms and presumably in the case of oceanic atolls on the sides or tops of volcanoes, because so far as known all oceanic islands are volcanic.[3] The finding of more than a hundred atolls in several adjoining groups of the southwest Pacific with no exposed volcanic rock proved particularly puzzling.

Darwin (1842) proposed his hypothesis as an outgrowth of his extended voyages on H.M.S. *Beagle*. As indicated in Fig. 175 the hypothesis is remarkably simple, requiring first the formation of

[3] New Zealand, Fiji Islands, New Caledonia, and others in the vicinity are considered continental.

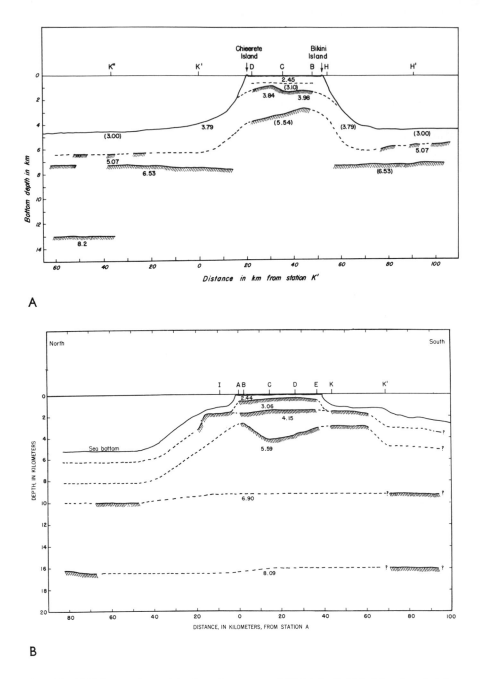

Fig. 174. (a) Velocity of sound in the substructure of Bikini Atoll. Velocities given in kilometers per second. From Raitt (1954). (b) Cross section beneath Eniwetok Atoll. Sound velocities in kilometers per second. After Raitt (1957).

fringing reefs on the sides of volcanic islands or along the margins of other islands and, second, the gradual subsidence of the land with the upgrowth of the corals along the outer margin keeping pace with the subsidence. First, a barrier would form with a lagoon on the inside, then eventually, if the entire island sank, the reef would form an atoll. It is often overlooked that Darwin postulated other ways in which atolls might form. He was the first to suggest that some atolls could

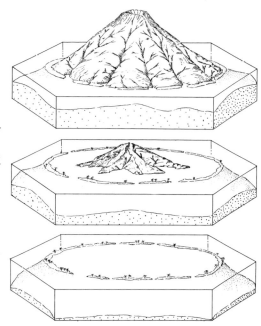

Fig. 175. The Darwin hypothesis of the submergence of a volcano and the upgrowth of the fringing reefs to form successively a barrier reef and then an atoll. Drawn by D. B. Sayner.

have been formed on flat, subsiding platforms and have grown into atolls without having passed through a barrier-reef stage; he went further, and suggested that a shallow bank might, by simple growth of the coral and without any subsidence, "produce a structure scarcely to be distinguished from a true atoll." It is now generally recognized that the atolls of the northern Marshalls originated in part on flat-topped banks and were converted into atolls by subsidence without going through a barrier-reef stage; thus Darwin anticipated the findings of modern studies in the area. The hypothesis was supported among others by Dana (1885) and Davis (1928). Both of them called attention to the numerous embayments into volcanic islands inside barrier reefs as evidence for submergence. Some of these embayments, however, are probably the result of volcanic collapse and others could be due simply to submergence of river valleys resulting from the rise in sea level at the end of the last glacial stage.

Daly (1910, 1915) first emphasized the importance of glacial control of sea level in the evolution of coral reefs, although the idea of glacial control was first suggested by Penck (1894). Daly considered that the lowering of sea level was accompanied by colder water killing many of the reefs and hence allowing erosion of the volcanic islands which had previously been protected by their coral fringes. He thought also that the lowered sea level led to the development of muddy water because it exposed the muds of the outer shelf and lower slope to wave turbulence. This also helped eliminate the corals because they live better in clear water. During these epochs of low sea level the reef-free volcanic shores would have been eroded by the waves, and wherever the islands consisted of soft volcanic ejectamenta, the erosion might have been very extensive. Daly thought that in this way one could account much better for the flatness and shallow nature of the lagoons than by submergence. It is now clear that he greatly overestimated the lagoonal flatness, but the hypothesis may help explain the relatively shallow nature of many lagoons which has been an embarrassment for the advocates of the Darwin hypothesis.

Davis appreciated that some of the islands in the marginal coral belt probably had their reefs killed during glacial stages, but he argued that most of the island shores inside lagoons were not cliffed as they would have been if the reefs were killed during the low sea level stages. This appears to be a well-taken observation and tends to minimize the influence of glacial control on the reefs.

Neither Daly nor Davis seems to have appreciated fully the importance of reef building and growth of *Halimeda* within the lagoons or the importance of wave action in providing sediment from the growing rim to help fill the lagoons. It is, however, rather surprising that submergence has not resulted in more deep lagoons because of the more rapid growth around the margins.

Daly also failed to appreciate the vast size of many of the atolls. It would not take long for open ocean waves acting on a cinder cone to produce a wave-cut platform a mile or more in width, but it is scarcely credible that atolls with diameters of 20 or 30 miles could have been truncated completely during glacial stages. It is as if the island of Hawaii were truncated by the waves during a small fraction of a million years. Surely no one familiar with the relatively slow attack of waves on most rock coasts would expect anything of the sort to happen.

The final test of the two hypotheses has been the borings. Daly considered that the Funafuti borings and even the Bikini borings had penetrated only the coral talus slopes on the sides of the volcanoes (Daly, 1948). This position was not well supported since the detailed study of the cores in both cases revealed only shallow-water organisms and almost none of the typical talus aspects, the core material being much more suggestive of lagoonal deposits than of the outer reefs, although both aspects were found. In any case the borings at Eniwetok seem to have proved definitely that there is no shallow wave-beveled platform under that island and the geophysical measurements on several of the islands have shown clearly that the coral lies far too deep below the surface to fit the Daly hypothesis.

Thus the evidence favors the ideas proposed by Darwin. It is remarkable that the actual sequence of events which led to the development of atolls such as Eniwetok and Bikini were anticipated by this great scientist. It seems clear that many of the volcanoes had been considerably truncated by erosion before the extensive submergence set in. The guyots (flat-topped seamounts described in Chapter XIII) form the base of several of the atolls, and the coral has grown up either on a portion of the flat surface or on what appears to be an eroded volcanic peak rising somewhat above the guyot (Fig. 176). The borings in the Great Barrier Reef also favor subsidence of a much smaller degree. The coarse sands and grits found beneath the reef at 250 m below sea level are too deep to be explained by glacial control.

**The Effects of Swinging Sea Levels.**    It is difficult to assess accurately the importance of the glacial control of sea levels in the development of the atolls. It is certainly possible that some of the lagoons have been beveled by low sea level erosion particularly in the marginal belt where reefs probably were killed by the colder water. Another important effect of lowered sea levels may have been the solution of the limestone within the reef caused by atmospheric water circulating in the exposed portions. Murray (1880) first suggested that solution was a cause of the lagoons although he did not appreciate that this might result from glacial control.  Hoffmeister and Ladd (1935) called attention to the importance of low stands of the sea in producing a moat inside the reefs and MacNeil (1954) further developed this hypothesis. The great irregularities within many of the atolls may be explained in part by this solution. Very likely the 10-fathom terrace found both in the lagoons and outside the atolls is a result of the lowered sea level. Further evidence is found in the weathered zones overlain by fresh coral growth in the upper portions of the Marshall Island borings.

In the first edition of this book it was suggested that a high stand of sea level in postglacial times allowed atoll rings to grow above the present surface and thus account for the coral islands of the atolls, an idea first brought out by Gardiner (1931). However, the detailed study of a number of atolls in recent years makes it evident that islands

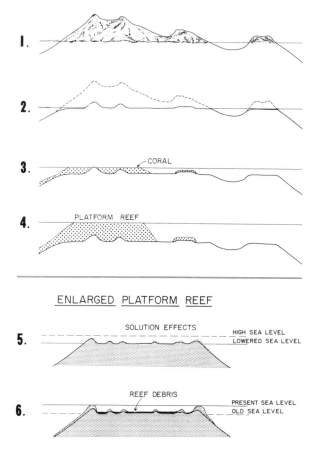

Fig. 176. The probable origin of such an atoll as Eniwetok by
a series of stages.

can develop as the result of piling up of coral debris by the waves
during unusually large storms (McKee, 1959). The considerable number of recently studied atolls that lack well-developed elevated reefs
is rather striking. It is possible that the occasional reefs of 2 to 12 ft
above sea level have been the result of postglacial high stands of sea
level, but we still lack proof of this suggestion from carbon-14 dating.
As this is being written, some of the shells from elevated reefs are
being analyzed to test the idea that they represent such recent growth
rather than being interglacial or the result of independent crustal
movements under the reefs.[4]

[4] First results from Oahu terraces at 5 and 12 ft have given average ages of 25,000 and
31,000 years and hence suggest a possible interstadial high stand corresponding to the
"Farmdalian" of Frye and Willman (1961). Probably diastrophism is partly responsible.

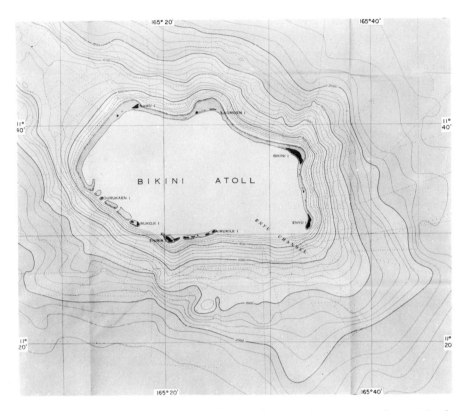

Fig. 177. Spurs extending down the slope beyond the projecting corners on the outside of Bikini Atoll. From Emery *et al.* (1954).

**Explanation of Irregular Outline of Atolls.** Atolls with a round shape are readily explained as conforming to the outline of a submerging volcano as in Fig. 175. Actually, the roundness of Eniwetok (Fig. 168) does not appear to be due to such an origin because the atoll has grown up on one side of an elongate beveled platform. The more common variety of atolls with projecting corners and concavities between are explained by Fairbridge (1950a) by landslides producing concavities in the sides of what would otherwise have been a more circular mass. As indicated by Fairbridge, concavities with such an origin should be matched by bulges on the sea floor near the base of the adjacent slope. An examination of the contours around the Marshall Islands (Emery *et al.*, 1954) does not provide much evidence in favor of this hypothesis, but the outer slopes are not well sounded so that landslide accumulations outside of the bights may not have been discovered. The bulging corners may be explained alternatively

as due to more active growth along portions of the atoll rim. Around
Bikini where the soundings extend to deep water some of the bulging
corners (Fig. 177) continue as submarine ridges to depths of as much
as 2000 fathoms. This appears to indicate that the reef has grown up
with an inheritance of projecting points.

# CHAPTER XIII

# DEEP OCEAN FLOOR TOPOGRAPHY

## Introduction

In recent years no phase of submarine geology has produced more spectacular results than has the study of the deep floor of the ocean basins. Notable contributions have come from the extensive investigations of the Atlantic by Lamont Geological Observatory (Heezen *et al.*, 1959) and of the Pacific by Scripps Institution of Oceanography (Menard, 1955b, 1959a,b,c; Menard and Fisher, 1958; Fisher, 1954, 1958). In addition very detailed and accurate mapping of portions of the deep Pacific has been conducted by the U.S. Coast and Geodetic Survey, and innumerable sounding lines have been obtained by the Hydrographic Office of the U.S. Navy particularly in the Atlantic. Some of the information is still classified as confidential although broad results have been released from which information of military importance is deleted. The Arctic Ocean was virtually unexplored until after World War II, but has since been rather widely sounded by a combination of ice breaker penetration into the ice pack along the margins, observations from floating ice islands (Crary and Goldstein, 1957), and cruises beneath the ice pack in submarines (Dietz and Shumway, 1961; Carsola *et al.*, 1961). The Antarctic was explored by many nations as a part of the International Geophysical Year program. The international exploration of the Indian Ocean is being conducted on a large scale as this is being written; by 1965 ships and marine scientists of more than fifteen nations will have participated.

## Topographic Features Defined

The results of deliberations by an international committee (Wiseman and Ovey, 1953) have led to a considerable degree of uniformity in the nomenclature of the topographic features of the ocean floor. In a few cases the rulings of the committee appear to have been subsequently disregarded by marine geologists and certain terms have become rather well established although they were not approved by

371

the committee. The following terms and definitions given alphabetically are, therefore, not entirely in accord with the committee report:

*Abyssal plain*   A very flat surface found in many of the deep ocean basins or adjacent seas.

*Archipelagic apron*   A fan-shaped slope around an oceanic island differing from deep-sea fans in having little, if any, sediment cover.

*Basin*   A depression on the sea floor that is more or less equidimensional.

*Continental rise*   A gentle even slope at the base of the steeper continental slope.

*Deep*   The well-defined deepest part of a depression, not used unless depths are in excess of 3000 fathoms.

*Deep-sea channel*   An elongate valley that cuts slightly below the surface of many of the deep-sea fans and may extend out to the basin floor.

*Deep-sea fan*   A gently sloping sediment-covered plain that borders the continental slopes in many places. The fans also occur in basins of intermediate depth on continental borderlands.

*Deep-sea terrace*   A benchlike feature bordering an elevation of the deep-sea floor at depths generally greater than 300 fathoms.

*Gap*   A steep-sided furrow which cuts transversely across a ridge or rise.

*Guyot*   A flat-topped seamount, also called a *tablemount*.

*Plateau*   An ill-defined extensive elevation of the deep-sea floor.

*Ridge*   A long elevation of the deep-sea floor with steep sides and irregular topography.

*Rise*   An elongate broad elevation of the ocean floor with gentler and smoother sides than those of a ridge.

*Seascarp*   An elongate and comparatively steep slope of the sea floor.

*Sill* and *sill depth*   A submarine ridge or rise that separates two partially closed basins. The greatest depth over the sill is called the sill depth.

*Seaknoll*   A submarine hill or elevation of the deep-sea floor less prominent than a seamount.

*Seamount*   An isolated or comparatively isolated elevation of the deep-sea floor with an elevation of 500 fathoms or more in relief and with comparatively steep slopes and relatively small summit area.

*Tablemount*   See Guyot.

*Trench*   A deep, long, and narrow depression of the deep-sea floor having at least relatively steep sides.

*Trough*   An elongate but relatively broad depression on the sea floor.

## Major Relief Features of the Oceans

All the oceans are interconnected, but there are submerged ridges which partially separate the three large oceans: the Pacific, the Atlantic, and the Indian. More pronounced barriers cut off three principal deep landlocked seas from the Atlantic Ocean, and the series of basins along the Asiatic coast from the Pacific. These seas are called mediterraneans or marginal seas. They include the North Polar Sea, the

Mediterranean, the Black Sea, the Gulf of Mexico, the Caribbean, and the seas inside the island festoons of eastern and southeastern Asia. For a general picture of the topography of the ocean floors the *Life* magazine maps of Nov. 7, 1960, are recommended. The general topography is also shown in the chart of the world (inside back cover).

**The Atlantic.** The Atlantic has an area of 31 million square nautical miles including the adjacent marginal seas and mediterraneans and of 24 million exclusive of the adjacent seas. The mean depth according to Kossinna (1921) is 2150 fathoms (3926 m) excluding the adjacent seas and 1820 fathoms (3332 m) including these seas. The Atlantic depths are only slightly less than the average for the entire ocean area.

The Atlantic is an elongate winding basin extending for about 7000 miles in a north-south direction with very much the same width (2000 ± miles) along its entire length. This is very different from the circular shape of the Pacific and the triangular shape of the Indian Ocean. The parallelism of the Atlantic coasts has led to the explanation that this ocean represents a great rift between a world continent known as *Pangaea*.

The topography of the Atlantic (Chart of the World, inside back cover) has been very extensively explored. The long continued work by Lamont Geological Observatory (Heezen *et al.*, 1959) has given us a very fine picture of the mountains, plains, and stepped plateaus in the North Atlantic, and the combination of Lamont work and the older soundings of the *Meteor* expedition (Stocks, 1933) give an almost equally valuable picture of the South Atlantic (Heezen and Tharp, 1962). No doubt this will be greatly improved when the soundings of the U.S. Navy Hydrographic Office are released for publication.

The most striking feature of the Atlantic is the Mid-Atlantic Ridge which runs almost the entire length and lies almost exactly equidistant from the Americas on one side and Europe and Africa on the other. The ridge rises about 1000 fathoms above the deep basins on either side (Fig. 178). The ridge is very mountainous although there are a few terraces on the sides. The highest parts of the ridge rise above the surface to form the Azores, St. Paul Rocks, Ascension, Tristan da Cunha, and Diego Alvarez Islands, all but the Azores and St. Paul Rocks being in the Southern Hemisphere.

The British as a result of their 1953 investigations first reported a deep valley cutting the northern portion of the Mid-Atlantic Ridge (Hill, 1956, 1960). Subsequently Heezen (1959b, 1960) referred to this as a "rift valley" and called for an extension of it for some 40,000 miles, stating that it not only can be traced along the entire Mid-Atlantic Ridge, but also that it extends east into the Indian Ocean

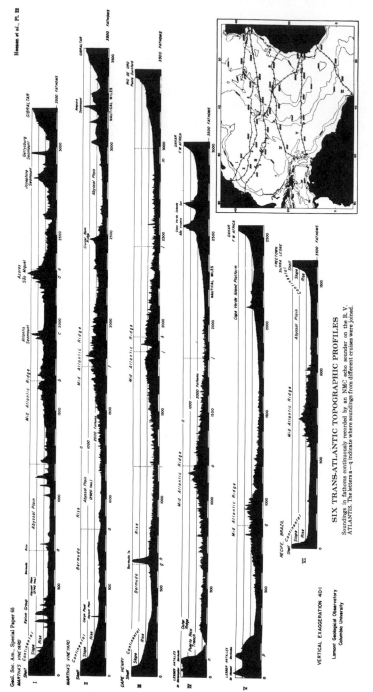

Fig. 178. Profiles across the Atlantic showing the Mid-Atlantic Ridge and the nature of the "rift" valley. Note that in some sections it is not easy to distinguish any valley. From Heezen et al. (1959, pl. 22).

and into the Pacific. This claim is difficult to confirm even in the Atlantic. For example, profiles partly from Lamont crossings (Fig. 178) show what could be interpreted as a rift valley in some crossings, but it is very difficult to recognize the rift in other crossings. Many valleys occur in the sections just as they do in profiles of land mountain ranges. Similarly, reported crossings by the Soviets on the *Lomonosov* (M. V. Klenova, personal communication) and by Dietrich (1956) south of Iceland showed no sign of a main rift valley. Some of the *Meteor* profiles in the south Atlantic (Stocks, 1933) show what may be the rift valley, but other profiles do not show any pronounced notch in the ridge. The profiles of the Indian Ocean (Fig. 191) (Ewing and Heezen, 1960) also show how difficult it is to determine whether there is a pronounced rift valley among the many jagged irregularities. Heezen's contention that the rift valley is continuous is based principally on the zone of earthquake epicenters found along the Mid-Atlantic Ridge (Gutenberg and Richter, 1954, Fig. 27). These distant epicenters, however, are not accurately located so that one can be sure only that the zone of epicenters follows the ridge rather than saying that it occurs along the supposed rift valley. Furthermore, many young mountain ranges have earthquake epicenters along their axis but lack continuous rift valleys. Thus, discounting for the present the hypothesis that the rift valley is 40,000 miles long, we can consider its character where it has been thoroughly studied by the British. Hill (1960) found the valley had a width of about 12 miles, a floor depth of 1800 to 2200 fathoms, with steep flanks rising to ridges with summit depths of 900 to 1200 fathoms. Hill also discovered with the use of temperature probes that the heat flow in the floor of the valley was about six times higher than usual for the deep sea and the continents. M. Ewing *et al.* (1959b) reported a high magnetic anomaly at the rift valley in the North Atlantic suggesting a "... subsurface body of high magnetic susceptibility." Hill (1960), on the other hand, found no large magnetic anomaly at the valley.

The rocks dredged from the Mid-Atlantic Ridge include basalt, gabbro, serpentine, and diabase (Shand, 1949). There have been reports, however, that the islands contain continental rocks (summarized in Gilluly, 1955). This evidence is based on hearsay and has never been clarified. The authenticity of the acidic types was seriously questioned by Teixeira (1950). He made the reasonable suggestion that ballast dropped from ships was responsible for these reports. Other rocks may have been rafted by ice or even kelp.

The greatest depth in the Atlantic is found in the Puerto Rico Trench where a depth of 5030 fathoms has been found. Profiles by Precision Depth Recorders show that the deep floor is very flat (Heezen

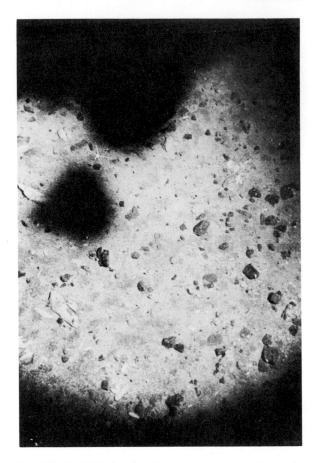

Fig. 179. Small blocks of rock on the floor of the Romanche Deep in the equatorial Atlantic. Photograph by Harold E. Edgerton, courtesy *National Geographic Magazine.* © National Geographic Society. The photograph covers an area approximately 3 by 4 ft.

*et al.,* 1959). The trench can be traced only about 600 miles, so that it is far shorter as well as much shoaler than the trenches of the western Pacific. Another trench is found at the south end of the Atlantic following the arcuate curve of the South Sandwich Islands (J. Ewing and M. Ewing, 1959b). This is also shoaler and less continuous than the Pacific trenches. The Romanche Trench, located on the east side of the Mid-Atlantic Ridge near the equator, is still less significant in dimensions. Photographs of the bottom of this trench (Fig. 179) show that the floor is irregular and partly covered with coarse sediments.

The South Atlantic has some transverse ridges, notably the Walvis

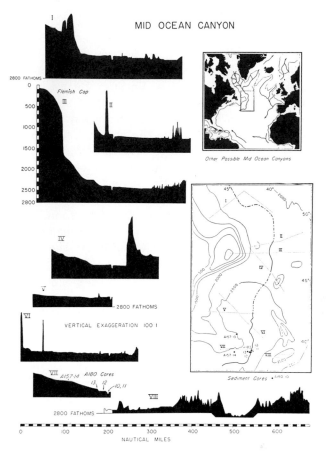

Fig. 180. The deep ocean channel extending down from Baffin Bay to the Nares Deep. From Heezen et al. (1959).

Ridge on the east and the Rio Grande Ridge on the west. These suggest possible sunken land bridges although they have not been explored to look for evidence of such connections. There are a number of seamounts and a few guyots in the Atlantic but not nearly as many as in the Pacific. One line of seamounts extends seaward from Georges Bank off the New England coast to Bermuda (Northrop et al., 1959). Many others are located on the Mid-Atlantic Ridge.

Deep-sea channels are found crossing the gently sloping continental rise off both the east and west side of the North Atlantic (Laughton, 1960). Another channel, called the Mid-Atlantic Canyon[1] (Fig. 180), was described by Heezen et al. (1959, Figs. 30, 31) as extending down

[1] A misnomer since it is not canyonlike in cross section and should be called a deep-sea channel or a trough.

from Baffin Bay, around the Newfoundland Rise and down the Atlantic Basin toward the Nares Deep. It has been suggested that this channel may have tributaries although this is not yet established. This Mid-Atlantic Channel is explained by the Lamont group as cut by turbidity currents. This idea was based on the finding of sand in a core taken in the channel, on finding a continuous slope to the south, and on what may be the existence of low levees on the sides. According to the Lamont map (Heezen *et al.*, 1959) the channel runs parallel to the Mid-Atlantic Rift Valley which suggests the possibility that the channel is due to faulting. The even gradient of the channel and the sand samples could be due to turbidity currents that flowed along the valley axis. The currents could also account for levees if these really exist, a point not at all well established by the sounding lines. That valleys of this type can be of tectonic origin seems to have been established by the report of another example on the continental rise running parallel to the Brazilian coast and the Mid-Atlantic Ridge (Heezen *et al.*, 1960). This could not be erosional or it would have extended down rather than along the slope.

**The Pacific.** The topography of the Pacific is strikingly different from that of the Atlantic. This largest of all oceans covers 52.5 million square nautical miles including the adjacent seas or 48.3 million excluding these seas. The average depth exclusive of adjacent seas is said by Kossinna (1921) to be 2340 fathoms (4282 m), slightly greater than the other oceans. Including the adjacent seas the depth is given as 2200 fathoms (4028 m). The depth differs so slightly from the Atlantic that there appears to have been no good reason for thinking that the Pacific is underlain by heavier rock than the Atlantic as was proposed by a number of geologists before geophysical shooting established that the crust is essentially the same under both oceans (see p. 425).

The most striking feature of the Pacific floor (see Chart of the World, inside back cover) is the series of trenches which virtually surround the basin. The trenches along North and South America extend in close to the lands but have a gap in their continuity along the west coast of the United States and Canada. This gap is indeed fortunate for the numerous west coastal cities of the United States that are located on low ground because the trenches are the world's greatest source of earthquakes and tsunamis. The east Pacific trenches are only slightly deeper than those of the Atlantic and not nearly as deep as those of the western Pacific. The latter, starting off Kamchatka, form a series of somewhat disconnected deeps extending in a general southerly direction as far as the Kermadec Islands, north of New Zealand. The greatest depths of these trenches are given in Table 10. The similarity of many of these depths is striking. The depths of the Mariana Trench and Tonga Trench are so close that we still do not know for sure which is the deepest although the evidence favors the former. The Challenger (Trieste) Deep in the Mariana Trench is now well sounded and the depth of 5933 fathoms is based on corrected echo soundings, on a wire sounding, and on corrected pressure readings taken on the trench floor in the bathyscaph *Trieste* during the descent by Jacques Piccard and Lt. Don Walsh in January 1960.

TABLE 10.  Depths of Pacific Trenches[a]

| Trenches | Depth in Fathoms | Meters |
|---|---|---|
| Aleutian | 4,200 | 7,679 (not accurate) |
| Kuril | 5,676 | 10,540 ± 100 |
| Japan (Idzu-Bonin) | 5,364 | 9,810 |
| Mariana | 5,933 | 10,850 ± 20 |
| Mindanao | 5,484 | 10,030 ± 10 |
| New Britain | 4,549 | 8,320 |
| New Hebrides | 4,940 | 9,035 ± 20 |
| Tonga | 5,905 | 10,800 ± 100 |
| Kermadec | 5,465 | 9,994 |
| Peru-Chile | 4,404 | 8,050 ± 10 |

Source: Information supplied by R. L. Fisher.
[a] See also Udintsev (1959) for Russian data.

Some of the trenches have a V-shaped bottom, but more commonly the profile indicates a relatively narrow flat floor several miles wide. Where the bathyscaph landed on the bottom of the Mariana Trench a diatomaceous ooze was encountered. The same type of bottom was reported by Petelin (1960) from both the Yap and Mariana trenches. Sand and gravel were found in the sample taken by the *Galathea* in the Mindanao Trench (Bruun *et al.*, 1956). Pillow lava was dredged from the walls of the Mariana and Bougainville trenches (Petelin, 1960).

The floor of the Aleutian Trench slopes quite evenly toward the west as far as Long. 180°. Farther west the slope is reversed. The even slope in the eastern portion is a strong indication that turbidity currents have been flowing along this trench. In the Mid-America Trench, off western Central America and Mexico, Fisher (1961) found V-shaped profiles to the south and generally flat-floored profiles to the north. The flat floor was shown by reflection shooting to have a roughly V-shaped rock floor under the sediment.

The trenches are bordered in many places by rows of volcanoes, and arc-shaped island chains like the Aleutians, Kurils, and Marianas. Virtually all of these occur on the concave side of arcuate trenches. Earthquakes also show a relation to trenches, the epicenters occurring near the surface in the vicinity of the trench but being found at

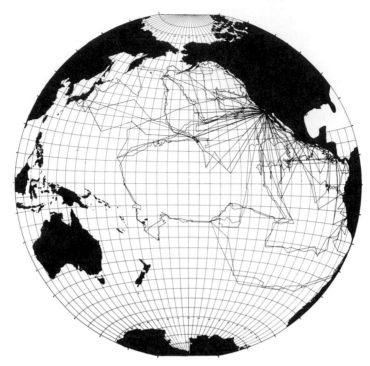

Fig. 181. Tracks of Scripps Institution expeditions in the Pacific up to 1961.

progressively greater depths in a direction towards the continents (Fig. 140).

Measurements of gravity have been made at many places over trenches in both the Atlantic, the Pacific, and in the Indian Ocean trenches (Vening Meinesz, 1929, 1955; Worzel and Shurbet, 1955). Here some of the greatest deficiencies of gravity in the world have been found. There is evidently a deficiency of mass at these places such as would be produced if the crust had been downbuckled and was being held down against isostasy by pressure from the sides, as suggested by Vening Meinesz (1929). The downbuckling is also indicated by the greater depth of the Mohorovičić discontinuity (see p. 425) under the Tonga Trench (Raitt *et al.*, 1955), under the Mid-America Trench (Shor and Fisher, 1961), under the Kuril Trench (Sisoev *et al.*, 1959, Fig. 2) and under the Puerto Rico Trench (Talwani *et al.*, 1959).

*Ridges and Seamounts.*    The North Pacific and part of the equatorial Pacific are now well sounded as a result of the extensive cruises of the Scripps Institution fleet of eight ocean going vessels (Fig. 181). A portion of the northeast Pacific has been surveyed in great detail by the U.S. Coast and Geodetic Survey. The results, contoured by Menard

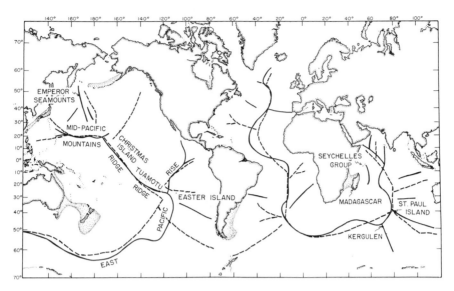

Fig. 182. Relationship between the various mid-ocean ridges (solid lines) and the middle lines between the continental shores. From Menard (1959c).

(Figs. 183, 185) and partly by Hurley (1960), show that there are numerous ridges in addition to a myriad of seamounts. As in the Atlantic some of the principal ridges follow close to the geometrical median line, equidistant from the continent margins as shown by Menard (Fig. 182). Thus the Emperor Seamounts of Kamchatka, the Mid-Pacific Mountains, and the Christmas Island and Tuamotu ridges continuing into the East Pacific Rise are all fairly close to these median lines.

Another series of ridges and seamounts extending out almost vertically from the west coast of North America are separated by rather even intervals (Fig. 183). These have been extensively surveyed by Menard (1955b) who has referred to them as *fracture zones*. The Mendocino fracture zone (Menard and Dietz, 1952) has a steep escarpment on the south side of the ridge that extends out beyond the Gorda Escarpment, thus reversing the steep side. The Mendocino fracture zone is also notable for its 2000-mile ridge. Farther south the recently discovered Pioneer Ridge also has a steep slope on the south side but does not have as much relief as the great escarpment off Cape Mendocino. The Murray fracture zone off the bend in the California coast has a continuous escarpment on the north side, but the ridge does not extend into the continental slope like that off Cape Mendocino. There is a series of seamounts extending parallel to the ridge. The Clarion and Clipperton fracture zones off Mexico

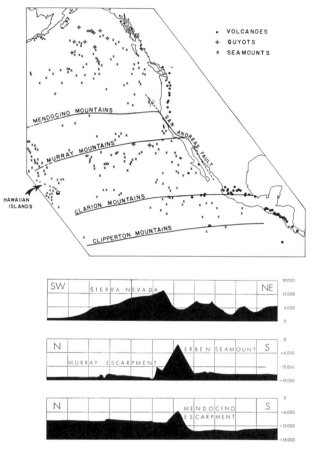

Fig. 183. The four main fracture zones off the west coast of North America, showing also the relation to volcanoes, guyots, and seamounts. The lower portion shows comparison of the Sierra Nevada with the Murray and Mendocino escarpments. From Menard (1955b).

and Central America consist of a string of seamounts in some places and continuous ridges elsewhere (Menard and Fisher, 1958).

Most of the fracture zones appear to have some connection with the structures or topography of the adjacent land. The Mendocino Escarpment lies off the point where what appears to be the northern end of the San Andreas fault system finally leaves the California coast and bends westward (Shepard, 1957), possibly splitting into several major faults. The Murray fracture zone occurs off the east-west ranges of southern California and off the place where the California coast shows a sharp bend to the north. The San Andreas fault bends toward the west along this line also, but farther north returns to the northwest trend. The Clarion fracture zone appears to connect with the east-west volcanic belt of southern Mexico and includes San Benedicto Island, where a new volcano first erupted in 1952 (Richards, 1959).

The magnetometer work of Mason (1958, 1960), Vacquier *et al.* (1959, 1961), and Mason and Raff (1960) has indicated that there is a left lateral slip along the Mendocino fracture zone of about 600 nautical miles. The Murray Escarpment to the south has a right lateral displacement of 84 nautical miles also shown by magnetometer (Vacquier *et al.*, 1961). Between them, Pioneer Ridge has a left lateral displacement of 138 nautical miles. The basis for these displacements is the matching of magnetic anamoly contours on the two sides of the fracture zones (Fig. 184). The displacements of the 2500-fathom contour at the ridges are almost the same as the magnetic displacements. The left lateral slip along the Mendocino Scarp is of special interest because this lies seaward of Gorda Scarp where a right lateral slip is indicated by the topographic offset of the continental slope and by the apparent relation to the San Andreas fault zone with its right lateral displacement (Shepard, 1957). Movements in relation to these fracture zones appear to have had vertical as well as horizontal components, as shown by the steep escarpments. Furthermore, the sea floor between the Mendocino and the Murray fracture zones is about 500 fathoms deeper than to the north and 200 fathoms deeper than to the south.

Minor lineations occur also in many areas of the Pacific (Menard, 1959a). These have in general a pinnate pattern. Elongate volcanoes are the most common type. These minor lineations extend out from either side of the major lineations like the barbs of a feather.

So far as is known, all the Pacific seamounts are volcanic in origin. The number of seamounts found in the Pacific grows with each expedition. Many of them were discovered by the wartime soundings of Hess (1946). As this is written H. W. Menard (personal communication) has listed 1400 of these Pacific seamounts (Fig. 185). Along certain lines many of them have flat tops. These guyots were first explained by Hess as being the result of Precambrian wave beveling followed by submergence resulting from sedimentation that weighted the ocean floor and caused a gradual subsidence. This hypothesis has had to be modified due to subsequent dredgings from seamounts that have shown that they have shallow-water forms ranging in age from Cretaceous to Miocene (Hamilton, 1953, 1956; Carsola and Dietz, 1952). Furthermore, according to available information the thickness of sediment on the Pacific Ocean floor has proved to be much too small to account for the submergence of the guyots to such characteristic depths as 800 fathoms. It seems far more likely that the flat

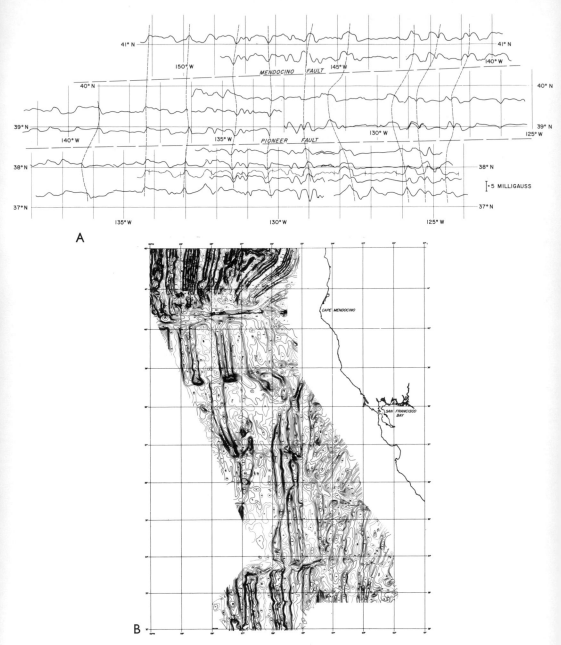

Fig. 184. (a) Variation in magnetometer readings in the east-west lines on either side of the Mendocino and Pioneer faults. Note that the sections have been shifted in such a way that the readings show a match of the character of the magnetometer variation. At the Mendocino fault there is an indication of a displacement of 600 nautical miles and at the Pioneer fault of 138 miles. From Vacquier et al. (1961). (b) Contouring of the magnetometer readings off the California coast that have been used as a means of indicating large horizontal strike-slip displacements on the sea floor. From Mason and Raff (1961).

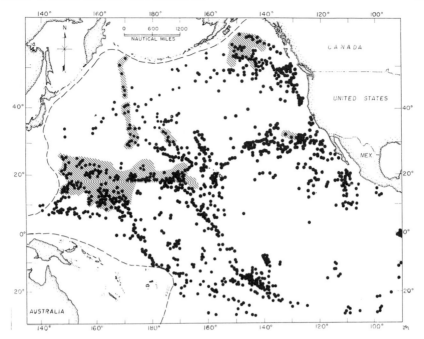

Fig. 185. The distribution of islands and seamounts in the Pacific rising 500 fathoms or more above their surroundings. Most of those in the shaded area are guyots. From Menard (1959c).

tops of the guyots are the joint product of wave beveling, or perhaps coral growth, at various times during the Cretacous and Tertiary followed by subsidence from various causes to their present depths. The history of the atolls such as Eniwetok and Bikini (p. 362) gives further confirmation of extensive subsidence. As an alternative the entire basin may have subsided accompanying the addition of water coming from great lava flows (Revelle, 1955). Large sources of carbon dioxide from these flows might account for the apparent increase in limestone deposition in the form of deep-sea ooze since the Cretaceous. The large-scale development of Globigerinidae and the other planktonic calcareous organisms that blanket the ocean floor requires large amounts of carbon dioxide. On the other hand, the guyots appear to occur along lines and in bands and therefore suggest local subsidence rather than worldwide deepening of the oceans. Evidence of subsidence of guyots comes also from the Gulf of Alaska where Menard and Dietz (1951) observed that a guyot in the Aleutian Trench has a greater depth than other guyots along a line to the southeast (Fig. 186). Finally, the finding of many depressions around guyots as well as around other seamounts and around island chains like the Hawaiian

Islands (Dietz and Menard, 1953; Hamilton, 1957) indicates subsidence rather than sea level rise.[2] The ridges and seamounts would be expected to subside because they form a burden on the earth's crust resulting from the piling up of lavas that must have come from a much more extensive area than now included in the highs.

The East Pacific Rise, also called Pacific Antarctic Ridge (Menard, 1960c) has been traced as a broad arch from a point near New Zealand to the coast of Mexico, a distance of 7000 miles. It extends southeast from New Zealand, then curves to the northeast to Easter Island.

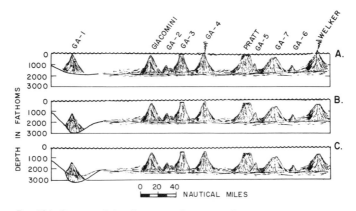

Fig. 186. Suggested development of a series of seamounts in the Gulf of Alaska. The first section, A, indicates supposed conditions before the formation of the Aleutian Trench. In section B a seamount has sunk into the trench, and in section C it has been partly buried by sediments in the trench. Redrawn from Menard and Dietz (1951).

At that place Sala y Gómez Ridge extends east from the rise and branches into the Nasca Ridge (Fisher and Norris, 1960; Rüegg, 1960) that runs in toward the coast of Peru. The East Pacific Rise (Pacific Antarctic Ridge) has a crest 1000 to 1600 fathoms above the deep Pacific. The Scripps Institution traverses of the Rise (Menard, personal communication) show that it is generally smooth with no indication of the rift valley predicted by Heezen (1960). The Rise, like the Mid-Atlantic Ridge, is the site of many shallow earthquakes. The heat flow from the ridge is several times higher than normal for continents and oceans (von Herzen, 1959). A series of eleven mountain belts bisect the Rise, all of them running approximately east and west. The Rise is offset by several of these. Menard (1960c) has suggested that the Rise may continue north through the Gulf of California, along the California borderland, and the California Coast Range. He suggests it returns to the sea floor again at Cape Mendocino, California, where it

[2] Recent dredging of Miocene corals around the islands confirms subsidence.

is represented by the shallow base of the continental slope along the coasts of Oregon, Washington, and British Columbia. Menard also suggests a genetic relationship of the east-west fracture zones to the East Pacific Rise since the Rise is offset by the fracture zones.

*Abyssal Plains and Channels.* The abyssal plains of the northeast Pacific (Fig. 187) have been described by Hurley (1960). These are sloping plains and seem to be somewhat comparable to what Heezen has called the continental rise in the Atlantic although they have lower slopes than the lower limit suggested by Heezen for the continental rise, but they are more sloping than the Atlantic abyssal plain. These Pacific abyssal plains slope gradually westward. Some of them are crossed by deep-sea channels with pronounced levees (Fig. 188). These channels have been found as far as a thousand miles away from the coast although their direct connections with channels on the lower continental slopes are not clear. Cascadia Channel crosses a submarine mountain range and has a much deeper gorge in the crossing than on either side. Hurley has pointed out that these channels are as much as 200 fathoms deep and 5 miles or more across. Since the levees suggest that they are at times filled with turbid sediment-laden water[3] the currents may have very high velocities, perhaps as much as 25 knots (using the Chézy formula), although as explained previously (p. 140) this does not necessarily refer to a bottom current. The westernmost abyssal plain is partly cut off from sources of turbidity current sediments from the east by a range of mountains and from the north by the Aleutian Trench. Since the other plains appear to be derived from turbidity current flows from the continental slopes, the assumption is that the mountains must have been raised up subsequent to the formation of this outer plain or that the Aleutian Trench was formed later than the plain and the sediments came from the Alaskan peninsula.

According to Menard (1956) many of the smooth portions of the Pacific Ocean are found as aprons around "groups of existing or ancient islands." These archipelagic aprons slope evenly away from the high areas, resembling fans, but through seismic refraction measurements (Shor, 1960) they are found to consist largely of lava flows with a rather thin covering of sediments, only sufficient to develop the extreme smoothness. These sediments like those of the continental rise and the abyssal plains were presumably introduced to a considerable extent by turbidity currents.

The preceding discussion has been concerned with some of the mountainous irregularities of the sea floor and with the smooth aprons, fans, and abyssal plains where sedimentation has developed remarkably

---

[3] Recent evidence from the channel off La Jolla suggests that the great depths may be due to rejuvenation and the deep channels may never be filled.

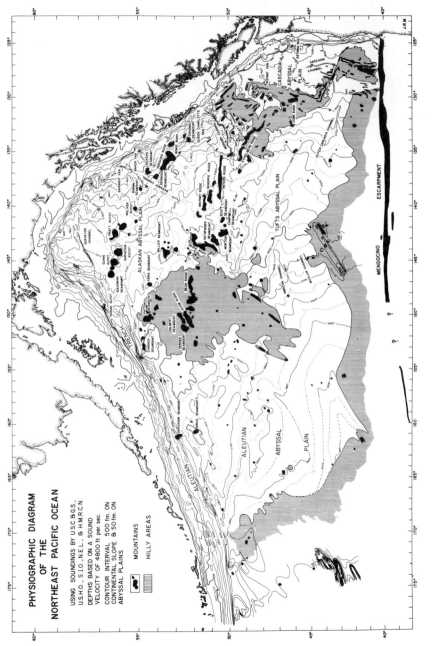

Fig. 187. Generalized contours of the northeast Pacific, north of the Mendocino Escarpment. From Hurley (1960). See also Fig. 188 and Chart of the World (inside back cover).

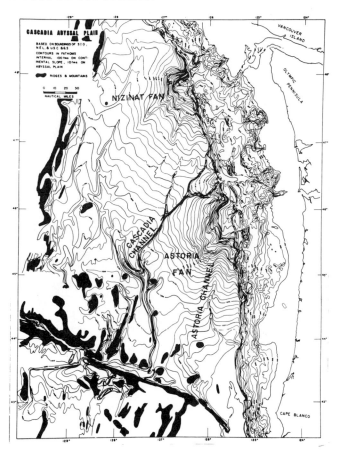

Fig. 188. Cascadia abyssal plain and the Cascadia and Astoria channels. Note that the connections between the channels and the canyons near shore are not very definite. The left hook of the channels emphasized by Menard (1956) is well illustrated. From Hurley (1960).

flat surfaces. Another type of topography covers the greater part of the Pacific floor as Menard has emphasized (1959b). This consists of a hilly terrain with relief of the order of one or two hundred fathoms. This type of topography (Fig. 189) is apparently much more common in the Pacific than in the Atlantic because in the former there are vast territories that are far removed from the influence of turbidity currents and from the lava flows of the seamounts and island ridges and, therefore, irregularities are not eliminated by burial.

**The Indian Ocean.** Only a few echo sounding lines are now published from the Indian Ocean although the information from the new expeditions should soon become available. The Indian Ocean is smaller than the Atlantic and contains 21.5 million square nautical miles without adjacent seas and 21.9 million with them. The mean depths were said by Kossinna (1921) to be 2180 fathoms (3963 m) without the adjacent seas, or 2140 fathoms (3897 m) with them. The deepest locality is the Java (Sunda) Trench extending up from west Australia past Indonesia. This is the only trench known in the Indian Ocean, and its maximum known depth of 4065 fathoms is even less than is found in the Atlantic trenches. It appears to be a

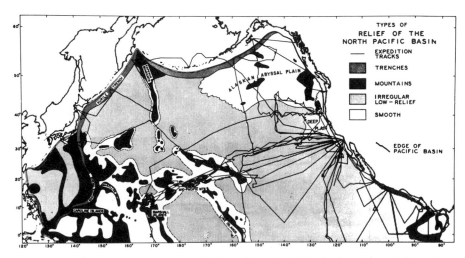

Fig. 189. Types of relief found on the floor of the North Pacific. From Menard (1959b).

westward continuation of the group of arcuate trenches of the western Pacific.

The ridges in the Arabian Sea are somewhat comparable to the Mid-Atlantic Ridge although they are not centrally located (Fig. 190 and Chart of the World, inside back cover). These were discovered largely by the soundings of the John Murray Expedition of 1933–1934. They extend largely in a north-south direction but at their northern end they curve to the northwest coming in at right angles to the African coast somewhat like the fracture zone ridges off western North America. The Kerguelen-Gaussberg Ridge extends south almost to Antarctica. A branch from this ridge extends west to the Mid-Atlantic Ridge and another east around Australia and up into the East Pacific Rise. Rocks have been dredged from the main ridge that were found to consist of basalt and some continental rocks (Wiseman, 1937).

Recent soundings of the ridge by Lamont's *Vema* (Ewing and Heezen, 1960) indicate the presence of some deep valleys (Fig. 191)

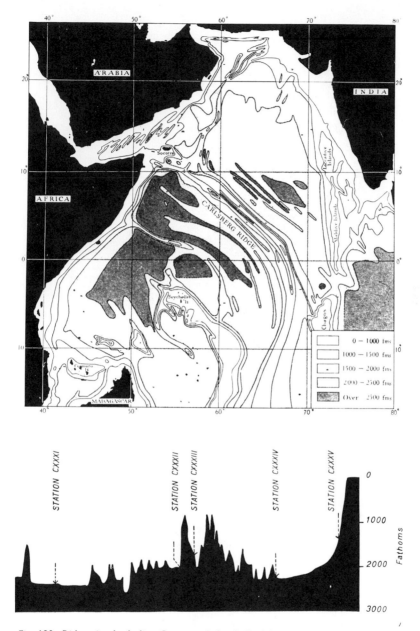

Fig. 190. Ridges in the Indian Ocean and the Gulf of Aden (upper left). Note the two dominant trends. After Wiseman (1937, Fig. 1A). A profile southwest of Kardiva Channel is shown below. See also Chart of the World (inside back cover).

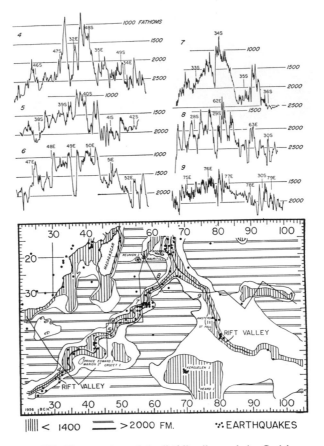

Fig. 191. The crossings of the "rift" valley and the Carlsberg
Ridge in the Indian Ocean made by Lamont Geological
Observatory. From Ewing and Heezen (1960).

that may extend along the ridge like the "rift valley" of the Mid-
Atlantic Ridge. As in the South Atlantic the evidence is not entirely
conclusive. According to R. L. Fisher (personal communication)
crossings of the ridges on the Scripps Institution *Monsoon* expedition
showed relief of 300 to 500 fathoms with no flat areas nor any obvious
rift valleys. The seamounts are apparently scarce in the south Indian
Ocean. The south central area, where no source of turbidity current
sediments is available, has hills with relief of 50 to 100 fathoms and
one or two broad shoal areas 800 to 1200 fathoms deep.

The soundings of the *Albatross* and *Galathea* expeditions show that
there is a southward sloping plain in the Bay of Bengal with probable
channels running along it extending out from the Ganges Trough.
These have been interpreted as turbidity current channels by Dietz

(1953) and as fault valleys by Koczy (1954). To settle this controversy more soundings are needed to tell whether the channels are continuous up to the Ganges Trough or whether they are local fault grabens. Available evidence favors Dietz because of the discovery by Gaskell (1960) of an abyssal plain in the area with sediment 1 to 3 km thick.

**The Mediterraneans.** The relatively small but deep basins that are largely surrounded by continents are called mediterraneans. Four of them attain rather large size including the Arctic that covers 4.1 million square nautical miles; the series of somewhat disconnected deeps extending from the Sea of Okhotsk south to the Coral Sea and containing 2.4 million miles; the Caribbean Sea and the Gulf of Mexico with a total of 1.2 million miles; and the Mediterranean and Black seas with a total of 840,000 miles.

The Arctic Ocean is roughly circular in outline. Most of the Arctic is covered with an ice pack so that the only way to explore it adequately has been to use submarines that dive under the ice. In addition soundings have been made from floating ice islands and by landing planes on the ice (Crary, 1956). Ice breakers have penetrated for some distance into the ice pack. About half of the Arctic consists of continental shelves, these being particularly wide off Europe and Asia. The deep portion (Fig. 192) contains two major basins separated by the Lomonosov Ridge extending from the New Siberian Islands to Ellesmere Island, west of Greenland, and rising to a truncated top at 700 fathoms (Dietz and Shumway, 1959). On the Alaska side of the ridge the flat basin has a depth of 2150 fathoms and on the Siberian side of 2230 to 2450 fathoms. In addition there are sharp mountain peaks and rolling hills. There is no striking difference between the general type of topography of the Arctic and the Atlantic. There seems to be little doubt but that the Arctic is of true oceanic character rather than related to the continents like the continental borderlands. The Arctic Ocean is separated from the Pacific by the shallow Bering Strait and from the Atlantic by the Faroe-Iceland Ridge with a sill depth of about 250 fathoms (Dietrich, 1956). The connections on the west side of Greenland are less known because of ice conditions, but apparently there are rather shoal sills leading into Baffin Bay.

The Gulf of Mexico and the Caribbean Sea, despite their juxtaposition, are quite different in character. The Gulf has a broad oval basin with a relatively flat floor despite the steep escarpments that occur along a portion of its margin (p. 285) (Fig. 193). The central basin, referred to as Sigsbee Deep, has soundings as deep as 2000 fathoms. The Lamont group has emphasized the importance of a great fan leading down into the central basin from the submarine trough off the west side of the Mississippi Delta (Ewing, M., et al., 1958).

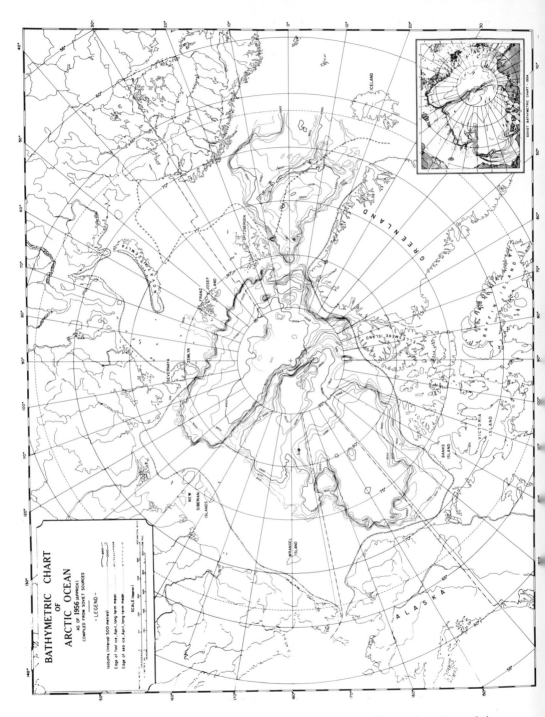

Fig. 192. Contours of the Arctic Ocean, showing the Lomonsov Ridge and positions of the sea ice margin. Compiled by Chief Cartographer, Surveys and Mapping Branch, Dept. of Mines and Technical Surveys of Canada, 1957.

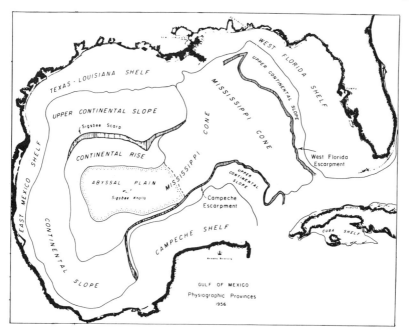

Fig. 193. Escarpments and fans in the Gulf of Mexico. From Ewing *et al.* (1958). See also Figs. 132 and 133.

Another branch of the fan extends down along the great west Florida Escarpment and appears to have supplied sediment to the lower portion of the deep submarine valleys at the south end of this escarpment. The Caribbean contains a series of trough-shaped elongated basins (Fig. 194). From west to east these include the east-west Yucatan Basin with a maximum depth of 2651 fathoms, the east-west Cayman Trough with Bartlett Deep having a sounding of 3798 fathoms, and then west and south of Jamaica a series of north-south basins and ridges including the Columbian Basin with depths up to 2280 fathoms, the Venezuelan Basin with a depth of 2987 fathoms, and the Grenada Trough with depths up to 2253 fathoms. On the east side of the Lesser Antilles lies the Tobago Basin separating the Grenadine Islands from Barbados. The latter island has often been referred to as containing elevated deep-sea deposits although the Foraminifera do not appear to have originated in depths much in excess of 500 fathoms (Beckman, 1954), which is comparable to the Tobago Channel. The West Indies are separated from Venezuela by only a shallow channel, about 100 fathoms deep, and from Nicaragua by a channel about 640 fathoms deep which compares with about 400 fathoms separating the Bahamas and Cuba from Florida.

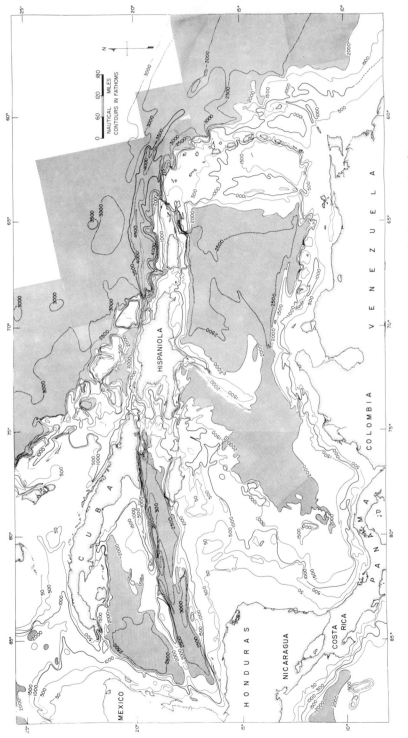

Fig. 194. The relief of the Caribbean and the series of basins and ridges which characterize this sea. Shaded areas represent depths in excess of 2000 fathoms. From U.S. Hydrographic Office charts.

The Mediterranean[4] and Black seas are comparable respectively with the Caribbean and the Gulf of Mexico. The Mediterranean, separated from the Atlantic by a sill of 155 fathoms, has a series of basins running mostly north and south and separated by sills, notably the Sicily Strait with its sill of about 160 fathoms. The Ionian Sea south of Italy and southwest of Greece has the deepest water with a maximum sounding of 2750 fathoms, this being found in a small trench off the Peloponnesos (Lacombe, 1960). The Tyrrhenian Sea west of Italy has been surveyed by the Italian Navy and special lines have been run across it by Lamont's *Vema*. From this area Segrè (1958) described several seamounts including one with a flattened top at 263 fathoms and a ringlike depression surrounding most of it.

The Black Sea, virtually landlocked, has a relatively smooth floor slightly in excess of 1100 fathoms (2000 m) in depth. It has been extensively sounded and sampled by the Soviet Union (Strakhov, 1947; Goncharov and Neprochnov, 1960). A small north-south rise separates an east and a west basin and apparently connects with a ridge on the south side.

The basins along the east coast of Asia are of diverse character. In some places there are trenchlike deeps, notably in parts of Indonesia and the Philippines. Elsewhere around Indonesia there are flat-floored troughs with steep walls such as the Lompok and Flores basins. The shapes and trends of the basins are irregular in most places. The greatest depths of most of the basins exceed 2000 fathoms and one of them near Bougainville attains at least 5000 fathoms. In general they are more like the Caribbean and the Mediterranean than like the Gulf of Mexico and the Black Sea. The basins in Indonesia have been investigated by the *Snellius* expedition (Kuenen, 1935) and most recently by Scripps Institution's *Monsoon* expedition.

**Small Landlocked Deeps.**    At least three deep gulfs have straight, parallel sides and no appreciable bordering shelves. These are the Gulf of Aden, the Red Sea, and the Gulf of California. Knowledge of the Gulf of Aden comes from the John Murray Expedition (Sewell, 1935–1936). The echo sounding chart shows that there are a series of diagonal ridges and deeps running northeast-southwest. These are at right angles to the ridges of the Indian Ocean to the east. The ridges rise about 400 fathoms above the deeps. The latter have depths which attain between 1500 and 2000 fathoms.

The Red Sea is more uniform in depth with a maximum of about 1200 fathoms. The sides form escarpments with some irregularities. A sill of about 40 fathoms separates the Red Sea from the Gulf of

[4] A series of contour maps of the western Mediterranean have been published by the Oceanographic Institute of Monaco (see Pfannenstiel, 1960).

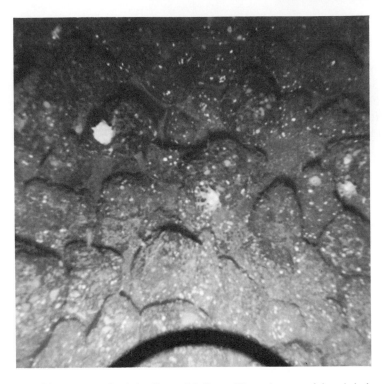

Fig. 195. Photograph of the floor of Ballenas Channel, west of Angel de la Guarda, Gulf of California, at a depth of approximately 400 fathoms. These large boulders about 4 m across are kept free of sediment by the powerful currents which move through this channel. Photo by C. J. Shipek, U.S. Navy Electronics Laboratory.

Aden, but outside the sill a channel 100 fathoms deep extends for 90 miles into the Red Sea. Along the shoal margins of the Red Sea there are numerous coral pinnacles. The chart notations of rock bottom from many localities in the center of this trench are surprising, and the matter should be investigated.

The Gulf of California which separates the Mexican states of Sonora and Sinaloa from Baja California is smaller than the Red Sea, being 700 miles long and 100 miles across. This Gulf has been explored by a series of expeditions from Scripps Institution. The report of the 1939 and 1940 expeditions has been published (Anderson *et al.*, 1950) and the topography known at that time was described (Anderson *et al.*, 1950, pt. III). Subsequently a closely spaced network of soundings has crossed the Gulf bringing out much more detail. The greatest depth is to the south where one of the basins shows soundings of 2030 fathoms. The basins are arranged somewhat en echelon with principal trends northwest-southeast but subsidiary trends at right angles. On the western side of the Gulf there are several small trenches with essentially V-shaped bottoms. The most spectacular of these lies to the north between Baja California and Angel de la Guarda and San Lorenzo islands. This trench has a floor in places over 800 fathoms deep and is in large part scoured clean by the strong tidal currents of the area. A series of photographs taken by C. J. Shipek show that large boulders virtually cover the deep floor in some sections (Fig. 195).

# CHAPTER XIV

# DEEP OCEAN DEPOSITS AND STRATIGRAPHY

**Deep-Sea Sediments**

Much recent progress has been made in the investigation of deep ocean floor sediments. Cores up to about 100 ft in length have been obtained. Many cores have penetrated far enough to give insight into the subocean stratigraphy of the Pleistocene and even the late Tertiary.

**History of Investigations.** Samples of the deep oceans were not obtained until the middle of the nineteenth century. Little was learned about these sediments until the famous voyage of H.M.S. *Challenger*, 1872 to 1876, which traversed all the main oceans and provided information of a revolutionary nature. The description by Murray and Renard (1891) of 12,000 samples, many deep water, obtained by the *Challenger* and other nineteenth century expeditions is contained in their classic report. The foundation of the greater part of our knowledge of the deep ocean deposits was built on this report. Much additional information came from samples taken during the many cruises of the United States Fish Commission ship *Albatross* (Agassiz, 1892, 1906). Shortly after World War I the German ship *Meteor* made extensive collections of deep-sea deposits, particularly in the Atlantic and Indian oceans, and these have been described principally by Correns *et al.* (1937), Córrens (1939), and Schott (1939). The last cruise of the *Carnegie* (1928 to 1929) yielded a considerable number of new samples which have been described by Revelle (1944). The *Snellius* expedition to Indonesia in 1929 and 1930 yielded valuable material from the deep basins of that area. These have been the subject of reports by Kuenen (1942) and Neeb (1943). The cruise of the *Discovery II* around southern South America and the adjacent portion of the Antarctic added important information from that area (Neaverson, 1934). Somewhat revolutionary information has come from the study of the Piggot cores taken across the Atlantic in 1936 from the cable ship *Lord Kelvin*. These cores are described by Bradley *et al.* (1942).

After World War II a great increase in knowledge of the sediments of the deep-sea floor has come from the numerous expeditions of oceanographic institutions. Much of the information is still unpublished and many of the recent reports have been in Russian and are as yet untranslated. The International Oceanographic Congress of 1959, however, has published rather lengthy abstracts that are helpful in getting this Russian information together. Summary reports of the American work in the Atlantic have been given (Ericson *et al.*, 1955) as well as for the Pacific (Revelle *et al.*, 1955). The work of Arrhenius (1961) has brought up to date both the field and laboratory investigations with special emphasis on the chemistry of the sediments. Perhaps the most notable advance in the study of deep-sea sediments in recent years has come from the recognition of turbidity current deposits over wide areas of the sea floor beyond the continental slopes. The long cores taken in the various oceans have also yielded information relative to climatic changes during the Pleistocene. Other notable contributions have come from the chemical studies of the sediments that are described in Chapter XVI.

**Classification of Deep-Sea Deposits.**   The classification of deep-sea deposits by Murray and Renard (1891) is still used widely along with the minor changes suggested by Revelle (1944) but is now subject to revision to bring it in line with recent discoveries. The older classifications included principally *red clay* and various types of organic ooze along with terrigenous muds of various colors. The first and much needed revision should be to abolish the term red clay. There are a few localities in which deep-sea deposits low in carbonates are red, but these are certainly rare and aside for some reddish brown silty layers deposited by turbidity currents (Ericson *et al.*, 1961, p. 203) reddish clays are apparently confined to portions of the south Indian Ocean. The typical deposit to which the name red clay has been applied is predominantly a clay in most places but the color is usually a shade of brown, particularly a chocolate color indicative of an oxidizing environment. Therefore, we might better call this *brown clay*, or *brown lutite* as suggested by Ericson *et al.* (1961), although clay seems more appropriate since lutite is generally defined as consisting of silt and clay whereas very little silt is present in the material in question. Some of the deposits formerly called red clay are not even clay since they have been largely altered to zeolites (Arrhenius, 1963).

Another difficulty with the older classifications is the failure to include turbidites. This resulted both from the short length of the early cores and from the failure to recognize fine-grained turbidites until recent years. Similarly, until the time of the Piggot cores across the Atlantic (Bradley *et al.*, 1942), the importance of ice-rafted sediments in the deep-sea deposits of high latitudes had not been realized.

Another serious difficulty in the older classification of the deep-sea sediments is in defining *pelagic sediments*. Concerning the meaning of this name many heated debates have been held. Therefore, without hope that any broad agreement can be reached on the definition, pelagic sediments will be considered here as those sediments of the deep part of the open ocean that settled out of the overlying water at a considerable distance from land and in the absence of appreciable currents so that the particles are either predominantly clays or their alteration products or consist of some type of skeletal material from plants or animals. The clays may be derived from the land either by water or by wind or may come from volcanic dust or meteorites.

A classification that appears to be fairly satisfactory is as follows:

Pelagic
  Brown clay (having less than 30 percent biogenous material)
  Authigenic deposits (consisting dominantly of minerals crystallized in
      sea water, such as phillipsite and manganese nodules).
  Biogenous deposits (having more than 30 percent material derived from
      organisms).
    Foraminiferal ooze (having more than 30 percent calcareous biogenous,
        largely Foraminifera, particularly common in cores penetrating
        Tertiary, usually called *Globigerina* ooze).
    Diatom ooze (having more than 30 percent siliceous biogenous, largely
        diatoms).
    Radiolarian ooze (having more than 30 percent siliceous biogenous
        largely radiolarians).
    Coral reef debris (derived from slumping around reefs)
      Coral sands
      Coral muds (white)
Terrigenous
  Terrigenous muds (having more than 30 percent of silt and sand of definite
      terrigenous origin)
    Green muds
    Black muds
    Red muds
  Turbidites (derived by turbidity currents from the lands or from submarine
      highs)
  Slide deposits (carried to deep water by slumping)
  Glacial marine (having a considerable percent of allochthonous particles
      derived from iceberg transportation)

**Brown Clay (Red Clay).**    The abyssal brown clays are found in the deep basins of all oceans far from land. They are characterized by their low carbonate and low silica content and they are usually soft, plastic, and greasy to touch. The color is usually chocolate brown. The median diameters run around one micron and material of silt size is rare. The chemical composition of the clays is discussed in Chapter XVI.

There is still considerable uncertainty as to the source of the brown clay but there is a growing opinion that in the Pacific it is derived to a considerable extent from the Gobi Desert in Mongolia (Goldberg and Arrhenius, 1958) and is transported by the wind and in part by ocean currents. Other portions come from volcanic ash, much of it altered to clay minerals, palagonite, and perhaps phillipsite (Revelle *et al.*, 1955). In the South Pacific a large portion of the clay of all origins has been altered to the hydrogenous mineral phillipsite (Arrhenius, 1963) and hence is excluded from the brown clays. Meteoritic dust is probably an important contributor to brown clay (Pettersson, 1960; Laevastu and Mellis, 1955). Magnetic spherules of probable meteoritic origin have been obtained from deep-sea cores, particularly from the Swedish Deep-Sea Expedition. These show a decrease in abundance with depth in the core. From the nickel content of dust collections made on Haleakala Volcano in the island of Maui of the Hawaiian group, Pettersson concluded that about five million tons of meteoritic dust fall on the earth per year. This appears to agree with the nickel content of the deep-sea clays. Rex and Goldberg (1958) found a latitudinal relation of quartz content in pelagic clays from the eastern Pacific with a high at about 30° N. They consider that this relationship is brought about by the atmospheric introduction of the quartz, more of it coming from the desert areas which center around 30° of latitude than from other areas. They also found that quartz decreased in depth in the cores and concluded that this was explained by the major climatic changes of the late Tertiary.

Brown clay was first explained as due principally to decomposition of volcanic ejecta (Murray and Renard, 1891). This idea was abandoned because of the failure to find progressive changes below the surface in brown clay cores such as would be expected by weathering. Furthermore, the clays contain a small quantity of Foraminifera and Radiolaria even in the deeper portion of the cores. The explanation for brown clay in the deep portions of the oceans now appears to be the greater solution of biogenous materials in the waters circulating in great depth that causes the removal of the calcareous debris along with some removal of the siliceous skeletal material. This removal takes place in part during the sinking of the particles but mostly by solution on the bottom. The slow deposition and high hydrostatic pressure and high partial pressure of $CO_2$ due to oxidation of organic matter favor the solution of calcite and aragonite in very deep water. The Pacific has a larger area with brown clay partly because the more widely separated lands cause slower deposition which exposes the biogenous material to solution for a longer period, and partly because of the more active circulation of the cold carbon dioxide charged Antarctic waters. The brown color is due to the oxidizing capacity of these deep waters.

**Authigenic (Hydrogenous) Deposits.** Since the reports of the *Challenger* expedition it has been known that phillipsite was an important constituent of deep-sea deposits (Murray and Renard, 1891). Arrhenius (1963) has made rather extensive studies of the Pacific sediments and has found that phillipsite constitutes the dominant mineral in large areas to the south. This mineral must have crystallized out of the sea water as the crystals are too large to have been transported by currents to the areas where they are formed. He calls such deposits *Halmeic* but they are here referred by the more familiar name authigenic.

**Manganese Nodules.** The most amazing authigenic deposit of the sea floor consists of manganese nodules. These were first discovered by the *Challenger* expedition, and were dredged from each of the large oceans. Their great abundance was first appreciated by Agassiz (1906), but their possible economic significance was not realized until extensive deep ocean dredging was conducted during the International Geophysical Year. During this work nodules rich in cobalt were recovered. In the Pacific dredging and bottom photography under the direction of Menard of Scripps Institution (Menard and Shipek, 1958) showed that vast areas had almost a pavement of the nodules (Fig. 50). Since 1957 Mero (1960) has been working on these deposits and their economic significance. The following summary comes from his early publications and from a paper delivered at the Pacific Science Congress in Honolulu in 1961.

Mero believes that the maganese nodules constitute "the most common form of hardrock found at the surface of the lithosphere of the earth." The manganese occurs as "grains, nodules, slabs, coatings on rocks, and impregnations of porous material." Whereas most nodules are not larger than 25 cm, one was discovered with a mass of 850 kg. The nodules apparently form around any hard object on the sea floor. They have concentric layers that indicate intermittent periods of deposition. Apparently accretion is stopped when the nodule is covered with sediment, and the movement of waves of sediment over the sea floor may re-expose a covered nodule and allow further growth.

Manganese nodules are the result of the essentially saturated condition of the sea water with manganese and iron, the manganese having come largely from streams and submarine volcanic eruptions. Additional manganese and iron dumped in the ocean are, therefore, forced to precipitate. They do so by forming colloidal particles, which, while filtering down through the seawater, scavenge nickel, copper, cobalt, molybdenum, lead, zinc, and other metals from solution. Manganese and iron sols are swept along the bottom by currents and attracted to centers of accretion on the bottom where the manganese, iron, and various other elements, such as nickel, copper, cobalt, molybdenum, and zinc (that have been scavenged by the manganese) are deposited. The average rate of nodule growth is thought by Mero to be about 1 mm per 1000 years. It seems quite certain that this represents a recent increase in the rate of deposition of the manganese relative to the rate of deposition of the associated sediments since cores invariably show a greater concentration of manganese deposits at the surface of the sediments than down in the sediments. If the present processes continue unabated, Mero believes that this recent development (perhaps in the last 15,000 years) is going to result in the covering of most of the ocean floor by a crust of manganese, incorporating other marine sediments.

The feasibility of mining the manganese nodules is discussed by Mero, who considers that it is quite possible to carry on such operations on a large scale. He points out that if the entire consumption of nickel in the United States were obtained from the nodules, as would be possible, the by-products would include about 300 percent of the annual consumption of manganese, about 200 percent of that of cobalt, and many times that of titanium, vanadium, zirconium, and other rare metals.[1]

**Pelagic Oozes.** The deposits in the deep ocean with more than 30 percent of organisms will be referred to as oozes. Like the deep-sea brown clay they are soft but contain myriads of microscopic animals including Foraminifera, pteropods, and Radiolaria, and microscopic plants including diatoms and coccoliths. Almost all these oozes have a considerable percent of brown clay, in fact some of the material called ooze in the past is found to have very small percents of organisms.

Most of the planktonic organisms contributing to oozes live in the upper waters of the ocean. After death they sink slowly to the sea floor. The descent, however, is apparently of sufficient speed so that the organisms do not move far from their surface habitat before getting out of the influence of the relatively strong surface and subsurface currents.

The type of organisms that reach the bottom depends considerably on their solubility. The calcareous organisms are more soluble than the siliceous, but are also much more abundant in most surface waters. In deep water areas where the carbonate shells are dissolved

[1] Manganese nodules are considered also in Chapter XVI, pp. 444–447.

and where the siliceous organisms are abundant in the surface waters, as for example in areas of high productivity due to upwelling, a siliceous ooze may develop unless it is masked by rapid deposition of terrigenous material. The coccoliths in bottom deposits are relatively rare at present but were apparently much more common in the Tertiary. At this time the ocean may have been warmed right to the bottom and therefore calcareous oozes in general were more widely distributed than at present. Some other calcareous sediments are introduced by the wind. Norin (1958) found that calcite was the most abundant mineral introduced by the wind into the Mediterranean.

**Terrigenous Muds.**   In the deep ocean around the borders of most of the continents the sediments are silty clays that are derived from the lands. They differ from the pelagic brown clays in having considerable silt and except for the red muds they are not oxidized. They contain rather small quantities of organisms because of the relatively rapid introduction of terrigenous material.

The muds vary in color according to source areas and local conditions. Blue colors are due to the presence of organic matter and to the alteration of ferric sulfate to ferrous oxide or ferrous hydrate under moderate reducing conditions. Black muds form in poorly ventilated basins due to high content of organic compounds and the presence of sulfide of iron. These black muds commonly but not always have a strong odor of hydrogen sulfide. Red muds contain an abundance of ferric iron oxide indicative of oxidizing conditions although the oxidizing probably occurred in rivers prior to the introduction of the muds into the ocean. Green muds are said to be characterized by the presence of ferrous iron, and, like blue muds, develop under mildly reducing conditions.  In fact, blue and green muds are virtually identical aside from color. The green color is due to ferrous iron and moderate amounts of organic matter. White muds are found in some tropical areas and consist predominantly of calcium carbonate, but unlike the oozes are relatively low in organisms and consist largely of the finely divided debris from reefs.

**Turbidites.**   The sand and coarse silt layers in the deposits of the deep ocean are generally ascribed to turbidity currents. Sands can be traced seaward for at least a thousand miles. The coarse layers occur at the surface but more commonly are found below a cover of terrigenous mud (Ericson et al., 1961). Most of the sands contain a considerable amount of silt and clay. In the Atlantic, according to the Lamont group, almost half of the sand layers are graded from fine above to coarse below (Ericson et al., 1955, Fig. 1). Our detailed studies at Scripps Institution have shown that roughly graded bedding in the turbidity current sands is common both in the Atlantic and in

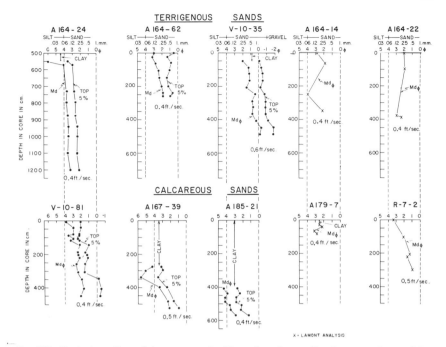

Fig. 196. Typical grading of deep-sea sands. Note that the grading is not perfect and in some cases does not exist at all. Where two curves are indicated, the left-hand one shows the median diameter of analyses along the length of a sand layer, and the right-hand one shows the median diameter of the coarsest 5 percent. Data from analyses of Lamont Geological Observatory's cores made by Scripps Institution (·) and by Lamont Geological Observatory (x).

the Pacific (Fig. 196). Many of the sands, however, show alternations between coarse and fine as if the turbidity currents alternately increase and decrease in speed or move out like the puffs of smoke from a volcano or the surges in a rip current. The sand sizes are mostly less than one-fourth of a millimeter in diameter, although locally much coarser material including gravel is found (Shepard, 1961a, 1962). Curiously the coarseness does not seem to change progressively in going out across the fans at the lower end of submarine canyons, but shows pockets of coarse mixed in with fine. The source of some of the coarse material is difficult to trace.

The constituents of the deep-sea sands include almost everything found in shallow water sands. In some areas mica and wood fragments are very common and suggest relatively weak currents. In the deposits at the foot of escarpments topped by calcareous banks the sands are also calcareous (Emery, 1960; Ericson *et al.*, 1961). Some forms appear to be screened out during the descent, notably echinoid spines that are usually much more common in shelf deposits than in the adjacent deep-sea sands. In many of the sands the Foraminifera are very scarce in contrast to both the shelf deposits and the normal deep-sea deposits of the area.

The presence of turbidite layers of sand in the deep ocean can often be detected by sound velocities of the surface sediments (Frye and Raitt, 1961). The typical deep-sea deposits show a slightly lower velocity than the deep-sea water, whereas the sand layers have a slightly higher velocity.

Turbidites of silt and clay size have been recognized (Ewing *et al.*, 1958; Emery, 1958b). They are distinguished partly by the absence of Foraminifera in silty beds lying between clays with abundant Foraminifera. The change is abrupt at the base of the turbidite bed. A large silt percent is another indication of the turbidites, and burrows are confined to the top few centimeters (Ericson *et al.*, 1961, p. 205). A color contrast is also found in many cases (Ewing *et al.*, 1958, p. 1036). In the Puerto Rico Trench the turbidite layers contain 37 percent $CaCO_3$ in contrast to 1 percent in the brown clay (Ericson *et al.*, 1961, p. 252). The same is true to a smaller degree of the turbidites in the Hudson fan area (Ericson *et al.*, 1961, p. 253).

**Glacial Marine Sediments.**   In both the Antarctic and the Arctic, deep-water sediments have been found which contain an abundance of coarse material, in which the mud is dominantly silt rather than clay. These sediments have been termed *glacial marine*, and they are considered to have been ice-rafted from glaciers. They were first described by Philippi (1912) from the Antarctic, where they extend to the margin of the ice pack, but they have been found farther north under the diatom oozes in the South Atlantic and South Indian oceans (Hough, 1956). In the North Atlantic, glacial marine deposits were found under the *Globigerina* ooze in many of the Piggot cores. Glacially transported material was also dredged by Menard (1953) from sea-mounts in the Gulf of Alaska.

**Volcanic Sediments.**   Shards of volcanic glass are quite common in samples from various deep-sea areas. In the study of the Piggot cores it was determined that there were definite horizons where these volcanic shards were concentrated and it was believed that these horizons could be traced across most of the western Atlantic along the line of cores.

In Indonesia, where there are abundant volcanoes and where a number of huge ash eruptions have taken place in historical times, the volcanic sediments form an important element in the basin deposits. Studies by Neeb (1943) show that portions of the cores in this area can be correlated with known volcanic eruptions and that volcanic ash horizons can be traced far away from the volcanoes.

Volcanic sediments are carried to the deep sea largely by the atmosphere. The well-known eruptions of Krakatoa in 1883 indicate how such deposits might become world wide, and the deposits which formed around Mt. Katmai in Alaska in 1912 indicate the appreciable thickness of ash which may accumulate hundreds of miles from the center of a volcanic explosion. Miss Neeb showed that some of the volcanic materials of Indonesia must have drifted a long distance to their place of deposition. Possibility of the drifting of fine volcanic dust for hundreds of miles can be readily understood. Porous materials like pumice can be carried for great distances on the sea surface before becoming waterlogged. The chart notation of pumice in deep deposits off Japan is not unusual.

The cores taken in the Mediterranean by the Swedish Deep-Sea Expedition (Pettersson, 1948; Norin, 1958) were found to have two ash horizons. One of them studied by Mellis (1954) seems to be very persistent and was correlated with ash from Santorin Volcano where a very large eruption took place somewhere between 1500 and 1800 B.C.

In the Pacific, Worzel (1959) found an ash layer in the deep-sea cores over a large area. This is indicated as a sub-bottom reflection in the Precision Depth Recorder records and could be traced from 11° N. to 12° S. Lat. in a zone extending a few hundred miles off Central and South America. M. Ewing *et al.* (1959a) have considered the possibility that this may be a worldwide ash fall that is better preserved in this area where Worzel discovered it.

The investigations of Menard (1960b) in the eastern Pacific have thrown new light on ash deposits that is not favorable to a worldwide ash of the same age. Menard has found through dredging and bottom photographs, partly supplied by the Soviet oceanographers, that there are many localities with angular consolidated slabs at or near the surface (Fig. 197). Dredgings show that these are coated to varying degrees with manganese crusts with thicknesses indicating ages of thousands to tens of thousands of years since their formation. The slabs consist largely of the alteration product phillipsite but also contain some unaltered volcanic minerals and volcanic glass. The slabs decrease in thickness to the west. Menard thinks that they represent the bottom-altered remnants of an ash once much more continuous and coming from various submarine volcanoes. The stirring of organisms and various physical-chemical processes are thought to have left the present discontinuous remnants. Menard does not think that these slabs are related to the Worzel ash. He has found that echo soundings west of the area in which the Worzel ash was discovered show similar layers at various depths, but that no one layer appears

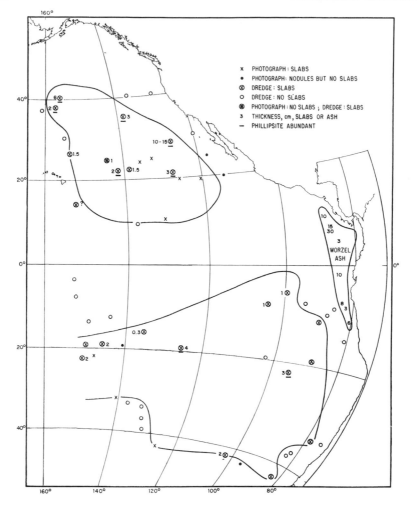

Fig. 197. Distribution of consolidated slabs found in dredgings and photography in the eastern Pacific. From Menard (1960b).

to be continuous. Ash discovered by Nayudu (1959) in cores of the Gulf of Alaska apparently is older than the Worzel ash.

**Distribution of Deep-Sea Sediments.**    The distribution of the principal types of sediments in the ocean is given in Fig. 198. There is still a vast amount of speculation involved in any map of this type. A considerable number of changes have been made from the widely reproduced map that appeared in *The Oceans* (Sverdrup *et al.*, 1942). Thus the diatom ooze extent is greatly restricted in the North Pacific and the radiolarian ooze in the high productivity zone just north of the equator in the eastern Pacific is considerably narrowed. A sharp

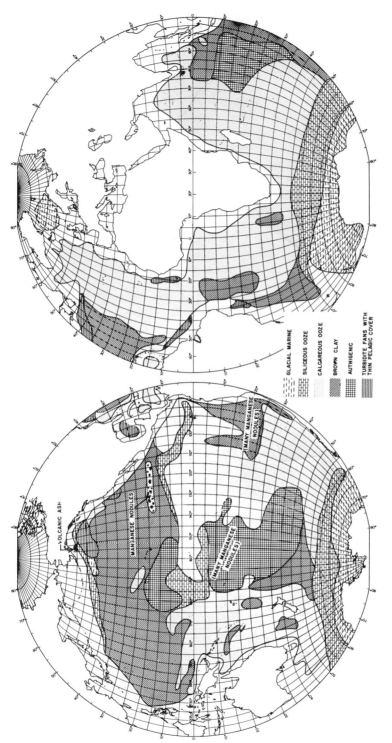

Fig. 198. Distribution of deep-sea sediments. Compiled from information by Arrhenius (1961) and Nayudu (1959) and from suggestions by D. B. Ericson, H. W. Menard, and W. R. Riedel. It is quite likely that the areas with abundant manganese nodules cover more territory than shown and that there are many more areas where turbidite layers are interbedded with normal pelagic deposits. All boundaries should be considered as subject to extensive changes as information becomes more abundant.

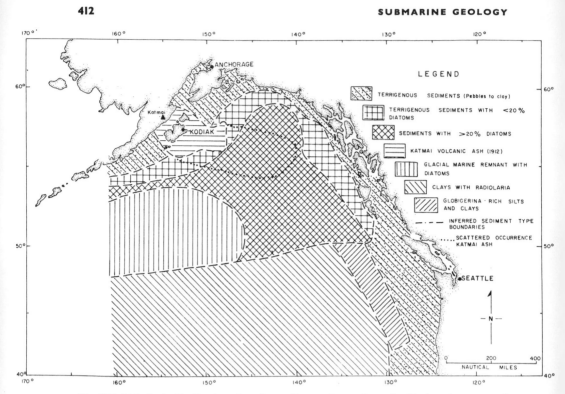

Fig. 199. Lithologic distribution of surface sediments in northeast Pacific, based on upper 5 to 10 cm of the cores taken by Nayudu (1959).

drop in the $CaCO_3$ content occurs at 5° N. Lat. and it is almost lacking in the sediments north of 9° N. Lat. (Arrhenius, 1963). Furthermore, extensive areas of terrigenous sediment are now included in both the Atlantic and the Pacific and areas of glacial marine sediment are shown bordering the Antarctic continent.

The area formerly called red clay in the South Pacific is found by Arrhenius (1963) to consist dominantly of the alteration product phillipsite making it an authigenic deposit in contrast to the more extensive brown clay area in the North Pacific which was also included in the red clay zonation.

A map of the sediments in the northeast Pacific has been supplied by Nayudu (1959). Based on 150 cores, he has shown that there are seven well-defined zones (Fig. 199) including terrigenous sediments around the margins, a large zone with Katmai volcanic ash from the 1912 eruption, glacial marine sediments with diatoms, clays with Radiolaria, *Globigerina*-rich silts, and diatom-rich sediments.

**Nondepositional Surfaces of the Deep Sea.** The results of the *Challenger* expedition (Murray and Renard, 1891) led to the suspicion

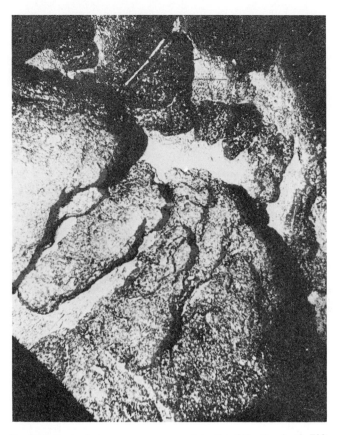

Fig. 200. Rocky bottom on a seamount in the Atlantic, depth 700 fathoms. Note debris lodged in the depressions. From Heezen et al. (1959, pl. 15).

that high areas of the ocean floor are apt to be free of sediments because only manganese nodules were found on a number of sea-mounts. Since the *Challenger* expedition almost all other expeditions have strengthened this early indication. Ericson *et al.* (1961, p. 234) report that "one out of every 10 cores in the Lamont collection contains pre-Pleistocene sediment." Volcanic rock of various types, but mostly basalt, has been dredged from the highs, and coring has generally resulted in bent core tubes or at best very short cores in contrast to the usual long cores from the flatter portions of the sea floor. Numerous photographs on seamounts have shown rock outcrops (Fig. 200). These photographs also show that ripple marks are common on seamounts (Fig. 49). As yet there are almost no measurements of the bottom currents, but the small amount of pelagic sediment and the presence of bare rock surfaces suggest that currents are relatively strong. Eocene calcareous ooze was discovered just beneath the cover of recent sediments on a Pacific seamount (Hamilton, 1953). Some of the ripples undoubtedly consist of foraminiferal sand that is transported more easily than terrigenous sand, but still is indicative of currents of the order of 16 cm/sec or more (Laughton, 1959). A change in direction of currents around an Atlantic seamount was discovered by Lamont cores (Ericson and Heezen, 1959). In the areas of little deposition winnowed sands develop. Ericson *et al.* (1961, pp. 215–217) show how these can be distinguished from turbidite sands. The winnowed sands are poorly sorted but lack very fine material, and are not graded. Also they lack the mixture of shallow and deep water organisms characteristic of turbidites. Furthermore, the lag deposits are likely to have coatings of manganese oxide.

It has been evident since the *Meteor* expedition (Wüst, 1936) that appreciable currents exist on the deep-sea floor. Photographs have shown what appear to be current scour marks (Fig. 50). The first evidence that relatively large areas may be kept free of a sediment cover over long periods was obtained from the cores of the *Albatross* expedition (Riedel, 1952, 1954, 1959). From a study of the Radiolaria in the cores of this expedition and in cores from the *Challenger* expedition and Scripps Institution Mid-Pacific expedition, Riedel found that there were assemblages at or near the surface that can be correlated with Oligocene and Miocene radiolarian assemblages in the Caribbean area. These are found over a wide area in the equatorial Pacific. Studies of the Foraminifera from the same material by Frances L. Parker and the Coccolithophoridae by Bramlette (Riedel and Bramlette, 1959) gave further support of the Mid-Tertiary age of the sediment. Thus since the cores come from the deep basins, there seems to be little doubt but that deposition has been negligible in this area for many millions of years or, alternatively, deposits of younger age have been subsequently eroded.

**Deposits of Deep Marginal Basins.** There appear to be two types of basins in which depositional conditions are quite different. These were described by Ström (1936) and Woolnough (1937), and a good summary was given by Fleming and Revelle (1939). In one type, circulation is inhibited, and there is very little ventilation or replacement of the water, thereby resulting in a stagnant basin. The best example of this type is the Black Sea which, as we have seen, is separated from the Mediterranean by a long shallow channel. In the deep waters of such a basin, oxidation will soon deplete the oxygen supply, and the decomposable organic material settling from the upper water will accumulate on the bottom and hydrogen sulfide will be dissolved into the bottom waters and the pH of the deep water will become very low. Only anaerobic bacteria will live here, and the bottom will become covered with black stinking mud. Such bedding or lamination as occurs will be preserved, since the bottom churning organisms that disturb the stratification in most other areas cannot live in the stagnant basins. Organic carbon will be unusually high.

The Black Sea sediments have been extensively studied by Soviet geologists (Archanguelski, 1927; Strakhov, 1947). These studies were summarized by Smirnow (1958), and Caspers (1957). The Black Sea water is said to contain oxygen only to a depth of about 160 m in most places. This prevents benthic organisms from inhabiting the bottom except when there are occasional penetrations of oxygenated waters. Several types of desulfurizing and denitrifying bacteria are found on the bottom. The high organic contents of the sediments are partly due to the usual absence of oxygen and oxydizing bacteria but are related also to the organic productivity of the surface waters which is quite variable in time and place. There seems to be some difference of opinion as to the extent of black-colored sediments in recent deposits. Some of the muds are highly calcareous with white calcareous layers alternating with dark clayey sapropelitic layers (Caspers, 1957).

In the deep Norwegian fiords, another type of stagnant basin, an occasional overturn takes place by relatively heavy saline water coming in over the sill and sinking below the brackish water inside. This causes a mixing of the sulfureted bottom water with the oxygenated surface waters and results in a catastrophic killing of the surface fauna. The result is the formation of a layer high in organic matter. Future exposure of such layers will reveal a wealth of fossil material.

Where the sill to a basin is wide, rather than narrow and tortuous, there is likely to be considerable renewal of the water in the basin, and the foul condition will not develop. The basins off the California coast are sufficiently ventilated by the currents so that very little hydrogen sulfide is found in the sediments obtained from these places. Therefore, it is significant that layering is not well developed in most of these basins. An exception is found in Santa Barbara Basin (Emery, 1960; Hülsemann and Emery, 1961) where many of the cores are well laminated and where the oxygen content of the bottom waters is very low. Considerable organic material accumulates in most of the California basins, as is shown by their high nitrogen content (Revelle and Shepard, 1939; Emery, 1960). The same conditions were found in the basins of Indonesia (Kuenen, 1942) as to both nitrogen and scarcity of stratification. On the other hand, some of the basin deposits in the Gulf of California show stratification, with alternating deposits of diatomaceous ooze and clay.

### Deep-Sea Stratigraphy

In the near future cores from the Mohole borings of the deep oceans may revolutionize geological knowledge of submarine stratigraphy. They may even provide information from periods of time for which nothing is now known. Meantime, we have to be content with the information coming from cores of the order of 10 m in length.[2] These have yielded considerable information concerning the Holocene and Pleistocene, and in some cases have extended down into Tertiary deposits.

The first indication that the sediments of the ocean floor had an interesting stratigraphic record came from the study of the short cores of the German South Polar Expedition of 1901–1903 (Philippi, 1912). These cores showed the glacial marine sediments that surround Antarctica as existing beneath a cover of diatom ooze which indicated that the glacial marine sediments were more continuous during an earlier period. Schott (1939) in studying the *Meteor* cores found a change in the faunas of the *Globigerina* ooze at a depth of 48 cm that was also indicative of a colder climate in the earlier deposits. In the South Atlantic Braun (1913) had previously reported "red clay" beneath *Globigerina* ooze and considered this as an indication of the change from the last glacial stage. The Piggot cores taken in a line across the North Atlantic led to more complete interpretations since their 8- to 10-ft lengths showed a series of alternations both of Foraminifera assemblages and of stratigraphy (Bramlette and Bradley, 1942). The four layers with glacial marine pebbles in these cores have been interpreted either as representing the four glacial stages or the subdivisions of the Wisconsin-Würm. Since the top foot represents the Holocene (Recent) or perhaps only the last five to seven thousand years at the end of the Holocene, the total of 10 ft would seem more likely to represent the Holocene and the Wisconsin-Würm because the latest information tends to extend this last stage back to as much as 70,000 to 115,000 years before the present (Flint and Brandtner, 1961; Ericson *et al.*, 1961; and Émiliani, 1955).

Perhaps the most satisfactory records of the Pleistocene have come from the Lamont cores (Ericson *et al.*, 1961). In addition to the change in Foraminifera in the east Atlantic the warm stages are identified by a brown color of the sediment in contrast to a gray color for the cool climate stages (Ericson *et al.*, 1961, p. 245). These may be explained by a desiccation of the north African climate resulting in brown sediments whereas pluvial climates cause the gray due to a carbonaceous

---

[2] The experimental Mohole drilling near Guadalupe Island off western Baja California is an exception (see p. 47).

pigment (Ericson *et al.*, 1961, p. 246). A considerable number of these cores have been tested for cold and warm stages by examination of the planktonic Foraminifera by Ericson and by $O_{16}$—$O_{18}$ counts by Emiliani (1955). According to Ericson the results as shown in Fig. 201 indicate the following sequence; the Holocene, the last glacial with a small warm period break near the bottom, the last interglacial, and an earlier glacial stage. The end of the last glacial occurred somewhere between 11,000 and 17,000 years before the present according to carbon-14 determinations on several cores taken in association with the temperature scales. As indicated previously, the evidence from sea level rise suggests about 18,000 years for the beginning of the Holocene and thus is in fair agreement. By interpolating the carbon-14 dates back into the older material Ericson concluded that the warm stage during a portion of the Wisconsin-Würm glacial ended about 60,000 years ago. In contrast, most other students of continental evidences of glaciation consider 30,000 to 70,000 as a maximum age for the last major glaciation (Flint, 1957; Flint and Brandtner, 1961; Frye and Willman, 1961). The end of the last interglacial according to Ericson was somewhat more than 100,000 years ago.

The work of Emiliani (1955) using $O_{16}$—$O_{18}$ interpretations for temperatures of the planktonic Foraminifera along the length of the same Lamont cores and Rosholt *et al.* (1961) supplementing the carbon-14 by $Pa^{231}/Th^{230}$ age determinations has produced somewhat different interpretations from those of Ericson. They are indicated in Fig. 201 allowing a comparison of the two time scales. Rosholt and others put the entire Wisconsin-Würm in the time allotted to the last glaciation stages 2–3 by Ericson and others. The Illinoisan-Riss is placed in the same position as Ericson's stage 1 of the Wisconsin-Würm. These most recent interpretations of the cores appear to be more in line with the latest evidence from land glaciation (Flint and Brandtner, 1961; Frye and William, 1961). It seems quite certain that the study of Foraminifera by Ericson failed to reveal a warming of the climate in the vicinity of 25,000 years B.P. that is now shown by various lines of evidence (Curray, 1961). More well-studied long cores would help resolve this difference of interpretation. Meantime some doubt is cast on the $O_{16}$—$O_{18}$ ratios because of evidence presented by Ericson *et al.* (1961, p. 227) that the Foraminifera may pass part of their life cycle below the photic zone where they may secrete an important part of their tests in a zone of lower temperatures than exist at the surface. Also doubt is cast on some $Pa^{231}/Th^{230}$ datings because of contamination by reworked clay due to deep ocean currents (Rosholt *et al.*, 1961).

In general the cores in the Pacific do not show the same alternations

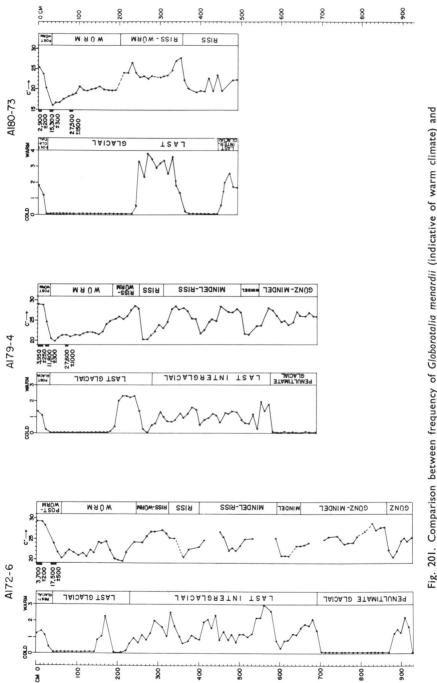

Fig. 201. Comparison between frequency of *Globorotalia menardii* (indicative of warm climate) and paleotemperature curves. Carbon-14 dates in years B.P. are included. From Ericson and Wollin (1956). See also Fig. 215.

# SEDIMENTATION IN THE EQUATORIAL CURRENT SYSTEM

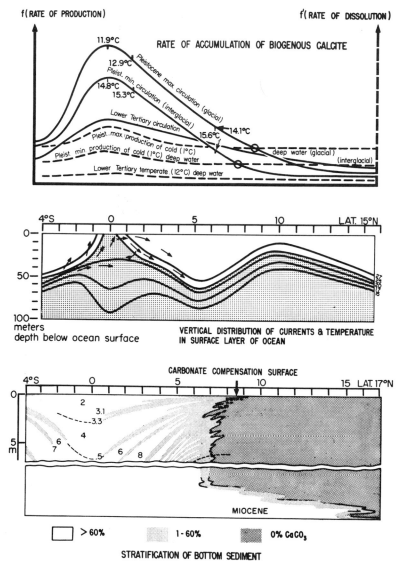

Fig. 202. Meridional profile at approximately Long. 130° W., showing the distribution of temperature and vertical motion in the surface layer of the ocean (middle graph), the stratification of the bottom sediment (lower graph), and the interpretation of the sedimentary record in terms of paleotemperature and rates of production and dissolution of calcium carbonate from planktonic organisms (upper graph). From Arrhenius (1961).

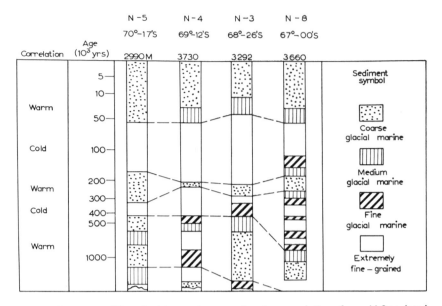

Fig. 203. Lithology of Ross Sea, Antarctic cores, showing correlation of core N-8 to dated cores N-3 to N-5. From Thomas (1959).

indicative of warm and cool periods. In many places the clay cores are continuous without any apparent change through what must represent a time equal to the entire Pleistocene. In the Gulf of Alaska, however, the last ice stage is indicated by the presence of glacial marine sediments at a depth of 50 cm or more in the cores. In the latitudes of the eastern Pacific between about 5° N. and 4° S. Arrhenius (1952), working with the *Albatross* cores, found an alternation of layers with high and low carbonate content of biogenous origin (Fig. 202). The top layer was low in carbonate with a high carbonate layer beneath. Hence Arrhenius concluded that the interglacial stages in this equatorial Pacific were times of low carbonate deposition and the glacial stages times of high carbonate. This he explained as due to more active circulation due to increased trade wind intensity in the glacial stages producing more nutrients in the surface waters and hence higher productivity and therefore more carbonate in the sediments. Using this interpretation Arrhenius found nine major carbonate maxima in the Pleistocene overlying Pliocene sediments at the bottom of some of the cores. The interpretation is somewhat puzzling since the carbonate content in the Atlantic changes inversely, being higher during interglacial stages and lower during glacial. The possibility exists that Arrhenius' cores had lost a thin top layer which is not unusual in piston core operations. In the Pliocene sediments oxygen isotope measurements indicate that bottom temperatures were about 10° C in contrast to 1° to 2° C in the Pleistocene (Emiliani, 1954, 1956). This caused a much greater northward extension of the carbonate sediments than during the Quaternary. The extent of the carbonate zones in the stratigraphic record of the Pacific should tell the extent of polar wandering in past ages as Arrhenius (1963) has indicated.

The sequence in the Ross Sea near Antarctica has been determined by Hough (1950) and Thomas (1959). Using ice-rafted sediment as an indication of the cold epochs they found a sequence illustrated in Fig. 203. Organic deposits high in Radiolaria in the glacial stages alternate with the clays free of organisms. The sequence shows three relatively warm stages with cold intervening periods. The cores also show that the past 6000 years was a period of climatic amelioration, providing evidence that the Holocene was a worldwide period of warmer climate rather than having the warming confined to the northern hemisphere as has been suggested.

Cores in the Arctic studied by Ericson and Wollin (1959), Hunkins (1959), and Laktionov (1955) have shown that there are distinct changes in content of Foraminifera with depth in core. The upper layer contains relatively abundant Foraminifera, largely *Globigerina pachyderma*, and a lower layer has few if any Foraminifera. This is interpreted by Ericson and Wollin as indicating that sediments of the last glacial stage underlie the Holocene. If this is the case, a further argument against the glacial stage ice-free Arctic proposed by Ewing and Donn (1956, 1958) is introduced (see also p. 270). The presence of a continuous ice pack would have prevented the entering of oxygen into the Arctic Ocean and hence would have restricted the productivity of Foraminifera, whereas an ice-free Arctic should have had greater productivity.

The Quaternary sediments in parts of the equatorial Pacific have been found to have thicknesses of as much as 10 m (Bramlette and Riedel, 1959). In the middle latitudes on either side, the thickness of the Quaternary is more difficult to establish because of the clay sediments but it appears to be much thinner, and the Radiolaria have shown that Tertiary is often present at or near the surface.

The cores in the northeast Pacific were studied by Nayudu (1959). No changes are found in these cores to represent the change from glacial to postglacial time. In one core the diatomaceous-rich sediments continue down to a layer dated as 25,800 B.P. and below these is a Foraminifera-rich sediment. Another shows *Globigerina*-rich silts and clays extending without change well below a layer dated as 19,300 ± 950 B.P.

# CHAPTER XV

# SUBOCEANIC LAYERS AND ORIGIN
# OF THE BASINS

## Layers Under the Deep Ocean

The use of explosives has produced a considerable amount of information concerning the nature of the material below the ocean floor. Both reflection and refraction shooting (p. 28) have been used, the latter producing the best results. With this information a fairly good idea of the thickness of ocean floor sediments has been obtained. In addition two other layers have been definitely recognized in the earth's crust above the uniform interior (outside the core) known as the mantle.

**Sediment Thickness.** Under the ocean the top layers of the earth's crust have an average seismic velocity of about 1.5 to 2 km/sec (Fig. 204). Velocities of this order are assigned by all geophysicists to unconsolidated sediment. Kuenen (1946) made extensive estimates of the average thickness of ocean floor sediments. These were based (1) on the rates of sedimentation during the Holocene which run on the average at about 1 cm/1000 years,[1] (2) on the quantity and composition of continental sediments which indicate amounts lost to the ocean, (3) on the sodium content of sea water, (4) on the loss of $TiO_2$ and $P_2O_5$ between sources and sediments, (5) on estimates of the amount of material that has been removed from the continents, and the total of volcanic products. Kuenen figured that the age of the ocean was about two billion years. He corrected for compaction and figured that present rates were faster than most of the past rates when continents were smaller. Rather good agreement was reached from estimates made by the various methods so that it seemed rather probable that the measurement of sediment thickness would yield figures that were close to Kuenen's estimates. Actually this has not proved to be true. Kuenen estimated there would be about 3 km of sediment on the average. The figures from the first layers of the Pacific

[1] The Atlantic cores taken by Lamont have an average thickness of 8.8 cm/1000 years (Ericson *et al.*, 1961, p. 274) but the rate in the Pacific must be much slower.

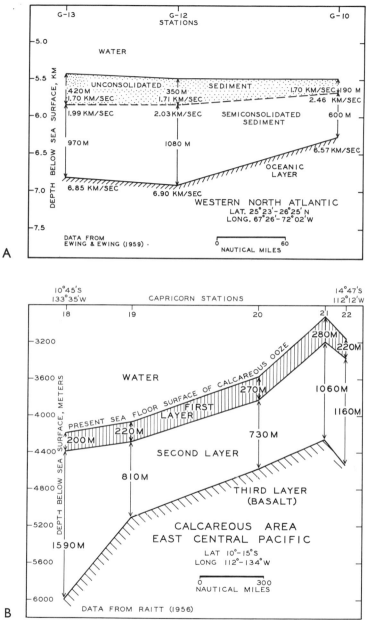

Fig. 204. (a) Seismic refraction section across the south end of the Hatteras Abyssal Plain in the Western North Atlantic. From Hamilton (1960); data from Ewing and Ewing (1959). (b) Seismic refraction section across part of the calcareous area of the East-Central Pacific. From Hamilton (1959); data from Raitt (1956).

average about 300 m and 600 m from the Atlantic (Hill, 1957; Raitt and Shor, 1959). Less well documented are thicknesses of about 600 m for the Indian Ocean and 100 to 300 m for the Arctic (Crary and Goldstein, 1957). According to Kuenen's estimates this sediment should have accumulated in about 400 million years, or since the late Cambrian according to uranium time scales.

The preceding computations might indicate that the ocean did not extend well back toward the beginning of geological time, generally supposed to be about three billion years (Bullard and Stanley, 1949); that early sedimentation rates were unusually low; or that sediments earlier than Mesozoic had disappeared (Revelle, 1955). A very reasonable alternative has been suggested by Hamilton (1959, 1960). He considers that layer two with velocities of 3.5 to 6.0 km/sec consists largely of consolidated sediment.[2] The gravitational consolidation of both clay and calcareous ooze can be shown by soil mechanics techniques to take place at a depth of from about 150 to 700 m. This consolidated product would produce the velocities of the second layer. If this reasonable suggestion is correct, the thickness of layer two should be included in the calculation of total sediment thickness. The combination of the two layers gives a total of about 1.3 km (Hess, 1960).

Hamilton (1960), employing soil mechanics concepts, has computed the original amounts of sediments necessary in several localities to consolidate to the present thicknesses. Assuming that the second layer is consolidated equivalent of the first layer, he finds that it would require about 2.8 km of sediments to form the present section (Fig. 204a) in the western Atlantic at Lamont Stations G-10, 12, and 13 (J. Ewing and M. Ewing, 1959a); at Lamont Station A-157-29 in the western Atlantic it would take about 3.7 km of original sediments to form the present section; other sections are computed for the Pacific and Indian oceans. Hamilton concluded that these amounts of original sediments required are in line with Kuenen's estimates, and this brings the requirements of the geochemical balance, the concepts of soil mechanics, and the recent findings of seismic exploration in line, and hence there may be *no* anomalous shortage of sediments.

An important consideration relative to the thickness of oceanic sediments has been stressed by Menard (1961). He has shown what a large volume of sediment exists in the abyssal plains off a few rather restricted areas. These, he believes, are largely the result of turbidity currents, which in turn can supply the ocean basins with large quantities of sediment only where no intervening geosynclinal troughs

---

[2] The experimental Mohole drilling off Guadalupe Island proved that in this area layer two is volcanic (AMSOC, 1961).

prevent the spreading of the sediment to the deep ocean. Apparently the present conditions with expanded continental boundaries are more favorable for the growth of abyssal plains than were conditions during most of the past when there appear to have been numerous marginal troughs.

Hamilton (1960) also applied soil mechanics techniques and laboratory tests to estimate the compaction of both *Globigerina* ooze and deep-sea clay and compared values of thickness found in various areas with rates of sedimentation for the same area, correcting by dividing by three for slower rates in pre-Pleistocene time, and for the probability that *Globigerina* ooze deposition does not extend back further than the late Cretaceous (about 100 million years ago). Therefore, the earlier deposits would probably be clay. Hamilton's results suggest that the sediments of the deep oceans have been accumulating for very long periods of time. For example, in an Indian Ocean locality he figured the basin was from 335 to 670 million years old, for the eastern Atlantic from 412 to 824 million, for the eastern equatorial Pacific from 536 to 1190 million, and for the western Atlantic from 556 to 2780 million years. As Hamilton admits, there are too many unknowns to allow more than the roughest estimates. Here again we are faced with some evidence suggesting that the oceans may not extend nearly back to the beginning of geological time.

**Thickness of Sediments Along Oceanic Margins.** There is some evidence to show that the deep ocean sediments are thicker near the continental slopes than out in the central basin areas. The Lamont scientists have found the existence of very thick sediment fills in troughs along the east coast of the United States (Fig. 205). The thickest reported to date is about 6000 m, almost as large as in some ancient geosynclines. Off southern California on the other hand only about 2700 m of sediment were reported from the base of the slope (Shor and Raitt, 1958). This smaller thickening can be interpreted as the result of the greater part of the sediments from southern California being deposited in the basins of the continental borderland.

**Deeper Layers and the Mohorovičić Discontinuity.** The third layer under the ocean has a velocity ranging from 6.4 to 6.8 km/sec. This has usually been considered as basalt. Hess (1960) calls attention to the fact that the layer could contain other types of rock such as serpentinized periodotite which was dredged from the fault scarps of the Mid-Atlantic Ridge (Shand, 1949). Layer three is remarkable for its uniform thickness with 81 percent ranging between 4 and 5.5 km. This uniformity has led Hess to consider that the layer represents "the position of an isotherm or past isotherm." If it were due to lava flows, it would be much thicker near the source vents than elsewhere. This

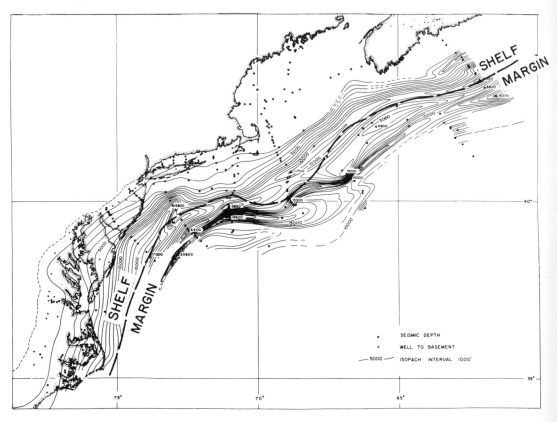

Fig. 205. The thickness in feet of the unconsolidated and semiconsolidated sediment off the east coast. The rise in the basement rock at the edge of the continental shelf is indicated and a basin is shown underlying the continental slope and adjacent deep ocean floor. From Drake *et al.* (1959). See also Fig. 139.

layer is found under the continents as well as under the ocean basins.

The base of layer three represents the Mohorovičić discontinuity, commonly referred to as the Moho. Here the sound velocity increases to slightly more than 8 km/sec. The depth to the Moho is somewhat better known under the oceans than under the continents because the crust is so thick under the continents that the Moho is difficult to pick up. On the average the Moho occurs at a depth of 6.5 km below the ocean floor (Raitt, 1956), whereas it averages 35 km under the continents. Along the margins between the oceans and the continents the Moho has intermediate depths (Fig. 206) and under marginal trenches where the Moho is deeper than under the adjacent ocean floor (see p. 380).

Under most of the mediterranean types of sea the Moho occurs at

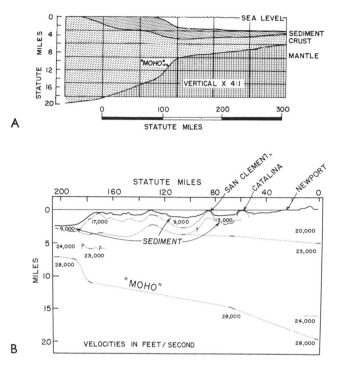

Fig. 206. (a) Generalized diagram showing the relation of the overlying sediment (layers 1 and 2), the crust (layer 3), and the Moho to the continental shelf, continental slope, and deep ocean basin off the east coast. From Worzel and Shurbet (1955). (b) Cross section of the sea floor off Newport, southern California, showing the thickness of the sediment under the basins and the travel velocities in feet per second in the underlying rocks. Note the progressive increase in the depth to the Moho in approaching the continent. From Shor and Raitt (1958).

depths somewhat comparable to the deep oceans. Under the Gulf of Mexico the Lamont investigation found the Moho is appreciably deeper than the average for the main ocean basins (J. Ewing *et al.*, 1960a). The same group investigating the Caribbean found that the Moho was near oceanic in depth under parts of the Columbia and Yucatan basins and true oceanic under the Cayman Trough in contrast to the nearby Puerto Rico Trench where the Moho is much deeper. The ridges that cross the Caribbean have a Moho that was too deep to detect. In fact, wherever the mediterranean seas are relatively shallow the Moho is relatively deep. Under the Black Sea, for example, where water depths are about half those of the major oceans, the Moho was found by the Soviet scientists to lie between 22 and 30 km (Goncharov and Neprochov, 1960). Above the Moho in the Black Sea the Soviets found the usual 6.4-km/sec layer and then a sediment layer 8 to 15 km in thickness, the latter having an average velocity of 3 km/sec. The Norwegian Sea, another relatively shallow portion of the ocean, also has a greater thickness overlying the Moho although the exact depth of the Moho has not yet been determined (J. Ewing and M. Ewing, 1959a). It is noteworthy that the California continental borderland has thicknesses to the Moho that are comparable to other intermediate depth areas (Fig. 206b).

Despite the inverse relation of depth to Moho and elevation shown by the preceding evidence, the Moho under the ocean varies directly with some topographic features. The most notable case is the down bend of the Moho beneath trenches, a fact that is now well established. Also several narrow ridges of the ocean floor show a rise of the Moho underneath. However, thick crust was found under the well-defined Nasca Ridge (Fisher and Norris, 1960). Also the broad Mid-Atlantic Ridge and the East Pacific Rise appear to have a greater Moho depth beneath them than under the adjacent deep ocean floor. In both cases there is a zone with velocities of somewhat over 7 km/sec at depths comparable to that at which the Moho occurs under the deep oceans (Raitt and Shor, 1959; J. Ewing and M. Ewing, 1959a). The velocities of 8 km/sec are not reached in any of the records. Under the Hawaiian Ridge the Moho is also depressed, and there is a thickening of the third layer (Shor, 1960). The same thing occurs under the Aleutian Islands, and in both cases a thick layer of probable volcanics is found (Raitt and Shor, 1959).

### Origin and History of the Ocean Basins

Ideas of the diastrophic history of the earth are changing so fast as this is written that it might be the part of prudence to omit mention entirely of the origin and history of the ocean basins. The best that can be done is to call attention to some of the current ideas and show how radically different they are from those discussed in the first edition of this book. Here also we can attempt to give some of the significant facts which appear to be emerging from the many fruitful new studies of the oceans.

**Comparison of Deformational Forces of Continents and Oceans.** Some authors have differentiated between tectonism of the oceanic areas and tectonism of the continents. Wegener (1924), for example, considered that the ocean basin was underlain by simatic rocks that were much weaker than the sialic rock underlying the continents so that the continental masses could drift over the ocean basins. Bucher (1952) pointed out, however, that the ocean floor has somewhat the same sort of deformed zones as are found on the continents. Thus, there are great arcuate ridges and bordering trenches in the oceans very much like those of the continents except that the continental trenches have far thicker masses of sediments because of deposits in land trenches, like the Ganges-Indus Trough, that come from the erosion of the adjacent ranges. Profiles across the land masses look very much like those across the oceans (Fig. 207). A difference may be the apparent lack of folded ranges under the ocean although there is no proof that folding is missing and the islands of the Mid-Atlantic Ridge have some evidence of compressional forces. In any case the trenches of the ocean floor must have considerable strength or they could not maintain their depths against the large deficiencies in mass which are indicated by their large negative gravity anomalies.

**Nature of Forces of Deformation of Ocean Floor.** Only a small amount of evidence is now available concerning the nature of the forces that deform the ocean floor. The existence of suboceanic strike-slip faults is now apparently well established (p. 383 and Fig. 184). If we are correct in believing that displacements of the order of 600 miles have occurred off the California coast, a major factor in the deformation of the sea floor is available. The most puzzling feature of these large shifts is that they appear to give out in a short distance horizontally. As Menard (1960c) has pointed out, the left lateral movement along the Mendocino Escarpment, when traced to the east, changes to a right lateral movement along the Gorda Escarpment; whereas the right lateral movement along the Murray fracture zone also reverses to the east and becomes a left lateral fault in the Santa Barbara Islands. This raises an interesting problem for the tectonic experts. Tremendous vertical movements appear to be indicated at the junctures with the oceanic crust, and the faults may continue deep under the continents as suggested by Dietz (1961).

Evidence for compressional forces on the deep-sea floor is based on very speculative material. Since the trenches are underlain by down-folded Moho, support is given to Vening Meinesz (1955) in his contention that lateral compression has downfolded the crust and is exerting continued pressure to hold the crust down against the force of gravity. Evidence for compressive forces comes also from the sheared anorthosites found in the islands of the Mid-Atlantic Ridge. Compression is also indicated by folds in some of the island arcs of the western Pacific. Reflection profiles on the north side of the Puerto Rico Trench also show probable folding (Ewing, J., and M. Ewing, 1962).

Evidence for tensional forces is also scanty. The great outpourings of lava forming the numerous volcanic islands and lava flows of the ocean floor suggest tensional forces as forming the openings for the

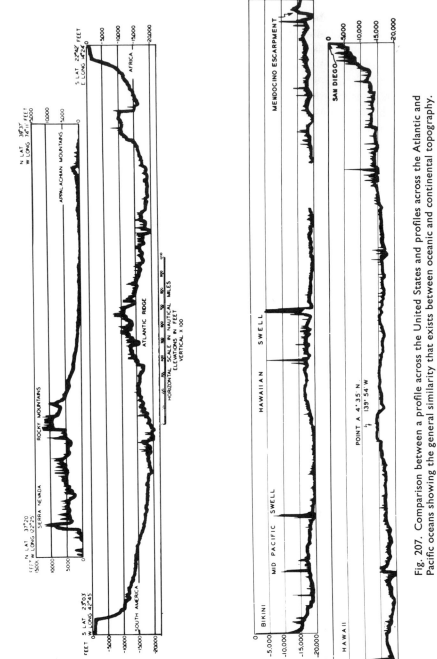

Fig. 207. Comparison between a profile across the United States and profiles across the Atlantic and Pacific oceans showing the general similarity that exists between oceanic and continental topography. Vertical exaggeration times 100 for all profiles.

lava escape. The great valley of the Mid-Atlantic Ridge, if comparable to the rift valleys of Africa as maintained by Heezen (1960), may indicate tension. Similarly the numerous fault scarps and block fault patterns found in all the oceans may suggest tension provided the faults are of the normal type, as is usually the case in similar topographic features on land.

Concerning causes for these forces acting on the crust of the ocean floor we must also resort to poorly confirmed speculation. Perhaps the most accepted hypothesis at present is that of convection currents. These currents according to Hess (1960) exert a drag on the bottom of the crust. This may produce compression in some localities, tension elsewhere, and even strike-slip faulting. The possibility that there is a rising convection current operating under the East Pacific Rise has been suggested by Bullard et al. (1956) as a result of their discoveries of excessively high heat flow along this ridge. More recently the same order of heat flow has been found under the Mid-Atlantic Ridge. This suggests upward convection here also although the heat is thought to be due to vulcanism (Hill, 1960; Simmons, 1961). Heezen (1960) has called upon this convection as an explanation of the rift valley of the Mid-Atlantic Ridge. He considers that the crust is flowing outward from the area of convectional rise and hence the rift in the center of the ridge. As indicated previously, however, H. W. Menard failed to find a similar rift valley in his extensive studies of the East Pacific Rise.

A good summary of the evidence for and against convection currents is given in the book by Jacobs et al. (1959, pp. 349–353).[3] Their feeling of skepticism concerning the hypothesis and their statement that "there is no direct evidence at all for any convection currents . . ." seem to the writer to be a healthy attitude toward this hypothesis.

**Permanency of Ocean Basins and Continents.** In recent years very little has been learned that would help decide the long existing controversy over the permanency of oceans and continents. However, a few discoveries have been made that may help slightly in deciding the issue. In the first place the cores and photographs of the deep ocean floor have shown that it is not very easy to distinguish deep from shallow water deposits along continental or insular margins. Turbidity currents and submarine slumping transport so much relatively coarse material to the deep ocean floor along with the remains of shallow-water organisms that it is easy to confuse the deposits. On the other hand, the deep ocean floor where separated from the continental margins by ridges has deposits that are very distinctive.

[3] They were not aware that one of their arguments against convection, namely, that the crust does not bend down beneath trenches, has been disproved.

If such an area were elevated into a continent, it should be relatively easy to recognize it from a study of the formations. However, no such deposits are known to exist on the continents. The supposed deep-sea formations of Barbados Island, as indicated previously, are now considered as having formed in intermediate depths. Similarly the supposed deep-sea red clays of Timor and other parts of Indonesia have never been ascertained to represent deep ocean deposits. In fact, the only evidence that now exists of change from deep water to land is found in some of the mountain ranges of the world, such as the Alps, and in parts of southern California where troughs or basins of inter-mediate depth appear to have existed during the depositional stages.

Perhaps the most convincing argument in favor of permanence of continents is that the layering under the continents is so different from that under the oceans. As Gaskell (1960, p. 213) has written recently, "the structure that has been found by seismic measurements for the oceans is not that to be expected from a sunken continent."

**Land Bridges.** The question of possible land bridges across the oceans has intrigued geologists for several generations. It was believed for a long time that the Mid-Atlantic Ridge was above water in the past, possibly accounting for the Greek fable of "The Lost Land of Atlantis." Dredging of the ridge, however, has not yet yielded clear evidence of any former land mass. One possible piece of evidence has been referred to by Kolbe (1955), who reported fresh water diatoms from the east flank of the equatorial portion of the ridge. He contended that this must indicate a former land mass, denying that the diatoms could have been introduced by turbidity currents since they occur on the flank of the ridge well above the basin floor. The discovery of large numbers of wind-transported diatoms in eolian dust (Radczewski, 1937a, b) has provided another possible explanation, as suggested by Arrhenius (1963). Possible trans-Atlantic bridges were referred to by Willis (1932) as "Isthmian Links." The faunal evidence of a connection between South Africa and South America might be explicable by a former elevation of the Walvis Rise extending from the Mid-Atlantic Ridge to Africa, and a formerly elevated, relatively shoal area extending in to the coral reefs off the Brazilian coast at Lat. 21° S. For such a connection we have as yet no substantial evidence and the degree of similarity of the faunas on the two sides is a moot question so far as paleontologists are concerned.

The floras and molluscan faunas of the Pacific islands have often been referred to as evidence for former land bridges (see, for example, Pilsbry, 1916). A reasonable interpretation of the evidence has been suggested by Ladd (1960). He has called attention to the growing evidence that the guyots and atolls represent relatively high islands of the early Tertiary and Cretaceous. There are so many of these features and they are spaced closely enough that they may have constituted stepping stones allowing the rather easy spreading of the faunas and floras, particularly with the help of typhoons, which are known to spread insects, plants, and mollusc shells over wide stretches of sea.

**Continental Drift.** Drifting continents were in general disrepute among geologists until recent years when the whole question was reopened partly because of the growing evidence of a gradual shift of the magnetic poles (Irving, 1958). Since the paleomagnetic studies show evidence that indicates the northward drift of the eastern hemisphere at a rate that would place Africa, India, and Australia in a south polar position for the Permo-Carboniferous (the time at which they were glaciated according to most authorities) and would also place these land masses in approximately the right place so that the great salt deposits of the early Mesozoic could have formed in the 30° latitudes where present deserts are found, the hypothesis can be seen to have much appeal. Furthermore, the rate of movement along the San Andreas fault, if as large as indicated by Hill and Dibblee (1953), and many other geologists, would seem to have been of somewhat the same order of magnitude as that required by the magnetism studies. The shift of scores or even hundreds of miles along the San Andreas and of a possible 300 miles along the Alpine fault of New Zealand (Wellman, 1954) certainly suggests something in the nature of continental drift. The evidence for polar shifts has been summarized by Day and Runcorn (1955) and Collinson and Runcorn (1960) and is discussed critically by Munk and Macdonald (1960, pp. 253–262).

The importance of the matching borders of the Atlantic and the parallelism of the Mid-Atlantic Ridge to the margins have been used for generations as one of the most important arguments favoring continental drift. This has been re-emphasized by Carey (1958) after careful comparison of the 2000-meter isobase on the two sides of the Atlantic. This depth curve, halfway down the continental slope, provides a much better fit than the land margins or the edge of the continental shelf. Carey explains the development of various basins oceanic and intracontinental by dilatation (stretching along cracks in the sial), or by the opening of wedges (sphenocochasm).

Against continental drift there are an equally impressive array of facts. The forces necessary for such movements seem to be beyond all reason. We have no good example of a recently exposed ocean floor. If we think of a continent as a great ship moving over the ocean basin, there should be freshly exposed ocean floor along the stern of the moving ship. Nothing of the sort has been discovered. This would be indicated by an absence of appreciable deep-sea sediments. For example, if North America is drifting westward, as often maintained, there should be an absence of deep-sea deposits off the east coast whereas the sediments are very thick there. The studies of paleo-climatic zones made by Chaney (1940) and more recently by Durham (1959) and Dorf (1960) give substantial evidence indicating that the climatic zones have moved only in such a way as would be expected by general warming or cooling of the earth's atmosphere. Similarly the faunal evidence favoring continental connections on the two sides of the Atlantic appears to be weak and misleading as has been recognized by numerous paleontologists. Therefore, all one can say now is that we should wait for more evidence before accepting any hypotheses of large-scale continental drift.

**Origin of the Ocean Basins.** The explanation for the great difference in elevation of the oceanic and continental tracts has been advanced little beyond the point that we know definitely that the crust is thin under the oceans and thick under the continents. It continues to be difficult to explain how a portion of the earth's surface should be covered with a thick crust which is absent on the rest. One explanation, now given some support, is that the earth is expanding (Halm, 1935; Egyed, 1956; Carey, 1958). If it has expanded to several times its former volume, it is conceivable that the crust once fitted the smaller earth and now covers only a little more than one-quarter of the earth. The gradual but fluctuating contraction of the seas that covered a large part of the continents during much of the Paleozoic, less during the Mesozoic, and still less during the Tertiary as shown by the paleogeographic maps of Termier and Termier (1952) and Strakhov (1948) impressed Egyed (1956) as evidence that the ocean rifts were widening during geological time and taking away more and more water from the continents. Most of the authors who follow this idea of an expanding earth have considered the cause as the radioactive heating of the interior of the earth following the early proposal by John Joly. The chief difficulty with the idea of an expanding earth is that it fails to explain the concentration of folded and, hence, compressed ranges around the Pacific where tensional forces should prevail although Carey (1958) has offered some possible interpretations of this anomaly.

The explanation offered first by George Darwin (1881) that the moon had been torn from the Pacific Ocean still has some appeal. The Atlantic Ocean could have been formed as the result of this catastrophic event because of the pulling apart of what was at first one large continent. It is difficult to see how Antarctica fits into this hypothesis. In contrast with George Darwin, Dietz (1959) has suggested that the original fragmentation of the crust may have happened through the impact of large asteroids dispersing the crust. The round shape of the Pacific and Arctic basins, which compare with the mare of the moon, is suggestive of such an origin.[4] If this hypothesis can be substantiated the Atlantic and some other parallel basins may be explained by continental drift in the formative stages following the asteroid impacts.

Another concept of ocean basin evolution has been suggested by Dietz (1961) called the Sea Floor Spreading Hypothesis. He considers that following the original fragmentation of the crust, thermal convection cells within the mantle have invaded the oceanic lithosphere so that the upper limbs of convection cells are fully exposed on the ocean floor. The median oceanic rises mark the ascending divergences while the convergences occur mostly under the continents, although the trenches mark the initiation of convergences. Unlike the ocean floor, the continents, being buoyant, are only partially coupled with convection forces as the mantle shears under them. Normally lying over a convergence, the continents are placed under compression and incline to buckle. Mantle forces determine the convective pattern, and the continents play a passive role. Initially, if a convective divergence happens beneath a continent, it is drifted along with the sima until it attains a position of dynamic equilibrium resting over a convergence. The concept presupposes that the Moho is a phase change, there being no world-encircling basaltic "crust." Some implications are: (1) a highly mobile ocean floor coupled with limited continental drift; (2) simultaneous development of compressional structures on continents and tensional structures under the oceans but with no volumetric change in the earth; and (3) the rocks and sediments of the ocean floor are much younger than those on the continents.

These hypotheses are interesting and may have true merit, but at present there is no adequate way to test them. Drilling to the Moho may provide a means of testing the ideas.

---

[4] A similar idea was presented by J. J. Gilvarry (1961). This was discussed critically by Goles *et al.* (1962).

# CHAPTER XVI

# MINERALOGY AND CHEMISTRY OF MARINE SEDIMENTATION
## BY EDWARD D. GOLDBERG

## Introduction

The oceans of the world act as a temporary reservoir for weathered rock material, volcanic emanations and extraterrestrial solid phases. The dissolved chemical species that enter the marine environment reside in the oceans for times that bear an inverse relationship to their reactivity in either biochemical or inorganic reactions, while the particulate phases generally remain a shorter time. The role of the oceans in the major sedimentary cycle is illustrated in Fig. 208.

Hence, one can classify the components of the marine sediments on the basis of the geosphere in which the solid phases were formed (Goldberg, 1954). Volcanic and rock weathering debris which undergo no chemical or physical change during their stay in the oceanic waters are classified as *lithogenous*. The skeletal building blocks of some of the plants and animals of the sea, apatite, opal, and calcium carbonate, with the organic phases in the sediments, constitute the *biogenous* fraction. The *hydrogenous* phases are composed of those solids which inorganically precipitate from sea water. Finally, the *cosmogenous* components are the solids which come to the earth from outer space and chemically resemble meteoritic material.

The classification of minerals into the above groups is generally clear cut on the basis of either crystal form, chemical or isotopic composition, size or geographical location, although there are instances in which distinctions are difficult to make. For example, a clay mineral derived from the continents may undergo partial changes in its structure while passing through the hydrosphere to the ocean floor or while in the sedimentary deposits (Griffin and Goldberg, 1963). Compartmentalization of such a phase into either the hydrogenous or lithogenous groups is impossible.

Insight into the geochemical behavior of a given element in the major sedimentary cycle can be found in considerations of the length

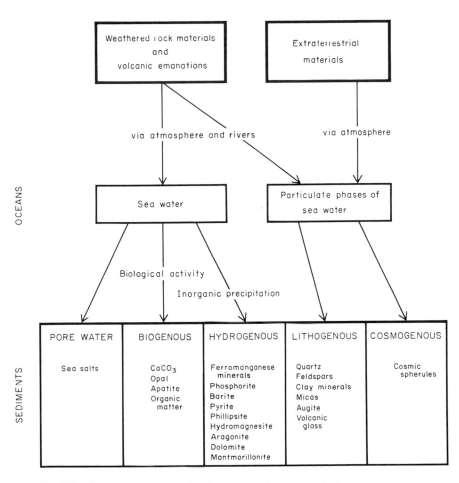

Fig. 208. The migration of dissolved and particulate materials through the ocean.

of time it spends in the oceans. A drastically oversimplified model of the cycle assumes that there is but one oceanic domain and that the presently observed chemical composition of the oceans reflects a steady state system in which the amount of any element entering per unit time is compensated by an equal amount deposited as sediments. A further assumption is that there is a complete mixing of the element in the oceans in times that are short with respect to its stay in the oceans. We can then define and calculate the residence time of an element in sea water as the total amount of the element in sea water divided by the amount introduced by the rivers or precipitated into the sediments per unit time. Barth (1952) used the river influx and

TABLE 11.  Residence Times and Abundances of the Elements in Sea Water

| Element | Concentration (mg/l) | Residence Time (years) |
|---------|---------------------|------------------------|
| H | 108,000. | |
| He | 0.000005 | |
| Li | 0.17 | $2.0 \times 10^7$ |
| Be | 0.0000006 | 150 |
| B | 4.6 | |
| C | 28. | |
| N | 0.5 | |
| O | 857,000. | |
| F | 1.3 | |
| Ne | 0.0001 | |
| Na | 10,500. | $2.6 \times 10^8$ |
| Mg | 1,350. | $4.5 \times 10^7$ |
| Al | 0.01 | 100 |
| Si | 3. | $8 \times 10^3$ |
| P | 0.07 | |
| S | 885. | |
| Cl | 19,000. | |
| A | 0.6 | |
| K | 380. | $1.1 \times 10^7$ |
| Ca | 400. | $8.0 \times 10^6$ |
| Sc | 0.00004 | $5.6 \times 10^3$ |
| Ti | 0.001 | 160 |
| V | 0.002 | $1.0 \times 10^4$ |
| Cr | 0.00005 | 350 |
| Mn | 0.002 | 1400 |
| Fe | 0.01 | 140 |
| Co | 0.0005 | $1.8 \times 10^4$ |
| Ni | 0.002 | $1.8 \times 10^4$ |
| Cu | 0.003 | $5.0 \times 10^4$ |
| Zn | 0.01 | $1.8 \times 10^5$ |
| Ga | 0.00003 | $1.4 \times 10^3$ |
| Ge | 0.00007 | $7 \times 10^3$ |
| As | 0.003 | |
| Se | 0.004 | |
| Br | 65. | |
| Kr | 0.0003 | |
| Rb | 0.12 | $2.7 \times 10^5$ |
| Sr | 8. | $1.9 \times 10^7$ |
| Y | 0.0003 | $7.5 \times 10^3$ |
| Zr | | |
| Nb | 0.00001 | 300 |
| Mo | 0.01 | $5.0 \times 10^5$ |
| Tc | | |
| Ru | | |
| Rh | | |
| Pd | | |

Goldberg and Arrhenius (1958) the sediment deposition in computations and a remarkable agreement is observed between the two sets of data. A compilation of residence times is given in Table 11, calculated by the second technique.

The longest residence times belong to the alkali and alkaline earth elements, Na, K, Mg, and Ca, which are also members of the major rock-forming element group, with values an order of magnitude or

TABLE II. (*continued*)

| Element | Concentration (mg/l) | Residence Time (years) |
|---|---|---|
| Ag | 0.0003 | $2.1 \times 10^6$ |
| Cd | 0.00011 | $5.0 \times 10^5$ |
| In | <0.02 | |
| Sn | 0.003 | $5.0 \times 10^5$ |
| Sb | 0.0005 | $3.5 \times 10^5$ |
| Te | | |
| I | 0.06 | |
| Xe | 0.0001 | |
| Cs | 0.0005 | $4 \times 10^4$ |
| Ba | 0.03 | $8.4 \times 10^4$ |
| La | 0.0003 | $1.1 \times 10^4$ |
| Ce | 0.0004 | $6.1 \times 10^3$ |
| Pr | | |
| Nd | | |
| Pm | | |
| Sm | | |
| Eu | | |
| Gd | | |
| Tb | | |
| Dy | | |
| Ho | | |
| Er | | |
| Tm | | |
| Yb | | |
| Lu | | |
| Hf | | |
| Ta | | |
| W | 0.0001 | $10^3$ |
| Re | | |
| Os | | |
| Ir | | |
| Pt | | |
| Au | 0.000004 | $5.6 \times 10^5$ |
| Hg | 0.00003 | $4.2 \times 10^4$ |
| Tl | <0.00001 | |
| Pb | 0.00003 | $2 \times 10^3$ |
| Bi | 0.00002 | $4.5 \times 10^4$ |
| Po | | |
| At | | |
| Rn | $0.6 \times 10^{-15}$ | |
| Fr | | |
| Ra | $1.0 \times 10^{-10}$ | |
| Ac | | |
| Th | 0.00005 | 350 |
| Pa | $2.0 \times 10^{-9}$ | |
| U | 0.003 | $5 \times 10^5$ |

two less than the presumed age of the oceans, several billion years. These elements are relatively unreactive in the marine environment. Silicon, aluminum, iron, and titanium, the remaining four major rock-forming elements, possess quite short residence times. These elements in part enter the oceans as lithogenous materials, the clay minerals, quartz, feldspars, augite, etc., and are also the reactants in the formation of such authigenic substances as the ferromanganese minerals, the zeolite phillipsite, etc. Thus, their entry into the oceans as solids and their high chemical reactivity probably account for their low residence times. It should be noted that the absolute values for such residence times are somewhat tenuous as the assumption that such times are small in comparison with mixing times in the oceans is not upheld.

The dissolved species with extremely short residence times (thorium, tungsten, niobium, beryllium, and chromium) may well exhibit ocean-to-ocean variations in their concentrations owing to incomplete mixing of water masses. Such a situation has been encountered in the case of thorium (Goldberg *et al.*, 1958) whose marine chemistries will be developed in the geochronology section.

The elements enriched in pelagic sediments, manganese, nickel, copper, cobalt, lead, and the rare earths (Goldberg and Arrhenius, 1958), have intermediate values for their residence times. Manganese has a markedly low value (1400 years) compared to other elements with similar chemistries which exist in sea water in divalent states, copper, nickel, cobalt, and zinc. This situation undoubtedly results from the incorporation of large amounts of this element into the ubiquitously distributed ferromanganese minerals. Silver and gold spend more time in the oceans than their periodic table associate copper. The two coinage metals exist in seawater as the anions, $AuCl_4^-$ and $AgCl_2^-$, while copper is present predominantly in the cationic state as $Cu^{++}$ (Goldberg and Arrhenius, 1958). Thus the complex forms of silver and gold give these elements stability in seawater.

## Lithogenous Components

The nature of the lithogenous components of marine sediments, coupled with size and geographical distributions, can be diagnostic of source areas of such materials as well as the modes of introduction into the marine environment. The mineral quartz has provided one of the most useful entries into such studies. Besides being one of the major constituents of crustal rocks (12–20 percent by weight on the average), it is one of the most resistant minerals to weathering. Its common occurrence in nearshore sediments is well documented.

**Quartz.** Radczewski (1937a) realized that the most probable source for some of the nonvolcanic material in the Cape Verde Basin was the Sahara Desert. A search for an indicator of such materials converged about the so-called Wüstenquarz, quartz grains coated with a red-brown hematite. These particles constituted between 3.1 and 39 percent of the total quartz in the 10- to 50-micron size range and between 5 and 22 percent in the 5.5- to 10-micron size range. On

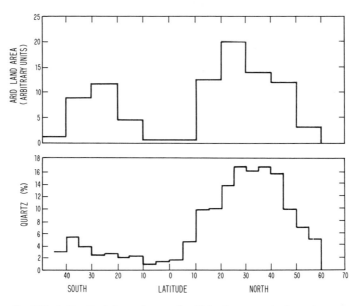

Fig. 209. Latitudinal dependence of arid land areas and of quartz contents of the Pacific pelagic sediments (on a calcium carbonate free basis).

the basis of their concentrations which decreased in these deposits with distance from shore and were highest in the inshore coarse fractions, and their geographical distribution, Radczewski suggested this material was transported by the equatorial easterly winds to the deposit site.

In the Pacific, Rex and Goldberg (1958) found a marked latitudinal dependence of quartz concentrations in surface sediment samples on a calcium carbonate-free basis (Fig. 209). The mineral occurred in the deposits as chips and shards, primarily in the silt range with 2- to 10-micron particles being most abundant. Maximum concentrations were found around 30° N. and somewhat less distinctly at about 35° S. Highest concentrations, about 25 percent, occur in regions north of Hawaii, farthest from the continents. The correlation of quartz concentrations and exposed arid land areas directed these same authors to the conclusion of an eolian path from the desert regions with the jet streams, whose highest intensities are at mid-latitudes, as the transporting agency. Further, filter-feeding plankton, collected from a number of mid-Pacific areas, contained mineral debris, including quartz, mica, and feldspars in their gut regions, apparently obtained from atmospheric fallout.

**Clay Minerals.** The clay mineral assemblages in the North Pacific and in the Atlantic can be interpreted in part on the basis of terrestrial

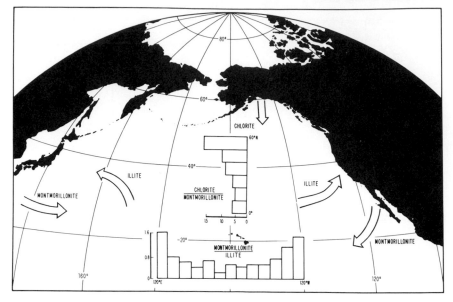

Fig. 210. Distribution of clay minerals in the North Pacific. Arrows indicate direction of decreasing concentration.

sources. The mid-North Pacific shows marked concentrations of illite, normally in association with high quartz concentrations (Griffin and Goldberg, 1963).

The nonauthigenic, continental origin of such illite is emphasized by recent potassium-argon age determinations. Hurley *et al.* (1960) found the clay components from a near-surface sample of an eastern Pacific deposit (Scripps Institution of Oceanography Core Y5P; 20°49′ N.; 125°15′ W.; 4550 m deep) to be at least 80 million years old, showing that they could not be of recent authigenic origin.

Griffin and Goldberg (1963) noted in North Pacific coastal deposits an enrichment in a "montmorillonite type" mineral which showed evidences of being either a stripped illite or chlorite. Such minerals are apparently transported to the oceans in the water from coastal continental areas. The chlorite contents of the North Pacific pelagic sediments decrease going from high polar regions southward, resulting from a chlorite source in the high latitudinal land areas. On the other hand, the South Pacific showed little terrestrial influence in clay mineral assemblages with montmorillonite always the predominant clay mineral, forming from the alteration of volcanic materials (Fig. 210).

In the Atlantic, Heezen *et al.* (1960b) describe similar regional

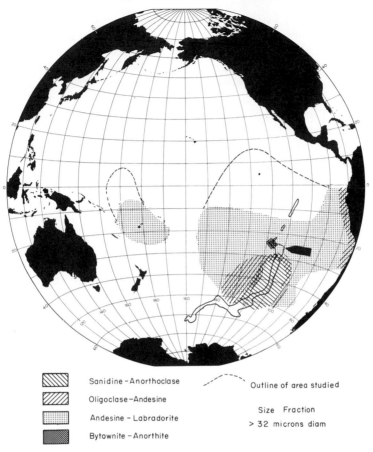

Sanidine – Anorthoclase

Oligoclase – Andesine

Andesine – Labradorite

Bytownite – Anorthite

Outline of area studied

Size Fraction
> 32 microns diam

Fig. 211. Feldspar distribution in the Pacific Ocean. Dark arrow points to bytownite-anorthite area.

occurrences of clay minerals. The sediments off the Brazilian coast are characterized by equal parts of illite, montmorillonite, and kaolinite. The abyssal plain of Sohm contains illite and chlorite with small amounts of kaolinite, while the abyssal plain of Hatteras and the continental shelf off the United States contains besides these minerals some montmorillonite. Hurley *et al.* (1960) find ages for these clay components to be between 85 and 464 million years.

**Feldspars.** Two major sedimentary provinces in the South Pacific have been delineated upon the basis of their feldspars, most probably derived locally from volcanic activity and the submarine weathering of lithospheric phases (Peterson and Goldberg, 1962). An area about the Society Islands (Fig. 211) is characterized by large amounts of labradorite in association with augite. Weathered hydrogenous products, montmorillonite, and phillipsite, derived from the direct alteration of basaltic ash, have bracketed the parent material to a quite basic nature. A rhyolitic province encompasses the East Pacific Rise where the sediments contain large amounts of quartz (especially in large size range of 24 to 40 microns), together with the feldspars sanidine and orthoclase. In this area the formation of phillipsite and montmorillonite is lacking or trivial and no clay mineral assemblages have evolved (Griffin and Goldberg, 1963). The associated unweathered volcanic glasses reflect the parent substances: high refractive index (1.58) glasses in the basaltic region and low refractive index (1.49) in the rhyolitic area.

## Hydrogenous Components

**Ferromanganese Minerals.**   The ferromanganese minerals, often in the form of nodules, are ubiquitously distributed over the open ocean floor where oxidizing conditions at the sediment-water interface prevail. Their importance can be ascertained from the estimate of

TABLE 12.   Typical Analysis of a Ferromanganese Nodule. *Challenger* Station 248. Lat. 37°41′ N.; Long. 177°04′ W.; depth 5304 m[a]

| Oxide | Weight Percent | Oxide | Weight Percent |
|---|---|---|---|
| $Al_2O_3$ | 6.04 | NiO | 0.53 |
| BaO | 0.58 | $P_2O_5$ | 0.30 |
| $B_2O_3$ | 0.010 | $K_2O$ | 1.45 |
| CdO | 0.0011 | $Sc_2O_3$ | 0.0015 |
| CaO | 2.10 | $Ag_2O$ | 0.0016 |
| CoO | 0.17 | $Na_2O$ | 3.37 |
| CuO | 0.80 | SrO | 0.18 |
| $Ga_2O_3$ | 0.0029 | $Tl_2O$ | 0.009 |
| $GeO_2$ | 0.0007 | $SnO_2$ | 0.03 |
| $Fe_2O_3$ | 21.4 | $TiO_2$ | 0.56 |
| $La_2O_3$ | 0.02 | $WO_3$ | 0.006 |
| PbO | 0.15 | $V_2O_5$ | 0.071 |
| MgO | 0.90 | $Y_2O_3$ | 0.003 |
| MnO | 31.62 | ZnO | 0.70 |
| $MoO_3$ | 0.06 | $ZrO_2$ | 0.015 |

Source: Data from J. P. Riley and P. Sinhaseni, *J. Marine Research* 17, 466–82 (1958).

[a] Data are given in weight percent of the oxide in the soluble fraction of the nodular material.

Menard and Shipek (1958) that between 20 and 50 percent of the deep-sea floor in the southwestern Pacific is covered with these accretions. Their unique chemical composition (Table 12), unlike any terrestrial material, has strongly indicated their authigenic character. A marine formation has been further substantiated by a clear-cut relationship between the collecting sites of the minerals and their lead isotopic composition (Chow and Patterson, 1959) where the lead is presumably derived from the waters overlying the sediments.

Little was known about the structure of the ferromanganese minerals until the rather elegant experiments of Buser and co-workers (Buser and Grütter, 1956; Grütter and Buser, 1957). They found the structure elements, which all of the ferromanganese minerals possess in common, consist of layers of $MnO_2$ in an irregular pile of quasi-two-dimensional crystals. The x-ray diffraction pattern of this structural unit is

$$3MnO_2 \rightleftharpoons Mn(OH)_2 \times H_2O$$

and is related to the mineral lithiophorite. By analogy with previously made structural analyses of lithiophorite, Buser suggests a structure with two $MnO_2$ layers, 10 A apart, separated by an in-between layer, consisting of $Mn(OH)_2$, $Fe(OH)_3$, and possibly sodium ions. Since many of the nodules contain more iron than can be accommodated in the in-between layer, the excess iron appears in the form of goethite, which remains in the residuum from a dilute hydrochloric acid leach.

The in-between layer accommodates a group of cations, such as nickel, copper, cobalt, and zinc, found in rather high concentrations in the ferromanganese minerals. Buser also noted in the residuum of the nodules the presence of fine quartz particles.

The rates of build-up of the ferromanganese minerals in the marine environment are extremely low—of the order of hundredths of millimeters to millimeters per thousand years. Perhaps this chemical growth, representing one of the lowest chemical reaction rates ascertained in nature, can better be expressed in terms of atomic layers per day, in which the results range between 1 and 100. The first direct determinations of the rates gave values between 0.7 and 65 mm/$10^3$ years (Pettersson, 1943; von Buttlar and Houtermans, 1950; Kröll, 1955) and were based upon the decrease in radium concentration with depth in the sediment. This chronology is based upon the assumptions that the radium is unsupported, i.e., derived directly from seawater, and that the decrease in radium concentration is determined solely by its half-life. Such assumptions, however, have been criticized by Goldberg and Arrhenius (1958) as probably being much too high. The unusually high amounts of thorium in the ferromanganese minerals (Goldberg and Picciotto, 1955) ranging between 30 and 100 ppm by weight, suggest that ionium, an isotope of thorium and a parent of radium in the $U^{238}$ decay series, is collected from the seawater along with normal thorium. If all the radium in the ferromanganese minerals is ionium-supported, that is the extreme case, the rates of deposition given by the radium method are too high by a factor of 50, the ratio of the ionium to radium half-lives. Two nodules analyzed by the ionium/thorium technique (Goldberg and Koide, 1958) indicate these suggested slow rates. Results on a nodule from the Blake Plateau (29°18′ N. and 52°20′W.; depth 5400 m, Lamont *Theta* Trawl No. 4) indicated a rate of accumulation of 0.1 mm/$10^3$ years, while the *Horizon* nodule from the Pacific (40°14′ N., 155°15′ W.; 5500 m) showed a recent accumulation (the ionium/thorium

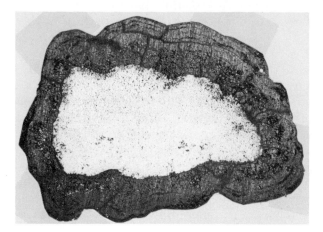

Fig. 212. Cross section of a manganese nodule, illustrating laminar growth, from Sylvania Seamount (12° N., 165° E.). The core material is phillipsite. Nodule is $3\frac{1}{2}$ cm across.

methodology defines a recent, measureable age as less than half a million years) only at a surface removed by slightly touching it with a dental drill, a depth under 1 mm. All surfaces greater than 1 mm in depth in the nodule were older than half a million years. It should be noted that such accretions do not grow uniformly or continuously as is indicated by the laminae present in most accretions (Fig. 212).

A large number of hypotheses concerned with the mechanisms of formation of the ferromanganese minerals have been advanced, yet most have been concerned with the immediate origins of the components rather than the physicochemical considerations.

Thermodynamic considerations provide a satisfying entry into the problem of ferromanganese mineral formation. The most reasonable oxidizing agent to convert the ionic divalent manganese in seawater to the tetravalent state is the dissolved oxygen gas. The reaction $2 \, OH^- + Mn^{++} + \frac{1}{2} O_2 = MnO_2 + H_2O$ has a free energy of $-9$ kcal at a pH of 8, a manganous ion concentration of $10^{-9}$ molar and a partial pressure of oxygen of 0.25 atmosphere. All these concentrations are similar to those in near-bottom waters.

Since tetravalent manganese is not found in seawater, although from the above data it would be the stable form, a reaction site or surface is apparently necessary for the occurrence of the reaction. The well-known catalytic properties of iron oxides, coupled with the observations that iron exists in seawater primarily as particulate species such as $Fe(OH)_3$ and that iron is one of the major components of the concretions, suggest the importance of iron in the formation process. The accumulation of iron oxides on surfaces, where either the bottom topography or the lack of sediment source material does not allow any appreciable accumulation of solid phases, would initiate the formation. In areas of rapid deposition, where nodules or accretions are not found, the burial of any oxide surface by other sediment components minimizes mineral formation. Where an excess of iron is accommodated, the mineral goethite appears. Finally, the formation of the mineral most probably results in the existence of further sites for the oxidation reaction, i.e., the reaction becomes autocatalytic.

The recent and significant observation by Graham (1959) that these ferromanganese minerals contain appreciable amounts of organic matter has resulted in the revival of the hypothesis of a biological origin for them. However, the direct uptake of organic matter upon the rather extensive surfaces of these minerals (6–190 $m^2/g$, Buser and Grütter, 1956) appears much more reasonable. This organic matter may be derived directly from solution in seawater or from benthic organisms or bacteria on the mineral surfaces.

**Dolomite.** Studies on the inorganic formation of carbonates from dissolved species in marine waters have not as yet fully defined the conditions for precipitation. The direct precipitation of dolomite has been observed in one general area, the shallow-water lagoons at the closed end of the Coorong in the southeast of South Australia (Alderman and Skinner, 1957; Alderman, 1959; Skinner, 1960). The carbonates, collected from suspensions in the waters, are mixtures of magnesian calcite ranging in composition from $(Ca_{0.84}Mg_{0.16})CO_3$ to $(Ca_{0.77}Mg_{0.23})CO_3$ and calcian dolomite of essentially constant composition $Ca_{0.56}Mg_{0.44}$. Celestite, $SrSO_4$, accompanies the precipitates in minor amounts not exceeding 3 percent. Hydromagnesite has been observed in the surface layers of the sediments where its concentration equals that of aragonite. It disappears with depth in the deposits (Alderman and von der Borch, 1960).

The precipitation in the lagoons takes place during spring and early summer when plant growth is most vigorous and carbonate suspensions are observed in the waters containing large amounts of photosynthesizing plants. The pH of the waters from which the carbonates form is around 9.0 although one value as low as 8.5 was observed. The uptake of carbon dioxide by the photosynthesizing biomass and the consequential increase in pH apparently provides in part the necessary conditions for the carbonate precipitation. The salinities of the waters vary between 15 and over 140‰.

**Oolites.** (See also p. 483) The inorganic precipitation of calcium carbonate is apparently limited to coastal waters in tropical or semi-tropical environments in which the solubility product of calcium carbonate can be exceeded. The extensively studied oolitic aragonitic sands of the Great Bahama Bank are widely distributed over a 100,000-square-mile area of the continental shelf between Florida and Hispaniola (Newell *et al.*, 1960) and provide the classic example for understanding the details of deposition. The oolites are composed of a nucleus, usually an abraded shell fragment, a recrystallized fecal pellet or a mineral grain, surrounded by concentric bands, either as a thin layer or as a rather thick coating. Newell *et al.* distinguish two components in the aragonitic envelope: oriented aragonitic lamellae which are relatively unpigmented, regular in thickness of about 1 to 3 microns, and consist of submicroscopic crystals of aragonite with their $c$ axes oriented tangential to the lamination; and unoriented crypto-crystalline aggregates, more heavily pigmented. They suggest that the oriented lamellae result from the inorganic crystallization of aragonite at the grain surface while the unoriented aragonite probably results from interstitial recrystallization. The oolites contain large amounts of organic substances both as perforating filamentous algae and as a mucilaginous phase most probably accommodated in the oolite during its growth.

The oolites precipitate from fairly shallow water—most of the area of the Great Bahama Bank is less than 5 m deep. Newell *et al.* (1960) indicate that oolite formation is most extensive in and just below the intertidal zone. The physical and chemical parameters of the environment are influenced not only by topography and temperatures of the area but also most probably by the intense biological activity. The cool, $CO_2$-rich water that enters the shoals from the open sea is heated by sunlight in the depositional sites. Further, the photosynthesis in the area results in a reduction in the carbon dioxide and the consequential increase in carbonate concentration. Both effects increase the concentrations of the reactants in the formation of aragonite.

The Bahama oolites possess a distinctive chemical composition, undoubtedly related to the inorganic precipitation process. Their strontium and uranium concentrations are markedly higher than most biogenous carbonates [2.4 percent $SrCO_3$ and 3 ppm of uranium (Tatsumoto and Goldberg, 1959)]. The isotopic ratios $C^{13}/C^{12}$ and $O^{18}/O^{16}$ are in general higher than aragonitic needles from marine algae and extend over a more restricted range (Lowenstam and Epstein, 1957). Oolites can be dated by either of two radiochemical techniques: carbon-14 (Newell *et al.*, 1960) or uranium-ionium (Tatsumoto and Goldberg, 1959).

**Apatites (Phosphorites).**   Authigenic marine phosphorites have the general formula $Ca_{10}(PO_4,CO_3)_6F_{2-3}$ in which the excess positive charge resulting from the substitution of carbonate for phosphate is balanced by excess fluorine or hydroxyl groups. This carbonate-fluorapatite is a hexagonal network composed of phosphate tetrahedra with the anion fluorine and hydroxide and the divalent cation calcium within the structure (Altschuler *et al.*, 1958).

Extensive deposits exist on the sea floor off the southern California coast where a total area of about 6000 square miles contains phosphorite in the forms of nodules, slags, and oolites (Emery, 1960, pp. 68–73). Emery points out that 98 percent of the material is in water depths from 100 to 1000 ft. Foraminiferal sands are often found in association with the phosphorite.

The physicochemical conditions for the formation of phosphorite have been postulated by Krumbein and Garrels (1952), who point out that it probably forms in restricted basins in which the pH is relatively low, i.e., environments near or at anaerobism and with pH values around 8, slightly lower than those of normal sea water. Several recent investigations tend to confirm this hypothesis. Altschuler *et al.* (1958) find that the uranium in the southern California phosphorites exists in the tetravalent state to the extent of 55 to 74 percent of the total uranium. In seawater uranium is in the hexavalent state, complexed with carbonate to form the anion $(UO_2)(CO_3)_3^{4-}$. The reduced uranium occurs in the apatites substituting for calcium in the lattice while the uranyl ions are apparently taken up by adsorption on the surfaces of the apatite crystallites (Sheldon, 1959). It is evident from an inspection of the stability relations among uranium species as a function of Eh and pH (Garrels, 1960, pp. 187–188) that the tetravalent uranium will not be stable in a marine environment in which the Eh is positive. A log dredged from a 410-m terrace in the Gulf of Tehuantepec, mineralized by phosphorite intrusions, apparently derived its apatite under the conditions cited above (Goldberg and Parker, 1960). The seawater in contact with the mineralizing log was depleted in oxygen and contained maximal values of phosphate ions. The deficiency in oxygen results from the combustion of the rather large amounts of organic matter falling from the surface waters which are notably productive of plant life in this area.

These observations coincide with the geologic evidence on the deposition of phosphorite (McKelvey *et al.*, 1953). Marine apatites are found in eastern oceanic coastal deposits where upwelled waters give rise to the high productivity of organic matter. The rapid accumulation of this organic matter on the sea floor not only produces an environment free of oxygen but also furnishes phosphate from the decomposition processes for mineral formation (McKelvey *et al.*, 1953).

**Barium Deposits.** Barite often occurs as a constituent of Pacific pelagic sediments (Goldberg and Arrhenius, 1958), but of greater significance, perhaps, is the fact that the gross content of barium in deep-sea sediments is unusually high in biologically productive oceanic areas. Barium concentrations in the oceanic water column have been shown to increase with depth (Chow and Goldberg, 1960). This phenomenon has been attributed to the conveyance of barium by organic phases, known to be enriched in barium relative to seawater, from surface to deeper waters. The oxidation of the organic matter results in the subsequential release of the barium. If the organic phases reach the sea floor, the regeneration of the barium can initiate the formation of barite or the incorporation of barium in other authigenic minerals.

In the eastern Pacific the barium/clay mineral ratio was twenty times higher in the sediments below the zone of high organic productivity at the equatorial divergence (10° N.) to 10° S. than at higher northerly or southerly latitudes. In the sediments from the equatorial region the barium concentrations rose to 1 percent or even higher in the dried samples (Goldberg and Arrhenius, 1958).

In siliceous deposits from the Bering Sea the barium concentrations appear to be covariant with the opal, originating from the tests of diatoms (Goldberg, 1958). Here the barium is probably associated with the organic debris accompanying the skeletal remains of the phytoplankton.

**Glauconite.** Of the authigenic marine clay minerals, glauconite is probably the most studied and also the most enigmatic with respect to its formation. It is found on bank tops, ridge crests, hills that rise above shelves, and some slopes at depths that range from 50 to more than 2000 m (Emery, 1960). The mineral glauconite is a single-layer monoclinic mica, often disordered and interlayered, with the distinguishing chemical characteristics of 7–8 percent $K_2O$ and an iron content of 20–25 percent whose $Fe^{+++}/Fe^{++}$ ratio varies between 3 and 9. Burst (1958a) emphasizes the dual connotations of the term "glauconite"; a blue-green micaceous mineral and a rock term for small green earthy pellets, containing varying amounts of the mineral. The concern here will be primarily with those materials which possess the structural properties, determined by x-ray diffraction analyses, attributed to the mineral.

Burst (1958b) points out four possible paths for the formation of glauconite pellets: (1) the transformation of fecal pellets or coprolites; (2) the conversion of materials filling foraminiferal tests; (3) the conversion of biotite booklets which yield rounded pellets retaining some of the booklike laminations of the parent material; and (4) the agglomeration of shale pellets or bottom clays and transformation to glauconite. Although a vast and often contradictory literature exists on the subsequent glauconization process, it seems preferable to seek out those parameters that may be influential or indicative of the physicochemical environments which give rise to the mineral.

First of all, glauconite is often in association with phosphorite, a mineral hypothesized previously to form under reducing conditions. Although the environments in which glauconite is most abundant are areas in which the overlying seawater is oxygenated (Emery, 1960), large amounts of organic matter can serve as a buffer against intrusion of oxygen into the formation site. The parameter common to glauconitic environments is the presence of such organic matter. The existence of ferrous iron in the structure of all glauconites can be explained only by a reduction of the normally present ferric iron in marine waters. Hence, one is directed to a reducing microenvironment for glauconitization—the interior of a foraminiferal shell, a fecal pellet, or a clay agglomerate containing organic phases.

The variations in the $Fe^{+++}/Fe^{++}$ ratio, magnesium, and potassium contents in glauconites probably stem not only from the relative redox potential of the environment but also from the amounts and types of organic matter that can complex the species of iron and the relative availability of magnesium and potassium ions. Further, the character of the argillaceous progenitors will strongly influence the chemical composition of the resultant mineral as Burst describes in his rather extensive studies.

**Clay Minerals.**   Clay mineral assemblages in the surface deposits away from land in the South Pacific show little terrestrial influence and, according to Griffin and Goldberg (1963), the commonly found montmorillonite arises from the alteration of volcanic materials. The formation of montmorillonite from volcanic ash is well documented in the literature (Ross and Hendricks, 1945). Furthermore, a few samples examined by electron microscopy and diffraction showed halloysite tubes, also reported from volcanic ash degradation (Hathaway, 1957).

The recent North Pacific surface sediments possess no readily identifiable authigenic clays—the layer-lattice minerals being most readily interpreted on the basis of terrestrial sources (see section on lithogenous components). However, the Tertiary pelagic deposits of the north mid-Pacific are enriched in montmorillonite and the

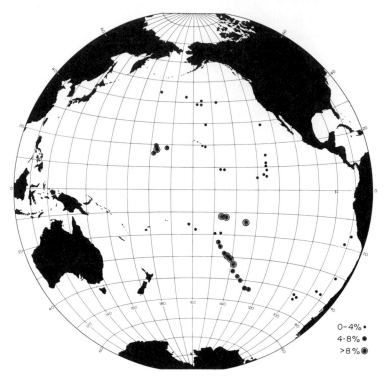

Fig. 213. Phillipsite concentrations in the Pacific on a calcium carbonate free basis.

zeolite phillipsite and resemble both mineralogically and chemically those of the present-day South Pacific. These observations have led Griffin and Goldberg to suggest that the North Pacific during the Tertiary times was similar as a depositional environment to the South Pacific today, i.e., an area that receives small amounts of detrital minerals and high amounts of pyroclastics.

**Phillipsite.** The distinctive microliths of the zeolite phillipsite were recognized by Murray and Renard (1891) as significant components of some pelagic deposits. Semiquantitative analyses on a marine phillipsite gave the following results: Si, 25.0 percent; Mg, 0.04 percent; Al, 8.8 percent; Ca, 0.21 percent; K, 5.1 percent; Na, 5.5 percent; Ti, 0.02 percent, and P, 0.09 percent. These values may be compared with the literature composition range of $KCa_3Si_9Al_7O_{32}$–$K_3CaSi_{11}Al_5O_{32}$ (Winchell, 1951, p. 343). These results are comparable to those of Murray and Renard (1891), who found the high sodium values, but also high iron values, quite clearly resulting from a surface coating which the authors state was not removed prior to analysis.

The high Si/Al ratio in the marine form accounts for the increased alkali metal/alkaline earth ratio.

The high concentrations of phillipsite in pelagic deposits are found in such areas as the Society Islands region in the South Pacific which are further characterized by feldspars and volcanic glasses apparently derived from basaltic materials (Fig. 213). The clay mineral in association with phillipsite is montmorillonite. At the present time it is tempting to relate the formation of phillipsite to the existence of basaltic volcanic debris. Whether such materials are necessary precursors of phillipsite or whether their degradation results in a physicochemical environment that accommodates the crystallization of the zeolite is at present unknown.

## Cosmogenous Components

In 1876 Murray initially described certain spherical particles in deep-sea sediments having a highly magnetic nature. These spherules were composed of an inner metallic nucleus surrounded by a mantle of iron oxides. They most commonly occur in the size range of 30–60 microns, seldom exceeding 0.2 mm in diameter. The rather unexpected occurrence of elemental metals in the sediments led Murray to consider a relationship with iron meteorites and an extraterrestrial origin for these spherules.

TABLE 13.  Some Elemental Ratios in Metallic Cosmic Spherules and Iron Meteorites (Smales et al., 1958)

|  | Ni/Cu | Ni/Co | Cu/Co | Ni/Fe |
|---|---|---|---|---|
| Magnetic spherules | 1400; 1100 | 17; 13 | 0.012; 0.012 | 0.08; 0.13 |
| Iron meteorites | 210–1650 | 7.3–43.4 | 0.013–0.069 | 0.06–0.17 |

This deduction of Murray found confirmation through chemical analyses of the metal phases some eighty years later (Smales et al., 1958; Castaing and Fredriksson, 1958; Hecht and Patzaic, 1957). Typical compositions of the metallic phases were remarkably similar to those of iron meteorites (Table 13.) X-ray powder analysis revealed the presence of magnetite and $\gamma$-ferric oxide as the major crystalline components of the oxidized phases (Hunter and Parkin, 1960).

Depth distribution studies on the spherules larger than 30 microns were made by Pettersson and Fredriksson (1958) on a series of Pacific sediments. Particles with diameters under 30 microns, difficult to count and easy to overlook, were not significant compared to the total weight of spherules. The number of counted spherules varied between hundreds and thousands per kilogram in salt- and carbonate-free sediments. Higher concentrations were found in the upper levels of the deposits, and Pettersson and Fredriksson (1958) suggested that the accretion of such particles by the earth has been higher now than in the past.

On the basis of ionium-radium chronology (see section on geo-chronology) for determining the rates of sedimentation of pelagic sediments, these authors calculate the total accruement of the spherules to the earth's surface to be of the order of 2500–5000 metric tons annually.

Hunter and Parkin extracted from both Atlantic and Pacific sediments some gray-black stony spherules which show a dendritic structure, attributed to a very rapid cooling from a liquid state. These stones are essentially a magnesium-rich, fine-grained olivine which according to refractive index determinations contain about 6 percent fayalite. Further, they occur in much larger sizes than the irons, and in some cases depart from the spherical shape. Around 15 to 20 percent have oblate or prolate shapes, and a few were even pear-shaped. It is tempting to relate these stones to their meteoritic counterparts; however, confirmation of an extraterrestrial origin awaits further chemical and mineral analyses.

### Biogenous Components

The three solid phases in marine sediments which have their origin in the skeletal building blocks of plants and animals are calcium carbonates, silicon dioxide (opal), and calcium phosphates (apatites). The chemical compositions and mineralogy of these materials can often provide a record of the nature of the environments in which they were formed.

**Calcium Carbonates.** The two important carbonate minerals are rhombohedral calcite and its orthorhombic polymorph aragonite. A variety of organisms contributes these forms to the inshore environment: mollusks, algae, corals, Foraminifera, sponges, echinoids, asteroids, ophiuroids, crinoids, etc., while in pelagic areas the dominant biogenous carbonates arise from the Foraminifera, coccolithophorids, and pteropods.

The persistence of calcium carbonate fossils in the depositional sites is a function of a number of parameters. Experimental values and those derived on the basis of thermodynamic considerations indicate the solubility product of aragonite to be higher than that of calcite with the ratio of solubility products $K_A/K_C = 1.59$ (theoretical) and 2 (experimental; Revelle and Fairbridge, 1957). Thus, aragonitic

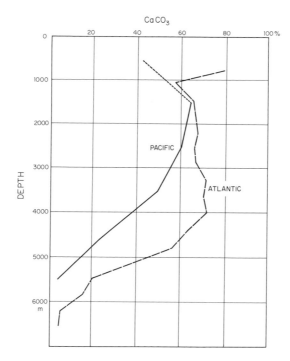

Fig. 214. The relationship between the calcium carbonate content of pelagic sediments and depth in Atlantic
and Pacific. From Revelle (1944).

pteropods are found less extensively and more often in a mottled
(slightly dissolved) condition than the calcitic Foraminifera.

Calcareous remains are rare or missing in deposits from depths
greater than 6000 m where the waters are apparently undersaturated
with respect to calcium carbonate (Fig. 214). The solubility of calcium
carbonate increases with increasing chlorinity and pressure and
decreases with increasing temperatures, and hence dissolution can
take place in such deep cold waters under high hydrostatic heads.

Lowenstam (1954) has extensively studied the role of temperature
in the role of calcium carbonate polymorphism in marine organisms.
In general, aragonite is associated with warm-water organisms. This
effect is reflected in three primary categories in which Lowenstam
classifies marine calcareous organisms. The first covers those orders of
organisms whose species have skeletons composed entirely of aragonite,
such as the madreporian reef-building corals. The number of species is
much greater in warm tropical waters than in those of higher latitudes.
The second group includes those classes or subclasses whose species
are composed entirely of either calcite or aragonite, but in which the

orders with aragonite-depositing species are confined to the warmer waters. The red algae and alcyonarians are typical members of this classification. Finally, the third category encompasses various genera and species, containing both aragonite and calcite; the ratio of calcite to aragonite is dependent upon the temperature at which the shell was laid down, the aragonite increasing with increasing temperature. This last group is typified by certain species of the molluscan genera *Brachindontes* and *Littorina*.

The magnesium concentration in calcareous skeletons is controlled in general by the crystal form (Chave, 1954). Aragonites generally have less than 1 percent magnesium carbonate whereas calcitic shells rarely contain less than 1 percent but can attain values as high as 20 or 30 percent. The phylogenetic level and the temperature of the water in which the organisms lived also directly influence the magnesium contents. Chave points out that there was always a positive correlation between the magnesium contents of the calcium carbonates and the environmental temperature for the groups of organisms he studied, which include algae, Foraminifera, sponges, alcyonaria, echinoids, asteroids, ophiuroids, crinoids, ostracods, decapods, and barnacles. Between the Foraminifera and the barnacles, groups increasing in organic complexity, a gradual decrease in total magnesium and of the slope of the temperature-magnesium content regression line were found. Lowenstam (1959) obtained excellent agreement between temperatures based on the magnesium content and those from $O^{18}/O^{16}$ and Sr/Ca ratios (see below) on the calcitic shells of recent articulate brachiopods. On the other hand, extensive studies on the magnesium contents of 131 genera of Foraminifera by Blackmon and Todd (1959) revealed that with this group' of organisms the family affiliation appeared to be the major control for magnesium content, whereas temperature entered to only a minor degree. Low temperatures resulted in a slight lessening of the magnesium concentrations, while high environmental temperatures showed no discernible effects.

Lowenstam (1959) derived an empirical relationship between the Sr/Ca ratios in calcitic brachiopods and their environmental temperatures and applied this ratio to ascertain temperatures in geologic time as far back as the Mississippian from fossil brachiopods.

Perhaps the most significant record of environmental temperatures which can be derived from calcareous shells is the $O^{18}/O^{16}$ ratio in the carbonates developed by Urey and his associates. The isotopic reaction

$$H_2O^{18}(l) + \tfrac{1}{3}CaCO_3^{16} \text{ (s)} = H_2O(l) + \tfrac{1}{3}CaCO_3^{18}(s)$$

results in an enrichment of the heavier oxygen isotope in calcareous

material essentially independent of pH of the solution, the poly-
morphic form of $CaCO_3$, the salinity of the solution, and apparently
of pressure (Epstein, 1959). The temperature dependence of the
equilibrium constant for the above reaction results in a 0.1 percent
increase in the $O^{18}/O^{16}$ ratio in carbonates for each 4.3° decrease in
temperature (Epstein et al., 1953). The stable carbon isotopes, $C^{13}$
and $C^{12}$, in marine shells do not log a temperature scale inasmuch as
they are not in isotopic equilibrium with the ocean bicarbonate (H.
Craig, quoted in Revelle and Fairbridge, 1957). Craig attributes the
cause of the lack of equilibrium carbon isotopic ratios to the admixture
of metabolic $CO_2$ with the carbon being laid down in the shells.

Pelagic Foraminifera have been extensively used in studies of
paleotemperatures by the oxygen isotopic technique (Wiseman, 1959;
Emiliani, 1954, 1957). Where the isotopic composition of the environmental waters is known, temperatures to an accuracy of one degree
are claimed. Reliable estimates on the isotopic compositions of past
seawaters clearly must be made for the paleomeasurements, and
possible changes in the $O^{18}/O^{16}$ ratio in ocean waters represent the
most serious limitation to the usefulness of the technique (Epstein,
1959). Other assumptions include that there has been no post-deposi-
tional recrystallization or ionic diffusion through the calcium carbonate
lattice. Finally, because of the deposition of calcium carbonate by
individual species of Foraminifera at different depths and different
seasons, single species are ordinarily analyzed to obtain a consistent
record for a given area. Emiliani has shown preference for *Globigerinoides rubra* and *Globigerinoides sacculifera* which inhabit surface levels
of the ocean, primarily because surface waters yield a temperature
record of greater amplitude and detail than deeper parts of the ocean.
Confidence in the technique can be seen in the rather consistent set
of temperature records for the Pleistocene (Figs. 201 and 215) and
the correlation with temperatures based upon pure paleontological
evidences (Emiliani, 1957).

**Siliceous Phases.**    Opal, a highly disordered form of silicon dioxide
generally containing less than 12 percent water, is a constituent of the
sediments which originates in the plant and animal life of the sea as
frustules of diatoms and silicoflagellates or as skeletal remains of
radiolaria and sponges. There is no evidence for the inorganic
deposition of opal in the marine environment. Quantitative assays of
biogenous silica have been limited to microscopic estimations, although
recently a method based upon the conversion of opal to crystobalite
and a subsequent x-ray diffraction analysis has been proposed
(Goldberg, 1958).

Riedel (1959) has systematized the factors controlling the preservation

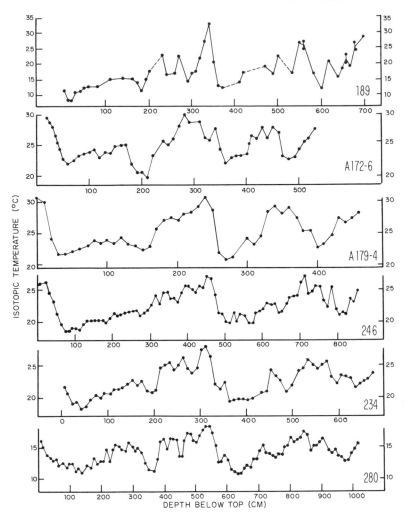

Fig. 215. Paleotemperature curves of six deep-sea cores from the Atlantic, Caribbean, and Mediterranean. From Emiliani (1958).

of opal in the deposit sites. Opaline phases persist in areas of high rates of sedimentation where the siliceous skeletons are well preserved. There is apparently no significant pressure effect upon the solubility of the biogenous opal, and diatomaceous sediments have been reported from depths as great as 9394 m in the Kurile-Kamchatka Trench. Riedel also suggests that in sediments containing large amounts of volcanic debris, the weathering of pyroclastic material introduces dissolved species of silicon into sediment waters which in turn reduce the rate of dissolution of biogenous silica. The author has observed that the existence of organic phases in the opal provides a measure of protection to the silica with respect to dissolving in slightly basic solutions. The isotopic composition and minor elements in opaline phases have received scant attention.

**Apatites.**   The calcium phosphates of biological origin are generally the teeth of fish and earbones of whales which can contribute a few percent by weight to slowly accumulating pelagic deposits. Not infrequently such skeletal debris forms the nuclei for ferromanganese nodules. These phosphates, while a part of the deposit, can accumulate heavy metals. Bowie and Atkin (1956) report high amounts of thorium and uranium in the skeletal remains of Devonian fish. The thorium occurs principally in the organic matter, while the uranium is concentrated in the apatite structure. Arrhenius *et al.* (1957) have examined material from the late Pleistocene to Recent and have found that it contains not only very high contents of uranium and thorium but also 0.6–1.5 percent of zinc, 0.1–0.5 percent of copper, 0.05–0.15 percent of tin, and 0.03–0.10 percent of lead. The rare earth elements, most of the strontium, and barium were found in the apatite structure, whereas the organic phases contained the zinc, tin, lead, titanium, copper, silver, magnesium, aluminum, chromium, and nickel. There were no significant differences in these elemental abundances between the Recent and Tertiary samples. Analyses of fish bones taken from living organisms did not reveal concentrations of any of the above-cited metals.

### Geochronologies

The determinations of the times of formation of sedimentary components by radioactive techniques have extended tremendously our knowledge of phenomena in the marine milieu. Radioactive clocks potentially cover the entire span of geologic time, and their applications will certainly increase in the coming years. Radioactive species on the earth's surface can be classified into three genetic groups: (1) those radioactive elements, or their radioactive daughters, which have half-lives of the order of the age of the earth, $4.5 \times 10^9$ years, and were an original part of our planet; (2) those species produced by the interaction of cosmic rays with atmospheric gases; and (3) the artificial radioactivities resulting from nuclear bomb detonations or nuclear reactors. The last group has not been used to any extent in marine geological studies.

Radioactive dating techniques have utilized both minerals separated from the deposits and isolates of the elements involved in the radioactive decay scheme from bulk samples. Certain requirements are common to all methods. First, there can be no gain or loss of the elements involved in the technique from the minerals or bulk sample subsequent to the time of formation of the solid phases. The time of formation of the solid phases must be short in comparison to the age of the sample. Finally, the modes of formation of the mineral or of the phases of the bulk sample should be known. For example, feldspars in a sedimentary deposit may have been derived from the continents, volcanic activity, or authigenic growth. Thus, the three groups of feldspars were most probably formed at different times. A geo-chronological technique using these feldspars would give a composite age, not the age of deposition.

**Carbon-14.** Radiocarbon, carbon-14, is produced by the reaction of cosmic ray neutrons with nitrogen gas in the upper atmosphere. Subsequent to its production, the radiocarbon is combusted in the atmosphere to form carbon dioxide. The half-life of carbon-14 is 5570 years, and a dating interval from the present to between 30,000 and 50,000 years can be covered.

The technique can be applied to calcium carbonates, organic carbon phases, and possibly to the structural carbonate in phosphorites. In age determinations in sediments from the southern California basin deposits, Emery (1960) obtained organic carbon and carbonate (primarily in the form of foraminiferal tests) ages and found the latter were 25 percent higher on the average. He attributed these differences to the erosion of old calcium carbonate from the shallow water areas and redeposition of it on the basin floors. Since the introduction of reworked organic carbon to the sediments was trivial in amount, age determinations using organic carbon appeared to be far less subject to error in these environments.

A second problem involves the zero age, i.e., the carbon-14 activity at the surface level of the deposit site. Emery (1960) found the extrapolated organic carbon ages of surface sediments from six basin deposits to have apparent ages between 1800 and 4200 years with respect to atmospheric carbon-14 measurements. These anomalous values arise from several phenomena. Surface waters from different parts of the world have "apparent ages," usually of the order of hundreds of years (Broecker et al., 1960) based on carbon-14 assays. Broecker et al. interpret such values on the basis of a steady state circulation model in which surface waters from a given oceanic water mass, defined as the waters above the thermocline, mix with deep waters from the same water mass and with adjacent surface waters. Such mixing processes result in surface waters having an apparent positive age. Further, fractionation of carbon isotopes can occur during photosynthesis, respiration, and the metabolic processes of animals and bacteria. Emery notes that a carbon-14 age from living benthos, mostly worms and echinoids, was 1670 ± 150 years. Since we are unaware of all the fractionations in the $C^{14}/C^{12}$ ratio that take place going from oceanic carbon dioxide to the shells of Foraminifera, or organic phases, the most expeditious way of obtaining ages of various levels in a marine deposit is to ascertain the lapsed times between the surface and the deeper strata by using the change in specific activity of the carbon isotopes.

One of the significant results from carbon-14 measurements in sedimentary deposits is the observation of nonuniformity in deposition rate. Initial work with the technique (Arrhenius et al., 1951) assumed a constant rate of accumulation of clay on the deep sea floor. However, extensive measurements of Broecker et al. (1958) in the mid-equatorial Atlantic indicated that deposition rates of both the clay and carbonate fractions decreased markedly approximately 11,000 years ago. The glacial to postglacial ratio of sedimentation rates was 3.7 for the clay fraction and 2.1 for the carbonates. Emery (1960) found uniform deposition rates in the Santa Barbara Basin to depths of about 3 m in the sediments with slower deposition rates for the older materials.

**Beryllium-10 and Silicon-32.**   Two other cosmic-ray produced isotopes appear promising for recording ages in the marine domain, beryllium-10 and silicon-32. Beryllium-10 is produced in the upper atmosphere by the cosmic-ray fragmentation of nitrogen and has a half-life of 2.7 years. Its discovery in nature was initially made in pelagic deposits from the Pacific (Arnold, 1956; Goel et al., 1957). Beryllium-10 comes to the land and the oceans in atmospheric precipitation but is so heavily diluted in the relatively large amounts of stable beryllium contained in continental surfaces that its detection there is extremely difficult. On the other hand, in the oceans the extremely low concentration of beryllium ($6 \times 10^{-4}$ parts per billion by weight in seawater) permits the specific activity of beryllium-10 to attain reasonably high values.

Preliminary results on the depth distribution of beryllium-10 in deep-sea cores emphasize the potentialities of the isotope (Merrill et al., 1960). In a near-equatorial eastern Pacific deposit an abrupt change in the beryllium-10 coincided with a discontinuity in the ionium-thorium values (see below) which should have decreased exponentially with depth in the sediment if uniform accumulation had taken place. These data also suggest that vertical migration of beryllium in sediments is unimportant. Several other cores gave uniform depth distributions of beryllium-10, which were attributed to homogenizing disturbances occurring during deposition.

Silicon-32 is formed through the interaction of cosmic rays with atmospheric argon and has a half-life of roughly 710 years. Like beryllium-10 it is brought to the earth's surface in rains and is most readily detected in seawater where its specific activity can rise to values that are readily detectable by modern low-level radioactivity counting instruments. On land surfaces the silicon-32 is so diluted by exchange and other chemical interactions with the exposed crustal materials that detection of the isotope would be extremely difficult. Silicon-32 was first discovered in nature in the spicules from siliceous sponges which had derived their silicon from surface seawater (Lal *et al.*, 1960). Although the isotope has not been utilized as yet in geochronological problems, the measurement of rates of rapidly accumulating sediments containing large amounts of hydrogenous or biogenous siliceous phases seems possible.

**Uranium and Thorium Decay Series.** The three naturally occurring radioactive families of uranium and thorium are characterized in seawater by a lack of radioactive equilibrium within them. Series members go from solution in seawater to the sedimentary components by different chemical paths, and this state of affairs has provided a rewarding entry into geochronological studies. The parts of the three series investigated are:

$$U^{238} \xrightarrow[4.5 \times 10^9 \text{ yr}]{} Th^{234} \xrightarrow[24.1 \text{ d}]{} Pa^{234} \xrightarrow[6.7 \text{ hr}]{} U^{234} \xrightarrow[2.5 \times 10^5 \text{ yr}]{}$$

$$Th^{230} \xrightarrow[8.0 \times 10^4 \text{ yr}]{} Ra^{226} \xrightarrow[1600 \text{ yr}]{} Rn^{222}$$

$$U^{235} \xrightarrow[7.1 \times 10^8 \text{ yr}]{} Th^{231} \xrightarrow[25.6 \text{ hr}]{} Pa^{231} \xrightarrow[3.43 \times 10^4 \text{ yr}]{} Ac^{227}$$

$$Th^{232} \xrightarrow[1.4 \times 10^{10} \text{ yr}]{} Ra^{228} \xrightarrow[6.7 \text{ yr}]{} Ac^{228} \xrightarrow[6.1 \text{ hr}]{} Th^{228} \xrightarrow[1.9 \text{ yr}]{} Ra^{224}$$

The first geochronological technique based upon disequilibrium in these natural series was the ionium/radium method which is based upon the precipitation of thorium-230 (ionium) to the sediments while its long-lived parent uranium-238 remained primarily in solution. Radium grows in from the unsupported ionium to a maximum and then decays with the half-life of its parent ionium of 80,000 years. The method's time span covers about 5 half-lives of ionium or 400,000 years. The initial applications of the technique (Urry and Piggot, 1942) appeared quite successful, but subsequent attempts indicated unreliable or unusable results owing to the migration of radium (Pettersson, 1951; Kröll, 1954; Arrhenius and Goldberg, 1955). A second assumption in the technique, the uniform deposition of ionium with time, is questionable.

In 1954 Picciotto and Wilgain proposed the ionium-thorium method, which was free of the assumption of a constant and uniform accumulation of ionium and did not involve two elements whose chemical species might behave differently in the sedimentary deposits. The technique is based upon the simultaneous removal of thorium-232 and thorium-230 from seawater. The decrease in the Io/Th ratio with depth in the sediment with an 80,000-year half-life should occur if the following assumptions are met: the Io/Th ratio in the waters overlying the sediment have to remain constant over the time intervals to be measured; the ionium and thorium must be in the same chemical forms in seawater; and the *analyzed* materials from the sediments must not contain significant amounts of either of these isotopes of thorium. The initial applications of the technique indicate the results are compatible with the above assumptions for pelagic sediments (Goldberg and Koide, 1958; Starik *et al.*, 1958; Almodovar, 1960). The work of Starik *et al.* established that the ionium was nearly completely supported by uranium in near-coastal deposits but, in areas distant from the coast, one or two orders of magnitude more unsupported than uranium-supported ionium were found in the Pacific and Indian surface samples.

The rates of accumulation of Pacific pelagic sediments have been extensively measured by the ionium/thorium technique and have values of 0.3–0.5 mm/$10^3$ years in the South Pacific with more varied and higher rates for the North Pacific deposits (Fig. 216).

The application of the method also revealed geographic variations in the value of the surface ratio, reflecting differences in the thorium-232 content of the overlying waters (Table 14). Uranium-238 has a residence time of the order of one-half million years, a time that is long with respect to oceanic mixing processes. Hence, one would expect and one does find a uniform content of uranium in seawater, a value around 3.5 micrograms/liter. Thus, the rate of production of its daughter ionium per unit volume of seawater is constant in all oceans. The ionium input from land is less than one-quarter of this oceanic production and is unimportant in these considerations. Hence, the variability in the surface ratios most probably results from differences in the thorium-232 content of the seawater from which the sediments derived their thorium isotopes.

The values appear reasonable when compared with the relative contributions of land runoff waters to the oceanic areas. Table 15 gives the areas of the oceans and the respective areas of land that are drained into the oceans. The Pacific receives but one-sixth of the amount of drainage waters that enter the Atlantic on an areal basis, which apparently accounts for the lower values of thorium, normalized to ionium, in the Pacific deposits. Similarly, the well-known

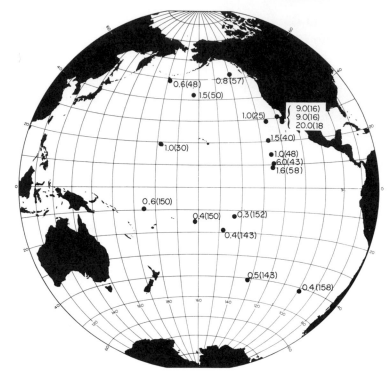

Fig. 216. Rates of deposition of deep-sea sediments in the Pacific Ocean as determined by the ionium/thorium technique. The units are millimeters per 10³ years. The numbers in parentheses are the ionium/thorium ratios at the surface in units of disintegrations per minute of ionium/disintegrations per minute of thorium.

TABLE 14. Surface Values of the Ionium/Thorium Ratios in Sediments in Units of Disintegrations per Minute of Ionium/Disintegrations per Minute of Thorium-232

| Oceanic Area | Io/Th at Surface |
|---|---|
| South Pacific | 143–158 |
| North Pacific | 16–58 |
| North Atlantic | 1.5–6 |
| South Atlantic | 9.4–19 |
| Indian | 20–27 |

observation that more and larger rivers drain into northern hemispheric marine areas is reflected in the higher ionium/thorium ratios in southern Pacific deposits as compared to their northern counterparts.

The uranium-ionium method has been applied successfully to calcium carbonates containing uranium in concentrations of several parts per million or higher. The technique is based upon the uptake of uranium by the crystallizing solid without any simultaneous accumulation of thorium isotopes. The growth of the daughter ionium results in uranium-238/thorium-230 ratios which are a function of the time since crystallization for dating intervals up to about 400,000 years. Barnes *et al.* (1956) clearly saw the build-up of ionium in coral limestones taken from a 200-ft drilling on Elugelab Island and concluded that the uranium/ionium ratios were clearly age indicative.

TABLE 15.   Oceanic Areas and Complementary Land
Areas Draining into Them. Units of Thousands
of Square Kilometers

| Ocean | Area | Land Area Drained | Percentage |
|---|---|---|---|
| Atlantic | 98,000 | 67,000 | 68.5 |
| Indian | 65,500 | 17,000 | 26.0 |
| Antarctic | 32,000 | 14,000 | 44.0 |
| Pacific | 165,000 | 18,000 | 11.0 |

Source: Adapted from John Lyman, Chemical considerations. In *Physical and Chemical Properties of Sea Water.* Natl. Acad. Sci.-Natl. Research Council Publ. No. 600, 1958.

Tatsumoto and Goldberg (1959) extended this technique to inorganic oolite samples (uranium concentrations were between 3 and 4 ppm by weight) and were able to assign ages to several samples. The uranium contents of most biogenous calcium carbonates, between 0.X and 0.0X ppm by weight (Tatsumoto and Goldberg, 1959) are too low for the ready utilization of this technique.

The protoactinium-ionium method has yielded apparently reliable rates of accumulation and absolute ages for strata for a group of pelagic sediments. The two nuclides, thorium-232 and protoactinium-231, are produced by isotopes of the same element, uranium. If these two daughter products are incorporated in the components of sediments without uranium, their ratio should give a unique age inasmuch as the two isotopes have different half-lives. Corrections can be made for any uranium-supported protoactinium and ionium by a measurement of the uranium content. One of the principal assumptions of the method is that the geochemical behaviors of protoactinium and thorium are similar and that there is no preferential uptake of either isotope in the analyzed samples.

The initial applications of the method to two deep-sea cores from the Caribbean (Rosholt *et al.*, 1961) and four deep-sea cores from the Pacific (Sackett, 1960) gave results that were consistent with age measurements by the carbon-14 technique.

**Potassium-Argon.**   Potassium-40 (a minor isotope of potassium) decays to argon-40, the principal isotope of argon (99.6 percent of atmospheric argon) and calcium-40. The 12.6-billion-year half-life of the potassium, coupled with the experimental work that allows ages of one million years or less to be determined, has made this technique extremely valuable for geological age determinations. It has been applied with considerable success to certain igneous minerals and to the sedimentary minerals sylvite and glauconite (Lipson, 1958; see also Curtis and Reynolds, 1958). The method requires a modest potassium content in the minerals.

The technique has been ingeniously applied to bulk samples and to clay isolates of deep-sea sediments of the Atlantic and Pacific by Hurley *et al.* (1960). Surface sediments gave ages of multimillions of years, indicating a continental origin for at least a part of the gross deposit. These ages are of course minimal for the nonauthigenic phases and are most probably averages. Nonetheless, these observations coincide with those of Rex and Goldberg (1958), Griffin and Goldberg (1963), and Peterson and Goldberg (1962) that at least for the North Pacific sediments, the illites, quartz, and feldspars, are land-derived.

**Rubidium-Strontium.** Rubidium-87 is naturally radioactive, constituting 27.85 percent of natural rubidium. It decays to stable strontium-87 with a half-life of 47 billion years. The method is quite often applicable to minerals datable by potassium-argon inasmuch as potassium-rich minerals are those that are liable to have high rubidium contents. Ages derived on this scheme have dated glauconites (Hurley *et al.*, 1958a,b). Where simultaneous potassium-argon measurements were made, it appears that the strontium-rubidium results are not nearly as consistent and have larger errors.

# CHAPTER XVII

# MODERN SEDIMENTS AND THE INTERPRETATION OF ANCIENT SEDIMENTS

## Introduction

For more than a century geologists have known that many, perhaps most, of the sedimentary rocks found on the continents were deposited in ancient seas. The marine origin of most petroleum has also been long recognized. Despite this knowledge it is only in recent years that marine research has begun to investigate the ecology of present-day marine environments as a means of interpreting the origin of sedimentary rocks. Most of the earlier studies in marine geology emphasized the deep-sea deposits that were and still are of great interest but have little bearing on sedimentary rocks because it is doubtful if any of these rocks were deposited in former ocean basins.[1] The first investigations of shelf sediments were also given little attention by stratigraphers because such a large part of the areas from which samples were obtained appeared to lack modern sediments. At first it did not occur to us that the coarse sediments of the outer shelves could represent a transgressive deposit related to the rise of sea level accompanying the last deglaciation. These sediments as a representative of the transgressive facies of ancient sediments assume a far more important role.

Since about 1950 a real impetus to the study of modern sediments as a guide in stratigraphic studies has resulted from the projects supported by petroleum geology. To date the largest of these has been the American Petroleum Institute Project 51 initiated in 1950 for the study of shallow Gulf of Mexico sediments and still continuing as a study of the sediments of the Gulf of California. Results of the first part have been largely published (summarized in Shepard *et al.*, 1960). During the same period the studies by K. O. Emery and

[1] Narrow basins and troughs of intermediate depth are excepted.

his associates of the relatively deep basins off southern California (summarized in Emery, 1960) have provided much helpful information from another important environment. Studying the structures of various shallow-water and coastal deposits has yielded valuable results (van Straaten, 1954, 1959b). Extensive studies have been made of the sediments around the Orinoco Delta (van Andel and Postma, 1954; Nota, 1958). Also the growing appreciation of the importance of turbidity current deposits in ancient sediments has come from the extensive investigations of Kuenen (1950, 1952, 1953b, and 1957), Crowell (1955), Carozzi (1957), and Ten Haaf (1959), and from the modern sediment collections obtained by Lamont Geological Observatory (Ericson *et al.*, 1955; Ewing *et al.*, 1958; Ericson *et al.*, 1961). The interpretation of coral reefs and other calcareous sediments has been considerably assisted by the studies of recent reefs by Ladd *et al.* (1950), Newell (1956), Emery *et al.* (1954), Cloud (1952), and McKee (1958). The two volumes on *Marine Ecology and Paleoecology* (Hedgpeth, 1957a; Ladd, 1957) contain a wealth of new information that can be used in interpreting ancient sediments. The symposium, *Habitat of Oil* (1958), contains a considerable amount of useful material. European symposia on sedimentation have appeared in *Geologische Rundschau* (1958), *Geologie en Mijnbouw* (1959), and *Eclogae Geologicae Helvetiae* (1959). Finally, *The First National Coastal and Shallow Water Research Conference* was published by the National Science Foundation (Gorsline, 1962).

In the preceding chapters descriptions of modern sediments in the various environments have been given. Here an attempt will be made to show the type of marine environments which appear to have existed during the deposition of various sedimentary rocks.

### Sandstones

Sands are the most common type of sediment on the continental shelves, but in their rock form they are clearly subordinate to shales and mudstones. The reason for this discrepancy is in part because so many of the ancient sediments were probably deposited in more enclosed and hence protected seas rather than on a typical present-day continental shelf and in part because most of the sands of the continental shelves appear to be transgressive and hence related to the relatively recent rise of the sea level. As a result the shelf is not yet in equilibrium. Several types of marine and marginal marine sandstones appear to have rather clear equivalents in present-day marine seashore deposits. These include sheet sands, shoestring sands, and sand lenses in deep water shales.

**Sheet Sands.**   Marine geologists have been mystified by the enormous extent of some of the ancient marine sands as, for example, the marine facies of the St.Peter or the Roraima of the Guianas. It seemed peculiar that sands could be carried so far out from the shore into ancient seas whereas the present waves seem capable of transporting the sands only for a few miles out from the coast. The explanation may be that slowly transgressing seas at various times during the past have reworked old alluvial sands into marine formations as the shoreline advanced. Similar widespread shelf sands have become reworked as the result of the melting of the last great glaciers. For example, the 100- to 200-mile wide strips of sand extending along much of the eastern Asiatic shelf (Shepard *et al.*, 1949) and off portions of the east coast of North and South America must be the relict deposits of the sea level rise. Some of these shelf sands are known to contain marine fossils, even several feet below their surface (Shepard, 1959a). Although these sands may grade downward into true continental deposits, there can be little doubt but that sandstone with this origin would be interpreted by geologists as marine because most of the fossils would be marine. In gently sloping areas with a gradually subsiding basin a series of transgressions and regressions should produce an equal number of transgressive and possibly also regressive sandstones of great lateral width.

Tides are a cause of another widespread sand formation both in tidal flats and on the present sea floor. Tidal flats may be very extensive. Thus the sea comes in across seven miles of flats at the Bay of Mont-St.-Michel on the west coast of France. Almost all the sediment in these flats is sand although it becomes high in calcareous content at the upper end of the bay (Bourcart and Boillot, 1959). The flats are extensively ripple-marked and are cut by numerous tidal channels. At Cholla Bay in Sonora on the Gulf of California another broad tidal flat is found. This is also covered with ripple-marked sand (McKee, 1957) and cut by many channels. Channels in such flats are likely to be filled with fine sediments. The ripples characteristic of the flats are current ripples with long parallel crests, whereas the ripples in the channels are more of a cusp type (Fig. 217). Trails are also common on the flats. The sediments of the southern end of the North Sea consist largely of sand (van Veen, 1936; Stocks, 1956). These deposits differ from the relict sands off the Asiatic coast in having a very irregular surface (Fig. 218). If turned into rock, the extensive longitudinal sand bars should contain well-developed cross-bedding, possibly resembling portions of the Tapeats sandstone of Arizona (McKee, 1940). Ripple marks should also be abundant. In general, sorting should be good since the currents prevent deposition of fine material

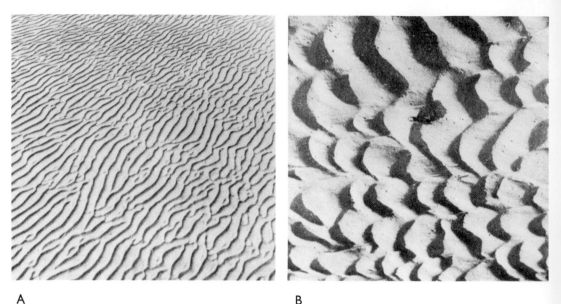

A                                                          B

Fig. 217. The two types of ripple marks in the tidal flats exposed at low tide at Cholla Bay along the northeast side of the Gulf of California. (*a*) represents ripples found on the exposed flats, and (*b*) ripples characteristic of the channels. Knife gives scale. From McKee (1957).

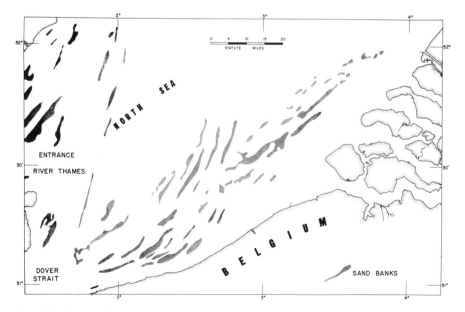

Fig. 218. Showing the elongate irregular sand banks which characterize the floor of the south end of the North Sea.

except perhaps in local depressions. A similar area occurs to the south of Cape Cod where the sands washed out from the retreating cliffs of Cape Cod have moved south to form the constantly shifting Nantucket Shoals. Farther east on Georges Bank another widespread sand area is found. At least the shoaler portions are coarse sands including some gravel and showing a remarkable degree of sorting and of grain rounding.

These tidally distributed sands are relatively free of marine organisms owing to the violent movement produced by the currents and waves operating over the shoals. Hence, the deposits of both of these areas might be difficult to recognize as marine in origin. In tropical areas, however, mollusk shell fragments are very common in sand bars and make it far easier to identify the environment of deposition in the ancient equivalents.

**Shoestring Sands.**    Oil operations have led to the recognition of a considerable number of elongate lenses of sandstone, called shoestring sands, that are found lying between masses of shale. In some places these have been traced for tens of miles as described by Bass (1934). The origin of some of the shoestring sands is a matter of discussion, some geologists favoring coastal sand barriers and, hence, a marginal marine origin, and others favoring river channels and, hence, fluvial subaerial origin. The investigation of the barriers along the Texas coast (Shepard, 1960b) has helped establish criteria for recognizing the former, and many studies have been made of river channel sands, notably by Fisk (1944, 1952) and Nanz (1954).

In ground plan, barriers are quite distinct from river channel deposits. Most of the former have a straight or smoothly curving front toward the ocean or other body of water and a lobate undulating face toward the lagoon on the inside, whereas the channels are likely to have roughly parallel margins with considerable sinuosity on both sides. In cross section (Fig. 219) the barriers could be expected to show the rather even bedding and lamination of the beach on the outside with the complex concave downward cross-bedding in the adjacent dunes, the horizontal bedding of the barrier flats, and perhaps a shell beach with brackish water shells at the inner margin. The stream channels should also have cross-bedding but of a more even type dipping downstream, and the bedding on the sides of the channel ordinarily dips toward the center of the channel and has many convolutions due to slumping from the sides. There should be no progressive change from one side to the other, but many alternations in grain size.

The barrier and stream channel sediments differ considerably in size and sorting. The barrier has well-sorted sand on the seaward

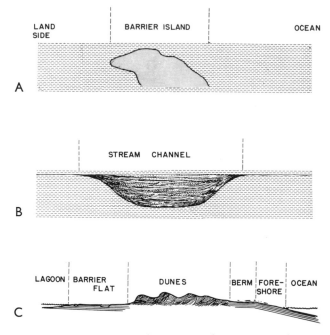

Fig. 219. Illustrating the contrast between typical cross sections of (a) barrier islands, (b) stream channels, and (c) the internal structures of a barrier island and adjacent areas.

beach and in the bordering dunes but rather muddy sand in the barrier flats on the lagoon side, whereas the stream channel has little well-sorted sediment and ordinarily displays many zones of muddy sediment along with lenses of sand and gravel. In a bird-foot delta, like the Mississippi, the only clean sand near the river mouths is found in the channel bars and in the reworked barriers (Shepard, 1956; Scruton, 1960; Lankford and Shepard, 1960). Up the Mississippi Valley the poor sorting extends across most of the valley fill because of the migration of the channels from side to side. Many barrier flat deposits have sand grains coated with calcium carbonate due to evaporation between the infrequent periods of overwash. Such coatings, however, may occur also in flood plains especially in arid areas. The sediment in barriers is likely to contain more shells than stream deposits, and the shells ordinarily decrease away from the oceanside, but may again increase near the lagoon shore usually showing a change from marine to brackish water types (Parker, 1960). The barrier sands are likely to show an increase in roundness and heavy minerals, and a decrease in mica in passing from the beach to the dune facies (Shepard and Young, 1961).

If it is possible to obtain oriented samples from the shoestring sand body, the preferred orientation of the elongate sand grains will be principally transverse to elongation, especially in the shoreface of the barrier sands (Curray, 1956) and roughly parallel in the river channels (Nanz, 1954).

Where it is possible to investigate the shale bodies on the two sides of the shoestring sand, differentiation between barrier sands and channel sands may be made because the lagoonal shales on the one side and the open marine shales on the other will ordinarily have a contrasting fauna whereas the same faunas are likely to be found in the shales on the two sides of a river channel.

**Deep Water Sands.**    Among ancient sediments, especially in geo-synclinal facies, there is a considerable number of layers or lenses of sandstone, many of them coarse-grained and even conglomeratic, found between thick masses of shale that have every indication of deposition in deep quiet water. Natland (1933) first pointed out that some of these ancient sediments contain deep water Foraminifera. At first considerable debate arose over the deep water origin of the Foraminifera because of the interbedded coarse sediments. It was not until turbidity currents and their sand-bearing capacity were estab-lished by Kuenen (Kuenen and Migliorini, 1950) that the anomaly was adequately explained. Now few people doubt that the sands were introduced by turbidity currents coming down valleys on the sides of old basins just as they move down into the deep California basins of the present day. Sands or other sediments of this origin are generally referred to as *turbidites*.

The recognition of turbidites is not always easy. A helpful criterion is the presence of graded beds which are commonly produced by turbidity currents (Fig. 196). This grading, however, is not always present, and the sand beds may show several gradations from coarse to fine in the width of an individual layer. Gradation is said to be formed in other types of marine deposits as the result of wave stirring (see for example Kingma, 1958, 1960), but has not been described from modern shelf deposits so far as the writer is aware.[2] Occasionally the upper portion of the turbidite layers is laminated, but this is not necesssarily indicative of turbidity currents. Mica is also abundant in the upper layers of the deep water sands (Shepard and Einsele, 1962).

The faunas of the turbidite sands may show a mixture of shallow and deep water forms, the shallow-water types having been trans-ported from the shelf margin or from a submarine canyon head, and the deep water forms having been picked up along the way. Many of

[2] Sands seen recently in Lamont cores from the shelf off Patagonia appear to form an exception.

the sands are virtually free of Foraminifera or other organisms such as echinoids, apparently because the currents tend to leave behind the light material that rises to the top of the flow and escapes into the overlying water mass. The finding of exclusively deep water Foraminifera in the intervening shales is perhaps the best means of recognizing Tertiary or younger turbidites.

A curious characteristic of sand turbidites of the present day is their rather high content of land vegetation. It is rather hard to understand how these plants get carried along with the flows, but they are definitely found even in the deep ocean off the Amazon and in the deep Caribbean off the Magdalena River. These were seen by the writer in microscopic examination of the coarse fraction of *Albatross* and *Vema* cores. Scattered plants are evidently introduced by sinking of waterlogged vegetation. Therefore, abundant plant fossils, generally considered as a criterion of nonmarine deposits, may be found in deep water marine environments.

It is not definitely known that present-day turbidites contain either cross-bedding or ripple marks,[3] but the Pliocene deposits of the Ventura, California, area, which otherwise closely resemble the deep-sea sands of the present-day California basins, have both of these sedimentary structures well developed (Natland and Kuenen, 1951). There is little reason to doubt that turbidity currents can produce such features, but the sand layers in cores are often so much disturbed and have such a narrow width that neither structure is likely to be recognized (see also p. 406).

The importance of turbidite sands as source beds of petroleum has been emphasized by Ericson *et al.*, (1961, p. 259). Their rapid deposition prevents mud feeders from devouring the organic material that is brought down abundantly by turbidity currents. Also the well-sorted sands should be ideal for reservoir rocks.

### Shales or Mudstones

Shales, also called mudstones, siltstones, or claystones depending on their composition, are the most common variety of sedimentary rocks despite the preponderance of sands over muds on the shallow sea floor of the present day. This may indicate either that the predominant seas of the past were more protected than those of the present, or it may indicate that many of the shales are the equivalent of the present intermediate depth deposits. The postglacial sea level rise may also explain the low mud content of the shelf sediments since the drowning of river valleys traps much of the mud in the resulting

---

[3] Both have been found recently in box cores.

estuaries and leaves relict sand on the shelves outside. On the other hand, the melting of the present-day Antarctic and Greenland ice caps, with a sea level rise of about 200 ft, would produce many large inland seas in all great lowland valleys in which mud should be the predominant sediment.

**Muds Deposited on the Shelf.**   There are extensive areas of mud, mostly silty clay according to available analyses, on the present shelves off large rivers. The broad mud zones on the inner shelves off eastern Asia and the mud zones east of the Mississippi Delta and the even greater extent of mud on the outer shelf west of the Mississippi Delta are examples. Some of the ancient shelf muds off the Gulf Coast of the United States have been buried and are now included as shales in the stratigraphic column (Lowman, 1949). The present-day shelf muds have little in the way of stratification due evidently to the activities of mud-churning benthic organisms, and in some places the muds contain rather discontinuous lenses of sandy sediments, the latter becoming more common near the shore. Another difference between the inner and outer shelf muds is the greater quantity of planktonic Foraminifera found in the latter. It seems likely that the direction of the shoreline could often be determined by tracing the planktonic to benthonic ratios along a shale outcrop. The shelf muds commonly contain echinoid fragments and glauconite in their sand fractions.

**Lagoonal Muds.**   The extensive lagoonal bays behind barriers that are found along many coasts of the world have a predominance of mud sediments. These muds differ from those of the open shelves in several respects. It is rare that glauconite or echinoids are found in the lagoons, most of the exceptions occurring where strong currents sweep sediments from the shelf in through the inlets.[4] Fecal pellets appear to be more common in lagoonal than in shelf deposits. Stratification is rare in the lagoons of humid areas (Shepard and Moore, 1955) but may be found more commonly in the lagoons of semiarid areas (Rusnak, 1960b). This difference may be due to the development of an algal coating on the sediments of very shallow lagoons of high salinity in the more arid regions. This coating causes a stagnation (lack of oxygen) in the underlying sediments so that burrowing organisms do not disturb the bedding. The semiarid lagoons are also likely to have sand grains coated with calcium carbonate or even may have oolites (Rusnak, 1960a). Gypsum deposits are also found in the semiarid lagoons or salt beds in areas of extreme aridity. The effect of the dry climate is less marked in the sediments if the barriers have large open passes.

---

[4] Echinoids live in enclosed bays where the salinity is close to that of the ocean (J. W. Durham, personal communication).

Most present-day lagoons inside barriers are elongate but relatively narrow, rarely more than a few miles across. It is likely that many ancient lagoonal deposits like those of the present day are elongated in a direction parallel to the ancient shoreline. However, transgression and regression may have given the older lagoonal deposits more width.

Oysters grow in the open ocean but they are much more common in the brackish water of bays with narrow inlets and a good supply of river water. Oyster reefs characterize many lagoons of the more humid climates. In ancient deposits these reefs might be observed cutting across the bay shales forming a type of bioherm. The thickness of oyster reefs along the Texas coast commonly reaches 10 m or more so that the reefs in old sediments may have considerable thickness.

The faunas of barred bays differ from those of the open shelf in having much less speciation, with only a few forms dominating. This is the result of the rather extreme changes in salinity and temperature which take place in most barred bays in temperate climates.[5] These contrasts inhibit the growth of all but a few euryhaline and eurythermal organisms which can stand the extremes. Echinoids are common in most shelf muds unlike the bay muds. The species of the various organisms which survive the extreme conditions have little competition and may grow very abundant so that the fossils in lagoonal deposits though containing few species may be more common than in shelf deposits. In the deposits of some humid bays the coarse fraction may be largely benthonic Foraminifera principally of two or three species (Phleger, 1960b). This situation appears to be rare in any environment other than a lagoon.

**Tidal Estuary Muds.** Where powerful tidal currents move up and down an estuary, the sediments are usually sand, particularly in the channels, but the tidal flats between channels commonly have sediments consisting of poorly sorted, rather sandy muds becoming finer with distance from the channels (Emery *et al.*, 1957, p. 730; van Straaten and Kuenen, 1957). Near the mouths of estuaries where strong tidal currents are common, little mud is deposited. The net upstream flow of the bottom waters of estuaries may keep the finer sediment in the channels.

Estuarine sediments are said to have low pH values and low oxygen content (Emery *et al.*, 1957). Such conditions may lead to the solution of shells so that ancient estuarine deposits may be unfossiliferous and low in calcium carbonate content. On the other hand, the bay deposits may be high in calcium carbonate if the contributing rivers are introducing abundant particulate calcium carbonate (Shepard and Moore,

---

[5] The temperature changes are, of course, much smaller in tropical bays.

1955, p. 1519) or if oyster reefs give large contributions to the total sediment.

**Delta Front Muds.** Rivers deposit their muds on their flood plains and at their mouths around the periphery of the delta except where the currents are strong enough to bypass all this fine sediment. If deposited at some distance from the river mouth, the sediment may be sufficiently diluted from other sources so that it is no longer recognizable as having a deltaic source. The flood plain deposits, being nonmarine, will not be discussed here except to say that they can often be differentiated from the marine deltaic series by their mud cracks due to desiccation and by their red or brown color due to oxidation.

Where the deltas of lowland rivers are building into seas with small tides and small waves, extensive mud deposits form along the periphery. The shallow platform that borders the subaerial portion of a delta like the Mississippi (Shepard, 1956) or the Orinoco (van Andel and Postma, 1954; Nota, 1958) has a mixture of mud and sand although in most places the mud (largely silt) predominates. In this environment and in the interdistributary bays such as those of the Mississippi bird-foot delta, the sediments are largely laminated and for the most part the laminae consist of relatively thick mud layers alternating with thinner layers of coarse silt or fine sand. This lamination is typical of many other marine delta topset beds. The lamination and interbedding of the sandy layers greatly decrease below the top of the foreset slopes, and the lower slopes are covered mostly with unstratified muds. No doubt, in older consolidated formations, however, the unlaminated muds develop a fissility parallel to the deposition slope. The lack of lamination and the high clay character continue out in the bottomset beds beyond the slope. The deltaic character of these foreset and bottomset beds can often be determined by their high content of wood fibers and of small orange or brown-colored aggregates, the latter having apparently formed in the marshes along the river channel margins. Mica is also unusually high in the deltaic facies as contrasted to shelf deposits formed at a distance from any large river mouth.

The organic remains in the deltaic facies are far lower than in other shelf deposits, although locally ostracods may be fairly abundant. Also productivity is high at a moderate distance from the river mouth (Phleger, 1960a, p. 284; Thomas and Simmons, 1960). As a result the water may contain many organisms although the rapid deposition will ordinarily mean a scarcity of fossils in the formations.

Around a large river mouth the formations are likely to show many alternations between subaerial and marine conditions because of the general subsidence found in many deltas and because of the shift in mouths. The resulting deposits may form a cyclothem type of sequence such as those of the Mississippian and Pennsylvanian periods (Weller, 1930; Wanless, 1950). In the marsh facies, developed between advancing channel deposits, tree growth may form peat deposits and, hence, produce coal beds between layers of shale.

**Deep Basin Muds.** It seems quite likely that geologists have misinterpreted as shallow-water deposits some of the deep geosynclinal basin muds because they were confused by the turbidity current sands which are interbedded with them. The study of the basins off southern California (Emery, 1960, p. 218) shows that the muds are very similar to those of the late Tertiary formations in the Ventura and Los Angeles basins. The muds and the shales are both dark green. The modern marine muds off California are laminated only in the Santa Barbara Basin (Hülsemann and Emery, 1961) where the bottom water has a low oxygen content. The other basins are partly ventilated by a slow circulation. The southern California basins contain a relatively high content of organic matter; locally the values exceed 10 percent by dry weight. The organic content is greatest in the basins that lie at intermediate distances offshore, where it is comparable but somewhat greater than that of the neighboring Tertiary basin deposits. The high content in intermediate basins is due to a high rate of sedimentation near shore masking the organic content and a very low rate in the outer basins allowing the organic content to become oxidized.

**Turbidite Muds.** Although it is relatively easy to recognize the coarser types of deep basin turbidity current deposits, it is more of a problem to identify the fine products except where they are definitely associated with graded sand layers. The problem has been partly solved by the work of Ericson (Ewing *et al.*, 1958). Ericson found that the cores taken from the Sigsbee Deep in the Gulf of Mexico had layers of dark gray silts with few Foraminifera and with burrow mottling only in the upper portions in contrast with the brown "foraminiferal lutite" which was full of mottled zones above and below. These characteristics are explained by the rapid emplacement of the gray silts by turbidity currents in contrast with the slow normal deposition which provided time for the planktonic Foraminifera to sift down from the overlying waters and become an important constituent. The organisms of the benthic fauna do not ordinarily bore into the sediments more than about half a meter so that a thick rapidly deposited turbidite mud would have borings only in its upper portion.

The investigations in Santa Barbara Basin off southern California (Orr *et al.*, 1958; Hülsemann and Emery, 1961) showed similar interbedded gray muds, but here they occur between green muds. The former are identified as turbidites in part by the sudden decrease in the pheophytin content of the individual gray mud layers and by a similar decrease in moisture content, $CO_3$, and nitrogen along with an increase in grain size from about 3 to 7 microns. Here, also, the Foraminifera were largely missing in the turbidite layers.

**Stagnant Basin Muds.** Stagnant basins are well represented among the fiords where they have been studied by Ström (1939) and Woolnough (1937). In some of these basins black mud is accumulating, and this suggests a possible origin for the black Chattanooga shale of Devonian age. The fiords are stagnant because of their high and relatively narrow sills and because of the fresh water from melting glaciers which flows out over the sill and develops a density stratification. As a result there is an exhaustion of the oxygen supply through the decay of organic matter which sinks to the bottom. During some winter periods the water at the bottom of the sill flows in from the open ocean, and because of its cold temperature sinks to the bottom and causes an overturn. This brings the stagnant water to the surface and causes a mass killing of the organisms in the upper layers with a resulting rapid sinking of their carcasses, and thus develops a layer high in organic remains on the bottom. This could account for the concentration of fossils such as the "bone beds" of some black shales. The deposits of the fiord basins are generally laminated because of seasonal changes and the absence of benthic boring organisms.

The deep basins of the Black Sea are also stagnant although some of the deposits are not black in color (Strakhov, 1947; Smirnow, 1958). No overturn takes place in the Black Sea although there is a very slow circulation which brings in small quantities of oxygen to the bottom. Most of the deposits in these stagnant and semistagnant basins show well-developed lamination.

The origin of the Chattanooga shale of the south and middle western United States (discussed extensively by Dunbar and Rogers, 1957, p. 207) raises a problem because of its black color, its lamination, and its usual lack of benthic fossils, all suggesting a relatively deep stagnant basin (Rich, 1951). The formation, however, according to Conant (1953),[6] overlies an angular unconformity, covers an area said never to have been deeply inundated during the Paleozoic, and is covered by limestones of supposed shallow water origin. A partial solution of this enigma may have been provided by Twenhofel (1939), who referred to shallow seas with luxurious growth of seaweeds that would damp out the waves, provide ample organic material, and, if enough fresh water were entering nearby, would cause conditions

[6] See also Conant and Swanson (1961).

inhospitable to benthic life. However, the width of the basin, several hundred miles, and the considerable thickness of the shale, 100 ft on the eastern margin, are rather difficult to explain under this idea. It seems likely, as Dunbar and Rogers have suggested, that no present-day environment is comparable to the conditions existing when the Chattanooga shale was deposited. More study should be made to see if the shallow water origin of the overlying limestone is well authenticated. As indicated previously, shallow water is often invoked on the basis of ripple marks or cross-bedding which we now know can form also under deep water conditions.

Basins where stagnation is less complete but where the oxygen is very low have sediments that contrast with those of better ventilated basins in having laminations. Some of these laminations in the Santa Barbara Basin are believed to represent annual layers with detrital clay deposited in the winter during the rainy season and diatom-rich layers in the spring when there is a high bloom of the siliceous plankton (Hülsemann and Emery, 1961).

### Limestones and Dolomites

Of the carbonate rocks, limestone is the most common and dolomite next in abundance. Limestone has more than 50 percent of carbonate as calcite or aragonite whereas dolomite has more than 50 percent of the carbonate as the mineral dolomite.

It has been widely believed among geologists that these limestones and dolomites were deposited farther from shore than the shales. The study of modern sediments, however, shows that this is not necessarily the case. In fact, in tropical areas calcareous sediments commonly extend in close to the coast and may even include the beach sands (see p. 185). On the other hand, there is little reason to doubt another current idea that marine limestone deposition implies, but does not prove, tropical or at least subtropical conditions. The chief exceptions exist in deep water where calcareous oozes extend well north and south of the tropics. Local estuarine limestone also occurs outside of the tropics in a few bays with high shell concentrations or where older limestones have been reworked.

**Fragmental Limestones.** In tropical areas there are numerous localities where samples of the bottom consist predominantly of broken shells, corals, or other calcified hard parts of organisms. On coastal charts these are often labeled as sand or sand and shells. The cementation of this material will produce a fragmental limestone with numerous fossil clastic shell fragments. Examples of areas where fragmental limestone has been accumulating include the western

Florida shelf (Fig. 107) (Gould and Stewart, 1955), the wide bank off Yucatan, the sea floor off Samoa (Bramlette, 1926), and the outer shelf of the South China Sea and the Sahul Shelf of Australia (van Andel *et al.*, 1962). Extensive zones directly adjacent to coral reefs also consist of fragmental calcareous material (Emery *et al.*, 1954).

As emphasized by Dunbar and Rogers (1957, p. 236) fragmental lime material is carried along the sea bottom by waves and currents very much like sand. Hence, it may develop ripple marks and cross-bedding resembling that of sandstone. In the process of dolomitization, however, fragmental limestone is likely to lose its sedimentary structures owing to recrystallization.

Fragmental limestone is certainly the most common calcareous type now forming on the continental shelves. Similarly, it is said to constitute the most common type among European limestones and quite possibly dominates all other types of limestone among the ancient formations elsewhere.

**Reef Limestones (Bioherms).**   Next to fragmental calcareous sediments in abundance on the present sea floor are reef limestones (described also in Chapter XII). The Australian Great Barrier Reef, extending for 1500 miles along the northeast Australian coast, is the most extensive of the present-day reefs. Coral reefs are favorable for oil concentration because of their cavernous nature. In the great oil fields of Alberta, for example, the oil accumulated in ancient coral reefs (Waring and Layer, 1950).

Ancient reefs can be recognized by their steep margins, their general lack of stratification, and the limestone breccias which border them on what were the sides most exposed to wave action. The El Capitan Reef of Texas, described by King (1948) and Newell *et al.* (1953) constitutes one of the most dramatic examples of an ancient reef (Fig. 220). The reef itself stands up in the towering cliffs of El Capitan, the highest peak in Texas. This is bordered on one side by talus similar to that around many of the modern reefs such as Bikini and Eniwetok. On the other side of the reef there was a shallow lagoonal basin bordering an arid land mass. Gypsum deposits formed here because of the excessive evaporation. The reef itself differs from typical present-day reefs in its high content of sponges. Algae, which are important reef formers today, were equally abundant in the El Capitan Reef.

The Dolomite Mountains of the eastern Alps have massive structureless dolomitic limestone. They are interpreted as ancient reefs with the corals largely recrystallized, although some corals are still preserved (Brinkmann, 1960, p. 76).

**Fine-Grained Limestone and Chalk.**   It was formerly believed that chalk was a deep-sea deposit like *Globigerina* ooze. This was based on the finding of numerous planktonic Foraminifera in the chalk formations. More careful study, however, showed that associated with the Foraminifera in the chalk are many organisms characteristic of shallow water conditions. The chalk beds are also bordered vertically and horizontally by formations which are considered as having formed in shallow seas. Bramlette (1958) found that some chalk

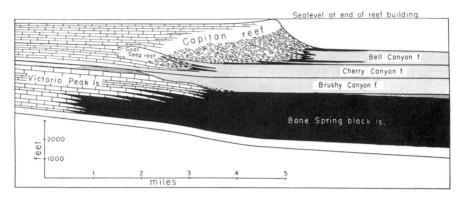

Fig. 220. Diagrammatic cross section of El Capitan Reef in west Texas. Talus deposits border the reef on what was the exposed side (to the right) and lagoonal lime deposits are found on the other side. From King (1948).

formations, such as those of the southeastern United States, have an abundance of coccoliths. The fossil structures of these small calcareous plants are easily destroyed by pressure so that where chalk formations have been metamorphosed into fine-grained limestones the coccoliths have disappeared. In Tunisia a chalk bed can be traced from an unfolded area to a folded area where it has turned into a fine-grained limestone.

Another important source of chalk and fine-grained limestone may be the chemical precipitation of calcium carbonate where currents of relatively cool water rise over shallow tropical banks and the calcium carbonate becomes supersaturated. Lime muds in the Bahamas are an example of such origin (Illing, 1954).

Aragonite needles have been reported from various shallow water carbonate oozes. These needles were thought at first to be inorganic in origin (Vaughan, 1917). However, investigations by Lowenstam and Epstein (1957) showed that the field relations were compatible with an origin of the needles from algal carbonates. Furthermore, needle-secreting algae show isotopic ratios in $O^{18}/O^{16}$ and $C^{13}/C^{12}$ that are in the range of those of algal carbonates and outside those of oolite and grapestone carbonates. Therefore, Lowenstam and Epstein conclude that the aragonite needles are probably of organic origin for the most part.

**Oolitic Limestones.** (See also Chapter XVI, pp. 448–449). The small round grains in limestones (less than 2 mm in diameter) called oolites or ooliths (from the Greek oo, a shortening of *oion* meaning egg) are quite common in limestones. The first studies of the Jurassic revealed so many oolites that in the early part of the last century the name *oolite series* was proposed for the period by the English geologist, William Smith. Later it was appreciated that the oolites were only of local importance so that the name was changed.

There are many modern oolites developing in shallow tropical seas, all having relatively high salinity. The best known oolites are from the Bahamas where they have been described by Vaughan (1916), Black (1933), Illing (1954), Newell (1955), and Newell et al., (1960). Flying over the Bahama banks one can see through the clear water extensive underwater bars called "dunes" or "giant ripples" (Fig. 221). These bars, often hundreds of feet across, are made almost entirely of oolite grains. The trends of these "dunes" are related to the currents. In general, they extend at right angles to the current, although locally where the currents are strong, as through the passages between islands, longitudinal bars are developed. The Bahama oolites are found in areas with very few associated organisms except for echinoids. Probably the bottom is inhospitable to most other organisms because of instability due to the migrating "dunes." On the Bahama Islands elevated oolite deposits are very common and many of these are cross bedded. The uplift of the present underwater "dunes" should reveal an extensively cross-bedded limestone formation.

Oolites are also forming over wide areas in Great Salt Lake (Eardley, 1938, pp. 1359–1387). Locally they occur in supersaline lagoons such as the Laguna Madre of the Texas coast where they appear to be related to evaporation in the very shallow water of the surf zone (Rusnak, 1960a).

The origin of oolites has been much debated. They are interpreted by most geologists as the result of chemical precipitation around various nuclei such as fecal pellets, worn shells, or even quartz grains. Newell et al. (1960) found clear evidence that the oolites south of Bimini were forming in shallow water probably less than 6 feet deep as the result of "cool $CO_2$-rich water [coming] into a shallow heated turbulent zone so rapidly that organic extraction of calcium carbonate does not keep pace with the increase in carbonate saturation due to $CO_2$ loss." The precipitation takes the form of aragonite in most

Fig. 221. Air view of underwater "dunes" on Bahama Banks, northwest of Great Exuma. Courtesy of N. D. Newell.

places. In the past some authors considered that the rounding of the oolites was caused by a snowball effect of rolling (Sorby, 1879), but the oolites are probably more largely due to precipitation (Newell *et al.*, 1960). The ovoid limestone described by Daetwyler and Kidwell (1959) from Batabano Bay in Cuba may be another example of chemical precipitation (see Chapter VIII, p. 221).

**Limestone Turbidite Layers in Deep Water Deposits.** The study of turbidity current deposits has shown a high probability that there should be limestone layers interbedded with the shales of a deep basin or trench, particularly in tropical areas where the lime deposits of the outer shelf and upper slope can have been transported to the basins. In recent sediments many such layers have been described by the Lamont scientists from the Bahamas and West Indies (Ericson *et al.*, 1961), with a notable example in the trench north of Puerto Rico. They are also found in the outer basins off southern California (Emery, 1960). It is quite possible that this type of limestone may have been misinterpreted by stratigraphers because of finding shallow-water fossils in the limestone layers. This would be true particularly if the shales on either side were essentially barren. Examination of the deep water calcareous layers shows little contrast with material obtained in nearby shallow water. Foraminifera, however, often contain some deep water benthonic species mixed with the shallow forms. The limestone is likely to be somewhat graded as to particle size (Kuenen and Ten Haaf, 1956), but so far as known this gradation is not as pronounced as in the terrigenous turbidity current deposits. An examination of several thick calcareous layers in the Lamont Geological Observatory cores revealed a certain degree of grading (Fig. 196).

### Marine Conglomerates and Breccias (Rudites)

It was formerly believed that marine conglomerates and breccias could form only in beaches and near shores outside cliffs. This idea has had to be modified as more and more rudites have been found interbedded with deposits containing deep water organisms or having other indications of deposition at considerable distance from shore. The most complete information on the marine rudites has come from the Alps where they are beautifully preserved in the deep water Flysch (Fig. 222). Here the rudites have both rounded and angular pebbles and angular boulders. Renz and others (1955) refer to submarine landslide blocks in northwest Venezuela up to 1 km in diameter. The huge blocks here were transported as much as 25 km. Blocks ranging in size up to 5 sq km have been found (Ten Haaf,

Fig. 222. Rudites from the Eocene Flysch of the western Alps showing the large boulders that have apparently slid into relatively deep trough deposits. The largest boulder is outlined. Photograph by Auguste Lombard.

1959). However, blocks more than a meter in diameter are rare. The overlying and underlying formations appear quite normal for deep trough deposits. The usual explanation is marine sliding on steep slopes bordering a depositional trough. Parts of these same beds have been attributed to turbidity currents (Kuenen and Carozzi, 1953). The latter interpretation may be applicable where the pebbles are small and where the rudite has graded beds. The formations with huge boulders could scarcely be interpreted as turbidity current deposits, and they are quite clearly of slide origin. The boulder beds are very badly sorted and are otherwise closely similar to landslide deposits on land.

Where there are scattered pebbles in a marine formation, several interpretations are possible. At the present time there are extensive areas where pebbles are found mixed with various types of muds and clays. All these are in areas bordering present or Pleistocene glaciation or off coasts where pack ice comes in to the shore during portions of the year. The pebbles are clearly transported by ice, either icebergs or drift ice. In the absence of active deposition from other sources the pebbles can make up a sufficient percentage of the formation so that it might be called a conglomerate or a breccia. The exotic blocks in marine formations of Permo-carboniferous age would seem to be explicable in this way since there is considerable evidence of glaciation during these periods (Wanless and Shepard, 1936; Wanless, 1960).

Kelp along the California and other coasts is an effective means of transporting cobbles up to a diameter of 40 cm (Emery and Tschudy, 1941). Scattered pebbles in the Pliocene of the Lomita quarry near San Pedro, California, suggest an origin by kelp transportation. The holdfasts (roots) of the kelp at La Jolla, California, are frequently armed with pebbles which are incorporated into the beach and near-shore deposits. To constitute an important item in marine formations other sources of sediment would have to be slight.

Tree-rafted pebbles have been described by many people as a source for erratics in marine formations. Tree rafts coming from tropical rivers often have terrigenous material although mostly smaller sized than pebbles. A tree dislodged by a flood will carry pebbles and even boulders out into the stream, and hence may reach the sea where the rocks can be deposited.

# REFERENCES

Adams, F. D., 1929, The geology of Ceylon. *Canadian Jour. Research*, v. 1, pp. 425–511.

Adams, K. T., 1939, On soundings. *U.S. Naval Inst. Proc.*, v. 65, no. 8, whole No. 438, pp. 1121–1127.

Agassiz, Alexander, 1888, Three cruises of the *Blake*. *Bull. Museum Comp. Zool.*, v. 14, 15.

Agassiz, Alexander, 1892, General sketch of the expedition of the *Albatross* from February to May, 1891. *Bull. Museum Comp. Zool.*, v. 23, p. 11.

Agassiz, Alexander, 1906, General report of the expedition steamer *Albatross* from October, 1904 to March, 1905. *Mem. Museum Comp. Zool.*, v. 33, pp. xiii, 77.

Airy, G. B., 1845, On tide and waves. *Encycl. Metropolitana*, v. 5, pp. 241–396.

Alderman, A. R., 1959, Aspects of carbonate sedimentation. *J. Geol. Soc. Australia*, v. 6, pp. 1–10.

Alderman, A. R., and C. C. von der Borch, 1960, Occurrence of hydromagnesite in sediments in South Australia, *Nature*, v. 188, p. 931.

Alderman, A. R., and H. C. Skinner, 1957, Dolomite sedimentation in the south-east of Australia. *Am. Jour. Sci.*, v. 255, pp. 561–567.

Allen, J. R. L., and J. W. Wells, 1962, Holocene coral banks and subsidence in the Niger Delta. *Jour. Geology*, v. 70, no. 4, pp. 381–397.

Almodovar, Ismael, 1960, Thorium isotopes method for dating marine sediments. Thesis, Carnegie Institute of Technology, Pittsburgh, Pa.

Altschuler, Z. S., R. S. Clarke, and E. J. Young, 1958, Geochemistry of uranium in apatite and phosphorite. *U.S. Geol. Survey Prof. Paper 314D*, 90 pp.

AMSOC, 1961, Experimental drilling in deep water at La Jolla and Guadalupe sites. *National Academy of Sciences—National Research Council*, Washington, D.C., Publ. 914, 183 pp.

Anderson, C. A., J. W. Durham, F. P. Shepard, M. N. Natland, and R. R. Revelle, 1950, 1940 *E. W. Scripps* cruise to Gulf of California. *Geol. Soc. America Mem. 43*.

Andrée, K., 1920, *Geologie des Meeresbodens. Bodenbeschaffenheit, nutzbäre Materialien am Meersboden*, v. 2, Leipzig, 689 pp.

Anonymous, 1946, The Decca system. *Aviation*, November.

Archanguelski, A. D., 1927, On the Black Sea sediments and their importance for the study of sedimentary rocks. *Soc. Naturalistes Moscou Bull.*, Sec. Geol. n.s., v. 35, pp. 276–277.

Arnold, J. R., 1956, Beryllium-10 produced by cosmic rays. *Science*, v. 124, p. 584.

Arrhenius, G., 1950, The Swedish Deep Sea Expedition. The Geological Material and its treatment with special regard to the Eastern Pacific. *Geol. Fören. i Stockholm Förh.*, v. 72, no. 2, pp. 185–191.

Arrhenius, G., 1952, Sediment cores from the East Pacific. *Swedish Deep Sea Expedition Rept. No. 5*, Göteborg.

Arrhenius, G., 1954, Significance of carbonate stratification in pelagic deposits. *Bull. Geol. Soc. America*, v. 65, pp. 1228–1229.

Arrhenius, G., 1961, "Geological record on the ocean floor," in *Oceanography*, Publ. No. 67, pp. 129–148, *American Assocation for the Advancement of Science*, Washington, D.C.

Arrhenius, G., 1963, Pelagic sediments, in *The Sea: Ideas and Observations*, v. 3, Interscience Publishers, New York, pp. 655–727.

Arrhenius, G., M. N. Bramlette, and E. Picciotto, 1957, Localization of radioactive and stable heavy nuclides in ocean sediments. *Nature*, v. 180, pp. 85–86.

Arrhenius, G., and E. D. Goldberg, 1955, Distribution of radioactivity in pelagic clays. *Tellus*, v. 7, pp. 226–231.

Arrhenius, G., G. Kjellberg, and W. F. Libby, 1951, Age determinations of Pacific chalk ooze, *Tellus*, v. 3, pp. 222–229.

Arthur, R. S., 1952, Class notes for a course in ocean waves. *Scripps Inst. Oceanog.*, Oceanog. 211(mimeo).

Bader, R. G., and R. G. Paquette, 1955, A piston coring device for sediment sampling. *Univ. of Washington, Dept. Oceanog., Tech. Rept. No. 41*, 18 pp.

Bagnold, R. A., 1937, The transport of sand by wind. *Geog. Jour.*, v. 89, no. 5, pp. 409–438.

Bagnold, R. A., 1942, *Physics of Blown Sands and Desert Dunes.* Methuen & Co., London, 265 pp.

Bagnold, R. A., 1954, Experiments on a gravity-free dispersion of large solid spheres in a Newtonian fluid under shear, *Proc. Roy. Soc. (London)*, A, v. 225, pp. 49–63.

Bagnold, R. A., 1956, The flow of cohesionless grains in fluids, *Philos. Trans. Roy. Soc. London*, ser. A, v. 249, no. 964, pp. 235–297.

Bagnold, R. A., 1963, Mechanics of marine sedimentation, in *The Sea: Ideas and Observations*, v. 3, Interscience Publishers, New York, pp. 507–528.

Barber, N. F., and F. Ursell, 1948, The generation and propagation of ocean waves and swell. I. Wave periods and velocities. *Philos. Trans. Roy. Soc. London*, ser. A, v. 240, pp. 527–560.

Barnes, J. W., E. J. Lang, and H. A. Potratz, 1956, Ratio of ionium to uranium in coral limestone, *Science*, v. 124, pp. 175–176.

Barth, T. F. W., 1952, *Theoretical Petrology*. John Wiley and Sons, New York.

Bascom, W. N., 1951, The relationship between sand size and beach face slope. *Trans. Am. Geophys. Union*, v. 32, pp. 866–874.

Bass, N. W., 1934, Origin of Bartlesville shoestring sands, Greenwood and Butler Counties, Kansas. *Bull. Am. Assoc. Petrol. Geologists*, v. 18, pp. 1313–1345.

*Beach Erosion Board*, 1941, A study of progress in oscillatory waves in water. *Tech. Rept. No. 1*, Office of Chief of Engineers, U.S. Army.

*Beach Erosion Board*, 1954, Shore protection planning and design. *Tech. Rept. No. 4*, 242 pp. Also 1961, Corrections, revisions, and addenda for Technical Report No. 4.

Beal, M. A., and F. P. Shepard, 1956, A use of roundness to determine depositional environments. *Jour. Sed. Petrology*, v. 26, no. 1, pp. 49–60.

Beckman, J. P., 1954, Foraminiferen der Oceanic Formation, Barbadoes. *Eclogae Geol. Helv.*, v. 46, p. 303.

Beckmann, W. C., A. C. Roberts, and B. Luskin, 1959, Sub bottom depth recorder. *Geophysics*, v. 24, pp. 749–760.

Berthois, Léopold, and R. Brenot, 1960, La morphologie sous-marine du talus du plateau continental entre le sud de l'Irland et Le Cap Ortegal (Espagne). *Jour. du Conseil Permanent Intern. Exploration Mer*, v. XXV, no. 2, pp. 111–114.

Berthois, Léopold, and Yolande Le Calvez, 1959, Deuxième contribution a l'étude de la sédimentation dans le Golfe de Gascogne. *Rev. Trav. Inst. Pêches Marit.*, v. 23, no. 3, pp. 325–377.

Bezrukov, P. L., 1960, Bottom sediments of the Okhotsk Sea. *Repts. Inst. Oceanology*, v. XXXII, Acad. Sci., USSR, pp. 15–95.

Bissett, L. B., 1930, Sediments from Barents Sea and the Arctic. *Trans. Edinburgh Geol. Soc.*, v. 12, p. 207.

Black, Maurice, 1933, The precipitation of calcium carbonate on the Great Bahama Bank. *Geol. Mag.*, No. 832, v. 70, no. 10, pp. 455–466.

Blackmon, P. D., and Ruth Todd, 1959, Mineralogy of some foraminifera as related to their classification and ecology. *Jour. Paleontology*, v. 33, pp. 1–15.

Blanc, J. J., 1954, Sédimentologie sous-marine du Détroit Siculo-Tunisien. *Études sur le seuil Siculo-Tunisien (suite)*, VII, pp. 92–126. *Voir Ann. Inst. Oceanog.*, v. XXXII, p. 233.

Böggild, O. B., 1916, Meeresgrundproben der *Siboga* Expedition. *Siboga-Expeditie Monographie*, v. 65, pp. 1–50.

Bourcart, Jacques, 1950, Le socle continental de Toulon a la frontière Espagnole. *Conf. Centre Recherches et Études Océanog.*, no. 3, 10 pp.

Bourcart, Jacques, 1954a, *Le Fond des Océans*, Presses Université de France, Paris, 108 pp.

Bourcart, Jacques, 1954b, Les vases de la Méditerranée et leur mécanisme de dépôt. *Deep-Sea Research*, v. 1, pp. 126–130.

Bourcart, Jacques, 1959, Morphologie du précontinent des Pyrénées a la Sardaigne. *Colloq. Intern. Centre Natl. Recherche Sci. (Paris)*, v. LXXXIII, pp. 33–50.

Bourcart, Jacques, Alain de la Bernardie, and Claude Lalou, 1948, Le rech Lacaze-Duthiers, canon sous-marine du Plateau Continental du Roussillon *Comptes Rendus Académie des Sciences*, v. 226, pp. 1632–1633.

Bourcart, Jacques, and G. Boillot, 1959, Sedimentation conditions in the Bay of Mont-Saint-Michel, abstract in *Preprints International Oceanographic Congress*, American Association for the Advancement of Science, Washington, D.C., pp. 602–605.

Bourcart, Jacques, Maurice Gennesseaux, and Éloi Klimer, 1960, Écoulements profonds de sables et de galets dans la grande vallée sous-marine de Nice. *Compt. Rend.*, 250, pp. 3761–3765.

Bourcart, Jacques, Francois Ottmann, and Jeanne-Marie Ottmann-Richard, 1958, Premiers résultats de l'étude des carottes de la Baie des Anges, Nice. *Revue de Geographie Physique et de Geologie Dynamique* (2), v. I, pt. 3, pp. 167–173.

Boutan, B., 1900, *La Photographie Sous Marine*. Schleicher Frères, Paris, 332 pp.

Bowden, K., 1955, Some observations of turbulence near the sea bed in a tidal current. *Quart. Jour. Roy. Meteorol. Soc.*, v. 81, pp. 640–641.

Bowden, K., and L. A. Fairbairn, 1956, Measurements of turbulent fluctuations and Reynolds stresses in a tidal current. *Proc. Roy. Society (London)*, A, v. 237, pp. 422–438.

Bowden, K., L. A. Fairbairn, and P. Hughes, 1959, The distribution of shearing stresses in a tidal current. *Geophys. Jour.*, v. 2, pp. 288–305.

Bowie, S., and D. Atkin, 1956, An unusually radioactive fish from Thurso, Scotland. *Nature*, v. 177, p. 487.

Bradley, W. H., *et al.*, 1942, Geology and biology of the North Atlantic deep-sea cores between Newfoundland and Ireland. *U.S. Geol. Survey Prof. Paper 196*, 163 pp.

Bramlette, M. N., 1926, Some marine bottom samples from Pago Pago Harbor, Samoa, *Carnegie Inst. Washington Publ. 344*, pp. 1–35.

Bramlette, M. N., 1958, Significance of coccolithophorids in calcium-carbonate deposition. *Bull. Geol. Soc. America*, v. 69, pp. 121–126.

Bramlette, M. N., and W. H. Bradley, 1942, Lithology and geologic interpretations. pt. 1 in Geology and Biology of North Atlantic Deep-Sea Cores, *U.S. Geol. Survey Prof. Paper 196*, pp. 1–34.

Bramlette, M. N., and W. R. Riedel, 1959, Stratigraphy of deep-sea sediments of the Pacific Ocean, abstract in *Preprints International Oceanographic Congress*, American Association for the Advancement of Science, Washington, D.C., p. 86.

Braun, G., 1913, Über marine sedimente und ihre Benutzung zur Zeitbestimmung. *Meereskunde, Sammlung volkstümlicher Vorträge*, 7 Jahrgang, no. 7, Berlin.

Bretschneider, C. L. and R. O. Reid, 1954, Modification of wave height due to bottom friction, percolation, and refraction. *Beach Erosion Board*, U.S. Corps of Engineers, Tech. Memo. 45, 36 pp.

Bretz, J. H., 1935, Physiographic studies in East Greenland. in *The Fiord*

*Region of East Greenland*, Louise A. Boyd, editor, *Am. Geog. Soc. Spec. Publ. No. 18*, pp. 159–266.

Brinkmann, Roland, 1960, *Geologic Evolution of Europe*. Translated from German by J. E. Sanders. Hafner Publishing Co., New York, 161 pp.

Broecker, W. S., R. Gerard, M. Ewing, and B. C. Heezen, 1960, Natural radiocarbon in the Atlantic Ocean, *Jour. Geophys. Research*, v. 65, pp. 2903–2931.

Broecker, W. S., K. K. Turekian, and B. C. Heezen, 1958, The relation of deep sea sedimentation rates to variations in climate. *Am. Jour. Sci.*, v. 256, pp. 503–517.

Bruun, A. F., Sv. Greve, Hakon Mielche, and R. Spärck, 1956, *Galathea Deep Sea Expedition*. English translation by Sprink, Reginald. George Allen and Unwin, Ltd., London, 296 pp.

Bucher, W. H., 1940, Submarine valleys and related geologic problems of the North Atlantic. *Bull. Geol. Soc. America*, v. 51, pp. 489–512.

Bucher, W. H., 1952, Continental drift versus land bridges. *Bull. Am. Museum Nat. Hist.*, v. 99, pp. 93–103.

Buffington, E. C., A. J. Carsola, and R. S. Dietz, 1950, Oceanographic cruise to the Bering and Chukchi seas, summer 1949, pt. I, Sea floor studies. *Navy Electronics Lab. Rept. No. 204*, 26 pp.

Bullard, E. C., A. E. Maxwell, and R. Revelle, 1956, Heat flow through the deep sea floor, in *Advances in Geophysics*, v. 3. Academic Press, New York, pp. 153–181.

Bullard, E. C., and J. P. Stanley, 1949, The age of the earth, in the publication dedicated to Ilmari Bondsdorff on the occasion of his 70th anniversary. *Veröffentlichungen des Finnischen Geodätischen Institutes* no. 36, pp. 33–40.

Burst, J. F., 1958a, Mineral heterogeneity in "Glauconite pellets." *Am. Mineralogist*, v. 43, pp. 481–497.

Burst, J. F., 1958b, Glauconite pellets: Their mineral nature and applications to stratigraphic interpretations. *Bull. Am. Assoc. Petrol. Geologists*, v. 42, pp. 310–327.

Buser, W., and A. Grütter, 1956, Über die Natur der Manganknollen *Schweiz. Mineral. Petrog. Mitt.*, v. 36, pp. 49–62.

Carey, S. W., 1958, A tectonic approach to continental drift, in *Continental Drift*, a symposium. University of Tasmania, Geol. Dept., pp. 177–355.

Carozzi, Albert, 1957, Tracing turbidity current deposits down the slope of an Alpine basin. *Jour. Sed. Petrology*, v. 27, no. 3, pp. 271–281.

Carrigy, M. A., 1956, Organic sedimentation in Warnbro Sound, Western Australia. *Jour. Sed. Petrology*, v. 26, no. 3, pp. 228–239.

Carrigy, M. A., and R. W. Fairbridge, 1954, Recent sedimentation, physiography and structure of the continental shelves of Western Australia. *Jour. Roy. Soc. W. Australia*, v. XXXVIII, pp. 65–95.

Carsola, A. J., 1954a, Recent marine sediments from Alaskan and Northwest Canadian Arctic. *Bull. Am. Assoc. Petrol. Geologists*, v. 38, no. 7, pp. 1552–1586.

Carsola, A. J., 1954b, Submarine canyons on the Arctic slope. *Jour. Geology*, v. 62, no. 6, pp. 605–610.

Carsola, A. J., 1954c, Microrelief on Arctic Sea Floor. *Bull. Am. Assoc. Petrol. Geologists*, v. 38, no. 7, pp. 1587–1601.

Carsola, A. J., 1954d, Extent of glaciation on the continental shelf in the Beaufort Sea. *Am. Jour. Sci.*, v. 252, pp. 366–371.

Carsola, A. J., and R. S. Dietz, 1952, Submarine geology of two flat-topped northeast Pacific seamounts. *Am. Jour. Sci.*, v. 250, pp. 481–497.

Carsola, A. J., R. L. Fisher, C. J. Shipek, and G. A. Shumway, 1961, Bathymetry of the Beaufort Sea, in *Geology of the Arctic*, First International Symposium on Arctic Geology, University of Toronto Press, Toronto, Canada, pp. 678–689.

Carson, R. L., 1951, *The Sea Around Us*. Oxford University Press, New York, 230 pp.

Caspers, Hubert, 1957, Black Sea and Sea of Azov, in *Treatise on Marine Ecology and Paleoecology*, v. 1, *Ecology. Geol. Soc. America Mem. 67*, pp. 801–889.

Castaing, R., and K. Fredriksson, 1958, Analyses of cosmic spherules with an x-ray microanalyser. *Geochim. et Cosmochim. Acta 14*, pp. 114–117.

Chamberlain, T. K., 1960, Mechanics of mass sediment transport in Scripps Submarine Canyon, California. Ph.D. thesis, University of Calif., Scripps Institution Oceanography, 200 pp.

Chaney, R. W., 1940, Bearing of forests on the theory of continental drift. *Sci. Monthly*, December, pp. 489–499.

Charnock, H., 1959, Tidal friction from currents near the sea bed. *Geophys. Jour.*, v. 2, pp. 215–221.

Chave, K. E., 1954, Aspects of the biogeochemistry of magnesium. I. Calcareous marine organisms. *Jour. Geology*, v. 62, pp. 266–283.

Chow, T. J., and E. D. Goldberg, 1960, On the marine geochemistry of barium. *Geochim. et Cosmochim. Acta*, v. 20, pp. 192–198.

Chow, T. J., and C. C. Patterson, 1959, Lead isotopes in manganese nodules. *Geochim. et Cosmochim. Acta*, v. 17, pp. 21–31.

Chute, N. E., 1946, Shoreline changes along the south shore of Cape Cod caused by the hurricane of September 1944, and the storms of November 30, 1944, and January 1, 1945. *Bull. 9, Massachusetts Dept. of Public Works* in cooperation with the U.S. Geol. Survey.

Cloud, P. E., Jr., 1952, Facies relationships of organic reefs. *Bull. Am. Assoc. Petrol. Geologists*, v. 36, no. 11, pp. 2125–2149.

Cloud, P. E., Jr., 1958, Nature and origin of atolls. *Proc. Eighth Pacific Sci. Congr.*, v. III-A, Oceanography and Zoology (A Progress Report), pp. 1009–1024.

Cloud, P. E., Jr., 1959, Geology of Saipan, Mariana Islands. Pt. 4, Submarine topography and shoal-water ecology. *U.S. Geol. Survey Prof. Paper 280-K*, pp. 361–445.

Colby, B. R., and Hembree, C. H., 1955, Computations of total sediment discharge, Niobrara River near Cody, Nebraska. *U.S. Geol. Survey Water-Supply Paper No. 1357*, 187 pp.

Collinson, D. W., and S. K. Runcorn, 1960, Paleomagnetic observations in the United States; new evidence for polar wandering and continental drift. *Bull. Geol. Soc. America*, v. 71, pp. 915–958.

Conant, L. C., 1953, Shallow-water origin of the Chattanooga shale (abstract). *Bull. Geol. Soc. America*, v. 64, no. 12, pp. 1529–1530.

Conant, L. C., and V. E. Swanson, 1961, Chattanooga shale and related rocks of central Tennessee and nearby areas. *U.S. Geol. Survey Prof. Paper 357*, pp. 1–91.

Cornish, Vaughan, 1934, *Ocean Waves and Kindred Geophysical Phenomena.* Cambridge University Press, Cambridge, England, 164 pp.

Correns, C. W., 1939, Pelagic sediments of the North Atlantic Ocean, in *Recent Marine Sediments.* American Association of Petroleum Geologists, pp. 373–395.

Correns, C. W., *et al.*, 1937, Die sedimente des Aquatorialen Atlantischen Ozeans. *Deutsche Atlant. Exped. Meteor* 1925–1927. *Wiss. Erg.*, v. III, pt. 3, 298 pp.

Cousteau, J. Y., 1958, *Calypso* explores an undersea canyon. *Natl. Geographic Mag.*, v. CXIII, pp. 373–396.

Cousteau, J. Y., and F. Dumas, 1950, *The Silent World.* Harper & Brothers, New York, 266 pp.

Crary, A. P., 1956, Arctic ice island research, in *Advances in Geophysics*, v. 3. Academic Press, New York, pp. 1–41.

Crary, A. P., and Norman Goldstein, 1957, Geophysical studies in the Arctic Ocean. *Deep-Sea Research*, v. 4, pp. 185–201.

Creager, J. S., 1953, Submarine topography of the continental slope of the Bay of Campeche, Oceanographic Survey of the Gulf of Mexico, *Texas Agr. and Mech. Research Foundation Tech. Rept. 10*, pp. 1–23.

Creager, J. S., 1958, A canyon-like feature in the Bay of Campeche. *Deep-Sea Research*, v. 5, pp. 169–172.

Creager, J. S., in press, Bay of Campeche.

Cross, E. R., 1954, *Underwater Photography and Television.* Exposition Press, New York, 258 pp.

Crowell, J. C., 1955, Directional-current structures from the Prealpine flysch, Switzerland. *Bull. Geol. Soc. America*, v. 66, pp. 1351–1384.

Cullies, C. G., 1904, The mineralogical changes observed in the cores of the Funafuti borings, in *The Atoll of Funafuti.* Royal Society of London, pp. 392–420.

Curray, J. R., 1956, The analysis of two-dimensional orientation data. *Jour. Geology*, v. 64, no. 2, pp. 117–131.

Curray, J. R., 1960, Sediments and history of Holocene transgression, continental shelf, northwest Gulf of Mexico, in *Recent Sediments, Northwest Gulf of Mexico*, F. P. Shepard, F. B. Phleger, and Tj. H. van Andel, editors. American Association of Petroleum Geologists, Tulsa, Okla., pp. 221–266.

Curray, J. R., 1961, Late Quaternary sea level; a discussion. *Bull. Geol. Soc. America*, v. 72, pp. 1707–1712.

Curtis, G. H., and J. H. Reynolds, 1958, Notes on the potassium-argon dating of igneous rocks. *Bull. Geol. Soc. America*, v. 69, pp. 151–160.

Daetwyler, C. C., and A. L. Kidwell, 1959, The Gulf of Batabano, a modern carbonate basin. *Fifth World Petroleum Congress*, Sect. 1, Paper 1, 20 pp.

Dahl, E., 1952, Some aspects of the ecology and zonation of the fauna on sandy beaches. *Oikos*, v. 4, pp. 1–27.

Daly, R. A., 1910, Pleistocene glaciation and the coral reef problem. *Am. Jour. Sci.*, ser. 4, v. 30, pp. 297–308.

Daly, R. A., 1915, The glacial-control theory of coral reefs. *Proc. Am. Acad. Arts Sci.*, v. 51, no. 4, pp. 157–251.

Daly, R. A., 1936, Origin of submarine "canyons." *Am. Jour. Sci.*, ser. 5, v. 31, no. 186, pp. 401–420.

Daly, R. A., 1948, Coral reefs—a review. *Am. Jour. Sci.*, v. 246, pp. 193–207.

Dana, J. D., 1885, Origin of coral reefs and islands. *Am. Jour. Sci.*, ser. 3, v. 30, pp. 89–105, 169–191.

Dangeard, L., 1928, *Geologie sous-marine de la Manche*. Blondel La Rougery, Paris.

d'Arrigo, A., 1936, Richerche sul Regime dei Litorali nel Mediterranneo. Richerche sulle Variazioni delle Spiagge Italiane. Consiglio Nazionale delle Richerche.

d'Arrigo, A., 1959, *Premessa Geofisica Alla Ricerca di Sibari*. L'Arte Tipografica, Univ. di Napoli, 192 pp.

Darwin, Charles, 1890, *The Structure and Distribution of Coral Reefs*, Ward, Lock & Co., London, 549 pp.

Darwin, G. H., 1881, On the tidal friction of a planet surrounded by several satellites and on the evolution of the solar system. *Philos. Trans. Roy. Soc. London*, v. 172, pt. II, pp. 491-535.

Davis, W. M., 1928, *The Coral Reef Problem. Am. Geol. Soc. Spec. Publ. No. 9*, 596 pp.

Day, A. A., 1959, The continental margin between Brittany and Ireland. *Deep-Sea Research*, v. 5, no. 4, pp. 249–265.

Day, A. A., and S. Runcorn, 1955, Polar wandering: some geological, dynamical, and paleomagnetic aspects. *Nature*, v. 176, p. 422.

De, S. C., 1955, Contributions to the theory of Stokes' waves. *Proc. Cambridge Phil. Soc.*, v. 51, pp. 713–736.

Deacon, G. E. R., 1958, Ocean waves. *Endeavour*, no. 67, pp. 134–139.

de Beaumont, Elie, 1845, *Leçons de géologie pratique*, Paris, pp. 223–252.

Dietrich, G., 1956, Uberströmung des Island-Faröer-Rückens in Bodennähe nach Beobachtungen mit dem Forschungschiff *Anton Dohrn* 1955/56. *Deut. Hydrograph. Z.* 9, pp. 78–89.

Dietz, R. S., 1952, Geomorphic evolution of continental terrace (Continental shelf and slope). *Bull. Am. Assoc. Petrol. Geologists*, v. 36, no. 9.

Dietz, R. S., 1953, Possible deep-sea turbidity-current channels in the Indian Ocean. *Bull. Geol. Soc. America*, v. 64, pp. 375–378.

Dietz, R. S., 1959, Point d'impact des astéroides comme origine des bassins océaniques: une hypothèse, in *La Topographie et la Géologie des Profondeurs Océaniques*, Centre Natl. Recherche Sci., Paris, pp. 265–275.

Dietz, R. S., 1961, Continent and ocean basin evolution by spreading of the sea floor. *Nature*, v. 190, no. 4779, pp. 854–857.

Dietz, R. S., and H. W. Menard, 1951, Origin of abrupt change in slope at continental shelf margin. *Bull. Am. Assoc. Petrol. Geologists*, v. 35, no. 9, pp. 1994–2016.

Dietz, R. S., and H. W. Menard, 1953, Hawaiian swell, deep, and arch, and subsidence of the Hawaiian Islands. *Jour. Geology*, v. 61, no. 2, pp. 99–113.

Dietz, R. S., and G. A. Shumway, 1959, Arctic basin geomorphology, abstract in *Preprints International Oceanographic Congress.* American Association of the Advancement of Science, Washington, D.C., p. 18.

Dill, R. F., 1958, Investigating the sea floor with diving geologists. *Geotimes*, v. II, no. 8, pp. 6, 7, 15.

Dill, R. F., 1961, Underwater photography. *McGraw-Hill Scientific Encyclopedia*, McGraw-Hill Book Co., New York.

Dill, R. F., 1962, Sedimentary and erosional features of submarine canyon heads, abstract in *Proc. First National Coastal and Shallow Water Research Conference*, D. S. Gorsline, editor. National Science Foundation and Office of Naval Research, p. 531.

Dill, R. F., R. S. Dietz, H. B. Stewart, 1954, Deep-sea channels and delta of the Monterey Submarine Canyon. *Bull. Geol. Soc. America*, v. 65, no. 2, pp. 191–193.

Dill, R. F., and G. A. Shumway, 1954, Geologic use of self-contained diving apparatus. *Bull. Am. Assoc. Petrol. Geologists*, v. 38, no. 1, pp. 148–157.

Dixon, W. J., and F. J. Massey, Jr., 1951, *Introduction to Statistical Analysis*. McGraw-Hill Book Co., New York, 370 pp.

Dobrin, M. B., 1960, *Introduction to Geophysical Prospecting*, 2nd ed. McGraw-Hill Book Co., New York, 446 pp.

Donn, W. L., W. R. Farrand, and Maurice Ewing, 1962, Pleistocene ice volumes and sea-level lowering. *Jour. Geology*, v. 70, no. 2, pp. 206–214.

Dorf, Erling, 1960, Climatic changes of the past and present. *Am. Scientist*, v. 48, no. 3, pp. 341–364.

Drake, C. L., M. Ewing, and G. H. Sutton, 1959, Continental margins and geosynclines: The east coast of North America, north of Cape Hatteras, in *Physics and Chemistry of the Earth*. Pergamon Press, London, v. 3, pp. 110–198.

Duboul-Razavet, C., 1956, Contribution à l'étude géologique et sedimentologie du delta du Rhône. *Mém. Soc. Géol. France*, v. 76, 234 pp.

Dunbar, C. O., and John Rodgers, 1957, *Principles of Stratigraphy*. John Wiley & Sons, New York, 356 pp.

Dunham, J. W., 1951, Refraction and diffraction diagrams. *Proc. 1st Conf. Coastal Engineering, Council on Wave Research*, pp. 33–49.

Durham, J. W., 1959, Palaeoclimates, in *Physics and Chemistry of the Earth*. Pergamon Press, London, v. 3, pp. 1–16.

Eardley, A. J., 1938, Sediments of Great Salt Lake, Utah. *Bull. Am. Assoc. Petrol. Geologists*, v. 22, pp. 1305–1411.

Eckart, Carl, 1952, The propagation waves from deep to shallow water, in *Gravity Waves, Natl. Bur. Standards Circ. 521*, pp. 165–173.

Eckart, Carl, 1953, The generation of wind waves over a water surface. *Jour. Appl. Phys.*, v. 24, pp. 1485–1494.

*Eclogae Geologicae Helvetiae*, 1959, Fifth International Congress of Sedimentology, 1958. v. 51, no. 3, 1172 pp.

Edmondson, C. H., 1928, The ecology of an Hawaiian coral reef. *Bernice P. Bishop Museum Bull.* 45, 64 pp.

Egyed, L., 1956, Determination of changes in the dimensions of the earth from paleogeographical data. *Nature*, v. 178, p. 534.

Ekman, V. W., 1904, On dead water, in *Norwegian North Polar Expedition 1893–1896, Scientific Results*, v. 5, no. 15.

*Electronics*, 1945, The Loran system. November, pp. 94–99; December, pp. 110–115.

Emery, G. R., and D. E. Broussard, 1954, A modified Kullenberg piston corer, *Jour. Sed. Petrology*, v. 24, pp. 207–211.

Emery, K. O., 1944, Beach markings made by sand hoppers. *Jour. Sed. Petrology*, v. 14, pp. 26–28.

Emery, K. O., 1945, Entrapment of air in beach sand. *Jour. Sed. Petrology*, v. 15, pp. 39–49.

Emery, K. O., 1950, A suggested origin of continental slopes and of submarine canyons. *Geol. Mag.*, v. LXXXVII, no. 2, pp. 102–104.

Emery, K. O., 1956, Sediments and water of Persian Gulf. *Bull. Am. Assoc. Petrol. Geologists*, v. 40, no. 10, pp. 2354–2383.

Emery, K. O., 1958a, Shallow submerged marine terraces of Southern California. *Bull. Geol. Soc. America*, v. 69, pp. 39–60.

Emery, K. O., 1958b, Southern California basins, in *Habitat of Oil*. American Association of Petroleum Geologists, Tulsa, Okla., pp. 955–967.

Emery, K. O., 1960, *The Sea off Southern California*, John Wiley & Sons, New York, 366 pp.

Emery, K. O., and Y. K. Bentor, 1960, The continental shelf of Israel. *Israel Geol. Survey Bull.*, no. 26, pt. 2, pp. 25–41.

Emery, K. O., W. S. Butcher, H. R. Gould, F. P. Shepard, 1952, Submarine geology off San Diego, California. *Jour. Geology*, v. 60, no. 6, pp. 511–548.

Emery, K. O., and A. R. Champion, 1948, Underway bottom sampler. *Jour. Sed. Petrology*, v. 18, pp. 30–33.

Emery, K. O., and Doak C. Cox, 1956, Beachrock in the Hawaiian Islands. *Pacific Sci.*, v. X, October, pp. 382–402.

Emery, K. O., and R. S. Dietz, 1941, Gravity coring instrument and mechanics of sediment coring. *Bull. Geol. Soc. America*, v. 52, pp. 1685–1714.

Emery, K. O., D. S. Gorsline, E. Uchupi, and R. D. Terry, 1957, Sediments of three bays of Baja California: Sebastian Viscaino, San Cristobal, and Todos Santos. *Jour. Sed. Petrology*, v. 27, no. 2, pp. 95–115.

Emery, K. O., and F. P. Shepard, 1945, Lithology of the sea floor off southern California. *Bull. Geol. Soc. America*, v. 56, pp. 431–478.

Emery, K. O., R. E. Stevenson, and J. W. Hedgpeth, 1957, Estuaries and lagoons, in *Treatise on Marine Ecology and Paleoecology*, v. 1, *Ecology*, J. W. Hedgpeth, editor. *Geol. Soc. Am. Mem. 67*, pp. 673–749.

Emery, K. O., and R. D. Terry, 1956, A submarine slope of Southern California. *Jour. Geology*, v. 64, no. 3, pp. 271–280.

Emery, K. O., J. I. Tracey, Jr., and H. S. Ladd, 1954, Geology of Bikini and nearby atolls, pt. I, Geology. *U.S. Geol. Survey Prof. Paper 260-A*, 265 pp.

Emery, K. O., and R. H. Tschudy, 1941, Transportation of rock by kelp. *Bull. Geol. Soc. America*, v. 52, no. 6, pp. 855–862.

Emiliani, C., 1954, Temperatures of Pacific bottom waters and polar superficial waters during the Tertiary. *Science*, 119, pp. 853–855.

Emiliani, C., 1955, Pleistocene temperatures. *Jour. Geology*, v. 63, no. 6, pp. 538–578.

Emiliani, C., 1956, On paleotemperatures of Pacific bottom waters. *Science*, v. 123, no. 3194, pp. 460–461.

Emiliani, C., 1957, Temperature and age analysis of deep-sea cores. *Science*, v. 125, pp. 383–387.

Epstein, S., 1959, The variations of the $O^{18}/O^{16}$ ratio in nature and some geologic implications, in *Researches in Geochemistry*, P. H. Abelson, editor. John Wiley & Sons, New York, pp. 217–240.

Epstein, S., R. Buchsbaum, H. A. Lowenstam, and H. C. Urey, 1953, Revised carbonate-water isotopic temperature scale. *Bull. Geol. Soc. America*, v. 64, pp. 1315–1326.

Ericson, D. B., W. S. Broecker, J. L. Kulp, and Goesta Wollin, 1956, Late Pleistocene climates and deep-sea sediments. *Science*, v. 124, no. 3218, pp. 385–389.

Ericson, D. B., Maurice Ewing, and B. C. Heezen, 1952, Turbidity currents and sediments in North Atlantic. *Bull. Am. Assoc. Petrol. Geologists*, v. 36, no. 3, pp. 489–511.

Ericson, D. B., Maurice Ewing, B. C. Heezen, and G. Wollin, 1955, Sediment deposition in the deep Atlantic, in *Crust of the Earth, Geol. Soc. America Spec. Paper 62*, pp. 205–219.

Ericson, D. B., Maurice Ewing, Goesta Wollin, and B. C. Heezen, 1961, Atlantic deep-sea sediment cores, *Bull. Geol. Soc. America*, v. 72, pp. 193–286.

Ericson, D. B., and B. C. Heezen, 1959, Distribution of fine sediment as an indication of deep current direction, abstract in *Preprints International Oceanographic Congress*. American Association for the Advancement of Science, Washington, D.C., p. 454.

Ericson, D. B., and G. Wollin, 1956, Correlation of six cores from the equatorial Atlantic and the Caribbean. *Deep-Sea Research*, v. 3, no. 2, pp. 104–125.

Ericson, D. B., and G. Wollin, 1959, Micropaleontology and lithology of Arctic sediment cores. *Geophys. Research Papers no. 63*, Scientific studies at Fletcher's Ice Island, T-3, 1952–1955. v. I, pp. 50–58.

Ewing, John, J. Antoine, and Maurice Ewing, 1960a, Geophysical measurements in the western Caribbean Sea and the Gulf of Mexico. *Jour. Geophys. Research*, v. 65, pp. 4087–4126.

Ewing, John, and Maurice Ewing, 1959a, Seismic-refraction measurements in the Atlantic Ocean basins, in the Mediterranean Sea, on the

Mid-Atlantic Ridge, and in the Norwegian Sea. *Bull. Geol. Soc. America,* v. 70, pp. 291–318.

Ewing, John, and Maurice Ewing, 1959b, Seismic refraction measurements in the Scotia Sea and South Sandwich Island Arc, abstract in *Preprints International Oceanographic Congress.* American Association for the Advancement of Science, Washington, D.C., p. 22.

Ewing, John, and Maurice Ewing, 1962, Reflection profiling in and around the Puerto Rico Trench, *Jour. Geophys. Res.,* v. 67, no. 12, pp. 2729–2739.

Ewing, John, Maurice Ewing, and C. Fray, 1960b, Buried erosional terrace on the edge of the continental shelf east of New Jersey. *Bull. Geol. Soc. America,* v. 71, p. 1860.

Ewing John, Bernard Luskin, Archie Roberts, and Julius Hirshman, 1960c, Sub-bottom reflection measurements of the continental shelf, Bermuda Banks, West Indies Arc, and in the West Atlantic Basins. *Jour. Geophys. Research,* v. 65, no. 9, pp. 2849–2859.

Ewing, Maurice, and W. L. Donn, 1956, A theory of ice ages, I. *Science,* v. 123, p. 1061.

Ewing, Maurice, and W. L. Donn, 1958, A theory of ice ages, II. *Science,* v. 127, pp. 1159–1162.

Ewing Maurice, and W. L. Donn, 1959, Discussion [of D. A. Livingstone, "Theory of Ice Ages"]. *Science,* v. 129, pp. 464–465.

Ewing, Maurice, D. B. Ericson, and B. C. Heezen, 1958, Sediments and topography of the Gulf of Mexico, in *Habitat of Oil.* American Association of Petroleum Geologists, Tulsa, Okla., pp. 995–1053.

Ewing, Maurice, and B. C. Heezen, 1960, Continuity of Mid-Oceanic Ridge and rift valley in the southwestern Indian Ocean confirmed. *Science,* v. 131, pp. 1677–1678.

Ewing, Maurice, B. C. Heezen, and D. B. Ericson, 1959a, Significance of the Worzel deep sea ash. *Proc. Natl. Acad. Sci. U.S.,* v. 45, no. 3, pp. 355–361.

Ewing, Maurice, Julius Hirshman, and B. C. Heezen, 1959b, Magnetic anomalies of the Mid-Oceanic Rift, abstract in *Preprints International Oceanographic Congress.* American Association for the Advancement of Science, Washington, D.C., p. 24.

Ewing, Maurice, A. C. Vine, and J. L. Worzel, 1946, Photography of the ocean bottom. *Jour. Optical Soc. America,* v. 36, pp. 307–321.

Ewing, Maurice, G. P. Woollard, and A. C. Vine, 1940, Geophysical investigations in emerged and submerged Atlantic coastal plain, pt. IV. *Bull. Geol. Soc. America,* v. 51, pp., 1821–1840.

Ewing, Maurice, J. L. Worzel, N. C. Steenland, and Frank Press, 1950, Geophysical investigations in the emerged and submerged Atlantic coastal plain, pt. V, Woods Hole, New York, and Cape May sections. *Bull. Geol. Soc. America,* v. 61, pp. 877–892.

Fairbridge, R. W., 1950a, Landslide patterns on oceanic volcanoes and atolls. *Geograph. Jour.,* v. CXV, pp. 84–88.

Fairbridge, R. W., 1950b, Recent and Pleistocene coral reefs of Australia. *Jour. Geology,* v. 58, no. 4, pp. 330–401.

Fairbridge, R. W., 1951, The Aroe Islands and the continental shelf north of

Australia. *Scope* (Jour. of Science Union Univ. of W. Australia), v. 1, no. 6, pp. 24–29.

Fairbridge, R. W., 1958, Dating the latest movements of the Quaternary sea level. *Trans. N.Y. Acad. Sci.*, ser. II, v. 20, no. 6, pp. 471–482.

Fairbridge, R. W., 1960, The changing level of the sea. *Sci. American*, v. 202, no. 5, pp. 70–79.

Fairbridge, R. W., 1961, Eustatic changes in sea level, in *Physics and Chemistry of the Earth*. Pergamon Press, v. 4, pp. 99–185.

*Fifth Congrès International de Sédimentologie, 1958*, 1959, Eclogae Geologicae, Helvetiae, v. 51, no. 3, 1172 pp.

Fisher, R. L., 1954, On the sounding of trenches. *Deep-Sea Research*, v. 2, pp. 48–58.

Fisher, R. L., 1955, Cuspate spits of St. Lawrence Island, Alaska. *Jour. Geology*, v. 63, no. 2, pp. 133–142.

Fisher, R. L., editor, 1958, Preliminary report on Downwind. *IGY General Rept. Ser. 2*. IGY World Data Center A, Washington, D.C.

Fisher, R. L., 1961, Middle America Trench: topography and structure. *Bull. Geol. Soc. America*, v. 72, no. 5, pp. 703–720.

Fisher, R. L., A. J. Carsola, and G. Shumway, 1958, Deep-sea bathymetry north of Point Barrow. *Deep-Sea Research*, v. 5, pp. 1–6.

Fisher, R. L., and Richard Mills, 1952, Sediment trap studies of sand movement in La Jolla Bay. Abstract, *Bull. Geol. Soc. Amer.*, v. 63, p. 1328.

Fisher, R. L., and R. M. Norris, 1960, Bathymetry and geology of Sala y Gomez, Southeast Pacific. *Bull. Geol. Soc. America*, v. 71, pp. 497–502.

Fisher, R. L., and R. R. Revelle, 1955, The trenches of the Pacific. *Sci. American*, v. 193, no. 5, pp. 36–41.

Fisk, H. N., 1944, Geological investigation of the alluvial valley of the lower Mississippi River. *Mississippi River Commission*, 78 pp.

Fisk, H. N., 1952, Geological investigation of the Atchafalaya Basin and the problem of Mississippi River diversion. *Mississippi River Commission*, 145 pp.

Fisk, H. N., 1956, Nearsurface sediments of the continental shelf off Louisiana. *Proc. Eighth Texas Conf. on Soil Mechanics and Found. Eng.*, pp. 1–36, University of Texas, Bureau of Engineering Research, Austin, Tex.

Fisk, H. N., 1959, Padre Island and the Laguna Madre flats, coastal south Texas. *2nd Coastal Geography Conf.*, Louisiana State University, Baton Rouge, La., pp. 103–151.

Fleming, R. A., and Roger Revelle, 1939, Physical processes in the ocean. In *Recent Marine Sediments*, P. D. Trask, editor. American Association of Petroleum Geologists, Tulsa, Okla., pp. 48–141.

Flint, R. F., 1957, *Glacial and Pleistocene Geology*. John Wiley & Sons, New York, 553 pp.

Flint, R. F., and Friedrich Brandtner, 1961, Climatic changes since the last interglacial. *Am. Jour. Sci.*, v. 259, pp. 321–328.

Forel, F. A., 1895, Les rides de fond. *Le Leman*, Lausanne, v. 2, pp. 249–274 (translation).

Francis, J. R. D., 1957, *Engineer*, 5 April, p. 159.

Fraser, G. D., J. P. Eaton, and C. K. Wentworth, 1959, The tsunami of March 9, 1957, on the island of Hawaii. *Bull. Seismol. Soc. America*, v. 49, pp. 79–90.

Frye, J. C., and R. W. Raitt, 1961, Sound velocities at the surface of deep-sea sediments. *Jour. Geophys. Research*, v. 66, pp. 589–597.

Frye, J. C., and H. B. Willman, 1961, Continental glaciation in relation to McFarlan's sea-level curves for Louisiana. *Bull. Geol. Soc. America*, v. 72, pp. 991–992.

Gardiner, J. S., 1931, *Coral Reefs and Atolls*. The Macmillan Company, New York, 181 pp.

Garrels, R. M., 1960, *Mineral Equilibria*. Harper & Brothers, New York.

Gaskell, T. F., 1960, *Under the Deep Oceans*. Eyre and Spottiswoode, London, 240 pp.

Gates, Olcott, and William Gibson, 1956, Interpretation of the configuration of the Aleutian Ridge. *Bull. Geol. Soc. America*, v. 67, pp. 127–146.

Gealy, Betty Lee, 1956, Topography of the continental slope in northwest Gulf of Mexico. *Bull. Geol. Soc. America*, v. 66, pp. 203–227.

*Geologie en Mijnbouw*, 1959, Sedimentology of Recent and old sediments, a symposium. NS, no. 7, pp. 185–230.

*Geologische Rundschau*, 1958, Die Heutigen Meere, v. 47, pt. 1, pp. 24–252.

Gibson, William, and Haven Nichols, 1953, Configuration of the Aleutian Ridge Rat Islands—Semisopochnoi I. to west of Buldir I. *Bull. Geol. Soc. America*, v. 64, pp. 1173–1181.

Gierloff-Emden, H. G., 1961, Nehrungen und lagunen. *Petermanns Geographischen Mitteilungen*, Quartalsheft 2, 3, pp. 82–92, 161–176.

Gilbert, G. K., 1885, The topographic features of lake shores. *U.S. Geol. Survey 5th Ann. Rept.*, pp. 69–123.

Gilbert, G. K., 1914, The transportation of debris by running water. *U.S. Geol. Survey Prof. Paper 83*, 263 pp. Abstract, *Washington Acad. Sci. J4*, pp. 154–158.

Gilluly, James, 1955, Geologic contrasts between continents and ocean basins, in *Crust of the Earth*, A. Poldervaart, editor, *Geol. Soc. America Spec. Paper 62*, pp. 7–18.

Gilvarry, J. J., 1961, How the sky drove the land from the bottom of the sea. *Saturday Review*, Nov. 4, pp. 53–58.

Ginsburg, R. N., 1956, Environmental relationships of grain size and constituent particles in some south Florida carbonate sediments. *Bull. Geol. Soc. America*, v. 40, no. 10, pp. 2384–2427.

*Glossary of Geology and Related Sciences*, 1957, American Geological Institute, Washington, D.C., 325 pp. Revised, 1960, with Supplement, 72 pp.

Godwin, H., and E. H. Willis, 1959, Radiocarbon dating of the late-glacial period in Britain. *Proc. Roy. Soc. (London)*, v. 150, pp. 199–215.

Godwin, H., R. P. Suggate, and E. H. Willis, 1958, Radiocarbon dating of the eustatic rise in ocean-level. *Nature*, v. 181, pp. 1518–1519.

Goel, P. S., D. P. Kharkar, D. Lal, N. Narsappaya, B. Peters, and V. Yatirajam, 1957, The beryllium-10 concentration in deep-sea sediments. *Deep-Sea Research*, v. 4, pp. 202–210.

Goldberg, E. D., 1954, Chemical scavengers of the sea. *Jour. Geology*, v. 62, pp. 249–265.

Goldberg, E. D., 1958, The determination of opal in marine sediments. *Jour. Marine Research*, v. 17, pp. 178–182.

Goldberg, E. D., and G. Arrhenius, 1958, Chemistry of the Pacific pelagic sediments. *Geochim. et Cosmochim. Acta*, v. 13, pp. 153–212.

Goldberg, E. D., and M. Koide, 1958, Ionium-thorium chronology in deep-sea sediments of the Pacific. *Science*, v. 128, p. 1003.

Goldberg, E. D., and R. H. Parker, 1960, Phosphatized wood from the Pacific sea floor. *Bull. Geol. Soc. America*, v. 71, pp. 631–632.

Goldberg, E. D., C. C. Patterson, and T. J. Chow, 1958, Ionium-thorium and lead isotope ratios as indicators of oceanic water masses. *Second United Nations International Conference on the Peaceful Uses of Atomic Energy*, Geneva.

Goldberg, E. D., and E. Picciotto, 1955, Thorium determinations in manganese nodules. *Science*, v. 121, pp. 613–614.

Goldstein, August, Jr., 1942, Sedimentary petrologic provinces of the northern Gulf of Mexico. *Jour. Sed. Petrology*, v. 12, no. 2, pp. 77–84.

Goles, G., H. C. Urey, V. R. Murthy, Walter Munk, H. W. Menard, A. E. J. Engel, and Tj. van Andel, 1962, A letter of complaint and protest from La Jolla. *Saturday Review*, April 7, pp. 42–43.

Goncharov, V. P., and U. P. Neprochnov, 1960, Geomorphology and tectonic problems of the Black Sea, in *XXI Intern. Geol. Congr., Reports of Soviet Geologists, Problem 10, Marine Geology*, pp. 94–104.

Goreau, Thomas F., 1959, The ecology of Jamaican coral reefs. *Ecology*, v. 40, pp. 67–90.

Gorsline, D. S., 1959, Sources and parameters of bottom sediments of the continental terrace off the southeastern United States, abstract in *Preprints International Oceanographic Congress*. American Association for the Advancement of Science, Washington, D.C., p. 615.

Gorsline, D. S., editor, 1962, *Proc. First National Coastal and Shallow Water Research Conference*. National Science Foundation and Office of Naval Research, Tallahassee, Fla., 897 pp.

Gould, H. R., and E. McFarlan, Jr., 1959, Geologic history of the chenier plain, southwestern Louisiana. *Trans. Gulf Coast Assoc. Geological Soc.* v. IX, 10 pp.

Gould, H. R., and R. H. Stewart, 1955, Continental terrace sediments in the northeastern Gulf of Mexico, in *Finding Ancient Shorelines. Soc. Econ. Paleon. and Mineral., Spec. Publ. 3*, pp. 2–19.

Graham, John, 1959, Metabolically induced precipitation of elements from sea water. *Science*, v. 129, pp. 1428–1429.

Granelli, N. C. L., 1959, Giant ripples in the Gulf of San Matias, Argentina, abstract in *Preprints International Oceanographic Congress*. American Association for the Advancement of Science, Washington, D.C., pp. 616–618.

Graton, L. C., and H. J. Fraser, 1935, Systematic packing of spheres—with particular relation to porosity and permeability. *Jour. Geology*, v. 43, pp. 785–909.

Griffin, J., and E. D. Goldberg, 1963, Clay mineral distributions in oceanic areas, in *The Sea: Ideas and Observations*, v. 3 Interscience Publishers, New York, pp. 728–741.

Grim, R. E., and W. D. Johns, 1955, Clay mineral investigation of sediments in the northern Gulf of Mexico. *Natl. Research Council, Proc. Second Annual Clay Minerals Conf.*, pp. 81–103.

Grimsdale, T. F., 1952, *Cycloclypeus* (Foraminifera) in the Funafuti boring, and its geological significance. *The Challenger Soc.*, no. 2, pp. 1–11.

Gripenberg, Stina. 1934, *Sediments of the North Baltic and Adjoining Seas. Havforsk-niningstitutes*, Skrift no. 96, Helsingfors, Fennia 60, no. 3.

Gripenberg, Stina, 1939, Sediments of the Baltic Sea, in *Recent Marine Sediments*. American Association Petroleum Geologists, Tulsa, pp. 298–321.

Gröba, Egon, 1953, Neue Ergebnisse morphologischer und geologischer. Untersuchungen in der mittleren und sudlichen Ostsee, 1952. *"Freiberger Forschungshefte,"* pt. C, pp. 41–46.

Grütter, A., and W. Buser, 1957, Untersuchungen an Mangansedimenten. *Chimia*, v. 11, pp. 132–133.

Guilcher, André, 1951, La formation de la Mer du Nord, du pas de Calais et des Plaines Maritimes Environnantes. *Bull. de la Société de Géographie de Lyon et de la Région Lyonnaise*, v. XXVI, no. 3, pp. 311–329.

Guilcher, André, 1958, *Coastal and Submarine Morphology*. Methuen & Co., London, 274 pp.

Guilcher, André, 1959a, Coastal sand ridges and marshes and their environment near Grand Popo and Ouidah, Dahomey, in *Second Coastal Geographical Conf.* Coastal Studies Inst., Louisiana State University, Baton Rouge, La., pp. 189–212.

Guilcher, André, 1959b, Les accumulations sous-marines du plateau de Molène et de la Chaussée de Sein (Finistère). *Centre Natl. Recherche Sci.*, LXXXIII, pp. 109–141.

Guilcher, André, Ph. H. Kuenen, F. P. Shepard, and V. P. Zenkovitch, 1957, Scientific considerations relating to the continental shelf. *United Nations Educational, Scientific and Cultural Organization, Conference on the Law of the Sea*, 13/2, 20 pp.

Gutenberg, Beno, and C. F. Richter, 1954, *Seismicity of the Earth and Associated Phenomena*. Princeton University Press, Princeton, N.J., 2nd edition, 310 pp. (originally published 1949).

*Habitat of Oil*, a symposium, L. G. Weeks, editor, 1958, American Association of Petroleum Geologists, Tulsa, Okla., 1384 pp.

Halm, J. K. E., 1935, An astronomical aspect of the evolution of the earth. Presidential Address, *Astronomical Society of South Africa*, v. IV, no. 1, pp. 1–28.

Hamilton, E. L., 1953, Upper Cretaceous, Tertiary, and Recent planktonic Foraminifera from mid-Pacific flat-topped seamounts. *Jour. Paleontology*, v. 27, no. 2, pp. 204–237.

Hamilton, E. L., 1956, Sunken islands of the Mid-Pacific Mountains. *Geol. Soc. America Mem. no. 64*, 97 pp.

Hamilton, E. L., 1957, Marine geology of the southern Hawaiian Ridge. *Bull. Geol. Soc. America*, v. 68, pp. 1011–1026.

Hamilton, E. L., 1959, Thickness and consolidation of deep-sea sediments. *Bull. Geol. Soc. America*, v. 70, no. 11, pp. 1399–1424.

Hamilton, E. L., 1960, Ocean basin ages and amounts of original sediments. *Jour. Sed. Petrology*, v. 30, no. 3, pp. 370–379.

Hamilton, E. L., G. A. Shumway, H. W. Menard, and C. J. Shipek, 1956, Acoustic and other physical properties of shallow-water sediments off San Diego. *Jour. Acoustical Soc. America*, v. 28, pp. 1–15.

Handin, J. W., and J. C. Ludwick, 1950, Accretion of beach sand behind a detached breakwater. *Beach Erosion Board, Tech. Memo No. 16*, 13 pp.

Hanna, G. Dallas, 1952, Geology of the continental slope off central California. *Calif. Acad. Sci. Proc.*, v. 27, no. 9, pp. 325–358.

Hansen, Kaj, 1951, Preliminary report on the sediments of the Danish Wadden Sea. *Meddel. Dansk Geol. Foren.*, Bd. 12, Hefte 1, pp. 1–26.

Hanzawa, Sheshiro, 1940, Micropaleontological studies of drill cores from a deep well in Kita-Daito Zima (N. Borodino Is.). *Jubilee Publication of Prof. H. Yabe's 60th birthday*, v. 2, pp. 755–802.

Hastings, C. E., 1947, Raydist—a radio navigation and tracking system. *Hastings Instrument Co., Hampton, Va., Bull. R-19*, 6 pp.

Hathaway, J. C., 1957, Observations on the genesis of clay minerals in the soils and limestones of Guam. *Sixth National Clay Conference.*

Hayter, P. J. D., 1960, The Ganges and Indus submarine canyons. *Deep-Sea Research*, v. 6, pp. 184–186.

Hecht, F., and R. Patzaic, 1957, Quoted by Smales, Mapper, and Wood, 1958, *Astronautica Acta*, v. 3, p. 47.

Hedgpeth, J. W., editor, 1957a, *Treatise on Marine Ecology and Paleoecology*, v. 1, *Ecology. Geol. Soc. America Mem. 67*, 1296 pp.

Hedgpeth, J. W., 1957b, Sandy Beaches, in *Treatise on Marine Ecology and Paleoecology*, v. 1, *Ecology. Geol. Soc. America Mem. 67*, pp. 587–608.

Heezen, B. C. 1956, Corrientes de turbidez del Río Magdalena. Bol. Soc. *Geograf. Colombia, Bogotá*, nos. 51, 52, pp. 135–142.

Heezen, B. C., 1959a, Submerged ancient beaches of the Atlantic, abstract in *Preprints International Oceanographic Congress*. American Association for the Advancement of Science, Washington, D.C., pp. 622–623.

Heezen, B. C., 1959b, Dynamic processes of abyssal sedimentation: erosion, transportation, and redeposition on the deep-sea floor. *Geophys. Jour. Roy. Astron. Soc.*, v. 2, no. 2, pp. 142–163.

Heezen, B. C., 1960, The rift in the ocean floor. *Sci. American*, October, pp. 98–114.

Heezen, B. C., Roberta Coughlin, and W. C. Beckman, 1960a, Equatorial Atlantic mid-ocean canyon (abstract). *Bull. Geol. Soc. America*, v. 71, p. 1886

Heezen, B. C., and Maurice Ewing, 1952, Turbidity currents and submarine slumps, and the 1929 Grand Banks earthquake. *Am. Jour. Sci.*, v. 250, pp. 849–873.

Heezen, B. C., and Maurice Ewing, 1955, Orleansville earthquake and turbidity currents. *Bull. Am. Assoc. Petrol. Geologists,* v. 39, no. 12, pp. 2505–2514.

Heezen, B. C., Maurice Ewing, R. J. Menzies, and Nestor Granelli, 1957, Extending the limits of the Congo Submarine Canyon (abstract). *Bull. Geol. Soc. America,* v. 68, no. 12, pt. 2, pp. 1743–1744.

Heezen, B. C., W. D. Nesteroff, and G. Sabatier, 1960b, Repartition des mineraux argileux dans les sediments profonds de l'Atlantique nord et equatorial. *Compt. Rend.,* v. 251, pp. 410–412.

Heezen, B. C., and M. Tharp, 1962, The Floors of the Ocean. II. South Atlantic. Physiographic Diagram.

Heezen, B. C., M. Tharp, and Maurice Ewing, 1959, The Floors of the Ocean. I. North Atlantic. *Geol. Soc. America Spec. Paper 65,* 122 pp.

Hersey, J. B., E. T. Bunce, R. F. Wyrick, and F. T. Dietz, 1959, Geophysical investigation of the continental margin between Cape Henry, Virginia, and Jacksonville, Florida. *Bull. Geol. Soc. America,* v. 70, pp. 437–466.

Hess, H. H., 1946, Drowned ancient islands of the Pacific basin. *Am. Jour. Sci.,* v. 244, pp. 772–791.

Hess, H. H., 1960, The AMSOC hole to the earth's mantle, *Am. Scientist,* v. 48, no. 2, pp. 254–263.

Hill, Mason L., and T. W. Dibblee, Jr., 1953, San Andreas, Garlock, and Big Pine Faults, California. *Bull. Geol. Soc. America,* v. 64, pp. 443–458.

Hill, Maurice N., 1956, Notes on the bathymetric chart of the N.E. Atlantic. *Deep-Sea Research,* v. 3, pp. 229–231.

Hill, Maurice N., 1957, Recent geophysical exploration of the ocean floor, in *Physics and Chemistry of the Earth.* Pergamon Press, London, v. 2, pp. 129–163.

Hill, Maurice N., 1960, A median valley of the Mid-Atlantic Ridge. *Deep-Sea Research,* v. 6, no. 3, pp. 193–205.

Hill, Maurice N., and W. B. R. King, 1954, Seismic prospecting in the English Channel and its geological interpretation. *Quart. Jour. Geol. Soc. London,* v. CIX, pp. 1–19.

Hinde, G. J., 1904, Report on the materials from the borings at the Funafuti Atoll. *Rept. Coral Reef Committee, Royal Society of London* (W. J. Sollas, *et al.*), London, pp. 186–360.

Hiranandani, M. G., and C. V. Gole, 1959, Formation and movement of mudbanks and their effect on southwesterly coast of India, abstract in *Preprints International Oceanographic Congress.* American Association for the Advancement of Science, Washington, D.C., pp. 623–624.

Hjulström, F., 1935, Studies of the morphological activity of rivers as illustrated by the River Fyris. *Bull. Geol. Inst. Univ. Upsala,* v. 25, pp. 221–528.

Hjulström, F., 1939, Transportation of detritus by moving water, in *Recent Marine Sediments,* P. D. Trask, editor, *Am. Assoc. Petrol. Geol.,* Tulsa, pp. 5–31.

Hodgson, E. A., 1930, The Grand Banks earthquake. *Seismol. Soc. America, Eastern Sec. Proc.,* pp. 72–79.

Hoffmeister, J. E., and H. S. Ladd, 1935, The foundations of atolls; a discussion. *Jour. Geology*, v. 43, no. 6, pp. 643–665.

Holtedahl, Hans, 1950, A study of the topography and the sediments of the continental slope west of Møre, W. Norway. *Univ. i Bergen Årbok, Naturvitenskap. Rekke*, no. 5, pp. 1–58.

Holtedahl, Hans, 1955, On the Norwegian continental terrace, primarily outside More-Romsdal: its geomorphology and sediments. With contributions on the Quaternary geology of the adjacent land and on the bottom deposits of the Norwegian Sea. *Univ. I Bergen, Årbok, Naturvitenskap. Rekke*, no. 14, 209 pp.

Holtedahl, Hans, 1958, Some remarks on geomorphology of continental shelves off Norway, Labrador, and southeast Alaska. *Jour. Geology*, v. 66, no. 4, pp. 461–471.

Holtedahl, Hans, 1959, Sur la geologie et la morphologie des plateaux continentaux glaciaires. *Centre Natl. Recherche Sci.*, v. LXXXIII, pp. 245–263.

Holtedahl, Olaf, 1940, The submarine relief off the Norwegian coast. *Norske Videnskaps-Akad. Oslo*, 43 pp.

Holtedahl, Olaf, 1950, Supposed marginal fault lines in the shelf area off some northern lands. *Bull. Geol. Soc. America*, v. 61, pp. 493–500.

Houbolt, J. J. H. C., 1957, *Surface Sediments of the Persian Gulf near the Qatar Peninsula*. Dissertation, University of Utrecht, Mouton & Co., The Hague, 113 pp.

Hough, J. L., 1950, Pleistocene lithology of Antarctic ocean-bottom sediments. *Jour. Geology*, v. 58, no. 3, pp. 254–260.

Hough, J. L., 1956, Sediment distribution in the southern oceans around Antarctica. *Jour. Sed. Petrology*, v. 26, no. 4, pp. 301–306.

Hough, J. L., 1958, *Geology of the Great Lakes*. University of Illinois Press, Urbana, Ill., 313 pp.

Hubbert, M. K., 1958, Permeability (fluid). *Encyclopaedia Britannica*, v. 17, pp. 531–532.

Hülsemann, Jobst, and K. O. Emery, 1961, Stratification in recent sediments of Santa Barbara Basin as controlled by organisms and water character. *Jour. Geology*, v. 69, no. 3, pp. 279–290.

Hunkins, Kenneth, 1959, The floor of the Arctic Ocean. *Trans. Am. Geophys. Union*, v. 40, no. 2, pp. 159–162.

Hunter, W., and D. W. Parkin, 1960, Cosmic dust in recent deep-sea sediments. *Proc. Roy. Soc. (London)* A, v. 255, pp. 382–397.

Hurley, P. M., *et al.*, 1958a, *Fifth Ann. Progr. Rept.* U.S. Atomic Energy Commission, Washington, D.C.

Hurley, P. M., *et al.*, 1958b, *Sixth Ann. Progr. Rept.* U.S. Atomic Energy Commission, Washington, D.C.

Hurley, P. M., *et al.*, 1960, *Eighth Ann. Progr. Rept.* U.S. Atomic Energy Commission, Washington, D.C.

Hurley, R. J., 1960, The geomorphology of abyssal plains in the northeast Pacific Ocean. Mimeographed Report, Scripps Inst. Oceanog. Ref. 60–7, 105 pp.

Hvorslev, M. J., and H. C. Stetson, 1946, Free-fall coring tube: a new type of gravity bottom sampler. *Bull. Geol. Soc. America*, v. 57, pp. 935–950.

Hydrographic Office, 1947, Manual of coastal delineation from aerial photographs. *U.S. Navy Dept., Hydrographic Publ. No. 592.*

Ijima T., *et al.*, 1958, Wave characteristics in the surf zone observed by stereophotography (for the case of short wind waves). Report of Transportation Technical Research Institute; *The Unyu-Gijutsu Kenkyujo Mejiro, Toshima-Ku*, Tokyo, Japan, Report no. 31, 30 pp.

Illing, L. V., 1954, Bahaman calcareous sands. *Bull. Am. Assoc. Petrol. Geologists*, v. 38, pp. 1–95.

Imamura, A., 1937, *Theoretical and applied seismology*. Maruzen, Tokyo.

Inman, D. L., 1949a, Sorting of sediments in the light of fluid mechanics. *Jour. Sed. Petrology*, v. 19, pp. 51–70.

Inman, D. L., 1949b, Sediment trap studies of suspended material near the surf zone. Scripps Inst. of Oceanography, Univ. of Calif. Quarterly Progress Rept. 2 to Beach Erosion Board, Corps of Engr. (Contract W-49-055-eng-3).

Inman, D. L., 1950, Beach study in the vicinity of Mugu Lagoon, California. *Beach Erosion Board, Corps of Engrs. Tech. Memo No. 14.*

Inman, D. L., 1952, Measures for describing the size distribution of sediments. *Jour. Sed. Petrology*, v. 22, no. 3, pp. 125–145.

Inman. D. L., 1953, Areal and seasonal variations in beach and nearshore sediments at La Jolla, California. *Beach Erosion Board, Corps of Engrs. Tech. Memo No. 39*, 134 pp.

Inman, D. L., 1957, Wave generated ripples in nearshore sands. *Beach Erosion Board, Corps of Engrs. Tech. Memo No. 100*, 42 pp.

Inman, D. L., and R. A. Bagnold, 1963, Littoral processes. In *The Sea: Ideas and Observations*, v. 3, Interscience Publishers, New York.

Inman, D. L., and A. J. Bowen, 1963, Flume experiments on sand transport by waves and currents. *Proc. 8th Conf. Coastal Engr.*, Mexico City, 1962, Univ. Calif., pp. 137–150.

Inman, D. L., and J. D. Frautschy, 1966, Littoral processes and the development of shorelines. *Coastal Engineering* (Santa Barbara Specialty Conf.), Amer. Soc. Civ. Engrs., pp. 511–536.

Inman, D. L., W. R. Gayman, and D. C. Cox, 1963, Littoral sedimentary processes on Kauai, a sub-tropical high island, *Pacific Sci.* v. 17, no. 1.

Inman, D. L., and N. Nasu, 1956, Orbital velocity associated with wave action near the breaker zone. *Beach Erosion Board, Corps of Engrs. Tech. Memo No. 79*, 43 pp.

Inman, D. L., and W. H. Quinn, 1952, Currents in the surf zone. *Proc. 2nd Conf. Coastal Eng.*, Council on Wave Research, Univ. Calif., pp. 24–36.

Inman, D. L., and G. A. Rusnak, 1956, Changes in sand level on the beach and shelf at La Jolla, California. *Beach Erosion Board, Tech. Memo No. 82.*

Irving, E., 1958, Rock magnetism: a new approach to the problems of polar wandering and continental drift, in *Continental Drift*—a symposium. University of Tasmania, Geol. Dept., pp. 24–61.

Jacobs, J. A., R. D. Russell, and J. T. Wilson, 1959, *Physics and Geology*. McGraw-Hill Book Co., New York, 424 pp.

Jarke, J., 1956, Eine neue Bodenkarte der südlichen Nordsee. *Deut. Hydro-*

*graph. Z.*, v. 9, I, pp. 1–8.

Jeffreys, H., 1925, On the formation of water waves by wind. *Proc. Roy. Soc. (London)*, A, v. 107, pp. 189–206.

Jelgersma, S., and A. J. Pannekoek, 1960, Post-glacial rise of sea-level in the Netherlands (a preliminary report). *Geol. en Mijnbouw*, 39e Jaargang, NR6, pp. 201–207.

Johnson, D. W., 1919, *Shore Processes and Shoreline Development*. John Wiley and Sons, New York, 584 pp.

Johnson, D. W., 1925, *New England—Acadian Shoreline*. John Wiley and Sons, New York, 608 pp.

Johnson, D. W., 1939, *The Origin of Submarine Canyons*. Columbia University Press, New York, 126 pp.

Jordan, G. F., 1951, Continental slope off Apalachicola River, Florida. *Bull. Am. Assoc. Petrol. Geologists*, v. 35, no. 9, pp. 1978–1993.

Jordan, G. F., 1954, Large sink holes in straits of Florida. *Bull. Am. Assoc. Petrol. Geologists*, v. 38, no. 8, pp. 1810–1817.

Jordan, G. F., and H. B. Stewart, Jr., 1959, Continental slope off southwest Florida. *Bull. Am. Assoc. Petrol. Geologists*, v. 43, no. 5, pp. 974–991.

Jordan, G. F., and H. B. Stewart, Jr., 1961, Submarine topography of the western Straits of Florida. *Bull. Geol. Soc. America*, v. 72, pp. 1051–1058.

Kalinske, A. A., 1943, Turbulence and the transport of sand and silt by wind. *Ann. N.Y. Acad. Sci.*, v. XLIV, Art. 1, pp. 41–54.

Kay, M., 1951, *North American Geosynclines. Geol. Soc. America Mem. 48.*

Kaye, C. A., 1959, Shoreline features and Quaternary shoreline changes, Puerto Rico. *U.S. Geol. Survey Prof. Paper 317-B*, pp. 49–140.

Keith, Arthur, 1930, The Grand Banks earthquake. *Seismol. Soc. America, Eastern Sec. Proc.*, Suppl.

Keulegan, G. H., 1950, Wave motion, in *Engineering Hydraulics, Proc. 4th Hydraulics Conference*, Hunter Rouse, editor. John Wiley and Sons.

Kiilerich, A., 1958, The Ganges Submarine Canyon. *Andhra Univ. Mem. Oceanog.*, ser. no. 62, v. 11, pp. 29–32.

King, C. A. M., 1959, *Beaches and Coasts*. Edward Arnold, London, 403 pp.

King, P. B., 1948, Geology of the southern Guadalupe Mountains, Texas. *U.S. Geol. Survey Prof. Paper 215*, 183 pp.

King, W. R. B., 1948, Geology of the eastern part of the English Channel. *Quart. Jour. Geol. Soc.*, v. 104, pp. 327–338.

Kingma, J. T., 1958, The Tongaporutuan sedimentation in Central Hawke's Bay. *New Zealand Jour. Geol. Geophys.*, v. 1, no. 1, pp. 1–30.

Kingma, J. T., 1960, The tectonic significance of graded bedding in geosynclinal sedimentary systems, abstract in *21st International Geological Congress*. Det Berlingske Bogtrykkeri, Copenhagen, pp. 218–219.

Klenova, M. V., 1940, Sediments of the Barents Sea. *Compt. Rend. (Doklady) Acad. Sci. USSR*, v. XXVI, no. 8, pp. 796–800.

Klenova, M. V., 1948, *Geology of the Sea*. 495 pp. (in Russian).

Klenova, M. V., editor, 1956, *Contemporary Sediments of the Caspian Sea*. Academy of Sciences, USSR, Moscow, 303 pp. Translation by American Geological Institute.

Klenova, M. V., 1960a, *The Geology of the Barents Sea*. Academy of Sciences, USSR, Moscow, 367 pp. (in Russian).

Atoll, Bikini and nearby atolls, Marshall Islands. *U.S. Geol. Survey Prof. Paper 260-Y*, pp. 863–903.

Ladd, H. S., and J. I. Tracey, Jr., 1957, Fossil land shells from deep drill holes on western Pacific atolls. *Deep-Sea Research*, v. 4, pp. 218–219.

Ladd, H. S., J. I. Tracey, J. W. Wells, and K. O. Emery, 1950, Organic growth and sedimentation on an atoll. *Jour. Geology*, v. 58, no. 4, pp. 410–425.

Laevastu, Taivo, and Otto Mellis, 1955, Extra-terrestrial material in deep-sea deposits. *Trans. Am. Geophys. Union.* v. 36, no. 3, pp. 385–389.

LaFond, E. C., 1961, The isotherm follower. *Jour. Marine Research*, v. 19, no. 1, pp. 33–39.

LaFond, E. C., and R. S. Dietz, 1948, New snapper-type sea floor sampler. *Jour. Sed. Petrology*, v. 18, pp. 34–37.

LaFond, E. C., R. S. Dietz, and J. A. Knauss, 1950, A sonic device for underwater sediment survey. *Jour. Sed. Petrology*, v. 20, no. 2, pp. 107–110.

Laktionov, A. F., 1955, The North Pole, summarized in *Recent Soviet Scientific Investigations in the North Polar Regions*, translated by K. R. Whiting, Air Univ. Documentary Research Study (AU-272-56-RSI), Maxwell Air Force Base, Alabama.

Lal, D., E. D. Goldberg, and M. Koide, 1960, Cosmic-ray produced $Si^{32}$ in nature. *Science,* v. 131, pp. 332–337.

Lamb, H., 1945, *Hydrodynamics*, 6th ed. Dover, New York, 738 pp.

Landes, K. K., 1959, Illogical geology. *GeoTimes*, v. III, no. 6, p. 19.

Langbein, W. B., and S. A. Schumn, 1958, Yield of sediment in relation to mean annual precipitation. *Trans. Am. Geophys. Union*, v. 30, pp. 1076–1084.

Lankford, R. R., and J. R. Curray, 1957, Mid-Tertiary rock outcrop on continental shelf, Northwest Gulf of Mexico. *Bull. Am. Assoc. Petrol. Geologists*, v. 41, no. 9, pp. 2114–2117.

Lankford, R. R., and F. P. Shepard, 1960, Facies interpretation in Mississippi Delta borings. *Jour. Geology*, v. 68, no. 4, pp. 408–426.

Laughton, A. S., 1959, Disturbance of the sediment surface in the deep-sea as observed by underwater photography, abstract in *Preprints International Oceanographic Congress*. American Association for the Advancement of Science, Washington, D.C., pp. 466–467.

Laughton, A. S., 1960, An interplain deep-sea channel system. *Deep-Sea Research*, v. 7, no. 2, pp. 75–88.

Lawson, A. C., 1893, The geology of Carmelo Bay. *Univ. Calif., Dept. Geol., Bull.* 1, pp. 1–59.

Lawson, A. C., 1897, The post Pliocene diastrophism of the coast of southern California. *Univ. Calif., Dept. Geol., Bull.*, v. 1, pp. 115–160.

LeBlanc, R. J., and W. D. Hodgson, 1959, Origin and development of the Texas shoreline. *Trans. Gulf Coast Assoc. Geol. Soc.*, v. IX, pp. 197–220.

Lesser, R. M., 1951, Some observations of the velocity profile near the sea floor. *Trans. Am. Geophys. Union*, v. 32, pp. 207–211.

Limbaugh, Conrad, and F. P. Shepard, 1957, Submarine canyons. *Geol. Soc. America Mem. 67*, v. 1, pp. 633–639.

Lipson, J., 1958, Potassium-argon dating of sedimentary rocks. *Bull. Geol. Soc. America*, v. 69, pp. 139–150.

Lisitzin, A. P., 1960, Bottom sediments of the eastern Antarctic and the southern Indian Ocean. *Deep-Sea Research*, v. 7, no. 2, pp. 89–99.

Lisitzin, A. P., and A. V. Zhivago, 1960, Marine geological work of the Soviet Antarctic Expedition, 1955–1957. *Deep-Sea Research*, v. 6, no. 2, pp. 77–87.

Livingstone, D. A., 1959, Theory of ice ages. *Science*, v. 129, pp. 463–464.

Longuet-Higgins, M. S., 1952, On the statistical distribution of the heights of sea waves. *Jour. Marine Research*, v. II, pp. 245–266.

Longuet-Higgins, M. S., 1953, Mass transport in water waves. *Phil. Trans. Roy. Soc. London*, ser. A, no. 903, v. 245, pp. 535–581.

Louderback, G. D., 1914, Preliminary report upon the bottom deposits in San Francisco Bay. *Univ. Calif. Publs. Zool.*, v. 14, pp. 89–97, 185–196.

Louderback, G. D., 1940, San Francisco Bay sediments. *6th Pacific Sci. Congr. 1939 Proc.*, v. 2, pp. 783–793.

Lowenstam, H. A., 1954, Factors affecting the aragonite/calcite ratios in carbonate secreting marine organisms. *Jour. Geology*, v. 62, pp. 284–322.

Lowenstam, H. A., 1959, $O^{18}/O^{16}$ ratios and Sr and Mg contents of calcareous and fossil brachiopods and their bearing on the history of the oceans, abstract in *Preprints International Oceanographic Congress*. American Association for the Advancement of Science, Washington, D.C., pp. 71–72.

Lowenstam, H. A., and S. Epstein, 1957, On the origin of sedimentary aragonite needles of the Great Bahama Bank, *Jour. Geology*, v. 65, pp. 364–375.

Lowman, S. W., 1949, Sedimentary facies in Gulf Coast. *Bull. Am. Assoc. Petrol. Geologists*, v. 33, no. 12, pp. 1939–1997.

Ludwick, J. C., 1950, Deep water sand layers off San Diego, California. Ph.D. dissertation, Scripps Institution of Oceanography, La Jolla, Calif., 56 pp.

Ludwick, J. C., and W. R. Walton, 1957, Shelf-edge, calcareous prominences in northeastern Gulf of Mexico. *Bull. Am. Assoc. Petrol. Geologists*, v. 41, pp. 2054–2101.

Luskin, Bernard, B. C. Heezen, Maurice Ewing, and Mark Landisman, 1954, Precision measurement of ocean depth. *Deep-Sea Research*, v. 1, pp. 131–140.

MacCarthy, G. R., 1935, Eolian sands, a comparison. *Am. Jour. Sci.*, v. 30, no. 176, pp. 81–95.

Macdonald, G. A., and C. K. Wentworth, 1954, The tsunami of November 4, 1952, on the island of Hawaii. *Bull. Seismol. Soc. America*, v. 44, no. 3, pp. 463–469.

Mackereth, F. J. H., 1958, A portable core sampler for lake deposits. *Limnol. and Oceanog.*, v. 3, no. 2, pp. 181–191.

MacNeil, F. S., 1954, Organic reefs and banks and associated detrital sediments and the shape of atolls: an inheritance from subaerial erosion forms. *Am. Jour. Sci.*, v. 252, pp. 385–401, 402–427.

Mahadevan, C., and M. P. Rao, 1954, Study of ocean floor sediments off the east coast of India. *Andhra Univ. Mem. Oceanog.* 1, pp. 1–35.

*Marine Ecology and Paleoecology, Treatise on*, v. 1, *Ecology*, 1957, J. W. Hedgepeth, editor, *Geol. Soc. America Mem. 67*, 1296 pp.

*Marine Ecology and Paleoecology, Treatise on*, v. 2, *Paleoecology*, 1957, H. S. Ladd, editor, *Geol. Soc. America Mem. 67*, 1077 pp.

*Marine Geology*, 1960, *Intern. Geol. Congr. XXI Session, Reports of Soviet Geologists, Problem 10*. Publishing House of Academy of Sciences, USSR, Moscow, 205 pp.

Mason, R. G., 1958, A magnetic survey off the west coast of the United States. *Geophys. Jour.*, v. 1, pp. 320–329.

Mason, R. G., 1960, Geophysical investigations of the sea floor. *Liverpool and Manchester Geol. Jour.*, v. 2, pt. 3, pp. 389–410.

Mason, R. G., and A. D. Raff, 1961, Magnetic survey off the west coast of North America, 32° N. latitude to 42° N. latitude. *Bull. Geol. Soc. America*, v. 72, pp. 1259–1266.

Mathews, W. H., and F. P. Shepard, 1962, Sedimentation of the Fraser River Delta, British Columbia. *Bull. Am. Assoc. Petrol. Geologists*, v. 46, pp. 1416–1437.

Mayor, A. G., 1924, Some posthumous papers relating to work at Tutuila Island and adjacent regions. Papers from the *Dept. Marine Biol. Carnegie Inst. Washington*, v. 19, pp. 1–90.

McAllister, R. F., 1957, Photography of submerged vertical structures. *Am. Geophys. Union*, v. 38, no. 3, pp. 314–319.

McClure, C. D., H. F. Nelson, and W. B. Huckabay, 1958, Marine Sonoprobe System, new tool for geologic mapping. *Bull. Am. Assoc. Petrol. Geologists*, v. 42, pp. 701–716.

McGill, J. T., 1958, Map of coastal landforms of the world, *Geog. Rev.*, v. XLVIII, no. 3, pp. 402–405.

McKee, E. D., 1940, Three types of cross-lamination in Paleozoic rocks of northern Arizona. *Am. Jour. Sci.*, v. 238, pp. 811–824.

McKee, E. D., 1950, Report on studies of stratification in modern sediments and in laboratory experiments. *Office of Naval Research* Project Nonr 164(00), NR 081 123, 61 pp.

McKee, E. D., 1957, Primary structures in some Recent sediments. *Bull. Am. Assoc. Petrol. Geologists*, v. 41, no. 8, pp. 1704–1747.

McKee, E. D., 1958, Geology of Kapingamarangi Atoll, Caroline Islands. *Bull. Geol. Soc. America*, v. 69, pp. 241–277.

McKee, E. D., 1959, Storm sediments on a Pacific atoll. *Jour. Sed. Petrology*, v. 29, no. 3, pp. 354–364.

McKelvey, V. E., R. W. Swanson, and R. P. Sheldon, 1953, The Permian phosphorite deposits of western United States. *19th Intern. Geol. Congr. (Algiers)*, C.R., sect. XI, pp. 45–64.

McMaster, Robert L., 1954, Petrography and genesis of the New Jersey beach sands. *State of New Jersey Dept. Conserv. Geol. Ser. Bull.*, *63*, 239 pp.

Mellis, O., 1954, Volcanic ash-horizons in deep-sea sediments from the eastern Mediterranean. *Deep-Sea Research*, v. 2, pp. 89–92.

Menard, H. W., 1953, Pleistocene and Recent sediment from the floor of the northwest Pacific. *Bull. Geol. Soc. America*, v. 64, pp. 1279–1294.

Menard, H. W., 1955a, Deep-sea channels, topography and sedimentation. *Bull. Am. Assoc. Petrol. Geologists*, v. 39, no. 2, pp. 236–255.

Menard, H. W., 1955b, Deformation of the northeastern Pacific Basin and the west coast of North America, *Bull. Geol. Soc. America*, v. 66, pp. 1149–1198.

Menard, H. W., 1956, Archipelagic aprons. *Bull. Am. Assoc. Petrol. Geologists*, v. 40, no. 9, pp. 2195–2210.

Menard, H. W., 1959a, Minor lineations in the Pacific Basin. *Bull. Geol. Soc. America*, v. 70, pp. 1491–1496.

Menard, H. W., 1959b, Distribution et origine des zones plates abyssales. *Colloq. Intern. Centre Natl. Recherche Sci.*, LXXXIII, pp. 95–108.

Menard, H. W., 1959c, Geology of the Pacific sea floor. *Experientia*, v. XV/6, pp. 205–213.

Menard, H. W., 1960a, Possible pre-Pleistocene deep-sea fans off central California. *Bull. Geol. Soc. America*, v. 71, pp. 1271–1278.

Menard, H. W., 1960b, Consolidated slabs on the floor of the eastern Pacific. *Deep-Sea Research*, v. 7, no. 1, pp. 35–41.

Menard, H. W., 1960c, The East Pacific Rise. *Science*, v. 132, no. 3441, pp. 1737–1746.

Menard, H. W., 1961, Some rates of regional erosion. *Jour. Geology*, v. 69, no. 2, pp. 154–161.

Menard, H. W., and R. S. Dietz, 1951, Submarine geology of the Gulf of Alaska. *Bull. Geol. Soc. America*, v. 62, no. 10, pp. 1263–1285.

Menard, H. W., and R. S. Dietz, 1952, Mendocino Submarine Escarpment. *Jour. Geology*, v. 60, no. 3, pp. 266–278.

Menard, H. W., R. F. Dill, E. L. Hamilton, D. G. Moore, G. Shumway, M. Silverman, and H. B. Stewart, 1954, Underwater mapping by diving geologists. *Bull. Am. Assoc. Petrol. Geologists*, v. 38, no. 1, pp. 129–147.

Menard, H. W., and R. L. Fisher, 1958, Clipperton fracture zone in the northeastern equatorial Pacific. *Jour. Geology*, v. 66, no. 3, pp. 239–253.

Menard, H. W., and C. J. Shipek, 1958, Surface concentrations of manganese nodules. *Nature*, v. 182, pp. 1156–1158.

Mero, J. L., 1960, Minerals on the ocean floor, *Sci. American*, v. 203, no. 6, pp. 64–72.

Merrill, J. R., E. F. X. Lyden, M. Honda, J. R. Arnold, 1960, The sedimentary geochemistry of beryllium isotopes. *Geochim. et Cosmochim. Acta*, v. 18, pp. 108–129.

Miles, J. W., 1960, On the generation of surface waves by turbulent shear flows. *Jour. Fluid Mech.* v. 7, pp. 469–478.

Miller, D. J., 1960, Giant waves in Lituya Bay, Alaska. *U.S. Geol. Survey Prof. Paper 354-C*, pp. 51–86.

Milne, John, 1897, Sub-oceanic changes. *Geog. Jour.*, v. 10, sec. 3, pp. 259–284.

Molengraaff, G. A. F., 1916, The coral reef problem and isostasy. *Proc. Akad. Wetenschap. Amsterdam*, v. 19, pp. 623–624.

Molengraaff, G. A. F., 1922, *De zeen van Nederlandsch Oest Indie.*

Molengraaff, G. A. F., 1930, The recent sediments in the seas of the East Indian Archipelago, with a short discussion on the condition of those seas in former geological periods. *Proc. Fourth Pacific Sci. Congr. Java*, v. 2B, pp. 989–1021.

Moody, J. D., and M. J. Hill, 1956, Wrench-fault tectonics. *Bull. Geol. Soc. America*, v. 67, pp. 1207–1246.

Moore, D. G., 1954, Submarine geology of San Pedro shelf, *Jour. Sed. Petrology* v. 24, pp. 162–181.

Moore, D. G., 1960, Acoustic-reflection studies of the continental shelf and slope off southern California. *Bull. Geol. Soc. America*, v. 71, pp. 1121–1136.

Moore, D. G., 1961a, Acoustic reflection reconnaissance of the Bering and Chuckchi Seas. *10th Pacific Sci. Congr.* (abstract). p. 380.

Moore, D. G., 1961b, Submarine slumps. *Jour. Sed. Petrology*, v. 31, no. 3, pp. 343–357.

Moore, D. G., 1961c, The free-corer: sediment sampling without wire and winch. *Jour. Sed. Petrology*, v. 31, no. 4, pp. 627–630.

Moore, D. G., manuscript, Geophysical evidence on structure of Cortes and Tanner Banks.

Moore, D. G., and J. R. Curray 1963, Structural framework of continental terrace northwest Gulf of Mexico. *Jour. Geophys. Res.*, v. 68, no. 6.

Moore, D. G., and George Shumway, 1959, Sediment thickness and physical properties: Pigeon Point Shelf, California. *Jour. Geophys. Research*, v. 64, no. 3, pp. 367–374.

Morgan, J. P., and W. G. McIntire, 1959, Quaternary geology of the Bengal Basin, East Pakistan and India. *Bull. Geol. Soc. America*, v. 70, pp. 319–342.

Morgan, J. P., L. G. Nichols, and Martin Wright, 1958, Morphological effects of hurricane Audrey on the Louisiana coast. *Coastal Studies Inst., Louisiana State Univ., Tech. Rept. no. 10*, 53 pp.

Müller, German, 1958, Die rezenten Sedimente in Golf von Neapel. I. Die Sedimente des Golfes von Pozzuoli. *Geol. Rundschau*, v. 47, no. 1, pp. 117–150.

Munk, W. H., 1949a, Surf beats. *Trans. Am. Geophys. Union*, v. 30, pp. 849–854.

Munk, W. H., 1949b, The solitary wave theory and its application to surf problems. *Ann. N.Y. Acad. Sci.*, v. 51, Art. 3, pp. 376–424.

Munk, W. H., and G. J. F. Macdonald, 1960, *The Rotation of the Earth, A Geophysical Discussion.* Cambridge University Press, Cambridge, England, 313 pp.

Munk, W. H., and M. C. Sargent, 1948, Adjustment of Bikini Atoll to ocean waves. *Trans. Am. Geophys. Union*, v. 29, no. 6, pp. 855–860.

Munk, W. H., and F. E. Snodgrass, 1957, Measurements of southern swell at Guadalupe Island. *Deep-Sea Research*, v. 4, pp. 272–286.

Munk, W. H., and M. A. Traylor, 1947, Refraction of ocean waves: a process linking underwater topography to beach erosion. *Jour. Geol.*, v. LV, pp. 1–26.

Murray, G. E., 1960, Geologic framework of Gulf coastal province of United States, in *Recent Sediments, Northwest Gulf of Mexico*, F. P. Shepard, F. B. Phleger, and Tj. H. van Andel, editors. American Association Petroleum Geologists, Tulsa, Okla., pp. 5–33.

Murray, H. H., and J. L. Harrison, 1956, Clay mineral composition of Recent sediments from Sigsbee Deep. *Jour. Sed. Petrology*, v. 26, pp. 363–368.

Murray, H. W., 1947, Topography of the Gulf of Maine, *Bull. Geol. Soc. America*, v. 58, pp. 153–196.

Murray, John, 1880, On the structure of coral reefs and islands. *Proc. Roy. Soc. Edinburgh*, v. 10, pp. 505–518.

Murray, John, and G. V. Lee, 1909, The depth and marine deposits of the Pacific, *Mem. Museum Comp. Zool.*, v. 38, no. 1, 169 pp.

Murray, John, and A. F. Renard, 1891, *Deep Sea Deposits, Scientific Results of the Exploration voyage of H.M.S. Challenger, 1872–1876. Challenger Reports,* Longmans, London, 525 pp.

Nanz, R. H., Jr., 1954, Genesis of Oligocene Sandstone Reservoir, Seeligeon Field, Jim Wells, and Kleberg Counties, Texas, *Bull. Am. Assoc. Petrol. Geologists*, v. 38, no. 1, pp. 96–117.

Natland, Manley, 1933, The temperature and depth distribution of some recent and fossil foraminifera in the southern California region, *Scripps Inst., Tech. Ser. Bull.*, v. 3, no. 10, pp. 225–230.

Natland, Manley, and Ph. H. Kuenen, 1951, Sedimentary history of the Ventura Basin, California, and the action of turbidity currents. *Soc. Econ. Paleontol. & Mineral. Spec. Publ. No. 2*, pp. 76–107.

Nayudu, Y. R., 1959, Recent sediments of the northeast Pacific. Ph.D. dissertation. University of Washington.

Neaverson, E., 1934, Sea floor deposits, general characteristics and distribution, in *Discovery Reports*. Cambridge University Press, Cambridge, England, v. 9, pp. 310–312.

Neeb, Ir. Gerda A., 1943, Bottom samples, the composition and distribution of the samples. *Snellius Expedition, 1929–1930*, v. 5, pt. 3, sec. II.

Nesteroff, W. D., 1958, Recherches sur les sediments marins actuels de la region d'Antibes. Ph.D. thesis, University of Paris, 347 pp.

Nesteroff, W. D., 1959, Attempt at a synthesis of present-day marine sedimentation along the French Mediterranean Coast (eastern part), abstract in *Preprints International Oceanographic Congress*. American Association for the Advancement of Science, Washington, D.C., p. 642.

Nevin, C. M., 1946, Competency of moving water to transport debris. *Bull. Geol. Soc. America*, v. 57, no. 7, pp. 651–674.

Newell, N. D., 1955, Bahamian platforms, *Geol. Soc. America, Spec. Paper 62*, pp. 303–315.

Newell, N. D., 1956, Geological reconnaissance of Raroia (Kon Tiki) Atoll, Tuamotu Archipelago. *Bull. Am. Museum Nat. Hist.*, v. 109, art. 3, pp. 311–372.

Newell, N. D., 1959a, Questions of the coral reefs. II. Biology of the reefs. *Natural History*. American Museum Natural History, New York, pp. 118–131, 226–235.

Newell, N. D., 1959b, West Atlantic Coral Reefs, abstract in *Preprints International Oceanographic Congress*. American Association for the Advancement of Science, Washington, D.C., pp. 286–287.

Newell, N. D., J. Imbrie, E. G. Purdy, and D. L. Thurber, 1959, Organism communities and bottom facies, Great Bahama Bank. *Bull. Am. Museum Nat. Hist.*, v. 117, art. 4, pp. 177–228.

Newell, N. D., E. G. Purdy, and John Imbrie, 1960, Bahamian Oölitic sand, *Jour. Geology*, v. 68, no. 5, pp. 481–497.

Newell, N. D., J. K. Rigby, A. G. Fischer, A. J. Whiteman, J. E. Hickox, and J. S. Bradley, 1953, *The Permian Reef Complex of the Guadalupe Mountains Region, Texas and New Mexico: A study in Paleoecology.* Freeman, San Francisco, Calif., 226 pp.

Newell, N. D., J. K. Rigby, A. J. Whiteman, and J. S. Bradley, 1951, Shoalwater geology and environments, Eastern Andros Island, Bahamas. *Bull. Am. Museum Nat. Hist.*, v. 97, art. 1, pp. 1–29.

Nichols, R. L., and A. F. Marston, 1939, Shoreline changes in Rhode Island produced by hurricane of September 21, 1938. *Bull. Geol. Soc. America*, v. 50, pp. 1357–1370.

Niino, Hiroshio, and K. O. Emery, 1961, Sediments of shallow portions of East China Sea and South China Sea. *Bull. Geol. Soc. America*, v. 72, no. 5, pp. 731–762.

Norin, Erik, 1958, The sediments of the Central Tyrrhenian Sea. Reports of the *Swedish Deep-Sea Expedition*, v. VIII, 136 pp.

Northrop, J., R. A. Frosch, R. Frassetto, and J. M. Zeigler, 1959, The Bermuda-New England Seamount Chain, abstract in *Preprints International Oceanographic Congress*. American Association for the Advancement of Science, Washington, D.C., p. 48.

Nota, D. J. G., 1958, *Reports of the Orinoco Shelf Expedition*, v. II. H. Veenman en Zonen, Wageningen, 98 pp.

O'Brien, M. P., 1931, Estuary tidal prisms related to entrance areas, *Civil Eng.*, v. 1, pp. 738–739.

O'Brien, M. P., 1933, Review of the theory of turbulent flow and its relation to sediment transportation. *Trans. Am. Geophys. Union*, pp. 487–491.

*Oceanographic Instrumentation, a symposium*, J. D. Isaacs, and C. O. Iselin, editors, 1952, sponsored by Office of Naval Research, *National Research Council Publ. 309*, 233 pp.

Odum, H. T., and E. P. Odum, 1955, Trophic Structure and Productivity of a Windward Coral Reef Community on Eniwetok Atoll. *Ecology Mon.*, v. 25, pp. 291–320.

Officer, C. B., and Maurice Ewing, 1954, Geophysical investigations in the emerged and submerged Atlantic coastal plain. VII. Continental shelf, continental slope, and continental rise south of Nova Scotia. *Bull. Geol. Soc. America*, v. 65, pp. 653–670.

Orr, W. L., K. O. Emery, and J. R. Grady, 1958, Preservation of chlorophyll derivatives in sediments off southern California, *Bull. Am. Assoc. Petrol. Geologists*, v. 42, pp. 925–962.

Ottman, François, 1959, Estudo das amestrov do Fundo Na Região do embocadura do Rio Amazonas. *Trav. Inst. Biol. Maritima* (Recife, Brazil), v. 1, no. 1, pp. 77–106.

Paige, H. G., 1955, Phi-millimeter conversion table. *Jour. Sed. Petrology*, v. 25, pp. 285–292.

Parker, R. H., 1960, Ecology and distributional patterns of marine macro-invertebrates, northern Gulf of Mexico, in *Recent Sediments, Northwest Gulf of Mexico*, F. P. Shepard, F. B. Phleger, and Tj. H. van Andel, editors, American Association of Petroleum Geologists Tulsa, Okla. pp. 302–337.

Parker, R. H., and J. R. Curray, 1956, Fauna and bathymetry of banks on continental shelf, northwest Gulf of Mexico. *Bull. Am. Assoc. Petrol. Geologists*, v. 40, n. 10, pp. 2428–2439.

Penck, Albrecht, 1894, *Morphologie der erdoberfläche*. 2 vols., Stuttgart.

Pepper, J. F., 1958, Potential mineral resources of the continental shelves of the western hemisphere, in *An Introduction to the Geology and Mineral Resources of the Continental Shelves of the Americas, Geol. Survey Bull. 1067*, pp. 43–65.

Petelin, V. P., 1960, Bottom sediments in the western part of the Pacific Ocean. *Oceanol. Researches*, X Section of the I.G.Y. Program, p. 45.

Peterson, M. N. A., and E. D. Goldberg, 1962, Feldspar distributions in South Pacific pelagic sediments. *Jour. Geophys. Res.*, v. 67, pp. 3472–3492.

Pettersson, Hans, 1937, Das verhältnis thorium zu Uran in den Gesteinen und im Meer. *Anz. Öst Akad. Wiss.*, no. 16, pp. 127–128.

Pettersson, Hans, 1943, Manganese nodules and the chronology of the ocean floor. *Medd. Oceanog. Inst., Göteborg*, v. 2, pp. 1–39.

Pettersson, Hans, 1948, Three sediment cores from the Tyrrhenian Sea. *Göteborgs Vetenskaps-och Vitterhets-Samhälles Handl.*, 6, Följden, ser. B, v. 5, no. 13, pp. 1–25, 89–94.

Pettersson, Hans, 1951, Radium and deep-sea chronology. *Nature*, 167, p. 942.

Pettersson, Hans, 1955, Manganese nodules and oceanic radium. *Deep-Sea Research*, v. 3, Suppl. pp. 335–345.

Pettersson, Hans, 1960, Cosmic spherules and meteoritic dust. *Sci. American*, v. 202, no. 2, pp. 123–132.

Pettersson, Hans, and K. Fredriksson, 1958, Magnetic spherules in deep-sea deposits. *Pacific Sci.*, v. 12, pp. 71–81.

Pfannenstiel, Max, 1960, Erläuterungen zu den bathymetrischen Karten des östlichen Mittelmeeres. *Bull Inst. Oceanog. Monaco, No. 1192*, 60 pp.

Philippi, E., 1912, Die Grundproben der deutschen Sudpolar Expedition. Drygalski, *Deutsche Sudpolar Expedition 1901–1903*, v. 2, Heft 6, pp. 431–434.

Phillips, O. M., 1957, On the generation of waves by turbulent wind. *Jour. Fluid Mech.* v. 2, no. 5, pp. 417–445.

Phleger, F. B, 1951a, Displaced Foraminifera faunas. *Soc. Econ. Paleontol. & Min. Spec. Publ. No. 2*, pp. 66–75.

Phleger, F. B, 1951b, Ecology of Foraminifera, northwest Gulf of Mexico. I. Foraminifera distribution. *Bull. Geol. Soc. America*, v. 46, pp. 1–88.

Phleger, F. B, 1955, Foraminiferal faunas in cores offshore from the Mississippi Delta. *Deep-Sea Research*, v. 3, Suppl. pp. 45–57.

Phleger, F. B, 1960a, *Ecology and Distribution of Recent Foraminifera*. The Johns Hopkins Press, Baltimore, Md., 297 pp.

Phleger, F. B, 1960b, Sedimentary patterns of microfaunas in northern Gulf of Mexcio, in *Recent Sediments, Northwest Gulf of Mexico*, F. P.

Shepard, F. B Phleger, and Tj. H. van Andel, editors. American Association of Petroleum Geologists, Tulsa, Okla., pp. 267–301.

Piccard, Jacques, and R. S. Dietz, 1961, *Seven Miles Down*, G. P. Putnam & Sons, New York, 249 pp.

Picciotto, E., and S. Wilgain, 1954, Thorium determinations in deep-sea sediments, *Nature*, v. 173, p. 632.

Pierson, W. J., G. Neumann, and R. W. James, 1955, Practical methods for observing and forecasting ocean waves by means of wave spectra and statistics. *U.S. Navy Dept., Hydrographic Office Publ. No. 603*, pp. 182–221.

Pilsbry, H. A., 1916, Mid-Pacific land snail faunas. *Natl. Acad. Sci. Proc.*, v. 2, pp. 429–433.

Pirsson, L. V., 1914, Geology of Bermuda Island; the igneous platform. *Am. Jour. Sci.*, v. 38, pp. 189–206, 331–334.

Powers, M. C., 1953, A new roundness scale for sedimentary particles. *Jour. Sed. Petrology*, v. 23, pp. 117–119.

Pratje, Otto, 1948, Die Bodenbedeckung der südlichen und mittleren Ostsee und ihre Bedeutung für die Ausdeutung fossiler sedimente. *Deut. Hydrog. Z.*, v. 1, pt. 2/3, pp. 45–61.

Pratje, Otto, 1949, Die Bodenbedeckung der nordeuropäischen Meere. *Handbuch der Seefischerei Nordsuropas*, v. I, pt. 3, 23 pp.

Price, W. A., 1951, Barrier island, not "offshore bar." *Science*, v. 113, pp. 487–488.

Price, W. A., 1953, The classification of shorelines and coasts, and its application to the Gulf of Mexico. Prelim. Rept., *Texas Agr. & Mech. College, Dept. Oceanog., Contrib. No. 15*, 111 pp. (mimeo.)

Price, W. A., 1955, Correlation of shoreline type with offshore bottom conditions. *Texas Agr. & Mech. Research Foundation Project 63*, pp. 1–8 (mimeo.).

Price, W. A., 1956, Environment and history in identification of shoreline types. *Quaternaria III*, pp. 151–166.

Price, W. A., and B. W. Wilson, 1956, Cuspate spits of St. Lawrence Island: a discussion. *Jour. Geology*, v. 64, no. 1, pp. 94–95.

Priestley, C. H. B., 1959, *Turbulent Transfer in the Lower Atmosphere*. University of Chicago Press, Chicago, Ill., 130 pp.

Prouty, W. F., 1946, Atlantic coastal plain floor and continental slope off North Carolina. *Bull. Am. Assoc. Petrol. Geologists*, v. 30, pp. 1917–1920.

Putnam, J. A., and J. W. Johnson, 1949, The dissipation of wave energy by bottom friction. *Trans. Amer. Geophys. Union*, v. 30, pp. 67–74.

Putnam, J. A., W. H. Munk, and M. A. Traylor, 1949, The prediction of longshore currents. *Trans. Amer. Geophys. Union*, v. 30, no. 3, pp. 337–345.

Putnam, W. C., D. I. Axelrod, H. P. Bailey, and J. T. McGill, 1960, *Natural Coastal Environments of the World*. Geography Branch, Office of Naval Research and University of California, Nonr-233(06), NR 388-013, pp. 1–140.

Putz, R. R., 1952, Statistical distributions for ocean waves. *Trans. Am. Geophys. Union*, v. 33, pp. 685–692.

Radczewski, O. E., 1937a, Eolian deposits in marine sediments, in *Recent*

*Marine Sediments*, P. D. Trask, editor. American Association of Petroleum Geologists, Tulsa, Okla., pp. 496–502.

Radczewski, O. E., 1937b, Die mineral fazia der sedimente des Kapverden-Beckens, *Wiss. Erg. Deut. Atlant. Expedition Meteor 1925–1927*, v. 3, pt. 3, pp. 262–277.

Raitt, R. W., 1952, The 1950 seismic refraction studies of Bikini and Kwajalein atolls and Sylvania Guyot. *Univ. Calif., Marine Phys. Lab. of Scripps Inst. Oceanog.*, SIO Ref. 52–38, pp. 1–25.

Raitt, R. W., 1956, Seismic-refraction studies of the Pacific Ocean Basin I, *Bull. Geol. Soc. America*, v. 67, pp. 1623–1639.

Raitt, R. W., 1957, Seismic-refraction studies of Eniwetok Atoll. Bikini and nearby atolls, Marshall Islands. *U.S. Geol. Survey Prof. Paper 260-S*, pp. 685–698.

Raitt, R. W., R. L. Fisher, and R. G. Mason, 1955, Tonga Trench, in *The Crust of the Earth. Geol. Soc. America Spec. Paper 62*, pp. 237–254.

Raitt, R. W., and G. G. Shor, Jr., 1959, Pacific oceanic crust, abstract in *Preprints International Oceanographic Congress*. American Association for the Advancement of Science, Washington, D.C., p. 49.

Rao, M. P., and C. Mahadevan, 1959, Studies in marine geology of Bay of Bengal along the East Coast of India, abstract in *Preprints International Oceanographic Congress*. American Association for the Advancement of Science, Washington D.C., pp. 655–656.

Raymond, P. E., and H. C. Stetson, 1932, A calcareous beach on the coast of Maine, *Jour. Sed. Petrology*, v. 2, no. 2, pp. 51–62.

*Recent Marine Sediments*, P. D. Trask, editor, 1939, American Association of Petroleum Geologists, Tulsa, Okla., 736 pp.

*Recent Sediments, Northwest Gulf of Mexico*, F. P. Shepard, F. B Phleger, and Tj. H. van Andel, editors, 1960, American Association Petroleum Geologists, Tulsa, Okla., 394 pp.

Redfield, A. C., 1958, Preludes to the entrapment of organic matter in the sediments of Lake Maracaibo, in *Habitat of Oil*. American Association of of Petroleum Geologists, Tulsa, Okla., pp. 968–981.

Reid, R. O. and K. Kajiura, 1957, On the damping of gravity waves over a permeable bed. *Trans. Amer. Geophys. Union*, v. 38, pp. 662–666.

Reineck, H. E., 1963, Der Kastengriefer. *Natur und Museum*, v. 93, no. 2, pp. 65–68.

Renz, O., R. Lakeman, and E. van der Meulen, 1955, Submarine sliding in western Venezuela. *Bull. Am. Assoc. Petrol. Geologists*, v. 39, no. 10.

Revelle, R. R., 1944, Marine bottom samples collected in the Pacific Ocean by the *Carnegie* on its seventh cruise. *Carnegie Inst. Washington Pub. 556*, pt. I, pp. 1–182.

Revelle, R. R., 1955, On the history of the oceans. *Jour. Marine Research*, v. 14, no. 4, pp. 446–461.

Revelle, R. R., M. N. Bramlette, G. Arrhenius, and E. D. Goldberg, 1955, Pelagic sediments of the Pacific. *Geol. Soc. America Spec. Paper 62*, pp. 221–236.

Revelle, R. R., and R. Fairbridge, 1957, Carbonates and carbon dioxide. in *Geol. Soc. America Mem. 67*, 1, 239–96.

Revelle, R. R., and F. P. Shepard, 1939, Sediments off the California coast, in *Recent Marine Sediments*, P. D. Trask, editor. American Association of Petroleum Geologists, Tulsa, Okla., pp. 245–282.

Rex, R. W., 1955, Microrelief produced by sea ice grounding in the Chukcki Sea near Barrow, Alaska, *Jour. Arctic Inst. North America*, v. 8, no. 3, pp. 177–186.

Rex, R. W., and E. D. Goldberg, 1958, Quartz contents of pelagic sediments of the Pacific Ocean. *Tellus*, v. 10, pp. 153–159.

Reynolds, Osborne, 1885, On the dilatancy of media composed of rigid particles in contact. *Philos. Mag.*, ser. 5, v. 20, pp. 469–481.

Rich, J. L., 1951, Probable fondo origin of Marcellus-Ohio-New Albany-Chattanooga bituminous shales. *Bull. Am. Assoc. Petrol. Geologists*, v. 35, no. 9, pp. 2017–2040.

Richards, A. F., 1959, Geology of the Islas Revillagigedo, Mexico. 1. Birth and development of Volcán Bárcena, Isla San Benedicto. *Bull. Volcanol. Union Géod. Géophys. Intern.*, ser. II, v. XXII, pp. 73–123.

Richards, H. C., 1940, Results of deep boring operations on the Great Barrier Reef, Australia. *Proc. Sixth Pacific Sci. Congr.*, v. 2, p. 857.

Riedel, W. R., 1952, Tertiary Radiolaria in Western Pacific sediments. *Medd. Fran Oceanog. Inst. I Göteborg*, Sjatte Foljden, ser. B, v. 6, no. 3, pp. 1–21.

Riedel, W. R., 1954, The age of the sediment collected at *Challenger* (1875) Station 225 and the distribution of *Ethmodiscus rex* (Rattray). *Deep-Sea Research*, v. 1, pp. 170–175.

Riedel, W. R., 1959, Siliceous organic remains in pelagic sediments, in *Silica in Sediments, Soc. Econ. Paleontol. and Mineral. Spec. Publ. No. 7*, pp. 80–91.

Riedel, W. R., and M. N. Bramlette, 1959, Tertiary sediments in the Pacific Ocean Basin, abstract in *Preprints International Oceanographic Congress*. American Association for the Advancement of Science, Washington, D.C., p. 105.

Riley, N. A., 1941, Projection sphericity. *Jour. Sed. Petrology*, v. 11, pp. 94–97.

Rivière, André, and Jean Laurent, 1954, Sur une méthode nouvelle et peu coûteuse de défense contre l'érosion littorale. *Compt. Rend.* v. 239, pp. 298–300.

Robinson, A. H. W., *et al.*, 1953, The storm floods of 1st February, 1953. *Geography*, pp. 132–189.

Rosalsky, M. B., 1960, The physiography of Cape Canaveral, Florida. *Rocks and Minerals*, March-April 1960, pp. 99–102.

Rosenan, E., 1937, *Fisherman's Chart—1:100,000 Scale in Four Sheets.* Government of Palestine, Dept. of Agr. and Fisheries Service.

Rosfelder, André, 1955, Carte Provisoire au 1/500,000ᵉ de la Marge Continentale Algérienne. *La Carte Géologique de l'Algérie* (Nfi), *Bull. No. 5*, pp. 57–106.

Rosholt, J. N., C. Emiliani, J. Geiss, F. F. Koczy, and P. J. Wangersky, 1961,

Absolute dating of deep-sea cores by the Pa[231]/thorium[230] method. *Jour. Geology*, v. 69, no. 2, pp. 162–185.

Ross, C. S., and S. B. Hendricks, 1945, Minerals of the montmorillonite group. *U.S. Geol. Survey Prof. Paper 205B*, pp. 1–77.

Rudnick, P., 1951, Correlograms for Pacific Ocean waves. *Proc. 2nd Berkeley Symposium Math. Stat. and Prob.*, University of California Press, Berkeley, Calif., 626–638.

Rüegg, Werner, 1960, An intra-Pacific ridge, its continuation onto the Peruvian mainland, and its bearing on the hypothetical Pacific landmass. *21st Intern. Geol. Congr., Copenhagen*, pt. X, Proc. sec. 10, pp. 29–38.

Rusnak, G. A., 1960a, Some observations of recent oolites. *Jour. Sed. Petrology*, v. 30, no. 3, pp. 471–480.

Rusnak, G. A., 1960b, Sediments of Laguna Madre, in *Recent Sediments, Northwest Gulf of Mexico*, F. P. Shepard, F. B. Phleger, and Tj. H. van Andel, editors. American Association Petroleum Geologists Tulsa, Okla., pp. 153–196.

Russell, R. C. H., and J. D. C. Osorio, 1958, An experimental investigation of drift profiles in a closed channel. *Sixth Conf. Coastal Eng.* pp. 171–183.

Russell, R. D., 1939, Effects of transportation on sedimentary particles, in *Recent Marine Sediments*, P. D. Trask, editor. American Association of Petroleum Geologists, Tulsa, Okla., pp. 32–47.

Russell, R. J., 1936, Physiography of Lower Mississippi River Delta, in *Louisiana Geol. Surv. Geol. Bull. No. 8*, pp. 3–199.

Russell, R. J., 1958, Geological geomorphology. *Bull. Geol. Soc. America*, v. 69, pp. 1–22.

Russell, R. J., 1959, Long, straight beaches. *Eclogae Geol. Helv.*, v. 51, no. 3, pp. 591–598.

Russell, R. J., and H. V. W. Howe, 1935, Cheniers of southwestern Louisiana. *Geog. Rev.*, v. 25, pp. 449–461.

Sackett, W. M., 1960, Protoactinium-231 content of ocean water and sediment. *Science*, v. 132, pp. 1761–1762.

Savage, R. P., 1953, Laboratory study of wave energy losses by bottom friction and percolation. *Beach Erosion Board*, U.S. Corps of Engineers, Tech. Memo 31, 25 pp.

Saville, Thorndike, Jr., 1956b, wave run-up on shore structures. *Jour. Waterways and Harbors Div.*, Proc. Am. Soc. Civil Engrs., Paper 925, v. 82, W.W. 2, pp. 925–1, 925–14.

Schalk, Marshall, 1946, Submarine topography off Eleuthera Island, Bahamas. *Bull. Geol. Soc. America*, v. 57, p. 1228.

Schenk, H. V., Jr., and Henry Kendall, 1954, *Underwater Photography*. Cornell Maritime Press, Cambridge, Md., 110 pp.

Schmidt, W., 1917, Wirkungen der ungeordneten Bewegung im Wasser der Meere und Seen. *Ann. Hydrograph Mar. Meteorol.*, v. 45, pp. 367–381, 431–445.

Schmidt, W., 1925, Der Massenaustansch in der freien Luft and verwandte Erscheinungen. *Probleme der Kosmischen Physik*, VII. H. Grand, Hamburg, 118 pp.

Schott, W., 1939, Deep-sea sediments of the Indian Ocean, and Rate of sedimentation of recent marine sediments, in *Recent Marine Sediments*, P. D. Trask, editor. American Association Petroleum Geologists, Tulsa, pp. 396–415.

Schumacher, A., 1952, Results of exact wave measurements (by stereogrammetry) with special reference to more recent theoretical investigations, in *Gravity Waves. Natl. Bur. Standards Circ. 521*, pp. 69–78.

Scott, Theodore, 1954, Sand movement by waves. *Beach Erosion Board Tech. Mem. No. 48*, 37 pp.

Scott-Russell, 1884, Report on Waves. *British Association Reports*.

Scruton, P. C., 1960, Delta building and the deltaic sequence, in *Recent Sediments, Northwest Gulf of Mexico*, F. P. Shepard, F. B Phleger, Tj. H. van Andel, editors, American Association Petroleum Geologists, Tulsa, Okla., pp. 82–102.

Segerstråle, S. G., 1957, Baltic Sea, in *Treatise on Marine Ecology and Paleoecology*, v. I, *Ecology. Geol. Soc. America Mem. 67*, pp. 751–800.

Segrè, Aldo, 1958, Observations generales sur l'Orographie sous-marine de la Mer Tyrrhenienne: La topographie et la geologie des profondeurs oceaniques. *Centre Natl. Recherche Sci.*, v. 83, pp. 53–59.

Sewell, R. B. S., 1935–1936, The John Murray Expedition, 1933–1934. *Scientific Reports 1935–1936*, v. 1, charts 1–3, Adlard & Sons, London.

Shand, S. J., 1949, Rocks of the Mid-Atlantic Ridge. *Jour. Geology*, v. 57, no. 1, pp. 89–92.

Sheldon, R. P., 1959, Geochemistry of uranium in phosphorites and black shales of the Phosphoria Formation. *U.S. Geol. Surv. Bull. 1084b*, pp. 83–115.

Shepard, F. P., 1937a, Revised classification of marine shorelines. *Jour. Geology*, v. 45, pp. 602–624.

Shepard, F. P., 1937b, "Salt" domes related to Mississippi Submarine Trough. *Bull. Geol. Soc. America*, v. 48, pp. 1354–1361.

Shepard, F. P., 1949, Terrestrial topography of submarine canyons revealed by diving. *Bull. Geol. Soc. America*, v. 60, pp. 1597–1612.

Shepard, F. P., 1951a, Transportation of sand into deep water. *Soc. Econ. Paleontol. and Mineral., Spec. Publ. No. 2*, pp. 53–65.

Shepard, F. P., 1951b, Mass movements in submarine canyon heads. *Trans. Am. Geophys. Union*, v. 32, no. 3, pp. 405–418.

Shepard, F. P., 1952a, Composite origin of submarine canyons. *Jour. Geology*, v. 60, no. 1, pp. 84–96.

Shepard, F. P., 1952b, Revised nomenclature for depositional coastal features. *Bull. Am. Assoc. Petrol. Geologists*, v. 36, no. 10, pp. 1902–1912.

Shepard, F. P., 1955, Delta-front valleys bordering the Mississippi distributaries. *Bull. Geol. Soc. America*, v. 66, no. 12, pp. 1489–1498.

Shepard, F. P., 1956, Marginal sediments of Mississippi Delta. *Bull. Am. Assoc. Petrol. Geologists*, v. 40, no. 11, pp. 2537–2623.

Shepard, F. P., 1957, Northward continuation of the San Andreas Fault. *Bull. Seismol. Soc. America*, v. 47, no. 3, pp. 263–266.

Shepard, F. P., 1959a, Sediment environments of the northwest Gulf of Mexico. *Eclogae Geol. Helv.*, v. 51, no. 3, pp. 598–608.

Shepard, F. P., 1959b, *The Earth Beneath the Sea*. Johns Hopkins Press, Baltimore, Md. 275 pp.

Shepard, F. P., 1960a, Mississippi Delta: marginal environments, sediments, and growth, in *Recent Sediments, Northwest Gulf of Mexico*, F. P. Shepard, F. B. Phleger, and Tj. H. van Andel, editors. American Association of Petroleum Geologists, Tulsa, Okla., pp. 56–81.

Shepard, F. P., 1960b, Gulf Coast barriers, in *Recent Sediments, Northwest Gulf of Mexico*, F. P. Shepard, F. B. Phleger, and Tj. H. van Andel, editors, American Association of Petroleum Geologists, Tulsa, Okla., pp. 197–220.

Shepard, F. P., 1960c, Rise of sea level along northwest Gulf of Mexico, in *Recent Sediments Northwest Gulf of Mexico*, F. P. Shepard, F. B. Phleger, and Tj. H. van Andel, editors. American Association of Petroleum Geologists, Tulsa, Okla., pp. 338–344.

Shepard, F. P., 1961a, Deep-sea sands. Repts. *XXI Intern. Geol. Congr.*, pt. 23, pp. 26–42.

Shepard, F. P., 1961b, Submarine canyons of the Gulf of California. Repts. *XXI Intern. Geol. Congr.*, pt. 26, pp. 11–23.

Shepard, F. P., and C. N. Beard, 1938, Submarine canyons: distribution and longitudinal profiles. *Geog. Rev.*, v. 28, no. 3, pp. 439–451.

Shepard, F. P., and G. V. Cohee, 1936, Continental shelf sediments off the Mid-Atlantic States. *Bull. Geol. Soc. America*, v. 47, pp. 441–458.

Shepard, F. P., and Gerhard Einsele, 1962, Sedimentation in San Diego Trough and contributing submarine canyons. *Sedimentology*, v. 1, no. 2, pp. 81–133.

Shepard, F. P., and K. O. Emery, 1941, Submarine topography off the California Coast: Canyons and tectonic interpretation. *Geol. Soc. America Spec. Paper No. 31*, 171 pp.

Shepard, F. P., K. O. Emery, and H. R. Gould, 1949, Distribution of sediments on East Asiatic Continental Shelf. *Allan Hancock Foundation Publ., Occasional Paper No. 9*, pp. 1–64.

Shepard, F. P., and U.S. Grant, IV, 1947, Wave erosion along the southern California coast. *Bull. Geol. Soc. America*, v. 58, pp. 919–926.

Shepard, F. P., U.S. Grant, IV, and R. S. Dietz, 1939, The emergence of (Santa) Catalina Island. *Am. Jour. Sci.*, v. 237, pp. 651–655.

Shepard, F. P., and D. L. Inman, 1950, Nearshore water circulation related to bottom topography and wave refraction. *Trans. Am. Geophys. Union*, v. 31, no. 2, pp. 196–212.

Shepard, F. P., and D. L. Inman, 1951, Nearshore circulation. *Proc. First Conf. Coastal Eng., Council on Wave Research*, pp. 50–59.

Shepard, F. P., and G. A. Macdonald, 1938, Sediments of Santa Monica Bay, California. *Bull. Am. Assoc. Petrol. Geologists*, v. 22, pp. 201–216.

Shepard, F. P., G. A. Macdonald, and D. C. Cox, 1950, The tsunami of April 1, 1946. *Bull. Scripps Inst. Oceanog., Univ. of Calif.*, v. 5, pp. 391–455.

Shepard, F. P., and D. G. Moore, 1955, Central Texas coast sedimentation:

Stocks, Theodor, 1933, Die echolotprofile Wissenschaftliche ergebnisse der Deutschen Atlantischen Expedition auf den *Meteor*, 1925–1927. v. II.

Stocks, Theodor, 1956, Der Boden der südlichen Nordsee. *Deut. Hydrog. Z.*, v. 9, pt. 6, pp. 265–280.

Stocks, Theodor, 1960, Zur Bodengestalt des Indischen Ozeans. *Erdkunde*, v. XIV, Lfg. 3, pp. 161–170.

Stokes, G. G., 1847, On the theory of oscillatory waves. *Trans. Cambridge Philos. Soc.*, no. 8, p. 441.

Stommel, Henry, 1958, *The Gulf Stream, A Physical and Dynamic Description*. University of California Press, Berkeley, Calif., 202 pp.

Strakhov, N. M., 1947, Zur Erkenntnis der Gesetzmässigkeiten und des mechanismus der marinen sedimentation. I. *Schwarzes Meer. Izv. Akad. Nauk SSSR, Geol. ser.*, no. 2.

Strakhov, N. M., 1948, *Outlines of Historical Geology*, Moscow.

Ström, K. M., 1936, Land-locked waters. Hydrography and bottom deposits in badly ventilated Norwegian fiords. *Norske Vidensk. Akad. Oslo, Mat. Naturv. Klasse*, no. 7, 85 pp.

Ström K. M., 1939, Land-locked waters and the deposition of black muds, in *Recent Marine Sediments*, P. D. Trask, editor. American Association Petroleum Geologists, Tulsa, Okla., pp. 356–372.

Sverdrup, H. U., M. W. Johnson, and R. H. Fleming, 1942, *The Oceans, Their Physics, Chemistry and General Biology*. Prentice-Hall, Englewood Cliffs, N. J., 1087 pp.

Sverdrup, H. U., and W. H. Munk, 1947, Wind, sea and swell—theory of relationships in forecasting. *U.S. Navy Dept., Hydrographic Office Publ. 601*, 44 pp.

Swallow, J. C., 1955, A neutral bouyancy float for measuring deep currents. *Deep-Sea Research*, v. 3, pp. 74–81.

Talwani, M., G. H. Sutton, and J. L. Worzel, 1959, A crustal section across the Puerto Rico Trench. *Jour. Geophys. Research*, v. 64, no. 10, pp. 1545–1555.

Tanner, W. F., 1960, Expanding shoals in areas of wave refraction (abstract). *Science*, v. 132, pp. 1012–1013.

Tatsumoto, M., and E. D. Goldberg, 1959, Some aspects of the marine geochemistry of uranium. *Geochim. et Cosmochim. Acta*, v. 17, pp. 201–208.

Teichert, Curt, 1958a, Cold- and deep-water coral banks. *Bull. Am. Assoc. Petrol. Geologists*, v. 42, no. 5, pp. 1064–1082.

Teichert, Curt, 1958b, Australia and Gondwanaland. *Geol. Rundschau*, v. 47, pt. 2, pp. 562–590.

Teixeira, Carlos, 1950, A propos d'une hypothèse sur la structure de l'Océan Atlantique. *Museo e Laboratorio Mineralógico e Geológico da Universidade de Lisboa*, Bol. no. 18.

Ten Haaf, E., 1959, *Graded Beds of the Northern Apennines*. V. R. B., Gröningen, pp. 6–102.

Termier, H., and G. Termier, 1952, *Histoire géologique de la biosphère*, Masson, Paris, 721 pp.

Terry, R. D., S. A. Keesling, and E. Uchupi, 1956, Submarine geology of Santa Monica Bay, California. Report to Hyperion Engineers, Inc., from Geol. Dept., Univ. So. Calif., 177 pp. (multilithed).

Terzaghi, Karl, 1956, Varieties of submarine slope failures. *Proc. 8th Texas Conf. on Soil Mech. and Found. Eng., Spec. Publ. 29*, Bureau of Engineering Research, University of Texas, Austin, Tex. 41 pp.

Terzaghi, Karl, and R. B. Peck, 1948, *Soil Mechanics in Engineering Practice*, John Wiley & Sons, New York, 566 pp.

Thomas, C. W., 1959, Lithology and zoology of an Antarctic Ocean bottom core. *Deep-Sea Research*, v. 6, pp. 5–15.

Thomas, C. W., 1960, Late Pleistocene and Recent limits of the Ross Ice Shelf. *Jour. Geophys. Research*, v. 65, no. 6, pp. 1789–1792.

Thomas, W. H., and E. G. Simmons, 1960, Phytoplankton production in the Mississippi Delta, in *Recent Sediments, Northwest Gulf of Mexico*, F. P. Shepard, F. B. Phleger, and Tj. H. van Andel, editors. American Association of Petroleum Geologists, Tulsa, Okla., pp. 103–116.

Thorndike, E. M., 1959, Deep-sea cameras of the Lamont Observatory. *Deep-Sea Research*, v. 5, pp. 234–237.

Tocher, Don, 1956, Earthquakes off the North Pacific coast of the United States. *Bull. Seismol. Soc. America*, v. 46, pp. 165–173.

Tokyo Imperial University, 1933, Papers and reports on the tsunami of 1933, Sanriku coast, Japan, T. Ogawa, editor. *Earthquake Research Inst. Bull.*, suppl. 1.

Torphy, S. R., and J. M. Zeigler, 1957, Submarine topography of Eastern Channel, Gulf of Maine. *Jour. Geology*, v. 65, no. 4, pp. 433–441.

Tracey, J. I., Jr., P. E. Cloud, Jr., and K. O. Emery, 1955, Conspicuous features of organic reefs. *Atoll Research Bull.*, no. 46, pp. 1–3.

Trask, P. D., 1932 (assisted by H. E. Hammar and C. C. Wu), *Origin and Environment of Source Sediments of Petroleum*, A.P.I. Gulf Publ. Co., Houston, Tex., 323 pp.

Trask, P. D., editor, 1939, *Recent Marine Sediments*. American Association Petroleum Geologists, Tulsa, Okla., 736 pp.

Trask, P. D., 1952, Source of beach sand at Santa Barbara, California, as indicated by mineral grain studies. *Beach Erosion Board Tech. Memo. No. 28*, 24 pp.

Trask, P. D., 1955, Movement of sand around southern California promontories. *Beach Erosion Board Tech. Memo. No. 76*, 66 pp.

Trefethen, J. M., and R. L. Dow, 1960, Some features of modern beach sediments. *Jour. Sed. Petrology*, v. 30, no. 4, pp. 589–602.

Truesdell, P. E., and D. J. Varnes, 1950, *Chart Correlating Various Grain-Size Definitions of Sedimentary Material*. U.S. Dept. of the Interior, Geological Survey, Washington, D.C.

Trumbull, James, John Lyman, J. F. Pepper, and E. M. Thomasson, 1958, An introduction to the geology and mineral resources of the continental shelves of the Americas. *U.S. Geol. Survey Bull. 1067*, pp. 1–92.

Tucker, M. J., 1950, Surf beats: sea waves of 1 to 5 min. period. *Proc. Roy. Soc. (London)* A, 202, pp. 565–573.

Twenhofel, W. H., 1939, Environments of origin of black shales. *Bull. Am. Assoc. Petrol. Geologists*, v. 23, no. 8, pp. 1178–1198.

Udden, J. A., 1898, Mechanical composition of wind deposits. *Augustana Library Publ.*, no. 1.

Udintsev, G. B., 1954, New data on the relief of the Kurile-Kamchatka Depression, *Doklady Acad. Nauk USSR*, v. 94, no. 2, pp. 315–318.

Udintsev, G. B., 1957, Relief of Okhotsk Sea. *Acad. Sci. USSR*, v. 22, 76 pp.

Udintsev, G. B., 1959, Relief of abyssal trenches in the Pacific Ocean, abstract in *Preprints International Oceanographic Congress*. American Association for the Advancement of Science, Washington, D.C., p. 54.

Udintsev, G. B., 1960, On the bottom relief of the western region of the Pacific Ocean. *Oceanological Researches*, no. 2, X Section of IGY Program (Oceanology), Moscow, pp. 5–32.

Ufford, C. W., 1947, Internal waves in the ocean. *Trans. Am. Geophys. Union*, v. 28, pp. 79–86.

Umbgrove, J. H. F., 1947, Coral reefs of the East Indies. *Bull. Geol. Soc. America*, v. 58, p. 733.

*U.S. Navy Diving Manual*, 1960, U.S. Government Printing Office, Washington, D.C.

*U.S. Waterways Exper. Station* (Vicksburg), 1935, Studies of river bed materials and their movement with special reference to the lower Mississippi River. Paper 17, 161 pp.

Urry, W. D., and C. S. Piggot, 1942, Radioactivity of ocean sediments. V. Concentration of radio-elements and their significance in red clays. *Am. Jour. Sci.*, v. 240, pp. 93–103.

Vacquier, Victor, 1959, Measurement of horizontal displacement along faults in the ocean floor. *Nature*, v. 183, pp. 452–453.

Vacquier, Victor, A. D. Raff, and R. E. Warren, 1959, Progress of the magnetic survey conducted by the Scripps Institution of Oceanography in the Northeastern Pacific Ocean, abstract in *Preprints International Oceanographic Congress*. American Association for the Advancement of Science, Washington, D.C., p. 60.

Vacquier, Victor, A. D. Raff, and R. E. Warren, 1961, Horizontal displacements in the floor of the northeastern Pacific Ocean. *Bull. Geol. Soc. America*, v. 72, no. 8, pp. 1251–1258.

Valentin, Hartmut, 1952, *Die Küsten der Erde*. Justus Perthes Gotha, Berlin, 118 pp.

van Andel, Tj. H., 1955, Sediments of the Rhone Delta. II. Sources and deposition of heavy minerals. *Koninkl. Ned. Geol.-Mijnb. Gen., Verh.*, Geol. ser., dl. 15, pp. 515–556.

van Andel, Tj. H., J. R. Curray, and J. J. Veevers, 1961, Recent carbonate sediments of the Sahul Shelf—northwestern Australia, abstract in *Proc. First National Coastal and Shallow Water Research Conference*, D. S. Gorsline, editor. National Science Foundation and Office of Naval Research, p. 564.

van Andel, Tj. H., and D. M. Poole, 1960, Sources of recent sediments in the northern Gulf of Mexico, *Jour. Sed. Petrology*, v. 30, pp. 91–122.

van Andel, Tj. H., and H. Postma, 1954, *Recent Sediments of the Gulf of Paria, Reports of Orinoco Shelf Expedition, I,* North-Holland Publishing Co., Amsterdam, 245 pp.

van Baren, F. A., and H. Kiel, 1950, Contribution to the sedimentary petrology of the Sunda Shelf, *Jour. Sed. Petrology,* v. 20, no. 4, pp. 185–213.

van Dorn, W. G., 1961, The source motion of the tsunami of March 9, 1957, as deduced from wave measurements at Wake Island, abstract in Tenth Pacific Science Congress, Honolulu, Hawaii, pp. 351–352.

Vanoni, V. A., 1946, Transportation of suspended sediment by water. *Trans. Am. Soc. Civil Engrs.,* v. 111, pp. 67–133.

Vanoni, V. A., 1953, A summary of sediment transportation mechanics. *Proc. Third Midwestern Conf. Fluid Mech.,* University of Minnesota, Minneapolis, Minn., pp. 129–160.

van Straaten, L. M. J. U., 1951, Texture and genesis of Dutch Wadden Sea sediments. *Proc. 3rd Intern. Congr. Sedimentology,* Netherlands, Excelsior, Den Haag, pp. 225–244.

van Straaten, L. M. J. U., 1953a, Megaripples in the Dutch Wadden Sea and in Basin of Arcachon (France), *Geol. en Mijnhouw,* NS., v. 15, no. 1, pp. 1–11.

van Straaten, L. M. J. U., 1953b, Rhythmic patterns on Dutch North Sea beaches. *Geol. en Mijnbouw,* NS., v. 15, no. 2, pp. 31–43.

van Straaten, L. M. J. U., 1954, The composition and structure of Recent marine sediments in the Netherlands, *Leidse Geol. Mededel.,* v. 19.

van Straaten, L. M. J. U., 1959a, Littoral and submarine morphology of the Rhone Delta. *2nd Coastal Geography Conference,* National Academy of Sciences–National Research Council, Washington, D.C., pp. 233–264.

van Straaten, L. M. J. U., 1959b, Minor structures of some recent littoral and neritic sediments. *Geol. en Mijnbouw,* NS., v. 21, pp. 197–216.

van Straaten, L. M. J. U., and Ph. H. Kuenen, 1957, Accumulation of fine grained sediments in the Dutch Wadden Sea. *Geol. en Mijnbouw,* NS., v. 19, pp. 329–354.

van Veen, Joh., 1936, *Onderzoekingen in de Hoofden.* 'S-Gravenhage, Algemeene Landsdukkerij, 252 pp.

Varney, F. M., and L. E. Redwine, 1937, Hydraulic coring instrument for submarine geologic investigations. *Natl. Research Council Ann. Rept.,* App. I, Sedimentation Comm., pp. 107–113.

Vaughan, T. W., 1916, On Recent Madreporaria of Florida, the Bahamas, and the West Indies, and on collections from Murray Island, Australia. *Dept. Marine Biol., Carnegie Inst. Washington, Year Book 14,* pp. 220–231.

Vaughan, T. W., 1917, Chemical and organic deposits of the sea. *Geol. Soc. America Bull.,* v. 28, p. 933.

Vaughan, T. W., and J. W. Wells, 1943, *Revision of the Suborders, Families, and Genera of the Scleractinia. Geol. Soc. America Spec. Paper 44,* xv, 363 pp.

Veatch, A. C., and P. A. Smith, 1939, *Atlantic Submarine Valleys of the United States and the Congo Submarine Valley. Geol. Soc. America Spec. Paper 7,* 101 pp.

Vening Meinesz, F. A., 1929, Results of gravity determination upon the Pacific and the organization of further research. *Proc. 4th Pacific Sci. Congr., Java*, IIB, p. 665.

Vening Meinesz, F. A., 1932, *Gravity Expeditions at Sea*. Waltmann, Delft, v. 1.

Vening Meinesz, F. A., 1934, *Gravity Expeditions at Sea*. Waltmann, Delft, v. 2, 208 pp.

Vening Meinesz, F. A., 1955, Plastic buckling of the earth's crust: the origin of geosynclines, in *Crust of the Earth*, A. Poldervaart, editor. *Geol. Soc. America Spec. Paper 62*, pp. 319–330.

Verstappen, Herman, 1959, Geomorphology and crustal movements of the Aru Islands in relation to the Pleistocene drainage of the Sahul Shelf. *Am. Jour. Sci.*, v. 257, pp. 491–502.

von Buttlar, H., and F. G. Houtermans, 1950, Photographic determination of the activity in manganese nodules of deep-sea origin. *Naturwissenschaften*, v. 37, pp. 400–401.

von Herzen, R. P., 1959, Heat-flow values from the southeastern Pacific. *Nature*, v. 183, pp. 882–883.

von Kármán, T., 1947, Sand ripples in the desert. *Technion Yearbook*, v. 6, pp. 52–54.

Waddell, Hakon, 1932, Volume, shape, and roundness of rock particles. *Jour. Geology*, v. 40, pp. 443–451.

Walker, Boyd W., 1952, A guide to the grunion. *Calif. Fish and Game*, v. 38, no. 3, pp. 409–420.

Walton, W. R., 1955, Ecology of living benthonic Foraminifera, Todos Santos Bay, Baja California. *Jour. Paleontology*, v. 29, no. 6, pp. 952–1018.

Wanless, H. R., 1950, Late Paleozoic cycles of sedimentation in the United States. *Rept. 18th Intern. Geol. Congr.*, Great Britain, 1948, pt. IV, pp. 17–28.

Wanless, H. R., 1960, Evidences of multiple late Paleozoic glaciation in Australia, abstract in *Rept. 21st Intern. Geol. Congr.*, Copenhagen, p. 106.

Wanless, H. R., and F. P. Shepard, 1936, Sea level and climatic changes related to late Paleozoic cycles. *Bull. Geol. Soc. America*, v. 47, pp. 1177–1206.

Waring, W. W., and Layer, D. B., 1950, Devonian dolomitized reef, D3 Reservoir, Leduc Field, Alberta, Canada, *Bull. Am. Assoc. Petrol. Geologists*, v. 34, no. 2, pp. 295–312.

Weatherby, B. B., 1948, History and development of seismic prospecting. *Geophysical Case Histories*, L. L. Nettleton, editor. Society of Exploration Geophysicists, Tulsa, Okla., v. 1.

Wegener, Alfred, 1924, *The Origin of Continents and Oceans*. English translation from German 3rd edition, E. P. Dutton & Co., New York, 212 pp.

Weller, J. M., 1930, Cyclical sedimentation of the Pennsylvanian Period and its significance. *Jour. Geology*, v. 38, no. 2, pp. 97–135.

Wellman, H. W., 1954, Active transcurrent faulting in New Zealand, (abstract). *Bull. Geol. Soc. America*, v. 65, p. 1322.

Wells, J. W., 1954, Recent corals of the Marshall Islands, Bikini and nearby atolls. II. Oceanography (Biologic). *U.S. Geol. Survey Prof. Paper 260-I*, pp. 385–486.

White, C. M., 1940, The equilibrium of grains on the bed of a stream. *Proc. Roy. Soc. (London)*, A, v. 174, pp. 322–334.

Wiegel, R. L., 1953, Waves, tides, currents and beaches: glossary of terms and list of standard symbols. *Council on Wave Research*, Univ. of Calif., 113 pp.

Wiegel, R. L., 1959, Theory of periodic waves, in *Oceanographic Engineering*, Chap. II. Notes for Civil Engin. 205, University of California, Berkeley (unpublished), 67 pp.

Wiegel, R. L., and R. A. Fuchs, 1955, Wave transformation in shoaling water. *Trans. Am. Geophys. Union*, v. 36, pp. 975–984.

Willis, Bailey, 1932, Isthmian links. *Bull. Geol. Soc. America*, v. 43, pp. 917–952.

Wimberley, C. S., 1955, Marine sediments north of Scripps Submarine Canyon, La Jolla, California. *Jour. Sed. Petrology*, v. 25, no. 1, pp. 24–37.

Winchell, A. N., 1951, *Elements of Optical Mineralogy*, pt. II, *Descriptions of Minerals*, John Wiley & Sons, New York.

Wiseman, J. D. H., 1937, Basalts from the Carlsberg Ridge, Indian Ocean. *The John Murray Expedition, 1933–34, Sci. Repts.*, v. 3, no. 1.

Wiseman, J. D. H., 1959, The relation between paleotemperature and carbonate in an equatorial Atlantic pilot core. *Jour. Geol.*, v. 67, pp. 685–690.

Wiseman, J. D. H., and C. D. Ovey, 1953, Definitions of features on the deep-sea floor. *Deep-Sea Research*, v. 1, pp. 11–16.

Woodford, A. O., 1951, Stream gradients and Monterey Sea Valley. *Bull. Geol. Soc. America*, v. 62, pp. 799–852.

Woodring, W. P., M. N. Bramlette, and W. S. W. Kew, 1946, *Geology and Paleontology of Palos Verdes Hills, California. U.S. Geol. Survey Prof. Paper 207*, 145 pp.

Woolnough, W. G., 1937, Sedimentation in barred basins and source rocks of petroleum. *Bull. Am. Assoc. Petrol. Geologists*, v. 21, pp. 1101–1157.

Worzel, J. L., 1948, Ocean bottom sampler for ships under way. *Geoph.* v. 13, no. 3, pp. 452–456.

Worzel, J. L., 1959, Extensive deep-sea sub-bottom reflections identified as white ash, *Proc. Natl. Acad. Sci.*, v. 45, no. 3, pp. 349–355.

Worzel, J. L., and G. L. Shurbet, 1955, Gravity interpretations from standard oceanic and continental crustal sections, in *Crust of the Earth*, A. Poldervaart, editor. *Geol. Soc. America Spec. Paper 62*, pp. 87–100.

Wüst, Georg, 1935, Die stratosphäre. Deutschen Atlantischen Expedition *Meteor* 1925–1927, *Wiss., Erg.*, v. 6, pt. 1, no. 2, 288 pp.

Wüst, Georg, 1936, Schichtung und Zirkulation des Atlantischen Ozeans. Deutschen Atlantischen Expedition *Meteor* 1925–1927, *Wiss. Erg.*, v. 6.

Wyrtki, K., 1953, Die Bilanz des Langstransportes in der Brandungszone. *Deut. Hydrog. Z.*, v. 6, no. 2, pp. 65–76.

Yamasaki, Naomasa, 1926, Physiographical studies of the great earthquake of the Kwanto District, 1923. *Jour. Faculty Sci.*, Univ. of Tokyo, sec. II, v. II, pt. 2, pp. 77–119.

Yonge, C. M., 1940, The biology of reef-building corals. Great Barrier Reef Expedition 1928–29. *Brit. Museum (Nat. Hist.)*, Sci. Repts., v. 1, no. 13, pp. 353–391.

Zeigler, J. M., 1959, Sedimentary environments on the continental shelf of northern South America, abstract in *Preprints International Oceanographic Congress*. American Association for the Advancement of Science, Washington, D.C., p. 670.

Zeigler, J. M., W. D. Athern, and H. Small, 1957, Profiles across the Peru-Chile Trench. *Deep-Sea Research*, v. 4, pp. 238–249.

Zen, E. -An, 1957, Preliminary report on the mineralogy and petrology of some marine bottom samples off the coast of Peru and Chile. *Am. Mineralogist*, v. 42, pp. 889–903.

Zenkevitch, L. A., 1955, Importance of deep-sea research. *Trudi Inst. Okeanol.*, 12, pp. 5–15. Translated from Russian by Admiralty Center for Scientific Information and Liaison.

Zenkovitch, V. P., 1946, *Dynamics and Morphology of Sea Coasts* (in Russian).

Zenkovitch, V. P., 1958, *The Coastline of the Black and Azov Seas* (in Russian), 371 pp.

Zenkovitch, V. P., 1959, On the genesis of cuspate spits along lagoon shores. *Jour. Geology*, v. 67, no. 3, pp. 269–277.

Zhivago, A. V., 1959, Types of bottom relief in the southern Indian Ocean, Abstract in *Preprints International Oceanographic Congress*. American Association for the Advancement of Science, Washington, D.C., p. 64.

# APPENDIX A. UNITS AND SYMBOLS (FOR CHAPTERS III AND V)

Because of the shortage of alphabetical letters, it was found necessary in several instances to employ the same symbols to denote different quantities. In the column following each symbol is an expression giving the dimensions of the quantity in terms of mass $(M)$, length $(L)$ and time $(T)$. Dimensionless quantities are shown with no units (0). These dimensions can be replaced by their equivalents in any dimensionally consistent system of units. For example, the coefficient of eddy viscosity $A_z$ has dimensions $ML^{-1}T^{-1}$ and thus can be expressed in grams per centimeter per second, or if necessary in pounds mass per foot per second. A note of caution in the use of the latter British units—the pound can be used both as a unit of mass $(M)$, as in the above expression, and as a unit of force $(ML^{-1}T^{-2})$.

### Combined List of Symbols for Chapters III and V

| Symbol | Dimensions | Introduced | Description |
|---|---|---|---|
| $A_z, A_s$ | $ML^{-1}T^{-1}$ | V, eqs. 3, 10 | Coefficient of dynamic eddy viscosity $(A_z)$; value applicable to sediment transfer $(A_s)$. |
| $a$ | 0 | V, eq. 11b | Coefficient of proportionality, $A_s/A_z$. |
| $a_2, a_3$ | 0 | V, eq. 8 | Shape coefficients; $\pi/4$, $\pi/6$, for spheres. |
| $C, C_d, C_s$ | $LT^{-1}$ | III, eqs. 1, 1a, 1b | Phase velocity of surface wave $(C)$; in deep water $(C_d)$; in shallow water $(C_s)$. Fig. 28, Chap. III. |
| $c$ | 0 | V, eq. 6 | Drag coefficient, $\tau/\rho\bar{u}^2$. |
| $D$ | $L$ | V, p. 103 | Grain diameter. |
| $d, d_0$ | $L$ | III, eq. 4 | Orbital diameter of water particle under wave motion $(d)$; near the bed $(d_0)$. Chap. III, Fig. 32. |
| $E$ | $MT^{-2}$ | III, eq. 7, ftn. 8 | Mean energy per unit surface area of a wave. |

| Symbol | Dimensions | Introduced | Description |
|---|---|---|---|
| $e$ | 0 | III, eq. 4a | Base of natural logarithms, $2.71 \cdots$. |
| $f$ | $MLT^{-2}$ | V, pp. 123, 126 | Fluid forces on a grain. Fig. 59, Chap. V. |
| $G$ | $LT^{-1}$ | III, p. 68 | Surface wave group velocity, $Cn$. Fig. 31, 36$b$, Chap. III. |
| $G$ | 0 | V, eq. 1 | Index of pore space geometry. |
| $g$ | $LT^{-2}$ | III, eq. 1 | Acceleration of gravity. |
| $H, H_d, H_s$ | $L$ | III, p. 49, eq. 4 | Whole height of surface wave ($H$); height in deep water ($H_d$); height in shallow water ($H_s$). Figs. 28, 32, 33, Chap. III. |
| $h$ | $L$ | III, eq. 1 | Water depth or flow depth. Fig. 28, Chap. III. |
| $i, i_b, i_s, i_\theta$ | $MT^{-3}$ | V, eq. 14 | Dynamic transport rate of sediment past unit width of flow ($i$); for bed load only ($i_b$); for suspended load only ($i_s$); for wave-induced transport ($i_\theta$). $i = [(\rho_s - \rho)/\rho_s]gmU$ |
| $K, K_b$ | 0 | III, eqs. 10a, 10b | Coefficient for the change in wave height due to refraction ($K$); for breaking solitary waves ($K_b$). |
| $K, K', K''$ | 0 | V, eqs. 20, 22, 22a | Ratio of sediment transport to available power ($K = i/\omega$); for wave-induced transport ($K'$); for solitary waves ($K''$). |
| $k$ | $L^{-1}$ | III, eq. 1 | Wave number, $2\pi/L$ |
| $k_0$ | 0 | V, eq. 5 | von Kármán constant. |
| $L, L_d, L_s$ | $L$ | III, eqs. 2a, 2b | Wavelength of surface wave ($L$); in deep water ($L_d$); in shallow water ($L_s$). Fig. 28, Chap. III. |
| $l$ | $L$ | V, eq. 4 | Prandtl's mixing length. |
| $l_1$ | $L$ | III, eq. 16 | Average separation between rip currents. Fig. 41, Chap. III. |
| $m, m_b, m_s$ | $ML^{-2}$ | V, eqs, 13, 16, 21 | Mass of sediment load over unit area of bed ($m$); for bed load only ($m_b$); for suspended load only ($m_s$). |
| $N$ | 0 | V, p. 110, eq. 10 | Grain concentration by volume; ratio of grain-occupied space to whole space. |
| $n$ | 0 | III, eq. 7; ftn. 9 | Ratio of wave group velocity to wave phase velocity, $G/C$. |

| Symbol | Dimensions | Introduced | Description |
|---|---|---|---|
| $P$ | $ML^{-1}T^{-2}$ | V, p. 132; eq. 12 | Dispersive grain stress normal to shear planes (transmitted from grain to grain). (Figs. 62, 63, Chap. V. |
| $q$ | $L^2T^{-1}$ | III, eq. 13 | Volume discharge of water in unit time per unit width of flow. Fig. 41, Chap. III. |
| $R$ | $0$ | V, p. 124; ftn. 5 | Reynolds number, $\rho\bar{u}h/\mu$ |
| $s$ | $L$ | III, eqs. 10a, 10b | Distance between wave rays Figs. 36$b$, 39, Chap. III. |
| $T$ | $T$ | III, eq. 1a | Wave period, Fig. 28, Chap. III. |
| $T$ | $ML^{-1}T^{-2}$ | V, p. 132, eq. 12 | Grain shear stress, transmitted from grain to grain. Figs. 62, 63; Chap. V. |
| $\mathscr{T}$ | $ML^{-1}T^{-2}$ | V, eq. 12 | Applied tangential stress by the fluid flow only. Fig. 63, Chap. V. |
| $U, U_b, U_s$ | $LT^{-1}$ | V, p. 136; eqs. 13, 16, 21 | Velocity of sediment transport $(U)$; for bed load only $(U_b)$; for suspended load only $(U_s)$. |
| $u, \bar{u}, \bar{u}_l$ | $LT^{-1}$ | III, eq. 16; V, eqs. 1, 2, 3 | Fluid flow velocity $(u)$; mean flow velocity $(\bar{u})$, Fig. 56, Chap. V; mean longshore current velocity $(\bar{u}_l)$, Fig. 41, Chap. III. |
| $u_m$ | $LT^{-1}$ | III, eqs. 3, 3a, 6a, 6b | Maximum horizontal component of wave orbital velocity. Figs. 32, 33, Chap. III. |
| $u_\theta$ | $LT^{-1}$ | III, eqs. 12, 14 V, eq. 22 | Fluid drift velocity, or wave drift current. Fig. 40a, Chap. III. |
| $w$ | $LT^{-1}$ | V, eq. 8 | Fall velocity of sediment grains. Fig. 58, Chap. V. |
| $x$ | $L$ | V, eq. 25 | Distance in direction of flow or travel. Fig. 56, Chap. V. |
| $z$ | $L$ | III, eq. 4 | Distance normal to bed surface, Fig. 28, Chap. III; Fig. 56, Chap. V. |
| $z_0$ | $L$ | V, eq. 5 | Roughness of bed boundary. Fig. 56, Chap. V. |
| $\alpha$ | $0$ | III, p. 72; eq. 16 | Angle between wave rays and a normal to the beach, or between wave crest and a bottom contour. Fig. 41, Chap. III. |
| $\alpha_\phi$ | $0$ | V, p. 107 | Phi skewness measure. Table 7, Chap. V. |

## Combined List of Symbols for Chapters III and V (*Continued*)

| Symbol | Dimensions | Introduced | Description |
|---|---|---|---|
| $\beta$ | 0 | III, eq. 16 | Angle of inclination of bed surface to horizontal, Fig, 41, Chap. III; Fig. 63, Chap. V. |
| $\beta_\phi$ | 0 | V, p. 107 | Phi kurtosis measure. Table 7, Chap. V. |
| $\gamma$ | 0 | III, eq. 15 | Relative wave height. $H/h$. Fig. 33, Chap. III. |
| $\epsilon, \epsilon_b, \epsilon_s$ | 0 | V, eq. 15a | Efficiency of sediment transport ($\epsilon = i \tan \phi / \omega$); for bed load ($\epsilon_b$); for suspended load ($\epsilon_s$). |
| $\theta_t$ | 0 | V, p. 129 | The stress ratio, $\tau_t / (\rho_s - \rho) g D$. Fig. 60, Chap. V. |
| $\lambda$ | $L$ | V, eq. 24 | Wavelength of sand ripple on bed surface. |
| $\mu$ | $ML^{-1}T^{-1}$ | V, eq. 2 | Molecular viscosity of fluid. |
| $\pi$ | 0 | III, eq. 1 | Ratio of circumference to diameter of a circle, $3.14 \cdots$. |
| $\rho$ | $ML^{-3}$ | III, p. 69 | Density of fluid. |
| $\rho_s, \rho'_s$ | $ML^{-3}$ | V, p. 109, eq. 8 | Effective density of sediment grains ($\rho_s$); dry bulk density of sand ($\rho'_s$). |
| $\sigma_\phi$ | 0 | V, p. 106 | Phi deviation measure. Table 7, Chap. V. |
| $\tau$ | $ML^{-1}T^{-2}$ | V, eq. 2 | Fluid shear stress. |
| $\tau_0$ | $ML^{-1}T^{-2}$ | V, eq. 6 | Fluid shear stress exerted at bed boundary. |
| $\tau_t$ | $ML^{-1}T^{-2}$ | V, eq. 9 | Threshold value of $\tau_0$. Fig. 59, Chap. V. |
| $\phi$ | 0 | V, p. 97 | "Phi unit," negative logarithm to base two of grain diameter in millimeters. Fig. 51, Chap. V. |
| $\phi$ | 0 | V, eq. 9 | Angle of solid friction, $\tan \phi = T/P$ Figs. 59, 62, Chap. V. |
| $\omega$ | $MT^{-3}$ | V, eq. 15a | Available power attributable to unit boundary area. In the case of waves, $\omega$ is the decrement of the transmitted power attributable to bed drag. |

# APPENDIX B.    CONVERSION TABLES

### Fathoms to Feet to Meters

| Fathoms | Feet | Meters | Fathoms | Feet | Meters |
|---|---|---|---|---|---|
| $\frac{1}{4}$ | 1.5 | 0.5 | $6\frac{1}{2}$ | 39.0 | 11.9 |
| $\frac{1}{2}$ | 3.0 | 0.9 | $6\frac{3}{4}$ | 40.5 | 12.3 |
| $\frac{3}{4}$ | 4.5 | 1.4 | 7 | 42.0 | 12.8 |
| 1 | 6.0 | 1.8 | 8 | 48.0 | 14.6 |
| $1\frac{1}{4}$ | 7.5 | 2.3 | 9 | 54.0 | 16.5 |
| $1\frac{1}{2}$ | 9.0 | 2.7 | 10 | 60.0 | 18.3 |
| $1\frac{3}{4}$ | 10.5 | 3.2 | 11 | 66.0 | 20.1 |
| 2 | 12.0 | 3.7 | 12 | 72.0 | 21.9 |
| $2\frac{1}{4}$ | 13.5 | 4.1 | 13 | 78.0 | 23.8 |
| $2\frac{1}{2}$ | 15.0 | 4.6 | 14 | 84.0 | 25.6 |
| $2\frac{3}{4}$ | 16.5 | 5.0 | 15 | 90.0 | 27.4 |
| 3 | 18.0 | 5.5 | 16 | 96.0 | 29.3 |
| $3\frac{1}{4}$ | 19.5 | 5.9 | 17 | 102.0 | 31.1 |
| $3\frac{1}{2}$ | 21.0 | 6.4 | 18 | 108.0 | 32.9 |
| $3\frac{3}{4}$ | 22.5 | 6.9 | 19 | 114.0 | 34.7 |
| 4 | 24.0 | 7.3 | 20 | 120.0 | 36.6 |
| $4\frac{1}{4}$ | 25.5 | 7.8 | 30 | 180.0 | 54.9 |
| $4\frac{1}{2}$ | 27.0 | 8.2 | 40 | 240.0 | 73.2 |
| $4\frac{3}{4}$ | 28.5 | 8.7 | 50 | 300.0 | 91.4 |
| 5 | 30.0 | 9.1 | 60 | 360.0 | 109.7 |
| $5\frac{1}{4}$ | 31.5 | 9.6 | 70 | 420.0 | 128.0 |
| $5\frac{1}{2}$ | 33.0 | 10.1 | 80 | 480.0 | 146.3 |
| $5\frac{3}{4}$ | 34.5 | 10.5 | 90 | 540.0 | 164.6 |
| 6 | 36.0 | 11.0 | 100 | 600.0 | 182.9 |
| $6\frac{1}{4}$ | 37.5 | 11.4 | | | |

## Statute Miles to Nautical Miles to Kilometers

| Statute Miles | Nautical | Kilometers | Statute | Nautical | Kilometers |
|---|---|---|---|---|---|
| $\frac{1}{4}$ | 0.21 | 0.40 | 9 | 7.84 | 14.50 |
| $\frac{1}{2}$ | 0.43 | 0.80 | 10 | 8.70 | 16.10 |
| $\frac{3}{4}$ | 0.65 | 1.21 | 20 | 17.40 | 32.20 |
| 1 | 0.87 | 1.61 | 30 | 26.16 | 48.40 |
| 2 | 1.74 | 3.22 | 40 | 34.80 | 64.50 |
| 3 | 2.61 | 4.84 | 50 | 43.50 | 80.50 |
| 4 | 3.48 | 6.45 | 60 | 52.20 | 96.50 |
| 5 | 4.35 | 8.05 | 70 | 61.00 | 113.00 |
| 6 | 5.22 | 9.65 | 80 | 69.60 | 129.00 |
| 7 | 6.10 | 11.30 | 90 | 78.40 | 145.00 |
| 8 | 6.96 | 12.90 | 100 | 87.00 | 161.00 |

# INDEX

*Bold face type indicates reference to an illustration on that page number.*

70 71 72 73    12 11 10 9 8 7 6